HISTORY OF
THE SECOND WORLD WAR
UNITED KINGDOM MILITARY SERIES

Edited by SIR JAMES BUTLER

The authors of the Military Histories have been given full access to official documents. They and the editor are alone responsible for the statements made and the views expressed.

Admiral Lord Louis Mountbatten and Lieut.-General R. A. Wheeler,
U.S. Army.

THE WAR AGAINST JAPAN

VOLUME III
The Decisive Battles

BY

MAJOR–GENERAL S. WOODBURN KIRBY
C.B., C.M.G., C.I.E., O.B.E., M.C.

WITH
CAPTAIN C. T. ADDIS, D.S.O., R.N.
BRIGADIER M. R. ROBERTS, D.S.O.
COLONEL G. T. WARDS, C.M.G., O.B.E.
AIR VICE–MARSHALL N. L. DESOER, C.B.E.

This edition of The War Against Japan: Volume III
first published in 2004
by The Naval & Military Press Ltd

Published by
The Naval & Military Press Ltd
Unit 10 Ridgewood Industrial Park,
Uckfield, East Sussex,
TN22 5QE England
Tel: +44 (0) 1825 749494
Fax: +44 (0) 1825 765701
www.naval–military-press.com

*In reprinting in facsimile from the original, any imperfections are inevitably reproduced
and the quality may fall short of modern type and cartographic standards.*

Printed and bound by Antony Rowe Ltd, Eastbourne

CONTENTS

APPENDICES

MAPS AND SKETCHES

Forest growth is shown only where it is considered necessary for the purpose of illustrating the text. Natural jungle is shown in neutral tint on black and white sketches. Conventional topographical symbols have been used on all maps. For economy in printing or for clarity, roads appear in black, red or brown.

MAPS

SKETCHES

PHOTOGRAPHS

Most of the photographs in this volume are Crown copyright and are reproduced by courtesy of the Imperial War Museum and the Ministries concerned. For permission to reproduce Nos. 5–9, 11, 26, 29 and 35 the authors are indebted respectively to the U.S. Foreign Histories Division, Tokyo, the Combined Historical Section, Simla, The Queen's Royal Regiment, Vandyk, New Bond Street, London W.1. and J. Russell & Sons, Queens Gate, London S.W.7.

PUBLISHED SOURCES

INDIA AND BURMA

Vice-Admiral The Earl Mountbatten of Burma, Report to the Combined Chiefs of Staff by the Supreme Allied Commander, South-East Asia, 1943–1945 (H.M.S.O., 1951).

Despatch by Field Marshal Sir Claude Auchinleck on Operations in the Indo–Burma Theatre based on India from 21st June 1943 to 15th November 1943.
(Supplement to the *London Gazette* of 27th April 1948, No. 38274).

Despatch by General Sir George Giffard on operations in Burma and North-East India from 16th November 1943 to 22nd June 1944.
(Supplement to the *London Gazette* of 13th March 1951, No. 39171.)

Despatch by Air Chief Marshal Sir Richard Peirse on air operations in South-East Asia from 16th November 1943 to 31st May 1944.
(Supplement to the *London Gazette* of 13th March 1951, No. 39173).

CALVERT, *Prisoners of Hope* (Jonathan Cape, 1952).

FERGUSSON, *The Wild Green Earth* (Collins, 1946).

SLIM, *Defeat into Victory* (Cassell, 1956).

ROMANUS and SUNDERLAND, *United States Army in World War II: The China-Burma-India Theater, Stilwell's Command Problems* (Washington, 1956).

CRAVEN and CATE, *The Army Air Forces in World War II: Volume IV, The Pacific – Guadalcanal to Saipan (August 1942 to July 1944)* (Chicago, 1950). *Volume V, The Pacific – Matterhorn to Nagasaki (June 1944 to August 1945)* (Chicago, 1953).

THE PACIFIC

MORISON, *History of United States Naval Operations in World War II:*
Volume VI, Breaking the Bismarcks Barrier, 22 July 1942–1 May 1944 (O.U.P., 1950).
Volume VII, Aleutians, Gilberts & Marshalls, June 1942–April 1944 (O.U.P., 1952).
Volume VIII, New Guinea and the Marianas, March 1944–August 1944 (Boston, 1953).

CROWL and LOVE, *United States Army in World War II: Seizure of the Gilberts and Marshalls* (Washington, 1955).

GILLESPIE, *The Official History of New Zealand in the Second World War: The Pacific* (Wellington, 1952).

HOFFMAN, *Saipan, The Beginning of the End* (Historical Branch, H.Q. U.S. Marine Corps, 1950).

HOUGH and CROWN, *The Campaign on New Britain* (Historical Branch, H.Q. U.S. Marine Corps, 1952).

KENNEY, *General Kenney Reports* (New York, 1949).

RENTZ, *Marines in the Central Solomons* (Historical Branch, H.Q. U.S. Marine Corps, 1952) and *Bougainville and the Northern Solomons* (Historical Branch, H.Q. U.S. Marine Corps, 1948).

SMITH, *United States Army in World War II: The Approach to the Philippines* (Washington, 1953).

WILLOUGHBY and CHAMBERLAIN, *MacArthur, 1941–1951* (Heinemann, 1956).

CRAVEN and CATE, *The Army Air Forces in World War II: Volume IV, The Pacific – Guadalcanal to Saipan (August 1942 to July 1944)* (Chicago, 1950).

ODGERS, *Australia in the War of 1939–1945, Air War against Japan, 1943–45* (Canberra, 1957).

INTRODUCTION

VOLUME I of this series of five recounted briefly the events which led to the outbreak of war with Japan and described the Japanese advance through Hong Kong, the Philippines, Malaya, Singapore and the Netherlands East Indies. Volume II told of the loss of Burma and the period of frustration which followed, during which the abortive attempt was made to recapture Akyab. It described how India Command set to work to reorganize, re-equip and train the army and air forces in preparation for the reoccupation of Burma, to build up India as a base and to improve the lines of communication to the north-eastern frontier. Like Volume I it is mainly a sombre record of disaster, lightened only by a description of the operations of the Chindits in the heart of enemy occupied Burma, by a brief account of the war in the Pacific, where the naval victories of the Coral Sea and Midway checked and then halted the Japanese advance, and of the dour fighting in the Solomons and in Papua which wrested the initiative from them.

The present volume has a brighter tale to tell. It begins with the planning in the autumn of 1943 for a general Allied offensive in 1944 to reoccupy Burma and the establishment of an Allied command in South-East Asia under a British Supreme Commander, Acting-Admiral Lord Mountbatten. It describes how the Eastern Fleet, steadily built up with ships freed by the surrender of Italy in September 1943, was eventually able to operate with impunity off the coast of Sumatra and Java from bases in Ceylon. It shows how the R.A.F. in India, greatly expanded and re-equipped with up-to-date aircraft and integrated with an enlarged American army air force, was able to challenge Japanese air supremacy with such effect that, by the middle of 1944, it had established air superiority over the whole of Burma.

It explains how one after another the plans for 1944 had to be abandoned owing to the withdrawal of most of the landing craft for the invasion of Europe, and to Generalissimo Chiang Kai-shek's refusal to allow the Yunnan armies to take the offensive, and how gradually, under American pressure, the main strategical object in South-East Asia became the capture of Myitkyina and the building of a road and pipeline to China to supplement the airlift over the Hump. It recounts in some detail how the enemy offensives in Arakan and into Assam brought about the decisive battles of the-war in South-East Asia which culminated in the defeat of the Japanese at Kohima and Imphal and the passing of the initiative to the Allies. It is therefore the key volume of the series.

A number of chapters have been devoted to the second campaign of the Chindits, now called Special Force and increased from two to six brigades. These operations, which were made much of in the contemporary press, are shown to have contributed less to the victories of 1944 than was popularly thought at the time. They underline once again that unorthodox forces or 'private armies' are wasteful and, though they can be of assistance to conventional forces, cannot by themselves win victories. These chapters also cover the final stages of Stilwell's advance down the Hukawng and Mogaung valleys, the capture of Kamaing and Myitkyina by the American/Chinese forces and of Mogaung, mainly by the Chindits.

The length of the lines of communication between the main bases in India and the north-eastern frontier, the lack of communications across the border between the Imphal plain and the Chindwin, the mountainous nature of the country on the borders of Assam and Burma and the climatic conditions which, during the monsoon, frequently made movement on land impossible and in the air extremely hazardous, created immense administrative problems. Including those of air supply, these have been described in some detail as they arose and it has been shown how they were solved.

As in previous volumes, the war in the Pacific has been described in outline, for, without a knowledge of events in that theatre, the reader would be unable to keep the war as a whole in proper perspective and grasp the significance of the overall strategy for the defeat of Japan. Unlike the previous volumes, this volume has devoted space to military events within China where some twenty-five Japanese divisions were tied down throughout the war. The Japanese offensive to wrest the airfields in south-eastern China from the Allies and the abortive Chinese offensive across the Salween are described.

We wish to express our gratitude to the relatives of the late Major-General Orde Wingate for permission to make use of his papers. We are indebted to Admiral of the Fleet Earl Mountbatten of Burma, Field Marshal Viscount Slim, General Sir George Giffard and to many other officers too numerous to mention here by name who have been good enough to read our drafts and send us their comments. We must also thank Mr. Gardner, Chief of the U.S. Foreign Histories Division and his staff for information from Japanese sources and for research carried out in Japan on our behalf, and Mr. Gavin Long, the General Editor of the Australian War History, who has kindly assisted us in connection with the New Guinea campaign.

We have had the advantage of using the Admiralty Staff History of the War against Japan written by Major C. S. Goldingham, R.M., the narratives written by Brigadier M. Henry and Lieut.-Colonel J. E. B. Barton of the Cabinet Office Historical Section and the narratives prepared by Squadron-Leader W. M. Gould and Mr. D. Craik of the Air Historical Branch, Air Ministry.

Our thanks are due to the Cabinet Office Mapping Section under Colonel T. M. M. Penney for the preparation of the many maps and sketches with which the volume is illustrated, to Miss M. M. Baird, Miss R. J. F. Hughes and Miss R. B. Harbottle for their careful research work and for the secretarial assistance given by Miss A. E. Davidson.

The quotation from *Allenby, Soldier and Statesman,* is reproduced by the kind permission of George G. Harrap & Company Ltd.

S.W.K.
C.T.A.
M.R.R.
G.T.W.
N.L.D.

"All plans in the dubious hazard of war must have . . . risks; the great commander is he who has both the courage to accept them and the skill to minimize them."

(Field-Marshal Viscount Wavell, *Allenby, Soldier and Statesman,* Harrap, 1946)

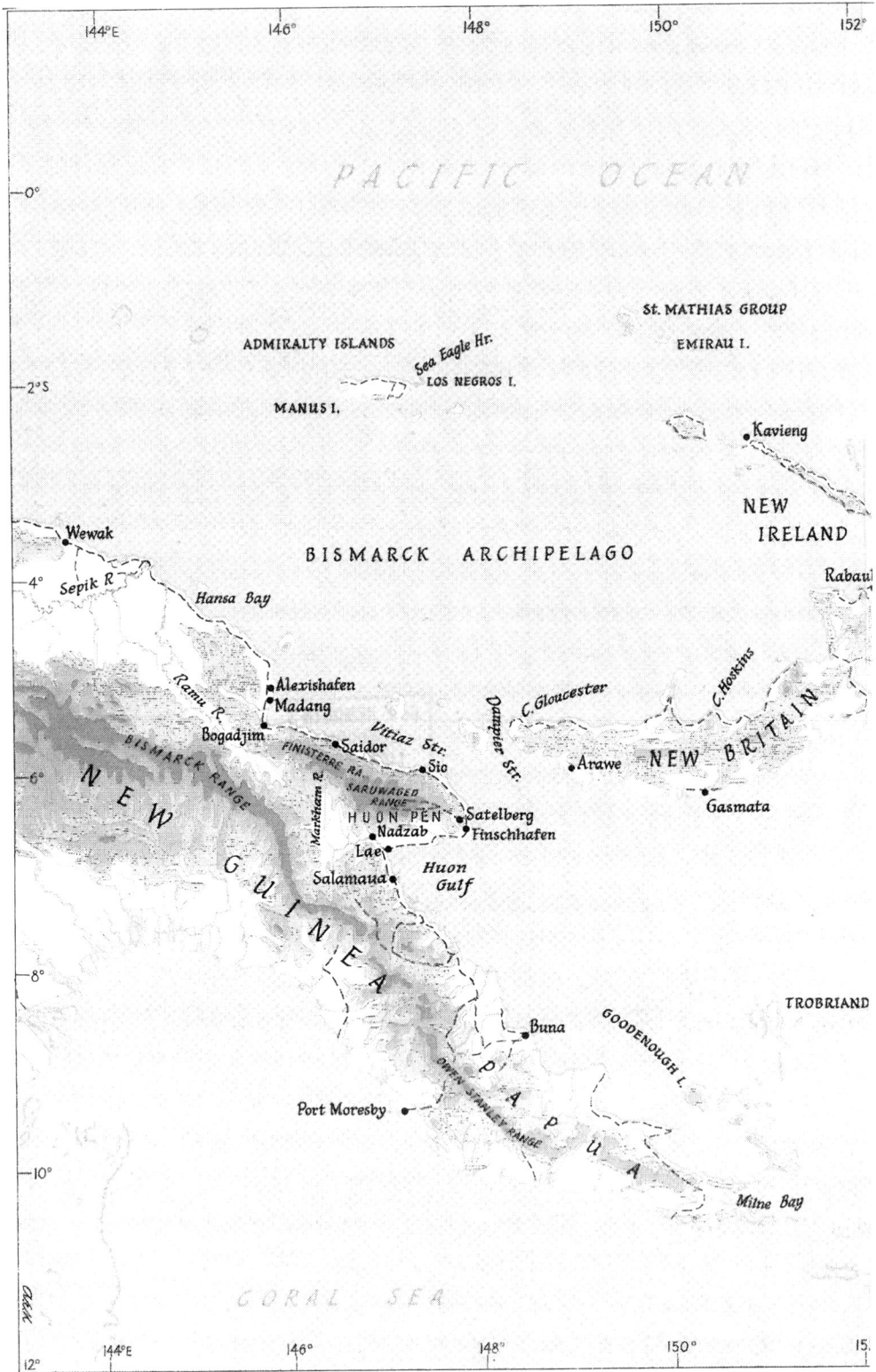

144°E 146° 148° 150° 152°

PACIFIC OCEAN

—0°

St. MATHIAS GROUP
EMIRAU I.

ADMIRALTY ISLANDS
Sea Eagle Hr.
—2°S LOS NEGROS I.
MANUS I.

Kavieng

NEW
IRELAND

Wewak
BISMARCK ARCHIPELAGO
Rabaul
—4° Sepik R.
Hansa Bay

Ramu R.
Alexishafen
Madang
C. Gloucester
C. Hoskins
Bogadjim
FINISTERRE RA.
Saidor
Vitiaz Str.
Dampier Str.
NEW BRITAIN
BISMARCK RANGE
—6° SARUWAGED RANGE
Sio
N E W
Arawe
Markham R.
HUON PEN.
Satelberg
Gasmata
Nadzab
Finschhafen
Lae
G
Salamaua
Huon
Gulf
U

I
TROBRIAND
—8°
N
Buna
GOODENOUGH I.
E
A
P
Port Moresby
A
OWEN STANLEY RANGE
P
—10°
U
A
Milne Bay

CORAL SEA

—12° 144°E 146° 148° 150° 15.

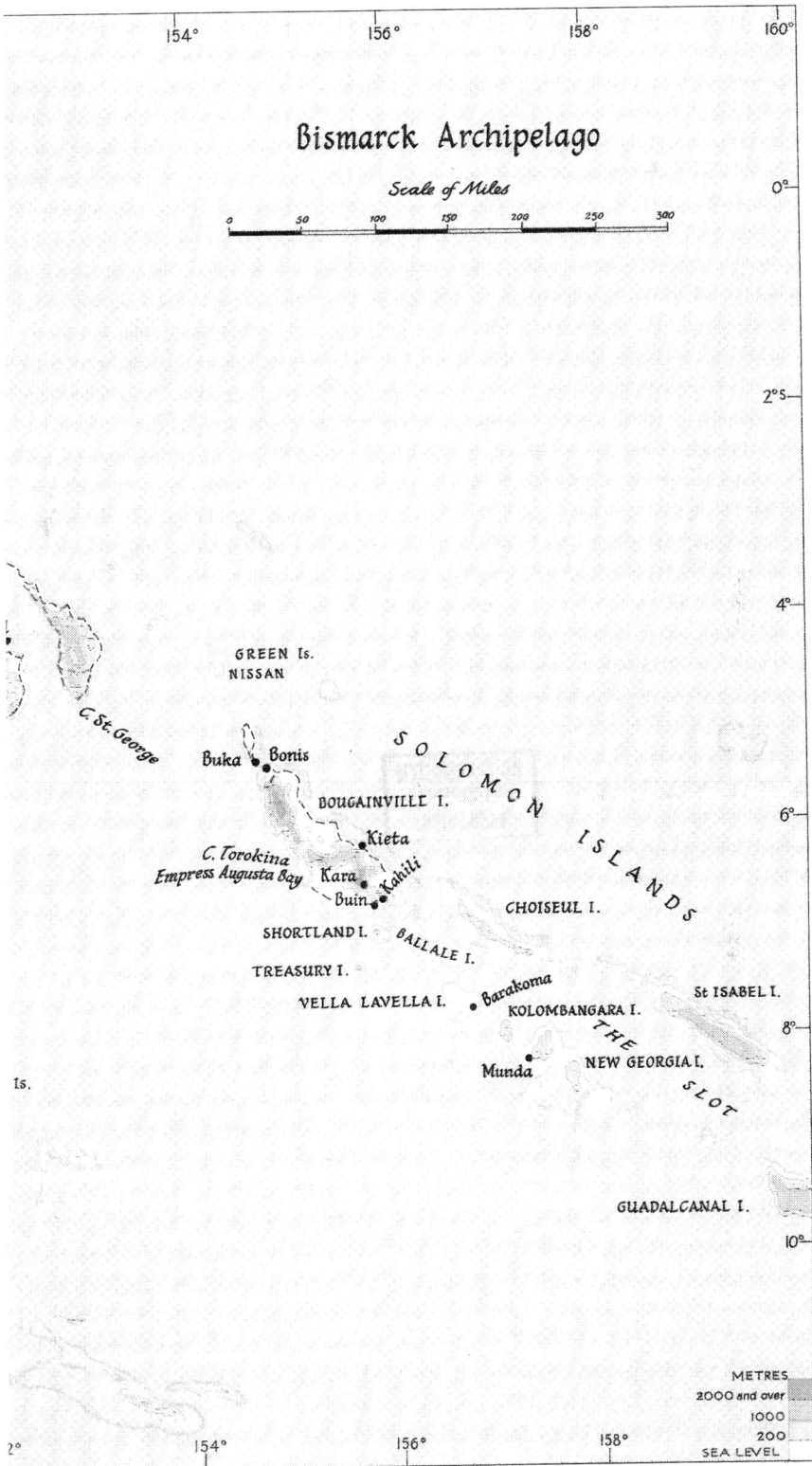

Bismarck Archipelago

Scale of Miles

0   50   100   150   200   250   300

154°   156°   158°   160°

0°

2°S

4°

GREEN Is.
NISSAN

C. St. George

Buka   Bonis

SOLOMON ISLANDS

6°

BOUGAINVILLE I.

Kieta

C. Torokina
Empress Augusta Bay   Kara   Kahili
Buin

CHOISEUL I.

SHORTLAND I.   BALLALE I.

TREASURY I.

VELLA LAVELLA I.   Barakoma

St ISABEL I.

KOLOMBANGARA I.

8°

Is.

Munda   NEW GEORGIA I.

THE SLOT

GUADALCANAL I.

10°

METRES
2000 and over
1000
200
SEA LEVEL

2°   154°   156°   158°

CHAPTER I

ALLIED PLANNING FOR 1943-44
(September – November 1943)

See Maps 1, 2, 3, 13, 14 and 15

BY the end of August 1943 the pattern of the war in the Pacific was beginning to take shape.[1] In every area the Americans had regained the initiative: in the north Pacific, the Japanese had been expelled from the Aleutians; in the central Pacific a great fleet of carriers and battleships was gathering at Pearl Harbour for a sweep westward by way of the Japanese-mandated islands to the Philippines; in the south, Vice-Admiral W. F. Halsey's advance up the Solomons chain had cleared the enemy from Guadalcanal and recaptured New Georgia; and in the south-west, with the fall of Buna, General D. MacArthur had regained Papua and, moving along the coast of New Guinea, had begun to close in on Lae and Salamaua.[2]

There was no counterpart of these victories in South-East Asia. In May 1942 the British forces in Burma had been forced to withdraw into India after a brief campaign; the Eastern Fleet had abandoned its bases in Ceylon and retired to the east coast of Africa, leaving command of the sea in the Bay of Bengal for a time in Japanese hands; and, with the loss of Rangoon and the closing of the Burma Road, China had been cut off from Allied help except by the hazardous air route from India.[3] An attempt at the end of 1942 to recapture Akyab, made by inexperienced troops with insufficiently developed communications, had by May 1943 ended in failure.[4]

The only other operation undertaken by India Command during 1943 had met with more success. Early in the year a long-range penetration (L.R.P.) brigade (the Chindits), under command of Brigadier O. C. Wingate, had penetrated deep into Burma, thereby proving that properly trained and organized groups supplied from the air, and thus independent of the normal lines of communication, could operate in the jungle far behind the enemy lines.[5] Although the operation had no immediate strategic value it had raised morale and to some extent offset the failure in Arakan and demonstrated that,

---

[1] See Maps 1 and 13, pages 1 and 438.
[2] See Volume II, Chapter XXV.
[3] See Map 15 in pocket at end of volume.
[4] See Volume II, Chapters XIX and XX.
[5] See Volume II, Chapter XVIII.

with air supply, an offensive across the grain of the country into Burma was possible. It had also had the unexpected effect of influencing the Japanese to alter their plans and turn from the defensive to the offensive for the protection of upper Burma.[1]

While these operations were taking place Allied plans for launching a counter-offensive to recapture Burma had been under consideration. At the Casablanca Conference in January 1943 the Combined Chiefs of Staff had recommended that an offensive for the reconquest of Burma (operation 'Anakim') should begin at the end of the monsoon in November. The main outline of the plan was an advance on Mandalay from two directions: by British forces from Assam and by Chinese forces from western Yunnan, while American/Chinese forces from Ledo advanced on Myitkyina. These operations were to be supported by amphibious operations at points of strategic importance along the coast of Arakan, culminating in an amphibious and airborne attack on Rangoon itself. It had soon become evident, however, that 'Anakim' was too ambitious and its timing premature.

When the Trident Conference met in Washington in May 1943, the Combined Chiefs of Staff recognized that no full-scale 'Anakim' could be carried out in the winter of 1943–44. But American and British opinion was divided on what was to take its place. Both were agreed that it was essential to keep China in the war and that they must go to her aid quickly. The Americans wished to do so by expanding the air route from India to China and opening up land communications with China by the recapture of northern Burma. The British wished, while maintaining the air route, to contain the Japanese armies in Burma until amphibious forces could be gathered for a break-through to the South China Sea by way of Sumatra and Singapore. The conference finally decided to give priority to increasing the air lift to China; to undertake vigorous offensive action from Assam into northern Burma, in step with an advance by Chinese forces from Yunnan, as the first stage towards opening a road to China; and to launch minor amphibious operations to capture Akyab and Ramree Island.[2]

The failure in Arakan and the desire for a more vigorous conduct of the war against Japan had led at the time of the conference to the acceptance in principle of a proposal to create a separate command in South-East Asia to control all operations in the area. This would relieve the Commander-in-Chief in India of some of his responsibilities and allow him to concentrate more on the organization and training of the Indian Army and the preparation of India as a base from which the counter-offensive for the recapture of Burma and Malaya could be launched.

---

[1] See Volume II, Chapters XVIII and XXVI.
[2] See Volume II, Chapter XXIII.

On the 18th June it was announced that Field-Marshal Sir Archibald Wavell was to succeed the Marquess of Linlithgow, whose term of office as Viceroy of India was due to expire in October, and that General Sir Claude Auchinleck would relieve Wavell as Commander-in-Chief in India.[1]

During July and August it was agreed that, as United States forces were already established in both China and India, the proposed new South-East Asia Command (S.E.A.C.) should be Anglo-American, under a British Supreme Commander assisted by an American deputy with an integrated British and American staff at all levels. The Supreme Commander would receive his orders and instructions from the British Chiefs of Staff, who would exercise jurisdiction over all operational matters, leaving the Combined Chiefs of Staff in Washington responsible for the general strategy of the war against Japan and the allocation of British and American resources to the new command and the China theatre. India was to remain a separate and independent command of equal status with the new command. The Commander-in-Chief in India was to retain responsibility for the development of India as a base, for her internal security and for the defence of her North West Frontier. He was to administer the Indian base for all forces within the boundaries of India, including those allotted to or destined for S.E.A.C., and be responsible for the training, equipment, maintenance and movement of such forces. He was also to provide the administrative services required in India for the S.E.A.C. air forces.

In the three months that followed the Trident Conference, which covered the peak of the monsoon period, it became evident that administrative difficulties would not allow the plans agreed on at the conference to be carried out in full. A further conference (Quadrant) took place at Quebec in August to reconsider among other things the Allied plans for South-East Asia in the light of these difficulties but in the knowledge that long-range penetration groups could operate effectively in jungle country. It was agreed that, for the dry weather of 1943–44, the capture of northern Burma, with the object of establishing land communications with China and securing the air route, should be given priority, although it was realized that administrative difficulties might reduce the scale or delay the start of the operations. It was also agreed that preparations should be made to launch, in the spring of 1944, amphibious operations on the scale of those contemplated at Trident for the capture of Akyab and Ramree. The Combined Chiefs of Staff, however, found it impracticable at the time to arrive at all the necessary decisions for the conduct of

---

[1] See Volume II, Chapter XXIII. Auchinleck became Commander-in-Chief on the 20th June 1943.

operations against Japan, and left the objectives for the amphibious operations to be decided later.

As regards the Pacific, it was decided that operations were to be carried out for the capture of the Gilbert and the Marshall Islands, Ponape and the eastern Caroline Islands, Palau (including Yap), Guam and the Japanese Marianas.[1] The current operations in New Guinea were to be extended with a view to the seizure or neutralization of eastern New Guinea as far west as Wewak and of the Admiralty Islands and the Bismarck Archipelago;[2] in particular Rabaul was to be neutralized if possible. Later, a step-by-step advance along the north coast of New Guinea would be undertaken.[3]

On the 25th August, the day after the Quadrant Conference ended, it was announced that Acting-Admiral Lord Louis Mountbatten was appointed Supreme Allied Commander, South-East Asia. Until he could set up his headquarters and assume control of operations, the Commander-in-Chief in India (Auchinleck) was left in charge of the preliminary planning for the operations which had been decided on by the Combined Chiefs of Staff, as well as of the reorganization and training of the Indian Army and the build-up of the long-range penetration force under Wingate's command.

In accordance with the Quadrant decisions the Chiefs of Staff told Auchinleck on the 26th that the main effort in South-East Asia was to be put into offensive operations to establish land communications with China and improve and secure the air route. He was therefore to submit plans for the capture of upper Burma by a three-pronged advance from Ledo, the Chindwin and Yunnan, with a target date of mid-February 1944.[4] Pending the selection of a particular objective, he was to prepare for an amphibious operation in the spring of 1944 on the scale of the operation contemplated at Trident for the capture of Akyab and Ramree. He was also to prepare India as a base for the operations eventually contemplated in S.E.A.C., and to continue to build up and increase the air route and air supplies to China with a view to keeping her in the war, equipping her armies, maintaining and increasing the American and Chinese air forces stationed there and intensifying air operations against the Japanese.

They directed him further to study and report on certain operations and their relation to one another. These were: an operation against northern Sumatra in the spring of 1944; operations southwards from northern Burma in November 1944; operations through the Moulmein area or the Kra Isthmus in the direction of Bangkok as early as practicable; and operations through the Strait of Malacca

---

[1] See Map 13, page 438.
[2] See Map 1, page 1.
[3] See Volume II, Chapter XXVI.
[4] See Map 15 in pocket at end of volume.

Map 2

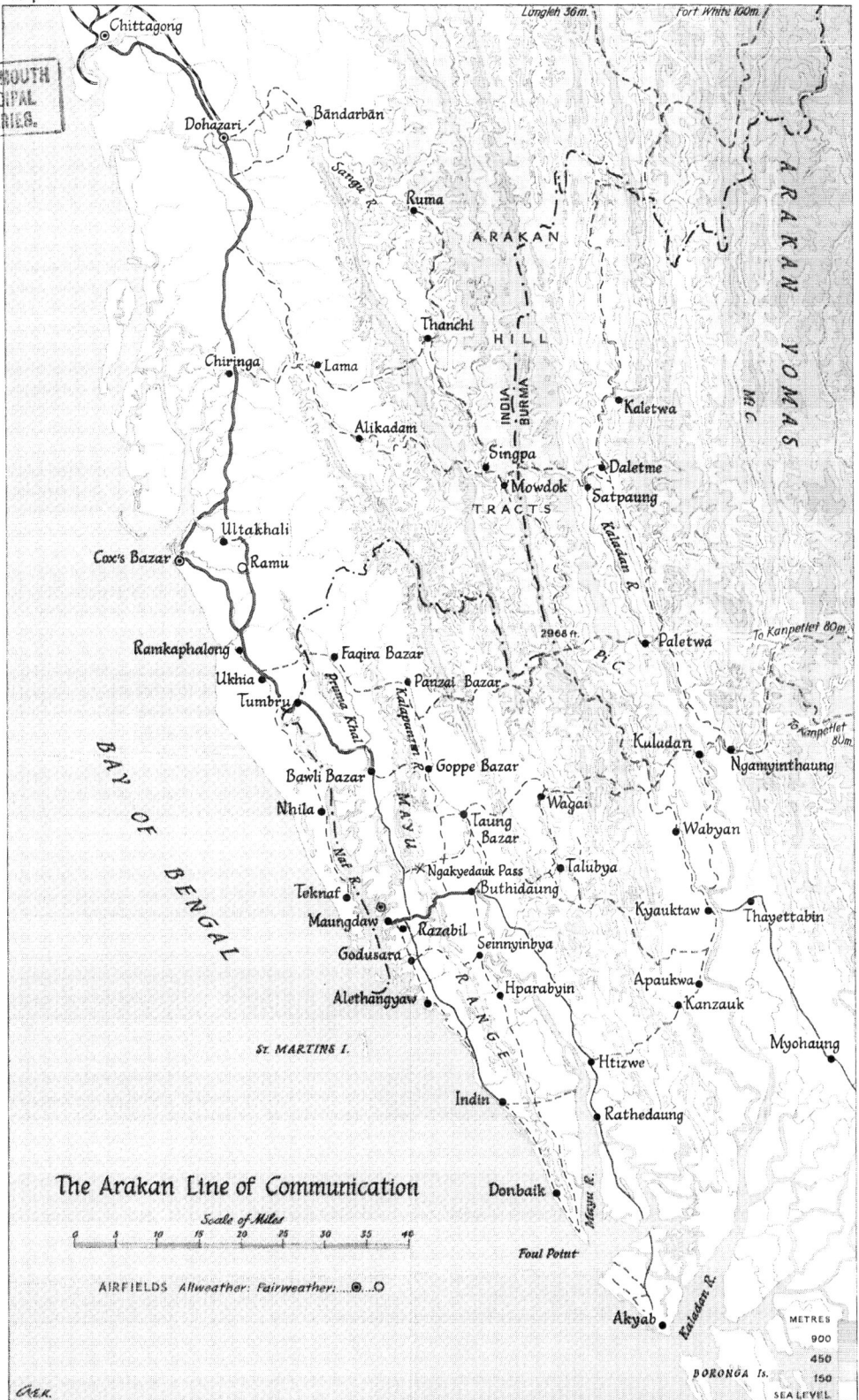

The Arakan Line of Communication

Scale of Miles

AIRFIELDS Allweather: Fairweather:

and Malaya for the direct capture of Singapore. He was also to determine whether the capture of Akyab and Ramree was necessary for the success of operations to capture upper Burma or any of those which were to be investigated. On the assumption that Germany would be defeated in the autumn of 1944, he was, in addition, to study the potentialities and limitations of developing the air route to China so that all the heavy bombers and transport aircraft likely to be available for the South-East Asia and China theatres in 1944–45 could be used.

In accordance with a directive which the Supreme Commander would be given and in consultation with the appropriate American authorities, Auchinleck was to take the steps necessary to develop the north-east India and Assam transportation systems, to increase the capacity of the line of communications to the Assam border from the 102,000 tons a month for which plans had already been made to 220,000 tons a month by the end of 1945, and to construct two 6-inch pipelines from Calcutta to Ledo, a 4-inch pipeline to Fort Hertz and a 6-inch pipeline along the Ledo–Myitkyina road.[1]

The Chiefs of Staff had already sent Auchinleck the principles formulated by Wingate governing the use of L.R.P. groups during the 1943–44 campaign.[2] These groups were to be used to pave the way for an advance by the main forces by disrupting enemy communications, finding targets for tactical air forces and creating such widespread confusion behind the enemy's forward areas that there would be a progressive weakening and misdirection of his main forces. They had suggested that, in the first instance, three groups might be used simultaneously but, since these would be capable of only some twelve weeks continuous operations, three more groups would be required as replacements. On the 25th August they told him to plan for a force headquarters to deal with organization and training, two wing headquarters and six groups, each of eight columns, to be ready for operations in northern Burma early in 1944. The ultimate number aimed at would be eight. The six were to be the existing 77th and 111th (L.R.P.) Brigades increased from six to eight columns and four newly-formed brigades. Since Wingate insisted that a high proportion of the groups should be British,[3] they directed Auchinleck to break up 70th British Division so that the existing brigades could be reorganized and brought up to strength and three new all-British groups formed. The sixth group was to be organized from 3rd Brigade of 81st West African (W.A.) Division when it arrived in India. If the remaining two groups were required

---

[1] See Appendix I for the directive.
[2] See Volume II, Chapter XXIV.
[3] Wingate refused to include any Indian troops in his organization which he originally wished should be made up entirely of British and Gurkha troops.

it might be necessary to break up 36th Indian Division, but no decision on this would be made until the study of the various alternative amphibious operations suggested at Quadrant had been completed.[1]

At the end of August 1943, the land front of India Command ran roughly in a 700-mile arc along the Burma frontier from the mouth of the Naf River in Arakan to the snow-clad mountains, rising in places to some 20,000 feet, which separate north Burma from China.[2] Geographically the front fell into three distinct sectors which became known as the Arakan, Central and Northern fronts. The Arakan front, based on Chittagong, stretched from the Bay of Bengal across the Mayu Range and the Arakan Hill Tracts to the Kaladan Valley; it was separated from the Central front by the northern end of the main chain of the Arakan Yomas which rise to some 9,000 feet. The Central front, based on Imphal, ran from the northern Chin Hills, which covered the approaches through Lungleh to eastern Bengal, in a north-easterly direction to the Naga Hills, which covered the approaches from the Chindwin by way of Tiddim, Tamu and Homalin to Imphal and Kohima. It was separated from the Northern front by the partly unsurveyed mountain mass of the northern Naga Hills which rise to over 12,000 feet. The Northern front was based on Ledo and covered the routes into north-east Assam from Myitkyina by way of the Hukawng Valley. The gap between this front and the Salween River was covered by the isolated outpost at Fort Hertz.

The responsibility for the Northern front, which the Americans called Northern Combat Area Command (N.C.A.C.), rested with Lieut.-General J. W. Stilwell, U.S. Army (Commanding General, China–Burma–India Theatre). It was held by 38th Chinese Division covering the construction of the Ledo Road over Pangsau Pass to the Hukawng Valley. The 22nd Chinese Division was in reserve.[3] In August operational control over the Arakan and Central fronts was vested in Eastern Army (General Sir George Giffard). The Arakan front was held by 26th Indian Division (Major-General C. E. N. Lomax) occupying monsoon positions on the general line Teknaf–Taung Bazar, with an independent battalion at Mowdok watching the Kaladan Valley.[4] The IV Corps (Lieut.-General G. A. P. Scoones) held the Central front with 17th Indian Light Division (Major-General D. T. Cowan), one brigade of which (63rd) was

---

[1] No action was ever taken to form the two additional brigades.
[2] See Maps 2 and 14, pages 5 and 452.
[3] Both these Chinese divisions had been accommodated at Ramgarh in India. They had been paid and fed by India Command and trained by Americans under General Stilwell's control.
[4] See Map 2, page 5.

south of Tiddim in the Fort White area and the remainder resting at Shillong, and 23rd Indian Division (Major-General O. L. Roberts) which covered the approaches to Imphal and Kohima from the Kabaw Valley. Headquarters XV Corps (Lieut.-General W. J. Slim) and 20th Indian Division (Major-General D. D. Gracey) were at Ranchi in Army reserve.[1]

Giffard had prepared a plan for operations during the dry weather of 1943–44 which provided for XV Corps assuming operational control in Arakan in the first week in October, when 7th Indian Division would have relieved 26th Division. The corps would then be brought up to strength by 5th Indian Division and, on its arrival in India, by 81st (W.A.) Division (less one brigade). The concentration would be completed by mid-December. At the end of January, 5th and 7th Indian Divisions were to capture the line Maungdaw–Buthidaung and then advance to the line Foul Point–Rathedaung. The 81st (W.A.) Division was to protect the left flank of the corps by advancing down the Kaladan Valley. The land advance in Arakan, which was given the code name of 'Cudgel', would be undertaken whether or no an amphibious operation against Akyab ('Bullfrog') were launched. On the Central front, IV Corps was to be reinforced by 20th Indian Division and 77th (L.R.P.) Brigade. One division was to reoccupy the Stockades on the Fort White–Kalemyo road, lost in May; another was to reoccupy the Kabaw Valley and the west bank of the Chindwin, which had been abandoned at the beginning of the monsoon, and then, in conjunction with an L.R.P. operation, raid eastwards to disrupt the enemy communications in the Shwebo area in order to bluff the Japanese into thinking that a large scale offensive across the river would follow.[2]

When Auchinleck received his instructions from the Chiefs of Staff on the 26th August, he saw that Giffard's plan for the Arakan front could stand with only minor modifications, but that the existing plan for the Central front would not materially assist the opening of a land route to China and would therefore need drastic revision. After discussions with Giffard and Scoones, he sent an outline of his proposals to the Chiefs of Staff on the 7th September. He explained that in Arakan the advance should take place whether or not the amphibious operation for the capture of Akyab were launched, but that in Assam he could plan only for operations within the capacity of the lines of communication, and that the forces used or the scope of operations could be increased only at the expense of other demands on the lines of communication, and in particular of the airlift to

---

[1] The 70th British Division was also at Ranchi, but since it was earmarked for conversion to L.R.P. groups was not available for Eastern Army.
[2] See Map 3, page 33.

China. For the employment of IV Corps from Assam there were two alternatives: an advance to secure the Kalemyo–Kalewa area to be followed by the capture of Yeu, thus threatening Mandalay and Shwebo, or an advance by way of Tamu and Sittaung to Indaw and the maintenance there of a force astride the main enemy line of communication to the north. In each case the advance of IV Corps would be assisted by L.R.P. groups which would distract the enemy and disrupt his communications. Although it made greater demands on the Assam lines of communication, Auchinleck himself favoured the first alternative since it directly threatened the whole Japanese position in northern Burma, covered its own line of communications and gave greater scope for the use of armour and artillery.

The Chiefs of Staff preferred the second alternative—the capture of Indaw—as being more in line with the Quadrant decisions, which demanded the capture of upper Burma in order to improve the air route and establish overland communication with China. They thought the first not only lacked the element of surprise but contemplated an advance along the direct route to the centre of the Japanese communications, which involved a frontal attack supported by tanks and artillery on prepared positions. The area of operations was too remote from that of the Chinese to give them definite support and encouragement to fulfil their part of the plan.

They felt that it was necessary to get away from orthodox methods and develop a fresh technique. The second alternative more nearly fulfilled the requirements of the object and agreed with their conception of the technique required. It would give greater scope for the employment of L.R.P. groups and, since it provided a greater element of surprise, would have a more direct effect on the Chinese advance. Moreover, as it would make fewer demands on the lines of communication, it would leave a greater balance of capacity for the airlift to China. On the 18th September they asked Auchinleck to examine whether his second alternative, elaborated on the lines suggested by Wingate's memorandum on the recapture of northern Burma,[1] was tactically and administratively possible.

Two days later Auchinleck received an appreciation from Scoones which showed conclusively that an overland advance to Indaw by IV Corps was not feasible. On the 27th he sent the Chiefs of Staff an entirely new plan (operation 'Tarzan'). Its broad outline was that the Chinese Yunnan armies would capture and hold the Bhamo–Lashio area; the N.C.A.C. forces from Ledo would seize the Myitkyina area and advance towards Katha and Bhamo; British airborne forces would capture Indaw and, supplied by air, remain there throughout the monsoon; and L.R.P. groups would be used to precede and assist each of these three advances. To contain as many

---

[1] See Volume II, Chapter XXIV.

enemy forces as possible there would be simultaneous advances by XV Corps in Arakan to the general line Indin–Kyauktaw and by IV Corps to the Chindwin from both Tamu and Fort White.

The main features of the British part of the operations would be the capture of the Indaw airfields by two battalions of parachute troops, at a time when the Japanese were already fully engaged by operations elsewhere. To hold the Indaw area a division (less one brigade) would then be flown in over a period of seven days, while its third brigade, equipped with mule and jeep transport, moved overland from Imphal. One L.R.P. group would operate by way of Haka towards Gangaw and Pakkoku, one from Homalin towards Katha and the Japanese line of communications to Myitkyina, one from Paoshan towards Bhamo and the Gokteik Gorge and one would be in reserve. In order to give the Indaw operation the best chance of success Auchinleck proposed to begin the Arakan offensive early in January 1944, to move the L.R.P. groups into Burma about the 15th February and to launch the airborne attack on the Indaw airfields about the 15th March. The division allotted to the Indaw area would have to come from the Arakan front and would probably not be available before mid-February. In addition to its primary task of gaining air superiority over the whole theatre, the air force would have to transport and maintain the L.R.P. groups and the Indaw force, as well as support the operations in Arakan and those of the two Chinese forces. He estimated that some eighteen to twenty-two squadrons of transport aircraft (450–550 aircraft) would be required.

The success of this plan depended on the Chinese from Ledo and Yunnan carrying out their share of the operation. It was to assist their endeavours as much as possible that Auchinleck now agreed that an offensive directed on Indaw was preferable to one directed on Yeu. There was a possibility, however, that the Chinese advance from Yunnan would not take place, in which case an isolated force established at Indaw with only limited powers of offensive action would be exposed to a prolonged Japanese counter-offensive. This danger might be lessened by the use of the L.R.P. groups which, coupled with British air superiority over Burma and sustained bombing of enemy airfields and communications, might very considerably reduce the Japanese ability to attack the Indaw force. The position of the force at Indaw would be very different from that of forces isolated during the Arakan campaign of 1942–43; as there would be no land line of communication, the Japanese would not be able to manoeuvre it out of position, but would be forced to attack positions which could be brought to a reasonably high state of preparedness. The determining factors might well prove to be the provision of fighter cover and an efficient warning system in the Indaw area. With adequate fighter cover there was, Auchinleck thought, a reasonable prospect of the force being able to hold the area throughout the monsoon until relieved by further offensive operations in the autumn of 1944.

On the 7th October the Chiefs of Staff replied that the possibility of obtaining aircraft on the scale he required was quite out of the question. They said that the plan he had submitted was very different from the type of operation they had envisaged, which was on a much lighter scale, demanding only one airfield at Indaw for occasional use by light aircraft. This telegram shows that they were thinking on the lines of the temporary occupation of Indaw by L.R.P. groups, constituted and trained for hit-and-run raids, rather than of the capture and permanent occupation of the area.

Since he could not count on the number of aircraft demanded by his original plan, Auchinleck was forced to recast it. He found that it would be possible to reduce his requirements in transport aircraft to an absolute minimum of 11 or 12 squadrons (275–300 aircraft) with a further 70 aircraft in reserve in India. He told the Chiefs of Staff on the 13th October that the resulting plan was feasible though not so satisfactory as his original, but made it clear that, unless the aircraft could be provided, the capture of Indaw should not be attempted. Since the number he required appeared to be still greatly in excess of what was likely to be available, he suggested that the solution might be to borrow aircraft from the air ferry route to China.

While planning for an offensive into upper Burma, Auchinleck had also been investigating the various amphibious operations suggested at Quadrant. He came to the conclusion that the capture of Ramree was not essential to the overall plan, but that the occupation of either Akyab ('Bullfrog') or the Andaman Islands ('Buccaneer') would be of considerable strategic value.[1] Since the occupation of Akyab would not only remove the threat to Chittagong but also provide advanced airfields from which heavier air attacks could be launched on enemy communications within Burma, he began to plan for 'Bullfrog'. He found that the five assault brigades left to him after the conversion of 70th Division to L.R.P. groups would suffice for the initial assault.[2] To transport the troops taking part in the operation he would need shipping to lift 50,000 men. The same resources would suffice for the capture of the Andamans provided that a fleet of five battleships and three aircraft carriers was made available to provide cover against interference by Japanese capital ships based on Singapore. He suggested that, if operations for the capture of northern Sumatra ('Culverin') in the dry weather of

---

[1] See Map 15 in pocket at end of volume.
[2] The three brigades of 2nd British Division and the two brigades of 36th Indian Division.

1944–45 were contemplated, it might be more advantageous to take the Andamans than Akyab. On the 17th October he told the Chiefs of Staff that the forces required for 'Culverin' would be roughly three times those needed for either of the other two operations and that, as all the aircraft allotted to India Command by the spring of 1944 would be required for the contemplated advance into northern Burma, none would be available for any other purpose. He therefore asked what prospects there were of anything being added to the resources already allotted to India Command for the capture of Akyab.

At Quadrant the American Air Planning Staff had put forward a plan designed to hasten the defeat of Japan by using very long-range bombers (B.29s) to bomb her industries. Maintained by a fleet of transport aircraft based on Calcutta and staging at Kunming, the aircraft would operate from central China. This proved to be administratively unsound, for it demanded the development of forty-five new airfields in the Calcutta area, for which no suitable sites existed, and a very considerable development of the port of Calcutta, which in itself was a long-term project. A modified plan, proposed by Headquarters China–Burma–India (C.B.I.) Theatre, by which the bomber aircraft would be based partly on China and partly on Calcutta, although it still required a vast increase in the port facilities and the construction of a special oil port on the Hooghly, reduced the number of airfields needed in the Calcutta area to seven, four of which would have to be ready by August 1944. It soon appeared that these airfields could not be ready by then, but a detailed examination was set on foot to see how much could be done. Since the port of Calcutta would have to be developed in any case, orders for the material required for the purpose were placed.

Admiral Mountbatten arrived at Delhi on the 7th October. He was followed by his Chief of Staff (Lieut.-General Sir Henry Pownall) and a nucleus staff, who were to arrange for the establishment of his headquarters in November, examine the planning undertaken in India to implement the Quadrant decisions and hold preliminary discussions with General Auchinleck and Mountbatten's three Commanders-in-Chief designate (Admiral Sir James Somerville, General Sir George Giffard and Air Chief Marshal Sir Richard Peirse). As the success of any offensive into northern Burma depended largely on the active participation of the Chinese Yunnan armies, Mountbatten paid an early visit to Generalissimo Chiang Kai-shek to establish personal relations with him and to ascertain to what extent the Chinese were prepared to co-operate in the proposed campaign. With Lieut.-General B. B. Somervell (Chief of the U.S. Services of

Supply), who had been sent out by President Roosevelt to present
the idea of South-East Asia Command to the Generalissimo and
secure his formal assent to its structure, and Lieut.-General G. E.
Stratemeyer (Commanding General 10th U.S.A.A.F.) he flew to
Chungking on the 16th October. There he met General Stilwell who
was to be his deputy and Major-General C. L. Chennault (Commanding General 14th U.S.A.A.F.).

Before Mountbatten met the Generalissimo, Stilwell told him that
the Chinese armies in Yunnan were in poor shape, mainly due to
malnutrition. If they were to be an effective force they would have
to be re-equipped and for this he would need 10,000 tons of equipment carried by the airlift by the end of the year, and thereafter
3,200 tons a month. He was unable to commit himself in any way to
an undertaking that the Chinese would, or were indeed able to,
conduct a major offensive into Burma. Chennault on his part said
that, for 14th U.S.A.A.F., he required a minimum of 4,700 tons of
supplies delivered by the airlift each month, rising to 7,000 and later
to 9,000 tons a month. These figures included the tonnage needed to
enable him to undertake the strategic bombing of Japanese shipping
in the China Sea, which he regarded as an essential part of any
strategy to recapture all or part of Burma. Any reduction in tonnage
delivered would prevent him from taking the offensive elsewhere in
China, lose him the initiative and possibly result in heavy damage to
his air force.

On the 19th, Mountbatten had a conference with the Generalissimo and Madame Chiang Kai-shek at which Stilwell and Somervell
were present. He outlined and explained the decisions reached at
Quadrant, which led to a discussion on the airlift to China and a
reminder from Madame Chiang Kai-shek that the Americans had
promised in March to lift 10,000 tons a month by the autumn of
1943.[1] Somervell explained the reasons why the promised figure had
not yet been reached and the steps taken to overcome the difficulties
encountered, and said that he hoped that the combined lift of Air
Transport Command and the China National Aviation Corporation
would reach some 8,500/9,000 tons in October.[2] Mountbatten
reminded the Generalissimo that the decisions of the Combined
Chiefs of Staff at Quadrant had been made in the clear knowledge
that the course they had adopted might lead to a reduction in the
airlift and said that he doubted whether these figures could be reached.
He would do everything in his power to ensure that the tonnage
carried to China reached the highest possible figure, but no one
could predict the course of a campaign and it might prove necessary
to divert aircraft to air supply duties or to bring reserves into battle.

---

[1] See Volume II, Chapter XVII.
[2] The actual lift was 8,632 tons. See Appendix 2.

He could not embark on the forthcoming campaign tied down to any specific figure and felt that he should be trusted to act in the best interests of the Allies. The Generalissimo fully accepted the position and said that Mountbatten need have no worry on that score since, if any change of policy seemed necessary, they could always consult each other.

The conference then turned to details of the proposed operations. Stilwell said that the Chinese forces in India were already concentrated at Ledo and ready to advance, and that he expected the Yunnan armies, consisting of fifteen divisions organized into five armies, to be equipped and concentrated by the 1st January 1944, with one division holding a bridgehead west of the Salween and the rest east of the river. The Generalissimo suggested that operations should start in mid-January. Mountbatten said that he would bear this date in mind but that it would be better to defer fixing the precise date until plans were more advanced; it was important that the main British objective—Indaw—should be captured only just before the monsoon broke so as to prevent a large scale Japanese counter-offensive. The Generalissimo accepted this argument and agreed that Mountbatten, assisted by Stilwell, should command all Chinese forces engaged in Burma.

At the conclusion of the conference, the Generalissimo said that he considered the British estimate of the Japanese strength in Burma—four or five divisions—was too low. He thought that by the spring of 1944 the Japanese could deploy some eight to ten divisions and seven hundred to one thousand aircraft. He finally laid great stress on the importance of a superior Allied fleet in the Bay of Bengal since there was need for a decisive victory at sea.

After inspecting units in Assam, Mountbatten returned to Delhi where on the 24th October he received his first directive from the Prime Minister. It drew his attention to the decisions taken at the Quadrant Conference by the Combined Chiefs of Staff and told him that 'pursuant to these decisions and acting in harmony with them' he was to assume his appointment as Supreme Allied Commander, South-East Asia, and conduct all operations against the Japanese within the limits of his command. His first duty was to engage the Japanese as closely and continuously as possible in order to consume and wear down their forces, especially their air forces, thus establishing Allied superiority and forcing them to divert forces from the Pacific theatre. His second duty, but of equal consequence, was to maintain and broaden Allied contacts with China both by means of the airlift and by establishing direct contact through northern Burma. He was, by utilizing to the full his sea and air power, to seize some point or points which would induce a powerful enemy reaction and thus provide opportunities for a counter stroke; plans for amphibious operations for 1944 should be drawn up with this object in view. At least four weeks before his first amphibious operation he would be furnished with a battle fleet based on Ceylon, strong enough to engage any forces which the Japanese could reasonably afford to detach from the Pacific. For this purpose the Eastern Fleet would be provided with at least ten escort carriers and any available fleet carriers. In preparation for whatever amphibious operation was eventually selected, and in anticipation of the arrival of the vessels promised, a start was to be made in forming a combined striking force which should include a naval squadron to undertake coastal bombardment, aircraft carriers, transports and the necessary types of assault craft and landing ships. The directive ended by stressing the importance of speed and instructed him to report what his plans were, the dates of his proposed operations and his requirements.[1] It will be noted that, while retaining the operation into northern Burma approved at Quadrant, great emphasis was laid in this directive on the use of amphibious operations as a means of drawing Japanese strength from the Pacific and producing suitable conditions for a decisive battle.

Mountbatten's staff had meanwhile been gradually taking over operational planning from India Command. In order to clarify the position regarding amphibious operations, he asked the Chiefs of Staff on the 27th October whether they could give any reply to Auchinleck's enquiry of the 17th about the possibility of additional forces being provided for the operation against Akyab,[2] only to be told that none could be provided though minor adjustments could be made. An attack on northern Sumatra was then clearly out of the question. The occupation of the Andamans would be possible with the forces available and appeared to offer a better objective for an amphibious operation than Akyab, since the islands would provide a forward base for photographic reconnaissance of Malaya and Sumatra and a refuelling base for submarines and naval light craft. Moreover, their capture would give the Japanese no clue as to the direction of any further advance. Mountbatten therefore ordered that planning for the capture of these islands ('Buccaneer'), already begun by Auchinleck, should be pressed ahead.

On the 1st November the Combined Chiefs of Staff asked Mountbatten for a summary of the situation in South-East Asia and his views on future operations. He replied that the Andamans would be the best objective for an amphibious operation. As regards northern Burma his proposed offensive would be a three-pronged advance by

---

[1] See Appendix 3 for the directive in full.
[2] See page 11.

British troops from the Imphal area, American-trained Chinese troops from Ledo and, if the Generalissimo kept his undertaking, Chinese troops from Yunnan. All three advances would be assisted by long-range penetration operations. In addition, to improve the defence of Chittagong, to divert enemy strength and to cause attrition, a subsidiary operation would take place in Arakan. The land operations would be accompanied by a continuous and intensive effort by Allied air forces in north-east India against Japanese air forces, communications and installations. The air forces would also act in direct support of the operations.

The scope of the proposed operations in Arakan, and of those from Ledo and Yunnan, was definite, though the timing had still to be settled. The operations from the Imphal area could, however, take a number of forms. He had considered three possible courses: an overland advance towards Yeu, the capture of Mandalay by an airborne operation and an airborne operation for the capture of Indaw. He discarded the overland advance to Yeu since it offered no prospect of linking up with the Chinese, made heavy demands on the Assam line of communications, contained no element of surprise, meant a frontal attack on strong Japanese defences and was unlikely to succeed before the end of the monsoon. Although it was strategically the most attractive, he also discarded the airborne operation for the capture of Mandalay on the grounds that his resources were insufficient, since it demanded the capture of the Shwebo group of airfields by parachute and L.R.P. troops, followed by the fly-in of two divisions and an advance overland by a third. He was left therefore with the airborne operation for the capture of Indaw ('Tarzan') which approximated very closely to the intentions of the Quadrant Conference. Although it would involve some diversion of tonnage from the airlift, it could be carried out with the resources at his disposal.

Mountbatten's plan differed from that submitted by Auchinleck in that, owing to the severe shortage of parachutes for supply dropping, the brigade which was to have moved overland to Indaw would now have to be flown in. This brought the number of transport aircraft required at the peak period of the operations (March and April) up to some 370. Since only some 140 British transport aircraft were expected to be available at that time, the balance of 230 would have to be found from elsewhere. Mountbatten therefore proposed, as Auchinleck had in October, that aircraft should be temporarily borrowed from the airlift, and a reduction in the tonnage carried to China accepted. A detailed examination of the problem showed that, if all the aircraft required were to be found at the expense of the airlift, the tonnage available for China during March, April and May would fall short of the minimum demands of the Yunnan armies and

14th U.S.A.A.F. by some 9,000 tons. In terms of carrying capacity this represented some thirty (C.46) transport aircraft over a period of four months. Mountbatten pointed out that to make the proposed operations possible the additional aircraft would have to be found from sources outside India, unless it was agreed by all concerned, including the Generalissimo, that the build-up of the American/Chinese air forces could be even further slowed down.

By mid-November Mountbatten had proposed that S.E.A.C. should carry out seven separate, but related, operations during the dry weather of 1943–44. These were:

(i) the capture of the Andaman Islands by amphibious assault ('Buccaneer');

(ii) an advance by XV Corps to secure the general line Maung-daw–Buthidaung–Kyauktaw and exploit towards Akyab;

(iii) an advance by IV Corps to the Chindwin;

(iv) an advance by the forces on the Northern front from Ledo to the Mogaung–Myitkyina area;

(v) an advance by the Chinese Yunnan armies towards Bhamo and Lashio;

(vi) the capture of Indaw by paratroops ('Tarzan') with the subsequent fly-in of a division to hold the area until the forces on the Northern front reached Mogaung, when the two would join forces on the railway;

(vii) operations by long-range penetration groups to cut enemy communications to Indaw and to assist the advance of the forces on the Northern front and the Yunnan armies.

The reader will note that the plans recommended by S.E.A.C. were very similar to those prepared earlier by India Command, the only changes being those necessitated by shortages of certain articles of equipment. In the chapters which follow it will be seen that the impact of events in Europe on the Far East and the failure of the Chinese to co-operate prevented most of these correlated operations being undertaken and forced the Supreme Commander to fall back on less enterprizing plans.

CHAPTER II

THE ADMINISTRATIVE
BACKGROUND
(September – November 1943)

See Maps 10, 14 and 15 and Sketch 12

BEFORE describing Auchinleck's administrative preparations for the operations approved at Quadrant for 1943–44, a brief outline of what had already been done in India in this respect since the outbreak of the war in Europe is necessary.[1] For nearly two centuries the only outside threat to India had been from the north-west through Afghanistan, and thus the defence of the North West Frontier had set the pattern for the defence of India as a whole. Administrative installations, workshops, supply, ordnance and ammunition depots had all been sited in depth along the line of communications to that frontier. The outbreak of war in Europe merely enhanced that threat and all new installations for the administration of India's rapidly expanding army and the maintenance of her formations in Egypt and Iraq were sited near to the ports of Bombay and Karachi or on the main railway lines feeding the North West Frontier.

The Japanese invasion of Malaya and Burma upset the traditional pattern of defence. The threat now shifted from the north-west to the north-east, and a complete reorientation of India's defence had to be undertaken. Her armies had now to be deployed along her eastern frontiers, and new bases and depots created to maintain them. New airfields had to be constructed with the least possible delay. Early in 1942 Wavell was forced to embark on a large building programme, including some two hundred airfields and new base installations near Benares which were sufficiently far inland to be secure yet with easy access to the coasts of Bengal and Orissa and to the railways leading to Assam and eastern Bengal.[2] During the year advanced bases were established at Dimapur and Gauhati in Assam and at Mymensingh, Silchar and Chittagong in eastern Bengal.

All this involved much administrative planning and placed a very heavy load on the engineering resources of India. The load became

---

[1] For details see Volume II, Chapters III, XI, XVII, XXI and Appendix 24.
[2] See Map 14, page 452.

heavier when, after the American naval victory at Midway, the threat of invasion receded and Wavell began to prepare plans for the overland and seaborne offensive against Burma ('Anakim') with Rangoon as its main objective. To maintain the forces required for 'Anakim' the base facilities in India had to be further expanded. In November 1942 it was planned that four reserve bases should be provided to enable the country to maintain the forces detailed for 'Anakim', those required for internal security and the defence of the North West Frontier, the new formations being raised and troops in training establishments throughout the country. In March 1943 it was decided that the bases would be so designed that they could be expanded if necessary to maintain one and a half times the forces required for 'Anakim'.[1]

This involved a vast amount of administrative preparation: the capacity of the ports and of the telephone and telegraph systems had to be enlarged, the railways and inland water transport system improved, new hospitals and new supply, ordnance and ammunition depots provided, and ordnance establishments built for the maintenance, supply and repair of vehicles, weapons and equipment. Provision had to be made for the import, storage and distribution of the increased quantities of petrol, oil and lubricants (P.O.L.) required and arrangements made to provide extra food and stores from indigenous sources or by import without undue interference with the economic life of the country. In many cases these preparations were complicated by the fact that the forces to be maintained were of mixed nationalities requiring different treatment, and included Allied forces whose organization and equipment differed in many respects from those of the British.

Work to increase the capacity of the ports at Chittagong, Calcutta and Madras, and to construct the four reserve bases, each to hold thirty days' supplies for the forces it was to maintain, was begun in April/May 1943.[2] Plans were made to develop the existing installations and depots at Lahore and Benares into Nos. 1 and 2 Reserve Bases to maintain the forces retained within India's frontiers, including those in Assam and eastern Bengal, and to build two new reserve bases to supply the forces to be maintained overseas through the ports of Calcutta, Madras and Vizagapatam—No. 3 at Panagarh (ninety-eight miles west of Calcutta) on an entirely new site and No. 4 at Avadi (twenty miles west of Madras) on the site of a small transit depot which had been established in 1940–41 to maintain Indian formations in Malaya. The two new bases were designed in such a way that they could be at least doubled in size if necessary.

---

[1] The forces required for 'Anakim' amounted to one armoured and ten infantry divisions, one tank brigade and seventy-six air squadrons.

[2] See Map 10, page 384.

New transit depots were also to be established at Calcutta and Vizagapatam since the bases serving these ports were some distance from them.

In January 1943 it was estimated that by the end of the year the Services' monthly requirement of P.O.L. would be twenty-three million gallons of aviation and motor spirit and one million gallons of oil and lubricants. Of this, local production could provide only four million gallons of aviation and motor spirit and 60,000 gallons of lubricants. The balance would have to be imported. Since the oil-fields of Burma and the Netherlands East Indies, from which India had imported much of her P.O.L. in peacetime, had been lost, all imports had to come from the Persian Gulf and, as far as possible, be landed at Bombay in order to save tanker tonnage. This threw an extra burden on the already overloaded railways, since the bulk of the P.O.L. had to be carried across India for the use of the forces in eastern India, Assam and eastern Bengal.

This had been foreseen and, in order to reduce the extra load, arrangements had been made in 1942 to build a 6-inch pipeline to carry 400,000 tons of petrol a year from Bombay over the heavy gradients of the Western Ghats to Bhusawal—a distance of some 275 miles. Storage tanks were to be built at Bhusawal to hold seven million gallons of petrol, and installations erected which would enable the terminal to handle four trains in and out a day (two of forty-five 5,000 gallon tank wagons and two carrying drums and containers). The pipeline and terminal installations were completed by May 1943, and from that date all P.O.L. for Bengal and Assam was sent by rail from Bhusawal.

It was calculated that, apart from the expeditionary forces, four months' reserves would be required for the forces based on India. An examination of the storage capacity showed that only three months' reserves could be held without building additional tanks. This smaller scale of reserves was accepted. As no bulk storage was likely to be available for the expeditionary forces in the area of operations, P.O.L. would have to be supplied to them in containers, and this would mean holding thirty-four million gallons of petrol and two million gallons of lubricants in containers at the Panagarh and Avadi bases. A review showed that India's monthly production of containers would not suffice even to meet monthly wastage, and so either the balance would have to be imported or production greatly increased. To save shipping, plant and steel plate were imported and containers were thereafter manufactured locally.

An important factor in the build-up of the Indian base, and one which gave cause for anxiety, was the carrying capacity of the Indian railway system. Among the ranks of the railway employees there were many of a low standard of education and some who were illiterate. They were trained to do a particular job under normal peacetime conditions but, since they were generally incapable of adjusting themselves quickly to changed conditions or using their initiative, slow and safety-first methods of operation had been adopted. This served the needs of a slowly developing subcontinent in peacetime, but did not lend itself to a rapid expansion of capacity under the stress of war. Even under peacetime conditions the railways had never had enough locomotives and wagons to meet demands in full, and peak traffic had been spread. To make matters worse, between September 1939 and December 1941, India had released a tenth of her railway equipment (excluding broad gauge locomotives and wagons) and specialist staff for service in other theatres of war.[1] Furthermore she had surrendered a considerable proportion of her coastal shipping to the Ministry of War Transport for use elsewhere. As a result, coal, which was normally carried by sea from Calcutta to Madras and the west coast ports, had perforce to be carried by rail. Thus when war with Japan broke out the railways, which in peacetime handled ninety per cent. of the internal traffic of India, were carrying, with fewer locomotives and wagons, about one million tons of coal a year in excess of their normal load, which represented nearly half of their net annual ton mileage.

As the Indian Army expanded and military movements increased, the load on the railways had steadily grown, and by July 1942 Wavell had to ask for 185 new broad gauge locomotives, the minimum necessary to meet India's war requirements.[2] But the world-wide demand for locomotives was so great that he was told he would receive only four in 1942–43 and forty in 1943–44, all of which had been ordered before September 1939. He could, however, place orders for spare parts and boilers to enable the existing stock to be repaired and retained in service. Between July 1942 and September 1943 orders were placed in the United States, Canada and Great Britain for 595 broad and 605 metre gauge locomotives and 25,649 broad and 29,480 metre gauge wagons. Of the metre gauge, 295 locomotives and 22,325 trucks were specifically earmarked for Assam and 108 for military use overseas. By the end of August 1943, however, only four broad and five metre gauge locomotives had reached India but it was confidently expected that a further 79 broad and 190 metre gauge would be shipped to India before the end of the year.

The shortage of locomotives in the first half of 1943 resulted in the stocks of coal for the railways throughout India, which should have

---

[1] This included 206 metre gauge locomotives and 8,000 wagons constituting $8\frac{1}{2}$ and $15\frac{1}{2}$ per cent. respectively of the total stocks.

[2] By the end of 1942 there were in India 5,321 broad gauge steam locomotives and 2,209 metre gauge locomotives. Of the former $16\frac{1}{4}$ per cent. and of the latter $13\frac{1}{2}$ per cent. were under or awaiting repair.

been maintained at forty-five to seventy-five days' supply, falling to an average of seventeen days' supply. So great was the shortage in industrial areas that many factories on war production subsisted on a day-to-day basis, and some had to close down temporarily. The situation became so serious that in July the Government of India found it necessary to ask the Ministry of War Transport for coastal shipping to lift 60,000 tons of coal a month from Calcutta to other Indian coastal ports. A breakdown was avoided by reducing passenger trains by some forty per cent., by increasing operational efficiency and by doubling tracks and improving signal communications where possible. These measures were but palliatives and, at least till the end of 1943, the railways remained the limiting factor in the build-up of India as a base.

Because there were no through roads in Bengal, the lines of communication from Calcutta to the north-east frontier of India depended entirely on the railways which were themselves hampered by a break in gauge and the unbridged Brahmaputra. Communications to the Central and Northern fronts depended primarily on the single-track metre gauge line, liable to be breached in the monsoon, which ran from Parbatipur on the broad gauge system north of Calcutta parallel to the foothills of the Himalayas to the Amingaon–Pandu wagon ferry and the river ports of Dhubri and Tezpur. East of the river a single-track metre gauge line ran from Pandu through Gauhati, Lumding and Dimapur to Tinsukia where it branched east to Digboi and Ledo and west to the river port of Dibrugarh.

Apart from the Sirajganj and Goalundo transhipment ferries with their long river haul to Chandpur, land communications to the Arakan front depended on the single-track metre gauge loop line which left the broad gauge system at Santahar and ran to the Tistamukh–Bahadurabad wagon ferry and to the Parbatipur–Amingaon line at Kaunia. East of the river, a single-track metre gauge line ran from Bahadurabad to Mymensingh where it branched to Dacca and Akhaura. At Akhaura it again branched, one line running south through Laksam and Feni through the port of Chittagong on the Bay of Bengal to the terminal at Dohazari, and the other north-east to Badarpur and Silchar. The two rail systems east of the Brahmaputra were linked by a line across the mountains between Badarpur and Lumding known as the Hill Section, but the steep gradients and sharp curves, necessitating special locomotives and short trains, limited the capacity of this link.[1]

The Assam Trunk Road, which by 1943 had been made to an all-weather standard, paralleled the railway system in the Assam Valley. It ran from Goalpara through Pandu, Gauhati, Silghat and Jorhat to Dibrugarh, Tinsukia and Ledo. It had a branch to Shillong and

---

[1] See Map 14, page 452 and Sketch 12, page 328.

Sylhet, and another from Jorhat to Golaghat, but the latter did not continue to the northern terminal of the Imphal Road at Dimapur. There was no access by road from India and all vehicles had to enter Assam by rail.

The area east of the Brahmaputra was one of the most backward parts of India. Its railways were designed solely to meet the demands of the seasonal tea and jute industries, the small output of coal and oil from north-east Assam and the negligible local requirements. Stations, the only places where trains could pass each other, were far apart and traffic control methods, though simple and foolproof, were inadequate. As a result, the capacity of the railways was limited and could not be easily expanded. Transhipment from broad to metre gauge and the restricted capacity of the wagon ferries across the Brahmaputra caused delay, while the lack of stone and gravel within a reasonable distance of most roads made their upkeep a matter of difficulty.

The Brahmaputra itself provided a secondary line of communication from the river ports of Khulna, Goalundo and Sirajganj (all served by broad gauge railways) and those at Tistamukh, Dhubri, Amingaon and Tezpur (served by the metre gauge railway) to the river ports on the east bank at Chandpur, Dacca, Jagannathganj and Bahadurabad, all connected to the eastern Bengal railway system, as well as those upstream from Goalpara, all of which were connected with either the Assam rail or road systems at Pandu, Silghat, Donaigaon, Neamati, Disangmukh and Dibrugarh. A fleet of river steamers and barges plied between the ports, but the capacity of the river route had been greatly reduced between 1939 and 1941 by the despatch of powered craft and barges to Iraq. The overall capacity of the river route was also limited by the behaviour of the river itself: its level fluctuated by as much as twenty-five feet and its course changed every monsoon with the result that jetties, roads and rail spurs at river ports were frequently washed away or left high and dry and had to be entirely reconstructed. In addition to the rail and river routes to the frontier, there was the route by sea to the port of Chittagong and thence by rail through Akhaura, Badarpur and Lumding to the Assam frontier or by road and coastal craft to Cox's Bazar and Maungdaw in Arakan.

These were the complicated communications which had to be expanded when the need to defend the north-eastern frontier arose in 1942. At that time the capacity of the railway from the junctions on the broad gauge system to Ledo did not exceed 600 tons a day. Steps were immediately taken to increase the capacity of the railways in Assam and eastern Bengal and the ferries across the Brahmaputra, to recover some of the river craft loaned to Iraq, to establish a road link between the railway at Bongaigaon and Jogighopa (a river port with a ferry service to the end of the Assam Trunk Road at Goalpara), to build a road from Golaghat (near Jorhat) to Dimapur in order to link the Imphal Road to the Assam Trunk Road, to double the road to Imphal and extend it first to Palel and eventually to Tamu on the frontier, to provide an access road for vehicles into Assam from Siliguri, which was on the broad gauge railway, to Jogighopa, and to construct a new river port at Neamati.

All these projects called for additional engineering resources and labour, both of which were scarce owing to the construction of the large number of airfields to which absolute priority had been given. They also added to the strain on the railways, which could be eased only at the expense of operations or the stocking of forward depots. They were seriously delayed by both the 1942 and 1943 monsoons. Nevertheless, by the end of June 1943 the capacity of the combined rail and river communications to Assam had been increased from 600 to 1,720 tons a day, the Assam Trunk Road had been improved to take heavy traffic, the Bongaigaon–Jogighopa and the Golaghat–Dimapur roads had been built to an all-weather standard and the Imphal Road had been doubled and extended as a single road to Palel, also on an all-weather standard. Further south, a fair-weather single-way road had been built from Dohazari to Ramu and Cox's Bazar and on to Tumbru at the head of the Naf River. The capacity of the port of Chittagong, which had been largely dismantled in the spring of 1942, had been extended to handle some 800 tons a day, exclusive of P.O.L. products.

Throughout 1942 there had been difficulty in getting adequate supplies through to IV Corps owing to the work on doubling the Imphal Road, wash-outs and landslides caused by heavy rains during the monsoon, shortage of vehicles, the inexperience of transport drivers and the ravages of malaria. In December 1942 Colonel R. J. Holmes, who had earlier run the traffic on the Burma Road, was given the task of reorganizing traffic on the Imphal Road. He introduced a system based on that previously used by the London General Omnibus Company (L.G.O.C.). Its adoption quickly reduced wastage in vehicles and improved the carrying capacity. During the six months from March to August 1943, which included the worst period of the monsoon, an average of nearly 17,000 tons a month was carried forward. The L.G.O.C. system was then replaced by an improved 'Round the Clock' (R.T.C.) system of running which obviated the faults of the former.[1] The adoption of these systems, together with the improvement of the roads, solved the problem of maintaining troops in the Imphal area and the tonnage carried from Dimapur to Imphal reached 30,000 in September and 40,000 in October.

From the time of its arrival at Imphal early in 1942 IV Corps had

---

[1] See Volume II, Appendix 24.

been responsible for the operation of traffic south of Dimapur and for the general administration in the area. In order to free it for its operational tasks forward of Imphal, Eastern Army assumed responsibility for these duties in March 1943. During the late summer an advanced echelon of General Headquarters, India, under Brigadier G. O. Jameson, began to take over responsibility for general administration on the Pandu–Dimapur–Imphal line of communication, working on the instructions of Eastern Army. On the formation of 14th Army in the middle of October, his organization became 14th Army Headquarters Advanced Echelon, Assam.

To lighten the load on the line of communication, all P.O.L. required east of the Brahmaputra was delivered by rail to the river port of Dhubri, from where it was carried by barge to river ports as far to the north-east as Dibrugarh. To facilitate distribution from these ports, work was begun in August 1943 on pipelines to connect the northern Assam airfields, all of which were fairly close to the river, to the river ports and on one from Tinsukia to Dibrugarh to carry the output of kerosene from the Digboi oilfields.

This left the railways to carry the bulk of the motor and aviation spirit required on the line of communication and on the Central front. To relieve them, work was also begun in August on a 4-inch pipeline from Chittagong along the alignment of the railway through Badarpur and Lumding to a bulk storage depot near Dimapur. It was proposed to extend it later as far along the Imphal Road towards the frontier as proved necessary.[1] Priority was given to the Tinsukia–Dibrugarh pipeline, the connections to the airfields from the river ports and to the 160-mile section of the Chittagong–Imphal pipeline between Chandranathpur (near Badarpur) and Dimapur. Those to the airfields were completed by the middle of November and those to Dimapur by the end of February 1944.

Mention has already been made of the 1942 airfield programme in India, which included the modernization of Dinjan airfield near Tinsukia and the construction of six new airfields in north-east Assam. Early in 1943 these had been completed and two (Jorhat and Tezpur) were taken over by the R.A.F. and five (Sookerating, Dinjan, Mohanbari, Chabua and Misamari) by the American Air Transport Command operating the airlift to China.[2] At the beginning of 1943 the plan was to increase the tonnage to be carried by the airlift to 4,000 tons a month by using these five airfields, but early in February at a conference in Chungking the Generalissimo insisted that, if he were to take part in any offensive into Burma during the dry weather of 1943–44, the airlift would have to be increased to 10,000 tons a month by November 1943. To operate the extra

[1] For details of the pipelines see Appendix 4.
[2] See Sketch 12, page 328.

transport aircraft required, 10th U.S.A.A.F. needed four or five more airfields in north-east Assam. Wavell accordingly arranged that it would take over the Jorhat and Tezpur airfields, that all the seven existing airfields would be enlarged and improved to take heavier aircraft, and that three new ones would be built at Moran, Nazira and Golaghat with runways constructed from steel planking imported from the United States.

The load which the Assam lines of communication would have to bear as the direct result of the increase in the airlift included not only the 20,000 tons of steel planking and the large quantities of other materials required for the construction work at the airfields, but also 10,000 tons of 100 octane petrol and the monthly maintenance requirements of the enlarged ground staffs and air-crews as well as the increased monthly lift to China.

To meet this situation Wavell formed in April 1943 the General Reserve Engineer Force (G.R.E.F.) which worked directly under the Engineer-in-Chief, General Headquarters, India,[1] and was responsible for the construction and upkeep of all the airfields, roads and pipelines in Assam east of the Brahmaputra. During the month he had told the Prime Minister that he could provide the three additional airfields only by abandoning all hope of undertaking operations into northern Burma during the dry season of 1943–44.

In May 1943, at the Trident Conference, the Combined Chiefs of Staff decided, as a matter of first priority, to raise the tonnage of the airlift to China to 7,000 tons a month by July and 10,000 tons by September, to undertake an advance into northern Burma during the dry weather of 1943–44 and to mount an amphibious operation for the capture of Akyab and other strategic points along the Arakan coast.[2] Auchinleck, who had succeeded Wavell as Commander-in-Chief in India in June, estimated early in July that, if the approved plans were to be carried out in full, the daily demand on the lines of communication to Assam would be some 4,300 against the existing capacity of 1,720 tons.

By further increasing the terminal and transfer capacities and improving the working of the railway systems to enable them to cope with heavier trains, by converting certain narrow gauge lines to metre gauge, by reducing the trains allotted to civil and industrial requirements by one train a day and by diverting to military use 54,000 tons of river shipping which was meeting civil needs, Auchinleck estimated that it was theoretically possible to increase the combined capacity of the rail and river routes to Assam to some 3,400 tons a day by the 1st November. By the end of August these changes were

---

[1] Major-General H. Roome had relieved Major-General R. L. Bond as Engineer-in-Chief on the 6th May 1943.

[2] See page 2.

well advanced. Work was also begun on increasing the capacity of the port of Chittagong from 800 to 1,200 tons a day by October/November 1943, and to 1,400 tons by February 1944. But, even with these very considerable improvements, the capacity of the communications to Assam was well below the theoretical requirements of the proposed operations and Auchinleck found that he had either to curtail their scope or severely reduce the tonnage available for the airlift.

At the end of July 1943 the main railway lines serving Calcutta were breached by the Damodar floods. This 'act of God' put back the date by which the capacity of the Assam lines of communication could reach 3,400 tons a day, delayed the construction of the airfields in north-east Assam and jeopardized the preparations for the offensives in north Burma and Arakan. Since full traffic could not be restored till December 1943, Auchinleck decided to move 5th and 7th Indian and 81st (W.A.) Divisions, which were to be concentrated by the end of the year in Arakan, by sea from Madras and Vizagapatam to Chittagong.[1] But the breaches in the railways had halved the supply of coal to Calcutta and there was none available from there for the shipping required for this move. It could not be supplied by the railways, whose stocks of coal had been reduced to the dangerously low level of twelve days' supply owing to the partial isolation by floods of the Bengal–Bihar coalfields.[2] On the 10th August he asked the War Office to send five shiploads of bunker coal from South Africa. The necessary shipping was diverted, the coal arrived and the move of the divisions to Chittagong took place.

There was, however, no way out as far as the Assam lines of communication were concerned, and by the middle of August Auchinleck reported that by March 1944 the lift to Assam would have fallen short of the desired amount by 128,000 tons. Even if the strictest economy were exercised, the deficit could be reduced by only 20,000 tons. Since major improvements entailing extensive engineering work, such as doubling railway tracks and enlarging the capacity of river ports, could not have any effect much before the autumn of 1944, the only solution lay in trying to improve the operational efficiency of the Assam railways and in introducing night navigation on the river.

An examination of the problem showed that, though with American help some small increase in the capacity could be made, a large overall deficiency would still remain. Auchinleck therefore advocated the adoption of a defensive rôle on the Assam frontier and the concentration of all administrative and engineering resources, surplus to the needs of the airlift to China, on making major improvements

---

[1] See Map 10, page 384.
[2] See Map 14, page 452.

in the lines of communication so that a full scale offensive could be launched in 1944–45. He suggested, as Wavell had before him, that the proper military course was to avoid wasting effort on such an unprofitable objective as northern Burma and to concentrate on preparations for a seaborne offensive against Japanese-held territory further south.

Meanwhile, in order that India could be prepared as a base to support offensive action by land and sea in 1944–45, Auchinleck had ordered a re-examination of his long-term administrative plans, and on the 7th August had issued a directive giving the data on which it was to be carried out. Plans were to be drawn up to enable India to handle the shipping required to launch a major amphibious operation and to receive, maintain, accommodate and train during 1944–45 a force equivalent to twenty-five divisions as well as those formations and units held for internal security and the defence of the North West Frontier.[1] The R.A.F. requirements for these forces, including coastal reconnaissance but excluding internal security, totalled 146 squadrons and 20 squadrons of the Fleet Air Arm, for which shore accommodation in Ceylon had to be found. He also directed that, until more definite figures were available, plans were to be prepared to increase the capacity of the Assam lines of communication to 6,300 tons a day, and to enlarge the capacity of the ports so that they could handle the despatch of an expeditionary force needing some sixty personnel ships, one hundred store ships and tankers and some fifteen hundred landing craft of various types, maintain the expeditionary force overseas and deal with the normal flow of imports and exports.

Early in September Auchinleck received the long-term planning committee's report called for by his directive of the 7th August. It showed not only that there were limiting factors in the supply of Indian manpower, of accommodation for men and stores and in movement and transport facilities, but that the number and capacity of the Indian ports were insufficient to keep the exports and imports needed to maintain India's war production and economy at a level which would enable her to provide a secure base, and at the same time launch and maintain amphibious operations on the scale envisaged. The committee said that three or four of the divisions earmarked for amphibious operations would have to by-pass India,

---

[1] The twenty-five divisions included two tank brigades, seven Indian and three Chinese divisions, two L.R.P. brigades, one brigade of the Burma Army and one parachute brigade, all for operations in Burma; eight and two-thirds amphibious divisions, two airborne divisions, and one armoured and one infantry division for the expeditionary force; and one brigade for the defence of Ceylon. There were in addition sixty-seven battalions for internal security and fifty-seven battalions and four armoured regiments for the defence of the North West Frontier.

and that the expeditionary force overseas would have to be main-tained partly by direct shipment from bases outside India. Urgent action would have to be taken to obtain additional broad gauge locomotives, develop road and rail approaches to the existing ports, increase the capacity of the ports themselves and, so as to ease the load on the railways, develop a number of smaller ports for use by assault craft and coastal shipping. Finally it showed that unless provisioning and other administrative action was taken at once, India could not be ready by the 1st October 1944, the date given for long-term planning to be put into effect.

On the 14th September Auchinleck told the Chiefs of Staff that work to enable India to maintain overseas the forces required for 'Anakim' was well advanced. He said that the two groups of opera-tions contemplated at Quadrant would, including the necessary reserves held in India, require the equivalent of 25 divisions, 146 R.A.F. squadrons and 20 Fleet Air Arm squadrons. Assuming that five divisions would go direct to the operational area from some other theatre, or would enter India only in replacement of others which had already gone overseas, the country would have to handle a total of twenty divisions as well as the air forces. Since a full examination of India's potential as a base might reveal that forces of this magnitude could not be handled, or handled only under certain conditions, he asked whether he could assume that the forces he had enumerated could be taken as a firm basis for administrative planning. Further, to ensure that long-term administrative projects would be closely correlated with the operations contemplated for 1944–45, he asked for an up-to-date operational forecast on which he could safely base his future administrative plans.

The Chiefs of Staff agreed to the forces as proposed with the alteration that the air forces would be increased to 154 R.A.F. and 30 Fleet Air Arm squadrons. Naval forces required for the amphi-bious operations would be based mainly on Ceylon, East Africa and western Australia. India would therefore be called on to provide for only minor naval requirements at Madras in addition to the amphi-bious training establishments in southern India. In view of India's precarious economic situation and the doubt whether she could cope with all the forces which might have to be based on her, they said that they would examine forthwith the possibility of using bases in East Africa and possibly western Australia so as to reduce the load.

Towards the end of October the Government of India reported to the India Office that not only were the demands likely to be made on India to implement the long-term plans under consideration beyond her ability, but that the continuance of the strain on her economy for another two years, even at the existing level, would in all probability lead to serious consequences. To ensure that the contemplated operations were not hindered or even frustrated by a collapse of India's internal economy, they recommended that measures should be taken without delay to relieve the existing dangerous situation and provide safeguards for the future.

These measures, they said, fell into two categories: the first designed to counter the menace of inflation and restrict or absorb surplus purchasing power in India, and the second to ensure that further demands on India for services and supplies for war purposes were reduced to safe limits. The first category therefore included the importation of specific consumer goods for the civil population, stores sufficient to absorb at least half of the purchasing power of the Allied troops coming into the country and enough silver to cover the pay and allowances of Allied troops, which should be restricted for American as well as Dominion troops. The second category included recommendations that sufficient transportation (by road, rail and river as well as by coastal shipping) should be reserved for civil use to maintain the country's internal economy and production at a reasonable level; that military demands from overseas on indigenous production of articles in short supply and essential to the civil population should be placed elsewhere; that India's existing volume of war production should not be exceeded; and that demands for supplies in 1945 should be drastically curtailed. They asked that these measures should be accepted in principle at the earliest possible date so that detailed proposals could be made. The Secretary of State for India replied on the 11th November that the proposals had been placed before a ministerial committee studying the Indian financial situation and were assured of urgent and sympathetic consideration. He asked for an estimate of the rolling stock, locomotives, ships, etc. required beyond those already on order, and for a clearer definition of the phrase 'to maintain India's internal economy and production capacity at suitable levels'. The problems involved were so complicated and had such wide repercussions that it was to be a long time before any action could be taken.

The fact that India's internal economy was reaching breaking point was shown only too clearly during the autumn of 1943 when hoarding of grain and other commodities became prevalent. This, coupled with a partial failure of the main crops, caused famine in various parts of India. Bengal, where the staple food was rice, was the most affected. Matters became so serious that at the end of October the Viceroy had to ask for military aid to relieve distress. Auchinleck appointed Lieut.-General A.G.O.M. Mayne as Supreme Military Liaison Officer between the Bengal Government and the military authorities, and Major-General A. V. T. Wakely as Director of Movement of Civil Supplies working under the Bengal Government, to organize the collection and transport of supplies to main distribution centres in Bengal. A field organization, under command of Major-General D. Stuart, was set up to assist the civil authorities to distribute supplies throughout the area and to provide medical relief.[1] Within a fortnight these measures began to show promising results. Though the situation was still serious, the despatch of relief supplies to the affected areas had been doubled, public confidence in the ability of the authorities to cope with the situation had been partly restored and the price of food grains and other foodstuffs had fallen substantially. But it was to be months before the situation returned to normal.

The problem of increasing the capacity of the lines of communication to Assam was also examined during the autumn by the civil and military transportation authorities in accordance with Auchinleck's directive of the 7th, as amended by the directive to the Supreme Commander of the 21st August.[2] The examination was based on the estimated load by the end of 1944 and on the assumption that the British oil pipelines already in hand would be completed in 1944, and that those authorized at Quadrant would, when completed, supply the Ledo Road and its eventual extension into China. The estimated load was: stores, 1,800 tons a day for Air Transport Command, 3,000 for the Ledo Road and 2,500 for the Imphal Road, making a total of 7,300 tons a day; oil, 1,200 tons a day for use by Air Transport Command at airfields in north-east Assam and 500 tons from Chittagong to the southern end of the pipeline at Chandranthpur, pending the construction of a pipeline between these two points, making a total of 9,000 tons a day.[3]

The river route could not be easily developed since the extra vessels required could neither be produced in India nor be provided from elsewhere in time. It was therefore planned to load it only to its existing capacity (1,500 tons of stores and 300 tons of oil a day from Calcutta and 300 tons of bulk oil from Dhubri to Dibrugarh and Neamati) and to expand the capacity of the Parbatipur–Tinsukia railway from its existing capacity of 3,400 tons a day to 6,900 tons (5,800 tons of stores and 1,100 tons of oil). This involved increasing the train paths from the existing fourteen to twenty-nine a day each way between Parbatipur and Dimapur, and to twenty-two beyond Dimapur to Mariani. To make this possible it was proposed that the broad gauge line southwards and the metre gauge line eastwards from Parbatipur should be doubled, and general improvements made in railway equipment and terminal facilities. It was also proposed that a bridge should be built over the Brahmaputra River at Amingaon and that the Assam Access Road from Siliguri to

---

[1] It included a brigade headquarters, eight battalions, a number of medical units and about one hundred medical and hygiene officers.

[2] See Appendix 1.

[3] See Sketch 12, page 328, and Appendix 5.

Jogighopa should be completed so that the number of transhipment points on the existing route could be reduced and time and manpower saved. Some 4,400 tons a day would, however, still have to be transferred from the broad gauge to the metre gauge at Parbatipur and, in order to act as a buffer and avoid delays to both systems, a transit establishment capable of handling this tonnage with storage accommodation for fifteen days (88,000 tons) would have to be built there.

These plans for the development of the Assam railways called for large quantities of steel, railway stores and equipment and the allocation of considerable engineering resources and labour, all of which were scarce. It was evident that they could not be carried out all at once and that it would be a long time before results could be expected. The development programme was therefore divided into two stages: the first, to be completed by October 1944, giving an estimated capacity of 4,400 tons a day; the second, to be completed by January 1946, to bring the capacity to the Combined Chiefs of Staffs' target of 7,300 tons a day.[1]

Meanwhile the capacity of the Assam lines of communication which by the end of October had reached 3,200 tons a day was clearly insufficient to meet the demands of the airlift and operation 'Tarzan', as well as to overcome the backlog caused by the Damodar floods. Since the contemplated long-term improvement would provide only 4,400 tons a day by October 1944, and no further increase of any sort could be expected till February 1944 when the completion of the pipeline from Chandranathpur to Dimapur would free train paths, some means had to be found of making an immediate increase in the capacity.

At Quadrant the United States Chiefs of Staff had offered to place some American railway units at the disposal of the Supreme Commander for use on the Assam railways. After discussion in September and early October, the War Office and General Auchinleck agreed that these railway units would be most welcome provided that they worked under the existing central control of the Indian railways. But, in view of possible political repercussions and the confusion inherent in a change-over, which might temporarily reduce the capacity, they asked that the units should be held in reserve till the end of the 1943–44 operational season, when the whole matter of the operation of the Assam railways would be reviewed. They could then be introduced if necessary.

During the conference at Chungking between Mountbatten and the Generalissimo early in October,[2] Somervell had expressed his conviction that the Assam lines of communication were capable of an

[1] See Appendix 5.
[2] See pages 11-13.

immediate increase and had held out hopes to the Generalissimo that the airlift would reach a total of 13,000 tons a month by April 1944. On the 23rd October an inter-command (S.E.A.C.–India) meeting was held to consider Somervell's proposals for achieving this increase. Somervell said that he was prepared to send 5,500 American railway troops by passenger ship immediately, and proposed that the Assam railway should be militarized from Parbatipur to Tinsukia. The improved operation of the railway under military control, together with a number of minor proposals for reorganizing the handling of goods at the ferries and a departure from the normal commercial methods of running, should, he thought, result in increasing the capacity by 500 tons a day almost immediately, working up to an eventual 2,700 tons a day. This would bring the total to 5,900 tons a day without having to undertake the proposed large engineering programme. The immediate increase of 500 tons a day in the capacity of the railway would make a further 5,000 tons a month available for the airlift, and the figures he had mentioned to the Generalissimo would then be reached without interference with the contemplated operations.

Mountbatten said that in view of the grave issues involved he would have to press for a fifty per cent. increase in the capacity of the railway by the 1st April 1944 and that, unless the Indian authorities could guarantee such an increase, he would have to recommend that the railways forward of Parbatipur should be operated by the Americans, who were confident that the increase in capacity could be achieved. Auchinleck agreed to investigate, with the help of experts from Britain and America, the way in which part of the Assam railway could be handed over to the control of the American units, the date by which the additional 500 tons a day could be carried, the possibility of a fifty per cent. increase by the 1st April 1944 and the necessity for American help to overcome weak links in the system.

Before this examination was completed further discussions with the Indian railway authorities and Mountbatten's staff took place, and on the 5th November Auchinleck told the Chiefs of Staff that he had come to the conclusion that the introduction of American control during the operational season need not cause dislocation and that he was now satisfied that, if it were introduced gradually, discontent among railway staff could be avoided. He was impressed, he said, by Somervell's guarantee and therefore recommended, as did the Government of India, that the American offer should be accepted and the troops moved as soon as possible. On the 14th November the offer was accepted; a week later Washington told the Chiefs of Staff that the railway units and their equipment would sail from the United States on the 10th December and that an advance party of fifteen officers would be flown to India.

Map 3

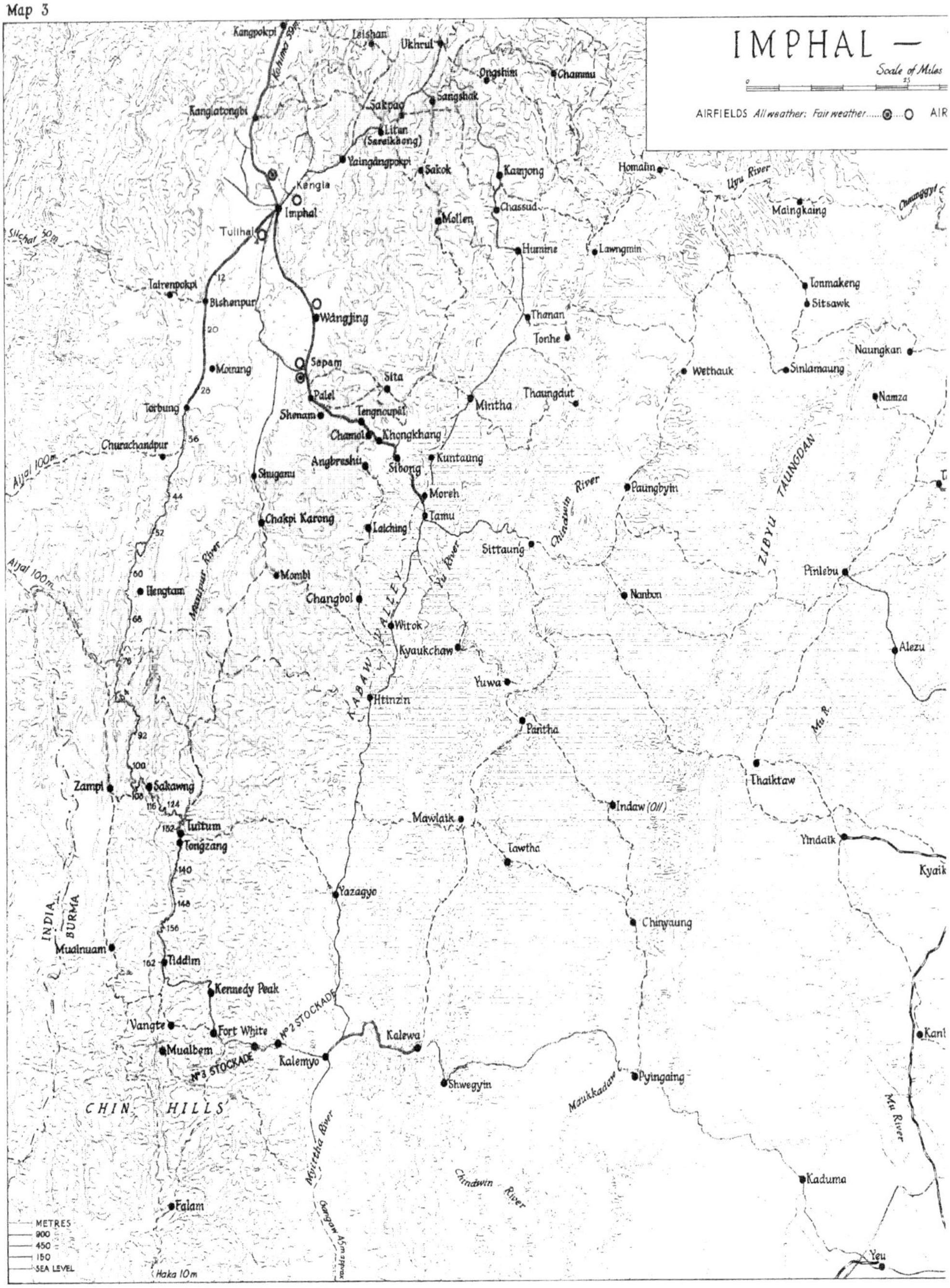

IMPHAL —

Scale of Miles

AIRFIELDS *All weather; Fair weather*......◎ O   AIR

Kangpokpi
Leisham
Ukhrul
Ongshim
Chamu
Kanglatongbi
Sakpao
Sangshak
Litan (Sareikhong)
Yaingangpokpi
Sakok
Kamjong
Homalin
Kangla
Tulihal
Imphal
Mollen
Chassud
Maingkaing
Humine
Lawngmin
Tatrenpokpi
12
Bishenpur
Wangjing
Tonmakeng
Sitsawk
20
Mbrang
Thanan
Wethauk
Sinlamaung
Naungkan
Sepam
26
Palel
Sita
Tengnoupal
Mintha
Thaungdut
Namza
Torbung
Shenam
Khongkhang
Kuntaung
Churachandpur
56
Chamol
Angbreshti
Sibong
Moreh
Paungbyin
Shugunu
44
Chakpi Karong
Laiching
Tamu
Sittaung
Pinlebu
52
Mombi
Changbol
Sittaung
Nankon
60
Hengtam
Witok
Kyaukchaw
Yuwa
Alezu
66
Httnzin
76
Paritha
Thaiktaw
92
Mawlaik
Indaw (Oil)
Yindaik
100
Zampi
Sakawng
Mualnuam
124
Tuitum
Tawtha
Kyaik
152
Tongzang
140
Yazagyo
Chinyaung
148
156
Tiddim
162
Kennedy Peak
No 2 STOCKADE
Vangte
Fort White
Kalewa
Kani
Mualbem
Kalemyo
No 3 STOCKADE
Shwegyin
Pyingaing
CHIN HILLS
Kaduma
METRES
900
450
150
SEA LEVEL
Falam
Haka 10 m
Yeu

INDIA
BURMA

KABAW VALLEY
ZIBYU TAUNGDAN
Chindwin River
Myittha River
Manipur River
Silchat 50 m
Aijal 100 m
Ugu River
Ma R.
Ma River

BHAMO

Myitkyina 26 miles

Myitkyina 55 miles

B A N G A W   R A N G E

Mansi

Meza River

Namkyaing

Aberdeen

Manhton

Pinbon

Nami

Nansiang

White City

Mawlu

Banmauk

Alegyun

Tonlon

Pinwe

aungmaw

Indaw

Naba

Katha

Legyin

Meza

Padeingon

Bongyaung

Pegon

Nankan

Aikma

Wuntho

Inywa

Chowringhee

Asugyi

Tawma

Tigyaing

Shweli R.

Hintha

Yanbo

Hintha C.

Taunggon

Hehtin C.

thin

Hinthaw

Hmaingdaing

Salin C.

Mabein

Tagaung

Baw

Htang Gyang

Molo

Man Mawk

Nayok

Kodaung Hill Tracts

Baw

Irrawaddy River

Alam Pan

Manton

Myitson

Pago

Nam Mte

Nabu

Mongmit

Mala

Mogok

Tantabin

Thabeikkyin

Shwebo 6m

alu

K A

Mohnyin

Kadu

Mawhan

Sinbo

Broadway

Kaukkwe R.

Namti

Piccadilly

Okkye

Irrawaddy River

Shwegu

Nahpaw

Sinaapa

Nalong

Templecombe

H I L L S

Taping R.

Myothit

Bham

Sinlumkaba

Kam Gintawng

H I L L S

Namhkam

Sikaw

Si-u

Stami River

K A C H I N

50

CHAPTER III

THE INDIAN ARMY PREPARES

FOR 1943-1944

(September – November 1943)

See Maps 2, 3, 10 and 14 and Sketch 12

WHILE operations were being planned and measures taken to prepare India as a base and improve the line of communications to the north-east frontier, General Auchinleck was preparing the Army in India for its coming offensive rôle. He knew that before any offensive could be launched the morale of the Army in India, which had been badly shaken by the failures in Arakan,[1] would have to be restored. He reorganized and enlarged the Intelligence School at Karachi,[2] which had up to that time concentrated on the study of the German and Italian armies more than of the Japanese. He appointed as Commandant, Colonel G. T. Wards, an officer who had a thorough knowledge of Japanese organization and training and who spoke their language and understood their mentality. Before long, trained intelligence officers with an up-to-date knowledge of Japanese methods were posted to formations in contact with the enemy and, for the first time since 1941, information from enemy sources could be properly collated.

Auchinleck ordered the recommendations of the Infantry Committee, India, to be put into effect so as to bring the training of British and Indian infantry to the necessary high standard, and to ensure that a flow of properly trained reinforcements was available to replace casualties from sickness or enemy action.[3] He impressed on all commanders of formations in contact with the enemy the importance of constant patrolling and the need to organize carefully-planned raids and ambushes in order to give the troops confidence and a sense of moral superiority over the Japanese and to kill the myth of Japanese invincibility, bred of the enemy's hitherto unbroken record of success. Before being sent to the front, all new formations which had not been in action were given battle training in jungle warfare under realistic conditions.

---

[1] See Volume II, Chapter XX.
[2] See Map 10, page 384.
[3] This committee sat in June 1943. See Volume II, Chapter XXIII.

More was needed, however, than training and the building-up of confidence to restore the morale of the army. Soldiers who are not physically fit or who are discontented with their lot have no stomach for battle. Auchinleck therefore began to improve the welfare, health and feeding of the army.

During 1942 the welfare of both British and Indian troops had perforce been somewhat neglected. Yet with soldiers of any nationality separated from their families and often employed on boring and uncongenial tasks away from the scene of action, sometimes in lonely and depressing surroundings, properly organized welfare services are of particular importance. British troops in India, far from their homes and their families, had begun to feel they were part of a forgotten army, while Indian troops were unsettled by the deterioration of the economic situation and consequent inflation which made it difficult for their families to meet the cost of living. The lot of the former could be bettered only by an improvement in the welfare services and by the introduction of some scheme whereby men who had been long away from Britain could be sent home and replaced by others, the lot of the latter by an adjustment of pay and allowances designed to meet the changed economic conditions, and by additional welfare facilities. By August 1943 welfare officers had been appointed to all formations and most of the larger units, and great efforts had been made to organize supplies of such items as books, games, sports gear and gramophones, to establish canteens and leave centres and to arrange concert parties and the showing of films. Voluntary organizations also gave devoted service to improve the lot of the soldier. The important work of family welfare was organized by a special staff of the S.S.A.F.A. which included a legal aid section set up in Calcutta. A scheme, introduced in 1942, whereby British troops could be sent back to Britain as shipping permitted after five years abroad, was brought up-to-date and speeded up. An increase in the pay of Indian troops was authorized towards the end of the year. By the time that S.E.A.C. was set up much had been accomplished with the very meagre resources then available, but much still remained to be done.

The maintenance of health in the forward areas and on the lines of communication was a pressing problem, since the exigencies of the campaign made it necessary for men to live and fight in malarial and typhus-infected areas. Added to this, dysentery was endemic and the heat and humidity of the monsoon aggravated the prevalent skin diseases. During the monsoon of 1943 for every wounded man of the Eastern Army admitted to hospital there were one hundred and twenty sick. Hospitals were overcrowded, doctors and nurses were overworked and none could be spared from other theatres of war. Both equipment and drugs required for the suppression of malaria were scarce. During the summer and autumn of 1943 much was done to reduce the incidence of disease: anti-malarial discipline was tightened up and, in areas where malaria was endemic, specially trained units carried out anti-malarial measures at staging points along the lines of communication and at hospitals, depots and reinforcement camps.[1] These measures, together with increased supplies of improved suppressive drugs, appreciably reduced the incidence of malaria but disease remained a more deadly foe than the enemy until 1944 when the measures adopted produced their full results.

The feeding of the vastly expanded army was a highly complex problem. Not only were there inadequate reserves of foodstuffs in the country, but the army and its huge non-combatant labour force composed of men of diverse race, caste and religion, often subject to stringent restrictions as to what they could eat, could have no standard ration scale. Moreover, the many different types of rations had to be sent over vast distances to Assam and eastern Bengal. Theoretically the ration scales were adequate, but the difficulties of supplying meat, eggs and vegetables resulted in substitutes being used and the actual ration was often unappetizing and monotonous. A diet of pumpkin, bully beef and soya link (an unpalatable sausage with a high content of soya bean meal, which was the invariable substitute for commodities in short supply) is calculated to try the constitution and temper of even the toughest soldier.

The most difficult problem was to ensure the supply of fresh meat to the troops on the north-east frontier. Train loads of cattle, sheep and goats were at first sent to the Assam and Arakan fronts from central India, but the distance involved, the unavoidable transfer from one train to another at the break of gauge and, in places, the long trek by road made the delivery of sufficient numbers in good condition so infrequent that this method had to be abandoned. To feed the British troops, arrangements were then made to import frozen meat from Australia and New Zealand, for which cold storage space was requisitioned in Calcutta. Plans were made to provide cold storage plants, fed by refrigerated rail and motor trucks, at key points on the lines of communication and in the forward areas. But before an efficient distribution scheme could be organized the problem was solved by air transport as it became available in 1944. To meet the requirements of the Indian troops, plants for the dehydration of suitable meat were set up and some dehydrated meats imported, but the supply did not meet the demand. Vegetables were grown and duck farms established in the forward areas to provide fresh vegetables and eggs, particularly for hospitals.

---

[1] Mobile malaria treatment units established close behind the forward divisions avoided light cases having to be sent to casualty clearing stations and so being struck off the strength of their units. This system ensured that men returned to their units with the minimum of delay.

Early in September 1943 Auchinleck set to work to create Special
Force (the name given to the L.R.P. organization to be under Wingate's command).[1] He estimated that, allowing for a tenth of the
infantry from 70th British Division proving unsuitable for L.R.P.
duties, there would be a deficiency of about one thousand men after
the transfer of all nine battalions together with their available reinforcements. He therefore proposed to transfer to L.R.P. duties one
battalion (7th Leicesters) from elsewhere in India, convert one
artillery regiment of the division to infantry and to call for volunteers
from other British units, keeping the remaining two artillery regiments of the division intact to meet the operational requirements of
his active corps. In telling the War Office and Air Ministry of these
proposals, he asked the former to send to India thirty staff officers,
sixty-four engineer and fifty infantry officers and one hundred and
fifty signals officers and men, and the latter to send two hundred and
fifty officers and men to work the R.A.F. wireless sets required by the
L.R.P. organization.

The War Office replied that requests for officers and men from
the United Kingdom had already been made by Wingate, then in
London, and would in general be complied with. Wingate had told
them that a proportion of men in the two existing L.R.P. brigades
would have to be replaced; they had also learnt (presumably again
from Wingate) that most of the infantry of 70th Division was not up
to the required physical standard, but that the artillery and armoured
corps units not immediately required for current operations contained a large proportion of high category men. Since the most
important rôle in the reduced campaign for 1944 was that of the
L.R.P. forces, they should have the best troops from the first. Therefore, though the War Office appreciated Auchinleck's desire to keep
artillery units for other purposes, they instructed him to make the
entire division available for selection for L.R.P. duties.

Auchinleck assured the War Office that every effort was being
made to produce an efficient L.R.P. force. He pointed out that the
information given them about the 70th Division was incorrect: it had
considerable battle experience and the standard of its infantry was
high. Moreover, he said, the War Office had entirely failed to
appreciate the situation since, quite apart from the formations
required for amphibious operations whose scope was not yet settled,
at least six divisions supported by armour would be operating in
addition to Wingate's force. He thus implied that he could employ
all the artillery and armoured units that were available, and that he
wished to keep them intact.

Nevertheless, in accordance with his instructions, he placed the
whole of 70th Division and 7th Leicesters at the disposal of Special

[1] See pages 5-6.

Force. After the transfer of all those considered fit for the arduous duties in an L.R.P. group, it was found by October that there would still be a deficiency of 1,850 men. To make this good, Auchinleck transferred another British battalion (2nd Duke of Wellington's), some 600 men from static anti-aircraft units and two armoured regiments (26th Hussars and 163rd R.A.C.).[1] He also agreed to volunteers, particularly officers, being accepted from all British units throughout India for service in Special Force. These transfers were in addition to the three battalions drafted to 77th Brigade after its return from operations in Burma. The raising of Special Force, on the scale demanded by Wingate and approved by the Chiefs of Staff, thus cost India Command one complete British division, eight other major units (the numerical equivalent of nearly another division) and many volunteers from units throughout the army in India. Some 200 officers and nearly 400 specialists had also to be sent from the United Kingdom.

Wingate, now promoted to Major-General, returned to India on the 16th September. He immediately set to work to organize Special Force (3rd Indian Division). The time was short and he threw himself into his task with his usual energy. It was far from easy for him to get what he wanted since many of the specialists as well as the stores he required were scarce and there was a long delay in the arrival of the new weapons which he had been promised while in the United States. He had, too, to overcome the natural disinclination on the part of General and Air Headquarters, India, to feed into a force, enlarged on orders from London far beyond what they considered necessary or advisable, reserves which were badly needed by 14th Army for the forthcoming operations. Wingate's insistence that in his force and his alone lay hope of victory, his disparaging remarks on the value of normally organized infantry, armoured and para-chute formations, his brusque manner often bordering on rudeness and even insubordination and his reiterated complaints that his plans were being deliberately baulked, tended to make enemies of those who were doing their best to co-operate with him. This did not ease his task. Yet by his drive and importunity he organized and trained Special Force in the short time available, despite an attack of typhoid fever which laid him low for some weeks.

The new British contribution to Special Force was concentrated in the Central Provinces by the 25th October and was joined by 3rd (W.A.) Brigade on the 15th November. An intensive training pro-gramme was then arranged to ensure that 16th, 77th and 111th

---

[1] In order to free two units for L.R.P. duties, 251st Indian Tank Brigade was disbanded. The 5th Horse (Probyn's) and 9th Royal Deccan Horse replaced 26th Hussars and 163rd R.A.C. in 255th Indian Armoured Brigade (part of 44th Indian Armoured Division), and 3rd Carabiniers was transferred to 254th Indian Tank Brigade.

Brigades would be ready for operations by the 15th January 1944 and the remaining brigades (14th, 23rd and 3rd West African) by the 15th April. Much of the special equipment ordered by Wingate before he returned to India did not, however, reach the force till the three leading brigades had arrived in Assam in January 1944.[1]

At Quadrant, on Mountbatten's suggestion, the American Chiefs of Staff had agreed to form an L.R.P. group.[2] They had also promised to raise a special air unit to assist in the maintenance of L.R.P. groups and increase their mobility by providing an airlift for them over difficult country where there was no tactical advantage in surface penetration. The L.R.P. unit—5307th Composite Unit (Provisional) —which became known as 'Merrill's Marauders' after its commander Brigadier-General F. D. Merrill, arrived in India at the end of October and began to train with Wingate's force, although it was not incorporated in it. The special air unit, which became known as No. 1 Air Commando, was formed early in September. It was a self-contained unit equipped with helicopters and gliders in addition to fighter, bomber, transport and light aircraft.[3] It was due to be concentrated and ready for operations in India by the end of 1943.

The maintenance by air of L.R.P. brigades operating deep in the centre of Burma, and possibly of an isolated division in the Indaw–Katha area, set India Command a number of administrative problems.[4] Air supply during the retreat from Burma had depended largely on improvisation. An air supply unit had been hurriedly formed from Army Service Corps and Pioneer units. Working in close co-operation with 31 Squadron R.A.F. and 2 Troop Carrier Squadron U.S.A.A.F., and using the small stock of parachutes available, it had fed and maintained refugees leaving Burma and part of V Chinese Army withdrawing to India. This scratch organization had then been used to maintain outlying detachments whose land communications had been cut by the 1942 monsoon.

As a result of the lessons learnt on these pioneering operations, India Command began towards the end of 1942 to improve supply dropping equipment and in December formed an Air Supply Training Centre at Chaklala (near Rawalpindi) to raise and train air supply units from the R.I.A.S.C., modelled on the earlier improvised unit. No. 1 Air Supply Company, R.I.A.S.C., was ready in time to form part of the organization which maintained 77th (L.R.P.)

---

[1] This equipment included Piats (projectors infantry anti-tank) and flame throwers.
[2] See Volume II, Chapter XXVI.
[3] No. 1 Air Commando consisted of thirty (P. 51) Mustang fighter-bombers, twelve (B. 25) Mitchell medium bombers, thirteen (C. 47) Dakotas and twelve (C. 46) Commando transport aircraft, one hundred (L. 5) light aircraft, six helicopters and two-hundred and twenty-five gliders.
[4] See Map 3, page 33.

Brigade during its operations in northern Burma in the spring of 1943.[1]

The function of an air supply company was to receive stores at the airfield, pack them in special containers, stow them (with parachutes attached) in the aircraft and, in co-operation with the aircrews, eject them over the dropping zone. A number of these units were raised during 1943 and by the autumn five were stationed at airfields in eastern Bengal. The 10th U.S.A.A.F. simultaneously set up a similar organization under the United States Services of Supply, consisting of air supply detachments at base airfields in Assam with central control at Dinjan.[2] British and American organizations, however, worked separately under their own administrative services.

As the operations contemplated for 1943–44 depended largely on air supply, it was evident that a very large number of parachutes would be required. On the 1st October 1943 Auchinleck estimated that 92,500 standard 18-foot parachutes would be needed each month up to the end of 1943, rising to 132,000 in January and 200,000 in February 1944.[3] The production of parachutes in India had begun on a small scale in 1941 but by October 1943 only some 35,000 a month were being turned out. It was believed that, at the expense of the civil economy, this output could be increased to some 65,000 a month by February 1944. If a large number of sewing machines were imported and considerable inroads made into the supply of cotton for civil requirements (which would aggravate the existing inflationary tendencies) the output could be raised to only some 132,000 by the end of March. Indigenous production, even if pushed to the utmost limits, could not therefore meet the foreseeable demands and, if the operations were to be carried out, parachutes would have to be obtained from elsewhere, but Auchinleck was told by the War Office on the 30th October that the prospect of obtaining them in any quantity from sources outside India was remote. Mountbatten thereupon took the matter up with the Chiefs of Staff and, since India's production would fall short of requirements for the period from November 1943 to June 1944 by some 700,000 (including a reserve of 300,000), he asked them to explore every possible external source and to cancel the contracts India had entered into to supply parachutes to the Middle East and elsewhere overseas.[4] As a result of his appeal, some 68,000 parachutes were supplied from the

---

[1] See Volume II, Chapter XVIII.

[2] See Sketch 12, page 328.

[3] Approximately twenty 18-foot cotton parachutes were required to drop one ton of stores.

[4] On the initiative of 14th Army an order was placed in February 1944 for 175,000 18-foot parachutes made of hessian instead of cotton (known as parajutes) and in March for 100,000 of an improved type. Both orders were completed by May, but the parajutes did not prove to be entirely satisfactory, especially in wet weather; they were therefore held as an emergency reserve.

United Kingdom and Canada. Although there were at times local shortages, the anticipated overall shortage did not materialize, for demands for parachutes fell short of the estimated figures and production in India was stepped up from 61,000 in January to 231,000 in December 1944, the total production over the year being 1.9 million.

During the autumn of 1943 Auchinleck made a number of changes in the organization and distribution of his forces and in the chain of command within India. Plans, based on the experience of the Arakan campaign of 1942–43, were made to alter once again the composition of the Indian divisions. A divisional headquarters defence battalion was to be introduced in place of divisional and brigade defence and employment platoons; the brigade light reconnaissance battalions in a light division were to be replaced by one divisional light reconnaissance battalion; one artillery regiment in each division was to be reorganized as a jungle field regiment, and equipped with 3.7-inch howitzers and 3-inch mortars, to give artillery support to the infantry in places where 25-pounder guns could not be used. Vehicles with less mobility than four-wheel drive 15 cwt. trucks were to be eliminated and the total number reduced to a minimum, only those which were required for the transport of essential fighting equipment being retained. Changes affecting the type and weight of equipment, the number and grouping of troops and the ranks of junior commanders were proposed for many formations and units.[1]

In preparation for the establishment of S.E.A.C. and the policy of relieving the Commander-in-Chief in India of responsibility for operations, Eastern Army was abolished on the 15th October. The 14th Army, under command of General Slim, was formed and took over its operational tasks and the security of Assam and Bengal east of the Meghna River. Eastern Command, India, was revived, under command of General Mayne, and became responsible for the internal security of Bihar, Orissa and Bengal west of the Meghna River. The 14th Army was eventually to be subordinate to S.E.A.C. through 11th Army Group, commanded by General Giffard.[2]

Meanwhile, as the monsoon abated, land and air activity had increased all along the north-eastern frontier. On the Arakan front, 7th Indian Division (Major-General F. W. Messervy) had relieved 26th Indian Division by the end of September and was disposed with

---

[1] See Appendix 6.
[2] The 11th Army Group was to be formed in Delhi at the same time as S.E.A.C. Headquarters was established.

114th Brigade (Brigadier M. R. Roberts) in the Kalapanzin valley and 89th Brigade (Brigadier J. C. Martin) west of the Mayu Range.[1] On the 1st November, Headquarters XV Corps (Lieut.-General A. F. P. Christison) assumed control of operations in Arakan,[2] and 5th Indian Division (Major-General H. R. Briggs) began, on the 9th, to take over the front west of the Mayu Range from 7th Division, which then concentrated in the Kalapanzin valley. The leading brigades of 5th and 7th Divisions steadily infiltrated forward and by mid-November were in contact with the Japanese outposts on a general line from Zeganbyin across the range to the point where the Ngakyedauk Chaung joins the Kalapanzin River, four miles south of Taung Bazar. Until a motor road had been built across Ngakyedauk Pass, 7th Division could be supplied only by pack mule across Goppe Pass and by sampan down the Kalapanzin River, and had to leave all its field artillery and motor transport west of the Mayu Range. As soon therefore as 5th Division began to arrive and there was adequate strength to defend the pass, work on the construction of this road began.

On the Central front, 20th Indian Division (Gracey), which had been relieved by 11th East African (E.A.) Division in Ceylon and concentrated at Ranchi, began to arrive in IV Corps area in October and relieved 23rd Indian Division (Roberts). The 100th Brigade was disposed with a battalion at Mombi and the rest of the brigade in the Kabaw Valley south of Tamu. The 80th Brigade was along the Yu River east and north-east of Tamu.[3] The 32nd Brigade had not yet reached Assam. The move into the Kabaw Valley was not opposed by the Japanese who continued to hold their monsoon positions on the general line Yazagyo–Mawlaik. The 23rd Indian Division, on relief, concentrated at Imphal and became IV Corps reserve.

Early in October the Japanese began to advance into the Chin Hills. The Chin Hills Battalion delayed them as best it could but, although some of the Chin Levies remained staunch, others had to be disarmed and sent back to their villages. During the month 63rd Brigade (Brigadier A. E. Cumming, V.C.) obtained identifications in the Fort White–Kennedy Peak area which indicated that the Japanese had elements of at least two and possibly three regiments in the Kalemyo area. By the beginning of November the Japanese had occupied Haka and Falam and had established two strong-points within six miles of the Kennedy Peak–Fort White road, from which they could not be dislodged. Anxious about the security of

---

[1] See Map 2, page 5. One brigade of 26th Division remained temporarily under command of 7th Division till the arrival of 33rd Brigade (Brigadier F. J. Loftus-Tottenham) at the end of October. The 26th Division then became 14th Army Reserve.

[2] XV Corps was temporarily commanded by Lomax till the middle of November.

[3] See Map 3, page 33.

Fort White which lay at the end of a tenuous line of communication from Kennedy Peak running parallel with the southern end of the Kabaw Valley held by the Japanese, Cumming asked for an extra battalion and was sent one from 23rd Division. The 63rd Brigade was then disposed with two battalions in the Kennedy Peak area, one as a garrison to Fort White and one guarding the road to it from Kennedy Peak.

As soon as Scoones (IV Corps) realized that the Japanese advance into the Chin Hills area was in strength, he ordered Headquarters 17th Division and 48th Brigade to move forward from Shillong. Divisional headquarters reached Tiddim on the 10th November and the leading unit of 48th Brigade on the 15th. On the 13th, however, although an attack on Fort White was repulsed, strong enemy columns succeeded in establishing themselves on the track between Fort White and Kennedy Peak and could not be driven off. Early on the 14th Cumming ordered his forward troops to withdraw to the ridge between Vangte and Kennedy Peak, and the garrison of Fort White to withdraw across country that night. The withdrawals were unopposed and the enemy made no attempt to follow up.

On the Northern front a regiment of 38th Chinese Division, moving forward to cover the construction of the road to the Hukawng Valley, was held up at the end of October by advanced parties of a regiment of *18th Division* near the junction of the Tanai and Tarung Rivers, some twenty-four miles east of Shingbwiyang.[1] Although it drove in some of the Chinese outposts, an enemy counter-attack early in November failed and by the middle of the month there was a temporary stalemate on this front. In the Fort Hertz area the Kachin Levies began guerilla operations against Japanese outposts screening Myitkyina.

The situation on the north-eastern frontier when the Supreme Commander assumed control of operations on the 16th November was that on every sector of the 700-mile long front from Arakan to Fort Hertz the Allies were in contact with the enemy. In Arakan XV Corps was in the process of concentration and had three brigades (one of 5th and two of 7th Division) in close contact with the enemy outpost line. The 26th Division was in reserve, and 81st (W.A.) Division, less the brigade allotted to Special Force, was shortly to join the corps. On the Central front IV Corps had 17th Division in contact with the enemy in the Tiddim area, 20th Division in the Kabaw Valley and 23rd Division in reserve. On the Northern front, two regiments of 38th Chinese Division were in contact with the enemy sixty miles across the Burma border, with the remainder of the division and 22nd Chinese Division in reserve. Intelligence reports indicated that in mid-November the Japanese had five

---

[1] See Map 14, page 452. The Chindwin in its upper reaches is known as the Tanai River.

divisions deployed in Burma: *55th Division* on the Arakan front, *31st* and *33rd Divisions* on the Central front from Tamanthi to the Falam area, *18th Division* on the Northern front and *56th Division* on the Salween front.[1]

In the autumn of 1943 the Japanese air force still held the initiative and, so long as it remained based beyond the reach of Allied fighters and had a wide selection of forward airfields from which to operate, was free to choose both the time and place for its attacks. It was therefore a constant threat to the air route to China and could harass airfields, communications and other military objectives in Bengal and Assam.

The Allied air forces in north-east India had to protect all these targets and at the same time disrupt enemy communications in Burma, give close support to the land forces on a 700-mile front and provide air supply wherever needed. To do all these tasks required more aircraft than were available. They were handicapped by a warning system which was only partly effective since there were many places where the intervening mountains made radar warning impossible. If they were to succeed, it was clearly essential that the Japanese air force should first be neutralized. Operations to that end therefore became of first importance.

The Japanese decided to use their air force in Burma to neutralize, as far as possible, offensive action by the Allied air forces.[2] They gave priority to attacks on Allied air bases and airfields used by transport aircraft operating the India–China ferry route. Towards the end of October they began a series of raids, usually by some twenty bombers with fighter escort, against airfields in north-east India, such as Agartala, Feni, Kumbhirgram, Palel and Imphal. Later they attacked the docks at Chittagong and the line of communication to Arakan in the Bawli Bazar–Cox's Bazar area. Casualties and military damage were slight, but at some places civilian labour disappeared.

About the same time there was a considerable increase in enemy air reconnaissance over the Bay of Bengal, as well as by flying-boats over Ceylon and Madras and by photographic reconnaissance aircraft over north-east India at too high an altitude to be intercepted by Hurricanes. Early in November the first Spitfire fighters arrived from the United Kingdom and three of the Hurricane squadrons were re-armed with these aircraft. The first Spitfire squadron to become operational (615 Squadron) was moved forward to Chittagong

---

[1] The Japanese had in fact six divisions in Burma at this time for *54th Division* had arrived and was in the coastal area south of Akyab. A seventh division (*15th*) was beginning to move overland from Siam to join *15th Army*.

[2] For organization of the Japanese air force in Burma in November 1943 see Appendix 7.

and, within a week of arrival, intercepted and shot down three high-altitude reconnaissance aircraft. Thereafter enemy reconnaissance flights over southern Bengal ceased.

The early Spitfires were not equipped with long-range fuel tanks and their short range restricted them primarily to a defensive rôle.[1] Although their advent greatly strengthened the defence, the air situation still remained unsatisfactory and, when S.E.A.C. took over control of operations, neither side could claim air superiority, although the Allies considerably outnumbered the Japanese.

---

[1] It was not until early in 1944 that long-range fighters arrived in India—first American Lightnings (P.38) and Mustangs (P.51) and later British Beaufighters.

CHAPTER IV

SOUTH-EAST ASIA COMMAND
TAKES OVER
(November 1943)

See Maps 10 and 14

AT midnight on the 15th–16th November 1943 S.E.A.C. came formally into being at New Delhi and Acting-Admiral Lord Louis Mountbatten became Supreme Allied Commander, South-East Asia, taking over from General Sir Claude Auchinleck, the Commander-in-Chief in India, responsibility for the conduct of all operations against Japan which were based on India and Ceylon and within the boundaries of S.E.A.C.[1] By agreement between the Supreme Commander and the Government of India, Assam and Bengal east of the Meghna River were also temporarily placed under Mountbatten's operational control.[2]

Lieut.-General J. W. Stilwell (U.S. Army) was appointed Deputy Supreme Allied Commander; Admiral Sir James Somerville (Commander-in-Chief, Eastern Fleet), Naval Commander-in-Chief; General Sir George Giffard, Commander-in-Chief, 11th Army Group; and Air Chief Marshal Sir Richard Peirse, who had been the Air Officer Commanding-in-Chief, India, Air Commander-in-Chief. Although on paper this organization appears comparatively straightforward, there were in fact several anomalies and complications which tended to militate against its efficient working and against harmonious co-operation between its various components.

On becoming Deputy Supreme Allied Commander, Stilwell remained Chief of Staff to Generalissimo Chiang Kai-shek, a post he had held since 1942, as well as Commanding General of all United States land and air forces allotted to the China theatre, the Indian theatre and those which happened to be in Burma; an area designated by the Americans as the C.B.I. Theatre.[3] All orders to American forces in India, including 10th U.S.A.A.F., had therefore to be passed through him in the latter capacity. He was also commander of the Chinese forces being raised and trained in India, and in this

---

[1] S.E.A.C. included the Indian Ocean between longitude 60 and 110 degrees east, Ceylon, Burma, Siam, Malaya and Sumatra. See Map 10, page 384.
[2] See Map 14, page 452.
[3] See Volume II, pages 153–54.

capacity he was Commanding General of N.C.A.C. in which they
were to operate.

As Deputy Supreme Allied Commander Stilwell owed allegiance
to Mountbatten and, in the latter's absence from the theatre,
became directly responsible to the Combined Chiefs of Staff through
the British Chiefs of Staff. But as Commanding General, C.B.I.
Theatre, he was directly responsible to the American Joint Chiefs of
Staff. As Chief of Staff to the Supreme Commander of the China
Theatre, he was responsible to Chiang Kai-shek. In this last capacity
he had not only to consider Chinese interests but to urge acceptance
of the Generalissimo's views, even though they differed from those
of S.E.A.C. As Deputy Supreme Commander S.E.A.C. he equally
had to press Mountbatten's views on the Generalissimo. Stilwell was
therefore placed in a most anomalous position. This had been pointed
out by the British at Quadrant, but the Americans had explained
that, since politically all United States forces in China or in S.E.A.C.
were regarded as being there for the sole purpose of supporting
China, Stilwell's appointment as Deputy Supreme Allied Commander was necessary to maintain close liaison with Chiang Kai-
shek and thus get as much support as possible for operations in
Burma.

Admiral Somerville also had a dual responsibility since, when he
became Naval Commander-in-Chief, S.E.A.C., he retained his
appointment as Commander-in-Chief, Eastern Fleet. His total area
of responsibility therefore covered areas outside as well as inside
S.E.A.C. and included Aden, the Persian Gulf, the east coast of
Africa and Madagascar. In all matters concerning the security and
support of land campaigns and amphibious operations in South-East
Asia, Somerville was subordinate to the Supreme Commander, but
in all matters connected with the security of sea communications in
the Indian Ocean, both inside and outside the area of S.E.A.C., he
was directly responsible to the Admiralty. This led to a series of
disagreements between Mountbatten and Somerville which, in
November, was referred to the Prime Minister who ruled that,
for all the purposes of S.E.A.C., the Naval Commander-in-Chief
and all his forces were under the Supreme Commander, and
therefore constituted a part of his Command. When any of the three
Commanders-in-Chief sat in consultation with the Supreme Commander he had the power of overriding decision. In other words,
within the limits and for the purposes of S.E.A.C., the Navy was on
exactly the same footing as the Army and Air Force.

To command the land forces in S.E.A.C., General Giffard was
appointed Commander-in-Chief of the newly-formed 11th Army
Group. This comprised Ceylon Army Command and 14th Army
which, under Slim, was responsible for the operational control of

British forces on the Arakan and Central fronts. Although Chiang-Kai-shek had agreed to place the American-trained Chinese formations allotted to the Northern front under Mountbatten's overall command, he had stipulated that they must be directly controlled by Stilwell. Stilwell would not, however, agree to come under Giffard's operational control, which would have been his logical position had the latter been an Allied land force Commander-in-Chief. Mountbatten, in his turn, was unwilling to assume direct responsibility for one section of the front. Eventually a compromise, approved by the Prime Minister, the President and the Generalissimo, was reached, whereby Stilwell agreed to place himself and his Chinese forces in Burma under the operational control of Slim personally until they reached Kamaing, when they would revert to Mountbatten's direct control. Giffard's command was therefore confined to British Commonwealth land forces in S.E.A.C. Thus, in theory, Slim owed allegiance to Giffard only in regard to the 14th Army front and not the Northern front. In practice, however, Slim's orders to Stilwell were based on Giffard's directives for the campaign as a whole. This compromise was made to work satisfactorily. The responsibility for formulating the general policy governing the organization, equipment and training of all forces within the boundaries of India Command assigned to S.E.A.C., including those which had not yet been actually transferred to his command, rested with Giffard but, as many formations had to be administered and trained by India Command, he and Auchinleck had to co-operate very closely.

On becoming Air Commander-in-Chief, S.E.A.C., Air Marshal Peirse kept command of the one Dutch squadron and all the Commonwealth air forces throughout India and Ceylon, with the exception of some Royal Indian Air Force squadrons which were left under the Air Officer Commanding, India Command, for the defence of the North West Frontier.[1] All Royal Air Force units and establishments in India were then transferred from the Indian to the British establishment. Peirse became responsible for the policy for the development of India, not only as a base for future air operations but as a training centre for the Allied air forces.[2] He assumed command of all the Allied air force squadrons (other than American) in S.E.A.C., including flying-boats, general reconnaissance and coastal striking force aircraft. The strategic control of aircraft operating over the sea was, however, vested in the Commander-in-Chief,

---

[1] On the formation of Air Command, S.E.A., a small new Air Headquarters, India, was formed to control and administer the Royal Indian Air Force. At this stage of its development the R.I.A.F. consisted of seven squadrons of which five (2, 3, 4, 6 and 8 Squadrons) were placed at the disposal of S.E.A.C. by the Commander-in-Chief in India.
[2] The actual development and training were carried out by India Command on his behalf.

Eastern Fleet, and their operational control exercised by the Air Officer Commanding 222 Group R.A.F., with headquarters in Colombo.

The 10th U.S.A.A.F. came under the command of the Supreme Commander only through Stilwell as Commanding General, C.B.I. Theatre. Since in November 1943 one-third of the combat aircraft in S.E.A.C. belonged to the American formation, this chain of command proved a source of embarrassment. Mountbatten considered it 'was certain to entail an overlapping of effort—or, worse, gaps in our air defence; that it would lead to a lack of co-ordination, and an impairment of general efficiency,' and that any of these might in a crisis have very serious consequences.[1]

During the Sextant Conference in Cairo early in December,[2] Mountbatten therefore discussed the matter informally with Air Chief Marshal Sir Charles Portal (Chief of the Air Staff) General G. C. Marshall (Chief of Staff U.S. Army) and General H. H. Arnold (Commanding General U.S. Army Air Force) who agreed that it was within his competence as a Supreme Commander to reorganize his command as he thought fit. Against the wishes of Stilwell, with whom Stratemeyer perforce agreed officially, he issued orders on the 12th December for the integration of the two air forces. Under the reorganization, Peirse became Allied Air Commander-in-Chief with Stratemeyer as his second-in-command. The latter was given the direct command of Eastern Air Command, which was formed to control those Allied air forces operating against the Japanese in Burma.[3] The 14th U.S.A.A.F. in China remained as before under Stilwell, but the co-ordination of its air operations with those of Eastern Air Command was to be effected through Stilwell and Peirse at S.E.A.C. Headquarters.

When the integration of the air forces took place, the Air Commander-in-Chief was made responsible under the Air Ministry for the air support of sea communications outside the boundaries of S.E.A.C., a position parallel to that of the Naval Commander-in-Chief. It was arranged that the Air Commander-in-Chief would work in the closest co-operation with the Naval Commander-in-Chief and that the disposition of the air forces to meet the strategic requirements of the Navy, in accordance with the maritime situation in the Indian Ocean as a whole, would be a matter for their mutual agreement.[4]

Lieut.-General Sir Henry Pownall was appointed Chief of Staff

---

[1] Mountbatten Report, Section A para. 37.
[2] For the conference see Chapter V.
[3] The American Chiefs of Staff in accepting the integration of the British and American air forces in S.E.A.C. reserved the right to re-assign units of 10th U.S.A.A.F. to 14th U.S.A.A.F. should their commitments in China make such a step necessary.
[4] The chain of command after the integration of the air forces is shown in Appendix 8.

to the Supreme Commander, with Major-General A. C. Wedemeyer (U.S. Army) as his deputy. Lieut.-General R. A. Wheeler (U.S. Army) became the Supreme Commander's Principal Administrative Officer, with Major-General C. R. C. Lane as his deputy. Since S.E.A.C. was dependent for all administrative services in India on the work of the administrative staffs at General Headquarters, India, Mountbatten requested that an officer should be appointed to co-ordinate administrative policy in India and act as an opposite number to Wheeler. This request was met and Lieut.-General Sir Wilfred Lindsell was appointed Principal Administrative Officer, India.

Air Marshal Sir Philip Joubert de la Ferté was appointed Deputy Chief of Staff (Information and Civil Affairs), Lieut.-General Sir Adrian Carton de Wiart, V.C. the Prime Minister's and the Supreme Allied Commander's representative with Generalissimo Chiang Kai-shek, and Mr. J. Keswick political liaison officer with Chungking. Mr. M. E. Dening became Chief Political Adviser, and Sir Archibald Rowlands Financial Adviser, to the Supreme Commander.

Since the demands of the Supreme Allied Commander, based on operational plans as they developed, might interfere with the economy of India and so lessen its value as a base, a conflict of opinion between the Supreme Commander and the Commander-in-Chief in India over the question of priorities could easily arise. The Viceroy (Field-Marshal Lord Wavell), acting on behalf of the War Cabinet, and not in his statutory capacity of Governor General, was therefore given the authority to take such measures and issue such instructions as he considered necessary to ensure harmonious co-operation between the two commanders. To assist him in this, Sir Archibald Rowlands, in addition to being Financial Adviser to the Supreme Commander, was appointed Adviser to the Viceroy on War Administration.

The Supreme Commander set up his own inter-Service and inter-Allied planning staff under his Chief of Staff. This became known as the War Staff. Its functions were to prepare, in broad outline, appreciations, plans and directives within S.E.A.C., to co-ordinate plans and operations with those contemplated in adjacent theatres and to maintain liaison with the planning staffs of the three Com-manders-in-Chief, in order to ensure that they were kept informed of the development of S.E.A.C. plans in their early stages. This system proved to have inherent disadvantages which, despite close liaison between the various planning staffs, soon made themselves apparent, mainly because, as will be seen, the lack of a firm directive from the Chiefs of Staff to the Supreme Commander after the Sextant Conference made it increasingly difficult to draw a line between long-term and short-term plans. This aggravated the tendency which inevitably existed for the work of the planning staff to overlap.

On the formation of S.E.A.C. the naval forces in the Indian Ocean consisted, apart from coastal forces, of the Eastern Fleet. This had been so reduced during 1943 by the demands from other theatres that it could only with difficulty act as a trade protection force. It consisted of one battleship—the *Ramillies*—one escort carrier, five cruisers of the 4th Cruiser Squadron, eleven destroyers, drawn from the 7th and 11th Destroyer Flotillas, and the 4th Submarine Flotilla which was being assembled at Ceylon.[1] Owing to the shortage of escort vessels, of which there were only a dozen on the station, all the cruisers and destroyers were employed on escort duties. The only force which could be used offensively was the 4th Submarine Flotilla, of which five submarines had arrived in Ceylon from the Mediterranean. There were in addition a considerable number of landing craft of various types, most of which had been transferred from the Mediterranean after the successful invasion of Sicily.

The surrender of Italy in September 1943 had freed a number of capital ships, and the Admiralty had ordered the battleships *Queen Elizabeth* and *Valiant*, the battle cruiser *Renown*, the aircraft carrier *Illustrious* and the aircraft carrier and repair ship *Unicorn* with seven destroyers to reinforce the Eastern Fleet in January 1944. They had directed that the battle squadron to be formed in the Indian Ocean should be known as the 1st Battle Squadron—a title which for years had been held by the British battle squadron in the Mediterranean. This change of title symbolized the transfer of British naval strength to the Far East. Admiral Somerville had moved his headquarters from Kilindini back to Colombo and Trincomalee was being built up as a fleet base.[2]

In addition to 14th Army, Giffard (11th Army Group), with his headquarters at New Delhi, had under his command Ceylon Army Command (Lieut.-General H. E. de R. Wetherall), the garrisons in the Indian Ocean bases and some Nepalese troops loaned to S.E.A.C. The 14th Army (Slim) consisted of XV Corps (Christison) on the Arakan front—5th and 7th Indian Divisions and 81st (W.A.) Division less one brigade; IV Corps (Scoones) on the Central front—17th, 20th and 23rd Indian Divisions; and 26th Indian Division and 254th Indian Tank Brigade in Army reserve. Slim also had temporary operational command over the Chinese-American divisions on the Northern front. The Ceylon Army Command comprised 11th (E.A.) Division, 99th Indian Infantry Brigade, the Mobile Naval Base Defence Organization, Royal Marines (M.N.B.D.O.), and local defence troops. A number of other formations were assigned to S.E.A.C. but remained temporarily under India Command. These were: XXXIII Corps (Lieut.-General

---

[1] See Appendix 9 for order of battle of the Eastern Fleet on the 16th November 1943.
[2] See Volume II, Chapter VII.

M. G. N. Stopford) consisting of 2nd British and 36th Indian Divisions, with 19th and 25th Indian Divisions and 50th Tank Brigade attached for administration and training; 50th Parachute (P.) Brigade; Special Force, and 3 Special Service (S.S.) Brigade, consisting of 5 Commando and 44 Royal Marine Commando.[1]

On the integration of the Allied air forces on the 12th December 1943, Air Command, South-East Asia, had sixty-seven operational squadrons (forty-three R.A.F., three R.I.A.F., one R.C.A.F., one Netherlands and nineteen U.S.A.A.F.) with an effective strength of some 850 aircraft of which 264 were American. It had directly under command 222 (Coastal) Group R.A.F. in Ceylon, 223 (Training) Group R.A.F. at Peshawar, 225 (Coastal) Group R.A.F. at Bangalore, 226 (Maintenance) Group R.A.F. at Delhi, 227 (Training) Group at Bombay and Eastern Air Command at Calcutta.

Eastern Air Command was organized into 3rd Tactical Air Force (Air Marshal Sir John Baldwin), a Strategic Air Force (Brigadier-General H. C. Davidson, U.S.A.A.F.), a Troop Carrier Command (Brigadier-General W. D. Old, U.S.A.A.F.) and a Photographic Reconnaissance Force (Group Captain S. G. Wise). The 3rd Tactical Air Force consisted of 224 Group R.A.F. in support of XV Corps, 221 Group R.A.F. in support of IV Corps, and Northern Air Sector Force in support of the Northern front. There were, in addition, twenty squadrons (twelve R.A.F., two R.I.A.F., and six U.S.A.A.F.) which were non-operational and in various stages of re-equipment and training.[2]

Headquarters S.E.A.C. was, as already stated, established in the first instance at Delhi: this was essential, since the only administrative machinery capable of serving the needs of the new command at short notice was there and, during the hand-over of command, very close liaison with India Command was essential. Mountbatten proposed, however, that his headquarters should be moved at the earliest possible moment to some suitable point outside India, since he was anxious that Headquarters S.E.A.C. should stand firmly on its own and be independent of General Headquarters, India.

When the formation of an Allied command in South-East Asia was under consideration, the Prime Minister had suggested Ceylon as the ultimate location of its headquarters. Mountbatten agreed with him, since Ceylon was well suited for the control of amphibious operations which, at that time, seemed to him likely to be of greater importance than operations on the India–Burma frontier. Moreover, it provided the main base and shore headquarters of the Eastern

---

[1] See Appendix 10 for order of battle of British and American army formations allotted or assigned to S.E.A.C. on the 16th November 1943.

[2] For order of battle of Air Command, S.E.A., on the 12th December 1943 see Appendix 11. The effective strength of the Japanese air force in Burma at this time was some 200 aircraft. See Appendix 7.

Fleet and it would therefore be possible for the Supreme Commander to have all his three Commanders-in-Chief alongside him.

Somerville and S.E.A.C. Headquarters staff favoured the move, but both Giffard and Peirse opposed it on the grounds that it would separate them from India Command on which they so largely depended, and would entail a great deal of travelling to and from Assam and eastern Bengal, where the greater part of their forces were engaged. Nevertheless, Mountbatten decided that the advantages of Ceylon outweighed the disadvantages and selected Kandy, the old capital of Ceylon, as the site for the new headquarters. He agreed to postpone the move till April 1944 so that the necessary buildings could be prepared and communications improved, and to allow time for the build-up of 11th Army Group Headquarters.[1]

---

[1] S.E.A.C. Headquarters moved to Ceylon on the 15th April 1944. Headquarters 11th Army Group remained in Delhi during the period covered by this volume.

Map 4

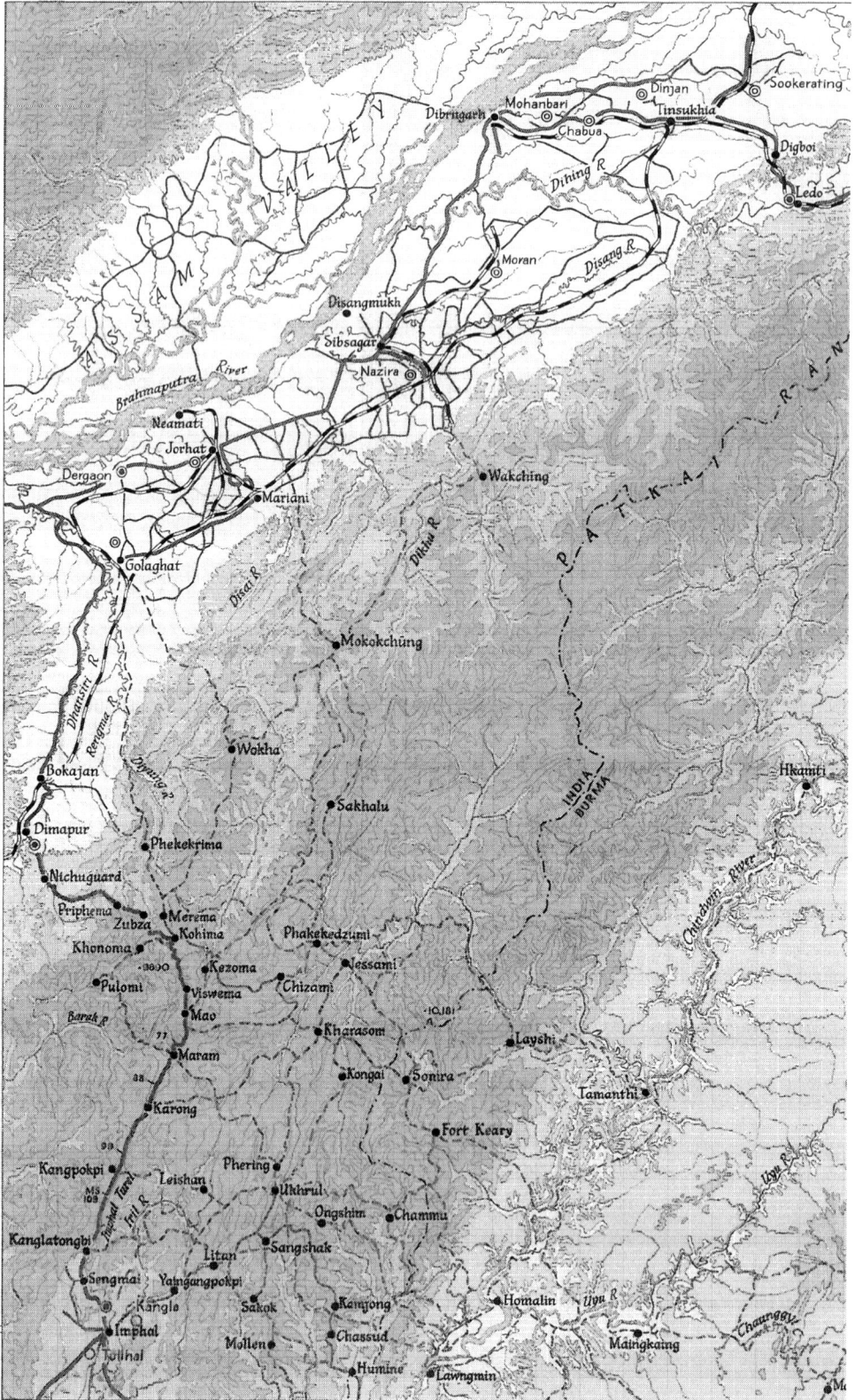

KOHIMA ~ MYITKYINA

Scale   0   25   50   Miles

Fort Hertz

Likhapani

Pangsau Pass

PATKAI-E

Tagap

Tarung R.

Nmai R.

Hkalak Ga

Shingbwiyang

Tanai R.

Lulum Nok

Taihpa Ga

HUKAWNG VALLEY

Tanai R.

Sumprabum

Taro

Maingkwan

KUMON RANGE

Tanai R.

Pabum   Naura Hkyet Pass

Walawbum

Taikri

JAMBU BUM

Nprawa

Shaduzup

Janpan

Ritpong

Nsopzup

Tingring   Hsamshingyang

Warazup

1725

Arang   Tingkrukawng

Inkangahtawng

Nhpum Ga

Wala   Auche

Lonkin

Mogaung R.

Nanyaseik

Lawa

Seingneing

Haingpa

Kamaing

Zigyun

Uyu R.

Seton

Tumbonghka

Namkwi

Irrawaddy R.

Lakhren

Myitkyina   Maingna

Sezin

Padiga

Panok   Mogaung

Waingmaw

Indaw C.

Sahmaw   Wajit

Tapaw

Indawgyi Lake

2171

Taungni   Mansen

Nam Tabet R.

Mokso

Kazu

Pinbaw

Fort Morton

Blackpool

Lamai

Kyusanlai Pass

Hopin

GANGAW RANGE

Templecombe

Nahpaw

Meza

Namyin C.

Naungpong

KACHIN HILLS

Mohnyin

Sinbo

Simapa

Kadu

Broadway

Nalong

Mawhan

Meza R.

METRES
900
450
150
SEA LEVEL

CHAPTER V

THE FINAL ALLIED PLANS FOR

1944

(December 1943 – January 1944)

See Maps 1, 2, 13, 14 and 15

WHEN Admiral Mountbatten assumed command in South-East Asia, the course of the war in both the West and the Pacific had taken a turn for the better. The battle of the Atlantic had been won and the toll taken of Allied shipping by German submarines had diminished very considerably. In May the successful conclusion of the North African campaign had re-opened the Mediterranean, and ships to India were able to use the shorter route through the Suez Canal instead of rounding the Cape, with a great saving in both time and tonnage. On the 9th July the Allies had invaded Sicily; on the 25th Mussolini had resigned; on the 3rd September an Allied landing had been made on the toe of Italy and five days later the Italians had surrendered. The Allies, having occupied southern Italy, began to advance northwards, and by the 1st October had captured Naples, but thereafter progress slowed down as they came up against stubborn German resistance between Naples and Rome.

During July and August three great battles had raged on the Russian front which forced the German army to retreat along the whole of its eastern front from opposite Moscow to the Black Sea. Early in October the pursuing Russian armies had crossed the River Dnieper and on the 6th November entered Kiev, thus laying the German front open and vulnerable to a winter campaign. In the Pacific the American counter-offensive had gathered way and the initiative had been finally wrested from the Japanese. Papua and Guadalcanal had been reoccupied and New Georgia captured,[1] and the enemy had been driven from his strongholds at Salamaua, Lae and Finschhafen.[2] Only in South-East Asia did stalemate continue. Both contestants were, however, preparing for battle as soon as the weather and administrative considerations allowed.[3]

The decision that the invasion of northern France ('Overlord')

---

[1] See Volume II, Chapters XVI, XXII, and XXV.
[2] See Map 1, page 1, and Chapter VII.
[3] See Volume II, Chapter XXVI.

would take place in 1944 had been confirmed during the Quadrant Conference in August 1943, and to ensure the success of this operation the Combined Chiefs of Staff proposed that a subsidiary landing in the south of France ('Anvil') should also be carried out. On the 19th August the Prime Minister and the President sent a joint message to Marshal Stalin urging the importance of an early meeting soon to discuss future strategy. It was some time before the President felt that his constitutional duties would allow him to travel as far as Teheran, the rendezvous suggested by Stalin, and while he deliberated he suggested that he and the Prime Minister should meet Generalissimo Chiang Kai-shek in North Africa. The Prime Minister agreed and on the 22nd November the Sextant Conference opened at Cairo. Mountbatten flew from Delhi to attend and the Generalissimo came accompanied by Stilwell and Chennault.

During the autumn the Chiefs of Staff had examined the relative merits of amphibious operations for the capture of either Akyab ('Bullfrog') or the Andamans ('Buccaneer'), and had agreed with the recommendations already made by both Auchinleck and Mountbatten that 'Buccaneer' was the better operation.[1] They had also come to the conclusion that the occupation of northern Sumatra ('Culverin') was the amphibious operation most likely to further the war against Japan in the spring of 1944, since its capture would provide the only air base from which effective blows could be struck direct at Japanese resources. It was almost certain to provoke a strong reaction, since an air offensive from this area would inflict shipping losses which the Japanese could ill afford and also contain and destroy air forces which would otherwise be available for the Pacific. Since it would need four divisions (three assault and one follow-up), strong naval forces and assault shipping and landing craft beyond those immediately available, it could be attempted only if their American colleagues were prepared to assist with material resources. On the 29th October they told the Joint Staff Mission in Washington their views and asked if the American Chiefs of Staff would be prepared to help. If not, they proposed to go on with preparations for the capture of the Andamans in the early spring of 1944.

When the Sextant Conference opened, the American Chiefs of Staff said that they were unable to provide the additional resources for an attack on northern Sumatra, but that the operation for the capture of the Andamans ('Buccaneer') should be mounted as early as practicable.

The strategy for South-East Asia as a whole was first discussed at a plenary meeting on the 23rd November. Mountbatten outlined his proposed land operation ('Tarzan') for the recapture of north

---

[1] See Map 15 in pocket at end of volume.

Burma in the dry weather of 1943–44,[1] and said that he would, as he had undertaken to do when he met the Generalissimo at Chungking, work up the airlift to China to 10,000 tons a month. The land operations would, however, entail a decrease in the amount carried of some 2,100 tons both in January and February 1944. The Prime Minister welcomed these proposals and told the Generalissimo that the surrender of Italy and other favourable events had enabled plans to be made for a formidable British fleet to be built up in the Indian Ocean. Its full strength would not however be reached until the late spring or early summer of 1944. By the spring Mountbatten would have formed an amphibious 'circus' for any operation decided on. No mention was made to the Chinese of the plans for 'Buccaneer', since the Combined Chiefs of Staff had first to consider them in relation to the needs of amphibious operations in the European theatre of war.

The Chinese reaction to Mountbatten's proposal was the old familiar one.[2] The success of any operations in north Burma, said the Generalissimo, depended on their co-ordination with naval operations to gain control of the Bay of Bengal; otherwise the Japanese would be able to reinforce Burma and the land operations would fail. It was explained to him that, though naval operations would not necessarily be linked with 'Tarzan', everything possible would be done to interfere with the enemy line of communications. Nevertheless he insisted that an amphibious operation must be carried out simultaneously with any land attack.

The Combined Chiefs of Staff met the Chinese delegation on the 24th. They were told that the Generalissimo was dissatisfied with the scope of 'Tarzan', and considered that it should be extended to cover the reoccupation of the whole of Burma, with the capture of Mandalay as its first and Rangoon as its final objective. He was not prepared, however, to allow the Chinese forces from Yunnan to advance beyond Lashio, their objective under Mountbatten's plans. Although he had told Mountbatten at Chungking that he accepted the fact that operations might interfere with the airlift, he now objected to its curtailment and insisted that, whatever the needs of the land campaign, the amount delivered must not drop below 10,000 tons a month.[3] The Combined Chiefs of Staff explained that the seizure of north Burma was but the first step towards the reoccupation of the whole of the country: 'Tarzan' was based on the principle that the initial advance should end with the onset of the monsoon to prevent Japanese counter-attacks. The capture of Mandalay was made impossible by administrative difficulties, and it was illogical for the

[1] See pages 8–10 and 15–16.
[2] See Volume II, Chapter XVII.
[3] See pages 12–13.

Chinese to insist that 'Tarzan' be extended and in the same breath demand that the airlift be maintained at 10,000 tons of supplies a month—a lift which, in any case, had not yet been reached.

During a meeting with the Prime Minister and the Supreme Commander on the morning of the 25th, the Generalissimo, despite his previous objections, agreed to participate in 'Tarzan' on condition that the Combined Chiefs of Staff provided the 535 extra transport aircraft needed if the plan were extended to include the capture of Mandalay, that the Eastern Fleet was in control of the Bay of Bengal and that an amphibious operation was linked with the land campaign. The Generalissimo also had talks with the President, who gave him a definite undertaking that there would be a considerable amphibious operation within the next few months.[1] That evening, however, the Generalissimo heard that the Combined Chiefs of Staff were unable to supply the extra aircraft required for the extended plan and immediately went back on his agreement to participate in 'Tarzan'.

With the approval of the Combined Chiefs of Staff, Mountbatten drew up a paper listing 'points on which the Generalissimo's agreement should be obtained'. These included:

(1) Since the aircraft needed for the Mandalay plan could not be provided, 'Tarzan' should be accepted.

(2) The Generalissimo's stipulation that an amphibious operation should be carried out would be considered by the Combined Chiefs of Staff when they reviewed amphibious operations in all parts of the world.

(3) The utmost would be done to increase the airlift tonnage to 10,000 tons a month by the late winter, and the Supreme Commander would have authority to divert not more than 1,100 tons a month to the land campaign.

The Prime Minister and the President had a final meeting with the Generalissimo on the 26th, when this paper was explained to him. Once again he changed his mind and agreed to every point. The following day the Prime Minister and the President flew with their staffs to Teheran and the first part of the Cairo Conference came to an end. But that morning, at a meeting of the S.E.A.C. representatives held by Mountbatten before he returned to India, Stilwell 'absolutely staggered' the Supreme Commander by saying that the Generalissimo had once again rejected everything he had previously agreed to. This new volte-face prompted Mountbatten to write in his diary: 'I am delighted that the Prime Minister and President and Combined Chiefs of Staff are at last being given first hand experience of how impossible the Chinese are to deal with'.

On the 30th November Mountbatten, now back in India, met the

---

[1] Churchill, *The Second World War*, Volume V (Cassell, 1952) page 290.

Generalissimo at Ranchi and went with him to inspect the camp at Ramgarh, the training centre for Chinese troops in India.[1] That evening the Generalissimo once again agreed to co-operate in Mountbatten's plans, subject to a synchronised amphibious operation. He appeared to accept the fact that there would be a temporary drop in the airlift tonnage and, when warned by Mountbatten that aircraft would have to be borrowed from the airlift to fly in the formations to Indaw and feed them, replied, 'I will trust you'. Thus by the end of November it seemed to Mountbatten that, provided 'Buccaneer' could be launched in the spring, the plans for the 1943–44 dry weather operations were as firm as any plans could be which relied on Chinese co-operation.

During the first part of the conference the Combined Chiefs of Staff reconsidered operation 'Matterhorn' (originally proposed at the Quadrant Conference) in which very long-range bombers (B.29s), based on Calcutta and on airfields in China, were to be used to strike at the heart of the steel industry in Japan in 1944. The project in its original form had been found to be impracticable and had been replaced by a modified scheme which required fewer airfields in the Calcutta area.[2]

The American Chiefs of Staff now reported that they had set up Headquarters 20th U.S.A.A.F. in Washington to prepare and control the operation and were forming 20th Bomber Command with two wings (58th and 73rd), each of 112 B.29 long-range bombers, to be sent to India. They were making arrangements through Stilwell for the construction of four airfields in the vicinity of Chengtu (200 miles north-west of Chungking) and for stocks of petrol and bombs to be built up in China. The control of the operation would rest with them and not with the Combined Chiefs of Staff. The aircraft would probably become available early in 1944 and would require four or five suitable airfields near Calcutta.

The Supreme Commander reported that preparations for this project would have to take priority immediately after land operations planned for northern Burma in the spring of 1944, since the only airfields which would be suitable were those in the Kharagpur area (65 miles north-west of Calcutta) and they would be required by eight R.A.F. heavy bomber squadrons employed in these operations. Furthermore, to take B.29s, the airfields would have to be improved, and the work could be completed by the desired date only at the expense of the Ledo Road and thus of the land operations. He proposed therefore that only such preparatory work on the airfields as

---

[1] See Map 14, page 452.
[2] See page 11.

would not interfere with the construction of the Ledo Road should be undertaken, pending the arrival from the United States of units, equipment and material specifically allotted to the project. Provided the preparatory work was started at once and the American units and material arrived in Calcutta by the 15th January, he estimated that the airfields should be ready for the reception of the B.29 aircraft by the middle of May 1944. The Combined Chiefs of Staff accepted these proposals and agreed to the diversion of equipment from the Ledo Road which would delay its progress by some six to eight weeks. It was also agreed that a base area should be prepared in Ceylon from which B.29s could attack the Palembang oilfields in southern Sumatra and that four airfields should be constructed in the island by mid-July 1944.

Before going to Teheran the Combined Chiefs of Staff had not been able to come to any agreement on 'Buccaneer'. Allied strategy was becoming increasingly hampered by the general shortage of assault shipping.[1] The British Chiefs of Staff considered that, if the second front in Europe ('Overlord') were to be launched in May 1944, 'Buccaneer' should be postponed or abandoned and the landing craft allotted to it brought back to the Mediterranean, so that the maximum Allied strength could be brought to bear on Germany to bring the war as a whole to an end as quickly as possible. In view of the President's promise to the Generalissimo, however, the American Chiefs of Staff were not prepared to agree to the postponement of 'Buccaneer'.

At the first plenary meeting at Teheran on the 28th November, Marshal Stalin said that Russia would enter the war against Japan the moment that Germany was defeated. As the conference progressed, it became quite clear that nothing could be achieved unless the Russians were given a firm date early in 1944 for the launching of 'Overlord'. On the 30th November Stalin was told that it would take place in May, in conjunction with the supporting operation ('Anvil') against the south of France on the largest scale permitted by the landing craft available.

The Combined Chiefs of Staff returned to Cairo on the 2nd December to work out the details of the undertaking they had given to the Russians. There they found awaiting them further news from the Supreme Commander on the subject of 'Buccaneer' and 'Tarzan'. He reported that, owing to the receipt of new information about Japanese strength in the Andaman Islands, the resources for 'Buccaneer' would have to be increased and a shipping lift provided for some 58,000 troops, and that further examination of 'Tarzan' had

---

[1] See Ehrman, *Grand Strategy*, Volume V (H.M.S.O., 1956).

shown that it would involve the Allies in much greater subsequent commitments in Burma than had originally been envisaged. This report resulted in a widening of the divergence of views on 'Buccaneer'. Although both the Prime Minister and the President agreed that it ought to be possible to capture the Andamans with far fewer troops than the number proposed by the Supreme Commander, Mr. Churchill was in favour of postponing the operation until after the monsoon so that the lift for 'Anvil', which he felt was dangerously low, could be strengthened, while Mr. Roosevelt considered that Mountbatten should be ordered to attack the Andamans with what he already had in his command. These opinions were reflected by their respective staffs. Any operation, said the British Chiefs of Staff, which prejudiced the success of 'Overlord' or 'Anvil' must be postponed or cancelled. The American Chiefs of Staff agreed that everything must be done to increase the strength of 'Overlord' and 'Anvil', but that military and political considerations made an amphibious operation in South-East Asia imperative.

To seek a way out of this impasse, the Supreme Commander was asked on the 5th December what operations on a smaller scale than 'Buccaneer' he could undertake if the bulk of his landing craft and assault shipping were withdrawn during the next few weeks. On the afternoon of the 5th, before he had time to reply, the difference of opinion over 'Buccaneer' came to a sudden dramatic end when the President sent the Prime Minister 'a laconic private message: "Buccaneer is off".'[1] With the concurrence of the Prime Minister he then sent a message to the Generalissimo telling him of the new development:

> 'Conference with Stalin', he said, 'involves us in combined grand operations on European continent in late spring giving fair prospect of terminating war with Germany by end of summer of 1944. These operations impose so large a requirement of heavy landing craft as to make it impracticable to devote a sufficient number to the amphibious operation in Bay of Bengal simultaneously with launching of 'Tarzan' to ensure success of operations.
>
> This being the case, would you be prepared to go ahead with 'Tarzan' as now planned, including commitment to maintain naval control of Bay of Bengal coupled with naval carrier and commando amphibious operations simultaneously with launching of 'Tarzan'. Also there is the prospect of B.29 bombing of railroad and port Bangkok.
>
> If not would you prefer to have 'Tarzan' delayed until November to include heavy amphibious operation. Meanwhile concentrate all air transport on carrying supplies over the Hump to air and ground forces in China.

---

[1] Churchill, *The Second World War*, Volume V (Cassell, 1952), page 364.

I am influenced in this matter by the tremendous advantage to be received by China and the Pacific through the early termination of the war with Germany'.

At the last plenary meeting on the 6th December, the Prime Minister and the President approved the Combined Chiefs of Staff's final report on the conclusions reached at the conference. The overall strategic concept for the prosecution of the war was still, in co-operation with Russia and other Allies, to bring about the unconditional surrender of Germany at the earliest possible date. Unremitting pressure would be maintained and extended against Japan. On the defeat of Germany, the full resources of the United States and Great Britain would, in co-operation with other Pacific powers and if possible Russia, be directed to bring about Japan's unconditional surrender.

For the war against Japan, the Combined Chiefs of Staff had approved in principle a plan which was to be the basis of further investigation. Its object was to gain places from where an intensive air bombardment of the Japanese homeland could be carried out, a sea and air blockade established and an invasion mounted against Japan if necessary. Within the Pacific, which was now to be the main theatre, the aim should be to advance along the New Guinea–Netherlands East Indies–Philippines axis and complete the capture of the mandated islands in the Central Pacific (the Gilberts, Marshalls, Carolines and Marianas) in time to launch a major assault in the Formosa–Luzon–China area in the spring of 1945.[1] Operations in the North Pacific, South Pacific, China and South-East Asia should be conducted in support of the main operations in the Central and South-West Pacific. Sufficient British naval forces should be kept in the Indian Ocean to act as a deterrent to the Japanese; all other available British naval units, as far as they could be supported and profitably employed, would be concentrated in the Pacific. As soon as possible after the defeat of Germany four British divisions should be based on Australia for service in the Pacific.

Within the terms of this basic plan, specific operations were to be carried out against Japan in 1944. These were:

(a) North Pacific: preparations for very long-range strategic bombing of the Kuriles and northern Japan.

(b) Central Pacific: capture of the mandated islands and very long-range strategic bombing of Japan proper from Guam, Tinian and Saipan in the Marianas.

(c) South and South-West Pacific: continuation of the advance along the New Guinea–Netherlands East Indies–Philippines axis concurrently with the capture of the mandated islands

---

[1] See Map 13, page 438.

and the intensification of bombing targets in the Netherlands East Indies–Philippines area, and the neutralization by air of Rabaul.

(d) China: the build-up of the American and Chinese air forces and the Chinese army to intensify air and land operations in and from China; the establishment of a very long-range bomber force at Calcutta with advanced bases at Chengtu to attack vital targets in the Japanese inner zone (Japan proper, Manchuria, Korea, North China, Japanese Sakhalin and Formosa).

(e) South-East Asia: operations to capture upper Burma in the spring of 1944 to improve the air route and establish overland communication with China, and an amphibious operation at approximately the same time; these operations to be continued during the autumn of 1944 to extend the positions held in upper Burma within the limits of the forces available.

Major amphibious operations in the Bay of Bengal were to be delayed until after the 1944 monsoon, and landing craft assigned to 'Buccaneer' diverted to the European theatre for 'Overlord' and 'Anvil'. The report went on:

'We have decided—
(a) To make all preparations to conduct 'Tarzan' as planned less 'Buccaneer', for which will be substituted naval carrier and amphibious raiding operations simultaneous with the launching of 'Tarzan'; and to carry out air bombardment of the Bangkok –Burma railroad and the harbour of Bangkok, in the meantime maintaining naval control of the Bay of Bengal.[1]

or alternatively

(b) To postpone 'Tarzan', increase to a maximum with planes available the air lift to China across the Hump and intensify the measures that will enable the B.29s [very long-range bombers] to be brought to bear on the enemy'.

Mountbatten had anticipated the question put to him on the 5th December, for in November he had been aware that the cancellation of 'Buccaneer' was possible and that it would inevitably lead to the collapse of 'Tarzan', since the Generalissimo had agreed to a reduction in the airlift tonnage and the co-operation of the Yunnan armies only if an amphibious operation were carried out. He had therefore consulted Giffard about an alternative operation whose object would be to achieve a greater measure of security for the air ferry route, obtain greater freedom of action for offensive operations in 1944–45, destroy the maximum number of Japanese on land and in

---

[1] See Map 15 in pocket at end of volume.

the air and gain some control over upper Burma by the employment
of L.R.P. groups.

On the 6th December he told the Chiefs of Staff that, with the
landing craft and assault shipping likely to be left at his disposal,
there appeared to be no worthwhile objective which he could seize
and hold: he was therefore examining the feasibility of hit-and-run
operations by carriers. Since, with the cancellation of 'Buccaneer',
'Tarzan' would probably not now take place, he proposed undertaking operation 'Gripfast', a modified 'Tarzan', in which IV Corps
would advance down the Kabaw Valley and through the Chin Hills
to the Kalemyo–Kalewa area in conjunction with operations by
L.R.P. groups.[1] The land advance in Arakan would remain as in
'Tarzan' and the Ledo force would continue its advance, if the
Generalissimo gave permission and it proved capable of doing so.
'Gripfast' would not enable him to fulfil the terms of his directive but
it had certain merits: it would enable L.R.P. groups to operate; it
would result in a certain amount of air fighting; and the occupation
of the Kalemyo–Kalewa area would provide a starting point for subsequent operations towards Mandalay, without definitely committing
14th Army to further operations in central Burma.

The Combined Chiefs of Staff at their last meeting on the 7th
December were unable to reach any decision on Mountbatten's
proposals until the Generalissimo's reactions to the President's telegram were known. They did decide, however, that a fresh directive
to Mountbatten should be prepared, but it was not, as will be seen,
until June 1944 that it was issued.

When the Generalissimo's reply was received on the 9th it did
little to clarify the situation. He said that he was inclined to accept
the recommendations in the President's telegram, though it would
make his task of rallying the nation infinitely more difficult. But
China's greatest danger was economic, and the solution therefore
was for the President 'to assure the Chinese people and the Army of
your serious concern in the China theatre of war by assisting China
to hold on with a billion gold dollar loan'. At the same time he
demanded that the American air force in China should be at least
doubled and the airlift increased from February 1944 to at least
20,000 tons a month to enable the additional aircraft to operate. On
the 17th he told the President that he thought that it would be better
to defer the 'amphibious all-out offensive' till November 1944, while
continuing preparations for a strong offensive against Burma so that
it could be launched at any favourable moment.

Aware that Chiang Kai-shek was wavering, Mountbatten again
reconsidered the various possibilities for amphibious operations. On
the 11th December he told the Chiefs of Staff that he was examining

---

[1] See Map 14, page 452.

a plan ('Pigstick') to land a division in the southern part of the Mayu peninsula behind the main Japanese forces holding the Maungdaw–Buthidaung area with the idea of destroying them. A week later, after a visit to Arakan and discussions with Giffard and Slim, he sent the Chiefs of Staff his plan: XV Corps was to advance astride the Mayu Range, with its left flank covered by two brigades operating in the Kaladan Valley and an L.R.P. brigade in the Lemro valley, while a division landed on the southern tip of the Mayu peninsula, crossed the Mayu River and cut the Japanese line of communication with Akyab, which was subsequently to be captured by an overland attack.[1] He explained that, since the earliest possible date for 'Pigstick' was the second half of February, it would clash with the proposed fly-in of a division to Indaw under the 'Tarzan' plan. He could not therefore undertake both operations. Of the two, he preferred 'Pigstick' which offered a chance of surrounding and destroying the Japanese and could be done with the resources at his disposal, provided that no more were removed, and might be accepted by the Generalissimo as fulfilling his condition. He asked that he might be given early permission to discontinue preparations for 'Tarzan' and substitute 'Gripfast' and 'Pigstick'.

At the same time he asked Stilwell and Carton de Wiart to tell the Generalissimo that he was proposing to undertake a decisive amphibious operation. While the Chiefs of Staff were examining 'Pigstick' on its merits and in relation to its effect on 'Anvil' and 'Overlord', they learnt that the Generalissimo had already been told about it. When on the 21st they expostulated with Mountbatten for having informed the Generalissimo he replied: 'I understood that it was your wish that an amphibious operation should be carried out in accordance with the known wishes of the Generalissimo. This was certainly the impression I gained from the telegram which the President sent the Generalissimo after Sextant'.

The same day that Mountbatten's plan for 'Pigstick' was sent to the Chiefs of Staff, Carton de Wiart telegraphed to the Prime Minister that Chiang Kai-shek would attack with his Yunnan forces only if a big amphibious operation took place, and that, if it did, he would be ready in either the spring or the autumn. He, however, placed the Chinese armies in India at Stilwell's disposal to use as he judged fit.

On the 20th the President told the Generalissimo that, while he fully appreciated the difficult situation in China, he thought the greatest contribution that the Chinese themselves could make to relieve it was to undertake operations to drive a land supply route across Burma in the forthcoming dry season. He hoped therefore that the Chinese Yunnan armies would begin operations to support those which Mountbatten was planning on as large a scale as his resources

---

[1] See Map 2, page 5.

permitted. It was evident that, until the line of communication and the ferry service could be improved, the air forces in China could not be increased beyond what had already been agreed upon. The airlift would, however, be built up to 12,000 tons a month as rapidly as possible. The matter of the loan to China would be examined by the Treasury. On the 23rd the Generalissimo made it quite clear to the President that he had no intention of launching an offensive from Yunnan.

Mountbatten's reaction to this news was to tell the Chiefs of Staff that he proposed to go ahead with his preparations for 'Gripfast' and 'Pigstick'. He felt that a limited advance by the Yunnan armies would help these operations; he therefore had asked Carton de Wiart to point out to the Generalissimo that such an advance was in China's own interest, and to try and get a firm undertaking that the Yunnan armies would move forward where possible. He was prepared, if the undertaking were given, to operate L.R.P. forces ahead of the Yunnan armies. He asked for an early reply so that alternative plans for the use of the L.R.P. forces could be made.

On the 27th Mountbatten reported to the Chiefs of Staff that, although it would be a race against time to launch the operation in the last favourable period (the third week in February), he could carry out 'Pigstick' with the resources already at his disposal, but had insufficient naval forces to cover, support and escort the operation. If these could not be provided or if any more shipping were removed from his command, he would have to cancel the operation. Two days later the Chiefs of Staff told him that, in view of the needs of 'Overlord' and 'Anvil' and other urgent operations in the Mediterranean, they had come to the conclusion that 'Pigstick' could not be carried out. Their final decision, however, depended on the agreement of the American Chiefs of Staff. Meanwhile, he was to sail three fast tank landing ships to the Mediterranean at once and make preparations for the despatch of certain other landing craft in his command.[1]

Mountbatten replied on the 30th that the three fast tank landing ships were being sailed and two slower but similar craft were waiting convoy. On the assumption that it was the need for the three fast ships that had made the Chiefs of Staff abandon 'Pigstick', he was examining the possibility of carrying out the operation if the two slower ships were retained and one on its way to Aden returned to him. If 'Pigstick' were abandoned, he said, any hope of the Generalissimo agreeing to the Yunnan forces advancing would finally disappear, and it would be too late to undertake the proposed fly-in to Indaw. He would then be forced back to 'Gripfast' and to the

---

[1] Mountbatten was ordered to return Force F which meant that, in addition to the three fast tank landing ships, he lost 1 L.S.C., 4 L.S.C. I., 4 L.S.M.T., 14 L.C.T. and a flotilla of L.C.I.

original very limited advance in Arakan to secure the line of the Buthidaung–Maungdaw road and the mouth of the Naf River ('Cudgel'), since there appeared to be nothing to be gained by merely repeating the previous year's operations down the Mayu peninsula. The result would be that no worthwhile offensive action against the Japanese would be undertaken during the first year from the formation of S.E.A.C., and he would be unable to comply with the Prime Minister's directive. Furthermore, the abandonment of 'Buccaneer', 'Tarzan' and now 'Pigstick' would be bound to have a bad effect on morale 'under the none too easy conditions existing out here'.

Meanwhile Mountbatten had been told by Carton de Wiart that, in spite of some initial weakening, the Generalissimo had finally taken the line that the Yunnan armies could not advance without heavy fighting. He was prepared to order an advance only if the Andaman Islands, Rangoon or Moulmein were taken by an amphibious operation or if Mandalay or Lashio were captured.[1] In a final attempt to persuade the Generalissimo to move, Mountbatten sent Wingate to Chungking to explain personally the proposed use of L.R.P. forces to assist the advance of the Chinese Yunnan armies. Wingate arrived in Chungking on the 30th but was unable to persuade Chiang Kai-shek to co-operate. The Generalissimo's attitude, as summarized by Wingate in his report, was, 'After you have completed the conquest of Burma I am prepared to advance across the Salween, and not before'. By the 2nd January 1944, therefore, both Carton de Wiart and Wingate had to acknowledge failure. The next day the latter left Chungking and flew to meet Stilwell at Shingbwiyang.

Having heard nothing further from the Chiefs of Staff, Mountbatten asked them on the 4th January 1944 for a definite and early decision on 'Pigstick' since the concentration for it had had to be begun and the alternative plans needed entirely different movements of troops and equipment. The Chiefs of Staff replied that they were still awaiting an answer from the American Chiefs of Staff. Realizing that it was now too late to catch the last favourable period in February and determined to see that the Arakan operations did not fall between two stools, Mountbatten told the Chiefs of Staff on the 6th that he had decided to stop the movements for 'Pigstick' and begin the concentration for the alternative Arakan operation 'Cudgel'. This elicited an immediate reply from the Prime Minister who said:

> 'I fully sympathize with all your difficulties which are caused by the clash of greater events. I am sure you should mark time for a day or two between Pigstick and Cudgel till we get matters

---

[1] See Map 15 in pocket at end of volume.

cleaned up. It is no good telling me that, with the energy and drive of which you and your staff are capable, these matters in this stage of their preparation turn on a single day. You have my full confidence.'

Mountbatten consequently gave instructions on the 8th that, should orders to undertake 'Pigstick' be received from the Chiefs of Staff, then the operation was to be carried out at all costs. On the 9th, however, the Chiefs of Staff told Mountbatten that 'Pigstick' was to be cancelled and the following day instructed him to go ahead with his plans for 'Cudgel'.

On the 14th January Mountbatten issued a directive to his Commanders-in-Chief cancelling all those previously issued and giving the operations to be carried out in the early months of 1944, irrespective of whether the Chinese Yunnan armies co-operated. These were an advance by N.C.A.C. forces from Ledo to Shaduzup and thence to the Mogaung–Myitkyina area to cover the construction of the Ledo Road and to provide additional security for the air ferry route; operations by IV Corps to contain and divert Japanese forces by gaining control of the area immediately south of the Imphal–Tamu road west of the Chindwin River, exploiting east of the river and giving vigorous support to L.R.P. groups across the river; and an advance in Arakan with the capture of Akyab as the ultimate object. L.R.P. brigades were to be used on a co-ordinated plan to assist these operations as best possible.[1] For these operations 11th Army Group was allotted 14th Army, 36th Indian Division (till the 31st May), Special Force, 50th (P.) Brigade, 3 S.S. Brigade and the N.C.A.C. forces. The air forces, in addition to the tactical support of the land forces (including L.R.P. brigades), were to attack the Japanese air force, roads, railway and maintenance installations.

Thus, after weeks of discussion at a high level, the far reaching plans for the 1943–44 campaign initiated by Auchinleck on the basis of the decisions taken at Quadrant, completed by the Supreme Commander and endorsed at Sextant came to nought. All major amphibious operations were abandoned and instead of the seven major related operations,[2] there were to be only four smaller operations: the overland advance in Arakan, a limited advance and exploitation by IV Corps, an advance on the Northern front and operations by L.R.P. groups.

From the time of his return to Delhi from the Sextant Conference, Mountbatten had given much thought to the long-term strategy for

---

[1] See Map 14, page 452.
[2] See pages 16.

S.E.A.C. He felt that, after the defeat of Germany, which the Combined Chiefs of Staff had told him was expected to take place before the winter of 1944, the numbers of landing craft, assault ships and aircraft freed for employment in the Far East would be so large that it would be difficult to find areas where they could be employed. He had been told by the Prime Minister, after the cancellation of 'Buccaneer', that preparations should go forward for 'Culverin' (the operation against north Sumatra). He therefore ordered his War Staff to determine, from the point of view of time and effectiveness, the courses of action open to S.E.A.C. He reminded them that the mission assigned to S.E.A.C., which was based on the Quadrant decisions and the Prime Minister's directive of the 24th October 1943, was to maintain and broaden contact with China by the air route and by establishing a land route, and to engage the Japanese in the way best calculated to reduce their forces and divert them from the Pacific. Furthermore, it had been decided at Sextant that the main theatre of war against Japan was to be the Central and South-West Pacific, and thus operations mounted in South-East Asia should be designed to help the Pacific drive as much as possible. He explained that, as the Generalissimo had refused to allow the Yunnan armies to advance, it would not be possible to establish overland communications with China within a reasonable period.

By the end of December the War Staff submitted their conclusions on future strategy. They said that the quickest contribution which S.E.A.C. could make in 1944 towards the defeat of Japan was to help the air offensive from China by delivering more supplies to 14th U.S.A.A.F.[1] The air route which supplied this force suffered, however, from competition with the Ledo Road. Military control of the area of Burma through which the road passed was essential in order to provide fighter defence and warning for the air route; thus a one-way road would in any case have to be carried across the Hukawng Valley and the work already done would not be wasted. But the Ledo Road could not be driven through to China in time to achieve the target deliveries before the Pacific drive resulted in far greater deliveries to China by the sea route.[2] To continue it beyond what was needed for the defence of the air route was therefore a waste of time and effort. Poor administration, inadequate equipment and training, as well as political considerations, all combined to make the Chinese armies unfit for sustained military operations and unlikely to take the

---

[1] During the previous nine months 14th U.S.A.A.F. claimed to have destroyed or damaged 269,000 tons of enemy shipping and about a thousand aircraft on an average monthly supply by air of some 2,500 tons.

[2] A two-way road from Ledo by way of Myitkyina was to be driven through to Wanting or Lungling, where it would join up with the old Burma Road to Kunming. Three pipelines were to follow the line of the road, which would be two-way gravelled all-weather as far as Shingbwiyang by February 1944. The estimated date for the completion of a one-way road to China was January 1946, and for the first 4-in. pipeline April/May 1946.

offensive from Yunnan against opposition. It followed therefore that only sufficient supplies to enable them to retain their defensive positions in China should be delivered to them.

The attrition and diversion of enemy forces could be achieved only by threatening the vital interests of Japan, and this could best be done by breaching the Japanese defensive perimeter and establishing within it bases from which to employ fully the sea and air power which would become available. One way to achieve this would be to reoccupy the whole of Burma, but for this Rangoon would first have to be captured. An essential preliminary was the occupation of the Andamans, but no expedition against them could now be launched before the end of 1944.[1] If Rangoon were to be captured before the 1945 monsoon heavy reinforcements would have to be provided from Europe. The main justification for the reoccupation of Burma was to establish land communications with China but, as already shown, this could not be accomplished in time to be effective.

Operations against Tenasserim and the Kra Isthmus leading to the capture of Bangkok would have considerable strategic value, but, because of the scale of air support necessary, should not be attempted until Rangoon had been occupied. Thus, at the earliest, Bangkok could not be attacked before the spring of 1946, which was too late to influence the course of the war.

Another alternative was to occupy northern Sumatra, which would provide a valuable base for air attacks on enemy shipping in the South China Sea and the Gulf of Siam and on bases as yet out of reach in Malaya and Siam, oil fields in Palembang and other important sources of strategic raw material. Most of the forces needed for this operation, which could be launched in October–November 1944, were available in S.E.A.C., provided that commitments in northern Burma were limited, but reinforcements in the form of assault shipping and aircraft would have to come from elsewhere. The occupation of northern Sumatra could stand on its own as an independent operation and, given additional resources, it could be used as a springboard for an advance into Malaya or the Sunda Strait in harmony with the Pacific advance.

The War Staff therefore concluded that:
  (i) The most immediate method by which S.E.A.C. could contribute towards the defeat of Japan in 1944 was to nourish the maximum air offensive from China. All the resources required should be diverted to increasing the airlift.
  (ii) The Ledo Road project was out of step with the Pacific strategy and should be limited in scope to the requirements for the defence of the air route to China.

---

[1] See Map 15 in pocket at end of volume.

2. Lieut.-General
J. W. Stilwell.

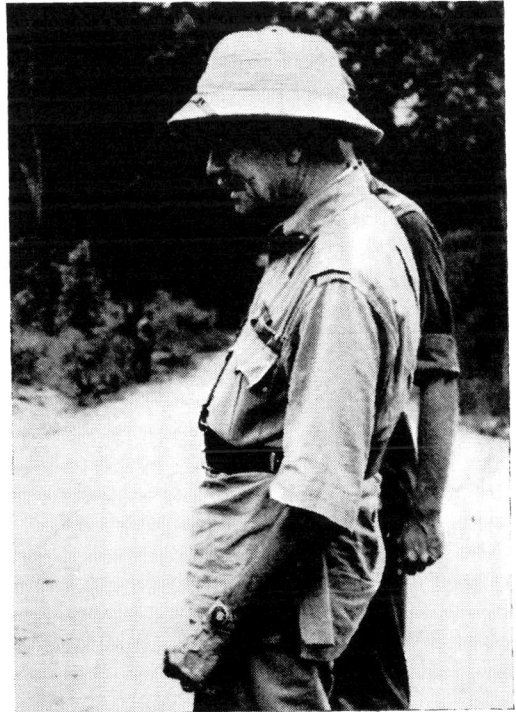

3. General Sir
George Giffard.

4. Lieut.-General
W. J. Slim.

5. Lieut.-General
M. Kawabe.

6. Lieut.-General
R. Mutaguchi.

7. Group taken at *15th Army Headquarters*.

Front row, *left to right*: Lieut-Generals G. Yanagida, S. Tanaka, R. Mutaguchi, S. Matsuyama, K. Sato.
Middle row, *centre*: Major-General H. Obata.

8. Lieut.-General
S. Sakurai.

9. Lieut.-General
T. Hanaya.

(iii) The reoccupation of Burma would absorb disproportionate resources, would prevent S.E.A.C. from taking timely decisive action against Japan and might prolong the war. The Japanese in Burma should therefore be contained by the minimum air and land forces required to deny them freedom of action, and the forces available to S.E.A.C. should be used to launch a major offensive elsewhere.

(iv) The conquest of northern Sumatra as soon as resources could be made available should be the first step, to be followed by operations against Malaya or the Sunda Strait. This operation should be launched towards the end of 1944 so that, with the thrusts in the Central and South-West Pacific, there should be a three-pronged threat against Japan.

Mountbatten was well aware that the operations envisaged were not in accordance with his directive on Burma. He felt, however, that they were in accordance with the general intention of maintaining and broadening contacts with China, and the quickest way of achieving this was by opening a port in the China Sea. The plan proposed would certainly assist operations in the Pacific, with which it would have to be carefully co-ordinated and synchronized. Moreover, the Prime Minister had said that 'Culverin' was the only worthwhile operation for South-East Asia and that he was determined to press for it day in and day out until all obstruction to it had been worn down.

Mountbatten therefore accepted the conclusions reached by his War Staff, and proposed that the new directive which he had been promised by the Combined Chiefs of Staff should be to:

(i) Conduct air and limited land operations in order to contain the enemy in Burma, provide reasonable security and facilitate the operation of the air route and support the maximum air offensive from China, thus encouraging Chinese resistance until a sea route could be opened.

(ii) Conduct progressive amphibious operations to establish offensive air bases, thereby accelerating the advance to the Chinese coast and hastening the defeat of Japan.

His three Commanders-in-Chief were in general agreement with these proposals, although they each expressed doubt in varying degrees whether the forces needed for the northern Sumatra operation could be assembled and prepared in time to carry it out in 1944. In the absence of Stilwell, who had taken personal command of the Northern front at the end of December, the matter had been discussed with his deputy, Lieut.-General D. I. Sultan, U.S. Army; it was not until the 31st January that Stilwell himself attended a meeting in Delhi. He straight away announced his complete disagreement with Mountbatten's proposals. He felt that to give up the present plans for S.E.A.C. and adopt others based on the early collapse of Germany was scarcely warranted. He queried whether the route to a port on the China Sea was shorter by Sumatra and Malaya than it was by Burma and Yunnan. He considered that an attack through Burma would raise the blockade of China and give direct access to the airfields from which the Allies could deploy their superior air strength most profitably, whereas an attack by way of Sumatra and Malaya would defer indefinitely the time by which this could be done and China, left blockaded, might collapse.

Despite the opposition of his deputy, Mountbatten decided to stand by his views. Since the effect of the new directive on the lines he desired would be far-reaching and would need careful study, he decided to send a special mission to the United Kingdom and America to discuss them with the Chiefs of Staff and the Combined Chiefs of Staff. On the 5th February a mission, known as the Axiom Mission, headed by his deputy Chief of Staff (Wedemeyer), left Delhi by air for London.[1] The mission was to put Mountbatten's views, together with dissenting views, before the Chiefs of Staff in London, and then go on to Washington.

---

[1] The composition of the Axiom Mission was: Major-General A. C. Wedemeyer (U.S. Army), Major-General D. Harrison (Engineer-in-Chief S.E.A.C.), Major-General M. W. M. Macleod (Head of Combined Operations), Brigadier G. Bourne and Captain M. G. G. Goodenough, R.N. (War Staff S.E.A.C.).

CHAPTER VI

THE JAPANESE PLANS FOR 1944
(September 1943–January 1944)

See Maps 1, 2, 3, 4, 12, 13 and 15

T HE Japanese plan on the outbreak of war in 1941 had been
to seize the Philippines, the Netherlands East Indies, Malaya,
Siam and Burma, which were to form a Greater East Asia
Co-Prosperity Sphere, and establish a strong defensive perimeter
around the newly-acquired territories.[1] This perimeter was to run
from the Kuriles, through Wake Island to the Marshall and Gilbert
Islands, the Bismarck Archipelago, New Guinea and Timor, Java
and Sumatra, Malaya and on to Burma. It was the intention to hold
this perimeter and, by the destruction of any Allied forces attempting
to penetrate it, destroy the Allies' will to fight, and compel them to
accept the occupation of the area conquered as a *fait accompli*.[2]

Carried away by the ease with which they had gained their perimeter in the Pacific, the Japanese decided in April 1942 to expand it
in order to give greater depth to their defences against an American
counter-offensive, and to try to bring the United States Pacific Fleet
to action before it had had time to rebuild its strength after its losses
at Pearl Harbour. The plan was to advance in the South-West
Pacific to the Solomons, and to Port Moresby in Papua,[3] and thus
gain forward bases from which an advance could later be made to
New Caledonia, Fiji and Samoa. At the same time the western
Aleutians and Midway were to be occupied, for it was thought that
the occupation of the latter, which would threaten Pearl Harbour,
would probably force a fleet action on the Americans.[4]

These decisions led to the naval actions of the Coral Sea and
Midway and to the fierce fighting in both the Solomons and New
Guinea, described in Volume II. In these battles the Americans
regained the initiative and the Japanese were thrown on the defensive, having suffered severe losses in ships and aircraft which they
could not replace.[5]

---

[1] See Map 13, page 438.
[2] See Volume I, Chapter V.
[3] See Map 1, page 1.
[4] See Volume II, page 225.
[5] For the distribution of Japanese forces in August 1943 see Appendix 12. For their losses
in merchant ships see Appendix 14 and in naval vessels Appendix 27.

The failure of the efforts to enlarge the perimeter in the Pacific and the alarming rapidity and intensity of the Allied counter-offensive forced *Imperial General Headquarters* to call a conference in September 1943 to reconsider Japanese strategy. The tripartite alliance of Germany, Italy and Japan had broken down with the collapse of Italy, and, with Germany deeply involved in Russia, Japan would have to continue to wage the war against Britain and America without any help from Europe. Although the Allies would probably give priority to defeating Germany, they had the means to prosecute the war in the Pacific at the same time. It could therefore be assumed that Allied forces would increase their pressure on all fronts in the Far East and that offensives might be expected on the south-west and north-east fronts as well as in the South-East Pacific. A large-scale offensive by the Americans in the Central Pacific was not, however, likely for the time being, though the Gilbert Islands, Nauru or Wake and Marcus Island might be attacked about the end of 1943.

The conference considered that the task of the Imperial military forces was to protect the homeland against invasion, secure the safety of the lines of communication from Japan to the occupied territories in the Southern Region and retain political and economic control of the major nations within the Greater East Asia Co-Prosperity Sphere, whose raw materials were essential to Japan's war effort and the maintenance of the minimum acceptable standard of living of her people.

In view of the great disparity between Japanese resources and those of the United States, there was no hope of holding the existing front in the South-East Pacific, even if reinforcements could be sent, which was doubtful. The conference therefore recommended that the main defensive zone should eventually be withdrawn to the general line Timor – Western New Guinea – Caroline Islands – the Kuriles. This line was to be firmly held since any further withdrawal would decrease the nation's capacity to conduct operations and to face a protracted war, and behind it the forces to launch counter-offensives would be built up.

The conclusions reached by the conference were that the Army and Navy, acting in close co-operation, should conduct operations to defend Japan, the oil-bearing areas in the Southern Region and the sea communications between the two; to continue preparations for war on the Manchurian front in the hope of preventing Russo-American co-operation and avoiding war with Russia; to make every effort to maintain peace in the occupied areas of China and exert pressure to crush the will of the Chinese to continue the struggle; to hold at all costs areas already occupied on the south-west front and crush any Allied offensives directed against Burma, the Andaman and Nicobar Islands, or Sumatra;[1] to defeat or delay to the utmost Allied offensives in the central and southern Pacific, and at the same time make every effort to prepare the Timor–Caroline Islands line for defence and build up forces for a counter-offensive with the object of retaining the initiative.

These conclusions were submitted as recommendations to a Liaison Conference in Tokyo on the 25th September and approved. They were confirmed at an Imperial Conference on the 30th.

In Burma, owing to the realization after the first Chindit operation that their defences east of the Chindwin could be easily pierced, and to the views of the forceful commander of *15th Army* (Lieut.-General R. Mutaguchi), the Japanese High Command had come to the conclusion during the summer of 1943 that, if they were to hold the country against the expected Allied offensive, they would have to advance into Assam and seize Imphal, the base from which any large-scale British offensive would have to be launched. The problem had been carefully studied at the end of June by *Burma Area Army* (Lieut.-General M. Kawabe) and *Southern Army* (Field-Marshal Count H. Terauchi), and early in July *Imperial General Headquarters* had given their consent for preparation for an offensive to begin.[2] On the 7th August, *Southern Army* instructed *Burma Area Army* to complete preparations for an offensive on the Imphal front (operation 'U-Go') to forestall a British offensive, while remaining on the defensive elsewhere in Burma, and told Kawabe that approximately seven divisions would be made available for Burma. The offensive was not, however, to begin without sanction from *Southern Army*, though preparatory operations could take place at the discretion of *Burma Area Army*. If the Allies took the offensive first, they were to be defeated and an advance to Imphal would follow.[3]

On the 12th August Kawabe issued his first operation instruction for the offensive. This stated that *56th Division* would remain responsible for holding the Chinese on the line of the Salween River or, if this were impossible, on the general line Pingka–Lameng–Tengchung,[4] *18th Division* for the defence of the Hukawng Valley, holding any Allied advance from Ledo well north of Kamaing, and that *15th Army* (*15th*, *31st* and *33rd Divisions*) was to advance on Imphal, gain control of the frontier mountain ranges and the passes through them and so provide a sure defence for Burma. In order to confuse the Allies and pin down the British formations in Arakan, an advance

---

[1] See Map 15 in pocket at end of volume.
[2] For the areas under control of *Southern Army* see Appendix 12.
[3] See Volume II, Chapter XXVI.
[4] See Map 12, page 398.

on the Akyab front by *55th Division* (operation 'Ha-Go') was to begin
two or three weeks before the Imphal offensive.

Mutaguchi prepared an outline plan based on these instructions
on the assumption that the operations would begin early in 1944 and
be completed within one month. The *56th Division*, assisted by a
detachment from *18th Division*, was to attack the Chinese troops on
the west bank of the Salween in October, destroy their advanced
bases and then, having driven them back across the river, stand on
the defensive on the river line itself. The main body of *18th Division*
was to be responsible for the defence of the Hukawng Valley north
of Kamaing; its detachment was to be returned to it as soon as *56th
Division's* operation was completed. As a preliminary to the offensive
against Imphal *33rd Division* was to occupy Fort White, Falam and
Haka (key localities in the Chin Hills) during November 1943.[1] The
15th Army plan for the advance on Imphal was that *33rd Division*, moving north up the Kabaw Valley and through the Chin Hills, isolated
and destroyed the forces there and then moved on Imphal, while the
main striking force, consisting of *31st* and *15th Divisions*, crossed the
Chindwin River between Homalin and Paungbyin and advanced on
Kohima and Imphal respectively. When it reached Kohima, *31st
Division* was to hold off any British reinforcements sent up from
India while *15th* and *33rd Divisions* conducted a pincer movement
on Imphal from the north and south. When Imphal had been occupied the army was to hold the passes over the mountains extending
from Kohima and thence west of Imphal and the Manipur River to
Falam and Haka.

General Mutaguchi considered that the fair-weather roads from
Wuntho and Indaw to Pinbon and thence through Sitsawk to
Paungbyin and Homalin would suffice to move *15th* and *31st
Divisions* secretly and quickly to their concentration areas on the
Chindwin, but, once the offensive was launched, would not be
adequate except in emergency to support the divisions.[2] The main
line of communication for the offensive was to be the motor road
which had been built from Shwebo through Yeu to Kalewa. As the
offensive progressed, the Kalemyo–Tamu road (which was erroneously considered to be an all-weather road) was to be used as an
extension of the main line of communication, and the Kalemyo–
Tiddim road as a subsidiary. In case there was a delay in gaining
control of the main all-weather road from Tamu to Imphal a road
from the north end of the Kabaw Valley to Ukhrul was to be built.[3]
He estimated that the first phase of the offensive would be completed

---

[1] See Map 3, page 33.

[2] These roads had been brought up to an adequate standard by early February.

[3] By the time the Japanese advance began IV Corps had built a fair-weather road on
this alignment capable of carrying light motor transport. See page 187.

in three weeks and therefore planned that each division would carry supplies and ammunition sufficient for that period.

Mutaguchi held a conference on the proposed operation between the 22nd and 26th December. The Vice-Chief of Staff of *Southern Army* (Lieut.-General K. Ayabe) and the Chief of Staff of *Burma Area Army* (Lieut.-General E. Naka) attended with two other staff officers. An appreciation of the Allied situation and intentions was placed before the conference. On the Arakan front it seemed that the British, despite their serious defeat by a much weaker force earlier in the year, were still clinging to the idea of recapturing Akyab and were concentrating two divisions on the Maungdaw–Buthidaung front with about two others in reserve.[1] They might be expected to open a large-scale offensive early in 1944. In Assam three divisions (17th, 20th and 23rd) had been concentrated, Imphal was gradually being developed into a major operational base and the Imphal–Tamu and Imphal—Tiddim roads were being made fit for motor transport. In north-east Assam (the Hukawng Valley front) reports showed that the newly-formed Chinese armies under General Stilwell's command were, particularly in organization, equipment and training, incomparably superior to the Chinese troops met during the earlier campaigns in Burma or in China. On the Yunnan front, although ten Chinese divisions were located on the east bank of the Salween River, preparations for an offensive were not so far advanced as elsewhere and the troops were of poor calibre; there was thus little danger from this flank for the time being.

The *Southern Army* had agreed that a decision whether the offensive should be launched would depend on the result of the conference and for that reason had arranged for Ayabe to attend. Ayabe came to the conclusion that, if the defence of Burma were to be ensured, it was essential that the general line of the Naga Hills–Kohima and the high ground west of Imphal should be held and that, even if there were risks inherent in the plan, it had to be carried out. The Commander-in-Chief, *Southern Army*, accepted his views and at the end of December sent him to Tokyo to obtain *Imperial General Headquarter's* sanction for the proposed offensive. There he was asked five questions: could the army deal successfully with an Allied seaborne attack from the Bay of Bengal; could the air force keep pace with the attacking divisions and support them throughout the operation; was the *15th Army* operational plan sound; was the supply position satisfactory; and, in view of the length of the front and the depth to which the attacking formations had to penetrate, was there sufficient strength to ensure success? Ayabe succeeded in satisfying his interrogators on these points. On the 7th January *Imperial General Headquarters* gave their assent to the proposed operation and issued an

---

[1] See Map 2, page 5.

instruction which read: 'In order to defend Burma the Commander-in-Chief, *Southern Army*, may occupy and secure the vital areas of north-eastern India in the vicinity of Imphal by defeating the enemy in that area at the opportune time.' *Imperial General Headquarters* had apparently some qualms on the wisdom of their action, for on the following day in a message to *Southern Army* they stressed the need for careful control of the operations and the desirability of bringing them to a conclusion and adopting the defensive in the new positions at the earliest possible moment. On the 15th January *Southern Army* instructed *Burma Area Army* to undertake the Imphal offensive.

The forces available to *Burma Area Army* at the beginning of January 1944 were *15th Army* (consisting of *56th Division* on the Salween front, *18th Division* on the Myitkyina–Hukawng Valley front, *31st* and *33rd Divisions* on the Chindwin front), *55th Division* on the Arakan front, *24th Independent Mixed Brigade* in Tenasserim, *54th Division* (which had begun to arrive and had been allotted to watch the coast from Ramree Island to the Irrawaddy delta) and *15th Division*. Although posted to *15th Army* in June 1943, *15th Division* was held by *Southern Army*, with *Imperial General Headquarters'* concurrence, in Siam as a reserve in case the Allies launched a seaborne offensive. It was not till mid-October, when *2nd Division*, reorganizing in the Philippines after its withdrawal from Guadalcanal,[1] was ready to move to Malaya, that *Southern Army* released *15th Division* to *Burma Area Army*. The division had meanwhile been training for jungle warfare in northern Siam and some of its units had been employed on the repair and improvement of the Chiengmai–Toungoo road, which was required as an alternative line of communication to Burma owing to the interruption of sea traffic in the Bay of Bengal and Allied air attacks on the railways in south Burma. The Siam–Burma railway being closed, the division early in November began its long journey of some 700 miles along the Chiengrai–Kengtung—Takaw road to the Mandalay–Shwebo area by route march, assisted by ten motor transport companies. Progress was slow and it was not till mid-January 1944 that *60th Infantry Regiment* (the leading formation of the division) began to arrive in *15th Army's* area, having left much of its equipment in Siam. It was then realized that the division could not be fully concentrated in northern Burma till early March.

Early in January Kawabe received a revised appreciation of the Allied situation and intentions. This followed closely the general lines of that of December 1943 but contained additional intelligence. On the Arakan front Allied forces were now in close contact with *55th Division* and their reserve divisions in the Chittagong area were well placed to move forward quickly; it was thought that their

---

[1] For the Guadalcanal campaign see Volume II, pages 279–86.

intention was to retake Akyab and that their preparations were nearly complete. On the Assam front an armoured formation had been identified at Imphal in addition to the three infantry divisions. Two or three Allied divisions were (erroneously) reported to be in the Dimapur and Shillong areas, and it was estimated that another division might be moved to Assam from the Chittagong area. Airfields on a large scale were being built at Imphal, Palel and Tamu. There were indications that an Allied offensive directed on Mawlaik might begin in the near future. In the Hukawng Valley, the road being constructed from Ledo had reached the Tanai River and an offensive by 22nd and 38th Chinese Divisions, assisted by a detachment moving by way of the upper reaches of the river, was about to be launched to cut *18th Division's* communications.[1] It was still felt that there was no immediate danger on the Yunnan front, although there had been signs of increased activity behind the Chinese lines.

It was estimated that the Allied air forces in India had a strength of 1,000 aircraft and this was expected to increase to 1,500 by the summer of 1944. Air superiority was more or less in the hands of the Allies; movement by road and rail was already becoming difficult during daylight and air attacks on airfields, strategic points on communications and important military installations in central and northern Burma were becoming all too frequent. Allied radio jamming had increased and was very active. Although the Allies were known to have a considerable number of transport aircraft available for moving men and stores, it was not considered that their forces once surrounded and cut off from ground supply could hold out for long. It was thought that supply by air would be extremely hazardous, if not impossible, in the monsoon and that the advent of the rains would reduce Allied resistance and act in Japan's favour. From all this information, the Japanese reached the conclusion that the Allies were planning to recapture the whole of Burma by attacking the Mayu peninsula, launching a main offensive into northern and central Burma which would converge on Mandalay and undertaking an amphibious operation on the south-west coast.

Despite the apparent increase in the strength of the British in Assam, Kawabe approved in principle the outline plan already submitted by *15th Army*, and on the 19th January issued his orders for the operation. While the Allied offensive preparations were incomplete, *15th Army* was to seize the opportunity to destroy the Allied forces at Imphal and build up strong defences covering Kohima and Imphal before the beginning of the monsoon. The offensive was to begin between the middle of February and early March so that it could be completed by mid-April, thus leaving a

---

[1] See Map 4, page 53.

month for consolidation and for assuming monsoon positions, but not enough time for Allied divisions to be brought from other fronts before the monsoon began. A complication arose when it became evident that *15th Division* could not complete its concentration east of the Chindwin till early March. Steps were therefore to be taken to accelerate its move by all possible means. To enable *Headquarters 15th Army* to concentrate the whole of its attention on the Imphal offensive, *56th Division* was to come under the direct command of *Burma Area Army*. By agreement with the provisional government of 'Free India', *1st Division* (some 7,000 men) of the so-called *Indian National Army* was placed under command of *15th Army*. The subsidiary offensive in Arakan (operation 'Ha-Go'), to mislead the British and contain their formations in that area, was to take place a short time before the beginning of the Imphal offensive.

As he proposed to allot all his formations either to the offensive operations or for frontier protection General Kawabe found himself without any reserve. He had therefore asked *Southern Army* for two extra divisions, and put forward a proposal that *Burma Area Army* should be reorganized. Assuming that the Allies would attack from China, from Assam and along the south-west coastline, and in view of the fact that *15th Army* was shortly to be involved in an offensive, he suggested that two additional army headquarters should be formed: one to take charge of north and north-east Burma, and the other of Arakan and the coastal area. This would leave *15th Army* free to deal with the Chindwin front. The *Southern Army* met his request for extra divisions in part and ordered *2nd Division* to move from Malaya to Burma, and accepted the necessity for the reorganization. On the 7th January *Imperial General Headquarters* sanctioned the immediate formation of *Headquarters 28th Army* to take control of the Arakan front and the coastal area and assume command of *55th*, *54th*, and *2nd Divisions*, and for *Headquarters 33rd Army* to be formed in April to take command of *18th* and *56th Divisions* and the control of the northern front. The *15th Army* would then be left with *15th*, *31st* and *33rd Divisions* and the *I.N.A.* division, and Mutaguchi could concentrate fully on the conduct of the Imphal offensive.

The *5th Air Division*, which commanded all the air forces in Burma, was under the direct control of *3rd Air Army* with its headquarters in Singapore. Kawabe therefore made an agreement with its commander by which *5th Air Division* would provide air support for operation 'Ha-Go' in Arakan from the 3rd February and, during the Imphal offensive, would maintain control of the air in the battle zone and attack Allied airfields and major tactical objectives. Should the Allies attempt an airborne landing in Burma, the division would use all available forces to attack it. The main bases for the division would be Kalaw and Meiktila with detachments at Toungoo and Rangoon.[1]

On the 21st January Lieut.-General S. Sakurai arrived in Rangoon and at the end of the month assumed command of *28th Army* with Major-General H. Iwakuro as his Chief of Staff. The army was given responsibility for the coastal area west of a line from Rangoon (exclusive) to Prome and then north-west across the Arakan Yomas to the Indo–Burma frontier. Sakurai ordered *55th Division* (Lieut.-General T. Hanaya) to be brought up to full strength, to undertake the defence of Akyab and carry out the 'Ha-Go' offensive on the Arakan front, *54th Division* to defend the line of communication between Akyab and Taungup and *2nd Division*, on arrival, to defend Sandoway, Gwa, Bassein and the Irrawaddy delta.[2]

When ordered to undertake operation 'Ha-Go' in January, Hanaya had decided to anticipate the imminent British offensive and render XV Corps impotent by cutting off and destroying the formations in the forward area and then occupying what he thought was the corps' operational base at Bawli Bazar.[3] To this end he proposed to pierce the British left with a strong mobile column moving through Taung Bazar on to Ngakyedauk Pass. Fearing that, in the event of an unfavourable turn in the battle, so deep a penetration might place *55th Division* in a position where it could not be assisted, General Sakurai (*28th Army*) told Hanaya that, while his general plan was approved, he was not to move north of an east and west line through Taung Bazar without permission.[4]

On the 25th January Mutaguchi held a conference, attended by the Chiefs of Staff of the three divisions under his command, at which he explained his plans for the Imphal offensive. By the end of February, *33rd Division* was to be concentrated in the Chin Hills west of Kalemyo and in the vicinity of Yazagyo in the Kabaw Valley.[5] On D-7 day the main body of the division was to take the offensive on the axis of the Fort White–Tiddim–Bishenpur road, and at the same time an armoured column (mainly composed of tanks, heavy field and anti-tank artillery) was to thrust north along the Kabaw Valley, seize Tamu and then, advancing along the Tamu–Palel road, attack Imphal in co-ordination with the attack of the main body of the division. It was hoped that, by launching this

---

[1] See Map 15 in pocket at end of volume.

[2] See Map 15 in pocket at end of volume. The defence of Akyab became the responsibility of *54th Division* on the 5th February.

[3] See Map 2, page 5. Hanaya succeeded General Koga, the victor of the first Arakan campaign, in command of *55th Division* in November 1943. (See Volume II, Chapters XIX and XX).

[4] Despite the fact that 'Ha-Go' had very limited objectives, the Japanese, for propaganda purposes, broadcast on the 4th February that the object of their offensive in Arakan was to capture Chittagong and advance on Calcutta.

[5] See Map 3, page 33.

division a week in advance of the other two, the Allied forces would
be drawn south and so facilitate the crossing of the Chindwin and
the subsequent advance of *15th* and *31st Divisions*.

By the beginning of March, these two divisions were to be deployed
on the eastern bank of the Chindwin River. On D-day *15th Division*
was to cross the Chindwin between Homalin and Sittaung in several
columns and, moving across country, seize the high ground north-
west of the Imphal plain. On reaching that area it was to send
detachments to cut the Imphal–Kohima road and the Bishenpur–
Silchar road, and prepare to assault Imphal. At the same time *31st
Division* was to cross the Chindwin between Tamanthi and Homalin
and, moving through Ukhrul and either Fort Keary or Layshi,
occupy Kohima and then protect the rear and flank of *15th Division*
till Imphal had been captured.[1] As soon as *15th* and *33rd Divisions*
were in position Imphal was to be assaulted from the north and south
and captured by the middle of April. Thereafter, the passes through
the mountain ranges east of Dimapur and Silchar and the Chin Hills
were to be held and preparations made for the monsoon.

On the 11th February (Japanese Empire Day) Mutaguchi issued
his operation orders confirming the plan which he had outlined at
the conference on the 25th January. It was now very desirable that
D-day should be before the end of the month, for operation 'Ha-Go'
had been launched in Arakan on the 4th. But, although every
available motor vehicle had been sent by *Burma Area Army* to accelerate the move of *15th Division* to its concentration area, it was now
plain that only two-thirds of the division could be in position by the
middle of March. Mutaguchi could not afford to delay his offensive
beyond that date and so accepted the risk of beginning it short of a
proportion of his already limited strength. He fixed D-day for the
15th March which meant that *33rd Division* had to begin its advance
on the 8th March.

The difficult problem of supplying *15th Army* once the offensive
had begun had, however, been only partially solved, for *Southern
Army* had allotted *Burma Area Army* only some two-thirds of the
administrative units it had requested and by no means all of those
allotted had been actually provided. It was considered that the
rations and ammunition which could be carried without loss of
fighting efficiency by the troops and animals accompanying them
was limited to twenty days' supply. Quick success in the offensive
was thus of supreme importance, for, with the administrative position as it was, any delay might result in the fighting divisions finding
themselves in inhospitable country, without a supply line and
opposed by a well-supplied enemy fighting on his own ground. To
ensure against delay, Mutaguchi arranged for five days' reserve

---

[1] See Map 4, page 53.

supplies for *15th* and *31st Divisions* to be held in the Indaw area, ready to be moved forward over the fair-weather roads to Homalin and Paungbyin. Despite these administrative weaknesses *15th Army* was apparently full of confidence in victory. In disregarding the precarious supply situation it was but following long-established Japanese military tradition and method.

CHAPTER VII

THE PACIFIC

(September–November 1943)

See Maps 1 and 13 and Sketches 1 and 18

AT the Quadrant Conference at Quebec in August 1943 two specific lines of approach towards Japan in the Pacific had been laid down.[1] General MacArthur's advance in the South-West Pacific was to continue in eastern New Guinea as far as Wewak; the Admiralty Islands were to be seized and the Bismarck Archipelago neutralized; and, with Rabaul rendered impotent, a further move westwards was to be made step by step along the New Guinea coast to the Vogelkop peninsula, its north-western extremity.[2] A second line of approach was to be opened in the Central Pacific, passing progressively through the Gilberts, the Marshalls, Ponape, Truk, Palau and northwards to the Marianas.[3] The two advances would be mutually supporting; they would divide the Japanese forces and keep them guessing where the next blow would fall. The central advance was to have priority: it would use the superior strength of the American Pacific Fleet to the best advantage to bring about the decisive defeat of the Japanese navy.

In the central Solomons, Munda, the linchpin of the Japanese defences, had fallen on the 5th August, and three weeks later all Japanese resistance in New Georgia had ended. Kolombangara, the next step in the Solomons ladder, had been successfully by-passed and American troops had landed at Barakoma on the south-east coast of Vella Lavella, where engineers were busy clearing the jungle and preparing an airstrip.

On the 18th September the Americans in Vella Lavella were relieved by 14th Brigade of 3rd New Zealand Division under command of Major-General H. E. Barrowclough. Three days later the New Zealanders began a two-pronged drive up the east and west coasts, and by the end of the month had driven the Japanese into a small pocket in the extreme north-west of the island.

By this time the Japanese had withdrawn their garrison from Kolombangara. Throughout September, patrols by American motor

---

[1] See Volume II, Chapter XXVI.
[2] See Map 1, page 1.
[3] See Map 13, page 438.

torpedo-boats and aircraft, and occasional night raids up 'The Slot' by cruisers and destroyers, had taken heavy toll of the barges carrying small parties of troops running the blockade, but had failed to prevent 9,000 men escaping. Having evacuated Kolombangara, the enemy had no further reason for maintaining the outpost on Vella Lavella, and on the 6th October six Japanese destroyers and a number of small craft were sent to rescue the survivors. They were intercepted by three American destroyers on the night of the 6th/7th. In the ensuing action an American destroyer was torpedoed and, out of control, was rammed by one of her sister ships. Five minutes later a torpedo blew the bows off the third. The Japanese lost only one ship which was set on fire and later sunk by torpedoes, but, instead of pressing home their advantage, they broke off the engagement and returned to Rabaul. Their object, however, had been achieved, as the New Zealanders discovered next morning; under cover of the action small craft had crept inshore and taken off the beleaguered garrison.

The battle of Vella Lavella, as it was called, ended the campaign in the central Solomons. Only Bougainville now remained to bar the way to Rabaul. The Japanese were well aware that an attack on the northern Solomons was imminent and doubted their ability to meet it. In the past eighteen months their naval and air losses had been very heavy,[1] and American submarines were taking an increasingly heavy toll of their merchant shipping. More than two million tons, nearly a third of the pre-war fleet, had already been sunk—a loss which Japanese shipyards were incapable of replacing.

In view of these losses, the impossibility of getting reinforcements through to the South-East front, and growing American strength, *Imperial General Headquarters* decided to abandon the Bismarck Barrier, and on the 30th September issued their new operational policy by which a new defensive perimeter was to be established from Timor through New Guinea and the Caroline and Mariana Islands to the Kuriles.[2] The New Guinea–Bismarck Archipelago–Solomon Islands triangle was thus relegated to the status of a delaying action area only, to be held by the divisions already there, without rein-forcement, as best they could. As a result of this Lieut.-General H. Imamura, Commander-in-Chief of *8th Area Army*, who controlled eastern New Guinea and the Solomons from Rabaul, issued new operation orders on the 7th October. The *4th Air Army* (*6th* and *7th Air Divisions*) was to support the forces in New Guinea and the Solomons and protect shipping; *17th Army* (*6th* and part of *17th Divisions*) was to hold the northern Solomons and particularly Bougainville; *18th Army* (*20th*, *41st* and *51st Divisions*) the Finschhafen

---

[1] See Volume II, Chapter XVI.
[2] See pages 72–73.

area and strategic areas along the coast of New Guinea west of the Vitiaz Strait; *17th Division* (less the part with *17th Army*) western New Britain; and *38th Division* Rabaul and strategic points in eastern New Ireland.[1]

In October Admiral M. Koga decided,[2] as Admiral I. Yamamoto had done with such poor results six months before,[3] to reinforce *11th Air Fleet* at Rabaul with aircraft from his carriers.[4] Disembarkation of these carrier aircraft was delayed by an abortive sortie of the *Combined Fleet* from Truk to intercept an American fast carrier task force from Pearl Harbour which raided Wake Island on the 5th October, and it was not till the 1st November that they reached Rabaul.

Bougainville, the largest island in the Solomons, was also the most strongly defended and its garrison of one division had been reinforced in September by one artillery and four infantry battalions from China. During the previous eighteen months the Japanese had built airfields in the extreme north at Buka and Bonis, on either side of the narrow channel which divides Buka from Bougainville, at Kara and Kahili in the extreme south and on the adjacent islands of Shortland and Ballale. The garrison of the group was estimated at about 40,000 troops, most of whom it was thought were concentrated around the southern airfields.

Admiral Halsey's first plan for the occupation of Bougainville had been a direct assault on Shortland Island as a stepping stone to the capture of the airfields in the south. To avoid the strongly defended airfields and to establish a beachhead where opposition would be weak and to build the airfields which he needed for the neutralization of Rabaul, Halsey later decided to by-pass the main Japanese centres of resistance as he had done so successfully at Kolombangara. Points on the east and west coasts were considered and Cape Torokina at the northern end of Empress Augusta Bay, half-way up the west coast of the island, was finally selected as the most suitable; it was a long way from the nearest Japanese forward base in the island and could be reached from inland only with great difficulty by narrow jungle tracks. Moreover, it was within air striking distance of Rabaul. The plan called for two preliminary landings: the first, to be undertaken on the 27th October, on the Treasury Islands half-way between the newly-captured airfield at Barakoma in Vella Lavella and Cape Torokina, so as to provide flank protection to the ocean supply route and an airstrip from which fighter cover could be maintained over Empress Augusta Bay; the

---

[1] See Appendix 12.
[2] Koga had succeeded Yamamoto as Commander-in-Chief, *Combined Fleet*, in April 1943.
[3] See Volume II, Chapter XXII.
[4] The remaining 200 land-based aircraft at Rabaul were reinforced by 172 aircraft from the carriers.

second, a diversionary landing on Choiseul Island, to be made at the same time, to lead the Japanese into believing that the main assault was coming on the east coast of Bougainville. The main assault was to take place on the 1st November.

The 5th U.S.A.A.F. from New Guinea pounded Rabaul whenever weather permitted, while aircraft of the South Pacific Command, operating from Munda and Barakoma, struck at the airfields in and around Bougainville to pave the way for the offensive. The strikes increased in frequency and intensity towards the end of October. The preliminary landing on the Treasury Islands led the Japanese to expect the main assault at the southern end of Bougainville and the defences in that area were consequently strengthened. A task force of four cruisers and eight destroyers under the command of Rear-Admiral A. S. Merrill bombarded Buka and Bonis airfields just after midnight on the 31st, and then turned south at 30 knots for Shortland Island and opened fire on the Japanese positions there. Aircraft from two fleet carriers, detached from the 5th Fleet to support the landings at Torokina, struck the Buka and Bonis airfields twice on the 1st November and twice more the following day, adding to the destruction wrought by the ships.

After a preliminary bombardment by escorting destroyers and aircraft, the first flight of assault craft carrying 3rd U.S. Marine Division touched down at Cape Torokina about an hour after sunrise on the 1st November. Since the Japanese had expected a landing in the southern part of Bougainville, no defences had been prepared on the west coast and only one platoon of infantry was defending the landing beaches. Owing, however, to heavy surf, the steepness and narrowness of the beaches and two enemy air attacks, which were beaten off by fighters from Barakoma, the unloading of troops and stores was not as rapid as had been hoped. Nevertheless, by nightfall a beachhead had been secured and over 14,000 troops had been landed.

The expected counter-attack by the Japanese Navy was not long in coming. At 2.45 a.m. on the 2nd November four cruisers and six destroyers, moving down from Rabaul with infantry reinforcements, were intercepted by Admiral Merrill's task force about fifty miles north-west of the beachhead. In a long and confused action fought in darkness and rain the Japanese lost the light cruiser *Sendai* and a destroyer and, shortly before daylight, turned back to Rabaul with many of their surviving ships hard hit. No American ship was sunk and damage to the force was comparatively light. Merrill's force was attacked next day by over sixty of the carrier aircraft of *3rd Air Fleet*, which had arrived at Rabaul on the previous day, but escaped with minor damage to one cruiser.

The battle of Empress Augusta Bay had parried the first Japanese thrust but a second and more serious one soon threatened. When Admiral Koga heard that Bougainville had been invaded, he ordered seven heavy cruisers and a division of destroyers to sail from Truk to Rabaul. They were sighted on the 4th when nearing the port, but Halsey had not a single heavy cruiser to pit against them. His capital ships were with the 5th Fleet preparing for the impending assault on the Gilbert Islands, but Rear-Admiral F. C. Sherman's carrier task force was still under his command. To send carriers to face the heavy concentration of land-based aircraft at Rabaul was to take a grave risk but he had nothing else to send. The whole success of the Bougainville landing was at stake. The carriers, which were refuelling at Guadalcanal after their strikes at Buka and Bonis, were ordered north to attack the ships in Rabaul harbour. At 9 a.m., when 230 miles south-east of the port, they began launching every available aircraft—forty-five bombers and dive-bombers escorted by fifty-two fighters. Although anti-aircraft fire was heavy and fighter opposition determined, six Japanese cruisers and two destroyers were hit, but all except one were able to leave Rabaul under their own steam.

Another carrier task group, commanded by Rear-Admiral A. E. Montgomery, was sent from the 5th Fleet to join Sherman, and Rabaul was struck again six days later by aircraft from five carriers operating in two separate groups. Most of the enemy ships damaged in the previous raid had left for Truk and the harbour was emptier. Visibility was poor, but a Japanese destroyer was sunk and a light cruiser and another destroyer heavily damaged. For the second time Sherman's force escaped detection. A heavy air counter-attack directed on Montgomery's carriers was driven off by fighter cover provided from Barakoma without a ship being touched. These raids brought to an end the Japanese use of their carrier aircraft for the defence of Rabaul. In the week since they had become land-based, nearly three-quarters had been destroyed and the remnants were withdrawn to Truk. The following day only a few destroyers could be seen in the harbour. Japanese heavy cruisers never again returned to Rabaul.

The success of these carrier-borne raids demonstrated to the Americans that, although hazardous, it was practical to operate carriers in the face of powerful land-based air attacks, if protected by ships' anti-aircraft fire and their own fighter cover. It encouraged their bold use in the campaign in the Central Pacific which was about to start.

Ashore at Torokina, despite counter-attacks on the 7th, the marines, reinforced from the 11th November onwards by 37th U.S. Division, were able to expand their bridgehead and by the end of the month had established a large and well defended perimeter, within which work on the construction of a fighter strip, a bomber airfield and a forward naval base went on. Japanese bombers made nightly harassing attacks but did not seriously impair progress, since the smothering of Japanese airfields reduced the scale, and air cover combined with anti-aircraft fire the effectiveness, of the attacks.

In the belief that Empress Augusta Bay was but a stepping stone to their northern airfields, the Japanese continued to reinforce Buka and Bonis.[1] On the night of the 24th–25th November five Japanese destroyers carrying over nine hundred troops were intercepted and engaged by five American destroyers half way between Buka and Cape St. George, the southernmost point of New Ireland. In a high-speed gun and torpedo action three of the Japanese destroyers were sunk without an American ship being hit. The battle of Cape St. George was the last of the long series of fierce naval engagements fought in the narrow waters of the Solomons. The Japanese made no more attempts to run reinforcements and supplies to Bougainville by destroyers. Henceforth the Japanese Navy dared not venture south of Rabaul.

In New Guinea at the end of August, 3rd Australian Division (Major-General S. G. Savige), consisting of 15th and 17th Australian Brigades and 162nd U.S. Regiment, had encircled Salamaua and was waiting to resume its assault on the town until the attack on Lae, the main objective, had developed. The 7th Australian Division (Major-General G. A. Vasey) was at Port Moresby and 9th Australian Division (Major-General G. F. Wootten) at Milne Bay.[2] The Japanese *18th Army* was disposed with *51st Division* in the Lae–Salamaua area, *20th Division* at Madang, with about one battalion finding the garrison for Finschhafen, and *41st Division* in Wewak.

General MacArthur's plan for the capture of Lae was to make a seaborne landing to the east of the town at the same time as an airborne force landed on a pre-war but derelict and overgrown airstrip at Nadzab in the Markham River valley, twenty miles north-west of Lae; the two forces were then to converge on the town.[3] A prerequisite to the success of the operation was local air superiority. The Papuan airfields were too far distant from Lae for fighters to cover the assault for long enough. Early in June, however, a reconnaissance party from Wau found a deserted airstrip, which had been used by gold miners, at Marilinan forty miles north-west of Wau. An Australian detachment and some American engineers were flown in and by the end of July fighters were able to use it.

[1] The reinforcements consisted of one artillery and three infantry battalions.
[2] See Volume II, Chapter XXV.
[3] See Sketch 18, page 420.

The sea and air landings were originally scheduled to take place on the 1st August, but delays in the arrival of transport aircraft and in training the troops had forced MacArthur to postpone the operation until the first week in September. During the interval, Allied aircraft had bombed the Japanese air bases and motor torpedo-boats had harried the barge convoys bringing supplies down the coast.

On the 1st September, 9th Australian Division embarked in transports and assault craft of the 7th Amphibious Force and, staging by way of Buna, was landed at dawn on the 4th about seventeen miles east of Lae under covering fire from the escorting destroyers. There was little opposition on the beaches, but the landing craft were attacked by Japanese dive- and torpedo-bombers and two L.S.Ts. were damaged as they withdrew. By nightfall, beachheads had been secured and 26th Australian Brigade had begun to move westwards along the coast.

The following morning 1,700 American paratroops and a detachment of Australian artillery were dropped at Nadzab. The drop, the first by Allied paratroops in the Pacific, was made without interference since fog over Rabaul kept the enemy aircraft grounded, and within two hours the area had been secured. Shortly afterwards, an Australian field company and a pioneer battalion reached the area by an overland advance. Next morning American and Australian engineers were flown in. The existing airstrip was improved and construction of two additional strips begun. On the 7th, transport aircraft began landing the leading troops of 7th Australian Division and its equipment on the airfield. Three days later 25th Australian Brigade was on its way to Lae.

Meanwhile troops and supplies for 9th Australian Division had been pouring ashore on the beaches east of Lae. As the two divisions converged on Lae from the west and from the east, American destroyers bombarded the town. The 9th Division's advance was held up by swollen rivers and Japanese delaying tactics, but on the 15th there were signs that they were evacuating Lae and on the following day the division entered the town, where it joined hands with the leading troops of 7th Division coming from the west.

At Salamaua 29th Australian Brigade had relieved the battle-weary 17th Australian Brigade, and Major-General E. J. Melford (5th Australian Division) had taken over control of the operations from General Savige (3rd Australian Division). On the 9th September the advance was resumed and, on the 11th, Salamaua and the surrounding country were in Allied hands. The capture of the two ports gave MacArthur control of the Huon Gulf. He was quick to make use of it. On the 21st, five days after the capture of Lae, landing craft of the 7th Amphibious Force embarked 20th Brigade

(Brigadier W. J. V. Windeyer) of 9th Australian Division and by mid-afternoon the convoy, escorted by ten destroyers, was on its way to Finschhafen which guards the eastern end of the Vitiaz Strait, dividing New Guinea from New Britain. An hour before dawn on the 22nd, after bombardment of the beach by destroyers, troops were landed six miles north of the town.

A landing at Finschhafen had been expected by the Japanese, but the fighting at Lae and Salamaua had seriously delayed their defensive preparations. The garrison had been reinforced by a regiment from *20th Division* and Major-General Yamada, expecting the attack to come overland from Lae, had disposed three-quarters of his force south and west of the port, leaving only one battalion in Finschhafen itself and a few hundred on the beaches. There was thus only slight opposition to the landing, but about noon half a dozen bombers escorted by fighters attacked landing craft as they were withdrawing. They were driven off with heavy loss by fighters of 5th U.S.A.A.F., four squadrons of which were covering the landing.

On the 23rd September, Japanese forces, entrenched along the south bank of the Bumi River, held up 20th Brigade's advance towards Finschhafen, but by the 26th a bridgehead had been established and that afternoon the advance was resumed. On the 1st October an assault, preceded by a heavy air attack and artillery bombardment, was made on the town and on the following morning it was learnt that the Japanese had withdrawn. By the end of the day Finschhafen was secured.

Before MacArthur could make use of the Vitiaz Strait he had first to secure his left flank by clearing the Huon Peninsula. The only practical route across the interior of the peninsula lay up the Markham and Ramu valleys to Bogadjim on the north coast. After the occupation of Nadzab early in September, an independent company had been landed on an improvised strip some thirty miles north-west of the village. It advanced up the Markham valley and on the 19th September captured the village of Kaiapit, where the Japanese had built an emergency landing strip. This strip was extended and two days later aircraft began to fly in 21st and 25th Australian Infantry Brigades, which had concentrated at Nadzab after the fall of Lae. From Kaiapit they crossed into the valley of the upper Ramu against little opposition and reached the village of Dumpu early in October, where General Vasey (7th Division) established his headquarters. The Japanese were holding the passes over the steep jungle covered mountains of the Finisterre Range, which blocked the approaches to Bogadjim north of Dumpu, with a regiment of *20th Division*. The Australians soon found that they could make no further progress until reinforcements and supplies were flown in. The 7th Division therefore contented itself with active patrolling to maintain contact with the enemy while airfields were built in the flat country round Dumpu. By the end of October bombers of 5th U.S.A.A.F. were using them for attacks on Japanese airfields at Madang and Wewak.

While 7th Division was driving inland across the peninsula towards Bogadjim, 9th Division at Finschhafen was preparing to take the longer route round the coast. By the 10th October, General Wootten had set up his headquarters at the port and, by the 16th, 20th Brigade had been joined by most of 24th Brigade. After withdrawing from Finschhafen General Yamada had concentrated his main force on the high ground round Satelberg, about six miles inland from the landing beaches, which overlooked the port and surrounding country. On the 5th October Lieut.-General S. Katagiri (*20th Division*) arrived from Madang with his headquarters and the remaining regiment and took over command. On the 16th, he began a series of attacks on the Australian positions, but, forewarned by the capture of an operation order, the Australians repulsed an attack from inland and sank two of the three barges which attempted a counter-landing north of Finschhafen on the 17th; the third was driven off by machine-gun fire from the beaches. The 9th Division was brought up to full strength on the 20th by the arrival of 26th Brigade and a tank battalion from Lae. On the night of the 25th/26th the Japanese abandoned their attacks and withdrew to the high ground to the north-west. Three weeks later the Australians began their advance, and by the 25th November were in possession of the area round Satelberg.

Thus by the end of November 9th Division had overcome the main obstacles to its advance and was about to begin its move forward along the coast, while inland 7th Division in the upper Ramu valley was building up its strength for an attack on the Japanese positions covering Bogadjim. In both sectors the goal was in sight, but there was still hard fighting ahead and it was well into the New Year before the Huon Peninsula could be reported clear of the enemy.

While in the South and South-West Pacific MacArthur and Halsey had been tightening their grip round Rabaul, Admiral C. Nimitz (Commander-in-Chief, Pacific Fleet) had been gathering his forces for the assault on the Gilbert Islands—the opening move of the advance through the Central Pacific. American building yards had been turning out ships, and particularly aircraft carriers, in large numbers during the summer, and by the autumn the U.S. 5th Fleet at Hawaii was more than a match for anything the Japanese could bring against it. It comprised the unprecedented number of nineteen aircraft carriers of various types (carrying a total of over eight hundred aircraft), twelve battleships and a commensurate number of cruisers and destroyers. Attached to the fleet, and forming part of it, was the 5th Amphibious Force which contained all the transports, cargo vessels, landing ships and assault craft needed to carry and supply troops employed in the assault.

The supply and maintenance of a fleet at long distances from its base must always be a major problem. It had been solved in the South and South-West Pacific by the construction of successive forward supply bases behind the advance which had been stocked with the fleet's requirements, and to which ships could return to replenish when necessary. MacArthur's advance in New Guinea had been to all intents and purposes land-based; Halsey's steps up the Solomons ladder had never been more than three hundred miles apart. Nimitz had, however, a different and far more complex administrative problem. The 5th Fleet was many times the size of Halsey's 3rd Fleet and the stepping stones across the vast ocean area of the Central Pacific were few and far apart. There could be no long drawn out struggle for the Gilberts and the Marshalls as there had been at Guadalcanal and Munda; the atolls were too small to hold two opposing bodies of troops for long. Before a forward base could become effective the tide of the advance would have swept on leaving it far behind. The support of the fleet would therefore have to be more rapid and more flexible than base development allowed. The answer was found in the provision of mobile service squadrons, consisting of supply and repair ships specially designed for the purpose— floating bases which enabled the fleet to remain at sea for months at a time and which gave it an endurance not known since the days of sail. A mobile supply base was no new idea, but it was one which was vastly expanded as the advance moved further westward from the main base at Pearl Harbour. Some forward bases were of course necessary. It was to obtain an air base from which to support the attack on the Marshalls, for example, that the Gilberts were to be seized.

Vice-Admiral R. A. Spruance, the victor of Midway, was appointed to command the 5th Fleet in August. He organized three main task forces: a fast carrier force which, to give tactical flexibility, was sub-divided into four task groups; an assault force; and a force which controlled both the mobile service squadrons and all shore-based aircraft within the area of operations. The fast carrier force was composed of the fleet and light fleet carriers, the new fast battle-ships, cruisers and destroyers. The battleships furnished the heavy gun support: their powerful anti-aircraft batteries gave protection to the carriers and their large fuel capacity enabled them to refuel the destroyers. The carriers furnished the air cover over the target area as well as long-range striking power. The assault force carried the expeditionary force. It was composed of ships and small craft of the

5th Amphibious Force, escorted by cruisers, destroyers and some of the older battleships to provide supporting fire, and escort carriers to give air cover to the troops ashore. Rear-Admiral **R. K.** Turner, who had commanded at sea at Guadalcanal, was given command of the 5th Amphibious Force and tactical command of the assault. This organization formed the pattern for all future operations in the Central Pacific.

The attack on the Gilberts was planned to take place on the 20th November. During September and October the fast carrier groups made preparatory raids on Marcus and Wake Islands as well as on the Japanese air bases in the Marshalls in order to soften up the Japanese defences and keep the enemy guessing where the first main attack would be delivered. The strikes did little damage but they served as useful training for the newly-formed task groups. In November shore-based aircraft from the newly-built airfields in the Ellice Islands, and from Baker Island which had recently been occupied, bombed islands in the Gilberts.

The atolls in the Gilberts selected for capture were Tarawa, Makin (a hundred miles to the north) and Abemama (sixty miles to the south).[1] The only fortified islands in the group were Butaritari in Makin where the Japanese had built a sea-plane base, and Betio in Tarawa which held an airstrip. These were to be the first objectives. Admiral Turner divided the assault force into two: a northern attack force for Butaritari and a southern for Betio. Each consisted of a transport group, a bombardment and fire support group and an air support group of escort carriers. One of the four fast carrier groups was assigned to each force, and the other two carrier groups were given the task of neutralizing enemy airfields within range during the assault.

The main body of the northern attack force left Pearl Harbour on the 10th November with transports carrying a regimental combat team and a battalion of 27th U.S. Division (6,742 troops). The southern attack force carrying the reinforced 2nd U.S. Marine Division (Major-General J. C. Smith), 18,600 strong, sailed from the New Hebrides two days later. The two forces sighted each other on the morning of the 19th as they made for their assigned targets. Ships carrying amphibious tracked vehicles from Samoa joined the southern force that evening.

The Japanese plan of defence for the Gilbert Islands had been based on the assumption that ships and aircraft would be available to repel invasion, but in the event the *Combined Fleet*, bereft of the ships and carrier-borne aircraft which Admiral Koga had sent to their critical south-east front, was unable to oppose the invading force.[2] Butaritari Island was lightly defended by a few guns and

---

[1] See Sketch 1, page 95.
[2] See page 85.

about eight hundred men, of whom less than three hundred were combatant troops. Shortly after daybreak on the 20th, aircraft from the northern carrier group made a concentrated bombing attack on the defences. The battleships, cruisers and destroyers of the fire support group then bombarded the island for nearly two hours. Finally, under cover of machine-gun and rocket fire from aircraft, the first wave of the assault craft went in. A beachhead was soon secured but, despite their overwhelming preponderence of thirteen to one, the attackers took three days to overcome the stubborn Japanese resistance.

Betio proved a much harder nut to crack. The little island, less than two miles long and only six hundred yards broad at its widest point, was heavily fortified. The defences included fourteen coast defence guns ranging from 5.5- to 8-inch, as well as field artillery and numerous heavy machine-guns. The beaches were barricaded, mined, and studded with obstacles of every description, but perhaps its most effective defence was the barrier reef which fringed the island and prevented continuous ship-to-shore movement of troops and supplies. The garrison consisted of about 4,500 troops, over half of whom were men of the *Special Naval Landing Force*.

The transports of the southern attack force reached their lowering positions in the early hours of the morning of the 20th November. As at Butaritari, the landings were preceded by a dawn air strike followed by bombardment by ships of the fire support group. For two and a half hours three battleships, four cruisers and a number of destroyers poured three thousand tons of projectiles on the tiny island. Nearly half the garrison was killed, but so well were the Japanese positions protected that, although nearly all the coast defence guns were silenced and the communication system disrupted, most of the field artillery and pillboxes were undamaged. The first three attacking waves were carried in amphibious tracked vehicles which were able to surmount the reef and land their troops on the beaches. The non-amphibious landing craft carrying succeeding waves could not reach the beaches, and had to disembark their troops on the reef to wade the four or five hundred yards to the beach in the face of murderous machine-gun fire. Casualties were very heavy and for a time victory and defeat hung in the balance, and half the divisional reserves had to be thrown in. Nevertheless by evening 5,000 men were ashore. They held no more than a precarious foothold on the island and a determined counter-attack could have driven them back into the lagoon. But the Japanese had suffered severely and, with their communications destroyed, were unable to organize any attack. With the arrival of reinforcements, guns and tanks unloaded at high water next day, the tide of battle turned and the marines were able to split the defenders into two

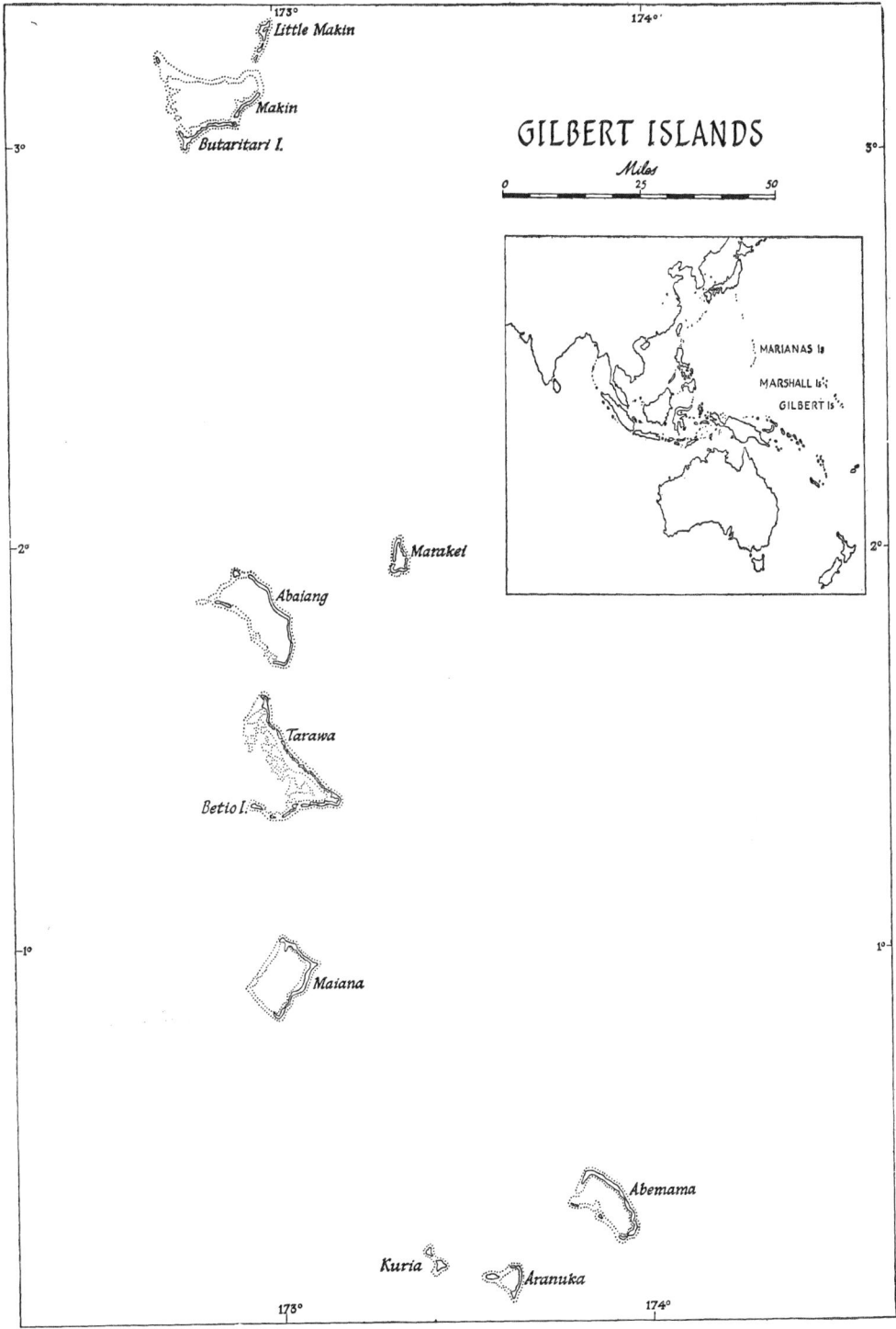

Sketch I

173° Little Makin 174°

Makin

Butaritari I.

3° 3°

GILBERT ISLANDS

Miles

0   25   50

MARIANAS Is

MARSHALL Is

GILBERT Is

2° Marakei 2°

Abaiang

Tarawa

Betio I.

1° 1°

Maiana

Abemama

Kuria Aranuka

173° 174°

groups. On the night of the 22nd/23rd the Japanese, as was their custom when defeat faced them, threw all their remaining troops into a suicidal counter-attack. It was their final effort and by noon on the 23rd Betio was won. The struggle for the island was one of the toughest and bloodiest of the smaller battles of the Pacific war. Nearly a thousand American marines and sailors were killed and over two thousand wounded. Of the Japanese garrison, only a hundred and forty-six allowed themselves to be taken prisoner, and a hundred and twenty of these were Korean labourers. The rest died fighting. During the next three days the remaining islets in the group, including Abemama, were secured, but not without fighting in which thirty-four marines lost their lives and fifty-six were wounded; the Japanese defenders numbering about two hundred and twenty-five were exterminated.

During these operations the Japanese Fleet had been unable to interfere. The American invasion had caught it off balance. The carriers, stripped of their aircraft for the defence of Rabaul, were all in home waters and the *Combined Fleet* at Truk (six battleships, four heavy cruisers, five light cruisers and three reduced destroyer flotillas) dared not venture so far from its base without its air cover. Land-based aircraft of *22nd Air Flotilla* from the Marshalls did what they could, but their number had been depleted to meet the needs of Rabaul; losses had been heavy and there were fewer than fifty in the entire area. They made several attacks on the American invasion force, but scored only one hit on a light fleet carrier at Tarawa on the 25th which did no vital damage. One of eight submarines, sent out from Truk, sank an escort carrier at Makin in the early morning of the 24th, but these were the only ship casualties.

The attack on Betio was the first seaborne assault on a heavily defended coral atoll. It was a costly victory but the price paid was not too high, since the lessons learnt were to prove of inestimable value in future operations and were to save countless American lives.

Map 5

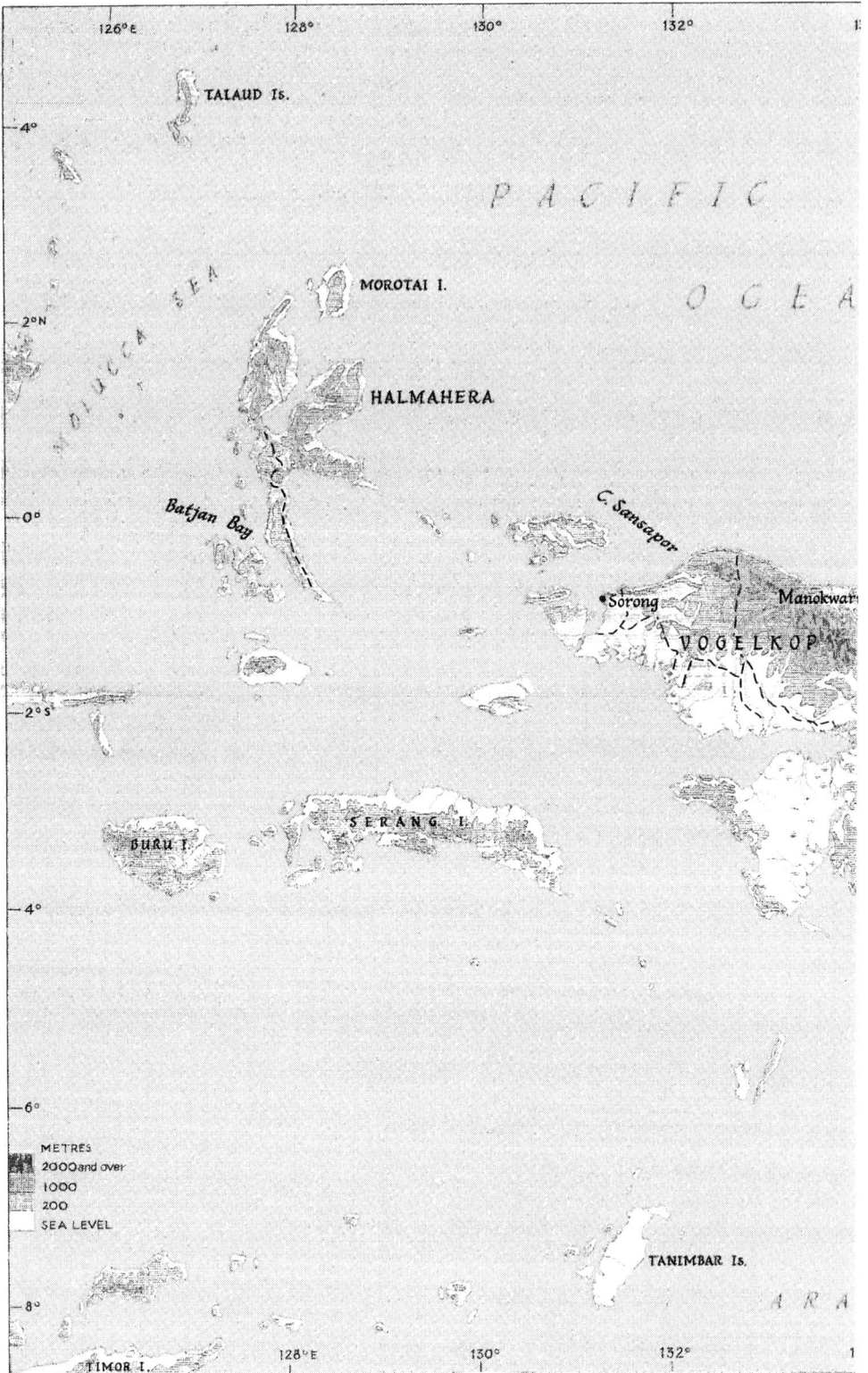

TALAUD Is.

MOLUCCA SEA

PACIFIC

OCEA

MOROTAI I.

HALMAHERA

C. Sansapor

Batjan Bay

Sorong

Manokwar

VOGELKOP

BURU I.

SERANG I.

METRES
2000 and over
1000
200
SEA LEVEL

TANIMBAR Is.

ARA

TIMOR I.

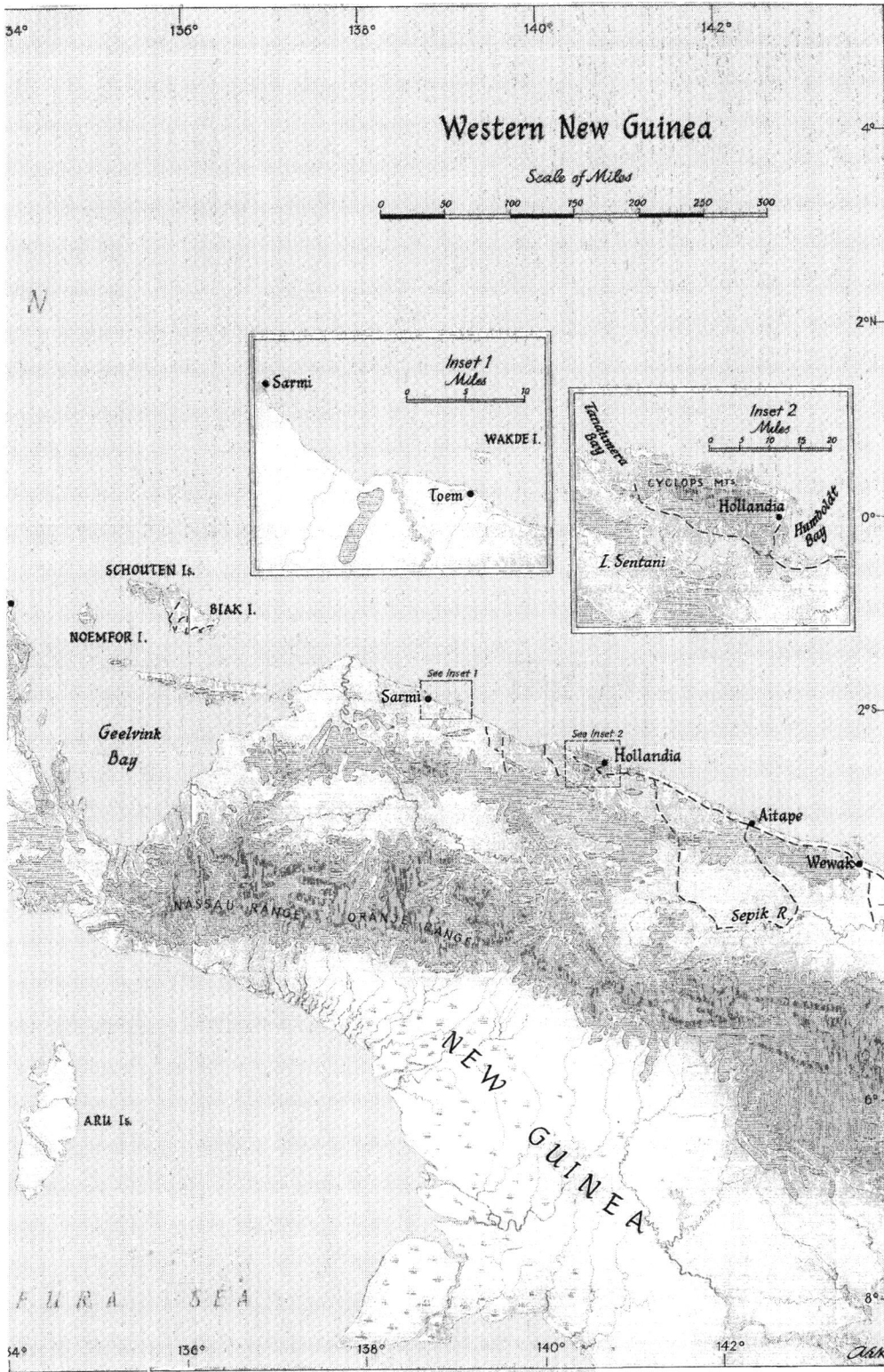

Western New Guinea

Scale of Miles

0   50   100   150   200   250   300

N

Inset 1
Miles
0   5   10

• Sarmi

WAKDE I.

Toem •

Inset 2
Miles
0   5   10   15   20

Tanahmera Bay

CYCLOPS MTS

Hollandia

Humboldt Bay

I. Sentani

SCHOUTEN Is.

BIAK I.

NOEMFOR I.

Geelvink Bay

See Inset 1

Sarmi

See Inset 2

• Hollandia

• Aitape

Wewak •

Sepik R.

NASSAU RANGE   ORANJE RANGE

ARU Is.

NEW GUINEA

ARAFURA SEA

Olik

CHAPTER VIII

THE PACIFIC

(December 1943 – March 1944)

See Maps 1, 5 and 13 and Sketches 2 and 18

AS soon as the decision of 25th September to withdraw to the new defensive zone had received formal approval from the Emperor,[1] *Imperial General Headquarters* accelerated the preparations already in hand for its defence. Among other measures, about twenty-five selected infantry battalions from *Kwantung Army* in Manchuria were hastily organized into detachments of varying strength for transfer to the Central Pacific.[2] The Marshall Islands, although outside the new defensive zone, received a considerable share of these, since *Imperial General Headquarters* were determined to make the Allied approach to the zone as slow and costly as possible. The *52nd Division* was moved from Japan to Truk. Losses at sea were heavy, but by January 1944 most of the reinforcements had arrived at their destinations. There, with the garrisons already in the Central Pacific, they came under operational control of the Commander-in-Chief, *Combined Fleet*.

Imperial General Headquarters had come to the conclusion during the autumn that the defences in the area north of Australia were not strong enough to hold a determined Allied offensive, particularly if it were combined with an offensive along the north coast of New Guinea. To strengthen this area they decided to send *Headquarters 2nd Area Army* and *Headquarters 2nd Army*, both at that time in Manchuria, to take over its defence. The *2nd Area Army* (Lieut.-General K. Anami) was, under the direct command of *Imperial General Headquarters*, to be responsible for western New Guinea as far east as the 140th meridian and for the Dutch islands as far west as a line drawn from the Strait of Makassar to the Strait of Lombok. It was to take over command from *Southern Army* of *19th Army*, already in Celebes, which consisted of *5th* and *48th Divisions* and was to be reinforced by *46th Division* from Japan. The *2nd Army*, consisting of *36th Division* brought south from China, was to provide the garrison for western New Guinea. *Headquarters 2nd Area Army* was established at Davao towards the end of November. The *46th Division*, half of

---

[1] See pages 72–73.
[2] See Map 13, page 438.

which was sunk in transit by Allied submarines, reached the Netherlands East Indies in December, and *36th Division*, having detached a regiment to garrison Biak Island in Geelvink Bay, reached Sarmi in western New Guinea about the same time.[1] The *7th Air Division* was transferred from the control of *8th Area Army* to that of *2nd Area Army* and set up its headquarters in Amboina.

The preparation of the new defensive zone required much more than the provision of adequate military garrisons. It demanded the build-up of air strength, the construction of a large number of new airfields in the western New Guinea–Celebes area and the transport by sea and stockpiling of huge quantities of ammunition, equipment and other material. The movement of troops and material required a vast amount of shipping.[2] But, owing to the heavy losses in the Solomons area and off New Guinea, and the depredations of American submarines, the ships were not available in the numbers required. The preparation of the new defensive zone, especially that part of it for which *2nd Area Army* was responsible, was thus seriously delayed.

It was not till late in 1943 that the Japanese paid any real attention to the protection of shipping against submarine attack. A *General Escort Command* was formed in November, but the number of suitable vessels allotted to it was completely inadequate and shipping losses continued to mount.[3]

The steady attrition of the Merchant Navy was only one of the many causes of concern to the Japanese leaders in the last quarter of 1943. In November the Gilbert Islands had been lost, and in the following month the Allies had landed in New Britain and cleared sufficient of the Huon Peninsula in New Guinea to open the gateway to the Bismarck Sea. At the end of December, *Imperial General Headquarters* reconsidered their overall operational strategy in the light of the decisions taken at the end of September and the progress of the Allied offensive in the Pacific since then. They recognized that the new perimeter was open to attack from any of the five Allied fronts: from the Aleutians on the Kurile Islands; across the Central Pacific on Formosa and the Philippines; from New Guinea and Australia on the southern Philippines; from the Indian Ocean on Sumatra and Java; and through Burma on Malaya and Siam. Special importance was attached to two of the five, namely Allied offensives in the Central Pacific and Burma. The former was of particular significance, since in their invasion of the Gilbert Islands the Americans had departed from their previous tactics of never advancing outside the range of

---

[1] See Map 5, page 97.
[2] The *2nd Area Army's* demands for shipping space amounted to 450,000 tons of large and 150,000 tons of smaller shipping a month for at least four months from December 1943.
[3] See Appendix 14.

their land-based fighter aircraft, and had delivered the attack under cover of carrier task forces only. This created a threat to the Central Pacific islands and even to Japan itself, and was one which could not easily be countered in view of the overwhelming material resources of the United States and the lack of adequate Japanese air power. An Allied offensive in Burma would, if successful, give fresh encouragement to China, and would be likely to cause unrest in Siam and Indo-China where Japanese forces were present only by agreement with the governments concerned and where there was no purely military administration. Defence against both these lines of advance had to be assured.

Whether the Allies would attack Japan direct or by way of the Philippines and Formosa could, of course, be only a matter of conjecture. But, considering the strategic value of the Philippines and the difficulties involved in making a direct attack against Japan, *Imperial General Headquarters* considered it probable that the Philippines would be attacked first, with a diversionary attack on the Kuriles. They came to the conclusion that of the two lines of approach to the Philippines, by way of the Marianas or from New Guinea and the north of Australia, the latter was the more likely. The decisive battles of the war, they foresaw, would take place somewhere in the region of the Philippines.

As a result of their deliberations, *Imperial General Headquarters* reached the conclusion that the United States would continue her offensive in the Pacific regardless of developments in Europe and that decisive battles were close at hand. It was therefore essential that the new defensive zone should be held at all costs so that there would be time to build up strength to take the offensive at some future date. They decided that the army garrisons in the Central Pacific should be further increased and the defences improved, a network of air bases constructed and the air force built up; and, so as to gain the greatest advantage from unity of command, *Headquarters Southern Army* should be moved to Manila to take command of all operations other than those on the South-East front.[1] To offset the appalling losses in shipping they agreed that operations in China should be directed towards opening up an overland supply route to the Southern Region, and that steps should be taken to strengthen convoy escorts, provide up-to-date radar equipment and anti-submarine devices, and increase the output of the shipyards. At the same time, Japanese air power would be greatly expanded by an increase in the production of aircraft and the provision of new air groups.[2]

---

[1] The South-East front (the Allied South-West Pacific), which was outside the new defensive zone, was placed under command of *Imperial General Headquarters* when *Southern Army* moved to Manila in April 1944.

[2] The production target was raised from 35,000 to 50,000 aircraft a year.

The operations in the Pacific, proposed by the Americans for 1944 and accepted by the Combined Chiefs of Staff at Sextant, differed little from those agreed at Quadrant four months earlier, except in the matter of timing. There was, however, one significant change: the capture of bases in the Marianas, from which the newly developed B.29 long-range bombers could strike directly at the Japanese homeland, took the place of the assault on the Palau Islands originally scheduled for October. Tentative dates had been allotted for the start of each operation, but the need for flexibility in planning and the seizure of opportunities for short cuts was emphasized in the event of the destruction of the Japanese Fleet, the early defeat of Germany or the entry of Russia into the war against Japan.[1]

After a slow and painful start, progress in the Pacific was at the end of 1943 beginning to gather momentum, but there were still formidable obstacles in the way. In the Central Pacific, the Gilbert Islands were but the first stepping stone across a vast expanse of ocean. The Marshalls and Marianas had yet to be seized. In the South-West Pacific, the Bismarck Barrier, though beginning to crumble, still barred the way to the approaches to Japan from the south. In order to break through it and use his amphibious forces to further his advance along the New Guinea coast and to complete the encirclement of Rabaul from the west, MacArthur decided that he would have to gain control over both the Vitiaz and Dampier Straits.[2] To do this he had to clear the Huon Peninsula in New Guinea and occupy the western end of New Britain.

In New Guinea, 9th Australian Division advanced steadily northwards during December from the Satelberg area and along the coast from Finschhafen against considerable opposition. By the 20th December the Australians had reached the Masaweng River (twenty miles north of Finschhafen).[3] The Japanese *20th Division* then began its retreat to Madang. The 20th Australian Brigade, ferrying tanks, artillery and stores in small craft between successive beaches, pursued it and occupied Sio on the 15th January 1944. There 9th Division was relieved by 5th Division and 20th Brigade by 8th Brigade, brought up from Australia.

Meanwhile, on the 2nd January, 126th U.S. Regiment had landed unopposed at Saidor seventy miles further west, thus isolating *20th* and *51st Divisions*. The *51st Division*, withdrawing from Lae and Salamaua, had reached the coast west of Sio in mid-October, after a march of about a hundred miles over the unexplored tracks of the Saruwaged mountains, during which it had depended for food on

---

[1] See Appendix 13.
[2] See Map 1, page 1.
[3] See Sketch 18, page 420.

what each man could carry and, when that was expended, on roots and herbs. Disease, starvation and exhaustion took their toll, and of the 8,600 who set out only about 6,500 reached the coast. After the American landing at Saidor, both divisions were ordered to fall back on Madang where they were to join *41st Division* which had been brought down the coast from Wewak. During the retreat along the coast American motor torpedo-boats played havoc with the barge traffic from Madang carrying supplies, with the result that another 2,000 of the troops perished on the march. Eventually the remnants of the two divisions, having by-passed the Americans at Saidor by taking to the mountains, struggled into Madang in mid-February. On the 10th February, 5th Australian Division made contact with the Americans. The task of clearing the Huon Peninsula and gaining control of the Vitiaz Strait had been completed. A fortnight later, in order to allow the greatest number of small craft to be concentrated at Finschhafen for use elsewhere, it was decided not to continue the advance towards Madang for the time being and 5th Australian Division was withdrawn to Sio.

In the Ramu valley, 15th and 18th Australian Brigades had been flown into Dumpu at the beginning of January and had relieved 21st and 15th Brigades of 7th Australian Division, which had been maintaining contact with the enemy positions on the passes over the Finisterre Range. A frontal attack on the enemy positions on the crest of the passes was launched by 18th Brigade on the 20th January, and four days later a battalion from 15th Brigade moving on its left threatened the Japanese communications. By the end of the month, the enemy had been driven from all his positions and the way to Bogadjim was clear. The ground gained was consolidated, but no further advance was attempted till the middle of March.

For his landings in New Britain MacArthur selected Cape Gloucester, in the north-west, where the Japanese were developing an airfield, and Arawe, in the south-west. New Britain is a mountainous, heavily wooded island about 250 miles long. In 1943 it was little developed except in the north-east round Rabaul where the only roads in the island existed. Thus, although the headquarters of *8th Area Army* was at Rabaul, the Japanese could reinforce other parts of the island only by air and sea or along jungle tracks. Till the autumn, western New Britain from Cape Gloucester to Arawe was defended by the *Matsuda Detachment*, the main strength of which was *141st Infantry Regiment* (less one battalion) and Gasmata was defended by *II/228th Battalion*. Early in October, part of *17th Division*, which had recently joined *8th Area Army* from central China, was sent by sea to Cape Hoskins on the north coast and its commander was made responsible for the defence of central and western New Britain.[1]

While American assault forces were being assembled at Milne Bay, Buna and Goodenough Island, Allied aircraft bombed Cape Gloucester and Gasmata. But, to avoid alerting the enemy, Arawe itself was not attacked until the day before the landing. On the 15th December a combat team of 112th U.S. Cavalry Regiment went ashore at Arawe, under cover of the guns of an Australian task force commanded by Rear-Admiral V. A. C. Crutchley, V.C. and aircraft of 5th U.S.A.A.F., and a beachhead was soon secured. Hoping to stop the invasion at the outset, the Japanese quickly organized a force of some 150 aircraft from Rabaul and Truk and within three hours of the landing attacked the transports, but with little effect. For the next ten days the follow-up convoys were subjected to determined and continual air attacks and a few ships were sunk or damaged. Nevertheless there was no serious interference with the build-up.

During the four weeks preceding the landing at Cape Gloucester, over 4,000 tons of bombs were dropped on the Japanese positions and, for the twenty-four hours prior to the attack, and on D-day, the airfields at Madang and Wewak were kept under bombing attack to prevent interference from that direction. On the 26th December, two regimental combat teams of 1st U.S. Marine Division, veterans of the fighting in Guadalcanal, were landed on beaches five miles from the airfield. As at Arawe, retaliation by the Japanese air force was swift and determined; but Rabaul, under heavy attack from American airfields in the Solomons, had the greater need of aircraft for its defence, and by the end of the month air attacks had virtually ceased. The two Japanese battalions defending the area fought with their usual stubbornness, and it was four days before the airfield was in American hands. Fierce enemy resistance, torrential rain and the swampy nature of the country hampered the establishment of a defensive perimeter, and it was not till the 23rd January, when the *Matsuda Detachment* gave up the struggle and retired, that western New Britain was securely in Allied hands.

With the clearance of the Huon Peninsula and the capture of Cape Gloucester, MacArthur had gained control of the Vitiaz and Dampier Straits, and so felt himself free to make his break-through into the Bismarck Sea. His first objective was the Admiralty Islands, which he wanted not only to complete the western side of the ring round

---

[1] The *Matsuda Detachment* was then reinforced by *53rd Regiment* (less one battalion), and *I/81st Battalion*. The *54th Regiment* (less two battalions) was sent to reinforce Gasmata. The *Matsuda Detachment* was then disposed with *53rd Regiment* responsible for the Cape Gloucester area, *141st Regiment* for the south-west coast and *I/81st Battalion* for Arawe.

Rabaul, but as a staging post on his road to the Philippines. The group had all the potentialities of a great advanced base. Manus, the largest island, had ample space for military installations, and Sea Eagle Harbour, fifteen miles long by four miles wide, enclosed by the encircling islands of the group, was an ideal fleet anchorage. Los Negros, forming its eastern side, already contained an airstrip and had room for others.

The Japanese had decided early in November 1943 to strengthen the skeleton defences of these islands. Their first attempt to send reinforcements, amounting to an infantry regiment and an artillery battalion, failed when the transports were sunk *en route* by American submarines. A second attempt to send two battalions fared little better since only one, carried in destroyers from New Ireland, reached its destination safely. Eventually a second battalion and a naval garrison unit reached the islands by the end of December.

Allied aircraft from New Guinea had been reconnoitring and bombing the islands for some time, but on the 23rd February a low-level attack failed to elicit any response from the Japanese defences and there were no signs of human activity. Seeing a chance to advance the date of the occupation of the islands, which was set for April, MacArthur at once ordered a reconnaissance in force. Within a few days, a thousand troops of 1st U.S. Cavalry Division had been packed into three transport destroyers at Buna, and on the 29th February landed on Los Negros, covered and supported by a task force of cruisers and destroyers. The troops in the first waves got ashore without encountering opposition, but when entering the harbour subsequent waves were subjected to heavy cross fire and some landing craft were sunk. By 10 o'clock one airstrip was captured and a defensive perimeter was quickly formed. That evening, MacArthur, who had been watching the landings from one of the cruisers, sailed with the task force, leaving two destroyers to give fire support when called for by the troops ashore. During the next two days determined Japanese counter-attacks and attempts at infiltration were repulsed. On the 3rd March reinforcements began to arrive, including a naval construction battalion (Seabees) to rebuild the airstrip and make the island habitable. On the 7th, troops crossed the narrow strait from Los Negros to Manus. By the 24th March Japanese resistance on Los Negros was broken and three weeks later all organized resistance in the Admiralties ceased.

While MacArthur was encircling Rabaul from the west Halsey was completing the encirclement from the east. In Bougainville, 3rd U.S. Marine Division and 37th U.S. Division had expanded and strengthened the perimeter round Torokina and by the 10th December a fighter strip was in use.[1] A runway suitable for bombers was completed on Christmas Day. Three weeks later Headquarters Solomons Air Command moved to Torokina from Munda and thereafter had the use of a fully equipped air base only 220 miles from Rabaul. At the end of the year the marines were relieved by the Americal Division and the command in Bougainville passed to XIV U.S. Corps.

The Japanese had been convinced that the landing at Torokina was but a preliminary to landings further north and in November had sent three infantry battalions and a battalion of artillery to Buka to protect their northern airfields. As time went on, they began to realize that the Americans were at Torokina to stay and at the end of December decided to make a supreme effort to retake the perimeter, using the whole of *6th Division* reinforced by two battalions and supported by *4th Air Army*. They hoped that the effect would be to divert forces from the South-West and Central Pacific, where Allied progress was causing alarm. So great did General Imamura (*8th Area Army*) consider the urgency that on the 21st January he himself paid a visit to Bougainville and thereupon ordered *17th Army* to launch an all-out attack on Torokina as early as possible, but at the same time to hold on to the positions in the north of the island.

While the Japanese in Bougainville were preparing for their big offensive, Halsey was looking for another link to forge in the chain round Rabaul pending the assault on Kavieng, not due to take place for at least three months, by which time it was hoped that the U.S. 5th Fleet would have completed the occupation of the Marshall Islands and could supply the necessary naval support. With MacArthur's approval, he chose Green Island, a group of coral atolls 37 miles north-west of Buka, since airfields in the islands would enable fighter escort to be given to bombers attacking Kavieng, and the final neutralization of Rabaul would be facilitated by the establishment of another base closer to it. Furthermore, motor torpedo-boats based on the islands could put a stop to the barge traffic from Rabaul, via New Ireland, to Buka.

A reconnaissance party of some 300 New Zealand troops, accompanied by American technicians, landed on the night of the 30th/31st January on Nissan (the largest atoll in the group) and reported that the strength of the garrison was not more than 100 men. On the 15th February, 3rd New Zealand Division (less one brigade group) made an unopposed landing. Elaborate precautions were taken against counter-attack from Rabaul; ample air cover was provided from Torokina, and two cruiser and destroyer task forces patrolled north and south of the island. The occupation of Green Island had the desired effect of cutting the Japanese communications between Rabaul and Bougainville. By that time, however, some Japanese

---

[1] See pages 87–88.

reinforcements had been brought in, mainly from Shortland and Choiseul Islands, and concentrated near Buin in the south.

From the middle of December onwards the airfields and shipping at Rabaul had been kept under attack by heavy bombers from Munda, escorted by fighters from the new airfield at Torokina. As soon as that airfield was ready to operate dive-bombers, these were used with more deadly effect. Despite heavy losses the Japanese naval air flotillas, constantly reinforced from Truk, were able to put up from thirty to eighty fighters to meet each attack. By the end of January, by which time some 300 American fighters and 100 light bombers were based at Torokina, Japanese resistance began to break. But there was no diminution in the fury of the American attack. In the first nineteen days of February nearly 3,000 sorties were flown over Rabaul and about 1,400 tons of bombs dropped on the airfields and such shipping as remained in the harbour. The last air battle over Rabaul took place on the 19th February, two days after the carriers and battleships of the 5th Fleet had made their first air and surface raid on Truk. The devastating effect of that raid caused the Japanese finally to abandon the air defence of Rabaul. All fighters were recalled to Truk, in anticipation of meeting further raids on the base, and Rabaul was left to depend on anti-aircraft fire alone for its own protection. Thus it was that, for its last desperate attempt to drive the Americans from Bougainville, *17th Army* could expect no air support from Rabaul. Nor could any help come from *4th Air Army* in New Guinea which had been so depleted during the previous months that it had insufficient aircraft either to support *18th Army* or defend its own airfields.

The attack on the perimeter at Torokina opened at dawn on the 8th March, supported by a heavy concentration of field artillery, laboriously dragged along jungle tracks during the preceding months and sited on high ground commanding the battlefield. In their first attack the Japanese gained some ground, but after nearly a week of fierce fighting were driven back. Three more attacks were bloodily repulsed by the Americans, but it was not till the 25th March that, on orders from *8th Area Army*, *17th Army* abandoned the offensive. In just over a fortnight *6th Division* alone had suffered 5,500 casualties, of which 2,400 had been killed. The total casualties in the island were more than twice that number.

The Japanese offensive was a course of despair. Without a single warship or aircraft to give it support, *6th Division* had no hope of defeating an enemy of more than twice its numbers, strongly supported by a locally based air force and a navy with complete control of the sea. The failure of the offensive sealed the fate of the Japanese in the island. Although some desultory fighting took place later in the year, Bougainville was virtually cut off from all supplies by the end of March 1944, leaving some 32,000 unfortunate men of *17th Army* to live as best they could off the country.

After the capture of Green Island, the campaign in the Solomons was complete for strategic purposes. The last rung in the long ladder from Guadalcanal had been reached. One final landing was to be made by the South Pacific forces to close the ring of airfields round Rabaul. On the 12th March the capture of Emirau Island in the St. Mathias Group, half-way between Kavieng and the Admiralty Islands, was substituted for the attack on Kavieng. On the 20th March, 4th U.S. Marine Regiment, which was to have carried out the Kavieng operation, landed unopposed on the island, while battleships and destroyers of the 5th Fleet bombarded Kavieng. With this landing the campaign in the Solomons was ended. The fortress of Rabaul was now powerless, and about 140,000 Japanese were cut off from playing any further significant part in the war.

While MacArthur and Halsey had been closing the pincers on Rabaul, Admiral Nimitz was securing with unexpected ease his first main objective, the Marshall Islands.[1] The seizure of the Gilbert Islands had never been intended as more than a curtain raiser to the occupation of the Marshalls where the stage was to be set for the drive westward across the Central Pacific.

The Marshalls have the same physical characteristics as the Gilberts. They consist of hundreds of low-lying coral atolls and islets scattered over more than 400,000 square miles of ocean. They lie in two roughly parallel chains, about 100 miles apart. In the north-east chain are the larger atolls of Mili, Majuro, Maloelap and Wotje. The south-west chain contains Jaluit, Kwajalein and Eniwetok. Japan had been given the mandate for the Marshalls, along with the other former German possessions in the Pacific, at the end of the First World War, under the Covenant of the League of Nations, by which she was prohibited from fortifying military and naval bases. In 1935, when she seceded from the League, she retained the mandate and closed the islands to foreign visitors. From then on, the extent and nature of Japanese activities in the islands were covered with a veil of secrecy. It is now clear, however, that systematic militarization of Truk and the Marshalls had already begun in 1940.

From the outbreak of the war until the autumn of 1943 the garrisons of the Marshalls had been entirely naval, but in September 1943, when the Japanese decided that the Carolines and Marianas were to become the main line of defence,[2] army units from the Philippines, Manchuria and Japan itself were sent to the main atolls. The defence

---

[1] See Map 13, page 438.
[2] See pages 72–73.

of the islands remained a naval responsibility, but the Navy could do little. Within a month the *Combined Fleet* at Truk was emasculated by the despatch of its aircraft to Rabaul; the *4th Fleet* was too weak to offer any real resistance and efforts to strengthen the air defences were brought to nought by American air power. *Imperial General Headquarters* were under no illusion that the islands, if attacked, could be held for long. The task of the garrisons was to hold out for as long as possible to give time for the strengthening of the inner defensive zone.

American planning for the invasion of the Marshalls had begun in the summer of 1943, but it was not until after the capture of the Gilberts that the final plan emerged. D-day was set for the 31st January 1944. The main assault was to be made on Kwajalein Atoll, the linchpin of the Japanese outer defensive perimeter and the centre of Japanese air power in the islands. Majuro, believed to be undefended, was first to be seized as an anchorage for the fleet and mobile service squadron. The occupation of Eniwetok, 330 miles north-west of Kwajalein, was to take place as soon as possible, but was dependent on the progress of the main assault and the number of troops available. Four strongly defended atolls, Wotje, Maloelap, Mili and Jaluit, each of which held an airfield, were to be by-passed, land-based aircraft operating from the Gilberts and the fast carrier force being relied on to keep them neutralized.[1]

Kwajalein is the largest true atoll in the world. It comprises no less than ninety-seven islands and islets with a total area of only $6\frac{1}{3}$ square miles surrounding a lagoon with an area of 839 square miles. The two points selected for capture were the twin islands of Roi–Namur in the north, the enemy's principal air base, and Kwajalein Island in the south, the main naval base and distribution centre in the islands. The organization of the invasion force was similar to that used in the Gilberts, improved and expanded in the light of experience gained. There were to be three attack forces instead of two, a northern, southern and reserve; each had its own transport group, bombardment and fire support group and air support group. The four groups of the fast carrier force, each with its quota of fast battleships, furnished the air striking power and could be quickly concentrated against the Japanese Fleet if it intervened. The invasion forces were placed under the tactical command of Rear-Admiral Turner, but Admiral Spruance, the Commander-in-Chief, U.S. 5th Fleet, was present, ready to assume command in the event of a fleet action.

The lessons of Tarawa had been taken to heart and very thorough preparations had been made for the assault. Air strikes had been made on the Marshalls before, during and after the capture of the Gilberts by carriers and land-based aircraft, strikes which had increased in

---

[1] See Sketch 2, page 111.

weight and frequency when the new airfields in the Gilberts came into use. Early in December, the fast carrier force had been recalled to Hawaii for training and much-needed rest, and for seven weeks land-based aircraft had continued the strikes alone, concentrating their attacks for the most part on the atolls to be by-passed. On the 27th January, the fast carriers came into action again and for three days made a devastating series of attacks on the Japanese air bases, the battleships, cruisers and destroyers adding weight to the bombardment with their broadsides. By D-day hardly a Japanese aircraft was left serviceable. Complete control of the air had been gained. A measure of that control was that, throughout the whole operation, not one ship in the vast armada gathered for the invasion was attacked from the air.

The seizure of Majuro, as was expected, gave little trouble, and at first light on the 1st February a battalion of 106th Regiment from 27th U.S. Division occupied the island without loss. Within a few days, the largest fleet of American tankers yet assembled in the Pacific was anchored in the lagoon.

The capture of Kwajalein followed the now familiar pattern. Roi–Namur and Kwajalein Islands were assaulted simultaneously by the northern and southern forces respectively. In each case islets flanking the main islands were first seized to site the divisional artillery and to secure an entrance to the lagoon. In each case the landings were preceded by intense and prolonged naval and air bombardment. During the morning of the 1st February, 4th U.S. Marine Division went ashore on beaches on the lagoon side of Roi–Namur and by the afternoon of the 2nd February all resistance had been overcome. The 7th U.S. Infantry Division assaulted Kwajalein Island on the 1st February, and by 4 p.m. 11,000 troops had landed. Although the island had received an even heavier pounding than had been given to Roi–Namur, many of the defences still remained intact, and the Japanese resistance continued with unabated determination until the afternoon of the 4th when, after several suicidal 'banzai' charges, there were no men left alive to resist.

Some twenty islands in the atolls still remained to be dealt with. The marines secured the northern section without difficulty. In the south, the soldiers met with some opposition, especially in the island of Ebbeye, where the Japanese had a seaplane base, but by the 7th the whole of Kwajalein Atoll was in American hands. When on the 2nd February it had become apparent that Kwajalein could be secured without committing the reserve force, it was decided to go ahead as quickly as possible with the capture of Eniwetok, covered by a carrier and surface raid on Truk.

On the night of the 12th/13th February, three of the fast carrier groups left Majuro lagoon under the command of Admiral Spruance for the attack on Truk. Refuelling from tankers north of Eniwetok, the force made its approach on the night of the 16th/17th. Shortly before dawn, when 90 miles E.N.E. of Truk, the carriers launched their first strike of seventy-two fighters. Hard on the tail of the fighters came the torpedo-bombers, loaded with fragmentation bombs and incendiaries, to plaster the airfields where aircraft, many of them under repair, were lying thick on the ground. In these first strikes, Japanese air strength was hard hit. Of the 135 operational aircraft in the atoll when the raids began, fewer than 80 remained undamaged. Throughout the day shipping in the harbour was kept under attack by dive- and torpedo-bombers while a task group of battleships, cruisers and destroyers patrolled outside, on the lookout for vessels attempting to escape. That evening the Japanese launched their only counter-attack, in which a torpedo-bomber penetrated the American screen and secured a hit on the carrier *Intrepid*, which put her out of action for several months.

Between midnight and dawn Spruance flew off a low-level night bombing attack on shipping in the harbour, the first of its kind to be made from carriers. The attack accounted for one-third of the total damage to shipping inflicted by the entire carrier force, and this success had a marked influence on future carrier operations. Bombing of airfields and shore installations began again at dawn and continued until noon on the 18th when Spruance withdrew his force.

The strike on Truk cost the enemy dear. Nearly 20,000 tons of merchant shipping, including five tankers, were sunk or damaged. Naval losses included two hundred and seventy aircraft, two light cruisers, four destroyers and a number of auxiliaries. They would have been very much heavier had not Koga, warned by a reconnaissance flight over the atoll, anticipated the attack. On the 10th he withdrew the *Combined Fleet* first to Palau, and later in the month to Singapore and Japan. The capture of Eniwetok could now proceed without fear of interference.

Eniwetok is a typical coral atoll with some thirty small islands rising from a circular coral reef surrounding a lagoon. The three main islands are Engebi in the north, which held an airfield, and Eniwetok and Parry in the south.[1] At the beginning of January 1944 about 2,500 men of *1st Amphibious Brigade* had been disembarked on the almost defenceless atoll, and set to work to fortify the islands against the expected American invasion, but the defences were still incomplete when the landings took place.

The American expeditionary force left Kwajalein lagoon on the 15th February carrying a mixed force of marines and soldiers, about 8,000 men in all, accompanied by a fast carrier group. It made the

---

[1] See Sketch 2, page 111.

approach to Eniwetok during the night of the 16th/17th. The mine-sweepers swept a passage into the lagoon at daybreak and the transports, led by one of the old battleships, then entered the lagoon. Bombardment by battleships and cruisers and bombing attacks from the carriers went on all day. During the afternoon and on the following morning 22nd Marine Regiment was put ashore at Engebi. The enemy resisted strongly, using well-concealed slit trenches, but by 4 p.m. the island was secured.

Although no sign of the enemy had been seen on Eniwetok and Parry Islands as the transports entered the lagoon, documents captured at Engebi indicated that there were at least 600 troops on the former and double that number on the latter. Simultaneous landings on the two islands, which had been planned, were therefore discarded. The strength of the landing force was doubled and the volume of naval gun fire directed on the islands increased. Two battalions of 106th U.S. Infantry Regiment were landed on Eniwetok on the morning of the 19th and by the evening of the 21st the island was secured. The following day Parry Island, after having been subjected to three days of heavy naval and air bombardment, was taken by the marines.

With the capture of Eniwetok, the campaign in the Marshalls was for strategic purposes over. The four by-passed atolls were kept neutralized and the unfortunate garrisons left to linger there until the end of the war. The remaining lightly defended or undefended atolls were all occupied by the end of April. The captured Japanese bases were quickly repaired, improved and enlarged, and provided airfields and harbours 2,500 miles nearer the Marianas than Pearl Harbour.

The easy capture of the key points in the Marshalls, coupled with the successful raid on Truk, brought about some changes in the conduct of the war in the Pacific.[1] The strike on Truk had revealed that the base was much weaker than had been supposed. The early end of the Marshalls campaign had freed a large body of trained troops for forthcoming operations. Nimitz was now able to recommend to the American Chiefs of Staff that the date of the invasion of the Marianas should be put forward to the 15th June and that Truk should be neutralized rather than captured. MacArthur, too, was able on the 5th March to suggest a method of speeding up his advance in New Guinea. After the capture of Manus in the Admiralty Islands earlier than originally planned, he proposed that Kavieng should be captured on the 1st April and that the proposed landings at Hansa Bay should be cancelled in favour of a direct jump to Hollandia.[2]

---

[1] See Map 13, page 438.
[2] See Map 5, page 97.

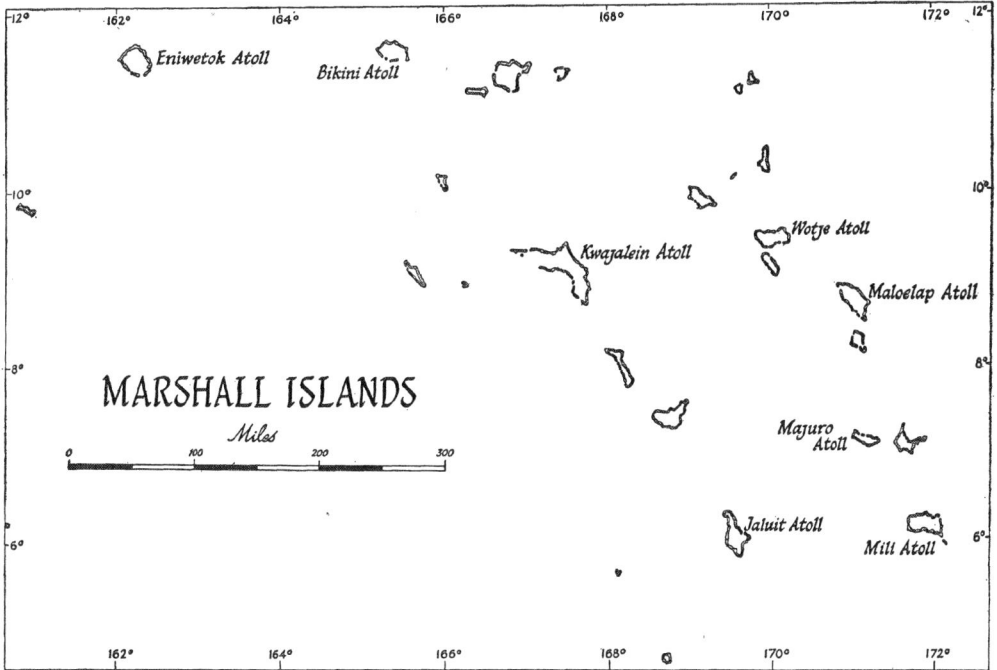

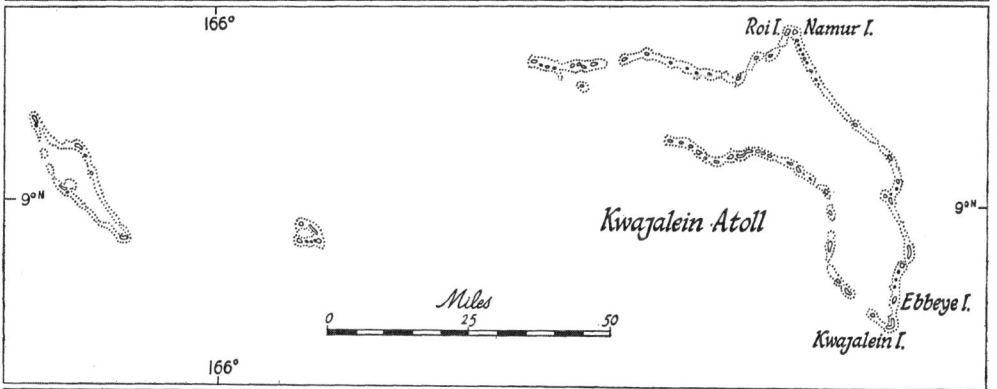

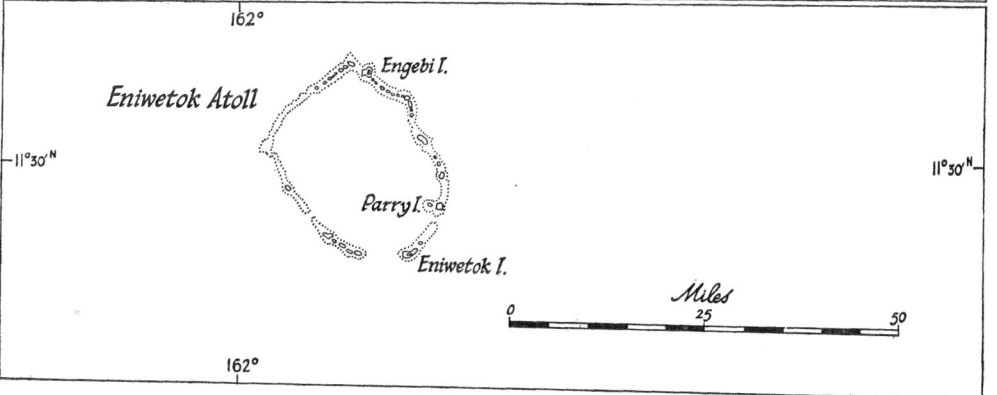

With these and other recommendations before them, the American Chiefs of Staff issued a new operational directive on the 12th March for action in the Pacific during the rest of 1944. MacArthur was ordered to cancel the Kavieng operation and complete the neutralization of Rabaul with the minimum of force. As soon as Manus, in the Admiralty Islands, had been developed as an air and naval base, he was to occupy Hollandia and continue his advance along the New Guinea coast with the invasion of Mindanao, the southernmost of the Philippine Islands, in view. Nimitz was ordered to keep Truk neutralized and conduct carrier strikes against the Marianas, Palaus, and Carolines and other profitable targets. The Marianas were to be invaded on the 15th June, after which Central Pacific forces were to move to the Palaus.

Map 6

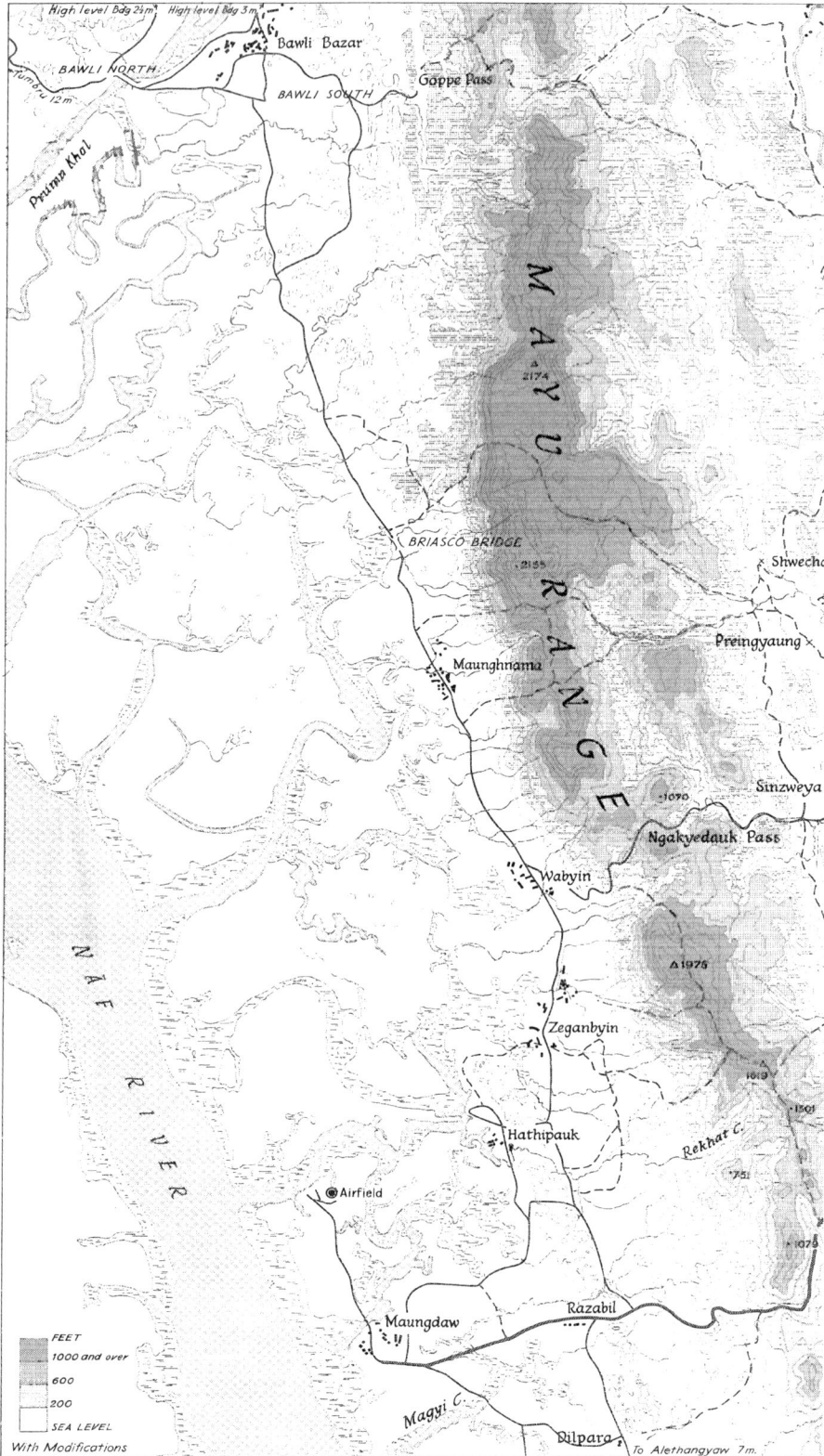

High level Bdg 2½m   High level Bdg 3 m

Bawli Bazar

BAWLI NORTH

Tumbru 12m

BAWLI SOUTH

Goppe Pass

Pruma Khol

M A Y U

·2174

R A N G E

BRIASCO·BRIDGE

·2165

Shwecho

Preingyaung

Maunghnama

·1070

Sinzweya

Ngakyedauk Pass

Wabyin

△1975

Zeganbyin

△
·1013

·1301

Hathipauk

Rekhat C.

·751

N A F

Airfield

·1075

R I V E R

Maungdaw

Razabil

Magyi C.

FEET
1000 and over
600
200
SEA LEVEL

With Modifications

Dilpara   To Alethangyaw 7 m.

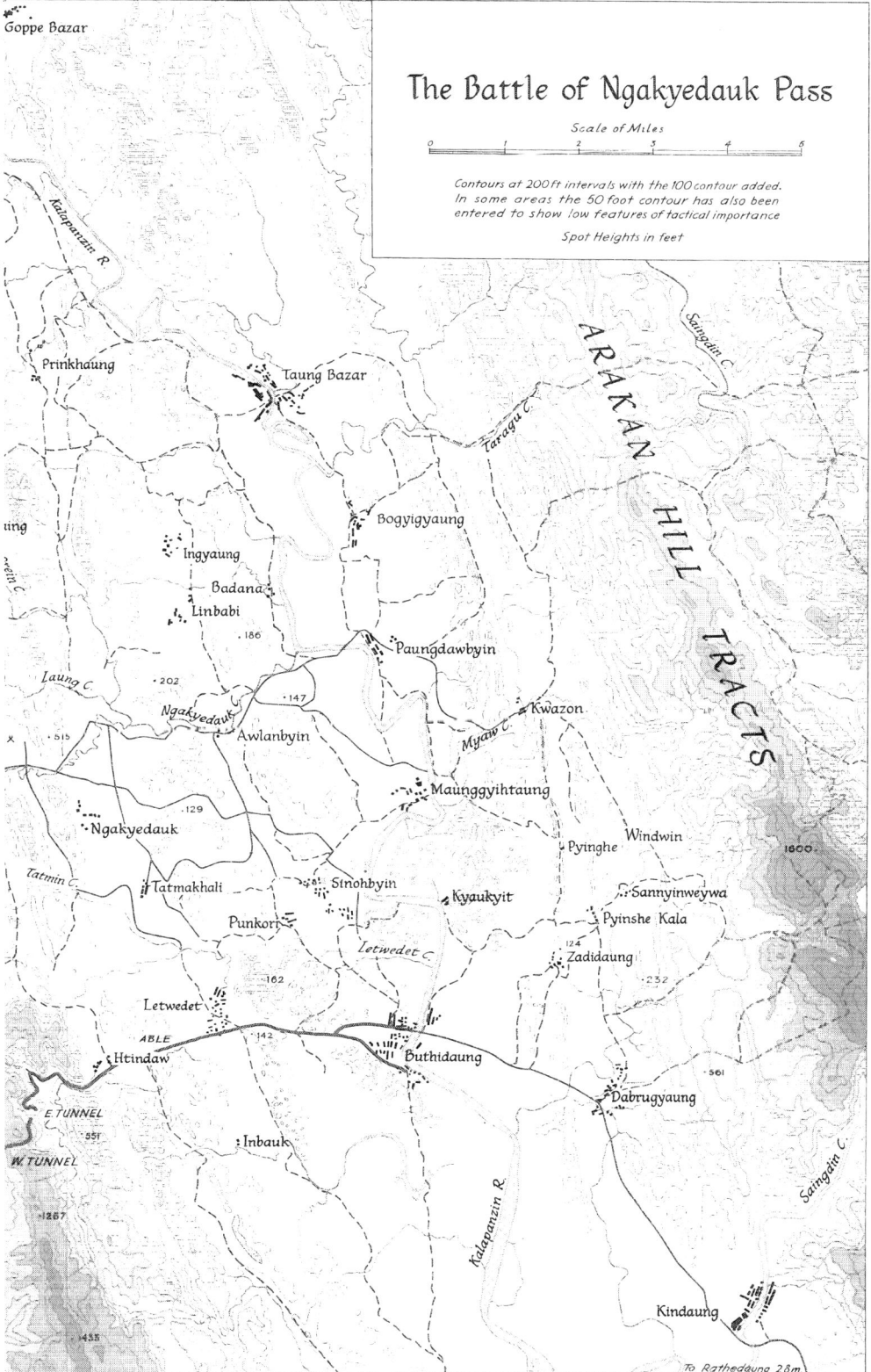

Goppe Bazar

Kalapanzin R.

The Battle of Ngakyedauk Pass

Scale of Miles

0   1   2   3   4   5

Contours at 200 ft intervals with the 100 contour added.
In some areas the 50 foot contour has also been
entered to show low features of tactical importance

Spot Heights in feet

Saingdin C.

ARAKAN HILL TRACTS

Prinkhaung

Taung Bazar

Taragu C.

Bogyigyaung

ung

Ingyaung

wein C.

Badana

Linbabi

.186

Paungdawbyin

Laung C.

.202

.147

Kwazon

Ngakyedauk

Awlanbyin

Myaw C.

X

.515

Maunggyihtaung

.129

Windwin

Pyinghe

1600

Ngakyedauk

Tatmin C.

Tatmakhali

Sinohbyin

Kyaukyit

Sannyinweywa

Punkorn

Pyinshe Kala

Letwedet C.

124

Zadidaung

.162

.232

Letwedet

ABLE

.142

Htindaw

Buthidaung

.561

Dabrugyaung

E TUNNEL

551

Inbauk

W. TUNNEL

.1287

Kalapanzin R.

Saingdin C.

Kindaung

.1433

To Rathedaung 28 m.

CHAPTER IX

OPERATIONS IN ARAKAN AND ASSAM

(November 1943 – February 1944)

See Maps 2, 3, 4, 6, 14 and 15

DURING the long period in which attempts were being made at the highest level to reach agreement on plans for the 1944 campaign, the Allied forces had been in contact with the enemy on all three fronts in Burma. Although no decision had been reached on the scope of operations on the Central and Northern fronts until the 14th January, it had long been accepted that, whatever the final overall plan, a land advance towards Akyab as planned in August 1943 would be the opening Allied move of the campaign. Giffard (11th Army Group) and Slim (14th Army) had therefore been concentrating XV Corps in Arakan so that an attack on the main enemy position along the Maungdaw–Buthidaung line could be made about the middle of January.[1]

The Japanese defences on the Maungdaw–Buthidaung line were of great natural strength and they were centred on the Tunnels and Point 551 with a forward strongpoint on Point 1301.[2] On the west, Razabil and, on the east, Letwedet were self-contained field fortresses in a maze of small hills and gullies covered in dense scrub and tiger grass, which provided perfect concealment and unlimited scope for mutually supporting positions. Both were under close range observation from the Tunnels area so that accurate artillery support was always available. A system of strong, mutually supporting positions east of the Kalapanzin covered the right flank and at Maungdaw the left flank. The field works were dug and tunnelled into the hillsides and were impervious to anything less than a direct hit from a heavy bomb or by a shell on the fire slit. Many were completely tankproof and no tank could venture into any part of the system without strong infantry escort. In mid-November 1943 the main position was held by *143rd Regiment* with a detachment east of the Kalapanzin and was covered by outposts at Awlanbyin and Hathipauk.

On the 19th November, three days after S.E.A.C. assumed control

---

[1] For order of battle of XV Corps see Appendix 15.
[2] See Map 6, page 113.

of operations, 5th Indian Division was disposed west of the Mayu Range with 123rd Brigade in touch with Japanese outposts on the general line Zeganbyin–Point 1619, and 161st Brigade in depth behind it; its third brigade was still in India. All three brigades of 7th Division were east of the Mayu Range supported by 25th Mountain Regiment and two batteries of 24th Mountain Regiment, and the leading brigade of 81st (W.A.) Division had reached Chiringa in readiness for its advance into the Kaladan Valley.[1] So that the appearance of tanks might come as a complete surprise to the enemy, 25th Dragoons (part of 254th Tank Brigade), armed with medium tanks, was secretly brought forward in landing craft and disembarked by night near Ukhia on the 2nd December. The tanks were hidden in the jungle which stretched right down to the beach, and engineers unostentatiously strengthened bridges along the track to Tumbru from where the tanks would move by barge to Bawli. On arrival of this armoured unit, XV Corps formed an armoured group under command of Colonel S. H. Persse.[2]

Work had only just begun on a road across Ngakyedauk Pass and, until the end of December, 7th Division had to operate without its motor transport and without the support of field artillery. Nevertheless, so that contact could be made with the enemy's main positions east of the Mayu Range, 114th Brigade was ordered to clear the Japanese from their two redoubts at Awlanbyin, while 33rd Brigade, less one battalion, occupied the two ridges running south from there towards Letwedet. The 89th Brigade on the right and 33rd Brigade in the centre were then to infiltrate forward towards the Tunnels–Buthidaung road, while 114th Brigade concentrated east of the Kalapanzin and moved forward to the Myaw Chaung. The 33rd Brigade succeeded in occupying its objectives after hard hand-to-hand fighting. The attack on Awlanbyin west redoubt, made from the rear through thick jungle, achieved complete surprise and valuable documents, including a comprehensive enemy order of battle in Burma, were captured. The attack on Awlanbyin east redoubt failed but, cut off from its main position by the successful advance of 33rd Brigade, the Japanese garrison withdrew on the 2nd December.

By the middle of December the Ngakyedauk Pass road was fit for jeep traffic and 139th (Jungle) Field Regiment, equipped with 3-inch mortars and 3.7-inch howitzers, was able to move into the Kalapanzin valley, where 33rd Brigade was being subjected to fierce counter-attacks. The 25th Mountain Regiment was placed in support of

---

[1] On arrival of 81st (W.A.) Division, XV Corps ceased to have any call on 26th Indian Division, which then became 14th Army reserve. For Chiringa see Map 2, page 5.

[2] The armoured group consisted of 25th Dragoons, one troop 401st Field Squadron, I.E. plus a bridging troop detachment, and one company 3/4th Bombay Grenadiers (motorized battalion), all part of 254th Tank Brigade, plus 81st (W.A.) Divisional Reconnaissance Regiment and the mechanized wing of the Gwalior Lancers (part of 7th Divisional Reconnaissance Regiment).

114th Brigade east of the Kalapanzin and the two batteries of 24th Mountain Regiment were returned to 5th Division. During the rest of the month both 5th and 7th Divisions infiltrated and fought their way forward to make contact with the enemy's main position in readiness for the main offensive, while the leading brigade of 81st (W.A.) Division moved from Chiringa across the hills towards Daletme in the Kaladan Valley.

Except for the fighting round Fort White in November there had been little activity on the Central front up to the 14th December, other than intensive ground reconnaissance. The 17th Indian Division was at Tiddim with 63rd Brigade forward holding Vangte and Kennedy Peak, 20th Indian Division (less 32nd Brigade) in the Kabaw Valley near Tamu and 23rd Indian Division in reserve at Imphal.[1] The Chin Hills sector south of Vangte was divided into two: the southern part covered the area west of Haka and was held by Barforce, consisting of the Bihar Regiment (less two companies) with a detachment from the Chin Hills Battalion and some Chin Levies; and the northern held by Hasforce, consisting of the Chin Hills Battalion (less a detachment) and some Levies. Both forces were under command of IV Corps.

The Japanese had made no further move forward after their capture of Fort White in November, but air reconnaissance reported increasing activity behind their front and on their line of communication. On the 14th December, an attack by 63rd Brigade on enemy positions astride the Kennedy Peak–Fort White road failed with some 200 casualties, including the commanding officers of both battalions.

The state of uncertainty over plans in S.E.A.C. after the cancellation of 'Buccaneer' was considerably eased on the 11th December when Mountbatten proposed operation 'Pigstick', which was on a sufficiently large scale to make its acceptance by the Generalissimo possible in place of 'Buccaneer'.[2]

Assuming that, if 'Pigstick' were undertaken, the Generalissimo would agree to the Yunnan armies taking the offensive, Giffard told Slim on the 14th December to prepare his plans on the basis of 'Tarzan'.[3] He placed at Slim's disposal 254th Tank Brigade, 50th (P.) Brigade, Special Force (3rd Indian Division) and 81st (W.A.) Division, less one brigade, in addition to his two corps. He was unable to give him any definite instructions on the subject of 'Pigstick', planning for which had only just begun, but indicated that the assault

---

[1] See Map 3, page 33.
[2] See pages 62–63.
[3] See pages 15–16.

landing on the Mayu peninsula would probably be made by 2nd British Division.

Although he could not yet give XV Corps specific orders, Slim was able to tell Scoones (IV Corps) to have plans ready by the 25th December to contain *31st* and *33rd Japanese Divisions*, assist the L.R.P. groups to cross the Chindwin and exploit any favourable opportunity created by their action, clear the Chin Hills, prevent the Japanese from establishing themselves between the Chindwin and the Yu Rivers and, finally, create the impression that the Allied main attack would be on the Kalemyo–Kalewa area. These tasks were confirmed in a written instruction on the 24th December. As the steady advance, being made by XV Corps under Giffard's original plan, to gain contact with the enemy main defences between Maungdaw and Buthidaung was well suited to the opening stages of 'Pigstick', there was no immediate need for Christison to be given fresh orders.

On the 27th December, Mountbatten, warned by his planners that if 'Pigstick' were to be carried out firm orders would have to be issued without delay, told his Commanders-in-Chief to press forward their preparations for it. Within a week, however, it became clear that the Chiefs of Staff considered that, subject to American agreement, it should be cancelled and that the Generalissimo was not going to accept it as a substitute for 'Buccaneer'.[1] In conference with his Commanders-in-Chief on the 3rd January, Mountbatten decided in the circumstances that it would be advisable to abandon the operation and undertake 'Gripfast' and 'Cudgel' instead. The following day he asked the Chiefs of Staff for a definite and early decision on 'Pigstick'.[2]

The uncertainty placed Slim in a difficult position since XV Corps might have to carry out either 'Pigstick' or 'Cudgel' and time was becoming short. On the 4th January he issued a carefully worded instruction to give Christison the detail necessary to enable him to plan his part in 'Pigstick' and the first stage of 'Cudgel', should it become the main operation in Arakan. The orders he had already given to IV Corps on the Central front could remain unchanged since they were equally suitable for 'Tarzan' and 'Gripfast'.

The instruction to XV Corps required Christison to advance southwards and destroy the Japanese forces in north Arakan with the ultimate object of capturing Akyab. His immediate objective was to be the general line Indin–Rathedaung–Myohaung, and he was to be ready to attack the Maungdaw–Buthidaung position by the 28th January.[3] The decision whether Akyab was to be attacked would rest with 14th Army and, as no decision had yet been reached, there was

---

[1] See pages 63–65.
[2] See page 65.
[3] See Map 2, page 5.

to be no mention of it as an objective in any corps orders to lower formations. The corps would have under command 5th and 7th Indian Divisions, 81st (W.A.) Division (less one brigade) and 50th (P.) Brigade (less one battalion). The 29th Brigade of 36th Indian Division with ninety-six landing craft of various kinds was to move to Cox's Bazar and be ready for action by the end of February. The Arakan Inshore Flotilla was to be in support of the corps for coastal operations,[1] and air support was to be provided by 3rd Tactical Air Force and the Strategic Air Force, using a maximum of four squadrons of heavy, and one of medium, bombers in any forty-eight hour period. The 81st (W.A.) Division in the Kaladan was to be supplied by air, half of the required lift being available from the 7th January and the full amount from the 14th. The roads from Dohazari to the river head at Tumbru and from Cox's Bazar to Ramu were to be brought to an all-weather one-way standard by the 1st April, and the road on from Tumbru to Razabil to fair-weather by the 15th May and to all-weather by the 1st July. An airstrip for fighters was to be built at Maungdaw and others for light bombers at Chiringa and Cox's Bazar. Airstrips for the evacuation of casualties were to be built at Taung Bazar and in the Kaladan.

The destruction of the Japanese forces in north Arakan was, in 'Pigstick', to be accomplished by landing 2nd Division in the southern part of the Mayu peninsula as an anvil for the XV Corps hammer; only after their destruction was Akyab to be surrounded and taken with the help of 29th Brigade of 36th Division and 50th (P.) Brigade. In the alternative ('Cudgel') the attack on Akyab would have to be direct, without the previous envelopment and destruction of the Japanese forces with the help of 2nd Division. It will be observed that the terms of the instruction to Christison covered both these operations. When 'Pigstick' was finally cancelled the only alteration asked for by Slim was that the whole of 36th Division should be allotted for the assault on Akyab instead of only one brigade, in order to compensate in some measure for the absence of 2nd Division.

By the 6th January, Mountbatten still had had no reply from the Chiefs of Staff on the subject of 'Pigstick'. Convinced that a final decision could no longer be delayed, he told them and his Commanders-in-Chief that he was cancelling it and ordering the mounting of 'Gripfast' and 'Cudgel' in its place. Three days later he was told by the Chiefs of Staff that 'Pigstick' was finally cancelled and that 'Cudgel' was to be adopted.[2] The cancellation of all major amphibious operations and the refusal of Stilwell to serve directly under 11th Army Group left Giffard, apart from the non-operational Ceylon Command and the Indian Ocean island garrisons, with only

---

[1] Motor launches manned by the Royal Navy.
[2] See page 66.

14th Army under his command. Nevertheless his headquarters remained a very necessary link in the chain of command, for it carried immense administrative responsibilities and was essential if further amphibious operations were to be planned for the future.

On the 9th Giffard ordered Slim to carry out 'Gripfast' and 'Cudgel'.[1] Allied land and air forces based on Ledo, Imphal and Chittagong were to conduct concerted offensive operations during 1944 to protect the construction of the Ledo–Myitkyina road, secure the air route from Assam to China and improve the tactical and administrative situation in Arakan. In addition to the forces already allotted to 14th Army in his order of 14th December, Giffard placed 11th (E.A.) Scout Battalion and the whole of 36th Indian Division under Slim's command, with the proviso that the latter was not to be used without his specific sanction. Slim's tasks were to secure the mouth of the Naf River, Maungdaw and Buthidaung as soon as possible and exploit success to the maximum; to clear the Chin Hills as far as the foothills in the Kabaw Valley, dominate the area south of the Tamu–Sittaung road between the Yu and Chindwin Rivers and contain Japanese forces in the Kabaw Valley[2]; to draw up plans for the L.R.P. brigades allotted to him, in consultation with Stilwell,[3] and exploit across the Chindwin if their operations created a favourable opportunity. On the Northern front the N.C.A.C. forces were to advance by way of Kamaing to Mogaung and Myitkyina.

Slim was also to bring the Palel–Tamu road and its continuations east to Pyinbon Sakan (on the crest of the range some fourteen miles west of Sittaung) and south to Kyaukchaw to a two-way all-weather standard before the monsoon. The road to Kyaukchaw was to be extended to Yuwa as a fair-weather shingled road if operations permitted.[4] The Imphal–Tiddim road was to be made fit to maintain a division in the Tiddim area throughout the 1944 monsoon. Eastern Air Command was to support 14th Army, provide photographic reconnaissance, move airborne and air transit forces, defend Calcutta and the industrial areas of Bengal and Bihar, protect the airfields in north-east India and maintain a strategic air offensive. No. 1 Air Commando was to be allotted to Eastern Air Command for the support of the L.R.P. brigades.

Although the bulk of the assault craft had been removed from S.E.A.C., the ninety-six landing craft allotted to 14th Army for 'Pigstick' were still available, and gave an assault lift in armoured craft for some 400 men and a follow-up in unarmoured craft for about

---

[1] Giffard's orders were finally confirmed on the 14th January when the Supreme Commander issued his directive for the 1943–44 campaign. See page 66.
[2] See Maps 3 and 14, pages 33 and 452.
[3] He was to consult Stilwell in the latter's capacity as Commanding General, N.C.A.C.
[4] See Map 3.

700. With these Slim planned to carry out, in exploitation of 'Cudgel', an amphibious assault on Akyab (to be known as 'Bulldozer') should a favourable opportunity arise, using 36th Division and 50th (P.) Brigade.

With 'Tarzan 'and 'Pigstick' cancelled, Slim had to decide how best to employ the L.R.P. brigades of Special Force, three of which would be concentrated forward, ready for action, by the second half of January 1944. After his visit to Chungking, Wingate had flown on the 3rd January to Shingbwiyang to see Stilwell,[1] who had asked him for the use of an L.R.P. brigade. In view of the Generalissimo's refusal to allow the Yunnan armies to advance, the fly-in of the American L.R.P. formation (Merrill's Marauders) to the Salween area was no longer necessary; Wingate therefore agreed to its reversion to Stilwell's control, subject to Slim's approval, but pointed out that it was not yet fully trained for L.R.P. operations. Stilwell on his part consented to the use of No. 1 Air Commando in support of all brigades engaged on L.R.P. operations and agreed to Wingate's request that one of the British L.R.P. brigades might be introduced into Burma from the vicinity of Shingbwiyang.

That night Wingate flew on to 14th Army Headquarters at Comilla and on the 4th a conference was held to consider plans for the use of Special Force.[2] Slim told Wingate that his rôle was to assist Stilwell's advance on the Northern front and afford a favourable opportunity both for the Chinese Yunnan armies to advance and for exploitation by IV Corps; of these tasks the most important was to assist Stilwell. Three brigades were in the first instance to operate: 16th Brigade in the Mu River valley (Pinlebu and Pinbon), moving into the area from Ledo by way of Shingbwiyang–Taro–Lonkin–Indawgyi Lake–Mohnyin and crossing the Chindwin about the 25th February,[3] 111th Brigade in the Meza valley–Wuntho–Indaw area, also crossing the Chindwin on the 25th at a spot to be selected by Wingate and Scoones, and 77th Brigade being flown in about the 5th March to an area lying north of the Irrawaddy in the Kaukkwe valley near Okkye.[4] Wingate was told that IV Corps could not cross the Chindwin and form a bridgehead for the passage of his brigades, but would assist the crossings by demonstrations and deceptive action. If by the end of March an airfield had been secured and a favourable situation created, the conference considered that a force might with advantage be flown in to take over from the L.R.P. forces. Slim therefore ordered 26th Indian Division, which was expected to be in IV Corps reserve by the end of March, to have one battalion ready to fly in, if required.

---

[1] See page 65.
[2] For order of battle of Special Force see Appendix 16.
[3] See Map 4, page 53.
[4] See Map 3, page 33.

The 16th Brigade was to concentrate at Margherita (near Ledo) and 77th and 111th Brigade at Silchar by the 25th January. Wingate was asked to get definite confirmation from Stilwell that No. 1 Air Commando would be at the disposal of Special Force and would provide fighter protection for both glider operations and supply dropping, operating from Lalaghat and Hailakandi airfields.[1] The 3rd Tactical Air Force would support the operations as necessary and 84 (Vengeance) Squadron would be earmarked to support the L.R.P. brigades up to the limit of its radius of action. These decisions were confirmed in an operation instruction issued by Slim to Special Force on the 9th January. Wingate was thus able to begin his detailed planning for the introduction of three L.R.P. brigades into Burma.

As soon as the monsoon was over the Japanese air force became much more active and in November 1943 began a series of offensive sweeps. Attacks by some 130 aircraft were made on the airfields in north-east Assam on the 8th and 11th but caused little damage. The next attack was the long contemplated raid on Calcutta with the object of destroying shipping and harbour installations and so delaying the Allied preparations for a counter-offensive. The *7th Air Brigade* had been given the task and had carried out rehearsals in Malaya in the middle of November. Towards the end of the month the brigade was reinforced by some aircraft of the naval air force and, as reconnaissance showed a large concentration of shipping at Calcutta, the Japanese decided to raid the airfields in the Chittagong area at the end of the month to draw the Allied fighters away from Calcutta which was to be attacked on the 5th December. The Allies reacted as expected by the Japanese: after attacks on the airfields at Feni and Agartala on the 28th and 29th November, the only Spitfire squadron available at that time for the defence of Calcutta was sent to reinforce the two Spitfire squadrons at Chittagong, leaving the air defence of Calcutta to two Hurricane squadrons and a night fighter squadron.

At 9.45 a.m. on the 5th December, after a radar warning, a force of sixty-five Spitfires and Hurricanes took off from Chittagong to intercept an enemy formation approaching over the Bay of Bengal. The Japanese launched their attack from Magwe airfield and took a course which gave Chittagong a wide berth. The R.A.F. fighters at extreme range were therefore unable to make contact. At Calcutta 67 and 146 Hurricane Squadrons, which had been held at instant readiness, had also taken off and at 11.30 a.m. intercepted the attackers. The Japanese force of twenty-seven medium bombers was

---

[1] See Map 14, page 452.

flying at 24,000 feet with about a hundred escorting fighters above and below it, and so the Hurricanes found themselves engaged at a tactical disadvantage with numerically superior enemy fighters. The docks were bombed and five Hurricanes were lost for only one Japanese fighter. Half an hour later a second wave of bombers with fighter escort approached the city. Both Hurricane squadrons were refuelling and re-arming after the first raid, and only six night fighter Hurricanes were immediately available. These intercepted the enemy but were themselves attacked from above. Three of the Hurricanes of 176 Squadron were shot down and the docks were bombed for a second time. In a final attempt to engage the enemy, two Spitfire squadrons took off from Chittagong in the hope that some of the raiders might be caught as they returned over the Bay of Bengal, but once again they passed out of range. Although the weight of bombs dropped on Calcutta was small, three merchant vessels and a naval ship were damaged, fifteen barges were set on fire and hits obtained on nine dock sheds, two of which were gutted by fire, and there were some five hundred civilian casualties. As had been the case in previous raids on Calcutta, many thousands fled from the city and only a tenth of the normal labour force in the docks remained at work. A false alert the following day did nothing to improve morale in the city. As a temporary measure a few Spitfires were moved back from Chittagong, partly to help in restoring morale, but the raids, which had little effect on military preparations, were not repeated.

After the raid on Calcutta the Japanese turned their attention to the air ferry route to China and, in doing so, achieved some success against supply-dropping aircraft in northern Burma. On the 10th December, enemy aircraft bombed the landing ground at Fort Hertz, but were intercepted by American fighters and five were believed destroyed. While returning to their bases from this raid, some of the enemy fighters encountered eight unescorted American supply-dropping transports and shot down four. Three days later a force of twenty bombers and twenty-five fighters raided Dinjan airfield, one of the main American bases serving the air ferry route, but did little damage to the airfield and caused only a few civilian casualties. Several further attacks of this kind, including two on the airfield at Kunming, were made during the month, but only eight transport aircraft in all were shot down on the ferry route. Though these losses were small, the attacks forced the Americans to maintain frequent fighter patrols and re-route their transport aircraft on a circuitous course over the higher mountains.

Towards the end of December the Japanese began to take an interest in shipping movements in and out of Chittagong and off the Arakan coast. On Christmas Day a raid on Chittagong by some fifty aircraft did little damage. Early on the morning of the 31st three

Royal Indian Navy motor launches, which had bombarded Japanese positions on Ramree Island, were sighted on their way back to Chittagong by an enemy reconnaissance aircraft and attacked at about 11 a.m. by some fifteen bombers with a fighter escort near St. Martin's Island off the Mayu peninsula. These aircraft were in turn intercepted by twelve Spitfires of 136 Squadron R.A.F., which had been held in readiness to provide cover for the naval force, and at least eight bombers and five fighters were believed to have been shot down and others damaged for the loss of one Spitfire. This success marked the first of several engagements between Spitfires and Japanese fighters which, in conjunction with long-range fighter operations, were soon to establish Allied air superiority over Burma.

It was not until the 15th January that enemy fighters again appeared in strength over Arakan. During that morning the Japanese launched a heavy air attack which was dispersed by two Spitfire squadrons. A careful check showed that for the loss of only two Spitfires sixteen enemy fighters were brought down, and it was estimated that many of the remainder were damaged.[1] Most of those destroyed were shot down over the corps forward area in sight of troops of 5th and 7th Divisions—an excellent fillip to morale. A few days later two Spitfire squadrons intercepted some thirty-five enemy fighters and an air battle took place over Maungdaw, in the course of which it was estimated that seven enemy aircraft were destroyed for the loss of two Spitfires. For the rest of January, except for reconnaissance, the Japanese air force remained largely inactive.

Meanwhile 224 Group R.A.F., with headquarters at Chittagong, had deployed nine squadrons for the direct support of XV Corps in the coming offensive.[2] In January several fair-weather strips in the area south of Cox's Bazar were brought into use, and a general forward movement then took place, in the course of which all but two of the Hurricane fighter squadrons (now numbering eight, having been reinforced by 30 and 134 squadrons from India) were located south of Chittagong.

From the 1st January to the 3rd February the two Vengeance squadrons, in support of 5th and 7th Divisions, made twenty-eight separate attacks (552 sorties) against enemy positions in Arakan in

---

[1] Radar plots disclosed the presence of some eighty aircraft at times. It is now known that some enemy formations turned back in the hope of drawing the Allied fighters southwards, where they could be attacked at the furthest limit of their radius of action.

[2] A Hurricane squadron (6 R.I.A.F.), responsible for tactical reconnaissance, was at Cox's Bazar. Two Vengeance dive-bomber squadrons (8 R.I.A.F. and 82 R.A.F.) were at Chittagong and Dohazari respectively. Six Hurricane fighter squadrons (11, 20, 60, 79, 258 and 261), combining the rôles of defence, escort, reconnaissance and ground attack, were at airstrips in the region of Chittagong, Comilla and Agartala. In addition the group had three Spitfire squadrons (136, 607 and 615), based at airstrips east of Cox's Bazar and at Chittagong, and two Beaufighter squadrons (27 and 177), at Agartala and Feni, for the air defence of Arakan and eastern Bengal. See Appendix 11.

which a total of 280 tons of bombs were dropped, but the results were disappointing. The hilly and broken country localized, and the jungle absorbed, the blast, and thus nothing but a direct hit on the target had much effect. Since it was almost impossible to pinpoint the target from the air owing to the thick vegetation, the chances of obtaining a direct hit on the small bunkers which constituted the Japanese defences were infinitesimal. The attacking infantry had to stand well back during the bombing and by the time they had reached their objective the dust and smoke had subsided and the defenders, more or less unshaken, were ready for them. To overcome this, a ruse was adopted of mixing delayed-action bombs with percussion bombs during preliminary bombing, to force the enemy to remain under cover till all had exploded. In the final bombardment before the attack, unfused bombs were used instead of delayed-action bombs in the hope that the infantry would be able to close in while the defenders kept underground until what they thought were delayed-action bombs went off. Though successful for a short time, the ruse became ineffective as the enemy grew accustomed to it.

On the Arakan front the road over Ngakyedauk Pass was fit to take 15 cwt. trucks by the 1st January.[1] The line of communication by mule and boat to units in the Kalapanzin valley was then abandoned in favour of the motor route over the pass, and the 7th Division Administrative Area and supply point was established at Sinzweya. The 5th Division was disposed with 123rd Brigade on the western slopes of the Mayu Range north of the Rekhat Chaung, 161st Brigade astride the Bawli Bazar–Razabil road north of Hathipauk and 9th Brigade in reserve. The 7th Division was on the general line Point 1619–Maunggyihtaung—Kwazon, with 89th Brigade on the eastern slopes of the range, 33rd Brigade facing Letwedet and 114th Brigade east of the Kalapanzin. Both divisions were in close touch with the main Japanese defences from the Naf River to the Arakan Hill Tracts and, it will be noted, 7th Division had no reserve brigade. The leading brigade of 81st (W.A.) Division had reached the Daletme area without meeting opposition.[2]

It was thought at the time that the Japanese *55th Division* was disposed with *143rd Regiment* plus *II/112th Battalion* and *II/214th Battalion* holding the Maungdaw–Buthidaung position, *112th Regiment* (less one battalion) on the coast between Maungdaw and Foul Point, a battalion of *213th Regiment* in the Kaladan Valley and the balance of the regiment at Akyab. Interrogation of prisoners captured by

---

[1] See Map 6, page 113.
[2] For Daletme see Map 2, page 5.

33rd Brigade in December had disclosed that a new Japanese division, understood to be *54th Division*, had recently arrived at Taungup to take over the defence of the coast line south of Akyab.[1] This was to some extent confirmed when air reconnaissance showed development of coast defences in this area consistent with the arrival of reinforcements.

On the night of the 6th/7th the Japanese, who had been stubbornly defending a redoubt close to Hathipauk (Point 124) despite the fact that it had been surrounded since New Year's Day, slipped away under cover of heavy rain and wind.[2] Two days later Maungdaw, threatened with isolation as a result of the abandonment of Point 124, was evacuated.

Meanwhile on receipt of 14th Army's orders to launch a general offensive before the end of the month,[3] Christison (XV Corps), whose divisions had already been ordered to infiltrate into, and if possible through, the enemy's main positions, issued fresh orders for a deliberate attack on Razabil and Buthidaung. It was to begin on the 19th January by which time the necessary ammunition would be in position and air support available.

The 7th Division (Messervy) was to capture Buthidaung and 5th Division (Briggs) Razabil, the operations being phased to enable the armoured unit (25th Dragoons) and the corps artillery to support each division in turn. The 7th Division, with the support of the corps artillery, was first to capture a feature known as Able overlooking the Tunnels–Buthidaung road east of Htindaw. The 5th Division, supported by 25th Dragoons and the Strategic Air Force, was then to capture Razabil. As soon as it had been occupied, the armour was to be transferred across the range and 7th Division was to advance on Buthidaung. The final phase was to be the mopping up of the Japanese isolated in the Tunnels and the Letwedet bastion and exploitation to the Indin–Rathedaung area. Simultaneously with these operations, 81st (W.A.) Division was to begin its advance down the Kaladan Valley.

Messervy's plan for the first phase was for 89th Brigade (Brigadier W. A. Crowther), supported by all the available divisional and corps artillery, to attack Able while 114th Brigade (Roberts), supported by 25th Mountain Regiment, infiltrated through the hills east of the river to the Dabrugyaung area, from where the Buthidaung –Rathedaung road could be cut when necessary. The 33rd Brigade (Loftus-Tottenham) was in the meantime to engage the Letwedet bastion so closely that its garrison could not interfere with the attack on Able. The enemy withdrawal from Maungdaw gave substance to

---

[1] See Map 15 in pocket at end of volume.
[2] See Map 6, page 113.
[3] See pages 116.

10. Major-General C. E. N. Lomax and Lieut.-General A. F. P. Christison.

11. Major-General
H. R. Briggs.

12. Major-General
F. W. Messervy.

13. Major-General
F. W. Festing.

14. Sinzweya, looking west from Ammunition Hill towards Ngakyedauk Pass.

15. Sinzweya, looking east from Ammunition Hill. Point 315 top left-hand corner.

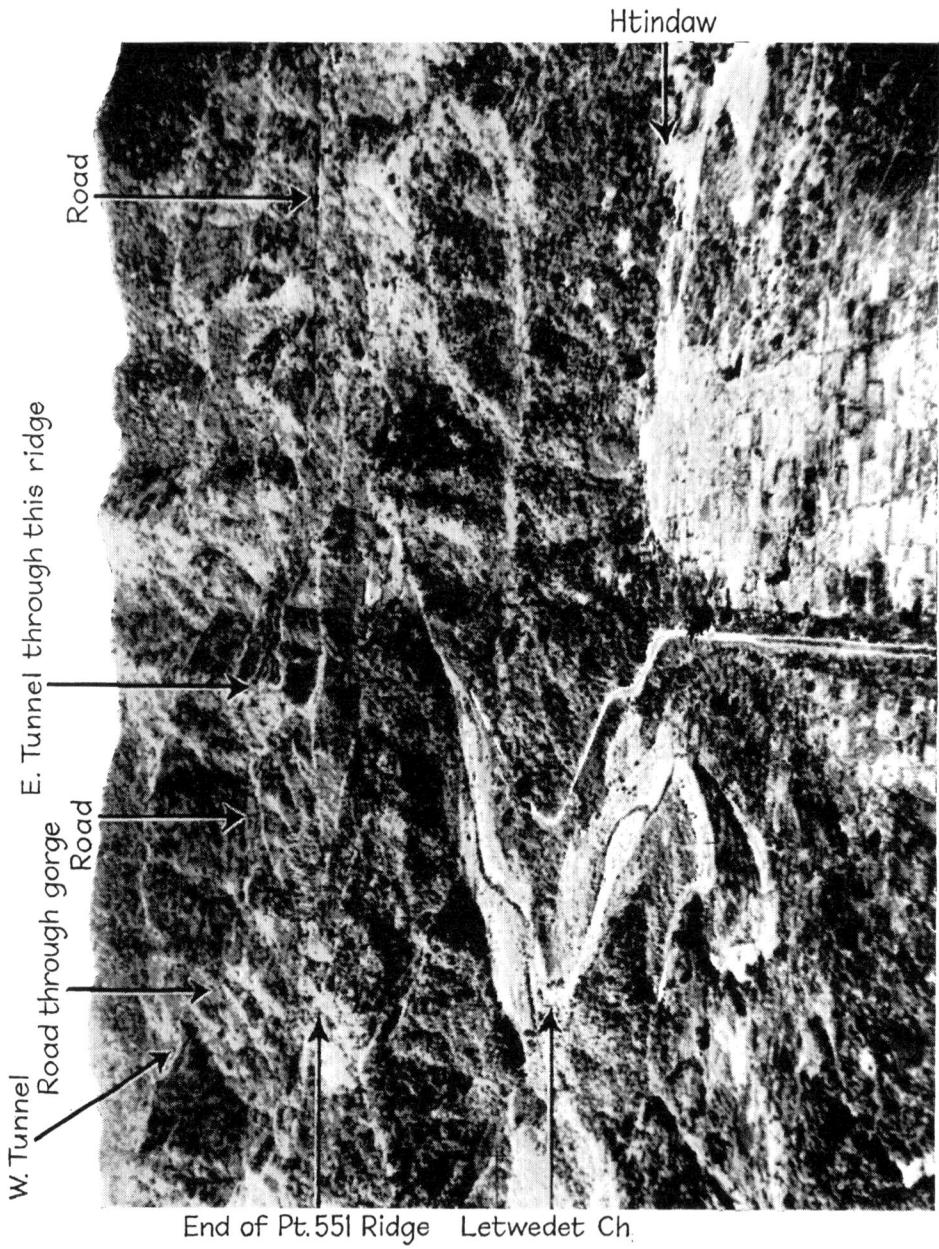

Htindaw

Road

E. Tunnel through this ridge

Road through gorge Road

W. Tunnel

End of Pt. 551 Ridge   Letwedet Ch

16. The Buthidaung–Maungdaw road, looking west from above Able.

Pt. 1267
↓

17. The Buthidaung–Maungdaw road, looking south from above the crest of the range. Dilpara top right-hand corner. West tunnel in foreground.

18. Tiger grass
at Razabil.

FAMOUS LAST
WORDS

"YOU CAN DRIVE
JEEPS ANYWHERE"
BUT GO SLOWLY

19. The western entrance
to Ngakyedauk Pass.

20. Point 1033 from Ngakyedauk Pass (for a time Colonel Tanahashi's headquarters).

21. The Kalapanzin River, looking south from Taung Bazar.

XV Corps Intelligence staff's belief that the Japanese might well withdraw, as they had done in 1942, from their forward position before the Allies attacked. In order to prevent them making an unmolested withdrawal, Messervy allowed 114th Brigade to begin its move forward on the night of the 14th/15th.

The 114th Brigade, relieved of the responsibility for protecting Taung Bazar, began to advance that night and, on the 15th, secured the general line Kyaukyit–Pyinghe–Windwin. On the night of the 19th/20th, 4/14th Punjab surprised a party of Japanese on the ridge east of Sannyinweywa and drove them off it at the point of the bayonet. Under cover of this attack 4/5th Royal Gurkhas moved south along the ridge, and on the 21st surprised an enemy party digging in on the hills about one-and-a-half miles north-east of Dabrugyaung and routed it. The enemy left three dead all belonging to *III/112th Battalion*; XV Corps Intelligence staff maintained that they were part of a reconnaissance (intelligence) group detached from *112th Regiment* which was itself believed to be still in the coastal sector south of Maungdaw. This deduction was surprising for the three men killed were from a party of over one hundred men who were digging in. In fact, the whole of *112th Regiment* had been brought up behind the right of the Japanese position in preparation for their 'Ha-Go' offensive. For the next few days there was heavy fighting east of the Kalapanzin as the Japanese made repeated attempts to cut the communications of the battalions working forward through the foothills. An attempt by the Somerset Light Infantry to isolate and capture the Pyinshe Kala redoubt failed with considerable loss.

West of the Kalapanzin at dusk on the 18th, after three days' 'softening up' by Vengeance dive-bombers, 89th Brigade attacked Able, and by the evening of the 19th after fierce fighting captured the eastern half of the feature and established a post overlooking the road east of Htindaw, but was unable to secure the centre and highest point of the feature. The struggle continued for several days and it was not till the 24th, by which time all three battalions had suffered severe casualties, that the whole feature was cleared and consolidated. Since it was under observed fire at close range from heavy howitzers in the Tunnels area, its retention, which was to be a decisive factor in the fighting that followed, was to prove costly and difficult.

As all the corps artillery which could be brought to bear had been supporting the attack on Able, the attack on Razabil by 161st Brigade had to be delayed until the 26th. It was opened by an air bombardment. Twelve Vengeance dive-bombers indicated the target; they were followed by sixteen Liberators (B.24) and seven Mitchells (B.25) of the Strategic Air Force and finally by another twelve Vengeance bombers. The bombing by the Strategic Air Force was not accurate and, despite the weight of artillery fire and the support of tanks, the infantry succeeded only in gaining a footing on the lower slopes of the northern end of the Razabil ridge.[1] During the next three days repeated attacks were made with artillery and tank support from different directions, the tanks concentrating on each enemy bunker position in turn. These, although apparently destroyed, came to life the moment the fire of the tanks was lifted and the infantry was unable to make progress. The attack was called off on the 30th, and both 161st and 123rd Brigades were ordered to consolidate the ground held.

Christison then decided to switch the axis of the corps' offensive to the east of the range and exploit the success already gained by the capture of Able. He proposed to use it as a point from which to break through towards Buthidaung, and isolate and then destroy the garrison of the Letwedet bastion. To give 7th Division the necessary reserve for the operation 5th Division's boundary was moved to take in the eastern foothills of the Mayu Range, and on the 1st February 9th Brigade (less a battalion left in Maungdaw) relieved 89th Brigade in that area. The 89th then moved to the Awlanbyin area to carry out a rehearsal with 25th Dragoons (less one squadron) for a break-through to Buthidaung on the 6th. A corps artillery group moved across Ngakyedauk Pass in close support of 7th Division during the first three days of February.[2] At the same time it was arranged that XV Corps should take over the divisional administrative area at Sinzweya to relieve 7th Division of administrative responsibility and provide a firm base for its forthcoming operation.[3] This was a most timely regrouping, for it brought about the concentration of a strong mobile reserve east of the Mayu Range one day before the Japanese launched their offensive.

To force the Japanese to lock up troops in protecting the Arakan coast, raids were made from time to time at various points along it. On the night of the 30th/31st January, a few hours before the regrouping began, one such raid was carried out on Alethangyaw by 81st (W.A.) Reconnaissance Regiment transported by 290th Inland Water Transport (I.W.T.) Company.[4] The Japanese, caught by surprise, fled, leaving the raiders to withdraw unmolested to their boats in daylight. Documents abandoned by the enemy showed that Alethangyaw was held by units of *144th Regiment* which had been in the Pacific and had not accompanied *55th Division* to Burma. This,

---

[1] The artillery supporting the attack consisted of 24th Mountain Regiment, 4th, 7th and 28th (Jungle) Field Regiments, one troop of 6th Medium Regiment and one battery of 8th (Belfast) Heavy Anti-Aircraft Regiment. The tank support was provided by 25th Dragoons equipped with medium (Lee/Grant) tanks.

[2] The group consisted of 6th Medium Regiment (less one battery), 7th Indian Field Regiment and a battery of 8th Heavy Anti-Aircraft Regiment.

[3] This changeover had not taken place when the Japanese isolated Sinzweya by cutting the pass. See Chapter X.

[4] See Map 2, page 5.

in conjunction with an identification made the previous night of a company of *II/112th Regiment* near Dabrugyaung and those obtained on the 21st January, might reasonably have been taken as an indication that a considerable part of *112th Regiment*, having been relieved by *144th Regiment*, was east of the Kalapanzin. The Intelligence staffs of both XV Corps and 14th Army did not, however, believe that there was more than one company in the area in addition to the reconnaissance group.

Thus, when on the 2nd February Giffard, on his way to inspect the Arakan front, visited 14th Army Headquarters to discuss the latest developments with Slim, they were sure that the Japanese were contemplating an offensive, but there was little to indicate its scope or direction although they thought that the enemy would probably attempt to outflank XV Corps. In order to ensure that there would be adequate forces to meet any contingency, Giffard decided that the move of 36th Division, already ordered to concentrate for 'Bulldozer' in the Chittagong–Calcutta area by the end of February, was to continue; a brigade of 26th Division, which had on the 31st January been ordered to join IV Corps in Assam, was not to move for the time being and a brigade of 25th Indian Division was to be sent to IV Corps instead; and 50th (P.) Brigade's allotment to 'Bulldozer' was to be cancelled, as all aircraft would probably be required for air supply purposes.

When he took command in Arakan at the end of the disastrous 1943 campaign, Slim had evolved a new method of dealing with Japanese infiltrating and encircling tactics. Realizing that, in a theatre where troops were few and the country was vast, lines of defence could always be turned, he planned to establish strong, well stocked and easily maintained pivots of manoeuvre covering areas which the enemy would be forced to attack to open up a line of communication for his advance, and from which mobile forces could operate not to hold or regain ground but to destroy the enemy forces.[1] When he assumed command of 14th Army in October 1943 he had made it clear that, in the event of their lines of communication being cut, forward formations and units were to stand fast, unless given orders to withdraw, and, supplied by air, were to form an anvil against which reserves could destroy the enemy forces in their rear. To make this a practical proposition he had warned Major-General A. H. J. Snelling, his principal administrative staff officer, that he must be prepared to maintain forward formations by air at any time. In consequence of this warning the air supply units at Agartala and Comilla had been reinforced and their training intensified.[2] Slim now told Snelling to start day and night packing

---

[1] See Volume II, pages 350–51.   [2] See Map 4, page 53.

in preparation for supplying XV Corps by air. With adequate reserves at hand and an air supply organization ready to go into action at short notice, he felt that the expected enemy offensive could be awaited with confidence.

Meanwhile in the Kaladan 81st (W.A.) Division (Major-General C. G. Woolner) had begun its advance down the valley on the 18th January, which it was believed was held by a battalion of *213th Regiment* based on Kyauktaw with a detachment about Paletwa and covered by a screen of Burmese irregulars.[1] The 6th (W.A.) Brigade (Brigadier J. W. A. Hayes), supported by the mortar troops of two light batteries, led the advance from Daletme along the track on the eastern bank of the Kaladan River. The 5th (W.A.) Brigade (Brigadier N. H. Collins), which had moved to Satpaung, began to prepare rafts to assist its onward move down the river to Paletwa. The division was to be supplied and casualties were to be evacuated by 62 (Transport) Squadron R.A.F. operating from Comilla, but arrangements were made to keep open a jeep track from Chiringa by way of Mowdok to Satpaung and beyond as an auxiliary line of land communication. The 7/16th Punjab was ordered to follow up behind the division to maintain and protect the track.

Shortly after leaving Daletme, 6th (W.A.) Brigade met slight opposition and captured two prisoners from *I/213th Battalion*.[2] On the 24th, just south of Paletwa, it encountered two small but well dug-in posts. In accordance with Woolner's policy of avoiding deliberate attacks in view of the lack of artillery support, the posts were surrounded and subjected to air bombardment. Two days later the enemy was found to have withdrawn. In order to outflank enemy defences reported near Kaladan village, Woolner ordered the advance to be continued on the 31st January on a broad front with 5th Brigade moving down the Pi Chaung, 6th Brigade down the Kaladan and 11th (E.A.) Scout Battalion on the left flank.[3]

On the Central front there were signs during January that the enemy forces opposing IV Corps were being reinforced and were taking an increased interest in the area west of the Chindwin River. Air reconnaissance in December indicated that the Siam–Burma

---

[1] See Map 2, page 5.
[2] These prisoners gave information that their battalion was leaving the Kaladan for Buthidaung.
[3] The 11th (E.A.) Scout Battalion had joined the division in place of 81st (W.A.) Reconnaissance Regiment which, being mechanized, was unsuitable for operations in the Kaladan Valley and was being used as corps troops for raids on the Mayu coast. See page 126.

railway was open to traffic and that there was intense activity on the enemy lines of communication in central Burma.[1] Patrols from 20th Division had discovered that enemy units belonging to *31st Division* had closed up to the Chindwin River, and there were unconfirmed reports that *15th Division* was being moved into Burma. About the middle of January enemy patrols began to probe the line of communication to 17th Division in the Tongzang area (fifteen miles north of Tiddim).[2]

In the Kabaw Valley the Japanese were found to have crossed the Chindwin and established a defended post at Kyaukchaw on the Yu River. Since this was in an area which 20th Division had been told to keep clear, 32nd Brigade was ordered to attack the post under cover of an air bombardment. There was a delay of several days because of unsuitable weather, but on the 17th January the post was bombed for one-and-a-half hours and then attacked by 1st Northamptonshire. It was not, however, till the 25th that it was cleared.[3] The effect of the aerial bombardment, which at first sight seemed to be considerable, was found to be much less than expected; no enemy bunker had received a direct hit and the near misses had done no damage. A prisoner later said that only one man had been killed by the bombardment and he had been standing above ground at the time.

On the 27th, a patrol from 80th Brigade ambushed and put to flight a Japanese detachment east of the Chindwin. Documents captured showed that at least one battalion of *60th Regiment* of *15th Division* was present in the area. It was already known that this division was being moved from Siam, but the presence of part of it on the Chindwin, together with increased activity behind the enemy front, made it evident that the Japanese were now being reinforced and were preparing to undertake an offensive.

The strategical outlook on IV Corps front was completely changed by this information and on the 3rd February Scoones made a fresh appreciation of the position. He concluded that *15th Army* was in a position to launch an offensive across the Chindwin from Homalin. He believed that one regiment of *15th Division* would be directed by way of Ukhrul to cut the Imphal Road in the Kohima area, that the rest of the division would move south down the Kabaw Valley to attack 20th Division from the north, while a regiment of *31st Division* attacked it from the east, and that the rest of *31st Division* would constitute a mobile reserve. The *33rd Division* would contain 17th Division in the Chin Hills. To counter this he proposed that the

---

[1] See Map 15 in pocket at end of volume.
[2] See Map 3, page 33.
[3] For his part in this action Lieut. A. G. Horwood, D.C.M., The Queen's Royal Regiment (West Surrey), attached The Northamptonshire Regiment, was posthumously awarded the Victoria Cross.

Kohima–Somra–Ukhrul area should be held by one brigade (if possible this brigade should be provided as a reinforcement to IV Corps),[1] that 20th Division should, if attacked, withdraw into and hold a secure base in the Tamu–Moreh area and that 23rd Division in corps reserve should be prepared to counter-attack in flank any enemy forces moving towards the Imphal–Kohima road or on Tamu.[2] The 17th Division's task of clearing the road to Fort White as a prelude to an advance to Kalemyo was to remain unaltered. Meanwhile the forward divisions were to carry out his orders to clear the Kabaw Valley and the Chin Hills.

On the Northern front Stilwell had personally taken command of all operations on the 21st December, intending to end the stalemate and get the drive towards Myitkyina under way.[3] By this time the whole of 38th Chinese Division had been concentrated in the vicinity of Shingbwiyang, and an attack with two regiments was launched on the 24th to break through the Japanese defences on the Tarung River.[4] It was not, however, till the end of the month and after considerable fighting that the river line was cleared. About the same time the Ledo Road reached Shingbwiyang.

Stilwell's next objective was the crossing of the Tanai River with its ferry at Taihpa Ga. Fighting, in which both 22nd and 38th Chinese Divisions were involved, continued throughout the second half of January 1944 and it was not until the 1st February that Taihpa Ga was occupied and the Japanese withdrew to positions covering Maingkwan. Two days earlier 65th Regiment of 22nd Chinese Division had occupied Taro and taken control of the Taro plain, thus securing Stilwell's right flank. The way was now clear for an attack on Maingkwan, the occupation of which would give Stilwell control of the whole of the Hukawng Valley.

To summarize the situation on the 3rd February: in Arakan, XV Corps had just completed regrouping for an assault on Buthidaung; on the Central front, Scoones had discovered that a third Japanese division was deploying opposite IV Corps and, believing that this portended an offensive, had prepared a fresh appreciation and plan; on the Northern front Stilwell, having secured the crossing of

---

[1] See Map 4, page 53.
[2] See Map 3, page 33.
[3] General Sultan was appointed Stilwell's deputy to deal with the administration of the C.B.I. Theatre. Stilwell was therefore able to devote more attention to operations on the Northern front.
[4] See Map 4, page 53.

the Tanai River, was planning to clear the whole of the Hukawng Valley and continue the advance to Myitkyina; and on the Salween front the Chinese Yunnan armies were still inactive.[1] The Japanese *28th Army* had ordered *55th Division* to launch operation 'Ha-Go' on the 4th February with the object of drawing Allied reserves to Arakan before *15th Army* launched the main offensive to capture Imphal in March.

---

[1] All the skirmishes and actions to date had cost the four Indian divisions involved (5th, 7th, 17th and 20th) just over 2,000 casualties, of which slightly more than half were incurred in Arakan. See Appendix 29.

CHAPTER X

THE BATTLE OF NGAKYEDAUK PASS

(February – March 1944)

See Maps 2, 6 and 7 and Sketches 3, 4 and 5

IN the darkness and mist of the early hours of the 4th February the Japanese launched their 'Ha-Go' offensive in Arakan which led to the Battle of Ngakyedauk Pass.[1] The ground over which it was fought was an area about ten miles square bounded on the north by an east-west line through Taung Bazar, on the west by the crest of the Mayu Range, on the south by the Tunnels–Buthidaung road and on the east by the Arakan Hill Tracts. Down the centre of this area from north to south runs the tidal Kalapanzin River, some fifty to a hundred and fifty yards in width with an eight-foot rise and fall, fordable in the dry season near Taung Bazar at low tide. South of the village its numerous tributaries were mostly unfordable to within about a mile of the foothills; the larger ones were tank obstacles at all times.

Within the battle area the Kalapanzin valley is about seven to eight miles wide and is intersected by jungle-clad ridges running from north to south; these vary in size and shape from single spine ridges, some two hundred yards wide rising to an elevation of two hundred feet, to tangled masses of steep jungle-covered hills over a mile in width intersected by deep ravines.[2] Between the ridges the flat valley floor was divided into large numbers of small rice-fields about thirty yards square, bordered by banks from one to three feet high. From November to March motorable tracks could be made by cutting through the banks and for a short time the hard-packed mud provided a good surface. During this period the rice-fields were covered with a two-foot stubble sufficient to give cover to a crawling man.

Sinzweya, the site of 7th Division's Administrative Area, which became the focal point of the battle, lay in an amphitheatre about a mile long and half a mile broad, surrounded by jungle-covered hills. The Ngakyedauk Chaung ran along its southern edge and to the west the ground rose steeply to the main ridge of the Mayu Range.

---

[1] Referred to by the contemporary press as the 'Battle of the Box'.
[2] See Map 6, page 113.

An isolated jungle-clad hill, known as Ammunition Hill from the ammunition dumps grouped round it, jutted out from the southern edge of the amphitheatre, almost dividing it into two.[1] By the 3rd February Sinzweya was connected with the forward posts west of the Kalapanzin River by a network of motorable tracks. There was, however, only one to the east of the river which ran from the Paung-dawbyin ferry to Kwazon where 114th Brigade had established its administrative area.

The influence of the country and the climate on operations was considerable. Throughout the dry season a morning mist with heavy dew formed daily in the small hours and, unless cleared by rain and wind, normally persisted till well after sunrise; the noise made by the dew falling from the trees on to the dry undergrowth was loud enough to drown the sound of footsteps so that, in the jungle, movement in the early morning could be unheard as well as unseen. The tides were an important factor in planning, for at high tide many of the chaungs were unfordable. The knife-edge ridges into which the Japanese so often dug their defences presented an unusual artillery problem. If guns were to bring effective fire to bear, they had to be sited on the line of the axis of a ridge, which was always difficult and sometimes impossible. Fire from any other angle meant that reverse slope defences were untouched and accurate ranging was extremely diffi-cult. The dense jungle covering the hilltops greatly restricted their use as observation points.

On the evening of the 3rd February, XV Corps (Christison) was carrying out the last stages of its regrouping for the deliberate attack on the Japanese defences east of the Mayu Range to take place between the 6th and 8th February.[2] Its advanced headquarters was established three miles south of Bawli Bazar. On and west of the range 5th Indian Division (Briggs), with headquarters at Wabyin, had one battalion of 9th Brigade guarding Maungdaw, which had been made the base for 81st (W.A.) Reconnaissance Regiment and 290th (I.W.T.) Company employed in raiding along the Arakan coast. The 161st Brigade (Brigadier D. F. W. Warren), with two battalions forward and one in reserve and 4th Field Regiment in support, was in close contact with the Razabil redoubt. To its left, 123rd Brigade (Brigadier T. J. W. Winterton) was deployed along the line of the Rekhat Chaung as far as the crest of the range at Point 1619, supported by 28th (Jungle) Field Regiment; the brigade was very dispersed with its four battalions forward and no mobile reserve.[3] In the foothills, on the east of the range, 9th Brigade (Brigadier G. C. Evans), less its battalion at Maungdaw, had just taken over from

---

[1] See Sketch 4, page 144.
[2] For order of battle of XV Corps see Appendix 15.
[3] It had been reinforced by the divisional defence battalion.

89th Brigade of 7th Division and was disposed with one battalion overlooking Htindaw and 2nd West Yorkshire (less one company with the forward battalion) in reserve immediately to the south of Sinzweya, alongside brigade headquarters. One of the divisional field companies was working on the Ngakyedauk Pass road and the others were with the forward brigades. The only corps reserve was the newly-formed reserve squadron of 25th Dragoons, which was alongside the maintenance centre at Briasco Bridge.

The 7th Indian Division (Messervy) had its headquarters one mile north-east of Sinzweya on the Laung Chaung. The division was disposed with 33rd Brigade (Loftus-Tottenham) holding a four-mile front between Able and the Kalapanzin River with three battalion groups: 4/1st Gurkhas on Able, 1st Queen's facing the Letwedet bastion and 4/15th Punjab continuing the line to the river. Brigade headquarters was situated near Tatmakhali with 136th Field and 139th (Jungle) Field Regiment alongside it. East of the Kalapanzin, 114th Brigade (Roberts) was poised to cut the Buthidaung–Rathe-daung road and had two battalions in the hills south of Sannyin-weywa, ready to attack on the 4th to secure the high ground over-looking the valley between Point 232 and Dabrugyaung. The former forward posts of the brigade from the Kalapanzin to Windwin were held by 1st Somerset Light Infantry, now little above half strength, headquarters and a company of 1/11th Sikhs and 421st Field Company. Brigade headquarters was on the Pyinshe Kala ridge about one mile north of the village with two batteries of 25th Mountain Regiment nearby. The horsed wing of the Gwalior Lancers was disposed in the low hills east of Taung Bazar watching the east and south-east approaches to it, with two dismounted troops on Point 1600. The 89th Brigade (Crowther), which had just been relieved by 9th Brigade, was in divisional reserve in the area south-east of Sinzweya, where it was to be joined on the 4th by 25th Dragoons and prepare for the attack on Buthidaung. The 7th Indian Field Regiment was to the south of the Ngakyedauk Chaung in the Point 147 area and 6th Medium Regiment, less one battery, was immediately north of the chaung just east of Sinzweya. The 24th Anti-Aircraft/Anti-Tank Regiment, with two of its batteries, was responsible for protecting the Sinzweya maintenance centre in which were the rear echelons of unit and brigade transport, brigade and divisional workshops, supply units, an ordnance field park and a main dressing station. The 258th (I.W.T.) Company and some medical and supply detachments were at Taung Bazar.

In the Kaladan Valley, 81st (W.A.) Division with 5th Brigade on the Pi Chaung, 6th Brigade on the Kaladan River and its left flank protected by 11th (E.A.) Scout Battalion had by the 3rd February reached an east-west line immediately north of Kaladan village.

The 7/16th Punjab was at Paletwa in touch with 'V' Force watching the tracks across the Arakan Yomas.[1]

Hanaya (*55th Division*) had formed the opinion that the Allies would launch an offensive against the Buthidaung–Maungdaw position with two or three divisions supported by armour in February or March, and might also launch separate amphibious attacks on Ramree and Cheduba Islands. The increasing pressure by XV Corps led him to the conclusion that a general offensive was imminent and that he must forestall it. As soon, therefore, as *28th Army* had sanctioned his plan,[2] he issued orders for the offensive to begin on the night of the 3rd/4th February.

At the end of January, *55th Division* was disposed with *143rd Regiment* holding the defences from Razabil to Sannyinweywa, *112th Regiment* in reserve in the Kindaung area, *144th Regiment* (less one battalion) holding the coasts of the Mayu peninsula and *111th Regiment* (less two battalions) with one battalion of *144th Regiment* providing the garrison for Akyab and Boronga Islands. The *I/213th Battalion* had just been relieved in the Kaladan by *55th Reconnaissance Regiment* and was moving to the Buthidaung area.[3]

For his offensive Hanaya divided his division into four columns: the *Koba* (*I/111th* and *III/144th Battalions*) to hold Akyab;[4] the *Yoshida* (*I/144th Battalion*) to guard the coast of the Mayu peninsula south of Godusara; the *Doi* (*I/143rd* and *III/143rd Battalions*) to hold the defences west of the Kalapanzin; and the *Sakurai* (*112th Regiment* with *II/143rd Battalion*, *I/213th Battalion* and *55th Engineer Regiment*) to break through the British left east of the river.[5] He kept one battalion (*II/144th*) in divisional reserve and left *55th Reconnaissance Regiment* to protect the Kaladan Valley. He ordered the *Sakurai Column* to pass through the British lines on the left bank of the Kalapanzin River and seize Taung Bazar. It was then to cross the river, block Ngakyedauk Pass and attack British formations which lay between the river and the crest of the Mayu Range from the north,

---

[1] See Map 2, page 5, and page 128. 'V' Force (see Volume II, page 192) had by this time been expanded and organized in two zones—Assam and Arakan. The Assam Zone had six groups operating on the Northern and Central fronts and the Arakan Zone three, one of which acted as a link between the two zones. Each group had platoons of Assam Rifles, or, in Arakan, Tripura Rifles, as a fighting element and up to 1,000 local men enrolled but not formally enlisted. Its main task was the collection of information and its officers were volunteers from the army, the police or civilians with local knowledge.

[2] See page 79.

[3] The strength of *55th Division* and attached troops at the end of January was approximately 14,600.

[4] The responsibility for the defence of Akyab and for the *Koba Column* was transferred to *54th Division* on the 5th February.

[5] Colonel T. Koba was the commander of *111th Regiment*, Colonel Yoshida of *144th Regiment*, Colonel Doi of *143rd Regiment* and Major-General T. Sakurai of *55th Divisional Infantry Group*. Colonel S. Tanahashi commanded *112th Regiment*.

while the *Doi Column* attacked them from the south.[1] The operation was to be covered by *7th Air Brigade*, which from the 4th to the 10th February was to attempt to gain air superiority over the battlefield.[2]

The spearhead of the Japanese offensive, the *Sakurai Column*, began its advance from Kindaung about 11 p.m. on the 3rd.[3] It moved north through Dabrugyaung and then, under cover of darkness and the thick early morning mist, passed in a tightly packed column sixteen men abreast up the centre of the four-hundred-yards-wide valley between Pyinshe Kala and Pyinghe, past Kwazon to Taung Bazar. The main body passed through the widely separated 114th Brigade's forward posts before suspicions were aroused and only the rearguard was intercepted and dispersed. Taung Bazar was occupied between 8 and 9 a.m. on the 4th, and an hour later the advanced guard (*II/143rd Battalion*) had crossed the Kalapanzin in captured boats and was followed later in the day by two other battalions.[4] The leading troops of these three battalions clashed with the advanced guard of 89th Brigade at Ingyaung that evening, and it was not until about noon on the 5th that the whole column was across.

That morning Sakurai issued his orders for the further advance of his column. The *I/213th Battalion* (less two companies) was to cross the Mayu Range to the Briasco Bridge area and cut the Bawli Bazar–Maungdaw road. Tanahashi was to send *I/112th Battalion* through Preingyaung to seize and hold the Ngakyedauk Pass road and with the rest of his regiment advance on Point 315. Sakurai, with the headquarters of the column and *55th Engineer Regiment*, proposed to follow behind *II/143rd Battalion*, which was to move towards Awlanbyin on the left of *112th Regiment*.

At about 4 a.m. on the 4th movement of men and animals was heard at 114th Brigade Headquarters and thought to be caused by ration parties moving to forward units. Shortly after this the Somersets reported that a patrol had heard a large number of men, talking in a strange language, and mules, moving north; these they had taken to be an Indian artillery ammunition party which had lost its way. Patrols sent out at once by brigade headquarters found nothing suspicious, but at 5.30 a.m. further movement was heard and patrols made contact with the enemy and identified *112th Regiment*. At about 7 a.m. the mist began to clear and a column of Japanese troops moving north with Arakanese porters was intercepted near Kwazon by a fighting patrol supported by bren carriers. Caught in the open

---

[1] See Sketch 3, page 140.
[2] The operational strength of *7th Air Brigade* was about forty-five aircraft at that time.
[3] The approximate strength of the *Sakurai Column* was 5,000 all ranks.
[4] Taung Bazar post was held by a few baggage guards and was the headquarters of 258th (I.W.T.) Company.

between Kwazon and brigade headquarters and subjected to artillery and mortar fire, the column dispersed. The porters dropped their loads and disappeared into the jungle. The infantry took up a position on the ridge overlooking 114th Brigade administrative area at Kwazon and beat off attacks by small local reserves until ejected the following day by troops recalled from a forward battalion. It was not at first thought that any large force was involved, and at about 7 a.m. Roberts told Messervy that he believed the column which had been engaged was composed of reliefs for Japanese forward positions which had lost their way. Meanwhile at 6.30 a.m. four miles to the south 4/5th Royal Gurkhas had successfully attacked the hill north of Dabrugyaung, its final objective before the assault on Buthidaung.

At about 9 a.m. the Gwalior Lancers reported to 7th Division by wireless that a column of Japanese about a hundred strong followed by another about eight hundred strong was approaching Taung Bazar. Messervy immediately ordered his reserve brigade (89th) to move north to locate and destroy them and asked XV Corps to speed up the arrival of the tanks. Christison thereupon ordered 25th Dragoons to send a squadron to Sinzweya and 5th Division to send an infantry detachment to prevent infiltration over Goppe Pass. The 89th Brigade moved north in two columns: the right column encountered the Japanese at about 4 p.m. near Ingyaung in hand-to-hand fighting, and the left reached the bend of the Prein Chaung east of Preingyaung. The right column then dug in at Ingyaung and Linbabi and the left on the Prein Chaung.

On the evening of the 4th, Slim, at Christison's request, ordered Lomax (26th Division) to place one brigade (71st) at the disposal of XV Corps immediately, and told Christison that his formations would be supplied by air if necessary. At the same time Snelling warned all concerned to be prepared to put the plan for air supply into effect.[1] Giffard, who was at 5th Divisional Headquarters, on hearing of the break-through, crossed the pass to 7th Divisional Headquarters where he spent the night of the 4th/5th. When he left to return to his own headquarters on the morning of the 5th the situation was still obscure, since 89th Brigade had not been able to assess the strength of the enemy south-west of Taung Bazar, and survivors from the garrison had been able to confirm only that the post had been overrun by a large Japanese column.

Throughout the 5th, 89th Brigade held its ground in the face of fierce attacks, but tanks of 25th Dragoons patrolling north from the Prein Chaung saw large numbers of enemy infantry moving westwards into the Mayu Range. By the afternoon it was clear that the Japanese force was much larger than had at first been supposed. In consequence Slim placed the whole of 26th Division at the disposal

---

[1] See pages 127–28.

of XV Corps and Christison ordered Lomax to move it forward to Bawli Bazar as quickly as possible. On arrival at 14th Army Headquarters from the forward area, Giffard arranged for the concentration of 36th Indian Division (Major-General F. W. Festing) at Chittagong to be speeded up.[1] Meanwhile Christison had ordered 71st Brigade (Brigadier R. C. Cotterell-Hill), on its arrival at Bawli North, to relieve the detachment from 5th Division on Goppe Pass and then attack the Japanese operating in rear of 7th Division.

By evening the situation seemed to be more or less in hand. Powerful reserves were moving forward. East of the Kalapanzin 114th Brigade was clearing its administrative area; 89th Brigade had maintained its positions at Ingyaung, Linbabi and on the Prein Chaung; and 25th Dragoons (less a squadron) had concentrated at Sinzweya. To the south the enemy had made no move.

In view of the satisfactory progress of the *Sakurai Column*, Hanaya ordered the *Doi Column* on the 5th February to take the offensive northwards with as strong a force as possible so as to be able to join in the attack on the British forces in the Sinzweya area which would be launched about the 10th. Accordingly *III/143rd Battalion* was ordered to attack on the following morning from Letwedet towards Tatmakhali.

During the 6th Sakurai reported that he had lost touch with *II/143rd Battalion* after the fighting near Ingyaung and that his headquarters was without infantry protection.[2] Hanaya thereupon ordered his reserve battalion, *II/144th*, to move north on the night of the 7th/8th to reinforce the headquarters of the *Sakurai Column* somewhere north of Awlanbyin. Early on the 7th, Sakurai sent a message by runner addressed to *II/144th Battalion* (Major Kato) instructing it to move to Point 147 and then help him to cross the Ngakyedauk Chaung. The runner, who also carried a list of the call signs and wireless frequencies of the *Sakurai Column*, was killed east of the Kalapanzin. The captured message was not translated in time to be of use to 7th Division, but 14th Army believed that the poor co-ordination of the Japanese operations during the battle may have been due to the fact that the call signs did not reach their destination.

During the 6th February the situation rapidly deteriorated. In the small hours of the morning a Japanese force of unknown strength

---

[1] See page 127.
[2] It appears that, after an engagement in the Ingyaung area, *II/143rd Battalion* moved to Point 202, crossed the Ngakyedauk Chaung and reached the Punkori area on the 8th, where it remained till the 11th.

appeared on the Bawli Bazar–Maungdaw road and raided 5th Division's administrative area at the Briasco Bridge. From then on convoys had to be escorted and the road constantly patrolled. East of the range at about 5 a.m., an enemy force, estimated at battalion strength, penetrated the widely separated posts held by the company of 24th Engineer Battalion defending 7th Division Headquarters, established machine-gun posts on tracks throughout the headquarters area and broke into the signal centre. In hand-to-hand fighting the attackers were driven out, but not before all communications had been cut and ciphers compromised. Tanks from Sinzweya moved to the sound of the fighting as soon as it was light but the ground prevented them from reaching the headquarters area; rain which set in about 8.30 a.m. further hampered them and they had to withdraw. At about 10 a.m. the signal centre was finally overrun. Messervy, unable to exercise command any longer, sent orders to all branches of his headquarters to destroy papers and equipment of value and make their way in small parties to Sinzweya. Most of them succeeded in doing so during the following twenty-four hours. Further south the Japanese had made a dawn attack on 33rd Brigade's front. Though all forward defences had held firm, enemy troops infiltrated into the gun positions near brigade headquarters and overran one of the mortar batteries of 139th Jungle Field Regiment.[1]

Having come to the conclusion that 7th Division Headquarters must have been overrun, Christison at 10 a.m. instructed 5th Division to tell Evans (9th Brigade) that he was to move at once to Sinzweya with what troops he could spare from his brigade sector, organize its defence and hold it to the last. Evans received this order at about 10.30 a.m. and, having given orders that 2nd West Yorkshire (less the company in the forward area) and 24th Mountain Regiment (less two batteries) were to follow as soon as possible, moved with his tactical headquarters. The three brigade commanders of 7th Division had meanwhile agreed that 33rd Brigade Headquarters should become the report centre until such time as divisional headquarters resumed control or corps headquarters issued other instructions, and that all brigades should stand fast and hold their respective areas.

Shortly after noon on the 6th Slim told Christison that the Japanese could probably maintain a force of about one regiment in rear of the forward troops, but only for a short period, and that he expected them to move from Taung Bazar towards Ngakyedauk Pass in the hopes of forcing a British withdrawal. It was therefore essential that 5th and 7th Divisions should stand fast while the reserves he was sending forward destroyed all the enemy who had

---

[1] The attack was made by *III/143rd Battalion* of the *Doi Column*. The mortars and ammunition were recovered later after a counter-attack.

THE JAPANESE HA-GO OFFENSIVE

February 1944

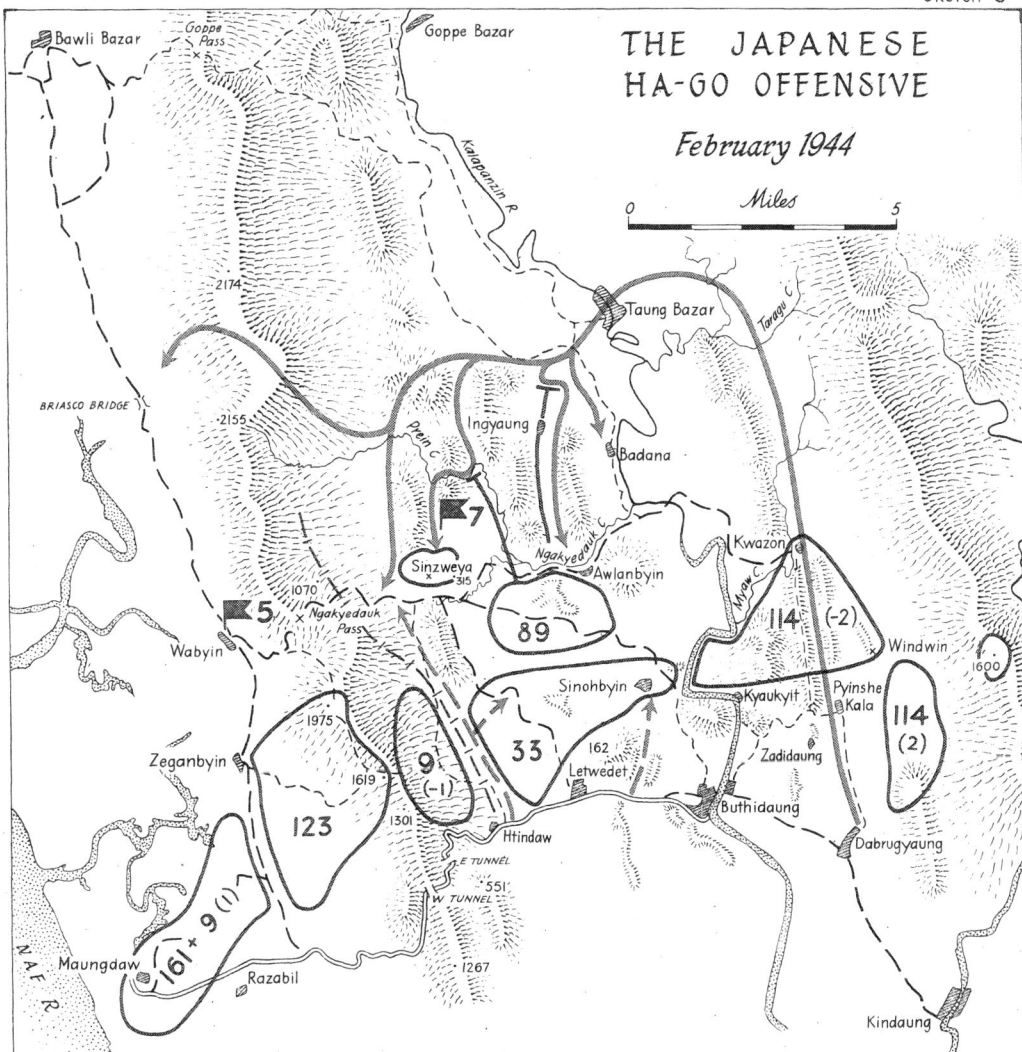

Miles

0 _____ 5

Bawli Bazar

Goppe Pass

Goppe Bazar

Kalapanzin R.

2174

Taung Bazar

Tarago C.

BRIASCO BRIDGE

2155

Prein C.

Ingyaung

Badana

7

Sinzweya
315

Ngakyedauk

Awlanbyin

Kwazon

5

1070

Ngakyedauk Pass

89

114 (-2)

Myaw C.

Windwin

1600

Wabyin

Sinohbyin

Kyaukyit

Pyinshe Kala

114 (2)

1975

9 (-1)

33

162
Letwedet

Zadidaung

Zeganbyin

1619

1301

Htindaw

Buthidaung

Dabrugyaung

123

E TUNNEL

551

W TUNNEL

161 + 9 (1)

N A F R.

Maungdaw

Razabil

1267

Kindaung

Legend

Line of advance of Sakurai Column .... ➤

Line of advance of Doi Column .... ➤

Position of 123rd Brigade 123

Position of 9th Brigade (less one Battalion) .... 9 (-1)

Position of two battalions of 114th Brigade 114 (2)

Boundary between 5th and 7th Division .... |—|—|—|

Division Headquarters .... ◀

ROADS Allweather ...... ══════

" Fairweather .... ─ ─ ─ ─

TRACKS ....

RIVERS .... ⟫⟫⟫

VILLAGES ....

HILLS ....

akk.

penetrated behind them. The first brigade (71st) of 26th Division would arrive at Bawli Bazar that day and the rest of the division would follow as soon as possible; the leading brigade of 36th Division would arrive in Chittagong by the 15th. He proposed to supply the forward divisions by air and by sea through Maungdaw. He suggested to Christison that it might be advisable to hold fast in the Kaladan Valley with one brigade of 81st (W.A.) Division, and bring the other across to the upper reaches of the Kalapanzin about Panzai Bazar to guard possible infiltration routes.

In the early afternoon Messervy suddenly appeared at Sinzweya with some of his staff. He told Evans to continue to command the garrison, and bring 6th Medium Regiment (less one battery) into it. He then set up a divisional tactical headquarters using wireless sets borrowed from 25th Dragoons. He ordered Crowther (89th Brigade) to withdraw his brigade less 4/8th Gurkhas to the Awlanbyin area to cover 7th Indian Field Regiment's gun positions and the rear of 33rd Brigade. The 4/8th Gurkha Rifles from the Prein Chaung was to move to Sinzweya and come under Evans' command. Crowther said that he was too closely engaged to break contact before darkness, but Messervy, knowing that the south-east corner of the Sinzweya defended area, where the track entered it at the southern end of the Point 315 feature, had only a detachment of a light anti-aircraft battery to hold it, had to insist that the Gurkhas moved at once.

By evening the situation did not appear to be quite so critical, since 114th Brigade had cleared the Kwazon area, 33rd Brigade had held the enemy attack and the greater part of 4/8th Gurkhas had occupied the southern half of the Point 315 feature.[1] A reserve in the shape of 71st Brigade of 26th Division had arrived at Bawli South, with the rest of the division coming up behind it.

By the morning of the 7th, 89th Brigade (less 4/8th Gurkhas) had established itself, though not without difficulty, in its new position south of the Ngakyedauk Chaung either side of Awlanbyin covering 7th Indian Field Regiment, and the defences of Sinzweya had been consolidated. The perimeter consisted of a series of small defended posts held, in the main, by administrative units, except at the south-east and south-west corners where the roads entered the area. These were held by 4/8th Gurkhas (less two companies) and a company of 2nd West Yorkshire respectively. There were insufficient troops to hold the whole of the Point 315 feature, and thus there was a deep re-entrant between the south-east and north-east corners of the perimeter extending back to the southern end of Ammunition Hill. Most of the artillery was disposed on the southern face with detachments holding perimeter posts. The 25th Dragoons was in mobile

---

[1] During the withdrawal one and a half companies of 4/8th Gurkhas lost direction and withdrew westwards over the ridge. They did not rejoin their battalion till the 12th.

reserve in two harbours held by a company of 3/4th Bombay Grenadiers, one each side of Ammunition Hill. The 2nd West York-shire (less two companies) constituted the infantry reserve and was located with divisional and garrison headquarters on the western side of Ammunition Hill. The main dressing station in the south-west corner was being moved to a more secure area.[1]

Though there was fighting in all the brigade sectors, there was no attack on Sinzweya on the 7th, but during the morning it became evident that the road over the pass was firmly blocked. The closing of the pass and the appearance of enemy parties on the Maungdaw–Bawli Bazar road made Christison call for air supply for all formations east of the range from the following morning, and place 9th Brigade under command of 7th Division. He ordered 71st Brigade, which was under orders to move over Goppe Pass to the Kalapanzin valley, to place two battalions under command of 5th Division to be used to keep open the road to Maungdaw; this meant that operations in any strength against the enemy forces behind 7th Division had to be deferred. In the afternoon, corps headquarters moved back to the north bank of the Pruma Khal at Bawli North. That evening Chris-tison told Lomax (26th Division) that when his division was concen-trated his task was to use two brigades to destroy the Japanese in the Kalapanzin valley in rear of 7th Division, leaving one brigade to maintain a firm base at Bawli South, keeping one battalion in hand as corps reserve.

During the night of the 7th/8th the Japanese launched their first attacks on Sinzweya. On the eastern side an attack was repulsed by 4/8th Gurkhas after heavy fighting, but another on the west overran the main dressing station. Most of the wounded had been removed during the previous afternoon because of enemy shelling, but a number remained. When the area was retaken thirty-six hours later only three were alive to tell the grim story of how they had been tied and beaten, kept without food and water, how those who cried for water had been shot, and finally how, when it was clear that the area could no longer be held, the enemy had opened fire on the survivors, killing all but themselves. The same night an enemy attack in the Sinohbyin area was repulsed, but the attackers dug in on a hill between the positions held by 1st Queen's and 4/15th Punjab, from which they were ejected three days later with the help of a squadron of 25th Dragoons. The unit making this attack was iden-tified as *II/144th Battalion* which Hanaya had ordered to move north to reinforce Sakurai.

By the 8th it was clear that the Japanese intention was to isolate and destroy 7th Division. The main body of the *Sakurai Column* had

---

[1] See Sketch 4, page 144.

cut the Ngakyedauk Pass road, invested Sinzweya from the west and
north, and established posts along the northern bank of the Ngakyedauk Chaung to the Kalapanzin and east of the river north of
Kwazon. The position held by 7th Division was now a rough rec-
tangle some seven miles wide and four miles deep, with 33rd Brigade
and one battalion of 9th Brigade holding the original forward posts
facing south, 114th Brigade east of the Kalapanzin guarding the left
flank and 89th Brigade (less one battalion) and the Sinzweya garrison
holding the line of the Ngakyedauk Chaung and Sinzweya facing
west and north. Each brigade and Sinzweya had its quota of artillery
and engineers. Movement between the various parts of 7th Division
remained possible, though subject at times to interference, but *55th
Division* could keep contact with and supply the *Sakurai Column* only
by infiltrating through 7th Division's position or round its left flank,
a task which became progressively more difficult in face of aggressive
patrolling. The 5th Division's forward posts along the Magyi and
Rekhat Chaungs to Point 1619 had not been attacked.

Orders had been issued that all troops east of the range were to be
supplied by air from the 8th. The 5th Division was to hold its forward
positions and clear both the Bawli–Maungdaw road and Ngakyedauk
Pass; 7th Division was to stand fast and prevent supplies reaching the
Sakurai Column, while 26th Division destroyed it by attacking from
the north.

When the Japanese opened their offensive they made a determined
effort to gain air superiority over the battlefield, using thirty-four
fighters and ten bombers. Between the 4th and 14th their fighters
flew some three hundred and fifty sorties, and bombers attacked the
Bawli and Briasco bridges and Sinzweya. Spitfires intercepted but
with less success than before. Japanese losses were believed to be
some fourteen aircraft destroyed and a number damaged, while
R.A.F. losses during the same period were eleven fighters.[1]

The presence of enemy fighters in such strength clearly made the
supply of 7th Division by air a hazardous and perhaps costly operation. Since supply dropping had to be undertaken, Hurricanes were
provided as escorts for the transport aircraft, and standing patrols
were maintained over the battle zone. But even so the first attempt
on the 8th February by aircraft of 31 Squadron R.A.F., led personally
by General Old of Troop Carrier Command, had to be abandoned
when half-completed, with the loss of one Dakota and one Hurricane,
and on the following day seven out of the sixteen transport aircraft
employed were forced to abandon their task.

---

[1] It is now known that Japanese aircraft were not equipped with self-sealing petrol
tanks. For this reason many of their damaged aircraft may have failed to return to their
bases.

To enable supplies to be dropped accurately inside the smaller posts and on the restricted dropping zone of Sinzweya, supply-dropping aircraft had to fly as low as two hundred feet and pass over enemy-held areas while approaching the dropping zone. They were thus vulnerable to light anti-aircraft and small arms fire. This and the presence of enemy fighters made it necessary for supply dropping to be carried out by night after the 9th. At Sinzweya, night dropping was not possible owing to the proximity of the Mayu Range, but special circuits were arranged to keep aircraft out of the range of enemy small arms fire. Air supply of Able had to be abandoned and the position supplied by pack mule from 33rd Brigade's dropping zone. As the days passed there was less and less interference by anti-aircraft and small arms fire; from the 14th there was a marked drop in enemy fighter activity,[1] and as a result it became possible to revert to daylight dropping.

Despite enemy interference, air supply was carried out daily from the 9th. No. 31 Squadron (dropping supplies for 7th Division) and 62 Squadron (for 81st (W.A.) Division) were reinforced on the 10th by 194 Squadron and on the 25th by 117 Squadron, recently arrived from the Middle East. Not only were 7th and 81st Divisions kept supplied with food and ammunition, but such amenities as cigarettes, rum, mail, razor blades and newspapers were delivered by air to the troops in increasing quantities as time went on. In five weeks Troop Carrier Command flew a total of 714 sorties and delivered nearly 2,300 tons of supplies.

Throughout the battle the Strategic Air Force and 224 Group gave constant close support to XV Corps. In addition to providing escorts for transport squadrons, Hurricanes so harried road, river and coastal transport on the Japanese lines of communication to Arakan that movement by day into the area virtually ceased. Tactical bombing of enemy positions was undertaken by two Vengeance squadrons which flew no less than 269 sorties in just over a week.

When the emergency in Arakan arose, the transport squadrons of Troop Carrier Command had not only to drop supplies to 81st (W.A.) Division and troops in the Chin Hills and at Fort Hertz, but at the same time carry out practice flights in preparation for the fly-in of the L.R.P. forces into northern Burma in March. If the crisis in Arakan were to continue into March these two major commitments for air supply would overlap, and so, unless additional transport aircraft could be made available, either the air supply to 7th Division would have to be abandoned or the fly-in of the L.R.P. groups postponed. But 7th Division had clearly to be supplied until

---

[1] The *7th Air Brigade* had been moved north in preparation for the Imphal offensive.

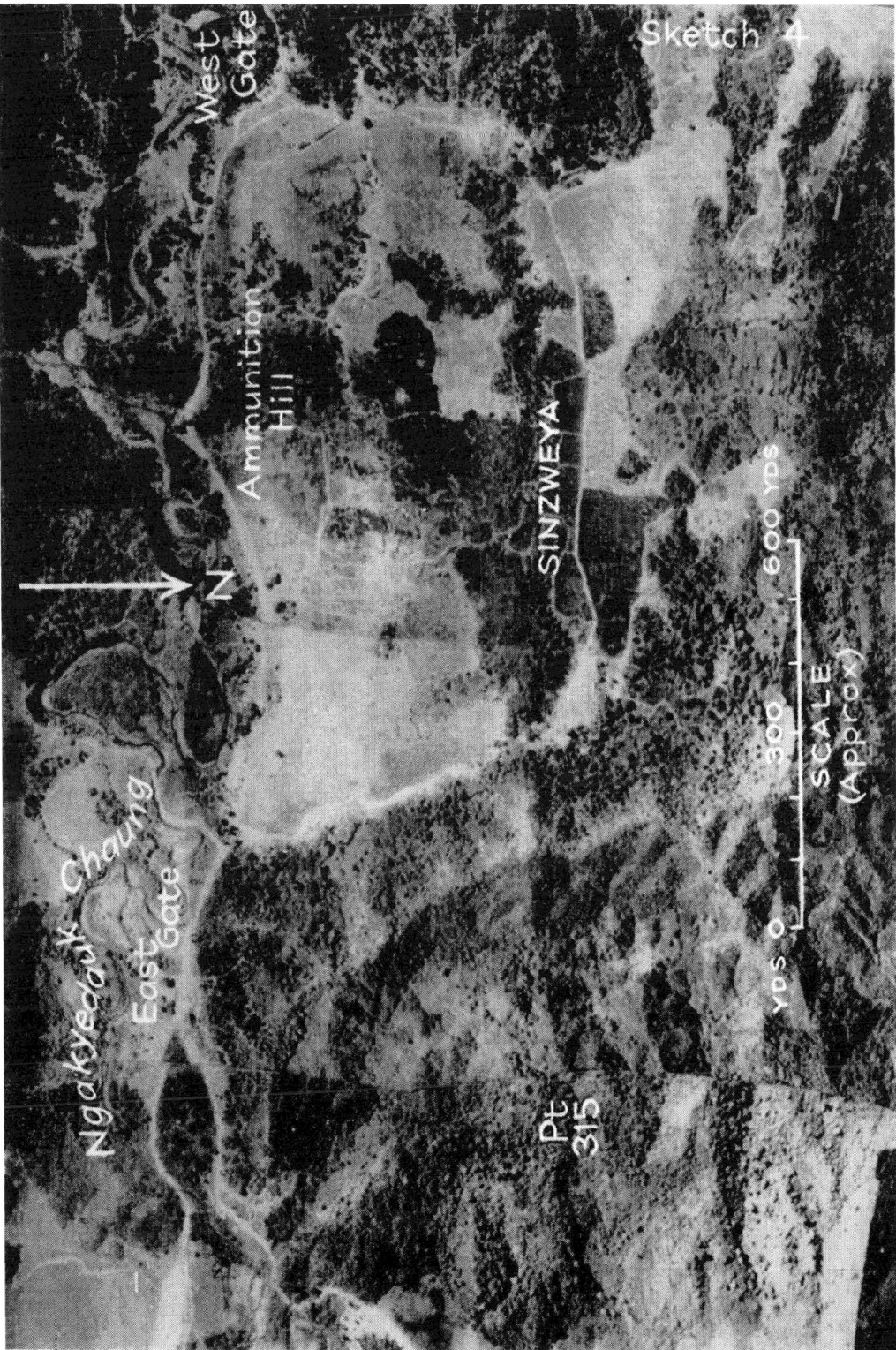

Sketch 4

West Gate

Ammunition Hill

N

SINZWEYA

Ngakyedauk Chaung

East Gate

Pt 315

YDS 0   300   600 YDS

SCALE (Approx)

the land line of communication was reopened, and therefore additional aircraft would have to be found for the fly-in of the L.R.P. groups. If both commitments overlapped, about thirty-eight extra Dakota (C.47) aircraft, or their equivalent in lifting capacity, would be needed and only Air Transport Command, which operated the airlift to China, could supply them quickly.

At the Sextant Conference in Cairo the Supreme Commander had been authorized to divert up to an average of 1,100 tons a month from the airlift over a period of six months to meet the requirements of the Burma campaign. Although the operations approved at the conference had not taken place, it had been accepted that it was within the discretion of the Supreme Commander to divert enough transport aircraft from the airlift within the authorized total lift in order to meet any unforeseen emergency arising in battle. Mountbatten considered that the situation which had developed in Arakan was such an emergency. On the 18th February he asked for the concurrence of the Combined Chiefs of Staff to the immediate diversion of up to thirty-eight Dakota aircraft from the airlift to China until such time as the emergency in Arakan ended. On the 24th the Chiefs of Staff authorized him to divert temporarily twenty-seven Commando (C.46) aircraft (the equivalent lift of some thirty-eight Dakotas) on the ground that the L.R.P. operations were essential to the security of the air route to China. The aircraft began to reach eastern Bengal the following day. As the pass had by that time been reopened, the need for them was over and they were returned between the 4th and 7th March.

To continue with the story of the battle; on the 8th Messervy reported that the Japanese were building up their strength on Ngakyedauk Pass, and Briggs reported the discovery of a roadblock near the top of the pass at the southern end of Point 1070. In the hope of quickly reopening communications between 5th and 7th Divisions, Christison gave permission for one of the battalions of 71st Brigade, which had been placed under command of 5th Division for operations on the Bawli–Maungdaw road, to be used on the pass.[1] At the same time, to create a diversion, he ordered 81st (W.A.) Division to by-pass enemy pockets of resistance in the Kaladan Valley, push boldly on to Kanzauk and threaten the Japanese right flank and rear.

On arrival at Bawli, Lomax (26th Division) told Brigadier L. C. Thomas (36th Brigade) to set up a firm base in the Bawli South area. This released the battalion which had been held in corps reserve under command of 71st Brigade and relieved that brigade of any operational responsibility west of the range, but for the time being

---

[1] The 1/18th Royal Garhwal Rifles.

left it with only one battalion (1st Lincolns) and a squadron of 81st (W.A.) Reconnaissance Regiment with which to begin exerting pressure on the enemy in the Taung Bazar area.[1]

Meanwhile in the 7th Division area Roberts, having been told to stop any further infiltration round the left flank, had withdrawn his two forward battalions and formed a strong mobile reserve in a secure base at Kwazon, ready to operate at short notice in any direction. The concentration, which involved the backloading of stores and ammunition dumped forward for the offensive, was carried out on the night of the 8th/9th with only minor interference from the enemy.

The same night the Japanese manhandled mountain guns to the top of a hill overlooking Sinzweya; at dawn they opened fire on Ammunition Hill at point-blank range and set the ammunition alight. A counter-attack by the infantry reserve supported by tanks drove them off, but it was late in the day before the fires and explosions were brought under control. A marked map found on the body of a dead officer gave details of the Japanese plan for several days ahead, and among other things showed that they were already far behind schedule. Further south the situation on Able, which was already precarious because of the difficulty of getting supplies to it, began to cause anxiety when the Japanese in the East Tunnel area opened fire at point-blank range with a medium howitzer, which neither counter battery fire nor air bombing could silence.[2] To the west, 5th Division's first effort to break the Japanese roadblock on the pass made no headway.

The ambitious Japanese plans disclosed by the captured map and the number and persistence of the enemy attacks made it clear to Giffard that there was no possibility of XV Corps being able to reach the Indin–Rathedaung line before the pre-monsoon swell made amphibious operations impossible. As the capture of that objective was a prerequisite of 'Bulldozer' (the assault on Akyab), he recommended to the Supreme Commander that planning for it should be abandoned. On the 10th he placed 36th Division, previously earmarked for 'Bulldozer', at the disposal of 14th Army, allotted 50th (P.) Brigade to IV Corps and ordered 25th Indian Division to Chittagong.[3]

Though Slim was in full agreement with the cancellation of 'Bulldozer', he realized that the Japanese plans had miscarried and that there was every advantage to be gained from continuing the land

---

[1] The diversion of two battalions of 71st Brigade to 5th Division (see page 142), one of which (1/18th Royal Garhwal Rifles) did not return to 26th Division throughout the battle, began a changeover of units between brigades of 26th Division which produced a situation in which it was unusual to find any battalion of the division serving with its own brigade.

[2] It was later found that the howitzer had been stabled in the Tunnels and moved out only to fire; hence its immunity.

[3] It had been intended to send 25th Division to reinforce IV Corps.

advance. On the 11th, he directed Christison to resume the offensive against the Tunnels–Buthidaung position as soon as he had cleared the land communications to his forward divisions. The following day Christison ordered 29th Brigade (the leading brigade of 36th Division) on arrival to take over the Bawli area from 36th Brigade of 26th Division. The 36th Brigade was then to become XV Corps reserve and clear the enemy from the area east of the Maungdaw road as far south as Maunghnama. The 26th Division (less 36th Brigade) was to destroy the enemy behind 7th Division in the Kalapanzin valley. Meanwhile 5th Division was to regroup in order to have a complete brigade available to clear the pass.

On the 13th, satisfied with the way the battle was developing, Slim told Giffard that he had every confidence in its outcome, but added that he thought the Japanese might be intending to follow the Arakan offensive by another on IV Corps front, as soon as they could switch their air force. Slim's confidence was well founded. Air supply was now firmly established; patrols of 26th and 7th Divisions had met near Taung Bazar; a second brigade of 26th Division was moving into the Kalapanzin; regrouping of 5th Division, to provide a complete brigade to attack Ngakyedauk Pass from the west, was nearly complete; 36th Division had begun to arrive at Bawli; and the enemy had failed to drive 7th Division from any of its defended positions.

Meanwhile on the 11th the Japanese had ordered *II/* and *III/143rd Battalions* to move north to the Sinzweya area.[1] The former was divided into three columns which were sent respectively to reinforce Ngakyedauk Pass, the detachment of *I/213th Battalion* operating in the hills south-east of Bawli Bazar and Sakurai's headquarters, while the latter moved to Point 315 and the area east of the Sinzweya perimeter.

On the 13th, 1st Lincolns, approaching Point 315 from the north, found the enemy in far greater strength than it had been led to expect. At the same time the pressure on Sinzweya increased and the small infantry reserve of 2nd West Yorkshire (less two companies), supported by elements of two squadrons of 25th Dragoons, was repeatedly called on to eject enemy parties which had succeeded in digging in between perimeter posts of the defences. The enemy offensive reached its climax on the 14th when a broadcast in clear called for an all-out attack at 7 p.m. that evening. As far as Sinzweya was concerned, the attack when it came was no better co-ordinated than the earlier ones. It included a courageous, but suicidal and unsuccessful, attempt by a Japanese tank destruction party to rush the tank harbour east of Ammunition Hill across the open from the direction of Point 315. Elsewhere attacks met with

---

[1] See pages 139 and 140 fns.

more success: Point 1070 fell into Japanese hands and part of the already constricted position on Able was lost.

Continuous infantry attacks by night and the constant harassing by day by mortars, artillery and aircraft were beginning to tell on the garrison of Sinzweya. In order to provide reliefs, Messervy decided, if it were possible, to bring the rest of 89th Brigade into Sinzweya. The 7/2nd Punjab, less one company left at Awlanbyin, was brought in on the 12th, and 114th Brigade was instructed to provide a force strong enough to take over the defence of 7th Indian Field Regiment's positions from 2nd K.O.S.B., if this could be done without seriously decreasing the brigade mobile reserve. On the night of the 15th/16th, Headquarters 89th Brigade and 2nd K.O.S.B. moved into Sinzweya, and Crowther took over responsibility for the eastern half of the perimeter.

Meanwhile the equivalent of two brigades of 26th Division had concentrated in the Kalapanzin valley. The 71st Brigade (Cotterell-Hill) was given responsibility for the Taung Bazar sector, and 4th Brigade (Brigadier A. W. Lowther) began to assemble three battalions north of Point 315, where the failure by 1st Lincolns to make progress had already shown that the position was strongly defended. On the 16th an attack by the Lincolns on the Point 315 area failed.[1] Tanks from Sinzweya, although unable to assist in the attack owing to the dense jungle and steep slopes, brought in the battalion's casualties, and physical contact was established between the garrison of Sinzweya and 4th Brigade. The same day an airstrip for light aircraft at Kwazon was brought into use, and during the following week some two hundred seriously wounded were flown out by light aircraft of No. 1 Air Commando.[2]

During the night of the 16th/17th patrols of 114th Brigade found that Kyaukyit had been abandoned by the enemy. On the 17th the Pyinshe Kala redoubt was occupied without opposition, and patrols reached the Rathedaung road and mortared Buthidaung from the east bank of the river. The extensive redoubt at Kyaukyit was not occupied since it would have tied up too many troops in a static rôle, but as much destruction as possible was carried out with the explosives available. The evacuation by the Japanese of positions on 114th Brigade's front, and the subsequent discovery that the strong position covering Punkori on 33rd Brigade's front had been abandoned, led to the belief that they might be contemplating a general retirement. On the 18th, Briggs ordered 5th Division to increase pressure on Ngakyedauk Pass, patrol deeply south and east and, should the enemy show any sign of evacuating them, seize Razabil and the

---

[1] Major C. F. Hoey, M.C., The Lincolnshire Regiment, gained a posthumous V.C. during this attack.
[2] The airstrip was built by 114th Brigade.

Tunnels. The following day Christison extended the scope of this to a corps operation in which 26th and 7th Divisions were to make an all-out effort to seize Point 315, and 33rd and 114th Brigades were to patrol southward to take advantage of any withdrawal.

By the time the corps order was issued, however, the idea of a general withdrawal from their main position had been discounted by the discovery that Japanese parties had dug in behind 33rd Brigade in the Point 129 area,[1] and on the ridge north of Kwazon behind 114th Brigade. The fact that the Japanese were trying to occupy areas covering the routes back to their main positions was taken as an indication that an early attempt was about to be made to extricate the *Sakurai Column*, which was known to be suffering from hunger and lack of ammunition.[2] On the 21st resistance on Point 1070 collapsed, though the enemy still clung to the now overlooked block on the Ngakyedauk Pass road. The same day a deliberate attack by 4th Brigade on Point 315 failed. The following day a fanatical attack by a comparatively small number of Japanese nearly reached 7th Divisional Headquarters in Sinzweya. It was clear from these desperate measures that the enemy commanders were facing a crisis.

Christison was now satisfied that he was within sight of achieving his first task—to clear the land communications to his forward divisions. On the 22nd he issued orders for the second task—the resumption of the offensive against the Tunnels–Buthidaung position. His plan was to resume the offensive as planned before it had been interrupted by the Japanese counter-stroke on the 4th February: it was to begin with the capture of Buthidaung by 7th Division as soon as possible after the road over Ngakyedauk Pass was open and end with a concentric attack by 5th and 26th Divisions to capture the Tunnels. To free 7th and 5th Divisions for the opening stages, 26th Division was to relieve 7th Division of the responsibility for Sinzweya and the eastern foothills of the Mayu Range, and a brigade of 36th Division was to take over the defence of the crest of the range from Point 1619 to the pass. As soon as 7th Division had taken Buthidaung, 26th Division was to take over the area west of the Kalapanzin River and prepare for the attack on the Tunnels.

On the 23rd, after a short but sharp action, a battalion of 89th Brigade from the east and 123rd Brigade from the west made contact on Ngakyedauk Pass and by evening had firmly secured it. The following day, as soon as the 500 casualties from Sinzweya had been evacuated, the pass was opened to normal traffic and air supply of 7th Division ceased.

---

[1] This was *II/144th Battalion*.

[2] Japanese records show that the shortage of supplies became a serious problem from about the 15th February.

It was on the 24th that, at the suggestion of Sakurai and with the approval of *28th Army*, Hanaya ordered the 'Ha-Go' offensive to be abandoned. Owing to the failure of his efforts to penetrate the Sinzweya defences, the loss of Point 1070 and the lack of food and ammunition, Colonel Tanahashi had already decided on the 22nd that he had no alternative but to make his way back to the main position. Accordingly, and without Sakurai's prior sanction, he ordered *112th Regiment* to withdraw southwards along the eastern foothills of the Mayu Range during the night of the 23rd/24th. The following night Sakurai ordered a general withdrawal, except for a rearguard which he left to hold the Point 315 feature until the units operating in the Briasco Bridge area had got back. But, on the night of the 25th/26th, as 4th Brigade closed in on it, the rearguard abandoned the feature under cover of a counter-attack. The occupation of Point 315 on the 26th completed the clearance of XV Corps' communications to its forward divisions, and the following day the forward flow of ammunition and supplies for the resumption of the offensive began.

The Battle of Ngakyedauk Pass cost XV Corps 3,506 casualties, of which more than half were in 7th Division and the corps troops under its command.[1] The battle, which took place on a not very important part of the Burma front, was of far greater importance than might at first appear. It marked the turning point in the war in South-East Asia. It was the first time that the Japanese met well trained British/Indian formations in battle and the first time that their enveloping tactics, aimed at cutting their opponents' line of communications, failed to produce the results they expected.

The ultimate object of the 'Ha-Go' offensive was to attract to and hold in Arakan 14th Army's reserves while *15th Army* overran the Imphal plain. The success or failure of the Japanese to achieve this object will be discussed later in the volume.[2] Here we are concerned only with the conduct and the outcome of the battle itself.

On the one hand Hanaya (*55th Division*) had come to the conclusion that to achieve his ultimate object he would have to forestall the imminent British offensive and, despite his inferior numbers, attack in such a way that XV Corps would be thrown into confusion. He therefore decided to make his immediate objective the isolation and destruction of 7th Indian Division in the area between the Mayu Range and the Kalapanzin River. He planned to use the same tactics which had proved so efficacious in the 1942–43 Arakan campaign and expected that, provided he isolated 7th Division by cutting its communications, he would not only succeed but could then attempt the destruction of 5th Division.

[1] See Appendix 29.
[2] See Chapter XXXII.

On the other hand Slim realized that, if the self-confidence of his troops were to be restored, an end would have to be put once and for all to the unbroken chain of success achieved by the enemy's infiltrating and enveloping tactics. He could not therefore risk even a minor defeat in the opening stages of the 1944 campaign. Expecting the enemy to take the offensive, he had already explained his policy of dealing with deep infiltration and, in order to make certain that it could be carried out, had impressed on all his commanders that, unless ordered to the contrary, any unit or formation whose communications were cut was to stand fast and attempt to cut those of its attackers. He would see that isolated formations were supplied by air and that reserves were brought up to destroy the enemy in their rear.

The Japanese attack of the 4th February was well planned and boldly and resolutely carried out. Partly owing to the failure of XV Corps to give sufficient heed to the information supplied by the forward troops in the third week of January, it achieved almost complete surprise and within twenty-four hours the *Sakurai Column*, some 5,000 men strong, was deployed in rear of 7th Division. Slim immediately put his policy into operation. But to bring forward and deploy reserve formations takes time, and in this battle the time was lengthened by the action of the small detachment of less than half a battalion sent by Sakurai to raid the Bawli–Maungdaw road. This detachment, by attracting to itself the first reserves to come forward, delayed for some days not only the concentration of an effective striking force in the upper Kalapanzin valley, but also the regrouping of 5th Division to enable it to launch an attack to reopen Ngakyedauk Pass from the west. It was not till the 16th February, twelve days after the battle began, that any serious pressure was brought to bear on the rear of *Sakurai Column* in the Kalapanzin valley and on the Ngakyedauk Pass road. As soon as it was applied the end was in sight, and ten days later Sakurai, short of food and ammunition owing to the precarious nature of his communications, was forced to withdraw the remnants of his exhausted column.

With 5th Division engaged in holding its positions west of the Mayu Range and regrouping to free a brigade to attack Ngakyedauk Pass from the west, and with 114th Brigade of 7th Division east of the Kalapanzin River ordered to guard the left flank against further attempts at infiltration, the early part of the battle was a straight fight between the *Sakurai* and *Doi Columns* and the two brigades of 7th Division in the area between the Mayu Range and the Kalapanzin River. The division, quickly recovering from the effects of surprise and the overrunning of its headquarters, reacted strongly. The course of the battle thereafter depended on its ability to hold its positions and at the same time cut the Japanese supply lines to the *Sakurai*

Column. Sinzweya became the focal point of the enemy attack. Its garrison, consisting largely of administrative troops, fought magnificently and, helped by the poor co-ordination of the Japanese attacks, repelled all attempts to break into its defences. Other small garrisons, such as the one on Able, fought with equal tenacity. Had 7th Division been overwhelmed the morale of 14th Army would have suffered a very serious setback, 5th Division would have become heavily involved and it would have been impossible to transfer major formations from Arakan to the Central front.

The outcome of the Battle of Ngakyedauk Pass was psychologically of immense value. It showed that there was an answer to the Japanese infiltrating and enveloping tactics which had hitherto been so invariably successful, and created in the troops confidence in their leaders and in their own ability to defeat the enemy in the jungle. It also raised, both in Britain and in India, civilian confidence in the ability of the Army in India to defeat the Japanese in the South-East Asian theatre of war.

We must now turn to events in the Kaladan Valley.[1] Realizing that the advance of the African division constituted a serious danger to his communications, Hanaya had between the 18th and the 21st formed a composite battalion and sent it to Myohaung.[2] On the 21st Sakurai (*28th Army*) relieved Hanaya of responsibility for the Kaladan, and formed the *Koba Force* under the command of *28th Army* for the defence of the valley.[3]

Meanwhile 81st (W.A.) Division had established a Dakota airstrip at Medaung on the 21st February, and occupied Kyauktaw on the 25th. The 7/16th Punjab had advanced to Paletwa and established forward posts near Kaladan. On the 26th Christison told Woolner that he was about to take the offensive on the main corps front; he expected the Japanese to delay his progress by rearguards and try to transfer their main effort to the Kaladan front where the advance of the West Africans constituted a serious threat to their communications. With the onset of the pre-monsoon swell, the Japanese, he considered, would be able to denude the Akyab defences and from the middle of March would probably be able to make a maximum of five battalions available for the Kaladan Valley. He expected that they would hold the Kanzauk–Apaukwa area and strike east of the

---

[1] See Map 7, page 278.
[2] This composite battalion consisted of headquarters and one company of *II/143rd Battalion*, from the Point 315 area, a company from *III/144th Battalion* and some officers from divisional headquarters.
[3] This force was to consist of *111th Regimental Headquarters, III/111th Battalion*, then en route to Myohaung from the south, the composite *II/143rd Battalion* from *55th Division*, *55th Reconnaissance Regiment*, and a composite unit (1,000 strong), under command of a Captain Honjo, formed out of reinforcements for *144th Regiment* which were at Myohaung.

river to recapture Kyauktaw. He instructed Woolner to protect the left flank of the corps, destroy as many of the enemy as possible, prevent them from gaining control of the Kaladan Valley north of Kanzauk and in any circumstances from establishing themselves at Kyauktaw. Subject to these general instructions, Woolner was to direct his main effort towards the Mayu River to cut the enemy line of communications between Akyab and Buthidaung. The 7/16th Punjab was to continue to patrol the Paletwa–Sami–Kaladan area.

Koba arrived at Myohaung about the same time that Woolner received his orders from Christison, so that the two opposing commanders were making their plans simultaneously. Koba decided that he would move up the eastern bank of the Kaladan and strike at Kyauktaw and attempt to surround and destroy the African division. He ordered the *Honjo Composite Unit* and *55th Reconnaissance Regiment* to oppose the advance of 81st Division south of Kyauktaw while he, with his main body (*III/111th* and *II/143rd Battalions*), moved on Thayettabin, seized Pagoda Hill, cut Woolner's communications from the north and attacked him from the rear.

Woolner calculated that *55th Reconnaissance Regiment* would not be a serious adversary after its long retreat and that the Japanese could not muster more than two battalions in the Kaladan till mid-March. Although fully aware of the need to hold the dominating Pagoda Hill overlooking the Kyauktaw plain, airstrip and ferry, he considered that a bold advance with both brigades, their left covered by 11th (E.A.) Scout Battalion, would ensure its safety and at the same time enable him to achieve his main task. In the event of a threat developing in the Pagoda Hill area, he felt he would have ample time to occupy the hill. On the 29th, therefore, he ordered an advance on Apaukwa and Kanzauk on a two-brigade front with Htizwe as the final objective, while the Scout battalion operated towards Myohaung east of the river.[1]

The main advance began well, and by the 2nd March the leading battalion of 6th Brigade had gained a footing in Apaukwa. Early that morning the Scouts reported that they had been pushed back to Thayettabin, which meant that the Japanese could get between them and Pagoda Hill. Woolner immediately ordered the rear battalion of 6th Brigade (1st Gambia) to send a company across the river to help the Scouts and secure the hill, and placed the rest of the battalion at one hour's notice to follow. Shortly afterwards he asked XV Corps for permission to use 7/16th Punjab in a counter-attack rôle and for a battalion to be flown to Pagoda Hill. A company of 1st Gambia crossed at 7.30 a.m. and, when about midday all communication with the Scouts ceased, the rest of the battalion followed.

About 6 p.m. that evening XV Corps told Woolner that no further

[1] For Htizwe see Map 2, page 5.

troops could be sent, but, of the tasks given him, the holding of Kyauktaw was the essential one. That evening Woolner ordered the rest of 6th Brigade to cross the river to restore the situation and hold Pagoda Hill at all costs, and 5th Brigade to maintain its pressure on the enemy until midnight and then withdraw to an area some four miles south-west of Kyauktaw.

During the night of the 2nd/3rd the Japanese infiltrated between the widely dispersed posts on Pagoda Hill and at dawn drove 1st Gambia off it in some disorder. When Woolner heard of the loss of the hill at about 11 a.m. on the 3rd he realized that 6th Brigade, now divided by the river and with 1st Gambia temporarily out of action,[1] would be unable to recapture it. He therefore ordered the brigade to withdraw all troops from the east bank and take up a position west of Kyauktaw to cover the withdrawal of 5th Brigade, which was to move north and establish a bridgehead on the Pi Chaung, near its junction with the Kaladan River. The 5th Brigade completed its withdrawal by midnight on the 4th and established its bridgehead early on the 5th. The Japanese had, however, already crossed into the area between the Kaladan River and the Pi Chaung and on the 6th attacked the bridgehead from the north. The fact that the enemy was behind them, coupled with the lack of cover to which they were accustomed, caused some unsteadiness among the African troops. Knowing that they would not recover their morale until they got back into the jungle, Woolner abandoned any idea of a counter-stroke from the north to retake Kyauktaw and on the 8th ordered the whole division to withdraw up the west bank of the Pi Chaung to Wabyan. By the 10th this had been carried out. The initiative had been lost and a withdrawal had begun which was not to end until the whole Kaladan Valley had been evacuated. ·

Colonel Koba, with his headquarters and *II/143rd Battalion*, had meanwhile moved up the east bank of the Kaladan and on the 9th had occupied Kaladan village, thus isolating the advanced company of 7/16th Punjab which was at Ngamyinthaung, while *III/111th Battalion* moved up the west bank to the vicinity of Kaladan. To cut off the retreating West Africans the latter battalion then moved across to the Pi Chaung, where it was ambushed and severely handled near Wabyan on the 11th. When the news of the ambush reached Koba, he withdrew the battalion to Kaladan and sent it by river to Kyauktaw, with orders to reinforce *55th Reconnaissance Regiment* which was following the Africans up the Pi Chaung.

On the 16th, 81st (W.A.) Division crossed the Pi Chaung and occupied a strong defensive position in the Kyingri loop with the broad tidal chaung on three sides. Within the loop an airstrip capable

---

[1] The 1st Sierra Leone had crossed during the night and 4th Nigeria was still west of the river.

of taking light aircraft, and later Dakotas, was constructed, casualties
were evacuated and supplies brought in. Meanwhile 7/16th Punjab
(Lieut.-Colonel J. A. Hubert) at Paletwa was unable to make contact
with its own forward company near Ngamyinthaung. Physical contact with 81st (W.A.) Division had been lost as a result of the change
of direction of its retreat, and having no rear-link wireless Hubert
could not discover what had happened to it after its withdrawal from
Kyauktaw, of which he had heard from stragglers. Believing his
forward company had been overrun and that the division had
suffered a disaster, he withdrew to Satpaung where there was a static
wireless post. He reported the situation to corps headquarters, who
told him he was to operate under their direct command and fall back
to Labawa. There the missing company rejoined, having fought its
way out of encirclement. On the 16th a rear-link wireless section
arrived from corps headquarters bringing with it orders that Hubert
was to return down the Kaladan, contact 81st Division and then
come under Woolner's command.

Christison refused to allow the reverses in the Kaladan Valley to
interfere with his offensive on the main front.[1] The initiative was
firmly in his hands, and by the 5th March his corps was deployed
ready to exploit the collapse of the Japanese offensive. The 7th Indian
Division (Messervy), with two brigades (33rd and 89th) on the west
and one brigade (114th) on the east bank of Kalapanzin, was in
position for its assault on Buthidaung; 5th Indian Division (Briggs)
was moving into position for its enveloping attack on Razabil; 26th
Indian Division (Lomax) had taken over the eastern slopes of the
Mayu Range with one brigade, and had two in reserve in the
Awlanbyin area ready to take over the Buthidaung area from 7th
Division as soon as it had been secured; and 36th Indian Division
(Festing) was disposed with 29th Brigade in depth along the crest of
the Mayu Range from Point 1619 northwards to Ngakyedauk Pass
and 72nd Brigade in reserve in the Bawli–Goppe area. On the 6th
March the B.G.S. 14th Army (Brigadier S. F. Irwin) visited XV
Corps headquarters and arranged that, from the 13th March, 25th
Division would begin to relieve 5th Division, which would then move
to the IV Corps area.

Messervy's plan was to use 33rd and 89th Brigades to break through
to Buthidaung, isolate the Letwedet bastion and then mop up the
garrison. The 114th Brigade, east of the Kalapanzin, was meanwhile
to press forward to prevent any Japanese forces east of the river from
intervening in the fighting around Buthidaung and Letwedet. In
order to form a corridor for the break-through to Buthidaung the

---

[1] See Map 6, page 113.

four features dominating the road on its southern side, from opposite Able eastwards to the col one mile west of Buthidaung, had first to be captured.[1] The 33rd Brigade (Loftus-Tottenham) with an extra battalion under command (to take the place of the battalion holding Able, which was the base for the attack) was given this task. Each of these features was to be attacked separately during the night of the 6th/7th March, and each attack was to be preceded by an intense bombardment of ten to twenty minutes by all the corps artillery which could be brought to bear—two medium and three field regiments and the howitzer batteries of a jungle field regiment, a total of about a hundred guns.

On the night of the 5th/6th, patrols found that all the objectives were occupied and the garrisons alert. At dusk on the evening of the 6th the assault troops (1/11th Sikhs and 4/15th Punjab) moved forward and, in bright moonlight, formed up north of the road in the open paddy fields just east of Able. At 10.15 p.m. the artillery bombardment opened on the two features called Rabbit and Poland and, as it lifted, the Sikhs moved forward. Success was complete and quick: a headquarters was overrun and two anti-tank guns captured. At 11 p.m. the artillery opened on Point 142 which was quickly overrun by 4/15th Punjab. At dawn the Punjabis seized the end of the ridge overlooking the main road east of Point 142, and 1st Queen's captured the feature to the south of the road immediately facing Able, meeting with practically no opposition. The total casualties in the night's fighting amounted to only sixty. That this figure was so low can be accounted for by the intensity of the artillery fire on the areas to be attacked, none of which was more than five hundred yards square; in four bombardments, aggregating some seventy-five minutes, 14,500 shells were fired.

By the evening of the 7th the captured positions had been consolidated and the brigade was firmly established on the south side of the road from Able to within a mile of Buthidaung. In view of the quick success of the first phase of the operation and the small losses incurred, Messervy decided to use 1/11th Sikh supported by tanks to speed up the break-through to Buthidaung instead of bringing up a battalion of 89th Brigade. The inevitable Japanese counter-attack, which began on the night of the 7th/8th, was beaten off after severe fighting. On the 9th raids were made on Dongyaung and Htinshabyin, and at 10 a.m. the assault on the col astride the road two miles west of Buthidaung was launched.[2] As they advanced the Sikhs came under heavy artillery and mortar fire, but counter-battery fire and a smoke screen became effective as the tanks moved forward to join the

---

[1] See Sketch 5, page 157.
[2] During the Japanese counter-attack, Naik Nand Singh of 1/11th Sikhs won the Victoria Cross.

infantry. At 10.30 a.m. the corps artillery brought down a concentration on the five-hundred-yards-wide objective on the col, while the tanks and the infantry moved in to the attack through the dense pall of dust and smoke caused by the bombardment and burning scrub. On reaching the col the tanks were held up by a minefield and an anti-tank ditch, but the infantry swept on to their objective to find that it had been abandoned and the Japanese were streaming away to the south and south-west. By nightfall fighting patrols had entered Buthidaung and were operating to the south of it. A battalion from 89th Brigade was then brought up and, by the evening of the 12th March, Buthidaung had been consolidated. Meanwhile east of the Kalapanzin the efforts of 114th Brigade to infiltrate forward had led to a series of actions, in one of which as many as one hundred casualties were incurred.

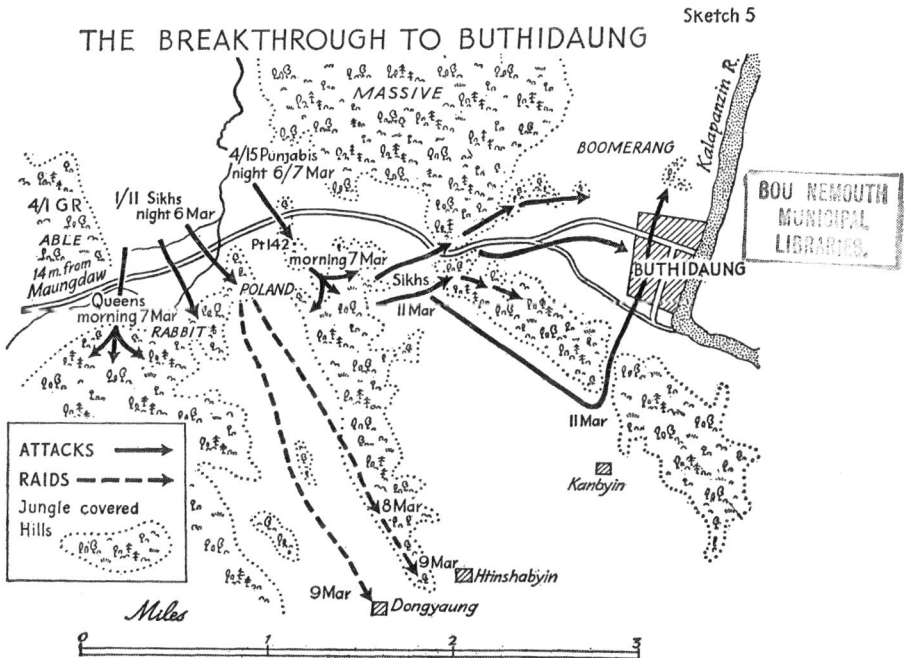

Sketch 5

THE BREAKTHROUGH TO BUTHIDAUNG

The capture of Buthidaung was the signal for 26th Division to relieve the two brigades of 7th Division west of the Kalapanzin, one of which was to continue the mopping up of the Letwedet bastion by steady pressure from the north, west and south. Accordingly 36th Brigade took over from Able to Buthidaung and, as 4th Brigade had already taken over the foothills on the eastern side of the range, 26th Division assumed operational control from the crest of the Mayu Range (where it linked with 29th Brigade near Point 1619) to the Kalapanzin at Buthidaung.

On the 9th, 5th Division had begun its attacks against Razabil and the Tunnels. Briggs' plan was that 81st (W.A.) Reconnaissance Regiment and 44 Royal Marine Commando should carry out raids in the Alethangyaw area south of Maungdaw to keep the enemy troops on the coastal plain pinned down. At the same time 161st Brigade, moving south past Maungdaw and then east into the hills, was to place itself south and east of Razabil, while 9th and 123rd Brigades closed in from the west and north respectively.[1] The attack from the north, to be carried out by 123rd Brigade, was to be supported by tanks, air and artillery to create the impression that a frontal attack on Razabil of the kind made in January was about to be repeated.

The move of 161st Brigade behind the enemy surprisingly met with no opposition and by the night of the 10th/11th it had reached its allotted position facing north, with its right resting on the Tunnels road about one and a half miles east and its left on the Alethangyaw road about a mile south of Razabil; a battalion of 9th Brigade had also moved forward to form a screen to protect its rear from enemy units known to be at Dilpara. That night a raid by 81st (W.A.) Reconnaissance Regiment was made immediately to the north of Alethangyaw, and on the following night 44 Royal Marine Commando landed at Alethangyaw and occupied the village. On the morning of the 12th, after a heavy artillery and air bombardment, 123rd Brigade succeeded in overrunning the main Razabil position from the north. The brigade then turned back to mop up the Rekhat Chaung, whilst 161st Brigade turned east and on the 13th advanced on the West Tunnel astride the Buthidaung road, in conjunction with 29th Brigade moving south along the crest of the range. Both brigades were held up by determined resistance at Points 1079, 731 and 1301. Deliberate attacks cleared the first two of these centres of resistance on the 15th, but Point 1301 held out against two more attacks. On the night of the 18th/19th, however, patrols found that the enemy had abandoned it.

As 29th and 161st Brigades converged on the West Tunnel, 123rd Brigade's front dwindled to nothing and, on the 14th March, it began its move back to railhead at Dohazari en route for the Central front. Two days later 51st Brigade of 25th Division began to arrive and took over from 9th Brigade, which left for Dohazari between the 19th and 21st. Command west of the Mayu Range passed from 5th to 36th Division on the 21st. East of the range, command had passed from 7th to 26th Division on the previous day; 7th Division, however, still retained operational control of the area east of the Kalapanzin. There 114th Brigade was preparing to drive the Japanese from Kyaukyit to cover the evacuation of the forward positions east of the Kalapanzin.

---

[1] On the 25th February Brigadier Evans replaced Brigadier Winterton in command of 123rd Brigade and Brigadier J. A. Salomons took over command of 9th Brigade.

The 89th Brigade was digging new positions at Taung Bazar for occupation during the coming monsoon in place of positions further south which would have to be evacuated. The last (161st) brigade of 5th Division began to leave Arakan on the 22nd on relief by 72nd Brigade of 36th Division.

This date marked the beginning of a new phase of operations in Arakan, where the aim was now to establish the positions to be held during the 1944 monsoon.

CHAPTER XI

THE AXIOM MISSION
(February – March 1944)

See Maps 13 and 15

WHILE the long-term strategy for S.E.A.C. was being reviewed in Delhi during January 1944, General Sultan (Deputy Commander C.B.I. Theatre) had kept the American Chiefs of Staff and General Stilwell (at that time directing operations on the Northern front from Ledo) informed of the trend of the discussions. It will be recalled that when Stilwell went to Delhi at the end of the month he found himself in complete disagreement with Mountbatten, who wished to contain the enemy in Burma while a sea route was opened to a port on the China coast by way of Sumatra. Stilwell thought that the correct strategy was to gain direct access to China through north Burma.[1] Although he was told that the Axiom Mission would represent his point of view in London and Washington, he sent his own mission to Washington without informing the Supreme Commander that he had done so.

On the 14th February, the Axiom Mission met the Prime Minister and the Chiefs of Staff in London and gave them a letter from Mountbatten explaining why he thought a change in long-term strategy was needed, together with a memorandum from Stilwell stating his reasons for disagreeing. The Prime Minister told the meeting that, although he was strongly in favour of the operations outlined, he had not only to find the best employment for the large land and air forces in India but to consider, in view of the heavy commitments in Europe, how the additional resources needed could be provided. The Chief of the Imperial General Staff thought that the 'Culverin' strategy should be tested by one question—would it help to shorten the war against Japan?

When the American Chiefs of Staff heard from Sultan of Mountbatten's proposal to attack Sumatra in the autumn of 1944, their immediate reaction was one of alarm. On the 14th, they told the British Joint Staff Mission in Washington that withholding forces from operations in Burma for 'Culverin' (for which resources were not yet in sight) was not, in their opinion, justified. It was essential to be able to use China as a base to support to the greatest extent

---

[1] See pages 69–70.

possible the advance on Japan from the Pacific. In order to prepare
such a base in time to support the forthcoming American advance on
the Formosa–China coast–Luzon area, as large scale operations as
possible should be carried out in north Burma. The capture of
Myitkyina that dry season was a minimum objective, and Stilwell,
they said, was confident that the Chinese-American forces from Ledo
could capture it and hold it during the monsoon, provided that IV
Corps crossed the Chindwin and seized and held the Shwebo–
Monywa area.[1] They feared that further delay in providing Mountbatten with his new directive would mean that little would be
accomplished in Burma before the monsoon in May and therefore
recommended that he should be directed 'to commence operations
without delay to seize and hold Myitkyina and Shwebo–Monywa
area, using all means at his disposal.'

The Chiefs of Staff could not agree to this suggested directive until
they had fully examined Mountbatten's proposals. Asked for his
comments on it, Mountbatten said that, in accordance with his existing directive, he was already carrying out the greatest offensive in
Assam and Arakan which the lines of communication could at that
time support. He was not withholding any forces for possible use in
'Culverin', although by maintaining the maximum offensive in
Burma he was probably prejudicing its being mounted in November;
moreover a stage had been reached in Arakan which made it doubtful whether two divisions could be relieved in time to take part in
'Culverin'. There were now eight Japanese divisions in Burma and
he did not consider it possible for IV Corps to seize the Shwebo–
Monywa area before the 1944 monsoon and, even if it did, administrative factors would make it impossible to hold the area during the
monsoon. Furthermore, he did not think that Stilwell's forces could
reach Myitkyina in time to enable the Ledo Road to be completed
across the Hukawng Valley before the monsoon, and without the
road Myitkyina could not be held. The problem was solely one of
lines of communication and could not be solved by adding to the
fighting troops or ignoring paramount logistic factors. He was already very short of transport aircraft and had been forced to borrow
from the ferry route; if further operations were to be undertaken in
Burma, still more aircraft would have to be provided. The views of
the American Chiefs of Staff must, he thought, be based on logisti-
cally unsound arguments, put forward by Stilwell who knew he dis-
agreed with them.[2] 'While I regret', he wrote, 'that General Stilwell
should have made representations in Washington without reference

---

[1] This was inspired by a report from Stilwell announcing his success in the Tanai River
area and asking when IV Corps would move forward to the attack.
[2] The American Joint Chiefs of Staff had in fact prepared their paper before the arrival
of Stilwell's mission.

to me and before General Wedemeyer had had an opportunity of presenting my proposals, I have complete confidence in General Wedemeyer and do not wish to change or add to his instructions in any way.'

By the 23rd February, the Chiefs of Staff had reached their conclusions on the 'Culverin' strategy. To enable it to be carried out at the end of 1944, the Americans would have to be asked to make good considerable deficiencies in resources. The cost to the Pacific operations would be two-fold; firstly, the American resources allotted to 'Culverin' would be lost to the Pacific for at least six months; and secondly, British naval assistance, which by mid-1945 might have amounted to about one-third of the American strength in the Pacific, would be delayed for at least one year. Even if 'Culverin' were postponed till the spring of 1945 and Germany had been defeated in the autumn of 1944, thus obviating the necessity for calling on America to make up the major deficiencies, the cost to the Pacific operations would be similar in degree though, of course, felt some months later. 'Culverin', attractive though it was, would thus seriously delay the Allied advance through the Central and South-West Pacific, and could not secure an entry into the South China Sea in time to assist the Pacific advance in any way. As a result, the penetration of Japan's inner zone would almost certainly have to be postponed and that would entail a risk of delaying her final defeat. They did, however, agree with Mountbatten that land operations in upper Burma could not open an overland route to China in time to have any military significance before the Pacific operations enabled far greater supplies to be delivered to China by a sea route. They therefore considered that S.E.A.C's efforts in Burma should be concentrated on the extension of the air operations into and through China. Since the 'Culverin' strategy would slow down the Pacific strategy, they concluded, on purely military grounds, that 'the Pacific strategy as recommended at Sextant offers the best opportunities for the earliest possible defeat of Japan'.[1] The Prime Minister and the Chiefs of Staff found themselves at loggerheads over this last point, since Mr. Churchill was not prepared to agree to the centre of gravity of British participation in the war against Japan being shifted from the Indian Ocean to the Pacific, and was none too sure that the Americans would welcome British naval assistance in that area.[2]

About this time information was received that the main Japanese fleet had arrived at Singapore. This move could either have been brought about by the American advance in the Pacific and the growing threat to Truk, or it could presage another raid on Ceylon and

---

[1] See pages 60–61.

[2] A full account of this difference between the Prime Minister and the Chiefs of Staff, which was not finally settled until the autumn of 1944, will be found in Ehrman, *History of the Second World War, Grand Strategy*, Volume V (H.M.S.O., 1956).

the Bay of Bengal. It was clear, however, that, so long as the fleet remained there, the despatch of major British naval units to the Pacific would have to be ruled out, and 'Culverin' could not be undertaken until a sufficiently large British fleet had been collected in the Indian Ocean to meet and defeat it.

On the 25th February, the eve of the departure of the Axiom Mission to Washington, Wedemeyer was asked to assure the Americans that no resources needed for operations in north Burma during 1944 would be diverted as a result of preparations for 'Culverin', and to explain the reasons which led the Supreme Allied Commander and the Chiefs of Staff to reject the prosecution of the Ledo Road strategy. He was also to say that the general strategy for the final defeat of Japan was still under consideration, but it was hoped that a decision would be reached within a fortnight. On the same day the President, instigated by a member of Stilwell's mission in Washington,[1] sent the Prime Minister a telegram saying that it was essential to make every effort to increase the flow of supplies to China, which could be done only by increasing the air tonnage or by opening a road through Burma. He was gravely concerned over the trend towards operations against Sumatra and Malaya; much more was to be gained by making an all-out drive in Burma. 'I most urgently hope, therefore', he ended, 'that you back to the maximum a vigorous and immediate campaign in Upper Burma'. The Prime Minister immediately assured the President that nothing had been or would be withheld from the operations in north Burma for the sake of 'Culverin' and that Wedemeyer, on arrival in Washington, would 'unfold the facts' about the Ledo–Burma Road, which showed that it could not be opened for traffic before 1947, and then for limited traffic only. He also informed Mountbatten that he had given the President his personal assurance that no forces would be withdrawn or withheld from the campaign in upper Burma for the sake of 'Culverin' or any other amphibious operation.

The Chiefs of Staff told Field-Marshal Sir John Dill in Washington that they were in complete agreement with Mountbatten that IV Corps was unlikely to be able to seize and hold the Shwebo–Monywa area during the monsoon.[2] While they agreed with the Americans that it was necessary to develop China as an air base to support the main drive on the Formosa–China coast–Luzon area, they upheld Mountbatten's views that the project for driving through the Ledo Road to Kunming could neither be completed early enough for the purpose nor, when finished, deliver more than an insignificant

[1] Romanus and Sunderland, *United States Army in World War II: The China-Burma-India Theater, Stilwell's Command Problems* (Washington 1956) page 164.
[2] Dill was the British representative in Washington and Head of the Joint Staff Mission. He represented the British Chiefs of Staff at meetings of the Combined Chiefs of Staff.

tonnage. They therefore considered that the instructions to Mount-batten should be 'to develop, maintain and protect the air link with China.'

On the 3rd March, the Axiom Mission met the Combined Chiefs of Staff in Washington. Wedemeyer outlined the situation in S.E.A.C. and the Supreme Commander's views on future operations, and told them that he was unable to say what the British Chiefs of Staff would decide. Turning to operations in north Burma, he said that Mount-batten proposed to continue to support to the maximum the air effort from China, increase the capacity of the air ferry route and undertake land operations to secure it and deny freedom of action to the enemy. A 4-inch oil pipeline from Ledo to Kunming was to be built by way of either Fort Hertz or the old Burma Road and, fantastic as it might seem, would take only some eight to ten months to complete. The Ledo Road to Burma passed over 'all but impossible' country, and to date 118 miles had been built. To reach Kunming another 1,000 miles would have to be constructed, including a ten-foot embank-ment along much of the Hukawng Valley which was flooded during the monsoon. The completion of this road would clearly take much longer than the pipeline.

On the 12th March, the American Chiefs of Staff issued a new directive for the Pacific which accelerated their 1944 programme:[1] the Palaus were now to be seized in the late summer and Mindanao in the autumn. The possession of these bases would enable a lodg-ment to be gained in Formosa early in 1945 or, at least, Luzon to be captured. Telling the British Chiefs of Staff of this new directive on the 21st March, they said that great efforts would have to be made to build up air strength in China and to continue to contain as many enemy forces as possible in South-East Asia. Their discussions with the Axiom Mission had in no way altered their opinions on the strategy to be adopted in that theatre—on the contrary, these meet-ings had shown more clearly than ever that the greatest contribution S.E.A.C. could make would be to provide timely and direct support of the Pacific advance to the China–Formosa–Luzon triangle. Once this area was under control, the value of operations in Sumatra and Malaya would be greatly reduced; in any case they could not supply the wherewithal for a major amphibious operation in South-East Asia that year. The increased capacity of the Assam lines of com-munication and the successful operations in Arakan and the Hu-kawng Valley,[2] together with the airborne operations of Special Force,[3] showed that the difficulties of operating in Burma might have been considerably overestimated. They therefore urged that

---

[1] See page 112.
[2] See Chapters X and XV.
[3] See Chapters XII and XIV.

Mountbatten should be directed to undertake vigorous action 'to capture upper Burma during the remainder of this dry season, throughout the monsoon, and next fall, in order to increase the capacity of the Air Transport line to China and expedite the laying of a pipeline to that country'.

On the 24th, the Chiefs of Staff forwarded the American views to Mountbatten, and said that they thought his directive should be 'to develop, maintain and protect the air link with China'. They told him that they still agreed with his opinion that IV Corps would be unable to seize the Shwebo–Monywa area and hold it throughout the monsoon, and that the Ledo force would be unable to capture Myitkyina in time to complete a road across the Hukawng Valley before the monsoon. They asked him whether he now wished to modify his opinion, bearing in mind the accelerated Pacific programme, the initial success he had gained in Arakan and especially the very satisfactory start to the airborne operations of Special Force, the extent to which the possession of the Myitkyina airfield was necessary for the protection of the air route to China, and the Prime Minister's injunction that he was not to withdraw or withhold any forces from the campaign in Burma for the sake of 'Culverin' or any other amphibious operation. They also asked him to report the resources he would need, particularly in transport aircraft, and to give an estimate of the extent to which the provision of these forces would affect the air ferry traffic.

At a meeting of the Combined Chiefs of Staff the same day, General Arnold said that, without interfering with the requirements for the defeat of Germany, the Americans would provide 400 additional transport aircraft to reach S.E.A.C. in groups of 100 a month, beginning on the 1st July 1944. He was also building up four additional air commandos, the first of which would reach South-East Asia in July and the rest by early autumn. The Combined Chiefs of Staff felt that the provision of these aircraft would make a great difference to the possibilities in north Burma, but decided that the British Chiefs of Staff and Mountbatten would have to be left to re-examine the situation in the light of these additional resources and then report to what extent they could meet the American wishes on a new directive to the Supreme Commander.

When the Axiom Mission was told of the offer of these additional aircraft, Wedemeyer, while agreeing that they would make a great difference, said that any directive to the Supreme Commander must be quite general in nature and merely tell him of the aircraft, leaving it to him to decide what could or should be done to increase the capacity of the air transport to China. He personally did not think that these additional aircraft would enable upper Burma to be reoccupied; he had been doing his best to advise moderation in

Washington on their estimate of the extent of Stilwell's success to date and the success likely to attend his future operations.

On the 29th March, the mission returned to London. We must now for a time leave the story of their future activities and deal with developments within S.E.A.C., for these influenced Mountbatten's answer to the Chiefs of Staff's telegram of the 24th March.

CHAPTER XII

THE SECOND CHINDIT
OPERATION IS LAUNCHED
(March 1944)

See Maps 3, 4, 14 and 15

WINGATE'S views on the employment of L.R.P. forces
had undergone considerable development when, having
won over the Prime Minister, the President and their
advisers by his brilliant advocacy, his force had been increased to six
brigades, and a balanced air force had been raised by the Americans
to work with them.[1] His original conception of the use of L.R.P.
forces had been penetration deep into enemy-held territory by small,
lightly equipped columns to raid lines of communication and direct
aircraft on to suitable targets, in co-operation with a main offensive.[2]
He now began to envisage a large increase in airborne and air-
maintained L.R.P. formations and their employment as the spearhead
of an offensive in which normal formations played a secondary rôle.
He did not at first press his views, for he realized that they were
unlikely to be accepted until the six brigades he had already been
given had proved their value. His ultimate aim of several L.R.P.
divisions operating well ahead of conventional forces is clearly shown
in his correspondence with the Supreme Commander in February
and March 1944.[3]

He had proposed at the time of the Quadrant Conference that three
of his L.R.P. brigades should move into Burma towards the end of
the 1943–44 dry weather and dominate the Katha–Indaw area on
the enemy line of communications. This would be followed almost
immediately by offensives on the Northern and Salween fronts and
by the fly-in to Indaw of an infantry division from 14th Army. The
L.R.P. forces would then be withdrawn. At the end of the monsoon
Stilwell's Chinese/American force, the Chinese Yunnan armies and
IV Corps, assisted by further L.R.P. operations and with the Indaw
force as a spearhead, would drive southwards toward Mandalay and
Rangoon. Wingate considered that the 'Tarzan' plan was a direct

---

[1] See Chapter I and Volume II, Chapter XXVI.
[2] See Volume II, Chapter XXIV.
[3] See pages 176–77 and 184.

outcome of the memorandum he wrote for the Chiefs of Staff at Quadrant in August 1943, and in this he was partially correct since Auchinleck had been forced by the Chiefs of Staff to adopt a plan based on the capture of Indaw.[1]

Wingate was in no way satisfied with the plan for operation 'Thursday' agreed to at the conference of the 4th January and confirmed by 14th Army order of the 9th,[2] under which three L.R.P. brigades of Special Force were to be placed astride the Japanese lines of communication to Myitkyina and the Hukawng Valley.[3] The plan he had submitted to the Chiefs of Staff at Quadrant had been abandoned, and his three brigades were now going to be projected into Burma in conjunction with an advance on the Northern front only. He felt therefore that, however powerful the immediate effect of their entry into Burma might be, they were likely to suffer the same fate as in the first Chindit campaign of 1943. He recorded these views in a memorandum to Giffard, and protested that his operations were being hindered by the lack of support he was receiving from higher authority. Having done this, he began to consider how to increase the weight of the blow which L.R.P. brigades could deliver without the aid of offensives by the main armies.

He realized that, with aircraft at his disposal, the difficult passage through the enemy lines and the long exhausting approach march to the area selected for operations could be avoided. Gliders could be used to land advanced parties in Burma, who would construct airstrips on which transport aircraft could land. The main body of the brigades could then be flown in, and sick and wounded from individual L.R.P. columns could be collected by light planes and evacuated to Assam. It would thus be possible for L.R.P. brigades to operate behind the enemy's lines for a much longer period than heretofore without relief or loss of morale.

It was evident that airstrips in enemy-held areas would be liable to attack from both the air and the ground and, since these would be the main bases for Special Force formations operating within Burma, they would have to be defended. Their defence could not, however, be carried out satisfactorily by the lightly-armed and guerilla-trained L.R.P. columns. Thus, if his formations were to remain in Burma unsupported for any length of time, they would have to be provided with artillery and infantry units of normal type to garrison their bases, which must be turned into strongholds. Since the number of troops available for their defence would be strictly limited, the bases would have to be located in areas too remote for the enemy to reconnoitre easily or to bring up artillery. In those

---

[1] See Volume II, Chapters XXIII and XXIV.
[2] See pages 119–20.
[3] See Map 3, page 33.

circumstances they would be capable of prolonged defence against superior forces. On these premises Wingate evolved a technique of operating L.R.P. brigades from carefully selected and well defended strongholds.

Slim agreed with these views but, aware that Wingate had little experience of Japanese tactics, told him to discuss with Scoones a method of defence, then being employed by IV Corps, of using mobile detachments hidden in the jungle outside the defended areas to fall on the flanks and rear of any attacking enemy units.

After his discussion with Scoones, Wingate wrote a Special Force Training Memorandum in which he directed that, on arrival in Burma, each of his brigades should select a stronghold, inaccessible to wheeled transport, but conveniently near where the brigade was to operate; it should cover, but not include, an airstrip and a separate dropping zone, both vital to the operation of Special Force formations. The enemy should be induced to attack L.R.P. columns in positions of their own choice, i.e. their strongholds; he was not to be attacked in defended positions if he could be met in the open. The garrison of each stronghold was to have a 'floater' company outside the perimeter to act as the eyes and ears of the defence and attack the enemy as he approached. If necessary, the brigade would detail a 'floater' column or columns to counter-attack the enemy from the flank or rear while he was attacking. As Wingate put it: 'If we look upon the Stronghold perimeter as the kid tied up to attract the enemy tiger, then we find the ambuscaded hunter in the shape of the floater columns on the grand scale, and the floater company on the minor scale. The floater columns are a strategical, the floater company a tactical, ambuscade.' The motto of each stronghold was to be 'No surrender'.[1]

By the middle of January, Wingate had received a report from Brigadier W. D. A. Lentaigne (111th Brigade) that the Japanese had moved forward to the Chindwin and were keeping a close watch on all crossing places from Homalin southwards, and that it would be impossible for his brigade to march into Burma as planned. Wingate had meanwhile formed the opinion that the Japanese would probably stage an offensive on both the Northern and Central fronts in the spring, with a subsidiary attack in Arakan. He had come to the conclusion that the best reply to any enemy move against IV Corps was an airborne L.R.P. operation directed against the enemy's main communications in the Pinlebu–Bhamo area. 'Such an operation', he said, 'will defeat the enemy's main effort, and even bring his plan to a disastrous end.'

By the 16th January he had prepared a revised plan: 111th Brigade was to be flown in about the 1st March to an area south of Pinlebu,

---

[1] The training memorandum was not actually issued until the 27th February.

with orders to cut the Wuntho–Pinlebu communications and the railway south of Wuntho, and later to operate in the Mu River valley north of Pinlebu. The 77th Brigade, with a garrison battalion attached, was to be flown into the Kaukkwe River valley between the 7th and 12th March to establish semi-permanent blocks on the railway between Mohnyin and Mawlu. The 16th Brigade, marching in if possible by way of Taro,[1] was to take advantage of the diversions caused by the other two brigades, attack Indaw and destroy the railway in the Bongyaung–Meza area. The plan assumed that there would be offensive action on the Northern front and that at least one brigade of IV Corps would cross the Chindwin to exploit as far as possible.

Wingate assessed the minimum additional forces required to hold the necessary strongholds in Burma at four battalion groups, each with a troop of 25-pounder guns and a light anti-aircraft troop. On the 18th January he placed his formal request for these additional troops before Giffard, who instructed him to discuss the matter with Slim. The next day he flew to see Slim at Ranchi. There are no records of their discussion, but that evening Slim sent a message to 14th Army Headquarters saying that he had seen Wingate. He had already agreed, he said, to have one battalion ready to fly in to hold a stronghold for 77th Brigade (Brigadier J. M. Calvert) as soon as it had secured a Dakota landing strip.[2] He now required 26th Division (Lomax) to train three more battalions forthwith for air landing to be ready to take advantage of possible opportunities developing later. The decision if and when the battalions were to be flown in would rest with him. He added that Wingate would arrive at Comilla that night and arrangements were to be made for him to meet Lomax the following morning. Two days later, in a telegram to Giffard, Slim said he was prepared to risk one battalion to ensure that Special Force remained in certain areas and to follow up by one brigade if there were a real opportunity for exploitation by IV Corps. He would decide on purely military grounds if and when any battalions were to go in, and could not accept the situation on any other terms. He added, 'Wingate realizes this'. These two messages are clear indications of the rulings given by Slim at the meeting on the 19th.

Although he had been given a copy of Slim's message to 14th Army Headquarters, Wingate placed a different interpretation on the discussion and, on the 20th, wrote to Mountbatten saying that Slim had 'agreed at once to the suggestion that he should put four battalions [of 26th Division] at my disposal for garrison purposes,'

---

[1] For Taro see Map 4, page 53.
[2] See page 119. The 3/9th Gurkhas from 26th Division had been earmarked for this purpose.

and had ordered Lomax to meet him at Comilla. On the 24th Slim met Wingate at Comilla and again told him that he would place one battalion (3/9th Gurkha Rifles) from 26th Division at the disposal of Special Force, which might be used for garrison duties should the circumstances envisaged arise, and would find the necessary artillery units for the garrisons. The other three battalions which Wingate required as garrisons would have to be found from within Special Force, and he suggested the use of 3rd (W.A.) Brigade for the purpose.

Wingate's immediate inclination was to propose to Mountbatten that the whole operation should be called off. On reflection, however, he wrote to Giffard on the 27th saying that, in spite of his strong objections to finding the bulk of the garrisons from L.R.P. sources, and his continued hope that, in the event of great success, British infantry from other sources in India might yet be available, he was of the opinion that the success of the operation need not be prejudiced unduly by the use of 3rd (W.A.) Brigade to supply the bulk of the garrisons. He therefore withdrew his request that the garrison battalions should be found by 14th Army except in so far as Slim had already agreed.

After preliminary discussions with Wingate on the 25th and 26th, Slim held a conference at 14th Army Headquarters on the 27th to consider the final plans for operation 'Thursday'. A joint 14th Army/Eastern Air Command instruction was issued on the 4th February. In this Wingate was told that, as far as was practicable, his operations would, in matters of equipment, maintenance, air supply and air transport, be given preference over other operations on the 14th Army front, and that 3/9th Gurkhas and the artillery detachments for garrison duties were placed under his command. He was given in order of importance three tasks: to help Stilwell's advance on Myitkyina by drawing off and disorganizing the Japanese forces opposing it and by preventing reinforcements reaching them; to create a favourable situation for the Yunnan armies to advance westwards; and to inflict the maximum confusion, damage and loss on the Japanese forces in north Burma. To achieve those tasks he was to operate in the Mogaung–Bhamo–Katha–Wuntho–Pinlebu–Lonkin area.[1] The 16th Brigade was to cross the Chindwin west of Taro about the 16th February and move by way of Lonkin to its operational area Indawgyi Lake–Mohnyin–Mu River valley—Pinlebu—Pinbon, destroying the enemy garrison at Lonkin if that were possible without causing undue delay. The 77th and 111th Brigades were to move to their operational areas under separate instructions issued by those concerned. Each brigade was to prepare a landing strip as soon as possible after its arrival in its operational area. Wingate was to arrange with 221 Group R.A.F.

---

[1] For Mogaung and Lonkin see Map 4, page 53.

and No. 1 Air Commando (Colonel P. Cochrane, U.S.A.A.F.) for the fly-in of 77th and 111th Brigades. The 14th and 23rd Brigades and 3rd (W.A.) Brigade (less two battalions) were to be in reserve for relief or exploitation, but they were not to move forward from India without the permission of 14th Army. The 3rd Tactical Air Force (Baldwin) was made responsible for all air operations on 14th Army front. The Strategic Air Force was told that the critical period for the successful entry of the L.R.P. forces would be from the 20th February to the 3rd March, and its operations at that time were to be designed to hamper any Japanese movements to oppose the brigades, and to break up any enemy concentrations in the areas in which they were to make their entry.

Wingate held a conference at Imphal on the 31st January and the 1st February which was attended by those concerned with the fly-in of 77th and 111th Brigades. He said that the governing principle of the operation was the concentration of effort at the decisive point, which he defined as an area within a circle of forty miles' radius from Indaw. Its occupation would effectively cut Japanese communications with their *31st* and *18th Divisions*, then operating on the Chindwin and in the Hukawng Valley respectively. The plan was based on his appreciation of the 16th January and was for 16th Brigade (Brigadier B. E. Fergusson) to approach the Indaw area from the north-west, 77th Brigade (Calvert) from the north-east and 111th Brigade (Lentaigne), which was to be flown in after instead of before 77th Brigade, from the south. The 16th Brigade, marching in from the direction of Ledo, was to deny to the enemy the Naba–Indaw and Banmauk areas. The 77th Brigade would be flown to two selected points in the Kyaukkwe valley where it was thought that gliders could land. These were named 'Broadway' (twenty miles east of Mohnyin) and 'Piccadilly' (thirty miles east of Mawlu). The first troops landed were immediately to prepare by hand an airstrip on which C.47 (Dakota) aircraft could land.[1] As soon as the airstrip was completed, the remainder of the brigade would be flown in. 'Piccadilly' was to be developed into a stronghold and a base for the brigade which, as soon as it was concentrated, would move westwards to cut the communications running north from Indaw. In addition to his stronghold troops, Calvert was to have under his command Morrisforce, consisting of 4/9th Gurkha Rifles (Lieut.-Colonel J. R. Morris) from 111th Brigade and Dahforce (Lieut.-Colonel D. C. Herring).[2] Both these would land with 77th Brigade

---

[1] Forty gliders were to land on each airfield on the first night. Training in the preparation by hand of airstrips to take Dakotas began on the 3rd February.

[2] Herring had reconnoitred the Kachin territory in the first Chindit operation. See Volume II, Chapter XVIII. Dahforce consisted of five British and two Burmese officers, a signals detachment, a British platoon and a few Kachin Levies. It was accompanied by two American liaison officers.

and, moving north-east, cut the Japanese communications between Bhamo and Myitkyina and raise a revolt among the Kachins north of the Taping River. The 111th Brigade would be flown in to the Tigyaing area near the junction of the Irrawaddy and Meza Rivers, the airstrip used for the fly-in being abandoned after it had landed. The brigade (less 4/9th Gurkhas) was then to move north-wards to its operational area, cut the communications between Wuntho and Indaw, and establish a stronghold south of Banmauk as a base for columns operating in the Nankan area.

During February the plan had to be altered when no area near Tigyaing suitable for an airstrip could be found. Wingate eventually decided that 111th Brigade would be landed at 'Broadway', and its stronghold battalion at 'Piccadilly', as soon as the landing of 77th Brigade had been completed; Morrisforce at 'Chowringhee' (an airstrip east of the Irrawaddy in the bend of the Shweli River); and Dahforce by gliders at 'Templecombe' (just west of the Bhamo–Myitkyina road, some fifty miles north of Bhamo). The 111th would move south-west and, passing north and south of Indaw, reach its operational area north-west of the line Indaw–Nankan. Both Morris-force and Dahforce would move east into the Kachin Hills.

The written orders based on this plan were not issued till the 28th February. They contained an entirely new feature: light bulldozers and earth scrapers were to be landed in the first flight of gliders so that the time taken to prepare the airstrip could be shortened. The night of the 5th/6th March was selected for the fly-in of 77th Brigade since the moon would then be full. By using both Piccadilly and Broadway, most of the troops could be landed before the Japanese reacted and it was expected that the build-up would take only three days. The fly-in of 111th Brigade could therefore begin on the night of the 9th/10th March. No. 1 Air Commando was to undertake the first phase (the landing of the advanced parties in gliders) and Troop Carrier Command, with four R.A.F. and two U.S.A.A.F. transport squadrons, would ferry the bulk of the troops to their operational areas.

During the period of preparation in February, the problem of getting the greatest number of loaded gliders to the landing area in the shortest possible time was carefully studied.[1] It would obviously be an advantage if each Dakota were to tow two loaded gliders at a time, but there was some doubt if this would be possible. For security reasons no large-scale rehearsal over mountainous country could be carried out east of Calcutta, but on the night of the 1st/2nd March a small-scale trial with four Dakotas, each towing two fully loaded gliders, was carried out. The aircraft took off from Lalaghat,[2] climbed

---

[1] The normal load for a glider was 25 fully equipped men or 4,500 pounds of stores or equipment.
[2] For Lalaghat see Map 14, page 452.

over the intervening range, flew over the Imphal plain at an average height of 3,000 feet and returned. Two of the aircraft with their gliders completed the flight satisfactorily, but the remainder had to turn back. It was so important that the greatest numbers should be flown in in the shortest possible time that it was decided to make the attempt with gliders in double tow, but, to lessen the strain on their engines, the towing aircraft were not to carry any load.[1]

Meanwhile on the 8th February the Supreme Commander, accompanied by his Deputy Chief of Staff and the commander of IV Corps, had paid a visit to Wingate's headquarters to discuss with him the preparations for 'Thursday'. That evening Mountbatten gave Wingate and Scoones a summary of the Combined Chiefs of Staff's strategy for the defeat of Japan. Wingate was extremely upset by what he was told, and questioned whether, in the light of the existing ideas on global strategy, operation 'Thursday' with its limited objective of helping the advance of Stilwell's forces should go on. In the circumstances Mountbatten felt constrained to write him a letter next day, in which he said he had come to the conclusion that Wingate's attitude arose from the fact that the global strategy as then planned was at variance with Wingate's own plans for a continental advance through Burma to Hanoi.[2] He pointed out that no such conception had ever been included in Wingate's directive, nor for that matter in his own. Mountbatten, however, invited him to prepare a written appreciation of his proposals so that they might be properly examined, and to give an assurance that he was prepared to carry on with 'Thursday' as planned.

On the 10th Wingate replied in a long and rambling letter, highly critical of the army and air force authorities in India, who, he alleged, were doing their best to thwart him by allotting equipment and aircraft to the 'useless' parachute brigade and to a non-existent airborne division,[3] and by refusing to allot him supply-dropping aircraft to train with his formations. He said that he had always insisted that it would be impossible to do two things at once and therefore that, if his plan for three L.R.P. brigades to soften up Japanese resistance in preparation for an advance by three main forces— IV Corps, Stilwell's N.C.A.C. forces and the Yunnan armies—were to be carried out, it would be essential to thin out and drastically diminish the strength of IV Corps and stop all new road construction in 14th Army area. The allocation of the three main forces to the operation had not been made, not because it was impossible but because no one was prepared to undertake the essential thinning out.

---

[1] The plan for the fly-in was based on the assumption, which proved correct, that the Japanese air force was unlikely to operate at night.
[2] See Map 15 in pocket at end of volume.
[3] The conversion of 44th Indian Armoured Division to an airborne division was under consideration at that time.

He was therefore faced with the choice of either abandoning the whole project or undertaking a modified operation. He had 'invented' the 'stronghold' method in order that he might perform with his own forces alone and unaided the rôle originally proposed for IV Corps, the Ledo forces and the Yunnan armies. To make this possible he had requested that his force should be provided with a tiny increment in the form of garrison troops. Despite the 'microscopic measure of support' which he had been given he was prepared to continue with the operation, provided that he was guaranteed the use of 14th and 23rd (L.R.P.) Brigades for exploitation, and would be supplied with the necessary supply-dropping and supporting aircraft. These last would, however, have to be definitely allotted to him and not removed under any circumstances whatsoever without his agreement, but this must not be used as an excuse for providing no more aircraft if it became necessary to fly in additional formations.

Wingate appended to this letter an appreciation of the prospects of exploiting 'Thursday'.[1] Next day he followed it up with a note on L.R.P. operations against Siam and Indo-China.[2] In these he maintained that, if 'Thursday' had any measure of success, further L.R.P. groups should be formed from a division of 14th Army, an army which 'can hardly be expecting ever to operate beyond the mountain barrier with its present establishment after the experiences of the past two years.' If 'Culverin' (the operation to capture northern Sumatra) were abandoned, and 'Thursday' proved to be an unqualified success, he proposed that a force of up to twenty-five L.R.P. brigades, some of which should be airborne, should eventually be formed to capture Hanoi and Bangkok. A chain of defended airports should then be built across China to the coast to link up with seaborne forces.

While Stilwell's forces were engaged in operations to clear the Hukawng Valley and the plan for flying in 77th and 111th (L.R.P.) Brigades early in March was being perfected, 16th (L.R.P.) Brigade began its long march of some 360 miles into Burma. Fergusson's orders were to march south down the western side of the Tanai River valley, cross the Chindwin on or about the 18th February and move on Haungpa.[3] Two columns were then to be detached to attack and hold Lonkin until replaced by troops flown in by Stilwell, while the remainder of the brigade moved down the Meza River valley to the Banmauk area. Fergusson decided to follow a track leaving the Ledo Road at Tagap which was said to go as far as Hkalak Ga.

---

[1] See Appendix 17.
[2] See Appendix 18.
[3] See Map 4, page 53.

From there he proposed to move as best he could through Lulum Nok to a point on the Chindwin some fourteen miles upstream from Hkamti, known to be garrisoned by Japanese. Having crossed the river he proposed to strike south-east towards Haungpa on the Uyu River from where he could launch his attack on Lonkin and then move the main body of his brigade down the Meza River valley.

Between the 5th and 11th February the brigade, supplied by air and preceded by an advanced party of engineers, moved off down the track in single file. The going was incredibly hard, the gradients often being as steep as one in two, and by the 16th the brigade had covered only the thirty-five miles to Hkalak Ga. After this, progress was quicker and the Chindwin was reached on the 28th, ten days behind schedule. On the 29th February a bridgehead was established without opposition, 250 men crossing on rafts improvised from packs, rifles and groundsheets, and a small party, found by 14th Brigade and called for by wireless, was successfully landed by light aircraft ten miles downstream from Hkamti to decoy its garrison away from the brigade's crossing point. At about 6 p.m. that evening two gliders, carrying assault boats and outboard motors, were landed on a sand bank at the river's edge; the boats were quickly launched and the brigade began to cross that night.

By noon on the 1st March the sand bank had been developed into a landing strip. That evening Wingate arrived and told Fergusson that the enemy's probable reaction to the operations of Special Force would be to reinforce Indaw from the south as well as from Pinbon and Banmauk. He explained that 111th Brigade was to prevent the arrival of reinforcements from the south by establishing road and rail blocks in the vicinity of Nankan, and that 16th Brigade, while moving down the Meza River valley, was to find a site for a stronghold sufficiently close to Indaw to enable columns operating in that neighbourhood to be maintained by light aircraft. It was to reach Banmauk by the 14th March, from where it was to prevent any enemy reinforcements reaching Indaw from the west and south-west. He did not, however, tell Fergusson that he intended the brigade to attack Indaw. Fergusson pointed out that with the best will in the world his leading troops could not reach the operational area until the 20th March. Wingate accepted this date but stipulated that not a moment should be lost. By the evening of the 1st March the advanced guard had moved off and by the 5th the whole brigade had crossed the river and begun the second part of its long march to the Indaw area.   .

On the afternoon of Sunday, the 5th March, Slim (14th Army), Old (Troop Carrier Command), Baldwin (3rd Tactical Air Force),

Cochrane (No. 1 Air Commando) and Wingate gathered at Lalaghat airfield to see 77th L.R.P. Brigade (Calvert) set off on its perilous mission into the heart of Burma. During the previous six weeks the Allied air forces had carried out an intensive air offensive to prevent any air activity over north Burma, by attacking enemy airfields at Heho, Toungoo, Magwe, Shwebo, Rangoon and Akyab as well as rail and road communications.[1] In these attacks it was estimated that at least eighty enemy aircraft had been destroyed, mostly on the ground. At Wingate's request no Allied aircraft had been allowed to fly near 'Broadway' and 'Piccadilly' for several weeks for fear of drawing the enemy's attention to the area east of Indaw. But that afternoon a photographic reconnaissance aircraft was sent without Wingate's knowledge to ascertain whether the two landing grounds were clear or had been interfered with. At about 4.30 p.m., half an hour before the first aircraft and its two gliders were due to take off, photographs, straight from the developing room, were delivered at the airfield. They showed that, although 'Broadway' and 'Chowringhee' were clear, 'Piccadilly' was obstructed by tree trunks throughout its length and that there were many tracks leading from it into the jungle.[2]

The immediate reaction was that the plan had been betrayed, that the Japanese had probably laid ambushes at 'Broadway' and 'Chowringhee' and that the operation would have to be called off. Reflection, however, suggested that, since photographs of 'Piccadilly' (used during the withdrawal after the first Chindit campaign) had appeared in an American magazine, it was possible that the Japanese, thinking the clearing might be used for future L.R.P. operations, had taken the precaution of obstructing it, and were unaware of the other two.[3] There was the danger that if the operation were cancelled, the morale of the troops, then keyed up to the highest pitch, might never again be brought back to the same level. Moreover, it was already late in the campaigning season and four weeks would have to elapse before the next full moon; by that time the Japanese might have begun their offensive. As there were strong reasons in favour of continuing with the operation, Wingate asked Calvert whether in the prevailing circumstances he would be prepared to go ahead with the operation. Calvert replied that, despite the risks involved, he considered that the plan, adjusted to meet the new situation, should be carried out. Wingate then discussed the matter with the Army Commander with whom lay the final decision.

Slim knew that a Japanese offensive across the Chindwin was

---

[1] See Map 15 in pocket at end of volume. From the 1st February to the 6th March forty such bombing attacks were delivered.

[2] See Map 3, page 33.

[3] The Japanese had already blocked all likely landing areas in central Burma.

imminent, and hoped that the appearance of Wingate's brigades in
the Indaw area would disrupt their communications and so hamper
their offensive. If he were to call the operation off, his plan for the
forthcoming campaign would be thrown out of gear and he would
be unable to keep his promise to Stilwell that the lines of communication to the Japanese *18th Division* in north Burma would be cut.
He did not believe that the obstruction of 'Piccadilly' necessarily
meant that the Japanese knew of the plan.[1] He therefore ordered the
operation to be carried out, subject to the tactical plan being adjusted
to meet the new circumstances.

Wingate then suggested that the part of 77th Brigade which was
to have been landed at 'Piccadilly' should be diverted to 'Chowringhee', but Calvert said he would prefer to fly his whole brigade
to 'Broadway' as he did not wish it to be split up and have one part of
it faced with a crossing of the Irrawaddy before undertaking its
allotted task north of Indaw. Cochrane was also opposed to a landing
at 'Chowringhee', for there was no time in which to brief the pilots
in the rather different lay-out of the proposed airstrip there. Since
Baldwin was also against the use of 'Chowringhee', Wingate agreed
that 'Broadway' alone should be used. Adjustments were then made
to meet the new situation and arrangements made to step up the
number of sorties during the night by a fifth if possible. The necessary orders were issued, the pilots diverted from 'Piccadilly' rebriefed,
and at 6.12 p.m., just over an hour behind schedule, the operation
began.

The advanced guard of four Dakotas, each with two gliders in
tow, took off in quick succession. The first glider to land at 'Broadway' carried the radio-telephone set and the ground control for the
landing strip. A flare path was quickly laid out and communications
established with Lalaghat. The landing strip, however, had several
deep ruts across it concealed in thick grass and, as a result, several
of the gliders crashed. The main body began to take off, at intervals
of a few minutes, an hour after the advanced guard. Things soon
began to go wrong: four gliders were forced to make crash landings
when, shortly after taking off, their nylon tow ropes broke; some
became unstable and had to break loose and land wherever they
could; and some had to be cast off when the pilots of the towing
Dakotas realized that the climb at full power was causing the engines
to overheat and that they would be unable to clear the mountains
with their heavy loads.[2] To make matters worse, the remaining
gliders began to arrive at the landing strip before the wrecks on it

---

[1] The obstruction was actually caused by Burmese forestry workers who had dragged
felled teak into the clearing to dry off.
[2] Many of the difficulties were caused by the glider pilots having insufficient experience
in double tow at night. Moreover, some gliders were incorrectly loaded or overloaded.

22. Major-General O. C. Wingate briefing Air Commando pilots.

23. The scene at Hailakandi airfield on receipt of the news that 'Piccadilly' was blocked. The three on the right are Brigadier J. M. Calvert, Major-General O. C. Wingate and Brigadier D. D. C. Tulloch (in shorts).

24. Gliders on Hailakandi airfield.

25. Light airstrip at 'White City'.

26. The 16th Brigade on the march to 'Aberdeen'.

27. Light plane of type used to fly out the wounded.

28. A supply drop.

29. Brigadier (later
Major-General)
W. D. A. Lentaigne.

could be cleared away and chaos resulted. Casualties began to mount and Calvert was compelled to send the code word 'Soya Link' meaning that there was trouble at 'Broadway'.[1]

Four Dakotas which were still airborne, each with two gliders in tow, were immediately ordered back to Lalaghat, since it was thought that the leading troops were being attacked and that after all 'Broadway' had been ambushed. Of the sixty-two gliders despatched that night, eight were recalled, eight crash-landed within the Allied lines, thirty-five landed at 'Broadway' (of which all but three were wrecked or damaged) and the remainder made forced landings at various points in enemy territory.[2] The casualties at 'Broadway' amounted to some thirty killed and thirty injured. Nevertheless, some four hundred men were landed during the night, together with sufficient mechanical equipment to enable an airstrip capable of taking Dakotas to be constructed.

By dawn on the 6th, order had been restored and work on the construction of a 1,400 yard airstrip begun. Calvert was then able to send the code word 'Pork Sausage' indicating that all was well, and a flight of light aircraft flew to 'Broadway' and took off the wounded. Engineers, assisted by all men who could be spared from protective duties, succeeded by evening in completing the airstrip and laying out landing lights. The first flight of American Dakotas took off from Lalaghat just before 6 p.m. and was followed by R.A.F. Dakotas from Hailakandi. During the night of the 6th/7th, out of a total of sixty-five aircraft despatched, sixty-two, of which only two were slightly damaged on the airstrip, touched down at 'Broadway', and landed some 900 men, 100 animals and 20 tons of stores. Wingate accompanied them to see for himself the state of affairs at the airstrip and discuss the brigade's future action with Calvert. On the following three nights, 272 Dakota sorties landed at 'Broadway' and thus completed the fly-in of the whole of 77th Brigade, together with its stronghold troops. There was no interference from the enemy throughout the whole operation.

To avoid too great a congestion at 'Broadway' and to get 111th Brigade to its destination before the enemy reacted, Wingate decided on the 6th that he would land it at 'Chowringhee'. On the night of the 6th/7th the advanced party, consisting of some American engineers and about 170 men, together with equipment and supplies, was sent forward in twelve gliders in single tow. All but one landed safely, but the glider which crashed carried the construction equipment and

---

[1] 'Soya Link' which represented the most disliked item in the rations was selected as an appropriate code word for this purpose. Calvert in using the code word was well aware that it would cause alarm at Lalaghat, but it was the only means at his disposal by which he could stop the arrival of further gliders.

[2] About half of the crews which landed in enemy-held territory managed to make their way back to Assam. These widely dispersed landings created a very useful diversion.

the advanced party was left to do its best to make the airstrip by hand. In answer to an urgent request, a bulldozer was sent forward by glider from Lalaghat and another from 'Broadway'. By midnight on the 7th/8th a strip was reported ready for use, though not fully completed. Twenty-four aircraft were immediately sent from Hailakandi, but, as the runway was too short for the more heavily loaded aircraft, seventeen had to be recalled. On the following two nights 118 aircraft landed advanced brigade headquarters, 4/9th Gurkha Rifles (Morrisforce) and 3/4th Gurkha Rifles (Nos. 30 and 40 Columns).

Wingate, who had visited 'Chowringhee' on the 8th, realized that continuous night flights over the enemy airfield at Katha would probably result in 'Chowringhee' being subjected to air attack. Moreover, it was inadvisable to concentrate the whole of 111th Brigade in the waterless area between the Shweli and Irrawaddy Rivers, with the latter to cross before the operational area could be reached. He therefore decided on the 9th that 'Chowringhee' should be abandoned the following day and that the remaining two battalions of 111th Brigade (1st Cameronians and 2nd King's Own) should be flown to 'Broadway' where the fly-in of 77th Brigade would be completed on the night of the 9th/10th. This turned out to be a very fortunate decision. All but four of the 129 aircraft carrying these two battalions were landed at 'Broadway' on the night of the 10th/11th. Lentaigne's brigade was now widely split: two battalions were at 'Broadway', while advanced headquarters and one battalion were at 'Chowringhee'. Owing to the lack of information about conditions at 'Templecombe', Dahforce was flown to 'Broadway' the following night, together with the remaining four aircraft loads of Lentaigne's brigade.

The fly-in of 77th and 111th Brigades, Morrisforce and Dahforce had been successfully completed without encountering enemy opposition. In seven nights some 650 Dakota and glider sorties had landed in the heart of Burma approximately 9,000 men, 1,350 animals and 250 tons of stores as well as a Bofors and a 25-pounder battery. Only complete air superiority over northern Burma had made possible the assembly of the large number of aircraft required for the operation and ensured the safety of the hazardous fly-in.

From the 1st to 13th March constant air reconnaissance had been maintained over all enemy airfields in Burma. When a considerable increase in the number of aircraft on the Shwebo airfields was noted on the 8th, No. 1 Air Commando succeeded in making a surprise low-level attack and destroyed some thirty enemy aircraft on the ground. This, and similar attacks during the period of the fly-in, largely accounts for the absence of enemy interference throughout the airborne operations.

On the 13th when the fly-in had been completed, Wingate issued an Order of the Day which read:

> 'Our first task is fulfilled. We have inflicted a complete surprise upon the enemy. All our Columns are inside the enemy's guts. The time has come to reap the fruit of the advantage we have gained. The enemy will act with violence. We will oppose him with the resolve to reconquer our territory of Northern Burma. Let us thank God for the great success He has vouchsafed us and press forward with our sword in the enemy's ribs to expel him from our territory. This is not a moment when such an advantage has been gained to count the cost. This is a moment to live in history. It is an enterprise in which every man who takes part may feel proud one day to say "I WAS THERE".'

Meanwhile, on the 8th Giffard had allotted 14th and 23rd (L.R.P.) Brigades to 14th Army to be used in a short penetration rôle to assist IV Corps, should the Japanese launch their expected offensive towards Imphal. That afternoon Slim called at Headquarters Special Force at Sylhet and, finding that Wingate was at 'Chowringhee', told Brigadier D. D. C. Tulloch (Wingate's Chief of Staff) that circumstances might arise which would make it necessary to use both of these brigades to assist IV Corps operations. When Wingate arrived at his headquarters on the 9th and was told that his reserve brigades might be diverted, he feared that his plan to establish and maintain a large L.R.P. force in the Indaw area might be brought to nought. He immediately flew to see Slim intending to tender his resignation, telling Tulloch to assume command of Special Force as soon as he had left.

Slim reminded Wingate that there had never been any question of Special Force using either of the two reserve L.R.P. brigades except as reliefs in some two or three months' time and thus, if it proved necessary to employ them at once to meet the Japanese offensive, no immediate effect on his operations would result. Wingate meanwhile had had time to think again and realized that, since these brigades were going to be in the forward area so much earlier than he had expected, they would be well placed to be used to exploit an initial success if he could persuade Slim to release at least one of them. Therefore, instead of tendering his resignation, he made his case for the use of 14th Brigade. Slim, who at that time was reasonably confident that IV Corps could deal with the enemy offensive, said that, although he could not place 14th Brigade at Wingate's disposal at once, he would let him have it for use in Burma should the situation on the main front develop satisfactorily. From that time Wingate made no secret of his intention to commit 14th Brigade in Burma with the least possible delay. On the morning of the 10th, so that it should be ready for action at short notice, Slim ordered the brigade (less two battalions) to move to Imphal, and the remainder as well as 23rd (L.R.P.) Brigade to Hailakandi.

It was perhaps with his conversation with Slim in mind that on the 13th Wingate sent him and Mountbatten a forecast of the possible developments of Special Force operations, and proposals for the use of 14th and 23rd (L.R.P.) Brigades. He said that 12,000 all ranks were embedded deep in enemy territory and that one stronghold ('Broadway') had been established. It was apparent from what had already occurred that the value of a stronghold which could be used by fighters and close support aircraft was enormous. He therefore proposed to establish a second stronghold in the Meza River valley ('Aberdeen'). Once that had been done, it would be necessary to consider how operations could be exploited by threatening Japanese communications south of Wuntho, thus affording an opportunity for IV Corps to advance and greatly increasing the effect of the L.R.P. operations. He suggested that a third stronghold might be established in the Simapa area north-east of Bhamo, that two columns from 14th Brigade should be put down in an area from which they could attack the Pinlebu–Wuntho road and that the rest of the brigade should be introduced into the Pakokku area to sever the communications of *33rd Division*.[1] An opportunity would thus be created for IV Corps to advance boldly down the Chindwin and establish a bridgehead in the dry zone before the monsoon. If 14th Brigade's operation were successful, it might later be possible to introduce his reserve brigade (23rd) into the Meiktila area so as to exploit the situation generally. If this were done, he said, 'we may confront the Japanese at the beginning of the monsoon with a front stretching from Pakokku to Lashio with almost the entire length of the Chindwin in our hands.' He concluded with these words:

> 'Needless to say, operations may develop in a very different and unexpected manner, and it is more than probable that a hard fight must first be fought before the Japanese will accept this startling measure of defeat. But in any case, the establishment of the three Strongholds and the introduction of 14 Brigade may be regarded as a practical certainty, unless we in turn are prepared to accept defeat'.

Wingate's forecast, taken together with his appreciation of the 10th and memorandum of the 11th February,[2] coming as they did after his complaint that, in carrying out operation 'Thursday', he was asked to operate unsupported, reveals very clearly his tendency to be inconsistent. Although he had himself laid down the principle that L.R.P. forces had to operate in close co-operation with an offensive

---

[1] See Map 14, page 452.
[2] See pages 176–77 and Appendices 17 and 18.

by the main forces, he was now prepared to abandon it. Pakokku and, in particular Meiktila lay in the open country of the dry belt in which the enemy could have quickly concentrated artillery and armour for the destruction of any forces landed there, and were so far beyond the reach of IV Corps that, even in the most favourable circumstances, the possibility of a link-up before such a force was overwhelmed would have been remote. It was unrealistic to suggest that the appearance of an L.R.P. column at Pakokku would create an opportunity for IV Corps to advance boldly down the Chindwin. It is hardly surprising that his suggestions were not accepted.

Although they had realized as early as the summer of 1943 that the Allies might attempt airborne operations in Burma, the landings at 'Broadway' and 'Chowringhee' took the Japanese completely by surprise. A report from *15th Division*, based on the interrogation of a captured glider pilot, that Allied airborne troops had landed west of the Irrawaddy ('Broadway') reached *15th Army Headquarters* on the 9th March. This gave a false idea of the strength of the landing and led Mutaguchi to think that garrison units in the area could cope with the situation. Accordingly he took no immediate action. Later reports from *5th Air Division* showed that the airborne troops which had been landed were in considerable strength and were being supplied and supported by air, but Mutaguchi still thought that they could be mopped up by local garrison units. Believing that the landings were the opening moves of an Allied offensive, he felt that it was all the more necessary to go ahead with the Imphal offensive. Kawabe (*Burma Area Army*) took a more serious view of the landings. Although, like Mutaguchi, he considered that the Imphal operation should be carried out as planned, he ordered *15th Army* to find an adequate force to destroy the Allied airborne troops.

On the 5th March there were only a few scattered administrative units and part of *5th Railway Unit* in the Indaw–Katha area, and *15th Army* had no reserves immediately available to deal with the threat to its communications. On the 10th, Mutaguchi formed a composite unit of two companies from men recently discharged from hospital and ordered *18th Division*, *56th Division* and *15th Division* each to send one infantry battalion to the Indaw area. On the 13th he sent Colonel Hashimoto, one of his staff officers, to Indaw to take command.[1]

On the 12th Kawabe, now aware of the strength of the airborne

---

[1] The *18th Division* selected *III/114th Battalion*, *56th Division II/146th Battalion* and *15th Division II/51st Battalion*. The composite unit arrived at Indaw on the 10th March and *III/114th Battalion* on the 17th. The *II/51st Battalion* did not reach Indaw till the 27th and *II/146th Battalion*, which had to move from the Salween front, was later directed to attack the airstrip at 'Broadway' and did not go direct to Indaw.

invasion, formed a special force under command of *15th Army* to conduct all operations against the airborne invasion. It consisted of the three battalions already allotted by Mutaguchi, *24th Independent Mixed Brigade* (a second-line formation of four battalions from garrison duty in Tenasserim), *4th Infantry Regiment* (less one battalion) from Malaya, and *II/29th Battalion* from lower Burma.[1] He placed it under command of Major-General Hayashi (*24th Independent Mixed Brigade*) who assumed command at Indaw on the 18th. Three of his battalions arrived at Indaw before the railway south of the town was temporarily interrupted by the demolition of a bridge on the 26th, and, with the exception of one battalion, the whole force was concentrated by the end of the month.[2]

---

[1] The *4th Infantry Regiment* and *II/29th Battalion* were part of *2nd Division*. The *II/51st Battalion* of *15th Division* was released to take part in the Imphal operation at the end of March as soon as Hayashi's force was concentrated.

[2] The commander and staff of *4th Infantry Regiment* arrived at Indaw on the 22nd, *II/29th Battalion* on the 25th, *24th Independent Mixed Brigade*, which had entrained at Moulmein, between the 26th and 31st, and *I/4th Battalion* on the 31st. The infantry strength of the force was equivalent to about a division by the end of March.

CHAPTER XIII

THE PRELUDE TO THE
BATTLE OF IMPHAL
(February – March 1944)

See Maps 3, 4 and 14 and Sketches 6 and 9

ON the Central front, in the first half of February, Scoones (IV Corps) was preparing to parry a Japanese offensive which he expected would be launched across the Chindwin through the northern end of the Kabaw Valley,[1] and at the same time attempting to clear the Kabaw Valley and the Chin Hills.[2] In the Tiddim sector, 17th Division, advancing towards Kalemyo, had surrounded enemy strongpoints covering Fort White. One was abandoned by the enemy on the 16th, but the main position astride the road at MS 22 held out. In the Kabaw Valley, the efforts of 20th Division to clear the track to Yuwa were meeting with stubborn resistance. The 23rd Division (less 49th Brigade) and 254th Tank Brigade (less one regiment) were in corps reserve on the Imphal plain. The 49th Brigade, with the Kohima garrison under command, was in the Ukhrul area preparing defensive positions covering the tracks from the Chindwin to Ukhrul and Kohima, and getting ready to counter-attack the flank and rear of any enemy force moving south down the Kabaw Valley towards Tamu. For this task, the track from Ukhrul by way of Chassud to the Kabaw Valley was being made fit to take light motor vehicles, work which unfortunately was to assist the enemy when he launched his offensive. On the 10th February, Slim ordered 50th (P.) Brigade to move as soon as possible to IV Corps area so that 49th Brigade could be released from its defensive rôle, thus giving Scoones the whole of 23rd Division as a mobile reserve.

During the second half of February it became evident that the Japanese were regrouping. There were definite signs that enemy strength in the Tiddim area and southern Kabaw Valley was steadily increasing. In addition to the determined resistance to any advance by 17th Division towards Fort White, there was a noticeable thinning out in the Haka area and it seemed that troops from there were moving north towards Tiddim. Entries in Japanese documents captured

---

[1] See pages 129–30. For order of battle of IV Corps see Appendix 19.
[2] See Map 3, page 33.

in the Yu River area indicated the presence of *213th Regiment* at the southern end of the Kabaw Valley. This, together with reports of a new unit in the area with fresh equipment and new tactics, led to the conclusion that the bulk of *213th Regiment* and *II/214th Battalion* had rejoined *33rd Division* from Arakan. Lastly, and perhaps most significant of all, documents captured in the Fort White area disclosed the presence in Kalemyo of *18th Heavy Field Artillery Regiment.*

Evidence of an enemy offensive across the Chindwin continued to accumulate. Patrols reported that Japanese motor transport moving along the Wuntho–Pinlebu track had reached Paungbyin. 'V' Force reported that rafts had been brought down the Chaunggyi Chaung from Mansi to within a few miles of the junction of the Uyu River with the Chindwin at Homalin, where there was already a considerable collection. By the third week in February patrols reported an increase in the number of country boats, and the appearance of power craft on the Chindwin at Pantha and Mawlaik. Finally, air reconnaissance showed that a pall of dust covering the jungle along the tracks leading to the Chindwin was steadily spreading, indicating extensive movement by night, and that the Sittang Bridge was in use for the first time since 1942.[1]

Such evidence could not be ignored and towards the end of the month Scoones ordered 23rd Division to send a brigade (1st) to the Kuntaung area at the northern end of the Kabaw Valley, and told his Chief Engineer to be prepared to withdraw the general reserve engineer force (G.R.E.F.) and labour units from the forward area. In the Tiddim sector, 48th Brigade of 17th Division tried to drive the Japanese from their positions at MS 22 on the Fort White road but, in spite of heavy bombardments on the 24th and 25th, failed to do so.

At the end of February Barforce and Hasforce to the west of the Manipur River were watching the tracks through the Chin Hills; east of the river the advance of 17th Division towards Kalemyo had come to a standstill between Kennedy Peak and Fort White; on the Chindwin, 20th Division was trying to clear the Yu River valley to enable the Yuwa road to be built and the advance on Kalemyo to be continued, and was pushing forward towards Sittaung, while 1st Brigade of 23rd Division watched the crossings further north; in the Imphal area 23rd Division was in reserve with 37th Brigade and 254th Tank Brigade (less the regiment in Arakan) on the plain and 49th Brigade in the Ukhrul area.

The Japanese had one division (*33rd*) in close contact with 17th Division and two others (*31st* and *15th*), standing back from the Chindwin, in positions favourable for an attack on 20th Division once 17th Division had been pinned and isolated. The situation was

---

[1] It had been demolished by 17th Indian Division during its retreat in February 1942. See Volume II, Chapter IV.

that two approximately equal forces faced one another, each manoeuvring for the initiative. The forward divisions of IV Corps were, however, widely separated and their communications were long and vulnerable. They were exposed therefore to defeat in detail unless they could quickly close on and destroy at least part of the enemy forces and then turn on the rest. It had become a matter of timing, and time, as a result of his stubborn resistance, was beginning to favour the enemy.

In view of the new threat apparent in the Tiddim area, and the fact that it now seemed probable that an enemy offensive would be launched very soon, Scoones came to the conclusion that his appreciation and plan of the 3rd February required modification. On the 29th he summed up the situation as follows: the enemy's probable line of action would be to cut 17th Division's line of communication, while further north a detachment of up to four battalions moved to cut the Imphal–Kohima road with the ultimate object of cutting the railway in north-east Assam. At the same time, converging attacks would be made on 20th Division from the north and south by *15th* and *31st Japanese Divisions* (less the detachment sent to cut the Kohima road). He foresaw the danger of 17th Division being defeated in detail and 20th Division being severely mauled. In the event of such an offensive he considered that his immediate object must be to secure the vital Imphal plain, and then counter-attack to destroy the attacking forces. His best plan would be to withdraw to the plain, hold vital points with the minimum forces and assemble as large a reserve as possible with which to destroy the Japanese by a counter-stroke delivered on ground of his own choosing. He therefore proposed that 17th Division should withdraw to Bishenpur and, leaving one brigade to hold the area, go into corps reserve; it was not to expect outside assistance and was to make a clean break with the enemy. The 20th Division, after covering the withdrawal of its technical, engineer and administrative units as well as the labour force, would withdraw to and hold the Shenam Pass south-east of Palel; if 49th Brigade in the Ukhrul area were relieved by 50th (P.) Brigade before the Japanese offensive began, then the whole of 23rd Division would be in mobile reserve. Thus, if all went according to plan, he would have for his counter-stroke 17th Division less one of its two brigades, the whole of 23rd Division and 254th Tank Brigade less one regiment.

Since the corps had been preparing for an offensive the proportion of administrative to fighting units in the forward area was high. If the Japanese attacked, the presence of numerous non-combatant units would clearly prove a serious embarrassment. Scoones therefore considered that it would be necessary to reduce the number of non-combatant and administrative units forward of Dimapur, and ensure that all such units remaining in the Imphal plain would be located in a series of self-contained defended areas sited to cover the all-weather airfields.

Slim, who had been in close touch with Scoones while this appreciation and plan were being prepared, agreed with it and early in March passed it to Giffard who accepted it and sent it on to the Supreme Commander. After paying a visit to Stilwell on the Northern front, Mountbatten intended to meet Slim and Scoones at Imphal on the 10th; for this reason he asked to be told by the 9th what arrangements 11th Army Group was making to reinforce IV Corps before the enemy offensive began.

The outline of the Japanese plan for their Imphal offensive was that *31st Division* (Lieut.-General K. Sato) on the right was to cross the Chindwin and move on Kohima; *15th Division* (Lieut.-General M. Yamauchi) in the centre, crossing the river further south, was to move south of Ukhrul to the Imphal Road immediately north of the plain; and *33rd Division* (Lieut.-General G. Yanagida) on the left was to advance along the Kalemyo–Tamu–Palel and Tiddim roads to Imphal.[1]

After crossing the Chindwin in the Tamanthi–Homalin area on the night of the 15th/16th March, *31st Division* was to close in on Kohima in three columns from north, east and south.[2] The right column was to move through Layshi and Phakekedzumi to the north of Kohima; the centre, which was to be followed by the main body of the division, through Fort Keary, Somra and Jessami to Kohima; and the left, under command of Major-General M. Miyazaki, through Ukhrul to Mao on the Imphal Road. The division was then to capture and hold Kohima, and be prepared to send a column to help *15th Division* in its attack on Imphal.

The *15th Division* was not up to strength when the offensive opened and consisted of six infantry battalions and mustered only eighteen guns.[3] It was to cross the Chindwin between Lawngmin and Thaungdut on the night of 15th/16th.[4] The divisional plan was for an advanced guard to move through Kamjong, Ukhrul and Leishan to cut the Imphal Road between Kangpokpi and Kanglatongbi, followed by the main body which was to seize the high ground in the vicinity of Kanglatongbi north of the Imphal plain, from where

---

[1] See Sketch 6, page 204.
[2] See Map 4, page 53.
[3] The *67th Infantry Regiment* (less *III/67th Battalion*), one battery *21st Field Artillery Regiment* and the main part of *15th Divisional Transport Regiment* were still on the way from Siam on the date selected for the opening of the offensive. The *II/51st Battalion* had been diverted to join the force collecting at Indaw to deal with the Chindits.
[4] See Map 3, page 33.

it would attack Imphal in co-operation with an attack from the south by *33rd Division*. The main body was to move in three columns: the right moving through Thanan, Humine, Chassud and Sangshak; the centre moving through Thanan, Sakok and Litan (Sareikhong); and the left moving to Mintha to cover the flank, and later through Thanan and Mollen to Yaingangpokpi. The divisional reserve was to follow behind the right column.

The *33rd Division* was to move forward a week earlier than the other two divisions in order to draw Allied reserves away from Imphal and Kohima. It was to advance from the general line Maw-laik–Yazagyo–Fort White in three columns; the right column, under command of Major-General T. Yamamoto, was to move on the 7th March along the Kalemyo–Tamu road and, after overcoming Allied resistance in the Witok–Tamu–Moreh area, advance on Imphal through Palel; the centre was also to move on the 7th from Yazagyo westwards with the object of striking the Tiddim road in the Tongzang area, in the rear of 17th Division; the left was to cross the Manipur River at Mualbem on the night of the 7th/8th and then turn north up the west bank of the river and block 17th Division's line of retreat in the area between MS 100 and the Manipur River bridge at MS 126. A reserve column was to hold the Fort White area until the centre column reached the Tongzang area, when it was to advance and co-operate with it; after the departure of the reserve column, a small garrison (a battalion, less two companies) was to look after the Falam–Haka–Fort White area until relieved by a battalion of the *Indian National Army*. Having surrounded 17th Division, the centre and left columns, assisted by the reserve column, were to destroy it and then advance to attack Imphal from the south.[1]

With the exception of the right (Yamamoto) and reserve columns of *33rd Division*, the three divisions all had to move along jungle tracks across high mountain ranges to reach their objectives, and were to carry supplies and ammunition with them for the three weeks it was estimated that *15th Army* would take to establish the main line of communication from Kalemyo through Tamu and Palel to Imphal.

Having watched the beginning of the fly-in of 77th (L.R.P.) Brigade on the evening of the 5th March, Slim went to IV Corps Headquarters at Imphal and on the 7th discussed with Scoones the plan to meet the expected offensive. He agreed to the withdrawal of 17th and 20th Divisions to the Imphal plain, provided that permission to withdraw was given to the divisional commanders personally by

---

[1] For the composition of the various columns see Appendix 20.

Scoones only when he was satisfied beyond all reasonable doubt that a major offensive had begun—a proviso that was to lead to the withdrawal of 17th Division being left until too late. Next day Giffard allotted 14th and 23rd (L.R.P.) Brigades, neither of which was involved in operation 'Thursday', to 14th Army to be used in a short penetration rôle to assist IV Corps. Meanwhile Slim had arranged on the 6th that in Arakan 25th Indian Division would relieve 5th Indian Division, which would then move to IV Corps area between the 13th March and the 14th April.

Scoones on the 7th set in motion his administrative plans. These included the stocking of supply points on the lines of withdrawal to the plain, their contents to be used up or backloaded as circumstances demanded; the movement of stocks of ammunition to Kohima and elsewhere on the Imphal Road for the defence of the lines of communication; the preparation of plans to withdraw non-combatant units and surplus motor transport to Dimapur in an emergency; and the preparation of a ring of self-contained administrative 'boxes' around the 'Citadel' (Imphal town) and the all-important airfields and landing grounds which were to maintain the corps as it fell back to the plain. These administrative boxes were to be garrisoned by detachments from the corps artillery, engineers, such infantry as could be spared, men of the R.A.F. Regiment and the administrative units concerned, all of whom had been trained to defend their installations. At first the boxes were numerous and dispersed as a precaution against air attack but, as the battle progressed and it was found that infantry raiding parties were a greater menace than air attack, they were amalgamated and concentrated more closely round the airfields.[1] There was in addition a large advanced base at Kanglatongbi, and a small one at Litan to supply the troops in the Ukhrul area, both of which had to be evacuated during the battle.

On the 9th, Scoones ordered 256 L. of C. Sub-Area (Colonel F. N. Elliott) to take over the administrative areas on the plain, put them into a state of defence and occupy them. He also gave orders for the preparation of a defended area some four miles north of Imphal into which corps headquarters could move in emergency. All G.R.E.F. units were to be withdrawn from the forward areas without delay and put to work on completing the roads north-west of Moreh and preparing defensive positions in depth on the Palel–Tamu road near Shenam, into which 20th Division could withdraw if forced to do so.

The IV Corps was at this time disposed with 17th Division on the Tiddim road, 20th Division in the Kabaw Valley south of Tamu, 23rd Division in reserve in the Imphal–Ukhrul–Kuntaung area and

---

[1] Imphal and its satellite Kangla, Palel with its satellite Sapam, Tulihal and Wangjing. See Map 9, page 374.

254th Tank Brigade in reserve on the Imphal plain. Three unbrigaded battalions (1st Assam Regiment, Shere Regiment (Nepalese) at Kohima and Kalibahadur Regiment (Nepalese) at Imphal) provided troops for the garrisons of the towns and detachments to watch the approaches from the Chindwin in the Jessami, Kharasom and Ukhrul areas.

Cowan's orders to carry out an offensive towards Kalemyo had not been cancelled, but he had been told that, if the enemy attacked, his division would be withdrawn to the Imphal plain and that he was to get it back without assistance from the corps reserve. He had therefore regrouped and formed a strong reserve: 48th Brigade (Brigadier R. T. Cameron) was in the Kennedy Peak–Vangte area; 63rd Brigade (Brigadier G. W. S. Burton) in mobile reserve between Kennedy Peak and Tiddim; divisional headquarters and divisional troops in the Tiddim area; and Tonforce (two battalions and some artillery) in the Tongzang area, covering the communications from Tiddim to the important bridge over the Manipur River at MS 126, an area which had been for some time harried by active and aggressive patrols from the east.

The 20th Division (Gracey) was disposed with 100th Brigade (Brigadier W. A. L. James) in the Witok–Htinzin area, 32nd Brigade (Brigadier D. A. L. Mackenzie) facing south-east astride the Yu River and 80th Brigade (Brigadier S. Greeves) further north facing east astride the track to Sittaung. All three brigades were patrolling actively and infiltrating forward. Divisional headquarters with some divisional troops and a squadron of tanks were at Tamu and the divisional administrative area was at Moreh. Aware that he might have to withdraw to Shenam Pass, Gracey had issued his plan of withdrawal to his brigadiers and senior staff officers with the proviso that no move was to take place except on his personal orders.

The 23rd Division was disposed with 1st Brigade (Brigadier R. C. McCay) near Kuntaung at the head of the Kabaw Valley with a battalion forward on the Chindwin at Tonhe simulating preparations for a crossing, 49th Brigade (Brigadier F. A. Esse) in the Ukhrul area watching the eastern approaches to the Imphal plain, and 37th Brigade (Brigadier H. V. Collingridge) at Kanglatongbi north of Imphal undergoing training with 254th Tank Brigade.

Early on the 9th, a report was received from a two-man patrol of 1/10th Gurkhas, which had been watching the crossings of the Manipur River in the Mualbem area, that a force of two thousand Japanese accompanied by guns and animals had crossed the river from east to west on the 8th. Since Barforce, Hasforce and 'V' Force covered all the tracks west of the Manipur River, early confirmation of this report was expected but, when by the 11th none had been received, its veracity began to be doubted. Meanwhile on the

10th, when the position held by Tonforce in the Tongzang area was attacked, Cowan told Burton (63rd Brigade) to reinforce it by 1/4th Gurkhas. On the 12th increased enemy pressure forced him to send back the rest of the brigade with orders to take Tonforce under command.

The same day Scoones received a delayed report, despatched on the 11th, from 'V' Force at Mualnuam that two enemy columns, each estimated to be 1,500 strong, were in that area moving north. Almost at the same time as the report was received, Japanese patrols appeared on the hills west of the Tiddim road near MS 108 to the north-west of the vital Manipur bridge. The appearance in these areas of the enemy, last seen on the 8th, constituted such a danger to 17th Division's line of communications that Scoones immediately ordered the corps machine-gun battalion (9th Jats) to move at speed to the Manipur bridge. It arrived, less one company, early on the 13th to find a detachment of Tonforce guarding the bridge.[1] It was by now evident that the greater danger lay to the north and the battalion was ordered back to MS 100 where its rear company was in position. Finding the road blocked at MS 107, the Jats took up a position to help the small garrison of administrative troops defend the supply dump at MS 109, on which 17th Division was dependent and which the enemy was clearly determined to capture. Meanwhile, the rear company at MS 100 had been surrounded. On the evening of the 13th, having heard from the Jats of the situation on the Tiddim road, Scoones decided that he must send a brigade, supported by armour, to the area.

In the Kabaw Valley enemy infantry, supported by armour, unsuccessfully attacked an outpost of 100th Brigade in the Witok area on the 11th. During the next two days further attacks in increased strength were made and repulsed, and it was clear that they were more than diversionary threats. These attacks, together with the rapid advance in strength around 17th Division's right flank and the attacks on its left flank at Tongzang, convinced Scoones that the expected offensive had begun. Consequently, during the morning of the 13th he gave Cowan permission to withdraw to the Imphal plain and told Gracey to speed up the evacuation of G.R.E.F. and other labour units from the Kabaw Valley. During the afternoon he told Slim by telephone that he had taken these steps, and at 9.30 p.m. he confirmed this, adding that he had ordered 37th Brigade from 23rd Division to move down the Tiddim road to the assistance of 17th Division, thus reducing his immediate reserves to one brigade and some armour.[2]

The 37th Brigade (less one battalion which was with 20th Division

---

[1] One engineer and three infantry companies supported by a battery of artillery.
[2] The 1st Brigade was still in the Kabaw Valley.

in the Kabaw Valley and did not join the brigade until later) embussed at dawn on the 14th and, followed by a squadron of light tanks from 7th Light Cavalry, moved to MS 82 on the Tiddim road. This was eighteen miles short of the point where the rear company of the Jat machine-gun battalion was in action, but no nearer rendezvous could be given since the eighteen miles forward from MS 82 were completely waterless.

The speed and depth of the Japanese penetration forced Scoones at midday on the 14th to order 49th Brigade (less one battalion) to be ready to move at twelve hours' notice from the Ukhrul area to MS 82. One battalion (4/5th Mahrattas) was to remain behind and come under command of 50th (P.) Brigade (Brigadier M. R. J. Hope-Thomson) on its arrival in the area.[1] At the same time he ordered 1st Brigade to concentrate at Kuntaung in readiness to move back to the Wangjing area to take over the task of watching the approaches to the plain from the east.

Although given permission on the 13th to withdraw 17th Division, it was not until 1 p.m. on the 14th that Cowan issued orders that the withdrawal, led by divisional headquarters, was to begin at 5 p.m. that day; the rearguard, consisting of a battalion and a half of 48th Brigade, was to begin its withdrawal from the Kennedy Peak area at approximately 7 p.m. and, in the few hours before the Tiddim area was evacuated, all the stores which could not be backloaded were to be destroyed. The orders to withdraw came as a complete surprise to most of the division. The move, which began uneventfully, was not followed up and the retreating forces reached Tongzang on the 15th. Meanwhile enemy pressure on that area had increased and, on the 14th and 15th, 63rd Brigade had repulsed several attacks from the east.[2] On the afternoon of the 15th it was found that the Japanese had occupied the Tuitum Saddle, over which the road passed between MS 128 and MS 132, and were thus blocking the way to the bridge over the Manipur River. There were now four roadblocks on the division's line of retreat to Imphal, and the detachments at MS 100, the important supply dump at MS 109 and the vital Manipur bridge were all isolated and threatened with destruction.

It was inevitable on the 12th that the road would be cut north of the bridge, but the failure of 63rd Brigade to secure the Tuitum Saddle, which was within a mile of and overlooked Tongzang, was an omission which might have had serious results. An attack with considerable artillery support was quickly mounted by 1/10th Gurkhas (which had two companies available in the area), but the leading company was soon held up by small arms fire. The

---

[1] The 50th (P.) Brigade had only two battalions.
[2] These attacks were made by the main body of the Japanese centre column (less *I/214th Battalion*).

importance of the ridge was still not appreciated and the battalion commander, who was about to put in his reserve company, was ordered to send it back to join the brigade reserve then being assembled to meet a Japanese attack from the east, which was making some headway.

The commander of the enemy unit holding the ridge (*I/214th Battalion*) had been ordered to attack Tongzang from the north by way of Tuitum. He, too, underestimated its importance. Finding that artillery fire from both the Manipur bridge area and Tongzang was inflicting casualties which he could ill afford, he decided to withdraw to the east.[1] That night 1/3rd Gurkhas was attacked while assembling to assault the ridge next morning, and it was not until the afternoon of the 16th that two of its companies occupied the right shoulder of the saddle. A company of 1/10th Gurkhas took the left shoulder, meeting scarcely any opposition. The way to the Manipur bridge was open.

The 37th Brigade had by then reached MS 82. On the afternoon of the 15th, 3/5th Royal Gurkha Rifles and a troop of tanks of 7th Light Cavalry were sent forward to rescue the hard-pressed Jat machine-gun company at MS 100. Two of the three tanks, confined to the road by precipitous hillsides, were destroyed, but two Gurkha companies, moving across country, linked up with the machine gunners soon after dark on the 15th. This small force held out against constant attacks for two days before withdrawing, carrying its seventy wounded across country to rejoin 3/5th Royal Gurkhas near MS 98. The situation at MS 109 had meanwhile been rapidly deteriorating. On the 17th the garrison commander asked permission to withdraw, but was ordered by IV Corps to hold on until help arrived. On the morning of the 18th, however, it was found that the administrative units had left their sector of the defences during the night and that the dump was in enemy hands. Without supplies and unable to reach its transport, the Jat machine-gun battalion had no option but to withdraw; carrying its guns, it moved through the hills and joined 37th Brigade without mishap.

The loss of the MS 109 dump was a severe blow, not only because a supply drop on the 16th had failed owing to enemy interception, but also because the Japanese *215th Regiment*, holding a ten-mile stretch of the Tiddim road, had now gained a plentiful source of supply. Thanks, however, to the rapid recapture of the Tuitum Saddle, 17th Division was able to continue its withdrawal. On the 17th, 48th Brigade crossed the Manipur River and began to close up to the southern end of the big roadblock from MS 100 to MS 109 which still barred its progress.

---

[1] Some thirty-three Japanese dead were found on the hill, most of whom must have been killed by shell fire on the 15th.

Meanwhile at Imphal the leading battalion (152nd) of 50th (P.) Brigade had arrived and, on the 15th, had moved out to Sheldon's Corner where it began to dig in, while 4/5 Mahrattas, left behind by 49th Brigade, was placed in reserve and moved to Kidney Camp to await the arrival of the rest of the parachute brigade.[1] That very night patrols from 20th Division found that the enemy was crossing the Chindwin on a wide front in the Thaungdut-Tonhe area, thus threatening the division's left flank. When Gracey reported this to Scoones on the morning of the 16th he was given permission to retire to Shenam Pass as planned. The same day 'V' Force gave warning that strong enemy columns had crossed the Chindwin and were approaching Ukhrul from the east.

While touring the Northern front on the 7th March Mountbatten received an eye injury and was taken to an American hospital at Ledo. Although he had both eyes bandaged, he was able to keep in touch with events and on the 9th received, through his Chief of Staff (Pownall), Giffard's proposals for reinforcing the Central front. On the 10th he asked Pownall what outside reserves could be moved up if IV Corps were attacked. Next day he was told that 14th (L.R.P.) Brigade, a brigade group of 5th Division and 23rd (L.R.P.) Brigade were moving in that order to IV Corps area, and that Giffard was intending to concentrate 5th Division behind IV Corps as soon as possible after its relief in Arakan, but could not yet give a firm date for the completion of the move. The only immediately available reserve outside 14th Army was 25th Division, but this was already on its way to Arakan to relieve 5th Division. Mountbatten told Pownall on the 12th to examine the possibility of using 19th or 36th Divisions, if he thought these reserves inadequate. Pownall replied next day that Giffard had instructed Slim to plan for emergency moves, which might include either the despatch of 36th Division to the Central front or for relief of the remainder of 5th Division, which would thus be freed earlier. He did not think that 19th Division, which was as yet neither fully trained nor equipped, could be got to Imphal in time to be of use.

Mountbatten left hospital on the 14th and flew back to Delhi by way of Comilla, where he met Slim and Baldwin about 10 a.m. on the airfield. Slim outlined the situation and, knowing that Scoones had already sent part of his reserves to help 17th Division to get back to the plain, asked for aircraft to expedite the move of 5th Division from Arakan to Imphal. Mountbatten told him that he would do his best to provide the extra aircraft, even if it meant taking them off the

---

[1] See Sketch 9, page 248.

air ferry route. That evening, on reaching Delhi, he discussed the question of reinforcements for the Central front with Giffard. The latter had already been in touch with Auchinleck with a view to moving forward part of XXXIII Corps, then in India carrying out training for amphibious operations. He pointed out, however, that he was faced with two serious administrative difficulties: those of getting another division to the Central front over the already over-crowded Assam line of communication, and of maintaining it there on arrival.[1] Mountbatten told him to accept all administrative risks and to lose no time in arranging for the reinforcement of 14th Army with Headquarters XXXIII Corps and at least one of its divisions.

The same evening, in a message to Mountbatten and Giffard, Slim gave the detail of his requirements for the move of 5th Division as 260 Dakota sorties for each brigade, and ended the message with the words, 'Press most urgently for these aircraft in view of the present situation'.

On the 15th, Slim went to Imphal, where he learnt that Scoones had had to order 49th Brigade as well as 37th Brigade to the Tiddim road, thus leaving himself without an infantry reserve, since 1st Brigade, which was being withdrawn from the Kabaw Valley, was needed to guard the approaches to the Imphal plain from the east.[2] The rapid move of 5th Division to Imphal was now imperative. In amplification of his earlier request, Slim sent a message to Mount-batten in which he reviewed the situation and asked urgently for the use of twenty-five to thirty Dakotas (C.47) from the 18th March to the 20th April. He received a reply the same evening that the aircraft would be placed at his disposal at once and that the Chiefs of Staff were being asked for immediate covering approval. Assured of the aircraft Slim gave orders for the air move to begin on the 19th.[3]

In a telegram to the Chiefs of Staff on the 15th, Mountbatten said that the first phase of the Japanese offensive, clearly aimed at the capture of the Imphal plain, had begun with a double encircling movement which threatened to cut 17th Division's line of communication, and that there were indications that their main offensive would begin by the 20th. The loss of the Imphal plain would give the Japanese two all-weather airfields and abundant supplies of food, would constitute a direct threat to the traffic on the air ferry route to China as well as to the Assam lines of communication and would jeopardize the whole air position in northern Burma. The

---

[1] The target figure for despatches along the Assam L. of C. for March was 4,368 tons a day. At this time the average daily shortfall was 918 tons. This meant that the British were getting only 76 per cent. of their requirements and the Americans 73 per cent. There was a 10 per cent. deficit of P.O.L., mainly due to the pipeline falling short of its expected capacity by 200 tons a day.
[2] See Map 14, page 452.
[3] See Appendix 25.

Japanese plan appeared to be similar to that adopted in Arakan, in that they were exploiting the ability of their troops to advance carrying all their needs for about three weeks, gambling on quickly capturing their opponent's supply dumps. An opportunity was thus offered of inflicting on them a defeat similar to that in Arakan, but on a much larger scale.

The success in Arakan, he continued, had been largely due to the fact that the troops, supplied by air, could be ordered to stand fast when encircled. Now, however, owing to the lack of reserves within striking distance of Tiddim and insufficient aircraft to bring up reinforcements and supplies, 17th Division had been ordered to withdraw towards the Imphal plain.[1] The plain had to be held since it was vital for the security of the ferry route and the line of communications which nourished it. It was therefore necessary to fly the operational portion of 5th Division from Arakan to reinforce IV Corps. The course of operations might also make it necessary to order encircled formations to stand fast, and might provide an opportunity for using Wingate's two reserve brigades (14th and 23rd) behind the enemy lines. In both these cases the formations would have to be supplied by air.

Since the operations in Arakan and Imphal were both part of the same Japanese plan, Mountbatten felt it was justifiable to regard the period of emergency, which had been accepted as existing in February, as still continuing. To meet that emergency the Chiefs of Staff had agreed that aircraft, which had since been returned, could be borrowed from the air ferry route.[2] He now proposed to borrow them again, since Troop Carrier Command was already fully committed to supporting operations elsewhere and could undertake no more. He asked the Chiefs of Staff to confirm that his interpretation of the situation was correct and said that unless he heard to the contrary thirty aircraft would be withdrawn from the air ferry route by the 18th for about a month. At the same time he raised with the Chiefs of Staff the general question of his authority to divert aircraft from the air ferry route to support forces engaged in its protection. He pointed out that at the time of the emergency in Arakan, after three days spent in a vain endeavour to get Stilwell's views, he had referred the matter to them and had not received a reply for a week. In the present circumstances it was fortunate that the general approval already received appeared to cover an extension of the emergency. But operational conditions could not be gauged from either London or Washington and would not always permit of

---

[1] This statement was not entirely accurate, for the division was to withdraw to the plain in any case in accordance with the pre-arranged plan as soon as the Japanese offensive began.

[2] See page 145.

delays such as had occurred in February. He therefore felt it was
essential that he should be given authority to divert aircraft for short
periods in an emergency, reporting the action he had taken to the
Combined Chiefs of Staff.

Two days later he received a telegram from Washington saying
that the United States Chiefs of Staff authorized him to divert, at
the discretion of Stratemeyer, thirty Dakotas or equivalent lift with
crews from Air Transport Command[1]; these aircraft were to be
returned at the earliest possible time. They could not agree, however,
to the Supreme Commander having the right to divert aircraft from
the China route without reference to them. They must remain
responsible for the Hump tonnage, since on it depended 14th
U.S.A.A.F., the equipment of the Chinese armies, the future operations of their very long-range bombers and the stability of the
Chinese Government itself.

On the 16th, Mountbatten told Field-Marshal Dill in Washington
and General Ismay in London that, had it not been for his enforced
stay in hospital, he would have initiated action to fly in 5th Division
at least four to seven days earlier. The same day he wrote Giffard a
letter, the burden of which was that Giffard had failed to grasp the
situation adequately during his (Mountbatten's) period in hospital.
He reminded Giffard that on the evening of the 5th he had asked
what steps were being taken about reinforcements to meet the threat
at Imphal, yet the movement of 5th Division had not even started by
road or rail when he visited Slim on the 14th. It was not, he said, till
he had questioned Slim closely on the dates by which reinforcements
were required that he had realized that he would have to take the
extremely difficult step of diverting aircraft off the Hump to ensure
that they arrived in time. No suggestion had reached him, or his
Chief of Staff in his absence, of how drastically the situation was
deteriorating or indicating the need for flying in reinforcements. He
ended by saying that he had had to act precipitately and thus
jeopardize the goodwill of the American Chiefs of Staff.

Giffard had in fact ordered forward all his available reserves
between the 5th and 13th March. The 25th and 26th Divisions had
already been allotted to 14th Army to relieve 5th and 7th Divisions.
By the 8th, 50th (P.) Brigade, 14th and 23rd (L.R.P.) Brigades and
5th Division had all been ordered to move to Assam,[2] and before the
14th Giffard had been considering the forward move of part of
XXXIII Corps.[3] The 5th Division was fully occupied in the renewed
offensive in Arakan and could not move until relieved, but it had
been ordered to begin moving out of Arakan on its way to the railhead

---

[1] Twenty Commandos (C.46), the equivalent lift of thirty Dakotas, were diverted.
[2] See pages 187 and 192.
[3] See page 198.

at Dohazari on the 16th.[1] Until the 12th Scoones was not certain
that the Japanese offensive had in fact begun, and not till the 13th
that 17th Division was endangered. It was not evident till midday on
the 14th that all the corps' available reserves would have to be sent
to assist the division to escape encirclement. Neither Slim nor
Giffard therefore had any grounds to press for an acceleration in the
move of 5th Division until the evening of the 13th. It was the cutting
of 17th Division's communications which completely changed the
situation and led to Slim's urgent request of the 14th for aircraft.
Without waiting for covering approval from the Chiefs of Staff,
Mountbatten diverted them from the air ferry to China the next day,
and the move of 5th Division began on the 19th.

On the 18th Giffard and Slim in conference decided that 2nd
British Division, now allotted to 11th Army Group, would be placed
in 14th Army reserve and moved to Chittagong, that 7th Indian
Division would follow 5th Indian Division to the Central front, and
that, if the Imphal Road were cut or a threat to Dimapur developed,
any brigade of 5th or 7th Division ready to move would be diverted
there. The destination of 14th (L.R.P.) Brigade (less two battalions)
was changed from Imphal to Hailakandi from where it could very
easily be flown to the Imphal plain.[2]

Meanwhile IV Corps' withdrawal to the Imphal plain was continuing. On the Tiddim road 17th Division from the south and 37th
and 49th Brigades (the latter less one battalion) from the north were
getting ready to break through the roadblock which *215th Regiment*
had established between MS 100 and MS 109.[3] The 17th Division
had crossed the Manipur River and, in preparation for an attack,
was disposed on the 18th with 48th Brigade reconnoitring the enemy
positions at Sakawng, which covered the MS 109 supply dump, while
63rd Brigade was in reserve near the Manipur River with one
battalion (1/10th Gurkha Rifles) as rearguard holding the Tuitum
Saddle. On the north side of the block 3/10th Gurkha Rifles of 37th
Brigade attacked the MS 100 position on the 21st and made some
progress, but the enemy countered by cutting the road behind it at
MS 96; the battalion was immediately put on air supply and was
ordered to hold its ground until the road had been reopened.

In the Kabaw Valley, Yamamoto, who had been in contact with
Allied forces at Witok since the 11th, had come to the conclusion by
the 15th that the Allied forces opposing him were preparing to
withdraw. He decided therefore to send the *Ito Column*, consisting of

[1] This date was brought forward to the 14th.
[2] See pages 183–84.
[3] See Map 3, page 33.

III/213th Battalion and some mountain artillery, through the hills by the Changbol–Laiching–Angbreshu track to cut the Tamu–Palel road about Tengnoupal. He intended to attack Witok on the 18th with his remaining infantry (three companies only) supported by tanks and artillery.

Gracey's plan for the withdrawal of 20th Division was to move 80th Brigade back to Khongkhang and Sibong at the eastern end of Shenam Pass, while 32nd Brigade (less one battalion temporarily placed under command of 100th Brigade) moved into the prepared defences at Moreh. The 100th Brigade, which was in close contact with the enemy in the Witok area, was to retire through 32nd and 80th Brigades to Tengnoupal at the top of Shenam Pass, while its detached battalion on the Mombi track carried out a fighting withdrawal to Chakpi Karong covering the southern entrance to the Imphal plain at Shuganu. These moves would, when completed, leave the division disposed in depth along the Imphal–Tamu road from the top of Shenam Pass to Moreh, with a battalion at Chakpi Karong protecting its right flank and the gap between it and 17th Division, while 1st Brigade (23rd Division) in the hills east of Wangjing covered its left flank.

The retirement of 32nd and 80th Brigades began on the 16th and went according to plan. Owing, however, to a last-minute change in 100th Brigade, the troops holding the position astride the road at Witok, through which the forward battalions were to fall back, were withdrawn without previous warning. Since these troops included all the armour and artillery, the two battalions could not fall back along the road, now dominated by enemy armour. They therefore decided to move through the jungle east of the road. Meanwhile the enemy, having succeeded in infiltrating to a position astride the line of withdrawal of the rearmost battalion, ambushed the transport of both battalions, creating great confusion. Despite this, the two battalions succeeded in extricating themselves and reached their allotted position without further loss. On the 20th a troop of tanks, sent south from Tamu to rescue a party of stragglers and wounded, met six enemy tanks on the road and destroyed four and captured two. At the same time an enemy column east of the Yu River was ambushed. These two setbacks slowed down the Japanese advance and it was not till late on the 21st that they made contact with the defences of Tamu. The first phase of the withdrawal had by then been completed and 20th Division was firmly established in depth along the road from Moreh to Tengnoupal.

In the Ukhrul area, Hope-Thomson with his headquarters, 50th (P.) Machine-Gun Company and 50th (P.) Field Squadron had reached Litan at 10 p.m. on the 18th. The 153rd (P.) Battalion, delayed by bad weather, was still on its way forward. At Litan he learned that a 'V' Force post near Ongshim had been attacked. Realizing that 152nd (P.) Battalion in position near Sheldon's Corner would shortly be attacked, and that there was nothing to prevent Japanese patrols from entering Ukhrul where forward supply and ordnance dumps had been established, he sent his machine-gun company there with orders to backload the stores and told his reserve battalion (4/5 Mahrattas), then at Kidney Camp, that it must be ready to counter-attack towards either Sheldon's Corner or Ukhrul.[1]

Next morning, 152nd (P.) Battalion, from its positions on Gammon Hill, Badger Hill and Point 7378 covering Sheldon's Corner and the tracks to Ukhrul, saw the enemy advancing from Ongshim and within a few hours was under attack. On the 20th, in spite of being reinforced by the Mahrattas, the 152nd found it increasingly difficult to maintain its forward positions. Point 7378 was lost and the enemy, now in control of the direct route to Ukhrul, began to work round the left flank of the position.

While the first shots of the action at Sheldon's Corner were being exchanged, the leading sorties of 5th Division's airlift from Arakan were beginning to touch down at Tulihal airfield, forty miles to the west, and by the 20th the infantry of 123rd Brigade had arrived. Scoones sent one battalion to Kohima and placed the rest of the brigade under command of 23rd Division (Roberts). To hold the east and north-east approaches to the Imphal plain, Roberts now had his own 1st Brigade in the Wangjing area, 50th (P.) Brigade in the Ukhrul area and 123rd Brigade, less one battalion, in reserve.[2]

On the 21st, Hope-Thomson with the newly-arrived 153rd (P.) Battalion, and 50th (P.) Machine-Gun Company recalled from Ukhrul, was eight miles to the south-west at MS 36. Acting on Roberts' advice, he decided to occupy a position at Sangshak, covering the junction of the Imphal–Ukhrul road and the motorable track from the Chindwin by way of Chassud and Sheldon's Corner, where there was water and where two companies of the Kalibahadur Regiment (Nepalese) were already in position. As the enemy had already occupied Ukhrul, thus outflanking his forward battalions at Sheldon's Corner, he ordered them to fall back that night on Kidney Camp while he himself with 153rd (P.) Battalion, less its support company, and 15th Mountain Battery moved to Sangshak. At the same time he sent a small garrison with his brigade transport to Litan with orders to hold it at all costs.[3]

About noon on the 22nd, Hope-Thomson ordered his two forward battalions, which had withdrawn during the night to Kidney Camp,

---

[1] See Sketch 9, page 248.
[2] Two brigades of 23rd Division (37th and 49th) were in the Tiddim road area.
[3] The garrison consisted of 50th (P.) Field Squadron, the support company of 153rd (P.) Battalion, and a platoon of 50th (P.) Machine-Gun Company.

to move at once to join him at Sangshak. At 2.30 p.m., as the leading troops of 152nd (P.) Battalion reached Sangshak from the east, an enemy column was seen advancing on it from the north down the road from Ukhrul. Further west, but unknown to Hope-Thomson, enemy patrols had already begun probing the defences at Litan, and Roberts had ordered 123rd Brigade to send a battalion (2/1st Punjab) there.

As it was now evident that heavy fighting on the Central front was imminent, Giffard and Slim, with a small operations staff, flew to Imphal on the 20th March to confer with Scoones. There they learned that the critical phase in the operation to extricate 17th Division from encirclement was about to begin in the MS 109 area on the Tiddim road, that 20th Division was withdrawing on Moreh closely followed by the enemy, and that 50th (P.) Brigade was under increasingly heavy pressure in the Ukhrul area. They also learned that Japanese columns had crossed the frontier north-east of Ukhrul and were advancing towards Kohima, thereby threatening the Imphal Road and IV Corps' communications with Dimapur, and that to the south-west enemy patrols might be making their way through the hills towards Silchar.

It was obviously advisable to have a corps headquarters available to take command at short notice of any forces that it might be necessary to concentrate to reopen the communications to IV Corps, should they be cut. Stopford (XXXIII Corps) was therefore ordered to move with his tactical headquarters to 14th Army Headquarters at Comilla. At the same time Kohima and the line of communications forward of it were placed under the command of IV Corps so that efforts to prevent the Imphal Road from being cut could be properly co-ordinated. To protect the vital advanced base at Dimapur, 1st Burma Regiment, then on its way to Fort Hertz,[1] was ordered to take up positions to cover the base and orders were issued that the next brigade of 5th Division to be flown from Arakan was to go to Dimapur to act as a mobile striking force. To cover the Silchar area the Mahindra Dal Regiment (Nepalese) was ordered to move there from north-east Assam, where it had for some time been employed on protecting the line of communication.[2] The minimum number of technical and administrative troops was to remain on the Imphal plain and the rest, together with all unarmed military personnel, were to be evacuated as quickly as possible. These measures it was believed would enable IV Corps to hold up the Japanese while a counter-stroke was prepared.

---

[1] See page 226.
[2] See Map 14, page 452.

The Japanese Imphal Offensive
March 1944

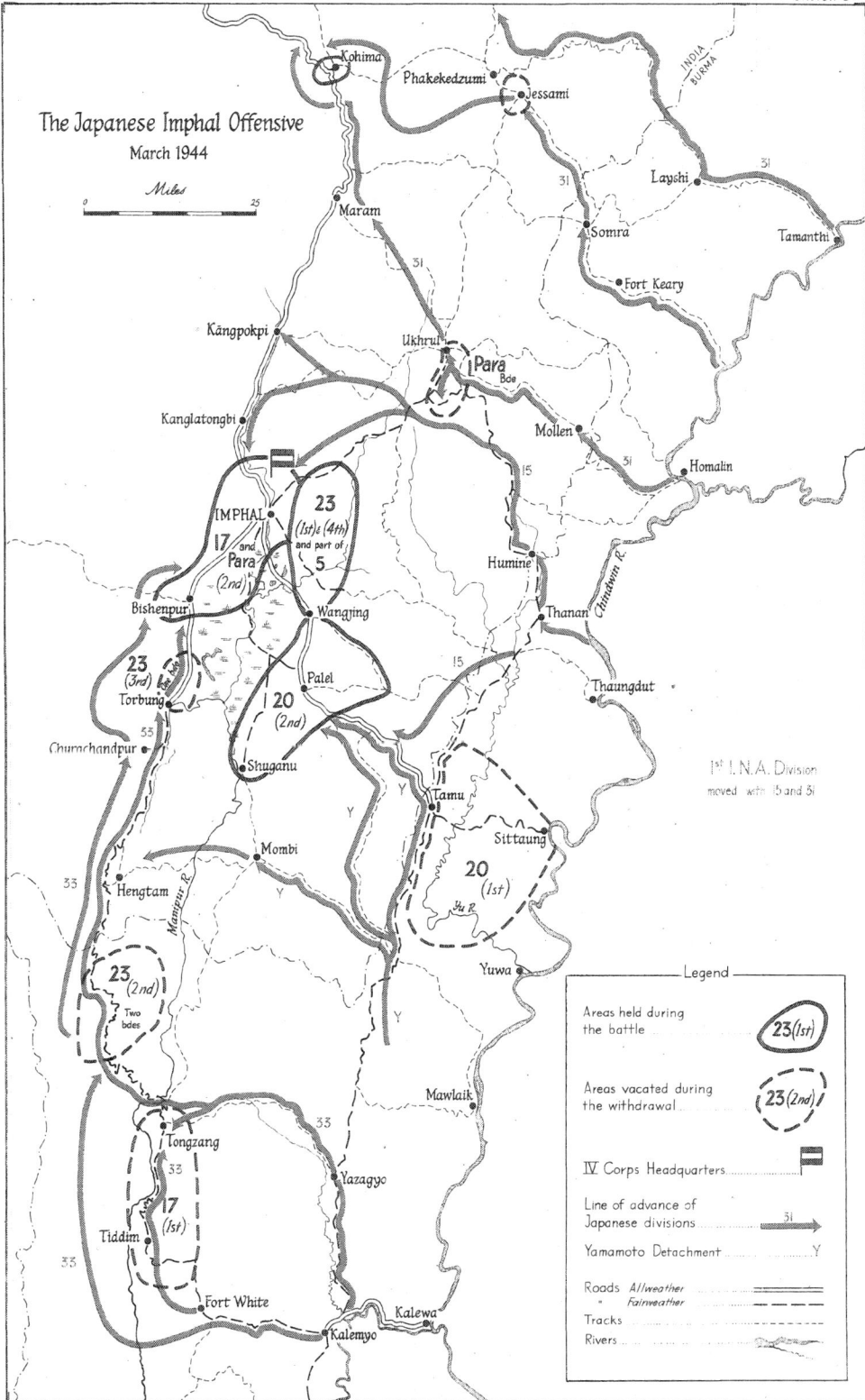

Miles
0 _____ 25

Kohima

Phakekedzumi

Jessami

INDIA
BURMA

31

Layshi

31

Maram

31

Somra

Tamanthi

Fort Keary

Kãngpokpi

Ukhrul

Para
Bde

Kanglatongbi

Mollen

15

31

Homalin

IMPHAL

23
(1st) & (4th)
and part of
5

17
and
Para
(2nd)

Humine

Bishenpur

Wangjing

Thanan

23
(3rd)

Palel

Thaungdut

Torbung

20
(2nd)

Churachandpur

33

Shuganu

15

Y

Y

Tamu

1st I.N.A. Division
moved with 15 and 31

Mombi

Y

Sittaung

Hengtam

33

23
(2nd)
Two
bdes

20
(1st)

Yu R.

Yuwa

Mawlaik

Tongzang

33

Yazagyo

33

17
(1st)

Tiddim

33

Fort White

Kalewa

Kalemyo

Legend

Areas held during the battle	23 (1st)
Areas vacated during the withdrawal	23 (2nd)
IV Corps Headquarters	
Line of advance of Japanese divisions	31 →
Yamamoto Detachment	Y
Roads *Allweather*	
" *Fairweather*	
Tracks	
Rivers	

CHAPTER XIV

THE CHINDITS IN BURMA
(March 1944)

See Maps 3, 4 and 14 and Sketches 7, 8 and 11

WHILE the Japanese offensive on IV Corps front was developing, the Chindits had begun to operate on the enemy lines of communication well within Burma. On the 9th March, Calvert (77th Brigade) set off from 'Broadway' to cut the road and railway north of Indaw. He left 3/9th Gurkha Rifles to establish the 'Broadway' stronghold and gave 1st King's (Nos. 81 and 82 Columns) the task of acting as a stronghold 'floater' defence battalion and of stopping all traffic on the Irrawaddy at Shwegu.[1] He ordered two battalions to establish a block on the main road and railway between Nansiang and Mawlu, and divided the remaining battalion into its two columns for the protection of his exposed flanks.

On the 12th Dahforce set off from 'Broadway' on its march towards Nahpaw, where Herring hoped to make contact with an officer of Special Operations Executive (S.O.E.) who was already working with Kachin and Chinese guerillas in that area, and crossed the Irrawaddy unopposed on the 18th. The two battalions of 111th Brigade also began their march on the 12th to join Lentaigne in the Nankan area; the King's Own crossed the railway between Indaw and Naba on the 20th and the Cameronians, moving round the north of Indaw, crossed the Banmauk road on the 22nd.

Some Bofors light anti-aircraft guns were flown into 'Broadway' on the 12th, after which six Spitfires with a portable radar set were based on the airstrip. The following day some thirty enemy fighters attacked it. The Spitfires intercepted and, although heavily outnumbered, broke up the raid, destroying a number of enemy aircraft for the loss of one Spitfire on the ground. On the 17th the Japanese again attacked; this time, owing to insufficient warning, the Spitfires were taken by surprise.[2] Only two were able to take off in time and one of these was shot down; the remainder were destroyed on the ground. Thereafter the air defence of 'Broadway' was based on fighter patrols flown from squadrons based on the Imphal plain.

---

[1] See Map 3, page 33.
[2] The portable radar set had insufficient range to give adequate warning of the approach of enemy aircraft.

Spasmodic enemy attacks continued until about the 21st, but failed to prevent the routine fly-in of supplies by transport aircraft at night, though stores were damaged and some Allied light aircraft were destroyed on the ground.

On the 15th Calvert, sending one column to attack Nansiang, used the remainder of the main body to establish a block on the railway just north of Henu.[1] On the 18th, before the block had been firmly established, a small enemy force attacked from the south.[2] The attack was driven off after savage hand-to-hand fighting and several bayonet charges, and the whole area secured. That night tools, barbed wire and ammunition were dropped and Wingate visited the block, which had been called 'White City' since the trees in and around it were draped with the remains of white parachutes. After three days of patrol activity, during which *III/114th Battalion* from *18th Division* was identified, the Japanese attacked from the north on the evening of the 21st. They succeeded during the night in occupying a small portion of the perimeter, but were evicted at dawn. Another attack during the morning failed to drive them away from the vicinity of the block, and it was not till they were heavily bombed at 5 p.m. on the 22nd that they withdrew to Mawlu, leaving sixty dead and four wounded behind them.[3] Wingate's first object had been achieved: the enemy's main line of communications to Myitkyina had been cut.

Meanwhile 'Chowringhee' had been abandoned early on the 10th March. Morrisforce then set off to cross the Shweli River on its long march to meet Dahforce north-east of Bhamo, and 111th Brigade Headquarters with 3/4th Gurkha Rifles (Nos. 30 and 40 Columns) moved to a point on the Irrawady some two miles south of Inywa. A few hours after the columns had moved off, the airstrip was heavily bombed; there was, however, nothing on it but damaged and abandoned gliders. Presumably under the impression that it was still in use, the Japanese continued to attack it for the next two days. These attacks on 'Broadway' and 'Chowringhee' were made by units of *5th Air Division* with some sixty fighters and thirty bombers—the total effective strength of the Japanese air force in Burma at that time. With the opening of the enemy offensive against the Imphal front *5th Air Division's* primary task became, from the 15th March, the close support of *15th Army*, and air attacks against the Chindits became of secondary importance.

In order to assist the Gurkhas to cross the river, four gliders containing collapsible boats and other equipment were landed on sand

---

[1] See Sketch 11, page 285.
[2] The attack was made by the composite *Nagahashi Unit*.
[3] Lieutenant G. A. Cairns, The Somerset Light Infantry, attached 77th Brigade, gained a posthumous V.C. during the actions to establish the 'White City' block.

banks on the eastern side of the Irrawaddy during the night of the
11th/12th. Two of the gliders were later snatched off. The crossing,
begun on the 12th under cover of fighter aircraft and the bombing
of Katha and Tigyaing, was considerably delayed by the failure of
some outboard motors and the stubbornness of the mules, and by
noon it was evident that it could not be completed that day. Since no
air cover could be provided on the 13th and it was believed that a
force was moving south from Katha, Lentaigne sent No. 40 Column
of 3/4th Gurkhas back to join Morrisforce east of the Shweli River,
and with his headquarters and the rest of the Gurkhas (No. 30 Column)
crossed the Irrawaddy and moved to the Meza River at Aikma,
where an airstrip for light planes was to be built and casualties
evacuated.

Lentaigne had hoped that 2nd King's Own would join him near
Aikma on the 18th and had planned that it and No. 30 Column
should cross the Meza River on a wide front and move on Bongyaung
and Nankan, while 1st Cameronians blocked the Nankan–Padeingon
road. But on the 20th, when he heard that the King's Own had been
delayed, he moved with No. 30 Column towards Nankan, and on the
26th blew up a railway bridge four miles south-west of the village.
Meanwhile a small detachment commanded by Major R. S. Blain
(Bladet), which had been landed by gliders at Aikma on the night
of the 19th/20th, had carried out demolitions on the Wuntho–
Tawma road. On the 30th March, it blew up a bridge on the railway
six miles north of Kyaikthin.

While these events were taking place 16th Brigade had been toiling
southwards towards its operational area. On the 10th March, when
nearing Haungpa, Fergusson detached two columns to move eastwards and attack Lonkin from the south.[1] On the 12th, by which time
the fly-in of 77th and 111th Brigades had been virtually completed,
Fergusson's orders were altered. He was told to make directly for,
and capture, Indaw with its two airfields and its important supply
dumps, establishing a stronghold to be known as 'Aberdeen' on the
way. The following day Fergusson reached Sezin and carried out an
air reconnaissance to find a suitable spot for his stronghold. He selected an area, which the enemy could approach in any strength only
from the south, near Taungle, to the west of Manhton at the junction
of the Kalat Chaung and the Meza River.[2] On the 18th Wingate sent
him a message saying that, as 77th Brigade was heavily engaged in
the Mawlu area, he was to go to its rescue and establish his stronghold en route. Accordingly, Fergusson ordered the main body of his
brigade to concentrate at Manhton and sent orders to the two
columns, which had occupied Lonkin on the 17th, to move on the

[1] See Map 4, page 53.
[2] See Sketch 7, page 209.

20th across the hills to Nami, whether or not the Chinese relieving troops had arrived.[1] Next day, however, Wingate found that the situation of 77th Brigade was not as serious as he had thought, and told Fergusson to continue his southward march towards Indaw.

On the afternoon of the 20th, after visiting 'White City', Wingate met Fergusson at Taungle and moved the site for the 'Aberdeen' stronghold some two miles nearer to Manhton. He told Fergusson that he proposed to use it as a base for 14th and 111th Brigades, as well as for 16th Brigade, and that he intended to fly in 14th Brigade as soon as the airstrip was ready. Fergusson then asked Wingate whether his brigade, which was widely spread out and extremely weary, could be given time to concentrate and have a short rest after its arduous march before it was committed to an attack on Indaw, which might by that time be well defended. Although the brigade had reached its operational area much later than planned, Wingate was apparently confident that the Japanese could still be surprised. He refused Fergusson's request and ordered him to attack Indaw on the night of the 24th/25th with the six columns which he could concentrate by that date, and told him that he could count on the support of the leading columns of 14th Brigade on their arrival at 'Aberdeen'. He arranged that the gliders carrying constructional equipment should be landed there on the 22nd so that 14th Brigade's fly-in could begin on the night of the 23rd/24th.

Although Wingate had told Fergusson that the leading columns of the brigade would, on arrival, support his attack on Indaw, he had other plans for it. He had in fact prepared an appreciation which led him to the conclusion that it should be used to disrupt the lines of communication of *15th Army*. In the appreciation he drew attention to the weakness of the Japanese lines of communication, which for *15th* and *31st Divisions* ran across the Zibyu Taungdan from Wuntho and Indaw by way of Pinlebu and Pinbon, and for *33rd Division* through Pyingaing. The Indaw communications had already been cut and L.R.P. forces could easily cut those passing through Wuntho and Pinlebu. With these lines of communication severed *15th Army* would, he thought, be compelled to withdraw. He proposed therefore that 14th Brigade should be flown into Burma without delay and directed to the Pinlebu area to complete the disruption of the communications to *15th* and *31st Divisions*. Two to four columns could then be spared to move south to cut *33rd Division's* communications at Pyingaing. He concluded his appreciation by saying, 'In my considered judgment this offers a complete answer to the Japanese penetration against IV Corps, and the only one which offers a reasonable chance of success. It is a choice between a major disaster and a major success.'

---

[1] See Map 3, page 33, and page 177.

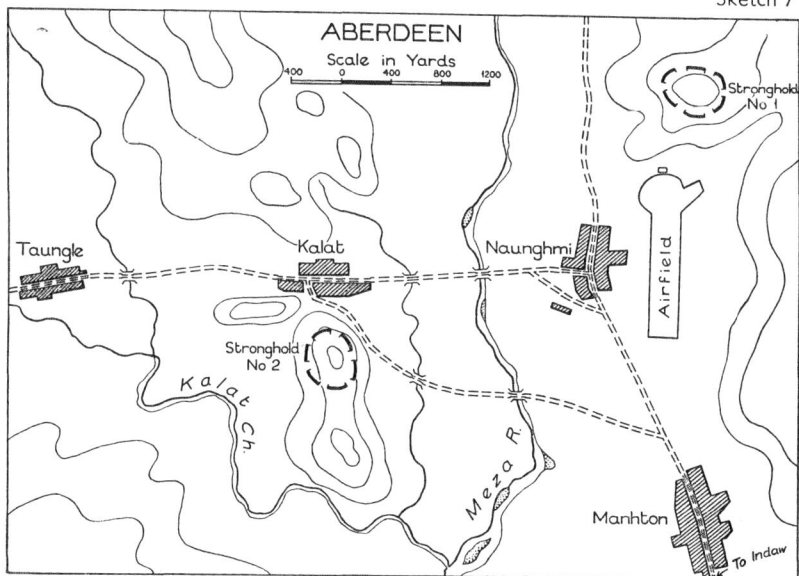

On the 21st Wingate flew to Comilla to ask Slim to place 14th
(L.R.P.) Brigade at his disposal. He had with him a copy of his
appreciation and undoubtedly used it as an *aide-mémoire*, but he
neither gave Slim a copy nor, as far as can be ascertained, anyone
else at Headquarters 14th Army. Satisfied that IV Corps, reinforced
by 5th Division which was already on its way to Assam, would be able
to deal with the Japanese offensive, Slim agreed to place 14th Brigade
at Wingate's disposal for use in Burma in accordance with the original
plan,[1] but he was not prepared at this stage to agree to it being used
to disrupt *15th Army's* communications, for its employment in that
way involved a change of policy which required Stilwell's agreement.[2]

Wingate, not satisfied with the rate at which 14th Brigade could
be flown into 'Aberdeen' with the thirty-three Dakotas at his disposal, demanded that additional aircraft should be made available.
When told by Slim that 14th Army was desperately short of aircraft
for the main operations about Imphal and that no more could be
provided for his operations, he said that he proposed to send a telegram to the Prime Minister on the grounds that his operations were
being thwarted by the shortage of transport aircraft. Slim told him
to do as he thought fit. That evening Wingate sent a telegram to

---

[1] The original plan of the 4th February was that 14th Brigade was to be held in reserve
to relieve a forward brigade or for exploitation. See page 174.
[2] The use of Special Force to disrupt the communications of *15th Army* was discussed at
the Jorhat Conference on the 3rd April. See pages 247–48.

Mountbatten for onward transmission without showing its contents to Slim. This was sent to London next day and read:

> 'Japanese have made mistake which can be made [to] prove fatal to them. But we are short of Dakotas. We want four more squadrons and your full backing . . . Success of L.R.P. operations means no more Hump and the complete destruction of four Japanese divisions. Get Special Force four transport squadrons now and you have all Burma north of twenty-fourth parallel plus a decisive Japanese defeat . . . General Slim gives me his full backing'.[1]

but Mountbatten had added:

> "While we all agree that we cannot have too many transport aircraft in this theatre particularly at this juncture neither Peirse, Giffard nor I know exactly why Wingate requires these extra squadrons . . . Giffard . . . tells me that he discussed the whole question with Slim and that their views are as follows:
> 'The expulsion of Japanese forces now West of the Chindwin in the very difficult country of the Chin and Naga Hills will be slow. It will take all our efforts between now and the monsoon to ensure their expulsion and they do not hold out any immediate hopes of conquering Burma North of the twenty-fourth parallel until the Japanese advance on to the Imphal Plain has been defeated. Since the only means of speeding up these operations is the use of transport aircraft for supply they support the request for additional Dakotas in principle'."

Although Slim had been pressing for additional aircraft for some months, he could neither support Wingate's request for 100 aircraft for the sole use of Special Force, nor was he able on the 21st to state precisely the number of additional squadrons required by 14th Army. Before flying with Giffard to confer with Scoones on the 20th,[2] he had told his planning staff to ascertain what extra transport aircraft would be required if the Imphal Road were cut. When, on the 21st, Wingate objected to the rate at which it was proposed to fly in 14th Brigade, Slim asked his planners to see whether the airlift of 5th Division to Imphal and 14th Brigade to 'Aberdeen' could be altered in order to speed up the fly-in of the latter. On the 22nd the planning staff advised Slim that no alteration of the existing plans for the fly-in of the formations was possible and that, in the event of the Imphal Road being cut, an additional 100 transport aircraft (four squadrons) would be required.

The same day Slim wrote to Giffard saying that it had long been his belief that the two essential arms for success in war in the Far

---

[1] Slim has stated that he did not give Wingate his full backing, and before he left on the morning of the 22nd took Wingate to task for using his name in vain.

[2] See page 204.

East were well trained tough infantry and air transport. The steady advance of Stilwell's forces, the success in Arakan and the promising situation of Special Force behind the enemy lines were all instances of the successful use of air transport. In the existing difficult operational situation in Assam, the main hope of a decisive success lay in the rapid move of reinforcing divisions by air. If, by using air transported reinforcements, the Japanese forces which had been committed across the Chindwin could be smashed west of the river, there would be an opportunity for exploitation which might easily lead to a major victory. An adequate pool of air transport was therefore essential, but the existing resources of Troop Carrier Command were only barely sufficient to sustain the present operations. The time had therefore arrived when he was forced to urge the provision of an increased allotment of squadrons to Troop Carrier Command. The minimum requirements were, he estimated, four R.A.F. transport squadrons (100 operational aircraft). On the 23rd, he followed up this letter with a telegram in which he again urged the provision of four R.A.F. transport squadrons. He regarded these, he said, as a necessity for a major success and an insurance against the possibility of a reverse demanding air maintenance on a large scale. Giffard immediately passed Slim's request for additional aircraft, with his full backing, to the Supreme Commander.

Mountbatten told the Chiefs of Staff on the 25th that Japanese forces were now apparently moving on Kohima and Dimapur and that both the Imphal Road and the Dimapur–Ledo railway might be cut.[1] It was thus possible that communications with IV Corps, Stilwell's formations on the Ledo Road and the Hump airfields would be severed. The Japanese were, however, operating well ahead of any reliable lines of communication and so it might be possible to turn a successful defence into a decisive victory. To achieve this, he had to be in a position to fly 7th Division quickly from Arakan, to fly in and maintain two additional L.R.P. brigades and to supply large forces which might be cut off from their base. The transport aircraft at the disposal of 14th Army (the equivalent of 130 Dakotas) were already operating as intensively as possible and could not be driven harder without entailing heavy wastage in aircraft and crews. To meet his requirements he had to have an additional 100 Dakotas. The retention of the twenty Commandos (the equivalent of thirty Dakotas) beyond the month for which they had been allotted to him would meet part of this total, but the balance of seventy Dakotas would have to be found from elsewhere.

The Chiefs of Staff agreed with Mountbatten's views on the threat facing the Allies and the need for these additional aircraft, but could do little themselves to help; they therefore asked the American Chiefs

---

[1] See Map 14, page 452.

of Staff to extend the period of loan of the twenty Commandos and to authorize a diversion of seventy Dakotas from the air ferry route. The Americans agreed to the retention of the Commandos until the middle of May, but would not agree to any further diversion of air-craft from the air route to China, and suggested that Mountbatten's requirements could best be met by the temporary transfer of aircraft from the Middle East. It was eventually agreed that one American group of sixty-four and one R.A.F. squadron of twenty-five Dakotas should be sent from the Middle East to S.E.A.C., the former to remain for about one month and the latter until the monsoon began during May. Mountbatten was therefore allotted eighty-nine Dakotas instead of the seventy for which he had asked. As the R.A.F. were able to send only fifteen instead of twenty-five aircraft, the number which reached India early in April was seventy-nine, and they immediately began to operate in support of 14th Army.[1]

After his interview with Slim, Wingate flew back to his head-quarters at Sylhet on the 22nd March and ordered 14th Brigade (Brigadier T. Brodie) to begin its fly-in to 'Aberdeen' on the night of the 23rd/24th. The following day he issued Brodie with written orders in which he said that 14th Brigade was to move south to Alezu and interrupt the enemy's communications between Wuntho and the Chindwin. He did not, however, tell Fergusson, who was expect-ing 14th Brigade to come to his assistance, of the change of plan. When he gave 14th Brigade its orders, Wingate either once again misinterpreted Slim's wishes, or deliberately decided to carry through his own plan for cutting the communications of *15th Army*. The same day that Wingate issued his orders to 14th Brigade, Slim gave orders that the fly-in of 5th Division would proceed as pre-viously decided and that 14th Brigade would be used as originally planned.

On the 24th Wingate flew to 'Broadway' and then paid a visit to Calvert at 'White City' and to 'Aberdeen', where he saw the leading column of 14th Brigade which had arrived during the night. In the early afternoon he returned to 'Broadway' and flew to Imphal to discuss with Baldwin the problem of air supply for 14th Brigade after it had reached Burma. Later that evening he left Imphal to return to his headquarters, but during the flight the American B.25 bomber in which he was flying crashed in the mountains west of Imphal. As soon as it was confirmed that all on board the aircraft had been killed, Slim appointed Lentaigne, who had greater experience of active operations and of the command of troops in the field than any other of Wingate's brigadiers, to command Special Force.

When Lentaigne was told on the 27th that he was to succeed Win-gate, he had just concentrated five columns of 111th Brigade north

---

[1] See Chapter XXII.

of Nankan in readiness to carry out its allotted task of interrupting the Japanese communications between Wuntho and Indaw. Tulloch (Chief of Staff of Special Force) told him that orders had been issued that Special Force was to cut the communications of *15th* and *31st Divisions* and that Wingate had directed 14th Brigade on Alezu to cut the Wuntho–Pinlebu road. Tulloch suggested that 111th Brigade might co-operate with it by cutting the enemy communications passing through Pinbon, which he believed had been Wingate's intention. Lentaigne agreed, placed Major J. H. Masters (his brigade major) in command of the five columns and ordered him to rendezvous early in April near Taungmaw and cut the track between Pinbon and Pinlebu. He then flew to Sylhet to take over control at Headquarters Special Force.

The leading battalion of 14th Brigade (2nd Black Watch) had meanwhile arrived at 'Aberdeen' between the 23rd and 27th. Its arrival had been delayed since it was found that the airstrip at 'Aberdeen' could not be used on moonless nights and the fly-in could, for security reasons, take place only for short periods in the half light at dusk and dawn.[1] The leading column (No. 73) left 'Aberdeen' on its way to Alezu on the 26th and by the 30th had reached Legyin.[2] The second column (No. 42) followed on the 29th.

Since its establishment early in March the stronghold at 'Broadway'—77th Brigade's base—had not been molested, except by air attack, but on the 27th it was attacked by the Japanese in strength. They succeeded in reaching a position which enabled them to prevent Dakotas using the airstrip and it was three days before they were forced to withdraw. Meanwhile, at 'White City', Calvert had decided to take the offensive, and on the 27th three columns (Nos. 36, 50 and 63) drove the enemy out of Mawlu, which proved to be an enemy administrative headquarters and a source of much useful information. By the end of the month 77th Brigade was in control of a corridor some thirty miles long astride the railway from Kadu in the north to Pinwe in the south and had blown up many bridges on both the road and railway; two anti-tank guns had been flown in to 'White City', its defences had been greatly strengthened and an intelligence system had been established in the surrounding country.

Dahforce had meanwhile crossed the Bhamo–Myitkyina road five miles south of Nalong on the 21st, and four days later reached Nahpaw. Food, clothing, arms, ammunition and equipment with which to arm a proportion of the guerillas collected by S.O.E. had been dropped on the 22nd at Simapa. The Japanese, who had seen

---

[1] Finding that twenty of the thirty-three Dakotas allotted to Special Force for the fly-in of 14th Brigade were not being used, Slim on the 25th ordered that they should be used temporarily for supply-dropping as required by 14th Army.

[2] No. 73 Column moving to Legyin crossed the path of No. 30 Column of 111th Brigade moving north-west to Taungmaw.

the supply-dropping aircraft, sent a patrol to the village on the 23rd. This was driven off by Chinese guerillas, but a strong enemy column returned on the 25th, occupied the village and then advanced on Nahpaw, which it attacked on the night of the 26th/27th. Herring had therefore to postpone his task of raising and arming a force of guerillas and interrupting communications between Bhamo and Myitkyina, and had to go into hiding in the hills until Morrisforce arrived.

Morrisforce, moving east from 'Chowringhee' towards the Kachin Hills, crossed the Shweli River just south of Asugyi on the 15th March and, after carrying out demolitions on the Bhamo–Si-u road near Sikaw, reached Bum Ghatawng at the end of the month where it destroyed bridges and culverts on the Bhamo–Namhkam road. There Morris received orders to move as rapidly as possible to Nahpaw to assist Dahforce. No. 40 Column, endeavouring to catch up with Morrisforce, was at this time still some five miles southeast of Sikaw.

As time was of importance, Wingate had ordered 16th Brigade to take the shortest route to Indaw. Fergusson's plan was that two battalions (2nd Leicesters and 45th Reconnaissance Regiment) were to attack from the north while one column of 2nd Queen's attacked from the south and the other blocked the Banmauk–Indaw road. He began his advance on the 22nd, unaware that Wingate had changed the orders of 14th Brigade and that in consequence it would not be coming to his assistance. When nearing Auktaw, he learnt from local inhabitants that, except in the valleys of the Nami and Ledan Chaungs, the area north of Indaw Lake was waterless,[1] that a British column which had recently moved west through Alegyun had told them that it was about to attack Indaw,[2] and that the Japanese garrison was some 2,000 strong and disposed in defences to the north of the town. At the same time an unexpected brush with the enemy at Auktaw destroyed any possible chance of obtaining surprise. The only covered approach lay down the Kyagaung Range but, as on this route water could not be found before reaching the lake, Fergusson considered he could not send both battalions along it. He therefore ordered 45th Reconnaissance Regiment to seize the northern end of the lake, while 2nd Leicesters moved in single file along the crest of the Kyagaung Range and occupied Inwa. They would then together attack the Indaw east airfield.

The Japanese had been warned by their intelligence to expect an attack from the north and had deployed *II/29th Battalion* to hold

---

[1] See Sketch 8, see page 215.
[2] On their way from 'Broadway' to rendezvous with 111th Brigade at Nankan, the Cameronians had given the local inhabitants this false information in the hope of misleading the enemy as to their movements.

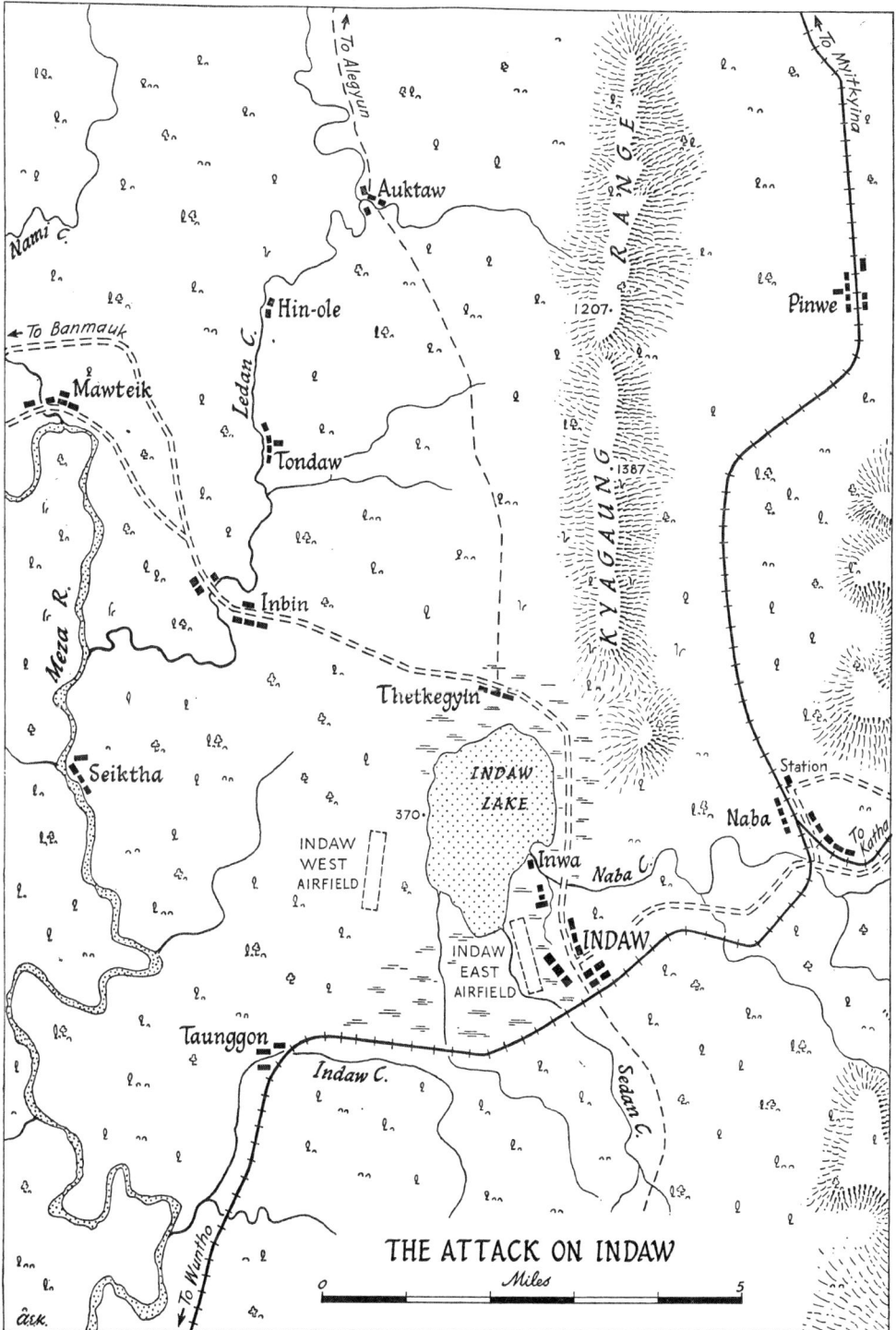

To Alegyun

To Myitkyina

Auktaw

Nami C.

Hin-ole

K Y A G A U N G   R A N G E

·1207·

Pinwe

To Banmauk

Ledan C.

Mawteik

Tondaw

·1387·

Meza R.

Inbin

Thetkegyin

Station

Seiktha

INDAW
LAKE

370·

Naba

To Katha

INDAW
WEST
AIRFIELD

Inwa

Naba C.

INDAW

INDAW
EAST
AIRFIELD

Taunggon

Indaw C.

Sedan C.

To Wuntho

THE ATTACK ON INDAW

0   Miles   5

Thetkegyin at the northern end of the lake, and had placed small detachments near Auktaw and on the crossings of the Indaw Chaung. As they arrived from the south, *II/51st Battalion* and *141st Independent Battalion* were disposed to cover the airfields and the town and to provide a reserve.

The Leicesters reached Inwa on the 26th without meeting with opposition, but the reconnaissance battalion ran straight into the enemy position at Thetkegyin and suffered heavy casualties. Unable to force its way to the lake, it moved west towards the Meza River to find water. Finding the enemy holding Inbin and Seiktha, it dispersed, but, owing to the loss of its wireless set, was unable to inform Fergusson. The leading column of the Queen's had meanwhile been ambushed on the Sedan Chaung south of Indaw on the 23rd, had suffered heavy casualties and had lost most of its mules with the mortars and ammunition reserves.

Realizing that the Leicesters at Inwa were unable to exploit their success until they were reinforced, and out of touch with the reconnaissance battalion, Fergusson tried to make contact with 'Aberdeen' in order to bring forward the leading columns of 14th Brigade. He was unable to get any reply and, when his rear headquarters in Assam told him that Japanese forces were advancing on the stronghold, it was apparent that no help would reach him from 'Aberdeen'. He decided therefore to break contact and withdraw his brigade to reorganize in the safety of the hills. On the 29th he ordered the Leicesters to withdraw northwards under cover of bombing attacks on Indaw, and the rear column of the Queen's, which had ambushed an enemy convoy on the 28th, to move on the 30th to Auktaw.

No sooner had the withdrawal begun than he regained wireless touch with 'Aberdeen', to learn that the stronghold had not been attacked, that 6th Nigeria Regiment and the leading battalion of 14th Brigade had arrived and that the remainder of the brigade and 12th Nigeria Regiment were due to arrive during the following week. He also learnt for the first time that 14th Brigade had been ordered to move south towards Alezu and not, as he had been led to believe, to support his attack on Indaw. Knowing that his stronghold was secure he ordered all his columns to concentrate there by the end of the month.

The failure of 16th Brigade at Indaw and the move of 111th Brigade north-west to the Pinlebu and Pinbon area meant that 77th Brigade at 'White City', already under heavy pressure, was open to attack by Japanese forces moving up from the south and in danger of being overwhelmed. Lentaigne therefore on the 30th rescinded Wingate's order to 14th Brigade to move south to cut *15th Army's* communications and ordered it to take over 111th Brigade's original rôle of preventing the Japanese from moving reinforcements to the

Indaw area. Brodie was to leave one battalion to block the Banmauk–Indaw road while the rest of the brigade attacked the road and rail communications in the Meza railway station–Bongyaung area. The southward movement of 2nd Black Watch was therefore stopped at Legyin until the rest of 14th Brigade had arrived at 'Aberdeen' and new orders could be issued. On the 31st March Lentaigne flew to Comilla to see Slim.

With the sudden death of Wingate, which came as a shock to the British and caused jubilation among the Japanese, an arresting and controversial figure disappeared from the Far Eastern stage. Since L.R.P. operations continued till August 1944 it is not appropriate at this point to offer any firm conclusion on whether Wingate's theories of long-range penetration were sound and whether the contribution made by Special Force in the 1944 campaign was commensurate with the resources it absorbed. It does, however, seem convenient here to assess his qualities as a commander and a leader, and to review the impact he had on the war in the Far East.

The task given to Wingate for the 1944 campaign was to assist the advance on the Northern front and to create a favourable opportunity for an advance by the Chinese Yunnan armies and for exploitation by IV Corps. Of these tasks he was told that the most important was to give assistance to N.C.A.C.[1] When planning his operation it is evident, however, that, in addition to cutting the enemy's communications to the Northern front, Wingate gradually came to have two other objects in mind—one, the capture of the Indaw airfields, and the other, the interruption of the communications of *15th Army*, when the Japanese, as he expected, launched their offensive against IV Corps. He therefore defined his object as the domination of the Indaw area, the control of which, he considered, would enable all these objects to be attained.

Wingate's plan of the 16th January was to land 111th Brigade south of Indaw to interrupt the road and railway in the Wuntho area, in order to prevent the enemy from rapidly bringing up reserves to counter the intrusion of Special Force, and at the same time to interfere with *15th Army's* communications.[2] The 77th Brigade was to land east of Indaw and establish a block on the railway to its north, while 16th Brigade, marching in from the Ledo Road, was to gain control of the area north-west of Indaw to prevent

---

[1] See page 119.

[2] It was known that the Japanese *18th Division* was fully occupied at the head of the Mogaung valley by Stilwell's numerically superior forces and in providing the garrison for Myitkyina, and that *56th Division* was holding a front of several hundred miles along the Salween. Wingate thought that *15th Army* was about to launch an offensive across the Chindwin. From this he could have deduced that the enemy could reinforce the Indaw area in strength only from the south.

reinforcements coming in from the west, and then occupy the town. The success of the plan depended on 111th Brigade carrying out its task quickly and efficiently; it was therefore to be flown in before 77th Brigade.

The new plan, as it eventually emerged on the 28th February, differed from that of the 16th January in that 111th Brigade was to land at 'Broadway' and 'Piccadilly' (which were far from its operational area) after, instead of before, 77th Brigade.[1] This decision made it inevitable that, although 77th Brigade could establish its block by about mid-March, 111th Brigade could not possibly concentrate south of Indaw till much later in the month.[2] Moreover, before the operation began, it was already clear that 16th Brigade, delayed and exhausted by its arduous march and reduced to three battalions by having to send a detachment to Lonkin, would not be ready to play its part till the latter part of the month. Thus, as it stood on the morning of the 5th March, the plan gave the Japanese time, if they reacted quickly, to reinforce the Indaw area before Special Force could either develop its full strength or interfere with the move of reinforcements from the south. The fact that 'Piccadilly' could not be used, and that 111th Brigade, entrusted with the most urgent task, had to be split up and a third of it faced with a major river crossing before it could concentrate in its operational area resulted in still further delay.

Although on the 12th March 16th Brigade was some ten days behind schedule, Wingate gave Fergusson a specific order to attack Indaw. On the 20th, by which time he knew that 111th Brigade had been seriously delayed and was unlikely to be able to cut the enemy's communications to Indaw from the south before the end of the month, he confirmed the order. He was clearly aware that, even if the Japanese reaction had been slow, they had had enough time to reinforce the threatened Indaw area, since he refused Fergusson's request for time to concentrate and rest his weary brigade before committing it to an attack. He was prepared, however, to take a considerable risk in the hope of taking the town by surprise, and gave Fergusson to understand that the leading troops of 14th Brigade, which was not at the time at his disposal, would be available to support him when they arrived at 'Aberdeen'. Having succeeded next day in obtaining Slim's permission to fly 14th Brigade into Burma, he ordered it to move south to Alezu contrary to Slim's wishes and failed to tell Fergusson that he had changed his plan—a very serious omission.

---

[1] See page 175.

[2] The 77th Brigade had to move some thirty-five miles from 'Broadway' to reach its objective. The 111th Brigade, which would be landed three days after 77th Brigade, had double that distance to move to its operational area.

The attack on Indaw was in any circumstances contrary to the precept, which he himself had laid down, that L.R.P. troops must never be committed to attack prepared positions. The 16th Brigade, understrength, exhausted by its long march, with no possibility of obtaining surprise and unsupported as a result of Wingate's change of plan, could not possibly have succeeded. It is clear that Wingate's obsession regarding Indaw led him to commit 16th Brigade to a task beyond its powers which could end only in failure.[1]

The move of 14th Brigade to the south, ordered by Wingate, and the subsequent diversion of 111th Brigade from the original task of cutting the Japanese communications south of Indaw, suggested by Tulloch in the belief that this was Wingate's intention, meant that there was nothing to prevent the Japanese from reinforcing Indaw, where 16th Brigade was in difficulties, and from concentrating a large force against 77th Brigade at 'White City'.

That Wingate was able to play such a prominent part in the war in the Far East was largely due to Wavell, under whose command he had served when conducting operations in Abyssinia. Wavell saw the possible value of similar operations by small mobile forces within Burma and considered that Wingate's ideas were worth pursuing. He raised the first L.R.P. brigade and decided that the value of such a formation justified the raising of a second L.R.P. brigade. He also allowed Wingate to try out his theories by making an incursion into Burma at a time when the operation could have little strategical value.[2]

Wingate's subsequent rise to prominence owes as much to the boldness of his theories as to the moment at which he propounded them. In a theatre of war where there had been little but retreat, disaster and frustration, Wingate offered a plan which meant action and attack. Whether his theories were sound or unsound, he appeared as a 'doer' at a time when something desperately needed to be done. The imaginative nature of his proposals and his claim to be able to kill once and for all the myth of Japanese invincibility appealed to the Prime Minister, who leaned towards the unorthodox in war. The timing of Wingate's proposals was opportune for they reached the Prime Minister at a moment when, as a result of the frustrations of 1943 and the failure of the first Arakan campaign, the prestige of British arms in the Far East was, in the view of the Americans, at its lowest. The Prime Minister grasped at the chance offered him, claimed Wingate as a genius, took him, a junior and comparatively

---

[1] The idea of capturing Indaw was stated in his appreciation of the 16th January and is inherent in his orders of the 28th February. See pages 171–72 and 174–75.
[2] See Volume II, Chapters XIV and XVIII.

unknown officer, to America and, with the agreement of the Chiefs of Staff, finally allowed him to propound his theories to the Combined Chiefs of Staff at Quadrant. Wingate's complete confidence in his ability to develop his theories to success, his unusual plan and his enthusiasm also captured the imagination of the American Chiefs of Staff. His proposals were then accepted by the Chiefs of Staff and relayed to the Commander-in-Chief in India as the foundation on which the plans for the 1944 campaign were to be built.[1]

High moral character, courage, self-confidence, forcefulness and determination, calmness in crisis and audacity are as much the mark of a great commander as an understanding of strategy, tactics and administration. Wingate had some but not all of these characteristics. He was clearly convinced of the righteousness of his cause and the soundness of his theories. He was, moreover, able to inspire others and kindle in them a sense of mission. Slim, in summing up the part played in Wingate's leadership by his Messianic and crusading zeal, has written:

> 'To see Wingate urging action on some hesitant commander was to realize how a mediaeval baron felt when Peter the Hermit got after him to go crusading. Lots of barons found Peter the Hermit an uncomfortable fellow but they went crusading all the same.'

Forcefulness and determination can, however, be carried too far. Wingate's belief that in his theories and plans and in them alone lay the chance of victory and his consuming fire of earnestness were such that, in a theatre where resources were limited, he relentlessly set about acquiring anything which he thought would further his own plans and made no effort to enlist the support of those whose help he would inevitably need. Instead of co-operating wholeheartedly with the army and air force commanders for the common good, he missed few opportunities of belittling them and questioning the value of orthodox forces. He appeared to revel in opposition and difficulties, and seems at times to have gone out of his way to create barriers in order to have another obstacle to overcome. The Supreme Commander, who gave Wingate his unstinted support throughout, was once constrained to draw Wingate's attention to his 'amazing success' in earning the dislike of people who were only too ready to be on his side.

Wingate had a flair for the flamboyant in military command and knew how to dramatize the operations he was about to undertake. He disguised the conventional language of war by using such terms as 'stronghold' to denote a firm base or pivot of manoeuvre, issued orders of the day which spoke of columns being inserted in the enemy's guts and sent messages which compared the feat of a battalion in

---

[1] See page 5 and Volume II, Chapters XXIV and XXVI.

crossing the Chindwin to that of Hannibal crossing the Alps. All this delighted the young men he selected to command his brigades and columns and turned the beastliness of war into an exciting adventure. By these methods, by the use of biblical quotations in his orders and by an appeal to the religious instincts which, though often latent, are present within most men, he created in Special Force a very high morale.

With the full backing of the Prime Minister and the Chiefs of Staff Wingate was able to overcome all difficulties. In a comparatively short space of time he raised and trained what can only be described as a private army with which to put his long-range penetration theories into practice. It must not be forgotten, however, that Special Force was formed only at considerable cost to the Army in India. An exceptionally fine British division was broken up: men in it not considered suitable were replaced by hand-picked men from other formations and the same procedure was applied to all units selected for operations with Special Force. As a result a very large number of units were robbed of their best officers and men.

The way in which his ideas on the use of long-range penetration forces grew in Wingate's fertile imagination would form an interesting psychological study. From his early conception of lightly armed troops penetrating behind the enemy lines and attacking communications as part of a larger operation by conventional forces, the operations of Special Force clearly became in his mind the one and only means by which northern Burma could be dominated. Subsequently, much increased in numbers, the force would become the spearhead of a victorious advance through southern Burma, Siam, and Indo-China to win the war against Japan. In February 1944, Wingate was already concerned lest the Combined Chiefs of Staff's global strategy should interfere with his own fast developing plans of reconquest, and even implied to the Supreme Commander that operation 'Thursday' should go on only if the existing world strategy were changed.[1]

It was inevitable that his continually developing ideas on the employment of long-range penetration forces should influence the planning and control of the operations he conducted to the point that his plans and his handling of his forces became unsound. In the first campaign his desire to prove his theories to the utmost by crossing the major river obstacle offered by the Irrawaddy led him to make an inflexible plan. This, after a period of indecision, caused him to commit his whole force across the river into a trap from which it was fortunate to escape.[2] In the second campaign he saw the capture of Indaw, with its airfields, and its retention throughout the

---

[1] See page 176.
[2] See Volume II, Chapter XVIII.

monsoon as the first step towards his future grand plans, and this led him into errors in both the planning and conduct of the early stages of the operation.

He was so obsessed by his theories that he entirely forgot that victory in Burma could be achieved only by the defeat of the enemy's main forces. His columns were neither equipped nor trained to do this. Although he served the Allied cause well by putting an almost forgotten army in the headlines and boosting morale, the very qualities which enabled him to win the support of the Prime Minister and the Chiefs of Staff and to create his private army in face of great difficulties reduced his value as a leader and a commander in the field. He was unwilling to co-operate with anyone not directly under his command and maintained an extraordinary degree of secrecy and furtiveness in his planning and in the conduct of operations. He carried this to such an extent that one of his brigade commanders observed that he often seemed to forget the difference between what he had planned and communicated to his staff and what he had merely thought of but not divulged.

No one can deny that Wingate understood the art of guerilla warfare, but he had no conception of the type of opposition he would meet if he became involved in a deliberate battle with well-trained Japanese regular army formations. The more his conception of the use of Special Force developed, the more was he driven into using his formations as conventional forces—a rôle for which they were not equipped—and the more widely he departed from the rules he had laid down for the employment of long-range penetration forces. He thus found himself facing problems which, by lack of experience, he was not equipped to solve. Always more determined on a course of action when he was opposed, he often rejected advice from those more experienced than himself, and so committed errors of judgment in tactical and technical matters as well as in planning. In the field it is evident that he tended to react too easily to the enemy's movements and at times laid himself open to the charge of order, counter-order, disorder.

Wingate had many original and sound ideas. He had the fanaticism and drive to persuade others that they should be carried out, but he had neither the knowledge, stability nor balance to make a great commander. He never proved himself to be the man of genius whom the Prime Minister wished to appoint as the Army Commander in charge of operations against the Japanese.[1] He did, however, make a valuable contribution to the development of the technique of air supply, particularly that of dropping supplies at short notice to columns operating in dense jungle in close proximity to the enemy. His 1943 operations were also a demonstration of the

---

[1] See Volume II, page 298.

practicability of maintaining troops in jungle country without a land line of communication.

What effect Wingate's sudden death had on the fortunes of operation 'Thursday' can never be determined. Just as timing played so great a part in his rise to prominence, so the moment of his death may perhaps have been equally propitious for him. He was killed at the height of his career and was not called upon to face the inevitable fact that his dreams and ambitions could never have been realized. Whether he would have accepted such a changed situation with good grace, or whether the qualities which helped to bring him into prominence would have produced his sudden eclipse, can never be known. Like Lawrence of Arabia, he is likely to remain a controversial figure.

CHAPTER XV

OPERATIONS ON THE
NORTHERN FRONT:
SIGNIFICANT EVENTS IN CHINA
(February – April 1944)

See Maps 4 and 11

SLIM had issued his first instructions for the Northern front to Stilwell on the 30th January. In these he had confirmed the plan already agreed upon—the advance of the Chinese–American troops on the general axis Shingbwiyang–Kamaing—Mogaung–Myitkyina, outlined the rôle given to IV and XV Corps and informed Stilwell of the general plan for the employment of Special Force in support of his advance.[1]

By the 1st February Stilwell had secured the crossings of the Tanai River at Taihpa Ga.[2] During the month he was reinforced by Merrill's Marauders and 1st Chinese Provisional Tank Unit, and by the 21st was in a position to resume his advance.[3] His object was now to encircle and destroy the Japanese *55th* and *56th Infantry Regiments* defending Maingkwan. To that end he ordered Merrill's Marauders to make a wide outflanking movement to the east and cut in on the enemy line of communication at Walawbum. The 22nd Chinese Division (less one regiment), supported by the armoured unit, was to make a frontal attack on Maingkwan while its third regiment moved eastwards from Taro to meet the Marauders in the Walawbum area. The 38th Chinese Division (less one regiment) was to follow up behind 22nd Chinese Division in reserve, while its third regiment moved on Maingkwan round the Japanese left flank.

The movement began on the 22nd February and by the 4th March the Marauders had succeeded in cutting the Japanese line of communication near Walawbum, where they tapped the main telephone line to Mogaung and gained valuable information on enemy

---

[1] See Map 4, page 53.
[2] See page 130.
[3] Merrill's Marauders had been training with Wingate's L.R.P. brigades in central India (see page 38). They reached Ledo on the 9th February and had concentrated forward by the 21st. The 1st Chinese Provisional Tank Unit was equipped with American tanks manned by Chinese. It was commanded by an American officer and stiffened with a platoon of American-manned tanks.

movements. The outflanking Chinese formations, however, moved too leisurely with the result that the Japanese were able to concentrate against the Marauders, drive them off the road after hard fighting in the Walawbum area on the 5th, and, avoiding encirclement, withdraw southwards, though not without difficulty. By the 7th March the whole of the Maingkwan–Walawbum area was cleared and the control of the Hukawng Valley secured. The Ledo Road could now be carried forward to Maingkwan to join the existing fair-weather road from Myitkyina through Mogaung to the Hukawng Valley, which had been improved by the Japanese. The first phase of Stilwell's advance to Myitkyina had, however, taken much longer than expected and only two months remained before the beginning of the monsoon.

Slim had meanwhile visited Stilwell on the 3rd March to discuss with him the plans for his further advance after the Hukawng Valley had been cleared, and to give him details of Special Force's operations to cut the enemy communications between central Burma and *18th Division* and thus speed progress towards Mogaung and Myitkyina.[1] They agreed that the Kachin Levies, assisted by British forces from Fort Hertz, should try to take Sumprabum in order to help the advance on the Northern front. To give the Levies the necessary backing, Slim asked 11th Army Group to fly a battalion of the Burma Regiment to Fort Hertz as soon as possible.[2] At this meeting Stilwell disclosed that he planned to make a sudden dash for Myitkyina at an appropriate moment, and descend on it from the north-west with a column which had crossed the Kumon Range by way of Naura Hyket Pass. He said that he had so far told no one else of this plan and asked Slim to keep it secret since any leakage would jeopardize it.

No sooner had Stilwell succeeded in clearing the Hukawng Valley and begun to consider how to open the way into the Mogaung valley than he received a message from Chiang Kai-shek calculated to slow down his advance:

'. . . 2. You are requested to report the operational plans of New 1st Army in advance.

3. In view of the operations of British forces and the preparations of our forces, the New 1st Army should not advance until there are advances in Arakan by the British forces. Before any advances are made by the friend [*sic*] forces, our army should stop at the present positions, so that we will not be attacked individually.

4. Please send a reply on the above mentioned two points'.

---

[1] See Chapter XII.
[2] The 1st Battalion Burma Regiment was earmarked for the task but the Japanese offensive caused it to be retained at Dimapur, and another battalion of the regiment was sent later.

Already well behind his schedule and with little time before the monsoon, Stilwell decided to make no reply, but to discuss the matter with the Generalissimo when next he visited Chungking.[1]

Meanwhile he proposed to continue his offensive. To gain an entry into the Mogaung valley he had first to cross the Jambu Bum ridge and seize the Shaduzup area, to which *55th* and *56th Japanese Regiments* had withdrawn after their defeat at Walawbum. He therefore ordered 22nd Chinese Division, supported by 1st Chinese Provisional Tank Unit, to attack the ridge frontally astride the Maingkwan–Kamaing road. Two outflanking columns were meanwhile to work round the Japanese right flank and establish roadblocks near Shaduzup and Inkangahtawng respectively, well to the rear of the main enemy position on the ridge. One column, consisting of a battalion of Marauders and 113th Regiment of 38th Chinese Division, was to move some fifty miles along tracks east of the main road to Nprawa before turning south-west to Shaduzup. The other, consisting of two Marauder battalions and a Chinese regiment, was to move east to Pabum and up the valley of the Tanai River to the watershed in the Nhpum Ga–Auche area, a distance of some eighty miles, before striking west for the road at Inkangahtawng. The outflanking columns were to begin their move on the 12th March and were expected to reach their objectives on the road between the 24th and 26th, by which time it was hoped that the Jambu Bum ridge would have been captured by the frontal assault.

The 22nd Division attacked on the 14th March with two regiments, keeping one in reserve, and by the 17th, after some sharp fighting, had reached the top of the ridge. There it found that the road south of the crest was mined and blocked with fallen trees and that the Japanese were holding a strong river line position half way between the ridge and Shaduzup. The road was cleared by the 19th, but repeated infantry attacks supported by armour failed to dislodge the enemy. Many tanks were lost, and on the 26th the reserve regiment had to be brought forward.

The Marauders' 1st Battalion, moving by the shorter route, had meanwhile reached Nprawa on the 20th followed by 113th Chinese Regiment. There, finding that all the tracks leading to the road between Jambu Bum and Shaduzup were blocked or ambushed, the battalion turned south-west with the intention of blocking the road near Warazup. On the 28th it surprised the Japanese occupying two camps on the road and, having put them to flight, established a roadblock. This was heavily counter-attacked the same afternoon but, with 22nd Division resuming its attacks from the north with a fresh regiment, the enemy withdrew on the 29th March. Shaduzup was occupied and 22nd Division made contact with 113th Regiment,

---

[1] Romanus and Sunderland, pages 176–77.

which by that time had taken over the roadblock from the Marauders. Entry into the Mogaung valley had been secured.

When the Marauders' 2nd and 3rd Battalions forming the second outflanking column moved off on the 12th March, they were not followed up by a Chinese regiment as planned. On the 18th, Stilwell ordered the column to halt and block the approaches to the Tanai River valley from the south in the vicinity of Janpan. On the 22nd, however, he told Merrill that the column was to move at full speed to its original objective. Merrill ordered 2nd Battalion and a combat team from the 3rd to establish the block at Inkangahtawng, while the remainder of 3rd Battalion moved to Auche to protect the left flank. The 2nd Battalion reached the Mogaung River on the 24th. Although it was known that 1st Battalion had not yet established its block further north, the column crossed the river and attempted to seize the village, but the Japanese counter-attacked and by evening it was forced to withdraw across the river. During the action a map was captured from which it appeared that the Japanese had sent a force of some two battalions from Kamaing along the Tanai River valley to outflank the Allied forces advancing southwards along the road.[1] In the circumstances Merrill ordered 2nd Battalion to fall back on 3rd Battalion at Auche as quickly as possible. By forced marches it reached the village on the 27th, where 3rd Battalion was already in contact with the enemy.

Merrill ordered both battalions to withdraw north on the 28th: 3rd Battalion to protect the airstrip at Hsamshingyang, and 2nd Battalion to establish and hold a defensive perimeter astride the track at Nhpum Ga five miles to the south. On the afternoon of the 28th, almost before 2nd Battalion was in position at Nhpum Ga, the Japanese attacked it. By the following night they had succeeded in cutting its communications with 3rd Battalion, and on the 31st began a series of attempts to overwhelm the defenders. Meanwhile on the 29th March, Lieut.-Colonel C. N. Hunter, having replaced Merrill (who was ill) in command of the Marauders, had ordered 1st Battalion to move to Hsamshingyang and had sent 3rd Battalion two 75 mm. howitzers by air. Since 1st Battalion could not arrive before the 7th April, 3rd Battalion, together with a few Kachin Levies, was then left with the task of relieving the besieged 2nd Battalion at Nhpum Ga, which by this time was short of water. By the 4th it reached a point only 1,000 yards north of the village but was unable to make further progress. By the 8th, after an exhausting march, 1st Battalion had arrived and was ready to join the battle and an all-out attack was planned for the 9th April.

---

[1] This force consisted of a battalion of *114th Regiment* (800 strong) from Myitkyina, organized as two columns each with four infantry guns, under command of Colonel F. Maruyama. Its primary task was to protect the right flank of *18th Division*.

That night, however, Maruyama's force, the sole reserve available to *18th Division*, withdrew and returned to Myitkyina. The action at Nhpum Ga was over. The 2nd Battalion had suffered some 360 casualties and by the 9th all three Marauder battalions were worn out. Although Stilwell wrote in his diary, 'GALAHAD is O.K.[1] Hard fight at Nhpum. Cleaned out Japs and hooked up. No worry there',[2] the fact was that Merrill's Marauders, on whom he relied to carry out his plan to capture Myitkyina, had been constantly in action for seven weeks and were almost completely exhausted.

On the 6th March, before the operations to gain an entry into the Mogaung valley had begun, Mountbatten visited Stilwell's N.C.A.C. Headquarters near Taihpa Ga.[3] Stilwell asked Mountbatten to urge the Combined Chiefs of Staff to persuade the Generalissimo to allow the Yunnan armies to take the offensive, since he felt that an immediate advance would contain the Japanese *56th Division* and might divert enemy troops which would otherwise be used to oppose his advance or that of the Chindits, or to support the expected enemy offensive against IV Corps.[4] He said that, when his advance reached the Mogaung–Myitkyina area, he would require an additional Chinese division and a second American L.R.P. formation.[5]

Next day Mountbatten received the eye injury which kept him in hospital till the 14th March.[6] This and the press of events on the Central front prevented him from doing anything about Stilwell's requests till the 17th. He then asked the Chiefs of Staff if the Prime Minister and the President would urge the Generalissimo to allow the Yunnan armies to take the offensive and to provide another division for the Northern front. He also asked whether the American Chiefs of Staff would consider supplying a second L.R.P. group.

Two days later the President sent the Generalissimo a strongly-worded request that he should launch an offensive across the Salween to co-operate with Stilwell's successful advance towards Mogaung and Myitkyina. The President's telegram crossed one from the Generalissimo saying that there had recently been significant developments which might affect the prosecution of the war in the Far East. These included indications that the Japanese would shortly

---

[1] Galahad was the code name for the Marauders.

[2] Romanus and Sunderland, page 191.

[3] This visit was made at Stilwell's invitation. He had been told by Washington that he was to take action to put his relationship with Mountbatten, spoiled by his sending his own mission to Washington, on a better footing. See Chapter XI.

[4] In addition to asking the Supreme Commander to approach the Combined Chiefs of Staff, Stilwell made a similar request through C.B.I. Theatre Headquarters direct to General Marshall in Washington.

[5] Romanus and Sunderland, pages 177–78.

[6] See page 197.

launch a large-scale offensive in the Loyang area on the Hankow–Peking railway, and that the Chinese communists in north Shansi might revolt against the Chungking Government.[1]

As soon as his offensive to open the way into the Mogaung valley had been launched, Stilwell felt himself free to visit Chungking to press the Generalissimo to allot additional Chinese formations to the Northern front so that the success already gained could be exploited and Myitkyina captured. The Generalissimo not only placed 14th and 50th Chinese Divisions from the Yunnan armies at Stilwell's disposal but agreed to their being flown to Assam as soon as the necessary arrangements could be made.[2]

The Generalissimo told the President on the 27th March that 'as long as our line of defences has not been adequately strengthened it is impossible for our main forces to undertake an offence from Yunnan'.[3] He fell back on the old argument that not until the Allies began large-scale amphibious operations on the Burma coast could he launch a vigorous offensive in Burma. He made it clear, however, that he was aware of the struggle which was developing on the Assam frontier and that his decision to send two divisions to reinforce the Northern front was his contribution towards the defeat of the Japanese in Burma.

Despite this refusal, the President made a further attempt on the 3rd April to persuade the Generalissimo to launch his Yunnan armies across the Salween by pointing out that the Japanese offensive was a threat to the line of communication on which the transport of supplies to China depended. The danger was being faced and heavy fighting was in progress from the Arakan coast to the Hukawng Valley but, as the Salween front remained quiescent, the Japanese had been able to withdraw troops from there to meet Stilwell's thrust into the Mogaung valley and the threat of the L.R.P. operations in north Burma. If the enemy offensive succeeded, he said, the Japanese would then be able to deal in turn with the Northern and Yunnan fronts at their leisure. He therefore again urged the Generalissimo to take the offensive with the Yunnan armies. An advance now would succeed, since the Chinese troops were provided with American equipment and were faced with only a shell of a Japanese division. With the situation as it had now developed and with seven Japanese divisions fully engaged in north and west Burma, the Yunnan armies should not be held back on the grounds that an amphibious operation

---

[1] See Map 11, page 394.

[2] The troops of 50th Chinese Division with their personal equipment had all been flown into the Maingkwan area by the 15th April. Those of 14th Division were flown into airfields in north-eastern Assam about the same date. Neither division was therefore in any way fit for battle and the training of the troops was of a much lower standard than that of the three Chinese divisions (22nd, 30th and 38th) trained at Ramgarh.

[3] Romanus and Sunderland, page 308.

against the south Burma coast was a necessary precursor to their advance.

A few days later Chennault (14th U.S.A.A.F.) confirmed the indications given earlier by the Generalissimo and reported that he believed the Japanese were about to launch two offensives in China, one to take Changsha and the other against the Hankow–Peking railway in Honan. He pointed out the weakness of the Chinese armies and said that, as he was engaged in building up supplies for operation 'Matterhorn', he was not in a position to meet a determined Japanese air attack and at the same time give proper air support to the Chinese armies if they were attacked. Unless 14th U.S.A.A.F. could be reinforced and supplies of aviation stores and petrol greatly increased in the near future, he would be forced to inform the Generalissimo that, if the Japanese took the offensive, no effective air cover for his armies could be provided. Since aircraft had had to be diverted from Air Transport Command to meet the situation in Assam, Stilwell was unable to do anything to increase the flow of supplies to Chennault and told him that he would 'simply have to cut down on activity to the point where you can be sure of reasonable reserves for an emergency'.[1]

While the President's message of the 3rd April was under discussion by the National Military Council in Chungking, a copy of a message from General Marshall to the C.B.I. Theatre was handed to the Chinese staff. This message told Stilwell that, unless the Yunnan armies took the offensive, he was to end all lend-lease despatches to them and divert the airlift so saved to supplies for 14th U.S.A.A.F., cancel the National Aviation Corporation's contract to fly lend-lease supplies to China, and return the corporation's lend-lease aircraft to Air Transport Command. The threat to cut off supplies succeeded in doing what all requests based on strategic grounds had failed to do, and on the 14th April General Ho Ying-chin (Chinese Minister of War and Chief of Staff) placed his 'Chop' on an order giving formal approval for the Yunnan armies to cross the Salween.[2]

Meanwhile preparations for operation 'Matterhorn' had been continuing. Chennault had proposed that the four airfields needed for B.29 bombers in China should be built in the Kweilin area which was closer to Japan than the area selected north-west of Chungking. Stilwell had, however, pointed out that to place the airfields so far east would be an invitation to the Japanese to take the offensive, to meet which he would require another fifty American-trained and equipped Chinese divisions. The American Chiefs of Staff accepted Stilwell's views and ordered four airfields to be constructed in the

---

[1] Romanus and Sunderland, page 312.
[2] The Chinese offensive began on the 10th May. See Chapter XXVIII.

Chengtu area, together with four fighter airfields in the immediate neighbourhood and three others on an arc further north-east. All these were completed and ready for use by the end of April. On the 10th April, the American Chiefs of Staff, no doubt influenced by the speedy progress of the Pacific offensive, decided to send only one of the two wings of B.29 bombers to India and retain the other in reserve in the United States for deployment in the Marianas as soon as that group of islands had been seized. By the 30th April, 58th Wing began to arrive in India and by the end of May was fully deployed and ready for action at the Kharagpur base near Calcutta.

The warnings given by the Generalissimo and Chennault that the Japanese were about to take the offensive in China proved correct. By the end of 1943 *Imperial General Headquarters* had decided to under-take an offensive in China with the objects of crushing the will of the Chinese people to resist, opening up an overland supply route to *Southern Army* by way of Indo-China,[1] and occupying the new Allied airfields in south-east China in order to protect shipping using the Formosa Strait and Japan itself from attacks by long-range American aircraft.[2] On the 24th January 1944, *Imperial General Headquarters* had ordered *China Expeditionary Force* (General S. Hata) to seize the south-ern portion of the Peking–Hankow railway in Honan,[3] the railways running south from Hankow to Canton and Liuchow and the Allied airfields in south-east China. They allotted Hata a number of re-inforcements from Manchuria, including *27th Division*, some artillery, engineer and transport units and three air regiments, all of which had to be returned to Manchuria by the beginning of 1945.[4]

Hata decided to divide the operation ('Ichi-Go') into two phases: the first, to capture Loyang and secure the use of the whole of the Peking–Hankow railway, which meant the clearance of Honan pro-vince between the Yellow and Yangtze Rivers; and the second, to capture in succession Changsha, Hengyang, Kweilin and Liuchow and, finally, Nanning, and the railway from Leiyang to Canton. The *12th Army* was to undertake the first phase, which was to begin in the latter half of April, assisted by *1st Army* which was to stage a diversion

---

[1] See page 99.

[2] See Map 11, page 394. These airfields were Hengyang, Lingling, Kweilin, Liuchow, Suichwan and Nanhsiung. Of these, Kweilin and Liuchow were capable of operating long-range bombers (B.29s).

[3] The control of the Peking–Hankow railway had become essential since the activities of 14th U.S.A.A.F. against shipping along the Yangtze River had made the river unreliable as a line of communication.

[4] In April 1944 *China Expeditionary Force* consisted of twenty-four divisions, one armoured division, eleven independent mixed brigades, fourteen newly-formed inde-pendent infantry brigades, and one cavalry brigade, supported by one air army. Its approximate strength was 800,000 men and some 200 aircraft.

west of Loyang.[1] The Japanese crossed the Yellow River on the 17th and two days later began moving south along the railway. Their offensive thus began only three days after the Chinese had at last agreed to launch the Yunnan armies across the Salween. By the 9th May the Peking–Hankow railway had been opened and by the 21st Loyang had been captured, thus securing the western flank.[2] Hata thereupon ordered *11th Army* to undertake the first part of the second phase of operation 'Ichi-Go' and begin its advance on the 27th May towards Changsha and Hengyang and the Allied airfields in southeast China.[3]

---

[1] The *12th Army* consisted of one armoured division (*3rd*), three divisions (*37th, 62nd* and *110th*), two independent brigades and one cavalry brigade. The *1st Army* consisted of two independent brigades and two unbrigaded battalions drawn from *26th Division*. One independent brigade from *11th Army* at Hankow co-operated by an advance northwards.

[2] This operation cost the Japanese some 3,000 casualties.

[3] The *11th Army* consisted of eight infantry divisions (*3rd, 13th, 27th, 34th, 40th, 58th, 68th* and *116th*), two independent infantry brigades and one independent infantry regiment. It was supported by *5th Air Army*.

CHAPTER XVI

THE BATTLES OF IMPHAL
AND KOHIMA
The Opening Phases
(March – April 1944)

See Maps 3, 4, 9 and 14 and Sketch 13

ON the 22nd March IV Corps was in contact with enemy forces converging on Imphal and Kohima on a 180-mile arc, stretching from Layshi in the north through Ukhrul and Tamu to Tuitum on the Tiddim road.[1] The most immediate threat, however, was from the Japanese columns approaching Sangshak, only thirty-six miles north-east of Imphal.[2] That day Scoones asked for 9th Brigade Group of 5th Indian Division, which Slim had ordered to be flown to Dimapur in accordance with the decisions reached on the 20th, to be diverted to Imphal.[3] One battalion (2nd West Yorkshire) had already reached Dimapur, but brigade headquarters and the rest of the group were landed at Imphal and Palel between the 23rd and 26th.[4] The West Yorkshires went straight to Kohima, but on the 28th, as soon as 161st Brigade (flown to Dimapur to replace 9th Brigade) began to arrive, the battalion moved by road to Imphal to rejoin its own brigade; it was the last unit to use the Imphal Road before it was cut.

The move by air of 5th Indian Division with its guns, jeeps, and mules from Arakan to the Central front, a distance of some 260 miles, was made between the 19th and 29th March. The whole operation was carried out by Dakotas of 194 (Transport) Squadron R.A.F. and twenty U.S. Commando aircraft in 760 sorties without a single mishap: no mean feat considering that the troops of the division had never before been moved by air, heavy rain had put Tulihal airfield out of action, enemy bombers with fighter escort were operating at intervals over the Imphal area, and the Palel airfield was within thirty miles of enemy forces in the Kabaw Valley.

On the 22nd, Scoones sent an operation instruction to Colonel

---

[1] See Maps 3 and 4, pages 33 and 53.
[2] See pages 203–204.
[3] See page 204.
[4] See Appendix 25.

H. U. Richards, who had just been appointed commander of the Kohima garrison. He said that two Japanese columns, each about a battalion strong, had crossed the frontier at midday on the 21st on the tracks leading from the Chindwin to Jessami and Kharasom and that a third column was at Layshi. It was his intention to keep the road open between Imphal and Kohima with 5th Division, less 161st Brigade, which was being flown to Dimapur to keep the Dimapur–Kohima road open. All troops in the Kohima area, including 1st Assam Regiment then holding the outposts at Jessami and Kharasom, were to come under Richards' command. His task was to hold Kohima and prevent the enemy from using the tracks through the area.

At 2.30 p.m. on the 22nd, just as 152nd (P.) Battalion arrived at Sangshak from the east along the track from Sheldon's Corner, an enemy column was seen approaching along the road from Ukhrul.[1] The Sangshak position was a continuous perimeter, about 600 yards long and 300 yards at its widest, shaped like an hourglass.[2] For its defence Hope-Thomson had three and a half battalions, a mortar and a mountain artillery battery and a detachment of engineers.[3] The key to the position was the north-west corner which was held by 152nd (P.) Battalion. The large number of pack mules with the brigade caused congestion within the perimeter and gave rise to a serious administrative problem during the action, since the two main water points were outside the perimeter and so could not always be used and it was impossible to dispose of the bodies of the mules killed.

The Japanese column approaching Sangshak was the leading battalion of the left column of *31st Division* which, under the command of Major-General Miyazaki, had been directed on Kohima by way of Mao.[4] On reaching Ukhrul on the 21st, Miyazaki heard that a British force was east of Sangshak astride the track which, until the Imphal–Tamu road could be cleared, constituted the only good line of communication to the Chindwin. Considering that it would be dangerous to continue his advance, leaving a strong British force astride his communications, he decided, despite the fact that it was in an area allotted to *15th Division*, to turn south and destroy it. At 4 p.m. *II/58th Battalion* unsuccessfully attacked a covering position north-west of the perimeter. A second attack in greater strength after dark broke through and it was not till about dawn on the 23rd that

---

[1] See Map 9, page 374, and page 204.
[2] See Sketch 13, page 346.
[3] The 152nd and 153rd (P.) Battalions, 4/5th Mahrattas, half the Kalibahadur Regiment (Nepalese), 15th Mountain and 583rd Mortar Batteries, a detachment of 4th Field Company and a field ambulance.
[4] See Map 4, page 53, and Appendix 20.

30. Lieut.-General
G. A. P. Scoones.

31. Major-General D. T. Cowan.

32. Major-General
D. D. Gracey.

33. Major-General
O. L. Roberts.

34. Lieut.-General
M. G. N. Stopford.

35. Major-General
J. M. L. Grover.

36. The Imphal Road near Nichuguard.

37. The Imphal–Ukhrul road near Litan.

38. The Tiddim road north
of the Manipur River bridge.

39. The Tiddim road blocked by
a landslide probably caused by
bombing.

Naga Village
Treasury Hill
D.I.S.
Gun Spur
Chedema
Jail Hill
Barracks Assam Rifles
Pimple

40. Kohima, looking east-north-east.

41. Kohima, looking south-west.

1. D.C.s Bungalow and tennis court.
2. Garrison Hill.
3. Kuki Piquet.
4. F.S.D. (Field Supply Depot).
5. D.I.S. (Detail Issue Section).
6. Jail Hill.
7. Road to Imphal.
8. Pimple.
9. Congress Hill.
10. G.P.T. (General Purposes Transport) Ridge.
11. Norfolk Ridge.
12. Rifle Range.
13. Two Tree Hill.
14. Jotsoma Track.
15. Pulebadze Peak (7532 ft).
16. South end of Pulebadze Ridge.
17. Top end of the Aradura Spur.
18. Japvo Peak (9890 ft).

42. Kohima, Garrison Hill after the battle.

43. Kohima, looking north-east from F.S.D.

the Japanese were ejected. There was a lull till the afternoon of the 24th, for Miyazaki waited until his column was concentrated and his artillery had arrived. Then, having ordered *I/58th Battalion* to advance on Mao, he renewed his attack at Sangshak.[1]

Fierce fighting continued for the next forty-eight hours, during which the Japanese broke into the perimeter from the north-west and overran the positions of 15th Mountain and 583rd Mortar Batteries. Attack and counter-attack continued till midday on the 26th when a determined onslaught by 153rd (P.) Battalion forced the Japanese to withdraw. Though artillery continued to harass the defenders throughout the rest of the day, it did not prevent them from reorganizing and replenishing their water which, for the previous three days, had been strictly rationed. During the fighting Hurricanes made a number of attempts to drop ammunition, supplies and water but, as they could not fly low enough to ensure accurate dropping within the perimeter without serious risk of damage from small arms fire, much fell outside.

At about 6 p.m. on the 26th a wireless message in clear, purporting to come from 23rd Division, was received saying: 'Fight your way out, go south then west, air and transport on lookout for you.' The message when challenged proved to be genuine, and had to be acted on without delay in case it had been intercepted by the enemy. Hope-Thomson therefore ordered the garrison to destroy its secret documents and anything of value it could not carry away, walk out of the southern face of the perimeter at 10.30 that night, move south in small parties till 6 a.m. on the 27th and then turn west towards Imphal. Each unit was to provide fifty men to help the field ambulance move the less seriously wounded; one hundred severely wounded had to be left behind. Heavy firing broke out soon after dark, under cover of which the troops carried out as much destruction as possible; they then walked out of the perimeter unmolested.

But for the lack of co-operation between the *Miyazaki Column* and the right-hand column of *15th Division* (Colonel Matsumura), 50th (P.) Brigade might have been more roughly handled than it was, for two battalions of *60th Regiment* were within striking distance of it throughout the 25th and 26th, one to the east and one to the south. The southern battalion did succeed, however, in rounding up some of the retreating parties and taking one hundred prisoners.[2] The survivors of the brigade were picked up on the Imphal–Yaingangpokpi road by the awaiting motor transport; the parachute units were taken to Imphal to be reformed, 4/5th Mahrattas was taken to

---

[1] The centre column of *15th Division* was preparing to attack Litan at this time.

[2] During the Sangshak action 50th (P.) Brigade lost 600 men of whom 400, including the 100 seriously wounded left behind and the 100 captured by *60th Regiment*, were missing. The Japanese state that out of a total strength of 2,180 men in the *Miyazaki Column* they lost 580, of whom 220 were killed.

Wangjing to rejoin 23rd Division and detachments were returned to their own units.[1]

On the 27th, Headquarters 5th Division (Briggs) took over operational control of the area north and north-east of Imphal from 23rd Division, with 123rd Brigade (Evans) on the Ukhrul road in the Yaingangpokpi area and 9th Brigade (Salomons) on its left holding Nungshigum Hill (Point 3833) and Kanglatongbi. When on the same day heavy fighting broke out at Litan, Briggs ordered its evacuation. This was successfully carried out, covered by 2/1st Punjab who held off strong enemy attacks while all stores and administrative units were being withdrawn.[2] The stand of 50th (P.) Brigade at Sheldon's Corner and Sangshak held up the advance of the greater part of *15th Division* and the left column of *31st Division* from the 19th to 26th March, and so not only delayed the cutting of the Imphal Road,[3] but gained valuable time for the deployment of 14th Army reserves at both Imphal and Kohima.

Fifty miles to the south in the Kabaw Valley, 20th Division was, on the 22nd March, disposed in depth along the Imphal–Tamu road with 32nd Brigade (Mackenzie) in the Moreh–Tamu area, 80th Brigade (Greeves) between Kongkhang and Sibong and 100th Brigade (James) at Moreh on its way to the Tengnoupal–Shenam area.[4] That day the rearguard of 32nd Brigade south of Tamu held off attacks by tanks and infantry, enemy patrols began to harass Moreh from the north, and 80th Brigade, while getting into position in the Kongkhang area, identified *III/213th Battalion* of Yamamoto's force and *I/60th Battalion* of *15th Division* in a series of skirmishes round Chamol and Sibong.[5] Having detached most of his infantry, Yamamoto was left with only three infantry companies to protect his large force of artillery and tanks, and therefore made no further attack fearing that he might provoke a counter-attack.[6] MacKenzie was thus able to retire at leisure to the strongly prepared defensive perimeter at Moreh, taking with him all the supplies from Tamu and withdrawing the civil authorities. On finding Tamu evacuated,

---

[1] See Map 3, page 33.

[2] See page 204. During the withdrawal *51st Regiment* of *15th Division* was identified. This regiment formed the centre column of the division (see Appendix 20) which had moved on Litan by a route taking it south of Sangshak.

[3] The *I/58th Battalion* reached the Imphal Road south of Mao on the 29th and *III/67th Battalion* at Kangpokpi on the 28th. The road was actually cut on the 29th.

[4] See page 202.

[5] The *I/60th Battalion* (less one company), the left column of *15th Division*, had been transferred to the command of the right column of *33rd Division* (Yamamoto) on the 20th March.

[6] Yamamoto had detached *II/213th Battalion* (less two companies) towards Mombi and *III/213th Battalion* (the *Ito Column*, see pages 201–202) towards Chamol. He was thus left with only two companies of *II/213th* and one of *I/215th Battalion*.

Yamamoto moved forward to the southern end of the Moreh defended area but, realizing that it was far too strong to be taken by storm with the forces at his immediate disposal, was content to wait for the operations of *III/213th Battalion* to take effect.

By the 25th, the detached battalion of 100th Brigade (14th F.F. Rifles), which was withdrawing from Htinzin through the mountains to cover the Shuganu entrance to the Imphal plain, had reached Chakpi Karong. It had broken contact with the Japanese battalion which had followed it as far as Mombi and had then turned west towards the Tiddim road. The same day Headquarters 100th Brigade, with 2nd Border Regiment, moved from Moreh to Shenam, unaware that *III/213th Battalion* was making its way to the same place by a parallel route through the mountains a few miles to the south.

Next day a weak attack on the northern end of the Moreh defences was driven off, but that evening a serious situation developed on Shenam Pass when a small enemy force from *III/213th Battalion* infiltrated on to the Tengnoupal ridge and dug in at its highest point, which thereafter became known as Nippon Hill.[1] From there it threatened but did not actually cut the road over the pass. Piecemeal attacks by companies and even platoons of 2nd Border Regiment, though supported by artillery, suffered the inevitable fate of such attacks, and the enemy remained in occupation of the hill. Fortunately the rest of *III/213th Battalion* was too involved with fighting patrols of 80th Brigade some two miles to the south-east to be able to exploit the success its detachment had gained. A temporary stalemate now arose on the front of 20th Division.

On the Tiddim road, an attack by a battalion of 37th Brigade on MS 100 was halted on the 22nd while an enemy column which had cut the road at MS 96 was driven off.[2] At the same time 48th Brigade was preparing to attack the southern end of the MS 109 block near Sakawng and recapture the supply dump; 63rd Brigade and the divisional transport were just north of the Manipur River; 1/10th Gurkhas, the rearguard, was holding the Tuitum Saddle and being attacked by *214th Regiment*, supported by tanks and heavy field artillery brought up from Fort White; and 4/12th F.F. Regiment, the divisional headquarters battalion, was holding off an enemy detachment which was attempting to cut in on the road between 48th and 63rd Brigades from the east.[3]

On the 22nd, 48th Brigade (Cameron) attacked Sakawng, and though by the evening 9th Borders had made some progress it had failed to dislodge the enemy. Next day 2/5th Royal Gurkhas, led by a screen of light machine-gunners firing from the hip, drove the

---

[1] See Map 9, page 374.
[2] See Map 3, page 33.
[3] See page 201.

enemy off the high ground near Sakawng in a brilliantly executed attack, and quick exploitation by the rest of the brigade recovered the supply dump which was found to be almost intact. On the 25th, in a hard fought action, the Japanese were driven from a strong position at MS 106 and next morning patrols from 37th and 48th Brigades made contact without further fighting. Meanwhile, Colonel Sasahara (*215th Regiment*), under severe pressure from north and south and deprived of his only source of supply by the loss of the dump, had sent his divisional commander (Yanagida) a message on the 24th explaining the situation, outlining his plans to recover the lost ground, and ending with an assurance that, if necessary, he would destroy the code books and defend the roadblock to the last. The message was sent in two parts, the second of which was delivered first. Yanagida, believing the situation of *215th Regiment* to be hopeless, ordered Sasahara to withdraw to the west of the Tiddim road. The last hope of encircling and destroying 17th Division had now gone and Yanagida recommended the abandonment of the Imphal offensive. Coming at a time when success further north seemed assured, this so incensed Mutaguchi (*15th Army*) that he took steps to have Yanagida superseded in command of *33rd Division*.

While 48th Brigade fought its way north, the rearguard of 17th Division (1/10th Gurkhas) was struggling against superior forces to hold the Tuitum Saddle. From the 21st to the 25th it repelled a series of attacks, supported by tanks (four of which were destroyed) and a great weight of artillery. On the morning of the 26th, as soon as it was known that the road to Imphal was open, the rearguard received permission to withdraw. By 2 p.m. it had broken contact, crossed the Manipur River and destroyed the bridge. At the same time 63rd Brigade began to move to the supply dump, which it took over by nightfall, thus freeing 48th Brigade to consolidate its contact with 37th Brigade. Meanwhile all available transport had been loaded to capacity from the dump and the engineers had begun to prepare what was left for demolition.[1]

On the 26th March, Giffard flew to Headquarters 14th Army to confer with Slim on the steps to be taken to deal with the now menacing thrust towards IV Corps' communications. That day orders were issued for the formation of a self-contained brigade of three regular battalions and detachments of the Assam Rifles and Chin Levies, with mule and porter transport, to be known as the Lushai Brigade (Brigadier P. C. Marindin). It was to take over watch and ward from the depleted Hasforce and Barforce on the approaches to the Surma

---

[1] The 17th Division had not been short of supplies during the fighting to recapture the supply dump as there had been a successful supply drop near the Manipur bridge.

valley through the Lushai and Chin Hills from Silchar southwards.[1] In the Assam Valley, pending the arrival of a divisional or corps headquarters, operational control of the Dimapur area as far south as, but excluding, Kohima was given to 202 L. of C. Area (Major-General R. P. L. Ranking), and 1st Burma Regiment as well as 161st Brigade (then beginning to arrive at Dimapur by air) was placed under his command. On the 27th, orders were issued for 2nd British Division to be diverted from Chittagong to Assam,[2] and Tactical Headquarters XXXIII Corps to move at once to Jorhat, where it was to be joined as soon as possible by its main headquarters from India.[3] Since the diversion of 2nd Division from eastern Bengal to Assam had deprived 14th Army of a reserve which could quickly reinforce Arakan, only one brigade (33rd) of 7th Division was to be moved to Assam for the time being.

On the afternoon of the 27th, Giffard returned to Delhi and early next day, taking Stopford (XXXIII Corps) with him, Slim flew to Dimapur to study with Ranking the immediate requirements in this vital area. By this time it was evident that all land communications north of Imphal were likely to be cut in the near future and that Scoones would no longer be able to exercise effective command over Kohima. It was therefore placed under operational control of 202 L. of C. Area. It was also decided that Dimapur was to be the destination of 2nd Division and Mariani that of 23rd (L.R.P.) Brigade (then on its way to Hailakandi).[4] Both were expected to begin to arrive about the 2nd April.

While the conference at Dimapur was taking place the situation in the field was developing rapidly. On the 28th the advanced guard of *138th Regiment (31st Division)* unsuccessfully attacked 1st Assam Regiment at Kharasom and Jessami.[5] In the evening *III/67th Battalion* crossed the Imphal Road near Kangpokpi but did not block it, and the following day after dark *I/58th Battalion* (Miyazaki's advanced guard) reached Maram and established a roadblock at MS 72. During the night of the 29th/30th transport on the road was fired on and turned back, and it became evident that the road was cut.

In the Kabaw Valley, Gracey, who had been ordered by Scoones to provide a brigade as the corps reserve at Palel, issued a warning order on the 28th for 32nd Brigade to start backloading stores from Moreh at once and prepare to evacuate its defences, destroying what stores could not be moved. On Shenam Pass the struggle for Nippon

---

[1] See Map 14, page 452. For composition of the Lushai Brigade see Appendix 21.
[2] See page 201.
[3] It was on the 27th that Mountbatten received permission to keep the twenty Commando aircraft on loan from the Hump. This meant that the strain on the Assam line of communication was reduced and the move of 2nd Division became a reasonable administrative risk.
[4] See pages 183–84.
[5] See Map 4, page 53.

Hill, destined to last till mid-April, had begun.[1] On the Tiddim road preparations were being made for the withdrawal of 17th Division, with 37th and 49th Brigades under command until the Imphal plain was reached.

On the 29th, 14th Army Headquarters began to put into effect the decisions taken between the 26th and the 28th. Arrangements were also made to fly 15/11th Sikhs from airfield protection duties at Agartala to Imphal on the 30th to undertake the close defence of IV Corps Headquarters, and to fly XXXIII Corps Signals to Jorhat on the 31st. The 11th Cavalry (armoured cars) and a squadron of 45th Cavalry (light tanks) were moved to Dimapur to protect XXXIII Corps Headquarters and the line of communications in that area;[2] and air priorities were allotted for the fly-in of 33rd Brigade of 7th Division to Imphal (later changed to Dimapur) and for the remaining brigade of 2nd Division from the 10th onwards.[3]

During the last days of March and the first few of April, operations on the Tiddim and Tamu roads followed their expected course and need only a brief description. The withdrawal of 17th Division from MS 109 to the Imphal plain was to begin on the 29th March.[4] The 37th Brigade was to act as rearguard, remaining in the MS 89–82 area till the division and 49th Brigade were clear of MS 82.[5] On arrival at Churachandpur the division was to move by motor transport to the north of Imphal, 49th Brigade was to revert to the command of 23rd Division and prepare the Torbung defile for defence, while 37th Brigade fell back slowly in order to cover the embussment and the preparation of the Torbung defences, reverting to the command of its own division as soon as 17th Division had moved north to Imphal. The withdrawal was comparatively uneventful, except that a battalion of 49th Brigade had to be used to prevent an enemy detachment which appeared at Hengtam from interfering with the move.[6] The 37th Brigade remained in the MS 89–82 area till the 3rd April under constant shelling but without being attacked, and then withdrew to its covering position in the MS 41 area. On the 5th, 17th Division moved north, 63rd Brigade going to Kanglatongbi to relieve 9th Brigade of 5th Division (which then moved east to the

---

[1] See Map 9, page 374.

[2] The 11th Cavalry was moved by broad gauge railway to Siliguri, thence by road to Dhubri and river steamer to Golaghat from where it could move to its destination by road. This move took a fortnight, but put the minimum strain on the heavily loaded line of communications.

[3] The 4th Infantry Brigade and 16th Field Regiment were moved by rail from western India to Amarda Road airfield (100 miles south-west of Calcutta) and were flown to Dimapur between the 10th and 15th April. See Appendix 25.

[4] See Map 3, page 33.

[5] The 49th Brigade had only two battalions; its third (4/5th Mahrattas) had remained in the Ukhrul area. See page 195.

[6] This detachment was *II/213th Battalion* (less two companies) which had moved from the Kabaw Valley by way of Mombi. See page 238 fn.

Nungshigum area) and the rest of the division going into corps reserve at Imphal.[1] The same day Roberts (23rd Division) took over operational control of the plain south of Imphal with 37th and 49th Brigades on the Tiddim road, and 1st Brigade at Wangjing covering the approaches to the plain from the east between the Tamu and Ukhrul roads.

The withdrawal of 32nd Brigade of 20th Division from Moreh was unmolested and by the evening of the 1st April it was concentrated at Palel with a battery of field artillery and a field company under command. On the 2nd it came under the command of 23rd Division, but remained at the disposal of IV Corps as a mobile reserve. The same day 80th Brigade began its withdrawal from the Kongkhang–Sibong area to join 100th Brigade on Shenam Pass.[2] This move met with little interference, though the rearguard fought a small action near Sibong on the 3rd and 4th April. Further piecemeal attacks on Nippon Hill failed, though on the 3rd, in a company attack by 4/10th Gurkhas, a few men succeeded in reaching the summit. These failures made it evident that nothing short of a carefully planned deliberate attack with considerable artillery support would have any prospect of success. On the Ukhrul road on the 4th April, 123rd Brigade (5th Division) repulsed an attack south-west of Yaingangpokpi. Next day, on relief by 63rd Brigade at Kanglatongbi, 9th Brigade moved towards Nungshigum where the enemy appeared to be taking an interest in Point 3833, a commanding feature overlooking the plain.

The withdrawal of IV Corps to the Imphal plain in accordance with the agreed plan for the conduct of the battle had now been completed. The corps was disposed in depth and firmly dug in on all the roads and main tracks leading to the plain, on a 90-mile arc from Kanglatongbi on the Imphal Road in the north through Nungshigum, Yaingangpokpi, Wangjing, Tengnoupal and Shuganu to Torbung on the Tiddim road in the south; 17th Division was in corps reserve at Imphal, but with 63rd Brigade holding Kanglatongbi; 5th Division had 123rd Brigade at Yaingangpokpi and 9th Brigade moving to the Nungshigum area; 20th Division (80th and 100th Brigades) was on Shenam Pass; and 23rd Division was holding the Wangjing area with 1st Brigade, the Torbung area on the Tiddim road with 37th and 49th Brigades and had 32nd Brigade in corps reserve at Palel. Along the whole of this front there was only patrol contact with the enemy. On the evening of the 5th, Scoones began to regroup IV Corps in readiness to mount his counter-offensive as soon as a favourable opportunity presented itself.

---

[1] See Map 9, page 374.
[2] One battalion of 100th Brigade was guarding the division's right flank in the Shuganu–Chakpi Karong area.

On the 30th March the concentration of XXXIII Corps in the Jorhat–Dimapur area was just beginning, and 161st Brigade (Warren) had moved up to Kohima and pushed detachments forward ready to cover the evacuation of the outposts at Jessami and Kharasom where 1st Assam Regiment was under increasing pressure and threatened with disaster unless it could be quickly extricated.[1] On this day 14th Army sent Ranking (202 L. of C. Area) a written directive, which detailed his tasks in order of priority as the defence of the advanced base at Dimapur, the protection of the railway, the retention of a firm base and a mobile striking force in the Dimapur area and, lastly, the defence of Kohima. The 161st Brigade, which on no account was to split up, was to be the mobile force, and 1st Burma Regiment was to hold its firm base. Stopford, who personally handed Ranking his directive, told him that, in view of the danger of 161st Brigade being cut off from Dimapur, the defence of which was his primary task, he was to get it back as soon as possible. Ranking ordered Warren to withdraw immediately and to have two battalions of his brigade at Nichuguard by 6 p.m. on the 31st March. Warren protested since, to get back to Nichuguard in time, his forward battalions, preparing to extricate the Assam Regiment from Jessami and Kharasom, would have to abandon it to its fate and break contact in daylight. Although Ranking overruled his protest, he was perturbed about the situation, and late on the night of the 31st, by which time two battalions were back at Nichuguard, telephoned 14th Army to ask whether he could leave the rest of the brigade at Kohima. Slim, having discussed the matter with Stopford who had returned to Comilla, replied that the original plan must be adhered to and the whole brigade concentrated at Nichuguard as soon as possible. There can be no question that this precipitous withdrawal was a mistake. The 14th Army order did not call for an immediate withdrawal and, although Stopford's warning on the need for speed placed Ranking in a difficult position, he might, without departing from his instructions, have interpreted the words 'as soon as possible' more broadly.

Wireless communication with Jessami had meanwhile broken down and a message dropped by an aircraft telling the garrison to retire to Kohima had fallen into enemy hands. It was only when an officer succeeded in running the gauntlet of the encircling Japanese that the commanding officer of the Assam Regiment learned that his orders to fight it out were cancelled and he was to retire. Only about one-third of the regiment, which was to have been the mainstay of the garrison, got back to Kohima; another two hundred men eventually made their way through the mountains to Dimapur.

By the evening of the 1st April, 161st Brigade, with 1st Burma Regiment under command, had reached Nichuguard, and the

---

[1] See Map 4, page 53.

depleted and somewhat dismayed garrison of Kohima had shortened its perimeter and was digging in for dear life on the Kohima ridge, with small patrols watching the lines of approach from the south and east. Thoroughly alarmed, the civilian population was clearing out of the area; Indians were seen going down the road to Dimapur and Nagas along the tracks to the north-east. This gave rise to rumours of troops fleeing from Kohima and of Japanese columns moving along the jungle paths towards the Assam Valley. By the evening of the 2nd there were still no signs of an enemy attack. That day the first formation of 2nd Division, 5th Brigade (Brigadier V. F. S. Hawkins), began to arrive at Bokajan, ten miles north of Dimapur; XXXIII Corps Headquarters opened at Jorhat and Stopford assumed operational command of all troops in the Assam and Surma valleys and Kohima.[1]

Air support for the operations on the Central front described above was provided by 221 Group R.A.F., with headquarters at Imphal, working in close co-operation with IV Corps. With the arrival of XXXIII Corps at Jorhat early in April the group had to co-operate with both corps. The control of close support aircraft was then decentralized to small air staffs attached to each corps headquarters, and Baldwin (3rd Tactical Air Force) arranged that the group could be reinforced if necessary from squadrons in the Bengal area.[2] By the end of March the group controlled fourteen squadrons, of which nine were located on airfields in the Imphal area, the remainder being based on airfields in north Assam.[3] These comprised nine Hurricane squadrons (four of which were equipped as fighter-bombers), three Vengeance light bomber squadrons for close support of army formations, and two Spitfire fighter squadrons for air defence. There was in addition a detachment of a Beaufighter squadron for night defence.

As their air effort was switched from Arakan, the Japanese increased their air activity on the Central front. From the 10th to the 19th there were attacks on the airfields and other objectives on the Imphal plain and on two occasions Imphal itself was bombed. These attacks were usually made at low level and, though they caused little material damage, inflicted casualties particularly among the civilian population. The enemy effort did not, however, reach the same intensity as it had a month earlier in Arakan.[4]

The interception of enemy aircraft proved difficult owing to the withdrawal of the wireless observer screen covering the plain, and to the blanketing of radar by the surrounding hills. There was therefore little warning of incoming raids and interceptions were infrequent.

---

[1] For order of battle of XXXIII Corps see Appendix 21.
[2] See Map 14, page 452.
[3] For order of battle of 221 Group R.A.F. see Appendix 22.
[4] According to Japanese records the total number of sorties flown was 200.

The intensive operations during February and March by British and American long-range fighters against enemy airfields in southern Burma were now clearly beginning to take effect. From the 19th to the 24th March, except for occasional sorties by reconnaissance aircraft, all Japanese air operations on the Central front ceased since most of their aircraft were grounded for repair and maintenance. There could be no clearer proof that air superiority had passed to the Allies.

During the first half of March 221 Group's main task was the close support of 17th and 20th Divisions in the Tiddim and Tamu areas where the Japanese pressure was steadily increasing. Later in the month the group provided protection for the air supply of 17th Division and attacked enemy armour and artillery following up 17th and 20th Divisions as they retired along the Tiddim road and up the Kabaw Valley. Hurricane and Vengeance aircraft persistently harassed the enemy lines of communication between their railheads at Yeu and Wuntho and the Chindwin and all traffic on the navigable rivers, until movement by day by both land and water was virtually brought to a standstill.

During March Hurricane fighter-bombers and Vengeance dive-bombers flew some 1,475 sorties in direct support of the army in which about 400 tons of bombs were dropped. In all other operations, including some 900 patrols by defensive fighters, 221 Group flew about 4,500 sorties in the course of which sixteen aircraft were lost.

While the momentous events of the last week in March were developing, Mountbatten had been considering their impact on the future strategy for S.E.A.C., so that he could comment on the views expressed by the American Chiefs of Staff after their discussions with the Axiom Mission.[1] On the 3rd April he set out to tour his various fronts in order to consult with his commanders.

At Jorhat that morning, Slim met Stilwell who, thoroughly alarmed at the way the threat to his communications was growing, suggested postponing his offensive towards Myitkyina and placing 38th Chinese Division at Slim's disposal to restore the position in the Dimapur–Kohima area. Believing that, with the arrival of XXXIII Corps and other reinforcements, he could hold the Japanese thrust towards Dimapur and being anxious that pressure on the Japanese *18th Division* should not be relaxed, Slim insisted that Stilwell should continue his advance on Myitkyina and gave a guarantee that, if the Japanese were to succeed in infiltrating into the Assam Valley, the communications to Ledo would not be interrupted for more than ten days. He accepted Stilwell's offer to take over responsibility for the

---

[1] See pages 165–66.

communications in north-east Assam, and to send a regiment of one of the two newly-arrived Chinese divisions to protect the airfields used by Air Transport Command. He then asked Stilwell when he proposed to put into effect the plan for the capture of Myitkyina which he had disclosed in March.[1] Stilwell replied that he was proposing to do so shortly and expected to reach the town about the 20th May.

In the afternoon Mountbatten held a conference at Jorhat which was attended by all land and air commanders on the Central and Northern fronts except those of IV Corps.[2] He gave them a brief outline of the situation in regard to transport aircraft and said that until the promised reinforcements arrived everyone must do the best he could with what was available.[3] It was stated that Stilwell was taking over responsibility for the north-eastern end of the Assam Valley, and that the Silchar–Bishenpur track was to be improved as an alternative route to Imphal. Each commander then gave a brief account of the situation on his front and the events which led up to it. Slim outlined the build-up of XXXIII Corps and said that the next five to ten days would be critical. He was using the only complete brigade on the spot (161st) to protect Dimapur, but Kohima had, if possible, to be held since it would be hard to recapture and its loss would undermine Naga loyalty. He had therefore instructed Stopford to reinforce the garrison as soon as he could do so without endangering the safety of Dimapur. Stilwell said he was satisfied that the build-up of XXXIII Corps would ensure the safety of his communications and that he felt justified in continuing his offensive towards Mogaung and Myitkyina. He did not, however, tell the Supreme Commander of his plan to make a sudden dash for Myitkyina and that he hoped to capture the town by the 20th May.

It was decided that two L.R.P. brigades would operate northwards to meet the forces advancing down the Mogaung valley. Subject to Lentaigne being able to overcome the difficulties of crossing the Zibyu Taungdan escarpment, where all the passes were held by the enemy, the other two brigades would operate towards the Chindwin to disrupt the communications of the Japanese *15th Army*.[4] As there seemed little possibility of an advance by the Yunnan armies across the Salween, it was agreed that there was no prospect of an early occupation of north Burma as far south as the Bhamo–Katha area. Baldwin pointed out that, in these circumstances and with the

---

[1] See page 226.
[2] Those attending included Slim (14th Army), Stopford (XXXIII Corps) and Lentaigne (Special Force); Stilwell and Brigadier-General H. L. Boatner (N.C.A.C.); Baldwin (3rd T.A.F.) and Old (10th U.S.A.A.F.). Giffard was represented by his chief planner Brigadier E. H. W. Cobb.
[3] See pages 211–12.
[4] See Map 3, page 33.

air-raid warning system in the Imphal area withdrawn, the air ferry to China had become very vulnerable. He urged that large-scale air attacks should be made on the Japanese air force in the Rangoon area. Mountbatten agreed to this as long as they did not interfere with more urgent tasks. The conference ended with Mountbatten giving Stilwell, Slim and Baldwin a memorandum produced by the S.E.A.C. Planning Staff on the American Chiefs of Staff's proposals for future strategy and asking for their comments as soon as possible.

The 3rd April had been a comparatively quiet day but, as the conference ended, the advancing Japanese were making contact with patrols from Kohima. Within a few hours its garrison was to get the first glimpse of their columns moving in single file along the tracks from Mao and Jessami.

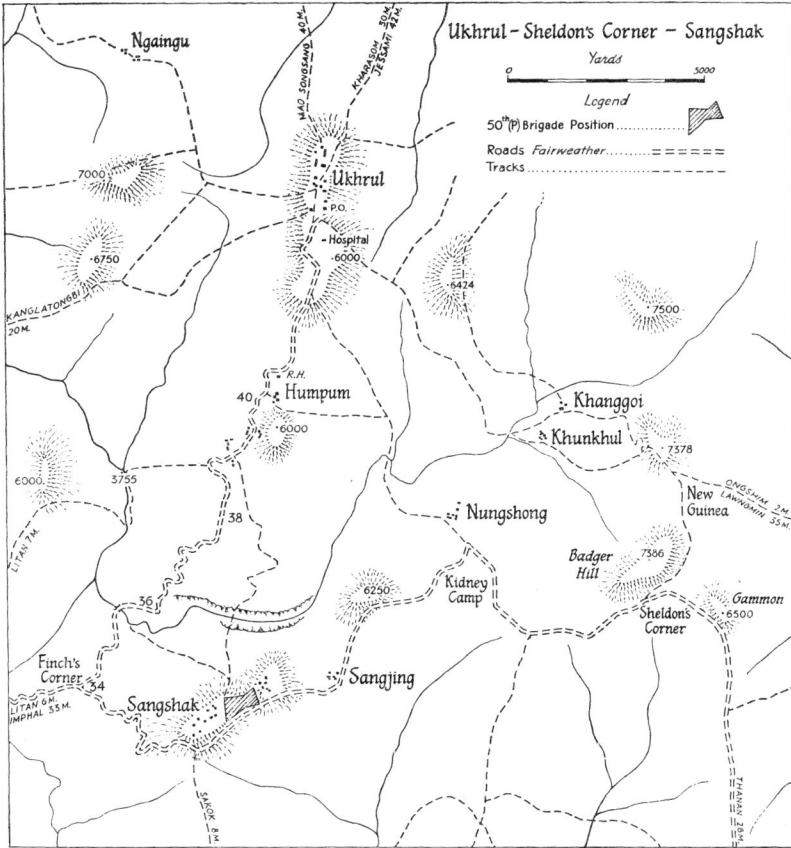

Sketch 9

Ukhrul – Sheldon's Corner – Sangshak

CHAPTER XVII

NEW DIRECTIVES FOR
SOUTH - EAST ASIA
(April–June 1944)

See Maps 13 and 15

A S soon as the conference at Jorhat ended, Mountbatten began a tour of all the battle fronts. After seeing Chinese units on the Northern front, British and American units in north-east Assam and making short stops at Jorhat, Sylhet and Imphal, he went to Comilla on the 9th April.[1] That afternoon, in conference with Slim and Lentaigne, he agreed that the decision made at Jorhat on the 3rd to use part of Special Force to disrupt the communications of *15th Army* should be cancelled and that the whole force should revert to its original primary task of assisting the advance on the Northern front.[2] After visiting the Arakan front and Calcutta, he returned to his headquarters in Delhi on the 12th and on the 14th sent his reply to the Chiefs of Staff's telegram of the 24th March.[3]

He told them that the capture of the Mogaung–Myitkyina area was already the object of Stilwell's forces from the north and four brigades of Special Force from the south, and confirmed the view he had previously expressed that IV Corps could not take the Shewbo–Monywa area before the monsoon.[4] The statement he had made in February about the capture of Myitkyina required modifying in the light of the advances made by Stilwell's forces, which were being assisted by the operations of Special Force and by the diversion of Japanese troops to the offensive on the Imphal front. It was now probable that an all-weather road across the Hukawng Valley would be completed before the monsoon to join up near Shaduzup with the existing fair-weather road to Myitkyina. He thought that Stilwell could reach Mogaung with the aid of Special Force and the two new divisions recently flown in from China, though these were not of the quality of the divisions trained in India. The capture of Myitkyina might well depend on the scale of co-operation given by the Chinese Yunnan armies; and its retention during and after the monsoon

---

[1] See Map 15 in pocket at end of volume.
[2] See pages 279–81 for the reasons for this decision.
[3] See page 166.
[4] See page 162.

would depend on the decisive defeat of the Japanese *15th Army* at
Imphal.

The acceleration of American operations in the Pacific put the
construction of a road and pipeline from India to China through
northern Burma more than ever out of step with global strategy;
neither could be completed in time to be of use in the attack on
Formosa and the China coast, and both would become unnecessary
once a sea route to China had been opened. He believed that the best
way for S.E.A.C. to help the Pacific advance would be to develop the air
route to China, so that the air forces operating from China could take
part in, and provide additional protection for, a landing on Formosa.

He had, he continued, made a preliminary examination of the
American proposals for the capture of the Mogaung–Myitkyina area
in July 1944, and the domination of north Burma down to the Katha–
Bhamo line by December 1944 or January 1945. This would require
all the aircraft promised to him, and possibly more, as well as reinforcements consisting of two divisions, a parachute brigade and an
L.R.P. brigade, all of which would have to arrive in India in the very
near future and be followed in the winter of 1944-45 by two relief
divisions. Since all his resources were fully employed in the battles
then taking place, none of these reinforcements could come from
within his command, and, even if they could be found from outside,
their maintenance might impose an impossible strain on the Assam
lines of communication. He concluded, therefore, that the American
proposals could not be implemented by the date given and that it
would be unsound even to try to complete them by a later date. The
best method of achieving the desired object would be to reoccupy
Burma by capturing the Rangoon–Prome area by a sea and airborne
operation, in order to isolate and destroy the Japanese armies in
Burma as a whole.

He understood that, if the air forces in China were to make an
effective contribution to the Formosa assault, a stockpile of some
60,000 short tons of P.O.L. would have to be accumulated on the
Chinese airfields. To achieve this he proposed that, when Myitkyina
was captured, it should be made into an oilhead served by two 4-inch
pipelines from India. Aircraft ferrying supplies to China could then
use the airfield as a staging post, and fly by the easier southern route
as well as by the direct route over the Hump. This would have the
double advantage of increasing the capacity of the air ferry from
12,500 to 14,000 tons a month and of relieving the congestion at
Kunming, since all petrol and supplies could be sent direct to forward
airfields in China by aircraft refuelling at Myitkyina.

He listed the many administrative actions which would have to be
taken to make this plan workable and forecast that, in addition to the
promised 400 aircraft which would be required to maintain his armies

in the field,[1] he would eventually need 230 long-range (C.54 or C.87) aircraft placed at his disposal. He ended,

> All the forces available to me are at present engaged in fighting on the Burmese perimeter. My aim is to seize the Mogaung-Myitkyina area with the object of developing it as an oilhead and an airbase for assisting in the movement of P.O.L. and other supplies to China. Whether this object will be achieved depends on the outcome of the battle [for Imphal].
> I propose that my directive in regard to North Burma should continue to be to develop, maintain, broaden and protect the air link to China and I shall leave no stone unturned to carry it out in the best way with all the resources at my disposal.'

On the 19th April, Mountbatten was told by Sultan that the American Chiefs of Staff now required an assurance that the 400 aircraft which they had offered could be maintained and would be used on a worthwhile mission. Mountbatten was faced with a dilemma. It seemed that the provision of the promised aircraft was to be conditional on the early preparation and approval of a plan of campaign, but he could not produce such a plan until he got his new directive, and in a telegram sent on the 17th the Chiefs of Staff had implied that this might be considerably delayed.

On the 21st April he told the Chiefs of Staff that to clear north Burma he would require all the formations in India, including 11th (E.A.) Division, then in Ceylon, 82nd (W.A.) Division, about to arrive in India, and 19th Indian Division, the only reserve at the disposal of General Headquarters, India; he could not therefore make any formations available for 'Culverin'. Since he could not produce a plan until he had some estimate of the formations which could be spared from the battle then raging around Imphal, he asked Giffard to let him have his views on the outcome of the battles at Kohima and Imphal and an estimate of the date by which a formation could be made available for operations in the Myitkyina–Mogaung area.

Giffard, replying on the 23rd April, said that, provided the enemy received no appreciable reinforcements, Slim hoped to defeat and disperse the three Japanese divisions operating west of the Chindwin with the resources at his disposal. From experience of operations elsewhere, the preliminary process of dispersing the enemy was bound to be slow and might take until the end of May, and the mopping-up of the dispersed formations would last well into the monsoon. It was possible, if operations went well, that one division could be released, at the earliest, by about mid-June. It was impossible at this stage to name a division, but, excluding the untried 11th (E.A.) Division, it would be either the 2nd, 20th or 36th. The 36th Division was most likely to be the first to become available, as it was

---

[1] See page 166.

due to leave Arakan about mid-May and would be ready for further operations by mid-July, but it would be weak owing to the shortage of British reinforcements. He warned Mountbatten that the brigades of Special Force operating in Burma would have to be withdrawn by about the end of June, though the two freshest could be left, if required, to co-operate with any Chinese or British division holding Myitkyina.

In the second half of April, while Mountbatten's telegram of the 14th was being considered in London and Washington, the Axiom Mission returned to South-East Asia, having completed its task. During the same period there was considerable direct contact between the American Chiefs of Staff and senior American officers in South-East Asia through Headquarters C.B.I. Marshall told Stilwell that, to provide the maximum aid for the proposed operations in the Pacific, a two-way all-weather road and a 4-inch pipeline would have to be driven through to China, and the tonnage carried by Air Transport Command increased to 20,000 tons a month. Myitkyina had therefore to be seized and a buffer zone created to the south so that the way for a road could be cleared. Commenting on this, Stratemeyer (Eastern Air Command) told Arnold (Commanding General, U. S. Army Air Force) that the key to any real increase in the tonnage carried by air to China was the establishment of an oilhead at Myitkyina, and that no ambitious plans in the China theatre could be made until this had been accomplished. Both Stratemeyer and Sultan reminded the American Chiefs of Staff that all plans for operations in Burma depended on a Combined Chiefs of Staff decision on strategy.

Sultan reported that there was reluctance within S.E.A.C. to support the main Pacific thrust as its primary mission, should that mean undertaking land operations in northern Burma, for these were not thought to be worth the effort. He said that he believed the Supreme Commander would advocate the expansion of the tonnage carried by Air Transport Command without any commitment of his ground forces into Burma, and that the present campaign to seize and secure the Mogaung–Myitkyina area would resolve itself into a purely Chinese–American affair unless a strong directive for the employment of British forces was issued by the Combined Chiefs of Staff. He backed this view by saying that the Chindits were to be withdrawn through the Mogaung valley, thus leaving Stilwell's right flank exposed. This report was very far from accurate, for Mountbatten had decided, after the receipt of Giffard's appreciation of the 23rd April, to allot 36th Indian Division to the Northern front to replace the Chindits when they were withdrawn.[1]

---

[1] The 36th Division began its move to Shillong on the 12th May and was concentrated there by about the 7th June. Armoured elements, beach groups and all special amphibious assault equipment were sent back to the amphibious warfare training establishment near Bombay and the division began to organize as a standard three-brigade division.

On the 3rd May the American Chiefs of Staff issued a new directive to Stilwell, in his capacity as Commanding General, China–Burma–India Theatre. In order to neutralize Japanese air action against the advance in February 1945 from the Mariana–Palau–Mindanao line to Formosa, the Pacific carrier-based aircraft were to be augmented by land-based aircraft from China.[1] Stilwell was therefore charged with the responsibility of providing air support from China against such targets as Formosa, the Ryukyu Islands, the Philippines and the China coast during the advance on Formosa. In the meantime he was to give what support he could during the attack on Mindanao in November 1944. In sending him this directive, the American Chiefs of Staff said they realized that the instructions would entail a major reduction in the tonnage carried by Air Transport Command for the support of the ground forces in China and for any other activities which did not directly assist the air effort required. The directive, with its long-term implications, made it abundantly clear to Stilwell that the early capture of Myitkyina was more than ever necessary.

On the day that Stilwell received his directive, Mountbatten was forced to remind the Chiefs of Staff that the absence of a clear-cut and up-to-date directive for S.E.A.C. was hampering initiative. They had, he said, agreed in general with his views on northern Burma and the air route to China, but it was evident that the Americans still held to the Quadrant decisions as modified at Cairo in December 1943.[2] He had now been informed that the additional aircraft necessary to carry out the operations proposed by the Americans were not likely to be forthcoming until some six to nine months after the defeat of Germany. In anticipation of any directive he might be given, he had therefore to consider what could be done without any additional resources. Assuming that nothing further would be sent to him except engineering and administrative units and material from America, and that victory in the battle for Imphal would allow of the redeployment of the forces he already had, he was preparing a plan to capture and consolidate the Mogaung–Myitkyina area by the 1st January 1945 and to construct a road and pipeline to, and establish air staging facilities at, Myitkyina. The fact that the offer of 400 transport aircraft had been made conditional on their being used 'in a manner which the American Chiefs of Staff consider more remunerative than elsewhere' must not be allowed to lead his command into undertaking operations in north Burma beyond the limits deemed advisable by the Combined Chiefs of Staff. All this emphasized the urgent need for a new directive; 'May I', he said, 'be informed as early as possible whether it is the intention of the Combined Chiefs of Staff that, as

[1] See Map 13, page 438.
[2] See pages 3 and 61.

soon as the present situation is cleared up, I should continue operations in North Burma with all my available forces and at the expense of any other operations in S.E.A.C.'

When the Prime Minister read this, he remarked that the American method of trying to force particular policies by withholding or giving certain weapons in theatres where the command belonged by right of overwhelming numbers to the British must be strongly opposed.[1]

The Chiefs of Staff had already drafted a telegram to Washington proposing that Mountbatten be issued with the directive he had himself suggested. Although the Prime Minister was in general agreement with the draft, he was still not prepared to exclude operations against Sumatra altogether. He felt he could not accept without 'searching scrutiny' the fact that India with 2,000,000 men under arms could support the equivalent of only ten divisions (200,000 men) on the Burma front, and pointed out that a return was being made to the old policy, condemned as foolish at the Trident and Quadrant Conferences,[2] of plunging about in the jungles of Burma.

The Chiefs of Staff explained that in preparing a draft directive they did not intend in any way to prejudice a major decision on strategy for the defeat of Japan: they would be quite content if words were inserted in it making it quite clear that the directive applied only to operations in Burma. They pointed out that unless a directive were sent to the Supreme Commander at an early date, an increasing number of forces would be drawn away into Burma and this would prevent any other operation in the Far East from being carried out. The Prime Minister replied that he would continue to press for operations to be undertaken which, while involving only small Allied commitments, would exhaust Japanese resources. Nevertheless, subject to words being inserted in the draft to make it quite clear that the directive was limited to operations in Burma, he was prepared to agree to a telegram being sent to Washington on the lines proposed. After months of argument a way was at last clear for the Combined Chiefs of Staff to reach agreement on the contents of a new directive for Mountbatten.

On the 9th May the Chiefs of Staff told the Joint Staff Mission in Washington that the problem was now to reconcile:

(a) The fact that land operations in Burma had to be carried out

---

[1] The Americans always insisted that requests for the assignment of equipment had to be linked with operations which had been approved. They would not agree to the earmarking of equipment for training purposes or for operations being planned but not yet approved. Although when S.E.A.C. was set up it was clearly understood that the command was to undertake amphibious operations, the Axiom Mission met with a blank refusal when it submitted the Supreme Commander's requirements for 'Culverin' and other amphibious operations for 1945 which included some landing craft to be delivered in 1944 for training the troops. The grounds for the refusal were that the operations under consideration were not approved and scheduled.

[2] See Volume II, Chapters XXIII and XXVI.

with the land and air forces now in, or earmarked for, S.E.A.C. and India.

(b) The agreed importance of getting as many supplies into China as possible, in particular for the build-up of the air force in that country.

(c) The time factor in relation to the Pacific advance, which showed that the maximum amount of supplies should be in China early in 1945.

With regard to (a), it had to be borne in mind that no additional land and air forces could be found from British sources until Germany had been defeated. This being the case, Mountbatten should not be directed to undertake operations which called for additional forces. With regard to (b) and (c), of the three possible ways of increasing the flow of P.O.L. and stores to China, the establishment of an air route direct from Calcutta to China was the best, since it did not depend on the early capture of Myitkyina and might be the only method of gaining substantial results in time for an attack on Formosa. If the capture of Myitkyina were made in time, it would provide another and better air route to China. They considered therefore that Mountbatten should be given the directive he had suggested, i.e. 'To develop, maintain, broaden and protect the air link to China in order to provide a maximum flow of P.O.L. and stores.' They would add to this, however, 'Operations to achieve this object must be dictated by the forces at present available or firmly allocated to S.E.A.C. and related in time to the Formosa operation.' Mountbatten would then be able to retain freedom of action to seize and hold Myitkyina, if he considered he could do this with the forces allotted to him. Finally, operations in Burma should have priority over any other operations in the command.

The capture of Myitkyina airfield on the 17th May came as a complete surprise to the Prime Minister and the Chiefs of Staff as well as to Mountbatten.[1] The possibility that Myitkyina itself would be captured in the very near future made it more than ever essential that the long-delayed directive should be issued. Nevertheless, it was not till the 27th that the American Chiefs of Staff replied saying they agreed with the Chiefs of Staff's views and had been considering plans for increasing the airlift to China by direct air route. It was not, however, within their capabilities to provide in time even a small number of the long-range transport aircraft needed. Hence any material increase of tonnage to China would have to come from the capture of the Mogaung–Myitkyina area. They therefore considered that the directive to Mountbatten must be so worded as to enable him to attain this; the capture of the area would in itself provide

---

[1] See page 294.

facilities for protecting an additional and lower altitude route from Assam to China. This would enable some increase in air traffic to be made even without using Myitkyina as an intermediate transport base. Subsequent operations for an advance further south into upper Burma, if feasible, would mean additional security for Myitkyina and its development as an intermediate transport base. They recognized that the gaining of either of these objectives must depend on the outcome of current operations and without any additional reinforcements, British or American, but were hopeful that continued pressure during and after the monsoon would bring the desired results.

They therefore agreed to the issue of a directive, on the lines proposed by the Chiefs of Staff, but they believed that the greatest possible air and ground effort should be made during the monsoon season: because of the enemy's exposed position and administrative situation, such operations, if pushed vigorously, might well result in a major disaster to the Japanese. If this happened, the Supreme Commander should be ready to exploit any advantage which would allow of overland communications to China being established and, in particular, of a pipeline being built. They therefore suggested an addition to the directive which would not preclude such exploitation.

By the 2nd June, the final wording of the directive was agreed, and the American Chiefs of Staff undertook to examine Stilwell's directive of the 3rd May to see whether it needed any amendment. On the 3rd June 1944, six months after it had been promised, the Combined Chiefs of Staff were at last able to send a new directive to Mountbatten; this, they said, was to be implemented forthwith. It read:

> 'To develop, maintain, broaden and protect the air link to China in order to provide maximum and timely flow of P.O.L. and stores to China in support of Pacific operations: so far as is consistent with the above to press advantages against the enemy by exerting maximum effort ground and air particularly during the current monsoon season and in pressing such advantages to be prepared to exploit the development of overland communications to China. All these operations must be dictated by the forces at present available or firmly allocated to S.E.A.C.'

CHAPTER XVIII

THE ORGANIZATION OF
SOUTH-EAST ASIA COMMAND

See Map 15

THE unsatisfactory nature of the organization of S.E.A.C. has been mentioned in Chapter IV. The point which gave rise to the greatest difficulty was the position of General Stilwell, who at one and the same time was Deputy Supreme Commander, Commanding General of all American troops in India and Chief of Staff to Generalissimo Chiang Kai-shek.[1] His presence was therefore required at S.E.A.C. Headquarters in Delhi and later Kandy, at Headquarters C.B.I. Theatre in Delhi, and at Chungking. When Stilwell decided to take charge of the operations on the Northern front himself and act as a corps commander, which demanded his continued presence at an advanced headquarters in Assam and later in the Hukawng Valley, the difficulties increased enormously.[2]

When Mountbatten visited the Northern front early in March 1944, Stilwell apologized for sending his personal mission to Washington.[3] The Supreme Commander said he was satisfied that any difficulties arising between them could be worked out provided they could maintain personal contact, but this would not be easy owing to Stilwell having to perform duties which required his presence in widely separated localities. General Marshall, to whom the difficulties arising from Stilwell's multiple appointments were subsequently referred, argued that Stilwell's prestige with the Chinese had to be maintained, and that made it difficult to remove him from any of his various offices. When asked if he could suggest a solution, Mountbatten replied that, at the Sextant Conference in Cairo in December 1943, he had told Marshall that the answer was to split the C.B.I. Theatre, placing Burma and India under Sultan or Wedemeyer and China under Stilwell, who could still remain Deputy Supreme Commander.

Later in the month Marshall told Stilwell that, as long as he considered it necessary to exercise personal command on the Northern front, he should delegate to Sultan the authority to act directly with

---

[1] See pages 45–46.
[2] See page 130.
[3] See page 229 and fn.

Mountbatten on practically all matters. Stilwell replied on the 29th that he had already delegated authority to Sultan so that action on all dealings with S.E.A.C. could be speeded up, and had given similar authority to Major-General T. G. Hearn in Chungking on all matters affecting the Chinese.[1] Neither of these two officers was restricted except in matters of established policy. There the matter rested, since Marshall felt that for the time being he could do no more.

Stilwell's delegation of authority did little to ease the situation, nor did the move in April of Mountbatten's headquarters to Kandy in Ceylon since Headquarters C.B.I. Theatre (Sultan) and 11th Army Group (Giffard) remained in Delhi, and Stilwell continued to spend the greater part of his time personally commanding operations on the Northern front.[2] The position was made much worse when, on the 13th April, Marshall sent a telegram to Stilwell on the subject of the four commando groups and four combat cargo groups which Arnold had offered S.E.A.C. on the 24th March,[3] which said,

> . . .'S.E.A.C. should realize that to furnish these air and service forces involves high cost to the United States in other operating theatres and at home. If operational requirements do not justify the necessary diversions and if logistic support cannot be provided, the allotment of these units to the theatre would be ill advised. Careful determination of the planned employment must be made by you so that we can be certain that their maximum potential capacity will be utilized.'[4]

To Mountbatten this telegram, as well as other direct communication between Washington and senior American officers under his command, appeared to make Stilwell the judge of whether his plans were adequate, and showed that the Americans were tending to view Headquarters C.B.I. Theatre as an operational as well as administrative headquarters.

It was only when the Chiefs of Staff sent Mountbatten the text of Stilwell's directive of the 3rd May and told him that they were unaware of the circumstances leading up to its issue,[5] that he realized that they were ignorant of the many direct enquiries being made by Washington to Headquarters C.B.I. Theatre about projects within S.E.A.C. still in the planning stage. He suggested that the Chiefs of Staff should be kept informed on these matters by Washington and not by him.

---

[1] Hearn was Chief of Staff U.S. Army Forces, C.B.I. Theatre, in Chungking.
[2] Giffard felt that even in Delhi he was too far from the scene of operations.
[3] See page 166.
[4] Sultan informed Mountbatten of the contents of this telegram on the 19th April. See page 251.
[5] See page 253.

By now a position had been reached which Mountbatten felt he could no longer accept. He therefore sent his Chief of Staff (General Pownall) to London to discuss it, among other things, with the Chiefs of Staff. In a letter, sent by the hand of Pownall, Mountbatten said that he was becoming increasingly embarrassed by a tendency on the part of the American Chiefs of Staff to treat with his Deputy as though, in his capacity as Commanding General of the U.S. Army Forces in the C.B.I. Theatre, he was the Supreme Commander of a theatre divorced from S.E.A.C., although the India–Burma section of that theatre was geographically identical with S.E.A.C.[1] This tendency, whether accidental or not, was inevitably being copied by the high-ranking American officers holding Allied responsibilities under his command, to the grave detriment of the integrity of that command and of Anglo-American co-operation in the theatre.

In the circumstances he found he could not properly fulfil the responsibilities with which, until recently, he had believed himself charged by the Quadrant decisions and his directive. From these he had understood that he was, with certain exceptions, in operational command of all forces in S.E.A.C., whether they were under the control of his Deputy or his Commanders-in-Chief. No mention had been made at Quadrant of the C.B.I. Theatre but only of the China Theatre and the S.E.A.C. Theatre, and it had in fact been expressly recognized in the Combined Chiefs of Staff's decision on S.E.A.C. that the rôle of his Deputy was dual and not threefold.[2]

He felt that these disruptive tendencies would increase to a dangerous extent unless the Chiefs of Staff could induce the Americans to accept that:

(a) There were only two theatres covering South-East Asia and China and only two Supreme Commanders—himself and the Generalissimo.

(b) All forces of whatever nationality in either theatre were commanded by the Supreme Commander within whose territory they were located.

(c) All communications whether from London or Washington about plans and operations of any forces of whatever nationality within S.E.A.C. must be addressed to the Supreme Commander and in no circumstances to his Deputy.

---

[1] As an example, Sultan had been under great pressure from the American Chiefs of Staff for an estimate of the practicability of providing support from China for the Pacific operations. This estimate clearly depended on the outcome of operations and future plans in S.E.A.C., but against his will Sultan had been forced to give it, including his own views on future planning for Mountbatten's forces, without awaiting consultation with Mountbatten.

[2] Section 8(a) of the decisions of the Quadrant Conference read:
'. . . General Stilwell will continue to have the same direct responsibility to Generalissimo Chiang Kai-shek as heretofore. This dual function under the Supreme Allied Commander and under the Generalissimo is recognized . . .'

(d) These provisions should also apply to the operations of the very long-range bombers (operation 'Matterhorn') from India or China.

Pownall met the Chiefs of Staff early in June and said that to simplify the complicated organization, which led to delays and misunderstandings, the first essential was to abolish the C.B.I. Theatre and have Mountbatten's four points established. At the same time Stilwell's functions should be simplified. If he were to continue as Chief of Staff to the Generalissimo, then another officer should be nominated to command N.C.A.C. and a full-time American Deputy Supreme Commander should be appointed with his headquarters at Kandy and his main administrative staff in Delhi as at present. The full-time Deputy, acting under orders of the Supreme Commander, would have administrative control of all American units in the theatre and advise as necessary on operational matters, especially from the American point of view. The American Air Transport Command, not being a fighting force, would be controlled from Washington through the Deputy Supreme Commander, or some other American officer as convenient.

The Chiefs of Staff decided to take the matter up personally with Marshall who, with the other American Chiefs of Staff, was in London in the middle of June for discussions on war policy. The interview was most unsatisfactory: Marshall, though admitting that the organization of S.E.A.C. left much to be desired, took the suggested changes as a criticism of Stilwell. He retorted that Stilwell was 'the one fighting spirit in South-East Asia', and suggested that 'the reason for his unpopularity was his efforts to galvanize less offensively minded people into activity.' In face of Marshall's attitude, the Chiefs of Staff had no alternative but to take the matter up officially through the normal inter-Allied machinery. They therefore sent a paper to the Joint Staff Mission in Washington for submission to the American Chiefs of Staff, which quoted the decisions made at Quadrant on the organization of S.E.A.C., explored the functions of the Deputy Supreme Commander and ended:

'We therefore propose that:

(a) It should be recognized that South-East Asia and China are two distinct theatres of war, and that the China–Burma–India theatre is only an administrative theatre:

(b) the appointments of Chief of Staff to the Generalissimo, Commander of the United States and Chinese Corps in North Burma, and Deputy Supreme Commander, S.E.A.C. should all be distinct;

(c) the Deputy Supreme Commander should continue to have his main administrative staff in Delhi, where he would, no doubt, require a senior officer in charge;

(d) the American Air Transport Command should be controlled from Washington through the Deputy Supreme Commander, or such other officer to whom the task is delegated.'

On the 4th July Marshall asked that the paper be temporarily shelved since another project—the appointment of Stilwell as commander of the Chinese forces in China—was afoot and this might solve the problem.[1]

Another aspect of the organization of the command arose about this time. At the Sextant Conference in Cairo in December 1943 it had been agreed that Stilwell, despite his position as Deputy Supreme Commander, would, in his capacity as Commanding General of the American and Chinese troops in N.C.A.C., place himself under the personal operational control of Slim until his forces reached Kamaing, when he would revert to Mountbatten's direct control.[2] By the middle of May 1944 Stilwell's forces were within twenty miles of Kamaing, and it was clearly only a short time before the town would be captured.

In these circumstances Giffard approached Mountbatten on the 19th and asked for information on the pattern of future operations and the chain of command so that he could issue fresh instructions to Slim governing the operations and his relationship with Stilwell. He suggested that either the existing arrangements should continue, or that Stilwell's command, which now included British troops, should be defined as another army and therefore logically come under the control of 11th Army Group, or that Stilwell should come directly under Mountbatten's command.[3] Mountbatten considered that, although it might be the best plan to leave Stilwell's forces under Slim's operational control, it would not be politically possible and that the only workable solution would be to form a new army under his own direct control, with Slim and Stilwell continuing to co-operate closely. He told Giffard on the 20th that the matter could best be settled by discussion between those most closely concerned, including the Generalissimo. He therefore arranged that Wedemeyer should go to Chungking to see Chiang Kai-shek and then consult with Stilwell, Giffard, Slim and Peirse.

Next day he received a message from Stilwell saying that after Kamaing was reached he would insist on keeping to the original agreement whereby the Yunnan armies and the forces on the Northern front would operate under his own command as Deputy

---

[1] For details of this proposal see pages 393–94.
[2] See page 47.
[3] Special Force had been placed under Stilwell's command from the 17th May. See Chapter XX.

to the Supreme Commander. 'I agreed', he said, 'to serve under Slim until we reached Kamaing because the question of rank was involved. Thereafter, I will not agree to this arrangement.' Mountbatten then told Wedemeyer that he entirely accepted Stilwell's wishes.

On the 29th May, Wedemeyer held a meeting at Calcutta with Giffard, Slim, Peirse, Sultan and Stratemeyer and told them that the Generalissimo had agreed to the Yunnan armies operating under Stilwell when they had crossed the Burma border,[1] and that Mountbatten had agreed to Stilwell's wishes. While accepting the situation, Giffard, Slim and Peirse wished it to be recorded that they considered Stilwell should be under the operational control of 11th Army Group.

In the circumstances Mountbatten had had no alternative but to accept the position that Stilwell should operate directly under him, although he knew it would be far from satisfactory: he himself had no purely operational staff, and any British troops operating under Stilwell's command had to be supplied and administered by 11th Army Group, which was the only headquarters able to do so. A conference was held to work out the necessary administrative arrangements between the C.B.I. Theatre and 11th Army Group, and, a suitable administrative *modus operandi* having been reached, the appropriate directives were issued to all concerned on the 9th June. The change of command was to become effective on the 20th.

On the advice of a committee which sat on the 9th and 12th June, and after obtaining the views of the Chief of the Imperial General Staff (through Pownall) and those of Stilwell and Slim, Mountbatten came to the conclusion that the best organization would be to turn 11th Army Group into an inter-Allied organization to control all land forces in S.E.A.C. On the 12th July he put his proposals to the Chiefs of Staff. He explained that since Stilwell, in accordance with the agreement at Cairo, had come under his direct operational control on reaching Kamaing, the command structure had become lopsided. To control Stilwell's operations directly, he would need additional operational and administrative staff and certain anomalies would arise. In dealing with Stilwell's forces in N.C.A.C. his staff would be acting parallel with 11th Army Group's in dealing with 14th Army, but would at the same time be issuing directions to the army group. The allocation of air support between Stilwell and 14th Army lay with Eastern Air Command (which was under his command), but any clash of priorities would have to be discussed with the army group as regards 14th Army and with himself as regards Stilwell's army—although he would in the end have to act as an impartial arbitrator. Finally, the allocation of British forces to

---

[1] The Yunnan offensive began on the 10th May. See Chapter XXVIII.

Stilwell raised administrative difficulties and although *ad hoc* arrangements had been made and appeared likely to work for the time being, difficulties would increase if more British forces were allocated.

He pointed out that any new system designed to avoid these difficulties would have to take into account the fact that sooner or later S.E.A.C. would have to undertake responsibilities outside Burma, such as re-entry into Sumatra, Malaya and presumably Siam and Indo-China. The organization had therefore to be framed so that when this occurred the added responsibility could be accepted with the least possible dislocation. There were three possible alternative organizations:

(a) The Supreme Commander dealing direct with 14th Army which would control Stilwell's forces in N.C.A.C. as well as its own corps, 11th Army Group being abolished and its staff divided between Supreme Headquarters and 14th Army. This organization, he thought, was unsound since it would remove the commander of 14th Army from his present close control of the battle and place on his shoulders many of the functions which had been performed up to date by the army group.

(b) The Supreme Commander controlling N.C.A.C. and 14th Army direct. This would involve the abolition of 11th Army Group Headquarters and a great increase in the Supreme Commander's operational and administrative work, making him in fact Allied Commander-in-Chief of the ground forces. Although Stilwell preferred this system, it was unsound for it would involve the Supreme Commander in far too close and detailed control of Burma and make it difficult for him to transfer control when S.E.A.C. had to undertake responsibilities outside Burma.

(c) The Supreme Commander dealing with an Allied ground force Commander-in-Chief who, with an Allied army group headquarters, would direct both N.C.A.C. and 14th Army. This system involved less reorganization than the others since 11th Army Group Headquarters would carry on, enlarged be a proportion of American officers. It would overcome the disadvantages of the existing lopsided system and would leave the Supreme Commander free of the detailed control of the fighting forces.

He therefore asked the Chiefs of Staff to agree to the introduction of the last of these three alternatives. He warned them, however, that it would be necessary to ensure that the Allied Commander-in-Chief was a man in whom both the Americans and the Chinese had confidence.

The Chiefs of Staff agreed that some form of reorganization of operational command was necessary, and said that they would discuss the matter with Mountbatten when he visited London during August to review future plans for South-East Asia.

The delay in the receipt of a long-term directive, uncertainty over resources in men and equipment likely to be available (particularly for amphibious operations) and the enemy offensives in Arakan and Assam all resulted in long- and short-term planning in the theatre becoming very much the same. In consequence the work of the War Staff at Supreme Headquarters began to impinge on that of the Commanders-in-Chief's planning staffs. The three Commanders-in-Chief therefore asked that planning be more closely integrated.

On the 11th May Mountbatten directed the War Staff and the Commanders-in-Chief's planners to work out a new system, but the two bodies failed to reach agreement. Eventually, with the unanimous agreement of his Commanders-in-Chief, Mountbatten set up an inter-Allied Joint Planning Staff (J.P.S.) which was responsible for all planning in the theatre, and contained separate sections for strategical and executive planning. A Director and Deputy Director of Plans were appointed from each of the three Services who bore separate responsibility to their own Commanders-in-Chief and, in conjunction with their colleagues, were jointly responsible, as the Joint Planning Staff, to the Supreme Commander. The J.P.S. as a whole worked at Supreme Headquarters at Kandy, but the executive planners had a section working in Delhi. Since there was henceforward no separate planning organization within Mountbatten's own staff, he received advice from his own senior staff officers on J.P.S. papers in the same way as his three Commanders-in-Chief received advice from their senior staff officers.

CHAPTER XIX

OPERATIONS IN ARAKAN
(April–July 1944)

See Maps 2, 6 and 7 and Sketch 10

EXPLOITATION after the Battle of Ngakyedauk Pass had resulted in the capture of Buthidaung by 7th Division and of Razabil by 5th Division.[1] By the 22nd March, control of the forward areas had been taken over by 26th and 36th Indian Divisions (Lomax and Festing). It had not been the intention to commit 36th Division, specially trained for amphibious operations, to inland fighting except in a reserve rôle, but Christison was authorized to do so in order to speed up the release of 5th Division for its move to the Central front. The 25th Indian Division (Major-General H. L. Davies) detailed to relieve the 5th had, on the 22nd, only one brigade in position in Arakan with another moving in. Two brigades of 5th Division had left, one of which had already reached Imphal.

The dividing line between the forward divisions of XV Corps on the main front was the spine of the Mayu Range. The 36th Division, with 3 S.S. Brigade and such troops of 25th Division as had arrived under command, was on the west of the range and 26th Division was between it and the Kalapanzin. The 114th Brigade covered the left flank east of the Kalapanzin, and the rest of 7th Division was in corps reserve under orders to follow 5th Division to the Central front. The forward troops west of the range were disposed with 5 Commando on the coastal plain at Godusara,[2] 51st Brigade (Brigadier T. H. Angus) south-east of Maungdaw facing east and south, and 74th Brigade (Brigadier J. E. Hirst) had just taken over Maungdaw from 9th Brigade, although all its battalions had not yet arrived. On the crest of the range 72nd Brigade of 36th Division (Brigadier A. R. Aslett) had relieved 161st Brigade in the West Tunnel area and 29th Brigade (Brigadier H. C. Stockwell) was in reserve in the Bawli area. The 26th Division was disposed with 4th Brigade (Lowther) facing Point 551 and the East Tunnel, 36th Brigade (Thomas) in the hills south and west of Buthidaung and 71st Brigade (Cotterell-Hill) in divisional reserve in the Awlanbyin–

---

[1] See Map 6, page 113, and Chapter X.
[2] See Map 2, page 5. The 44 Royal Marine Commando had just been withdrawn from Alethangyaw into divisional reserve.

Sinohbyin area. The 7th Division (Messervy) had 114th Brigade in close contact with the enemy at Kyaukyit and Pyinshe Kala, 33rd Brigade on both sides of the Letwedet Chaung, mopping up a very elusive Japanese force operating in the maze of low hills and tiger grass which had once formed the right bastion of the Japanese Mayu defences, and 89th Brigade preparing a new defended area near Taung Bazar for occupation during the coming monsoon, with a battalion at Sinzweya and a detachment at Goppe Bazar. In the Kaladan, 81st (W.A.) Division (Woolner) was building a Dakota strip within its defences in the Kyingri loop on the Pi Chaung, and patrols of 7/16th Punjab had reached Paletwa on the 23rd, on which day the battalion came under Woolner's command.[1]

On the 22nd March Christison issued his instructions for the operations to be carried out up to the beginning of the monsoon. Without recourse to air supply, all of which was needed for other fronts, 25th and 26th Divisions were to complete the capture of the Maungdaw–Buthidaung road and hold it during the monsoon, subject to the possibility that Buthidaung itself might be evacuated if holding it became either a tactical or administrative liability. This meant driving the Japanese from their strongholds on the Point 551 feature, the West Tunnel area and any other high ground giving observation over the road.[2] The 114th Brigade was to drive the Japanese out of the Kyaukyit area to prevent them from interfering with its withdrawal, due to take place within the next few days, and 26th Division was to be given 81st (W.A.) Reconnaissance Regiment for patrolling east of the Kalapanzin after the withdrawal of 114th Brigade.

The 36th Division and elements of 7th Division, or whichever formation relieved it, were to establish and hold a firm base until monsoon positions were taken up. This base was to include Sinzweya, Ngakyedauk Pass and the crest of the Mayu Range between it and the Tunnels, Taung Bazar, Goppe Bazar and Pass and Bawli North and South, since the retention of these areas was essential for the orderly withdrawal of surplus forces before the monsoon flooded the Mayu–Kalapanzin valley. Christison warned his divisional commanders that time was limited, for he would have to begin the withdrawal of the tanks from the Kalapanzin early in April, leaving only one squadron which would also have to be withdrawn when the heavy pre-monsoon showers began. Finally he explained that it was his intention to move 81st (W.A.) Division across the mountains from Kyingri in the Kaladan Valley to the vicinity of Taung Bazar to counter any Japanese close outflanking move.

When the monsoon positions were taken up, 25th Division was to

---

[1] See Map 7, page 278.
[2] See Map 6, page 113.

be based on Maungdaw and deployed along the axis of the Maungdaw–Buthidaung road with a battalion at Buthidaung so placed that
it could control traffic on the river, and 26th Division was to hold
Taung Bazar, Goppe Bazar, Goppe Pass and Bawli with a brigade,
leaving the bulk of the division in reserve north of the Pruma Khal.
The division sent to replace 7th Division was to remain in corps
reserve at Chittagong, and it was expected that 36th Division would
be withdrawn to India in May.[1]

On the 25th March Christison told Woolner that he was to
destroy the *Koba Detachment*[2] and then, having sent his guns and
wheeled transport away up the Kaladan Valley protected by 7/16th
Punjab and a battalion detached from his division, move to the
Kalapanzin. He was to debouch between the 20th April and 7th
May on the Saingdin Chaung and avoid any major action on the
way.[3] Woolner's first problem was to get his transport on to the jeep
track leading north to Paletwa and Satpaung, which ran eastwards
from Kaladan along the Mi Chaung for some miles before turning
north, for 'V' Force had reported that the Japanese were patrolling
the area and had sent a column towards Themawa—the point at
which he hoped to get his transport across the Kaladan. He ordered
5th (W.A.) Brigade to clear Kaladan village and push southwards
from there, and 6th Brigade to cross to the east bank of the Kaladan,
secure the crossings of the Mi Chaung between Kaladan and Ngamyinthaung and link up with 7/16th Punjab, which was to advance
south from Paletwa and clear the road between Themawa and the
Mi Chaung. Hubforce, consisting of 7/16th Punjab and 1st Gambia
under command of Lieut.-Colonel Hubert (7/16th Punjab), was
then to be formed. When the transport was clear of Themawa, 5th
Brigade was to begin its march to the Kalapanzin, followed by 6th
Brigade (less 1st Gambia). Hubert was to become responsible for the
Kaladan Valley as soon as the rearguard of the division had moved
away from the river. Heavy equipment and the wounded were to be
flown out between the 24th and 27th from the Dakota strip at Kyingri, and meanwhile every available man was to be used to improve
the track to Themawa. Kyingri was to be evacuated on the 28th.

While 114th Brigade was preparing to attack the Zadidaung-
Kyaukyit area, the Japanese abandoned the much fought over

[1] The 7th Division was not replaced. The 2nd Division was ordered to Chittagong to
replace it but was diverted to Assam (see page 241). The 11th (E.A.) Division was later
earmarked for Chittagong and began its move there in June, but it too was diverted to
Assam. See page 365.
[2] The *Koba Detachment* was believed to consist of *55th Reconnaissance Regiment, III/111th
Battalion* and a weak composite battalion.
[3] See Map 7, page 278.

Pyinshe Kala redoubt, and on the 25th Zadidaung and the low hills north and west of it were taken without much loss.[1] But at this moment a considerable Japanese force appeared once again on Point 315 near Sinzweya. The tanks were hurriedly withdrawn from 114th Brigade and sent back to Awlanbyin, and the attack on Kyaukyit was postponed. The Japanese occupation of Point 315 was, however, short lived, for 1/11th Sikhs (89th Brigade) forming the garrison of Sinzweya cleared the hill on the 26th, and after the action counted sixty enemy dead of *112th Regiment*, all with new equipment and clothing.[2]

On the 27th, it became clear that the Japanese troops facing 114th Brigade in the Kyaukyit area were changing their tactics. Fighting patrols began to appear in the hills south-east of Taung Bazar, and it seemed that the Japanese were evacuating the low ground near the river. They did not, however, abandon their strong positions at Kyaukyit. After considerable fighting, during which two tanks were disabled, the mopping-up of the Awlanbyin–Tatmakhali–Sinohbyin area was completed, and on the 28th the tanks were again placed at the disposal of 114th Brigade. A few days later Kyaukyit was taken without much difficulty.

Meanwhile on the 26th, after a series of heavy bombardments, 72nd Brigade had occupied the West Tunnel area, but, although the ground which commanded both its entrances was occupied, the enemy still held on inside the tunnel. It was not till the 4th April, when a tank succeeded in firing a shell into the west entrance which set an ammunition dump alight, that resistance ceased. Inside was a large quantity of stores and a serviceable heavy field howitzer. The known Japanese losses were sixty dead found in and around the tunnel, and it is clear that the rear party fought to the death.

By this time Davies (25th Division) had assumed command of the Maungdaw sector, and arrangements had been made for 53rd Brigade, which was just beginning to arrive, to take over the West Tunnel area from 72nd Brigade (36th Division) which was then to capture the East Tunnel in co-operation with an attempt by 4th Brigade (26th Division) to take Point 551.[3] On the 4th April, 33rd Brigade of 7th Division began to leave Sinzweya for Assam. The 114th Brigade evacuated the east bank of the Kalapanzin between the 4th and 6th, after which only patrols of 81st (W.A.) Reconnaissance Regiment remained east of the Kalapanzin, south of Taung. While the evacuation was taking place 4th Brigade made an unsuccessful attack on the north end of the Point 551 feature and

---

[1] See Map 6, page 113.
[2] Hanaya had ordered a general offensive on the 22nd. This effort by *I/112th Battalion* was the only one that made any impression.
[3] It was the loss of Point 551 in the spring of 1943 which had led to the British abandonment of the Maungdaw–Buthidaung position. See Volume II, Chapter XX.

72nd Brigade succeeded in capturing the East Tunnel, meeting with only slight opposition.

Japanese patrols were now becoming so aggressive at the southern end of the hills south of Buthidaung that Lomax decided to send forward 1st Lincolns from divisional reserve, supported by one and a half squadrons of medium tanks, to clear the area; this they succeeded in doing after a heavy airstrike and a bombardment by the whole divisional artillery. It was now becoming evident that the Japanese had lost interest in the Tunnels but intended to hold Point 551 and, if possible, regain Buthidaung.

With the capture of the Tunnels and the evacuation of the forward positions on the east bank of the Kalapanzin, the first phase of the pre-monsoon operations was completed and, on the 6th April, Christison held a conference with the commanders of 7th and 26th Divisions to decide on future operations east of the Mayu Range. They agreed not to hold Buthidaung during the monsoon but to defer fixing the date on which it was to be evacuated. Meanwhile 26th Division, supported by two regiments of medium artillery and the remaining squadron of tanks, was to capture Point 551, and 7th Division (less 33rd Brigade), while awaiting its move to the Central front, was to prepare new monsoon positions in the Taung Bazar–Goppe Bazar—Bawli area. On the 8th, 14th Army ordered 3 S.S. Brigade to move at once to Silchar.[1] Headquarters and 5 Commando left that evening, and 25th Division was ordered to release 44 Royal Marine Commando (then located south of Godusara) as soon as possible.

On the 13th, Lomax issued instructions for the deliberate attack on the Point 551 feature, where the garrison had frustrated all 4th Brigade's attempts at infiltration for ten days. The prolonged Japanese defence of this hill against superior forces was as determined as that of Sinzweya or Kohima. The hill was precipitous and 'T' shaped with the cross of the 'T' some 800 yards long, parallel to and overlooking the Tunnels–Buthidaung road, and the leg of it running due south, parallel to the main ridge, to a point nearly opposite Point 1433.[2] Point 551 itself was about 1,000 yards south along the leg. Along the cross there were five prominent but small peaks with defiladed reverse slope positions within close mutual supporting range of each other. The whole was a feature of immense natural strength and, as the Japanese had held it for nearly a year, the field defences on it were formidable. Knowing this, Lomax allotted all the artillery he had to support the attack; this comprised most of the divisional artillery, two medium regiments and two batteries of 36th Divisional artillery. In addition, one squadron of

[1] See page 302.
[2] See Sketch 10, page 274.

tanks of 25th Dragoons and one of 149th R.A.C. were available to help the attackers get on to the hill, the lower slopes of which were defiladed from much of the artillery. A diversionary attack was to be made by a battalion of 71st Brigade on features south of the road two miles to the east.

The attack went in at 8 a.m. on the 15th April after a heavy air and artillery bombardment. The 1st Wiltshire on the left succeeded in taking its objectives, the two left hand knolls, but was driven off them twice before, by the evening, it eventually consolidated one. The 2/13th F.F. Rifles was held up on a false crest short of its objective and got no further. The 2/7th Rajputs, ordered to attack features below and to the east of Point 551 itself, reached them without serious opposition. After the brigade had gained a footing on the cross of the 'T' it began to try and infiltrate southwards, with the result that fighting on the hill became continuous, attack and counter-attack following one another in rapid succession, with 4th Brigade gradually gaining ground.

Meanwhile, 25th Division had been endeavouring to assist the attack by forcing its way southwards along the apparently dominating main ridge towards Point 1433. But this had no effect whatever on the struggle for Point 551, and on the 20th Davies was ordered to give 26th Division direct assistance. Accordingly on the 25th, in co-operation with the next deliberate attack by 4th Brigade, a battalion of 25th Division (14/10th Baluch) attacked eastwards from the main ridge south-east of the West Tunnel with the object of getting on to the south end of the Point 551 ridge. In this attack 2/13th F.F. Rifles captured the three knolls which had been its objective in the earlier attack, but 1st Wiltshire made little progress, and 14/10th Baluch was stopped by well-sited positions covering the few negotiable ways up the precipitous west face of the feature. In a counter-attack supported by artillery and mortar fire on the 27th, the Japanese regained two of the three knolls taken by the 2/13th two days earlier, so that at the end of April the situation was almost the same as it had been before the attack of the 25th.

A corps instruction of the 20th April had outlined the final plan for the reorganization and distribution of forces for the monsoon, and it is interesting to note that, in a forecast of possible enemy action, Christison stated that the enemy could launch an offensive in the first week in May with three or perhaps four battalions and gave the probable objective as Maungdaw. It will be seen, as the story unfolds, that this forecast was accurate as regards intention and strength, but the objective proved to be Buthidaung. The monsoon reorganization was to be carried out in three phases. The first, from the 6th to 9th May, was to be the withdrawal of two brigades of 26th Division from the Buthidaung area, one of which was to take over the Taung Bazar–Goppe Bazar–Bawli area and the other to go into corps reserve.[1] This phase involved the evacuation of Buthidaung. The second, from the 10th to 13th May, was the consolidation of control by 25th Division of the Maungdaw–Buthidaung road as far as Point 551, and the positioning of 81st (W.A.) Division in the Taung Bazar area east of the Kalanpanzin to assist the small garrison until the arrival of the monsoon prevented any major attack on it. The inter-divisional boundary between 25th and 26th Divisions was to be an east-west line from the junction of the Ngakyedauk Chaung with the Kalanpanzin, thence westwards along the Ngakyedauk Chaung–Prein Chaung to its source and then along the track to Briasco Bridge. The change of the inter-divisional boundary from a north-south to an east-west line meant that the forward divisions would now face east instead of south. The third phase was the move into final monsoon positions, the date depending on when the monsoon began.

During the monsoon, 25th Division was to hold a firm base at Maungdaw and dispose its brigades in depth along the road from Maungdaw to Point 551. One battalion was to be at Wabyin and detachments were to hold all crossings of the spine of the Mayu Range between Point 1267 and the inter-divisional boundary. The 26th Division was to have one brigade with detachments of artillery in the Taung Bazar–Goppe Bazar–Bawli area, one brigade group at Tumbru, another at Cox's Bazar, and divisional headquarters at Ukhia. The 81st (W.A.) Division was to concentrate at Chiringa.[2] The armour was to start thinning out on the 23rd April, one squadron only remaining with 26th Division east of the Mayu Range until the evacuation of Buthidaung. After the 1st May, one troop of 25th Dragoons was to remain with 25th Division for counter-attacks but was not to be employed off an all-weather road.[3] All formations were warned that they must plan for their wheeled transport to leave the Kalapanzin valley by way of Ngakyedauk Pass because there was no guarantee that Point 551 would be taken before the monsoon broke and, until it was taken, the Maungdaw road could not be used east of the Tunnels.

Sakurai (*28th Army*) considered that it was no longer advisable to hold the Point 551 area and on the 17th April instructed Hanaya to be prepared to shorten his front to conserve his strength by falling back to the general line Seinnyinbya–Alethangyaw. Aware that

---

[1] See Map 6, page 113.
[2] See Map 2, page 5.
[3] The rest of 25th Dragoons went back to hard standings near Ukhia and all personnel except maintenance men went back to India.

there had been constant movement of British–Indian troops from front to rear in the Kalapanzin valley, Hanaya did not consider that a withdrawal was neccessary and decided to take the offensive to recapture Buthidaung. During the second half of April the Japanese attacked in the coastal plain and overran a company post near Dilpara, and in the Kalapanzin valley they captured the hill over-looking Sinohbyin. Both the lost positions were quickly recovered by counter-attacks. On the last day of April, when the first heavy pre-monsoon storm broke over Arakan, temporarily clearing the sultry air and laying the appalling dust on the tracks which had become almost unendurable, both sides were preparing to launch major attacks in early May, Hanaya against Buthidaung and Lomax in a final effort to take Point 551.

Meanwhile in the Kaladan, the positions which 6th (W.A.) Brigade had occupied at the end of March on the Mi Chaung east of Kaladan village had been under attack for some days until a counter-attack on the 7th April drove the enemy away. With the safety of the track along which the transport had to withdraw ensured, 5th (W.A.) Brigade began its move to the Kalapanzin. By the 10th, 6th Brigade was also on the move and its rearguard had taken up positions near Kaladan village.[1] Though attacked that night, it succeeded on the morning of the 11th in breaking contact and following the rest of 81st (W.A.) Division westwards. It was not, however, till the 13th that the enemy made contact with Hubforce whose rearguard was in position between Kaladan village and Themawa.[2] By this time, however, the transport was well away to the north and, finding Japanese patrols working round its flanks, Hubforce began a methodical withdrawal towards Satpaung forty miles to the north.

By the 16th April, 81st Division had gained touch with patrols from Taung Bazar at Wagai, and had established a standing patrol on the hill at Windwin. On the 22nd, patrols pushing south down the Saingdin Chaung encountered the Japanese five miles north-east of Kindaung. By the 24th, the main body of the division had concentrated at Talubya, where it remained until the end of the first week in May, when it moved to the Taung Bazar area. By the end of April Hubforce had reached Satpaung but, finding that a Japanese force was moving up the Pi Chaung pushing the Tripura Rifles before it, Hubert was forced to order a further withdrawal to Labawa to prevent his communications to Mowdok from being cut.

---

[1] See Map 7, page 278.
[2] The Japanese in the Kaladan consisted of *H.Q. 111th Regiment, III/111th Battalion* (less one company), *55th Reconnaissance Regiment* (less one company), *II/143rd Battalion* (a composite unit about 250 strong) and *Honjo Composite Unit.*

Except for the evacuation of the Satpaung–Daletme area, the operations of 81st Division and Hubforce had gone according to plan. For the next fortnight all interest was centred on the main front.

The choice of the night of the 3rd/4th May for another attempt to take Point 551 was a fortunate one, since Hanaya had by that time begun to assemble his force for his attack on Buthidaung and had withdrawn some of his outposts.[1] The 4th Brigade's attack was made by 1/8th Gurkhas and 2/7th Rajputs in place of the F.F. Rifles and Wiltshires, both of which had for more than a fortnight been clinging to their precarious foothold on the hill, now stripped of all foliage and pitted with bomb and shell craters. The attack began at 10 p.m. on the 3rd with an advance by the two battalions in seven columns of company strength, each with its own objective. The objectives were captured on the 4th, and orders were issued for 25th Division to take over the Point 551 feature the next day. This was the first step in the withdrawal of 26th Division from the Buthidaung area. At the same time 71st Brigade began to withdraw from the southern end of the ridge east of Inbauk.[2]

As the fighting on Point 551 died down, Hanaya's force, consisting of four columns under the command of Major-General Sakurai, moved into position for the attack on Buthidaung. One column about 900 strong (made up from *112th* and *143rd Regiment*) was to advance from the Inbauk area against Point 142 on the road south of Letwedet; a second, some 600 strong (*112th Regiment*), was to advance south from Sinohbyin (where during the previous four days it had twice captured and twice been driven off the hills overlooking the village) directed on the hills on the west edge of Buthidaung; a third (*I/213th Battalion*), about 450 strong, was to advance on the same objective as the second from the south of Buthidaung; while a fourth column (*III/143rd Battalion*), some 550 strong, was to hold Point 162 and converge on the same objective.

The first indication of the impending attack was the infiltration of a column, estimated at 300 strong, between 1st Lincolns and 1/18th Garhwal Rifles near Inbauk at about 9 p.m. on the night of the 3rd/4th May. This was followed at 4 a.m. on the 5th by a general attack on 71st Brigade from the south between Point 142 and Buthidaung. The attack from the north came in later in the day. There was heavy fighting throughout the 5th but, although the Japanese artillery support was on a greater scale than usual, the attack made little impression. The Japanese casualties must have

---

[1] See Map 6, page 113.
[2] The 71st Brigade had relieved the 36th in the Buthidaung sector on the 21st April. The 36th Brigade on relief moved back to the Awlanbyin–Sinohbyin-Letwedet-Tatmakhali area.

been severe because the squadron of 25th Dragoons under command of 71st Brigade caught enemy parties in the open on more than one occasion.[1] On the 6th the attack faded out, and on the 7th the evacuation of Buthidaung was carried out as planned, 71st Brigade moving north through 36th Brigade's covering position near Letwedet.

By the 8th, 71st Brigade had taken over the Taung Bazar–Goppe Bazar area from 114th Brigade, which then left for Assam.[2] During the night of the 8th/9th, 4th Brigade, which had been relieved on Point 551 by 2/2nd Punjab from 25th Division, withdrew by way of Ngakyedauk Pass to Tumbru, reporting before it left that the Japanese were still unaware that Buthidaung had been evacuated.[3] It was followed on the 11th and 12th by 36th Brigade which went to Cox's Bazar. As soon as the last troops of 36th Brigade had crossed Ngakyedauk Pass, 72nd Brigade of 36th Division evacuated Sinzweya and began to move out of Arakan to Shillong. The division's other brigade (29th) remained under command of 26th Division watching the tracks across the Mayu Range between the Tunnels and Goppe Pass until the 4th June when it too left for Shillong.

The only result of Hanaya's attack on Buthidaung was to delay its evacuation by one day. In spite of their losses in that action the Japanese decided to make one more effort, this time to recapture Point 551. The 2/2nd Punjab was having a most uncomfortable time, for the heat was intense, and as the shelling had stripped the trees bare there was no shade. Moreover, the Japanese knew exactly where the few remaining water points were, and shelled them steadily. On the 20th a determined Japanese attack just before dawn reached Point 551 itself, but an immediate counter-attack at 9 a.m. regained it. That evening it began to rain and frequent heavy pre-monsoon showers fell throughout the following week. By the 28th it was clear that the Japanese were pulling out all along the front.

Although events on the main front had gone according to plan during the second week in May, the situation in the Kaladan had begun to deteriorate. Between the 3rd and 7th, 7/16th Punjab had withdrawn to the Pi Chaung some seven miles west of Satpaung and 1st Gambia to the ridge east of Mowdok along which the India–Burma border runs. During the next few days the Tripura Rifles, retreating up the Pi Chaung, joined up with the Punjabis.[4] They were closely followed

---

[1] In the Garhwal Rifles area alone 170 Japanese dead were buried after the action.

[2] From its rest area near Bawli 114th Brigade had relieved 89th Brigade (7th Division) in the Taung–Goppe area, which had then left for Imphal on the 27th April.

[3] See Map 2, page 5.

[4] The Tripura Rifles was an Indian State Force battalion. It was equipped and trained only for internal security and reconnaissance duties.

The Tunnels and Point 551

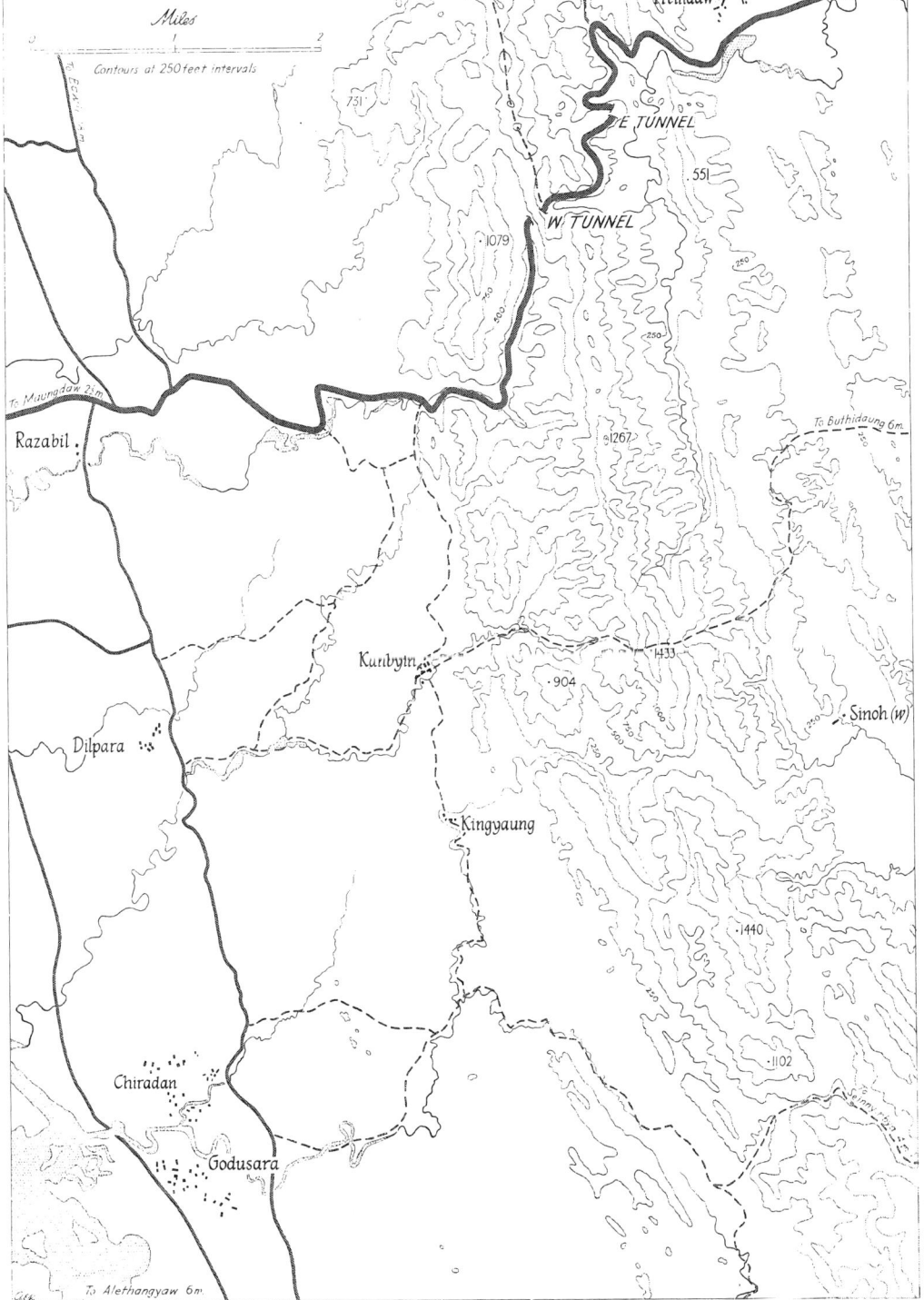

Miles

Contours at 250 feet intervals

To Buthidaung 3 m.

Htindaw

E TUNNEL

551

W. TUNNEL

1301

731

1079

To Eot...

To Maungdaw 2 m.

Razabil

1267

To Buthidaung 6 m.

Kuribyin

1433

904

Sinoh (w)

Dilpara

Kingyaung

1440

Chiradan

1102

Godusara

To Alethangyaw 6 m.

by a strong Japanese force, which immediately attacked the Punjabis. On the 14th, aware that there was a danger of the enemy interposing between his two battalions, Hubert withdrew the Punjabis to Mowdok in order to cover the village with his whole force. The Tripura Rifles, leaving small patrols on the Pi Chaung, took over the local defence of Mowdok and its supply dumps. By the 18th May, however, the situation had begun to cause anxiety, and Christison ordered Headquarters 6th (W.A.) Brigade (Brigadier R. N. Cartwright) to move at once with one battalion from the Kalapanzin to Chiringa. On arrival at Chiringa with 1st Sierra Leone Regiment, Cartwright was ordered to go to Mowdok and take command of the Kaladan force. On the 22nd the Japanese attacked the Hubforce positions covering Mowdok and gradually drove the defenders back to a close perimeter round the village.

In the meantime Headquarters 6th (W.A.) Brigade and 1st Sierra Leone Regiment, finding the track from Chiringa to the Sangu River valley flooded, had moved back to Bandarban and from there each day a company, the most the river route could take, moved up the Sangu by boat towards Mowdok. Christison's orders to Cartwright were that on arrival at Mowdok he was to ensure that at least the village, its supply dumps and communications to the Sangu at Singpa remained securely in his hands until the monsoon was fully established and the Japanese thereby forced to abandon their attacks. He was to drive the Japanese back, if possible, to the Kaladan. Six fighter aircraft were to support him. Once the monsoon had set in he was to withdraw to Bandarban and leave the Tripura Rifles to hold the Mowdok area. The operational control of the Sangu valley would then pass to Headquarters 404 L. of C. Area at Chittagong.

On the 27th Giffard sent Mountbatten an appreciation of the Arakan situation prepared by Slim with which he was in full agreement. Slim said that the withdrawal in the Kaladan had been premature but inevitable. On the main front, readjustment of positions for the monsoon had been based on the assumption that the 20th May was the latest date that tanks and medium artillery could remain in areas devoid of all-weather roads. Maungdaw was firmly established as a base, the Mayu Range to the east of it was firmly held and the road was in daily use.[1] Except perhaps for odd patrols there was no enemy north of Godusara or Point 1433. The Japanese *55th Division* was tired and understrength and there was as yet no sign of its relief by either *2nd Division* or *54th Division*, of which he believed one regiment might be on IV Corps front.[2] In the Mowdok area, 7/16th Punjab, 1st Gambia and the Tripura Rifles were opposed, he thought, by *55th Reconnaissance Regiment*, the *II/143rd*, two companies of the

---

[1] See Map 6, page 113.
[2] The *II/154th Battalion* was in the Bishenpur area of Imphal. See page 344 fn 5.

III/111th and an *I.N.A.* battalion. Headquarters 6th (W.A.) Brigade and 1st Sierra Leone were moving to reinforce Mowdok. In spite of the late arrival of rains and the reduction in XV Corps' strength, operations, except in the Kaladan, had gone according to plan and the corps held the initiative. From this report it is evident that Slim was not perturbed by the reverse in the Kaladan.

By the 1st June, Headquarters 6th (W.A.) Brigade and 1st Sierra Leone Regiment had reached Thanchi by boat from Bandarban, and Cartwright assumed command of all troops in the Sangu valley. Leaving two companies at Thanchi, the rest of the column set out for Mowdok, but at this stage a three-day downpour made the track almost impassable: the river rose in spate and no boat was safe on it. It was therefore not till the 5th that the troops reached Mowdok, although Cartwright managed to get through a day earlier. He at once took over command, and Hubforce ceased to exist. By the 6th the weather was so bad that a serious attack on Mowdok seemed to be most unlikely. Leaving the Tripura Rifles there with a large supply of rations and ammunition, Cartwright began to withdraw the rest of the force on the 7th to Thanchi, where 7/16th Punjab, followed by 1st Sierra Leone, took to boats for the move back to Bandarban. By the 11th, brigade headquarters, 1st Gambia and one company of 1st Sierra Leone were all that remained at Thanchi. On that day the Japanese drove the Tripura Rifles out of Mowdok and 1st Gambia was sent back to extricate them and take up a covering position through which they could fall back. Contact was made a few miles north of Singpa.

Christison then decided to leave a much stronger garrison in the Sangu River valley than had originally been intended. The 6th (W.A.) Brigade was to be disposed with one battalion (less a company) at Thanchi with its remaining company at Ruma, a second battalion at Bandarban and a patrol base at Alikadam supported by the remaining battalion of the brigade at Chiringa. The 7/16th Punjab was to move back to Chittagong. On the 15th June, 6th (W.A.) Brigade reverted to command of 81st (W.A.) Division, which had been withdrawn from Taung Bazar and was concentrating in the Chiringa area.

On the 24th June patrols found Mowdok deserted and the Tripura Rifles reoccupied it. The *55th Reconnaissance Regiment* and *II/143rd Battalion* had moved back to the Satpaung–Daletme area leaving a covering detachment at Labawa, while *I/29th Battalion* watched the tracks from the west to the Pi Chaung.[1]

---

[1] The *I/29th Battalion* had arrived in the Kaladan Valley late in April and both Koba and *III/111th Battalion* had returned to Akyab. With Koba's departure Colonel Sugimoto, who had relieved Kawashima in command of *55th Reconnaissance Regiment*, had assumed command in the valley. The *I/29th Battalion* was withdrawn late in July and sent to the Salween front.

The monsoon broke on the 15th June. The Sangu rose twenty feet in the night and eleven out of twelve boats loaded with stores were lost. On the Mayu front, troop movements other than patrols became impossible and even relief of forward troops could be made only with difficulty. Both sides had by that time withdrawn all but the bare minimum of troops from forward areas. And so the 1944 Arakan campaign ended with XV Corps in possession of the all-important road from Maungdaw over the Mayu Range to the vital Point 551, which overlooked the rest of the road to Buthidaung. It was the ideal position from which to launch an offensive down the Mayu valley as soon as the ground dried out sufficiently to allow movement of large bodies of troops. However, on the 14th July, Giffard recommended that any idea of an offensive in Arakan in the dry season of 1944–45 should be abandoned, since at least four divisions and possibly five would be required to ensure victory against the three divisions (*55th*, *54th* and *2nd*) available to *28th Army*. Moreover, the air force no longer needed Akyab as an advanced landing ground. He therefore advised that only enough forces should be left in Arakan to maintain an offensive-defensive there, and that the rest should be used to exploit the victory at Imphal by invading Burma. No immediate decision on this was necessary because not only was the monsoon at its height and would remain so for the next two months, but XV Corps was in a position from which it could carry out either a large scale or limited offensive as soon as movement once again became possible.

The three months of fighting to establish the monsoon positions cost XV Corps 3,362 casualties, of which more than half were in 26th Indian Division, making a total for the Arakan operations of 7,951.[1]

---

[1] See Appendix 29. The Japanese state that the strength of *55th Division* on the 4th February 1944 was 14,038, including 1,900 attached service units, and that their casualties from January to July 1944 were 3,106 killed, 100 dead of disease, 2,009 wounded and 120 missing.

Map 7
KALADAN VALLEY

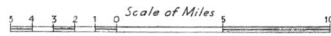

Scale of Miles

Contours at 500ft.

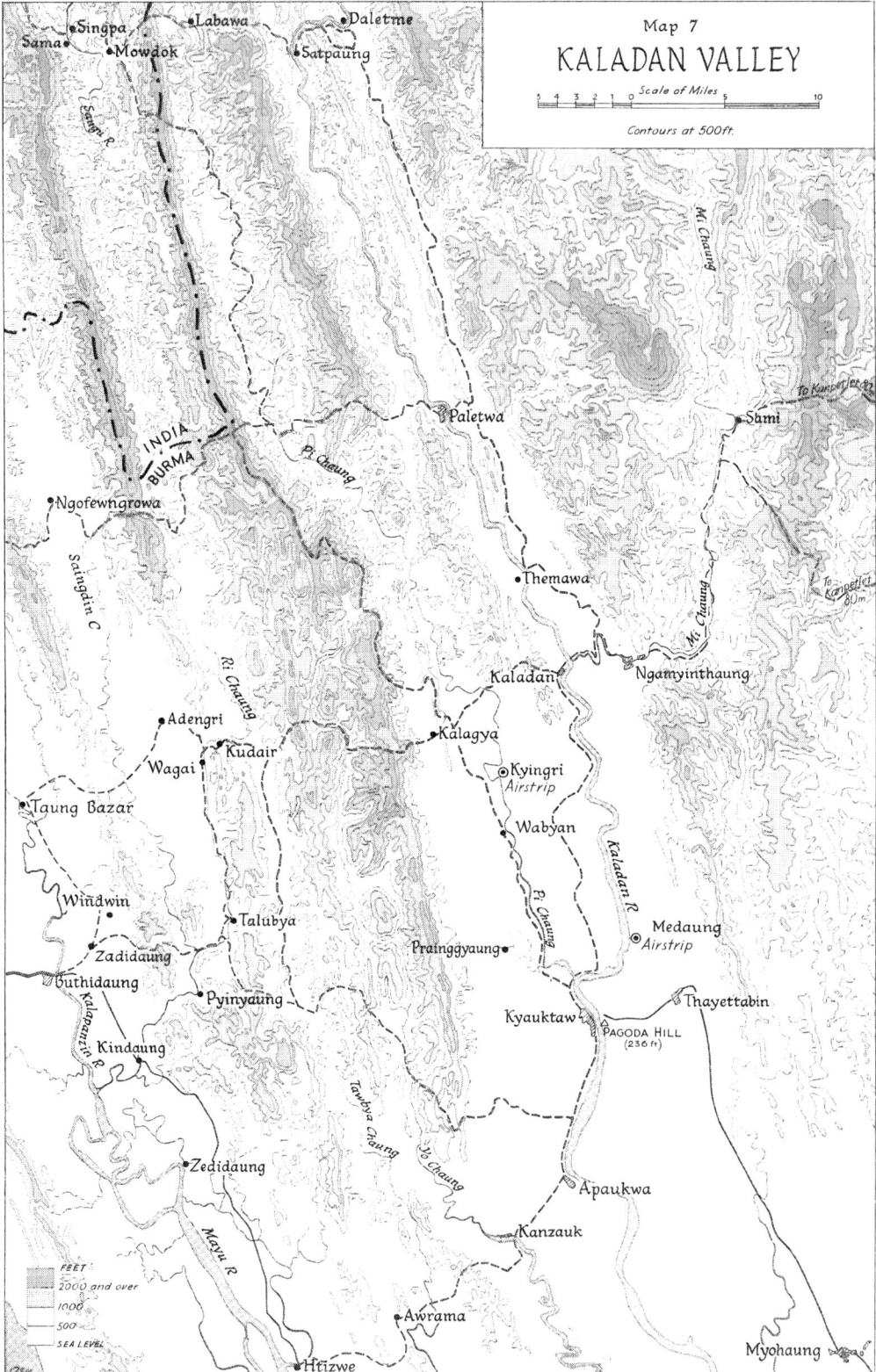

Singpa
Labawa
Daletme
Sama
Mowdok
Satpaung

Sangi R.

To Kanpetlee R.?

Paletwa
Sami

INDIA
BURMA

Pi Chaung

Ngofewngrowa

To Kanpetlet
& Um

Mi Pimwi

Mi Chaung

Saingdin C.

Themawa

Ri Chaung

Kaladan

Ngamyinthaung

Adengri
Kudair
Kalagya

Wagai

Kyingri
Airstrip

Taung Bazar

Wabyan

Kaladan R.

Windwin
Talubya

Pi Chaung

Medaung
Airstrip

Zadidaung

Prainggyaung

Buthidaung
Pyinyaung

Kyauktaw
Thayettabin

Kalapanzin R.

Kindaung

PAGODA HILL
(236 ft)

Tawbya Chaung

To Chaung

Zedidaung

Apaukwa

Mayu R.

Kanzauk

FEET
2000 and over
1000
500
SEA LEVEL

Awrama

Myohaung

Htizwe

CHAPTER XX

THE CHINDITS MOVE NORTH AND COME UNDER STILWELL'S COMMAND

(April – May 1944)

See Maps 3 and 4 and Sketches 11 and 17

AT the beginning of April Special Force was disposed with 77th (L.R.P.) Brigade (Calvert), based on 'Broadway', holding the 'White City' block and a strip of the railway to its north; 16th Brigade (Fergusson), worn out after its long march and temporarily disorganized by its failure to capture Indaw, assembling at 'Aberdeen'; and 111th (L.R.P.) Brigade (Masters),[1] based on 'Aberdeen', concentrating north of Pinlebu for operations against the Japanese communications to the Chindwin.[2] The 14th (L.R.P.) Brigade (Brodie) and 3rd (W.A.) Brigade (Brigadier A. H. Gillmore), less one battalion, were being flown into 'Aberdeen', the former under orders to operate against the road and railway serving Indaw from the south. The garrison for 'Aberdeen' was provided by 6th Nigeria Regiment and for 'Broadway' by 3/9th Gurkhas and 1st King's. Morrisforce was astride the Bhamo–Lashio road and Dahforce (Herring) was taking refuge in the Kachin Hills. The 23rd (L.R.P.) Brigade was no longer available as it had been allotted to 14th Army.[3]

On the evening of the 3rd April, after the close of the conference at Jorhat where he had been told that two of his brigades were to operate northwards in support of Stilwell's operations and two, if possible, towards the Chindwin, Lentaigne flew to 'Aberdeen' to meet and discuss the position with his brigadiers.[4] When he had described the Japanese offensive and the situation in IV Corps area around Imphal and had outlined the instructions he had received that day,[5] he asked for their views on future operations. Both Calvert

---

[1] When Lentaigne became commander Special Force, Morris was promoted to the rank of brigadier and given the command of 111th Brigade but, since he remained with Morrisforce, the actual command devolved on Masters. See page 213.

[2] See Map 3, page 33.

[3] See page 192.

[4] Fergusson, Calvert, Brodie, Gillmore and an R.A.F. representative were present.

[5] See page 247.

and Fergusson advised against any dispersion towards the Chindwin. Calvert recommended the strengthening of 'White City', the capture of Indaw and a demonstration towards Mohnyin with an eventual drive north to join up with Stilwell and open up the railway route to Mogaung before the monsoon broke. Fergusson stressed the importance of capturing Indaw and of maintaining a force in the Indaw–Katha area throughout the monsoon, as Wingate had originally intended, for he felt that the maintenance of a block in that area was the best way of assisting Stilwell.

Lentaigne himself considered that, if 23rd (L.R.P.) Brigade were placed at his disposal by the 12th April, he had a chance of taking Indaw and improving one of its existing airstrips to an all-weather standard before the monsoon broke. By staggering reliefs, it should then be possible to replace the L.R.P. brigades by normal formations and to hold Indaw throughout the monsoon. If on the other hand 23rd (L.R.P.) Brigade could not be made available, the capture of Indaw would not be feasible and it would be necessary either to construct an all-weather airstrip at 'Broadway' or 'White City', or capture an existing all-weather airfield in north Burma. The construction of an all-weather airfield at either 'Broadway' or 'White City' was in his opinion too hazardous a project to be contemplated, and in these circumstances his only course was to move north and, in co-operation with Merrill's Marauders, capture Myitkyina and its all-weather airfield.

He felt, however, that he could not decide on any plan until he knew whether he was going to be given the use of 23rd Brigade. His immediate task was to stabilize the existing position. It was clear that the Japanese, having defeated the attempt to wrest Indaw from them, were concentrating forces to make a determined attempt to overwhelm 'White City'. He therefore arranged to fly some field, anti-tank and light anti-aircraft artillery there as soon as the airstrip was ready to take Dakotas.[1] On the 6th April he ordered 3rd (W.A.) Brigade, less 6th Nigeria Regiment, to move to 'White City' and take over its defence, thus leaving Calvert free to operate outside the perimeter. To provide 'floater' columns for 'White City', he placed 45th Reconnaissance Regiment from 16th Brigade under Calvert's command and ordered Fergusson temporarily to lend 77th Brigade a second battalion (2nd Leicesters). The same day he transferred the control of Morrisforce from 77th Brigade to Force Headquarters, and ordered Morris to begin operations against the Bhamo–Myitkyina road at once.

A conference at Headquarters Special Force on the 7th April, attended by staff officers from 14th Army, agreed that any move by

---

[1] This artillery was flown in on the night of the 5th April.

L.R.P. brigades westwards towards the Chindwin would be hazardous and of little value, as it was now evident that the Japanese were
not using the lines of communication across the Zibyu Taungdan
north of Pinlebu. On the 9th, Lentaigne met Mountbatten and Slim
and they decided that the sole task of Special Force (less 23rd
Brigade being held by 14th Army for the Imphal operations) would
be to assist the advance of Stilwell's forces on the Northern front.[1]

Lentaigne had now to prepare a new plan. He felt that, with the
diversion in March of two brigades to interrupt enemy communications towards the Chindwin and the failure to take Indaw, the operations of Special Force to date had not, despite the 'White City' block,
inconvenienced the Japanese as much as had been hoped. The *18th
Division* was, he thought, making use of occasional supply columns
which were by-passing 'White City' and dumps already established
in the Mogaung area, and its fighting qualities appeared to be as good
as ever. The maintenance of his brigades in the Indaw area and the
clearance of casualties could be carried out only by Dakotas which
would need all-weather airstrips during the monsoon. Unless such an
airstrip could be captured or built before the monsoon and a fresh
formation flown in to hold it, the Indaw area would have to be given
up. There were neither sufficient aircraft to bring in materials to
build an airfield, nor, owing to the battle raging around Imphal, was
a fresh formation available. Moreover, it was evident that 'White
City' could not be held indefinitely, for its position was known and
the Japanese could easily concentrate strong forces to attack it. So he
came to the conclusion that the evacuation of the Indaw area before
the monsoon was inevitable.

If Special Force were to influence the battle for Mogaung and
Myitkyina, Lentaigne thought it would have to be moved closer to
the Northern front.[2] Such a move would have the advantage that
light aircraft could operate between the brigades and existing all-
weather airstrips in the Hukawng Valley; this would enable casualties to be evacuated and his brigades to operate during the monsoon
and to be flown out to India when exhausted.[3] Moreover, a northward move would enable him to threaten and perhaps overrun the
Japanese forward dumps of food and ammunition in the Mogaung
area. He therefore decided to establish a new block near the railway
in the Hopin area ('Blackpool') some fifty miles north of 'White City'.
The 16th Brigade, which had been longest in the field and was almost
completely exhausted, would be flown back to India, after which
'Broadway', 'Aberdeen' and 'White City' would be evacuated. He

---

[1] See page 249.
[2] See Map 4, page 53.
[3] Wingate had always stated that the maximum period for which L.R.P. brigades could
operate efficiently was three months, and had originally intended that 16th, 77th and 111th
Brigades should be relieved by his reserve brigades after that time.

would then be able to concentrate his four remaining brigades (77th, 111th, 14th and 3rd West African) for an attack on Mogaung from the south while Stilwell's forces attacked from the north. The disadvantage of the plan was that it meant abandoning the friendly Kachins to the mercy of the enemy. He felt, however, that the Japanese would be kept far too busy to go into the hills to destroy the Kachin villages, and in any case military necessity demanded the northward move.

This plan was approved in principle by Slim, who told Lentaigne to see Stilwell and get his agreement to it. The visit took place in a friendly atmosphere on the 16th April, but Stilwell urged Special Force to 'keep the front door at Indaw open' while he forced 'the garden gate at Myitkyina and Mogaung.' After the meeting, Stilwell sent a message to the Supreme Commander saying that he had been told by Lentaigne that Indaw would have to be abandoned, unless a division could be flown into the area. He expressed the opinion that, if they moved north as proposed, the Special Force brigades would bring large numbers of Japanese with them into the Mogaung area. He therefore urged that 19th Indian Division should be flown into Indaw to give him the flank protection which he had been promised. Mountbatten could not agree to this, for not only was 19th Division his only reserve, and being fully mechanized quite unsuitable for use in the rôle envisaged, but there was no possibility at the time of flying any formation into Burma.

On the 25th April, Stilwell told Mountbatten that he thought Special Force should continue to hold the Indaw area. Since it had now been ordered to withdraw northwards, he had, he said, been put into the position of having to agree. Nevertheless he would co-operate with Lentaigne and assist him to carry out the withdrawal. He made it clear, however, that he refused to be in any way responsible for the change of plan and the consequent danger to his flank south-west of Mogaung. Mountbatten then suggested that Stilwell and Slim should meet and try to settle the differences in points of view, and on the 1st May Slim, Stilwell and Lentaigne met at Maingkwan. They decided that Stilwell's objective would remain the capture of the line Mogaung–Myitkyina, but that he could not count on an additional division being flown into Burma; that Special Force would attempt to hold 'White City' until the new block ('Blackpool') had been established near Hopin, after which the remainder of the force would move north and advance on Mogaung; and that Special Force (less 16th Brigade which was to be flown out) would, after the establishment of the 'Blackpool' block, come under Stilwell's operational control, but would probably have to be withdrawn to India during the monsoon. Since Stilwell telegraphed Mountbatten after the meeting saying, '. . . I had a conference with Lentaigne and Slim and we arranged everything', it was presumed that he had accepted the new plan. A combined 14th Army and 3rd Tactical Air Force Operation Instruction was issued on the 6th giving effect to the conclusions of the conference and, on the 15th, 14th Army ordered that the command of Special Force was to pass to Stilwell on the night of the 16th/17th May.

Meanwhile it had been decided on the 7th to make plans for the evacuation of Special Force's casualties by flying-boat from Indawgyi Lake, should the monsoon break before Special Force had made physical contact with the Chinese and American forces on the Northern front. Orders were issued for the preparation of two flying-boat anchorages at the north-east and south-west corners of the lake, a main base at Calcutta, where an anchorage existed on the Hooghly, and, in order to cut down the length of the flights and speed up the evacuation of casualties, an advanced base on the Brahmaputra River near Dibrugarh.

While the future of Special Force was being settled, there had been considerable activity in the Indaw area. Calvert (77th Brigade) had at his disposal at 'White City' 3/6th Gurkha Rifles, 1st Lancashire Fusiliers and 1st South Staffordshire Regiment.[1] Knowing that the garrison was about to be reinforced, he took the risk of sending out a striking force on the 4th April, consisting of the Gurkhas and one column of the Fusiliers, to seize Kadu and reconnoitre towards Mohnyin, intending to reinforce it as soon as he could. During the next two days 12th Nigeria Regiment from 'Aberdeen' reached 'White City', and six Bofors anti-aircraft guns, four 25-pounder field guns and two anti-tank guns were flown in from India.

On the night of the 6th/7th April the Japanese began their second attempt to overcome 'White City'.[2] Preceded by a short artillery bombardment, three battalions (*I/4th, II/29th* and *139th Independent*) made a series of uncoordinated attacks on the north-east and south-east sides of the perimeter but, held up by the barbed wire entanglements, they suffered severely and withdrew. Next morning Calvert, expecting further attacks, ordered the striking force to return as quickly as possible to the vicinity of 'White City'. That night the Japanese again attacked from the same directions as before and were once again repulsed. After this second failure there was a lull of several days.

Headquarters 3rd (W.A.) Brigade and 7th Nigeria Regiment reached 'White City' from 'Aberdeen' on the 9th and next day Gillmore assumed command of the garrison. On Lentaigne's orders,

---

[1] See Map 3, page 33
[2] See Sketch 11, page 285.

Calvert then took command of the striking force and moved outside the perimeter to prepare for a counter-attack on the enemy forces concentrating against it.[1] Since Special Force had been relieved of the task of cutting enemy communications to the Chindwin, Lentaigne was able on the 10th to order 111th Brigade to destroy enemy supply dumps in the Pinbon area and prevent reinforcements from moving towards 'White City' and 'Aberdeen' from the direction of Wuntho and Pinlebu.

That evening the Japanese began their third series of attacks on 'White City'. These were made by *24th Independent Mixed Brigade* with the same three battalions as before, reinforced by *141st Independent Battalion* and supported by tanks, mortars and artillery and, on the 14th, by aircraft. The attacks displayed a complete lack of originality and were no more successful than the previous ones. All broke down on reaching the barbed wire entanglements, until, in the early hours of the 16th, *II/29th Battalion* succeeded in breaking through a gap blown in the wire and gaining a foothold within the south-east corner of the perimeter. A counter-attack shortly after dawn threw the Japanese back, and heavy air strikes the next day on their gun positions and forming-up places forced them to withdraw. As a result of the seven days of fighting around the block, in which the Japanese losses were about 700, no further attacks were made on 'White City' until its evacuation early in May.

Calvert, who had meanwhile concentrated his striking force three miles south-west of Mawlu, attempted on the 13th to occupy Mawlu and Sapein (two miles further south). Although the former was occupied without difficulty, the attack on the latter broke down, and Calvert decided to withdraw southwards to the vicinity of Tonlon with the intention of blocking all lines of communication from the south until the Japanese were forced to break off their attacks on 'White City' and turn back to attack his brigade. On the 16th, however, Gillmore appealed for help and the following day, leaving part of his forces to hold the Tonlon block and threaten Sapein, Calvert moved north with two battalions. Although at first successful, his advance was held up east of Mawlu on the 18th and, finding that he could make no further headway and was incurring heavy casualties, he withdrew to Tonlon.[2] When they found their communications cut, the Japanese, as Calvert had foreseen, decided to attack Tonlon on the 25th with three battalions (*II/29th, I/4th* and *II/4th*), supported by an artillery battalion, and *139th Independent*

---

[1] The striking force now consisted of 77th Brigade Headquarters, 3/6th Gurkha Rifles, 45th Reconnaissance Regiment, 7th Nigeria Regiment and one column of 1st Lancashire Fusiliers. The garrison remaining in 'White City' consisted of 1st South Staffordshire, 12th Nigeria Regiment and one column of 1st Lancashire Fusiliers.

[2] The 77th Brigade's casualties were about 50 in the action at Sapein on the 13th and some 250 east of Mawlu on the 18th.

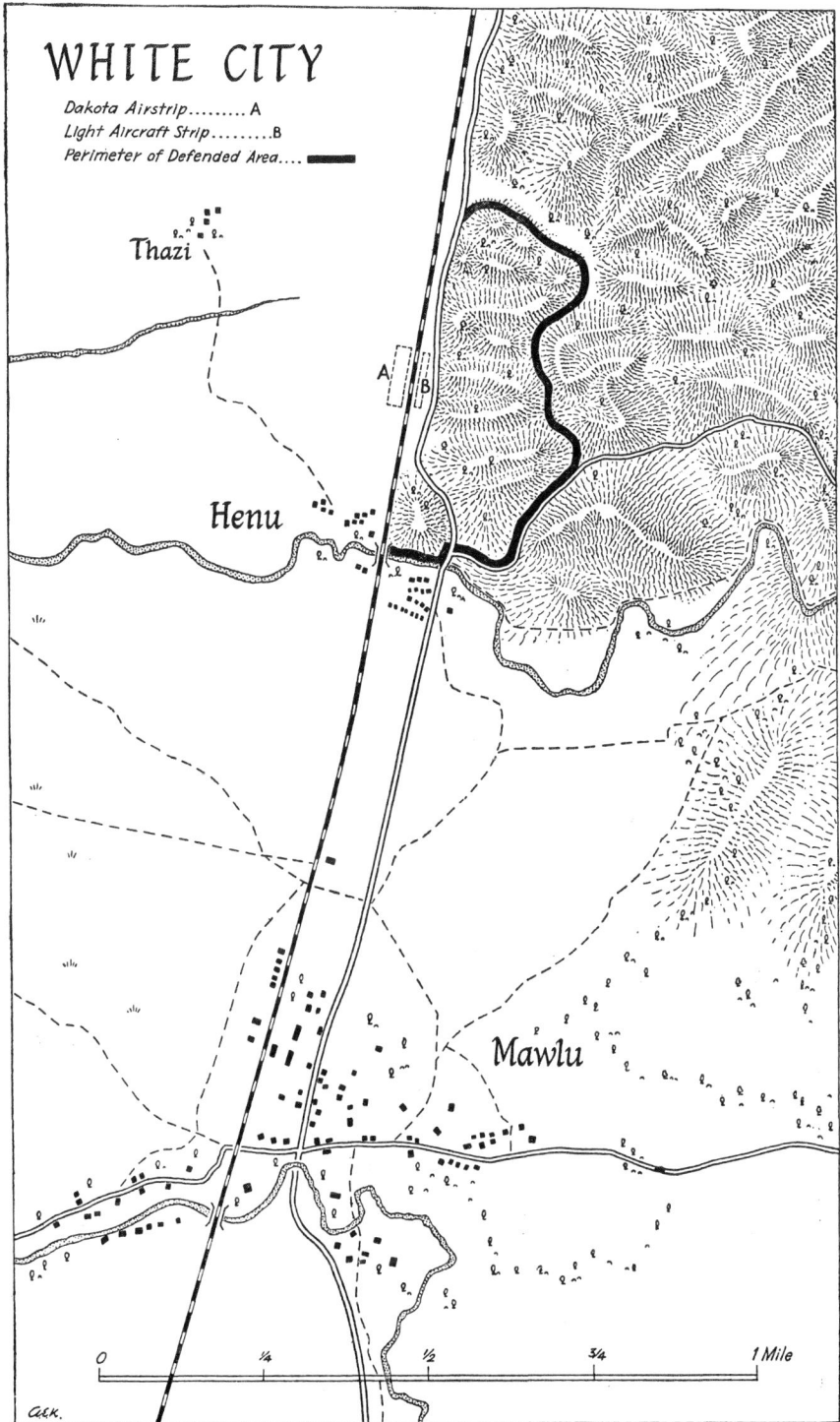

WHITE CITY

Dakota Airstrip.........A
Light Aircraft Strip.........B
Perimeter of Defended Area.... ▬▬

Thazi

A B

Henu

Mawlu

0   ¼   ½   ¾   1 Mile

a.&.k.

Battalion in reserve. The attack met with little resistance, for on the night of the 24th/25th Calvert had begun to withdraw to the Gangaw Range to the east of 'White City' in order to rest his brigade before its move to the north.

While the fighting was taking place around 'White City', 111th Brigade had destroyed several enemy supply dumps near Pinbon, 14th Brigade had demolished the main railway bridge over the Bongyaung gorge as well as several other bridges on the railway to Indaw and 2nd Leicesters from 16th Brigade had held a block on the Pinwe–Mawlu road. On the 18th, satisfied that the enemy's third attempt to reduce the 'White City' block had failed, Lentaigne decided after all to launch an attack to capture the Indaw West airfield, destroy all supply dumps in the Indaw area and inflict such damage and casualties on the Japanese that, in the event of a withdrawal to the north, their follow-up would be delayed. He therefore ordered an advance on Indaw by 16th Brigade from the north and 14th Brigade from the south, while 111th Brigade moved down the axis of the Banmauk road to protect the western flank and act as a general reserve. Between the 22nd and 27th April, 14th Brigade destroyed twenty-one dumps of supplies and ammunition, 15,000 gallons of petrol, cut the railway south of the town in sixteen places and left mines and booby traps throughout the area. The 16th Brigade occupied Indaw West airfield on the 27th without opposition to find, as Lentaigne had suspected, that the runway was neither drained, cambered nor surfaced. The brigade then wrecked all enemy installations in the area.

Further east, Morrisforce had destroyed the main road bridge over the Taping River at Myothit, captured and destroyed Nalong and several other villages in its vicinity and severely damaged the Bhamo –Myitkyina road. A Japanese battalion attacked a roadblock near Nalong on the 1st May and forced Morris to disengage and retire into the hills, but not before his force had inflicted considerable casualties. Dahforce too had been able to resume operations again in the Nahpaw area and had twice successfully ambushed enemy columns.

The future rôle of Special Force had by this time been determined and, on the 20th April, Lentaigne issued a warning order for the evacuation of 16th Brigade and the northward move of the remaining brigades; this he confirmed on the 28th. He hoped that, when 'Blackpool' had been established and the Japanese efforts to reduce it had been frustrated, at least two of his four brigades could be released to co-operate with Stilwell's forces on the Northern front. His hopes were not to be fulfilled.

The new plan was acted on without delay; 111th Brigade moved quickly north and on the 7th May occupied the area selected for the new block at 'Blackpool', two miles west of the road and railway on the bank of a small chaung five miles south-west of Pinbaw.[1] By then 16th Brigade had been flown back to India from 'Aberdeen', which had been abandoned, and its garrison (6th Nigeria Regiment) had moved north to join 111th Brigade. The 14th Brigade had meanwhile moved towards 'White City' to take up its task of protecting the block in place of 77th Brigade, which was to join up with the garrison of 'Broadway', less 1st King's, and then move north to protect 'Blackpool' from the east.[2] On the 7th the leading unit of 14th Brigade (2nd Black Watch) successfully ambushed an enemy column on a track which by-passed 'White City' on the east, and the following day blocked a track five miles south-west of Mawlu. A sharp action developed but, when the Black Watch found itself confronted by superior enemy forces, it withdrew.[3] On the evening of the 9th, when everything which could be of any use had been flown out, the 'White City' block was abandoned, four days earlier than Lentaigne had planned. Its garrison, 3rd (W.A.) Brigade (less 6th Nigeria Regiment) began to move north with 14th Brigade to protect 'Blackpool' from the west and keep open the tracks from it to Indawgyi Lake. Calvert, having time in hand, began a leisurely march towards Naungpong, where he had arranged to meet Colonel F. D. Rome after the evacuation of 'Broadway', and on the way made a successful raid on enemy posts on the road five miles north-east of Mawhan.[4] 'Broadway' was evacuated on the 13th and, when Rome joined Calvert on the 15th at Naungpong, 77th Brigade began its move to the north.

During April the Japanese had reorganized their forces in Burma. In accordance with a decision taken in January 1944,[5] *Headquarters 33rd Army* had been established at Maymyo on the 30th April, and Lieut.-General M. Honda had assumed command of *18th* and *56th Divisions* (on the Hukawng Valley and the Salween fronts respectively) and of all the forces engaged in operating against Allied airborne landings.[6] Because of the reverses suffered by *18th Division* and the situation created by the airborne landings in the Indaw area, *Southern Army* had decided on the 27th March to send its reserve

---

[1] See Map 4, page 53.

[2] The 1st King's was ordered to move north and become the 'floater' battalion of 111th Brigade.

[3] In this action, in which both sides had approximately fifty casualties, the Black Watch had come in contact with the advanced guard of *53rd Division* which was moving up towards 'White City'.

[4] Rome was second-in-command of 77th Brigade and the commander of the 'Broadway' garrison.

[5] See page 78.

[6] For Maymyo see Map 14, page 452.

division (*53rd*) to reinforce *Burma Area Army*. General Kawabe allotted this division, which had begun to arrive in Burma towards the end of April, to *33rd Army* and directed it to concentrate as quickly as possible at Indaw.

Headquarters and part of *53rd Division* reached the Indaw area early in May and the divisional commander, Lieut.-General K. Takeda, assumed command of *24th Independent Mixed Brigade, 4th Infantry Regiment, II/29th Battalion* and all other units in the area.[1] He decided to launch a further attack on 'White City' from the east and south-east on the 11th May with two regiments supported by a strong force of artillery. The evacuation of the 'White City' block on the 9th/10th instead of the 13th/14th, as originally planned, was fortunate since it might well have been overwhelmed by this very considerable force. When he learnt that the block had been abandoned, Honda ordered *53rd Division* to move up the railway in pursuit of Special Force, leaving *24th Independent Mixed Brigade* to hold the Indaw area under the direct control of *33rd Army*.[2]

Masters (111th Brigade) took the Cameronians and King's Own to garrison the new block at 'Blackpool', and left his animal transport at Mokso protected by No. 30 Column of 3/4th Gurkha Rifles. The Japanese, who had *II/146th Battalion* in the Pinbaw area, immediately reacted to the arrival of 111th Brigade. On the 7th May, the very first night of 'Blackpool's' existence, a weak enemy attack was repulsed and thereafter the garrison had to prepare its defences under sporadic small arms and artillery fire. Some American engineers with equipment were landed on the 9th by gliders, one of which was hit by small arms fire and crashed. Work on the preparation of a Dakota airstrip began immediately. It was brought into service on the 10th but proved unsatisfactory: of the first five aircraft which attempted to land on it, one crashed and two were severely damaged. Not till the 12th was it sufficiently improved to enable aircraft to use it safely. That day No. 81 Column of 1st King's from 'Broadway' arrived and was at once employed outside the perimeter to protect the airstrip, and both field and anti-aircraft artillery were flown in.

As there were no 'floater' columns operating outside the perimeter, the Japanese were free to reconnoitre the approaches to the block and establish their artillery observation posts without interference. On

---

[1] The portion of *53rd Division* which reached northern Burma in May consisted of *128th Regiment* (less *II/128th Battalion*), *I/151st Battalion*, *53rd Field Artillery Regiment* (less two battalions) and *53rd Engineer Regiment*.
[2] The *II/29th Battalion* was placed under command of *56th Division* on the 15th May to relieve *II/128th Battalion* which rejoined its regiment in *53rd Division* at Mogaung later in the month.

the night of the 14th/15th they began their first attempt to over-come 'Blackpool' with *II/146th* and *III/114th Battalions*. Heavy fighting followed, and they succeeded in gaining a foothold at the north-eastern end of the perimeter from which they were not ejected until the night of the 16th/17th. The Japanese then withdrew to a distance, and it seemed probable that 'Blackpool', like 'White City', could be held for some time.

On assuming command of Special Force on the night of the 16th/17th May, Stilwell told Lentaigne that his general plan was to close in on Mogaung from the north, south-west and south-east with 22nd and 38th Chinese Divisions and the bulk of Special Force to liquidate Japanese resistance there while retaining the base at 'Blackpool'. While awaiting the opportunity to attack Mogaung, Special Force was to undertake the active defence of 'Blackpool', maintain strong patrols on the railway to its north-east and south-west and attack any enemy forces by-passing it either on the east or west. The instruction ended, 'A reconnaissance in force, to consist of not less than 2 columns of the 77th Brigade, will move at once to develope [*sic*] enemy strength and dispositions in the Mogaung area, operating generally south and east of the railroad.'

On the night of the 17th/18th May, 77th Brigade moving north through the hills east of the railway reached Lamai, ten miles east of 'Blackpool'. Next day Lentaigne told Calvert that Myitkyina airfield had been seized and that it was vital to hold the 'Blackpool' block, and ordered him to protect it from the east and detach a battalion to carry out a reconnaissance towards Mogaung. Calvert immediately sent 3/6th Gurkha Rifles to Mansen with orders to reconnoitre towards Wajit, and directed his two other battalions to make their way down to the Namyin Chaung valley and operate against the enemy forces attacking 'Blackpool'. These battalions were delayed by the slippery state of the tracks and, when they reached the valley, were prevented by floods from assisting the garrison of the block.[1]

On the 21st, Calvert reported that the Gurkhas had ascertained that there were some 4,000 Japanese in Mogaung and that he was chary of ordering the battalion nearer the town without support. On the 24th, Lentaigne, acting on Stilwell's orders, told Calvert that the Gurkhas should attack Mogaung, withdrawing into the hills if strongly opposed, while the remainder of the brigade was directed against the enemy's line of communication around Hopin. Before the receipt of this order, Calvert, believing that 'Blackpool' could not after all be held for long, had already sent 1st South Stafford-shire north to support the Gurkhas and had begun to make

---

[1] A few patrols managed to cross the flooded chaung and attack an enemy gun position, forcing it to move.

preparations to follow with the rest of his brigade as soon as 'Blackpool' had been abandoned.

The 14th Brigade, accompanied by 3rd (W.A.) Brigade and the garrisons from 'Aberdeen' and 'White City', had already begun its move northwards through the hills west of the railway but was seriously delayed by the bad weather which had set in on the 17th. Its leading battalion (7th Leicesters) had been ordered to occupy and hold Kyusanlai Pass in order to protect the right flank of the brigades as they moved towards the Indawgyi Lake area. The Leicesters reached the pass on the 21st just in time to forestall the enemy. A struggle for the pass continued for the next five days, battalions of the two brigades being thrown in as they arrived.[1] On the 26th, by which time 'Blackpool' had been abandoned, the pass was finally secured and 14th Brigade was able to resume its northward march to the aid of 111th Brigade.

Meanwhile on the 20th May the garrison at 'Blackpool' had been reinforced by 3/9th Gurkha Rifles and No. 82 Column of 1st King's from 'Broadway'.[2] The same day the leading units of *53rd Division* reached the vicinity of Hopin and the weather suddenly deteriorated. Owing to dense cloud masses and heavy rain, neither close support air strikes nor night supply-dropping sorties could thereafter be flown. The Japanese were thus able to establish anti-aircraft and field artillery positions near the block. By the 22nd they had closed up to the edge of the airstrip, and on the afternoon of the 23rd launched their attack. Although it was repulsed, much ammunition was expended, all troops had to be withdrawn within the perimeter and the airstrip and two Bofors guns were lost. Several gallant attempts were meanwhile made by both R.A.F. and U.S. air crews to drop ammunition and supplies in face of heavy fire. On one occasion eleven out of the twelve transport aircraft employed were hit, and it was realized that not even the most determined flying could ensure the replenishment of the dwindling supplies of food and ammunition.

During the 24th, the Japanese established themselves round the southern half of the block, shelled it throughout the day and launched several attacks, all of which were repulsed though one gained a temporary foothold within the perimeter. After a night of fighting, the perimeter was again pierced at 5 a.m. on the 25th. Food supplies were by this time at an end, ammunition stocks very low and there

---

[1] The first identification of the Japanese *53rd Division* was obtained during this fighting.

[2] Just before 'Broadway' was abandoned Lentaigne ordered 3/9th Gurkha Rifles to reinforce 111th Brigade at 'Blackpool' instead of joining 77th Brigade; the battalion, together with No. 82 Column of 1st King's, began its move north on the 13th when 'Broadway' was evacuated. While crossing the railway near Hopin on its way north, No. 82 Column had become involved with an enemy formation moving north and split into two parts; one, consisting of some 150 men, was forced to move east and eventually joined 77th Brigade.

was no prospect of further supplies being dropped. When a counter-
attack failed to eject the enemy, Masters decided at 8 a.m. that he
had no option but to evacuate the block.[1] The withdrawal was successfully carried out under appalling conditions of rain and mud,
and, carrying 100 wounded with it, the brigade reached Mokso on
the 27th. The action at 'Blackpool' had cost 111th Brigade 210 and
53rd Division some 500 casualties. The Japanese were now free to
move into Mogaung and bring assistance either to their hard-pressed
garrison at Myitkyina or to *18th Division* at Kamaing, but Indawgyi
Lake, the only place from which Special Force's many casualties
could be evacuated, was secure.

The decision to abandon 'Broadway', 'Aberdeen' and 'White City',
and the movement of Special Force nearer to the Northern front were
inevitable; there was no other course open except to withdraw the
entire force to India. The block at 'Blackpool' was sited so close to
the enemy garrison at Mogaung that it was under attack from the
moment it was established, and there was no time to prepare it
properly for defence or to stock it with ammunition and supplies. If
a block so near to Mogaung were to be established, 111th Brigade
should have had support close at hand. But it seems that when the
new plan was drawn up neither the increasing difficulty of moving
along hill tracks nor the possible drastic reduction in air supply once
the monsoon had broken was fully appreciated. Torrential rain,
which made the hill tracks almost impassable, seriously delayed the
progress of the three weary brigades of Special Force which had been
ordered to protect the block. The fresh Japanese *53rd Division*, once
'White City' had been evacuated, was able to move entirely unopposed along the much shorter and easier route in the railway
corridor. The enemy was thus able to attack 'Blackpool' before 111th
Brigade could be properly supported. Without aid, and with its
ammunition and supplies running short, Masters had either to
abandon the block or be overwhelmed.

It is now necessary to turn back in time and describe the events on
the Northern front during April and May. After the Jorhat Conference, where to his relief he learned that Slim believed the Japanese
offensive could be held and the line of communications to the
Hukawng Valley secured,[2] Stilwell, already far behind his schedule,
was able to turn his full attention to the capture of Myitkyina. He
had told the American Chiefs of Staff that he could capture it with

---

[1] On the 19th, Lentaigne had given him discretion to evacuate 'Blackpool' in just such
an eventuality.
[2] See pages 246–47.

the forces at his disposal, and he was determined to prove that he was right. With the monsoon not far ahead, he felt that now was the moment to launch his long cherished plan to hold the Japanese *18th Division* in the Kamaing area by a direct attack down the Mogaung valley, the entrance to which he now held, while he sent Merrill's Marauders across the Kumon Range to make a sudden dash on Myitkyina from the north.[1]

At this time the Japanese were holding a position astride the road at Warazup with their right flank near Tingring. Stilwell ordered 22nd Chinese Division to attack astride the road with one regiment, sending the other two round the Japanese left flank, and 38th Chinese Division to move east of the Mogaung River on Tingring and Wala, keeping one regiment in reserve to cut in on the Kamaing–Mogaung road near Seton at an appropriate moment. He directed that these two divisions should reach the general line Nanyaseik–Lawa by the 27th April. He was unaware that Chiang Kai-shek had given orders to the Chinese divisional commanders to hold back until the result of the battle for Imphal was known, and had not taken into account the stubbornness of the Japanese resistance and the possibility that, despite the presence of Special Force in its rear, *18th Division* would be reinforced. The timing of his advance on Kamaing was therefore over-optimistic. The Marauders, weakened and exhausted after their earlier operations and in particular after their defence of Nhpum Ga,[2] were to be reorganized into three columns each strengthened by Chinese infantry or Kachin guerillas.[3] They were to move off towards the end of April and were to capture Myitkyina by the 12th May.

The *Burma Area Army* had ordered *18th Division* (Lieut.-General S. Tanaka) to hold Kamaing at all costs, and, to enable these orders to be carried out, had reinforced the division between the end of April and mid-May by four battalions: *146th Regiment* (less *I/146th Battalion*) from *56th Division* and *4th Regiment* (less *III/4th Battalion*) from the Indaw area, as well as some 2,000 reinforcements. Tanaka appreciated that there were two good defensive positions north of Kamaing. He thought that he could hold the first—from Tingring to Warazup —for about a fortnight, and the second—from Wala to a point on the road some four miles south of Inkangahtawng—for a considerable time, provided that the reinforcing regiments reached him as planned. He considered that, if the Allied forces could be held on the second of these two positions till the middle of May, the advent of the

---

[1] See page 226.
[2] See pages 228–29.
[3] These three columns were: 'H' Force, 1st Battalion and 150th Regiment of 50th Chinese Division (Colonel C. N. Hunter); 'K' Force, 3rd Battalion and 88th Regiment of 30th Chinese Division (Colonel H. L. Kinnison); and 'M' Force, 2nd Battalion and 300 Kachin Levies (Colonel G. A. McGee).

monsoon would bring their advance to a halt. Moreover, by that time he believed that the Imphal offensive would have been brought to a successful conclusion, and that he would be further reinforced and put in a position to launch a counter-offensive. He gave *55th Regiment* the task of holding east of the Mogaung River and ordered *56th Regiment* to hold the road.

To Stilwell's chagrin the Chinese advance began in a very leisurely manner: it was not until the 20th April that 38th Division succeeded in taking Point 1725, and the 4th May that 22nd Division captured Inkangahtawng and both divisions were in contact with the Japanese main position. When Tanaka received his reinforcing formations, he sent *146th Regiment* to reinforce his right flank, and *4th Regiment* to strengthen his left west of the road. Weeks of desultory fighting now ensued and, although on the 6th May 38th Division captured Wala and was able to infiltrate round the Japanese right flank, 22nd Division made very little progress and by the middle of May the Allied forces were still facing the Japanese main position.

By this time *18th Division* was experiencing administrative difficulties. Not only had its strength been reduced by a long fighting retreat without relief, but it was beginning to be seriously short of ammunition and supplies of all kinds. In order to accumulate stocks for *15th Army* in preparation for the Imphal offensive, *Burma Area Army* had on the 10th January stopped sending supplies to *18th Division*, intending to resume the flow as soon as *15th Army* had launched its offensive in mid-March. The Allied airborne landings and the establishment of a road and rail block at 'White City' had, however, cut the main line of communications to the north just as the flow was about to begin. From about the middle of January, the division had therefore been forced to live on the reserves accumulated in the Myitkyina–Mogaung–Kamaing area. All it had received during the four months ending mid-May had been some ninety tons of ammunition and stores sent as an emergency measure by *56th Division* to Myitkyina, since all efforts to send supplies northwards through Bhamo had failed. By mid-March *18th Division* had begun to suffer from shortage of petrol with the result that, during the retreat to the Kamaing area, the evacuation of casualties and vehicles had become a serious problem—a problem which was to increase as time went on, and which was aggravated when the Allies began to bomb warehouses and suspected supply dumps in jungle areas during April.

About the middle of May, the Chinese divisional commanders were at last told by Chiang Kai-shek that they might press forward energetically towards Kamaing.[1] The 38th Chinese Division (Lieut.-

---

[1] This was a corollary to the Generalissimo's decision to take the offensive on the Salween front with the Yunnan armies. See page 231.

General Sun Li-jen) drove in the Japanese right flank south of Auche on the 20th. The same day, Sun Li-jen directed 113th Regiment on Zigyun (on the Mogaung River opposite Kamaing), 112th Regiment on Seton to cut the road between Kamaing and Mogaung, and 114th Regiment on Tumbonghka in readiness to attack Mogaung.[1] The 22nd Chinese Division, with 149th Regiment of 50th Division under command, also began to increase the pressure on the Japanese positions astride the road some fifteen miles north of Kamaing and to develop the outflanking movement through Nanyaseik.

Further east there was a very different story. The 4th Burma Regiment and some Kachin Levies, working south from Fort Hertz, had captured Sumprabum on the 19th March, and by the end of April were in contact with the Japanese some fifteen miles north of Nsopzup. Merrill's Marauders could thus cross the Kumon Range knowing that their left flank was secure. On the 28th April, 'K' Force, followed on the 30th by 'H' Force, began to move by way of Naura Hkyet Pass across the range, while, to protect the right flank, 'M' Force moved on the 7th May to cross the range further south and occupy Arang. After a struggle lasting three days, 'K' Force drove a Japanese force out of Ritpong on the 9th and pursued it towards Nsopzup, only to be held up at Tingkrukawng. 'H' Force had meanwhile moved south through Ritpong without meeting any opposition. Merrill thereupon ordered 'K' Force to retrace its steps and follow 'H' Force southwards. Passing through Seingneing, 'H' Force reached Namkwi on the Mogaung–Myitkyina railway four miles north of the Myitkyina airfield on the 16th. At 10 a.m. on the 17th the column attacked and captured the airfield and the river ferry terminal at Pamati.[2] By 3.30 p.m. the airfield was ready to receive transport aircraft and, within thirty-six hours, a flight of eight P.40 fighters, an engineer battalion, a battery of light anti-aircraft guns and a battalion of 89th Regiment of 30th Chinese Division had been flown in, at the cost of only one aircraft shot down.[3] Stilwell's plan had so far succeeded but it was now necessary to occupy Myitkyina itself before Colonel Maruyama's garrison of *I/* and *II/114th Battalions* (less two companies) could be reinforced.[4]

Immediately after the airfield had been secured, 150th Chinese Regiment attacked the town but its units lost direction, fired on each other and fell back. 'K' and 'M' Forces were immediately ordered to hurry south and in the following two days the remainder of 89th

---

[1] For Lieut.-General Sun Li-jen see Volume II, page 168 fn.
[2] See Sketch 17, page 414.
[3] On the 17th, when 'H' Force captured the airfield, 'K' Force was near Seingneing and 'M' Force was at Arang.
[4] The total combatant strength of the Myitkyina garrison on the 17th was about 700, which included 100 men of *15th Airfield Battalion*. In addition there were some 300 administrative personnel and 300 patients in hospital.

Chinese Regiment and a battalion of 42nd Regiment of the newly-arrived 14th Chinese Division were flown in, together with some artillery. On both the 18th and 20th renewed attacks by 150th Regiment failed to make headway, and Merrill realized that he must wait until his forces were concentrated before making another attempt.[1]

On the 20th, Lentaigne proposed that Morrisforce, about to attack Kazu on the Bhamo–Myitkyina road, should be directed on Myitkyina. Stilwell, still confident that the town would be quickly overrun, declined the offer. On the 24th the first full-scale attack by 88th and 89th Chinese Regiments failed to overcome the stubborn Japanese defence. Next day Stilwell instructed Lentaigne to order Morrisforce to capture Waingmaw on the east bank of the Irrawaddy opposite Myitkyina. At the same time, he placed General Boatner in command at Myitkyina, and sent forward two engineer battalions from the Ledo Road and all the replacements for the Marauders he could find.[2] No further attacks could, however, be made before the end of the month.

The Japanese made full use of this breathing space. Despite the fact that *56th Division* was under attack by the Chinese Yunnan armies,[3] Honda (*33rd Army*) on the 17th May ordered it to send Major-General G. Mizukami (the divisional infantry group commander) with a battalion and other units from the division to Myitkyina to assume command of the garrison and hold the town at all costs.[4] He also reinforced the garrison with *III/114th Battalion*, then in the Pinbaw area. Mizukami reached Myitkyina on the 30th May and the two battalions between the 4th and 6th June. The arrival of these reinforcements brought the strength of the garrison up to about 3,000.

Stilwell's bid to take Myitkyina by a *coup de main* had failed.

---

[1] By the night of the 22nd/23rd, Merrill had at his disposal the whole of the Marauders and 150th Chinese Regiment (most of whom were debilitated or sick), 88th and 89th Chinese Regiments and one battalion of 42nd Chinese Regiment.

[2] By the 22nd the Marauders were wasting at the rate of 130 men a day. Stilwell ordered forward 2,600 reinforcements held for the Marauders in India, and brought pressure to bear on the hospital authorities to send back to their units any man who was fit to press a trigger.

[3] See Chapter XXVIII.

[4] The units sent to Myitkyina with Mizukami included *56th Infantry Headquarters, I/148th Battalion*, one rifle and one machine-gun company from *113th Regiment*, one battery of *56th Artillery Regiment*, one company of *56th Engineer Regiment* and some medical and administrative detachments.

CHAPTER XXI

THE BATTLES OF IMPHAL AND
KOHIMA
The Japanese Advance Halted
(April 1944)

See Maps 3, 4, 8, 9 and 14 and Sketches 13 and 15

WHEN on the 2nd April Stopford (XXXIII Corps) assumed operational control of all troops in the Assam and Surma valleys[1], Slim gave him three tasks: to prevent enemy penetration into the Assam and Surma valleys or through the Lushai Hills;[2] to keep open the line of communication to IV Corps between Dimapur and Kohima; and to be prepared to move to the assistance of IV Corps and help in all possible ways to destroy the Japanese forces west of the Chindwin. When Stopford made his appreciation and plan for the coming battle he expected to have at his disposal by the middle of April 2nd British Division, two brigades from Arakan (161st and 33rd), 23rd (L.R.P.) Brigade, the Lushai Brigade, a regiment of armoured cars, and a squadron of light tanks and possibly one of medium tanks.[3] At the end of March, however, apart from static garrisons only one brigade (161st) was in position, though the leading brigade of 2nd Division was expected to arrive on the 2nd April. He therefore had some cause for anxiety, since from the information at his disposal he estimated that the Japanese could attack Kohima by the 3rd April and infiltrate into the Dhansiri valley by the 11th, thus creating a serious threat to Dimapur.[4]

The information regarding the enemy available at that time was that the whole of *33rd Division* had been committed to battle on the Tiddim and Tamu roads but that contact had been lost with *215th Infantry Regiment*, which it was thought might be moving west of the Tiddim road towards the Bishenpur–Silchar track.[5] Two regiments of *15th Division* had been identified, one of which was in the Sangshak area and a battalion of the other with *33rd Division* on the Tamu road.

---

[1] See page 245.
[2] See Map 14, page 452.
[3] See Appendix 21, order of battle of XXXIII Corps.
[4] See Map 4, page 53.
[5] See Map 3, page 33.

Documents captured at Sangshak indicated that *58th Infantry Regiment* of *31st Division* had been ordered to cut the Imphal Road near Mao and that two regiments of the division had been committed.[1]

Stopford believed that the task of *15th* and *33rd Divisions* was to contain IV Corps at Imphal, while *31st Division* moved north and north-west on Kohima and into the Assam Valley. He knew that *58th Infantry Regiment* was moving to cut the Imphal Road and that a second, and unidentified, regiment was in the Jessami—Kharasom area, but he had no knowledge of the whereabouts of the third regiment.[2] He suspected that it might move north from Layshi into the Assam Valley with Golaghat and Mariani as its objectives.

The information about *31st Division*, which was Stopford's main concern, was accurate as far as it went, but it was of course incomplete. Sato had been given the task of capturing Kohima in order to prevent help reaching Imphal from the Assam Valley by way of the Imphal Road but had not been authorized to move into the valley. The enemy force in the Jessami–Kharasom area was *138th Regiment* (less *III/138th Battalion*) which had been given the area immediately north of Kohima as its objective. The column at Layshi was *III/138th Battalion* which had orders to cut the Imphal Road at Priphema between Dimapur and Kohima. The *124th Regiment* was Sato's divisional reserve and was moving forward behind *138th Regiment*, which was the reason why it had not been located.

Stopford knew that it would not be possible to prevent infiltration entirely. He did not believe that there was as yet a serious threat to the Surma valley and considered that the Lushai Brigade, then being formed, would be capable of meeting any infiltration in that area. In the Assam Valley it looked as if infiltration on a wide front might be attempted, and he decided that his best course would be to ensure the safety of the vital areas, which he defined as Dimapur, the all-weather airfields at Golaghat, Dergaon and Jorhat, the main railway line through the valley and the Digboi oilfields. Kohima had to be held if possible, but it was evident that he could not prevent the cutting of the Imphal Road, though he could re-open it once his corps was concentrated. He considered that his third task should be undertaken only when the threat to Dimapur and the Assam Valley had been completely eliminated. He had also to face two difficulties: the first, that 2nd Division was so highly mechanized that, if it were required to advance on Imphal, it would be completely bound to the main road from the time it entered the hills, unless it could in the meantime be provided with a proportion of pack transport and trained in its use; the second, that the civil telegraph and telephone lines were inadequate and it would take time for his corps signals to

---

[1] Confirmation that the road had been cut at Mao on the 29th was received on the 30th.
[2] See Map 4, page 53.

build up a wireless and cable network over the vast area of his command.

On the 3rd he issued an operation order in which he stated that his intention was to protect Dimapur, and prevent infiltration to the Surma valley and the railway between Badarpur junction (west of Silchar) and Margharita (near Ledo).[1] Headquarters 202 L. of C. Area (Ranking), with 161st Brigade under command, was to remain responsible for the local defence of Dimapur and Kohima, pending the arrival of 2nd Division, and for maintaining static garrisons and patrols along the railway within its area. Kohima was to be held for as long as possible, but Ranking was given authority to withdraw the garrison to Dimapur if he thought it was in danger of destruction. The 2nd Division was to concentrate between Bokajan and Golaghat, with a squadron of 45th Cavalry (light tanks) under command, and be prepared to clear the Dhansiri River valley should the enemy reach it, or to open the road between Kohima and Imphal. The corps reserve was to consist of 23rd (L.R.P.) Brigade at Mariani and 11th Cavalry, less two squadrons (one each to 2nd Division and 202 L. of C. Area). The Lushai Brigade was to prevent infiltration through the hills into eastern Bengal and 257 L. of C. Sub-Area was to hold Silchar and block the track from Bishenpur.[2]

It is evident from Stopford's appreciation and plan that Kohima, unlike Imphal, was not a deliberately selected battle ground. That a battle was fought at Kohima was due to the fact that it was the objective for *31st Division* and that the magnificent defence put up by the garrison gave time for XXXIII Corps to be deployed to protect it. The tactical importance of Kohima stemmed primarily from its position on the summit of a pass at an altitude of 4,700 feet between the precipitous massif to the west, rising to nearly 10,000 feet, and the less impressive but nevertheless formidable mountain ranges, rising to nearly 8,000 feet, which merged to the north-east into the wild unsurveyed regions of the India–Burma border. The pass was the only practical route for a highway between Assam and the fertile rice-growing Imphal plain in Manipur State and to the Chindwin River in Burma. Memorials erected at the summit of the pass to those who had fallen in its defence in by-gone years testify to its age-long importance as the gateway to north-east India.[3] Precipitous slopes and dense sub-tropical forest at the lower altitudes made the pass difficult to approach except along established tracks. The hillsides round Kohima itself were extensively cleared and terraced for

---

[1] See Map 14, page 452.

[2] The 257 L. of C. Sub-Area had under command the Nepalese Mahindra Dal Regiment (see page 204) and a company of 25th Gurkhas, the garrison battalion formed for protection duties at 14th Army Headquarters.

[3] The first recorded incursion into Assam from Burma dates back to 1229 when the Ahom kingdom was established. In the 18th century the East India Company found Kohima a trouble spot until the area was finally ceded to India by Burma in 1826.

cultivation. Naga villages crowned many of the mountain tops in its vicinity, including one east of the pass which overlooked the Kohima ridge (the summit of the pass itself). This, since it was traversed on both faces by the Imphal Road, was the key to the pass and was the area which the garrison prepared to defend.

When, on the morning of the 4th April, the garrison of Kohima had its first glimpse of the enemy approaching along the Imphal Road from Mao and along the track from Jessami,[1] 161st Brigade and 1st Burma Regiment were concentrated at Nichuguard, 5th Brigade (2nd Division) was arriving at its concentration area near Bokajan, 23rd (L.R.P.) Brigade was on its way to Mariani, and 1st Assam Regiment, split into small parties, was making its way back by devious routes to Kohima and Dimapur.[2] The Imphal Road entered the defended area between the two southernmost knolls of the Kohima ridge (G.P.T. Ridge to the west of the road and Jail Hill to the east).[3] The first attack on Kohima was launched after dark on the 4th by *II/58th Battalion* which had advanced northwards from Mao, and fell on G.P.T. Ridge. It was unsuccessful but, on the morning of the 5th, a second attack gained a footing on the ridge and part of the garrison was cut off. To the east *III/58th Battalion*, which had moved from Mao through Kezoma, entered Naga Village unopposed on the 4th, but next day moved on to Cheswema.[4]

The garrison on the ridge got a foretaste of what was to come when its only gun (a 25-pounder) was knocked out within a few minutes of opening fire on the morning of the 5th. Help, though belated, was however at hand for, on the evening of the 4th, Ranking had suggested to Stopford that, as 5th Brigade was now concentrating at Bokajan, it would be advisable to send a battalion of 161st Brigade with supporting arms to strengthen the Kohima garrison and try to clear the roadblock to its south. Stopford decided that the whole brigade should be sent forward. At dawn on the 5th, 4th Royal West Kents, 20th Mountain Battery and a section of engineers moved to Kohima in motor transport followed a few hours later by the rest of the brigade. As the West Kents and the mountain battery got into position during the afternoon, attacks developed on Jail Hill and, at the other end of the ridge, the Deputy Commissioner's (D.C.'s) Bungalow was steadily shelled and mortared.[5]

---

[1] The garrison consisted of 1,500 combatants and 1,000 non-combatants and was on the morning of the 4th engaged in preparing the defences of the ridge position.
[2] See page 244.
[3] See Map 8, page 360.
[4] The move of *III/58th Battalion* from Naga Village was ordered as a result of a report that Garrison Hill had been captured. The *I/138th Battalion*, the leading battalion of the centre column, reached Naga Village on the 6th, and on the same date *III/58th Battalion* was ordered back to Naga Village. Both battalions took part in the attacks on Garrison Hill from the 7th.
[5] See Sketch 13, page 346. The Deputy Commissioner was Mr. (later Sir) Charles Pawsey. It was largely due to his great influence over the Nagas that they remained staunch.

44. Bishenpur from Point 5846. Bishenpur village upper left; the Tiddim road runs through it from left to right. Note Silchar track through the trees in the lower right-hand quarter of the photograph, which was the water point area.

Road and Imphal Turel   Sengmai
Telegraph line   Kanglatongbi

45. Imphal airfield looking north.

46. Palel, looking north over the Imphal plain. Note the supply dump on the far hillside on the right.

47. The approach to Shenam Pass from the Imphal plain.

48. Scraggy, looking towards Crete and Tengnoupal.

49. Stuart tanks and infantry in action near Kanglatongbi.

50. Near Kangpokpi on the Imphal Road: 2nd British and 5th Indian Divisions meet on the 22nd June 1944.

51. Tank on transporter near the southern end of the Imphal plain.

52. Mopping up on Shenam Pass.

53. Nippon Hill from the Tamu road.

54. Air Marshal
Sir John Baldwin.

55. Japanese supply train on the Rangoon–Mandalay railway after attacks
by R.A.F. Beaufighters.

56. Bridge and temporary by-pass on the Rangoon–Mandalay railway
after Allied air attacks.

57. Bridge on the Bangkok–Singapore railway being bombed
by R.A.F. Liberators.

Warren (161st Brigade), realizing that there was not sufficient room on the Kohima ridge for the rest of his brigade, occupied a position near Jotsoma (some $2\frac{1}{2}$ miles north-west of Kohima) from which his artillery could support the garrison and from where he could assist it by counter-attack or at least by drawing off a proportion of the attacking forces. There is little doubt that the presence of the brigade at Jotsoma was one of the decisive factors in the defence of Kohima, for its guns provided the only artillery support for the garrison throughout the siege.[1]

By nightfall on the 5th the West Kents were in position on Garrison and F.S.D. Hills, and it was planned to re-occupy a previously prepared post on Treasury Hill and withdraw the two isolated companies from G.P.T. Ridge. Both operations met with opposition, and the troops involved were thrown into such confusion that some withdrew towards Dimapur instead of to Kohima. This loss of strength to the garrison was, to some extent, made good when, on the 7th, a company of 5/7th Rajput from Jotsoma got through to Kohima and, having evacuated some 200 wounded and non-combatants under the escort of a platoon, remained to reinforce the defenders. The loss of G.P.T. Ridge was serious, since the enemy soon found and cut the water mains from the reservoir. Thereafter the garrison had to rely on the meagre springs on Garrison Hill, augmented by the not very successful attempts to drop canisters of water by air. The enemy next attacked Jail Hill, and by the afternoon of the 7th its defenders had suffered about 100 casualties and had had to abandon some vital posts. A counter-attack by the West Kents having failed, Richards ordered its evacuation and the survivors fell back through D.I.S. to F.S.D.

The Japanese next turned their attention to the north-east corner of the contracted perimeter and, helped by the perfect observation from Naga Village which made their artillery support devastatingly effective, succeeded during the 8th and 9th in pushing the defenders back and reaching the tennis court in front of the heap of rubble which had been the picturesque Kohima Club.[2] It had been hoped that more wounded could be evacuated to Jotsoma during the 8th, but the enemy had blocked the road in the Piquet Hill area and closed all exits to the north. The same day patrols from 161st Brigade working back towards Dimapur to repair broken telephone lines found an enemy roadblock had been established near Zubza.[3] An

---

[1] Two of the mountain guns which accompanied the West Kents on to the ridge quickly suffered the same fate as the 25-pounder, and no positions could be found from which the remaining two could remain in action.

[2] Japanese records state that *III/58th* on the right and *I/138th Battalion* on the left carried out uncoordinated attacks on Garrison Hill beginning at dusk on the 7th.

[3] This block was formed by elements of *138th Infantry Regiment* which on the 7th Sato had ordered to cut the road near Zubza to prevent reinforcements from reaching Kohima.

attack on the 9th by a detachment of 1/1st Punjab failed to clear it, and five days were to elapse before road communications between 2nd Division and 161st Brigade were re-established.

Slim had meanwhile decided that it would be advisable to relieve XXXIII Corps of the responsibility for stopping infiltration through the Chin and Lushai Hills, and on the 8th April had placed the Lushai Brigade under his own direct command. At the same time he ordered 3 S.S. Brigade (Brigadier W. I. Nonweiler) with its two commandos to move from the Arakan coast to Silchar,[1] so that Stopford could entrust the security of that area to a fighting formation and be free to concentrate on meeting the dangerous threat to north-east Assam and the vital line of communication.

Stopford still had not the full use of 23rd (L.R.P.) Brigade (Brigadier L. E. C. M. Perowne), but had permission to use two of its battalions in a defensive rôle. One he deployed on the Golaghat–Phekekrima track to protect the left flank of 2nd Division, and the other with one column at Wokha and a second at Mokokchung to watch the main tracks from the Jessami area to the Assam Valley. He contemplated relieving them in due course by 33rd Brigade (7th Division) which had begun to arrive from Arakan. When, on the 9th, the decision of the Jorhat Conference was reversed and the whole of Special Force was ordered to assist the advance on the Northern front,[2] Mountbatten suggested that it might be advisable to compensate IV Corps for the fact that no part of Special Force would operate to the south-west of Indaw by giving Scoones 23rd (L.R.P.) Brigade to operate against the Japanese communications in the Kabaw Valley. Slim was not prepared, however, to allot the brigade to either corps until the Japanese *124th Regiment* was located. Thus Stopford still could not use it for the task he had in mind, which was to cut the communications of *31st Division*, now bringing its full strength to bear on Kohima and on 161st Brigade.

On the 10th April, Slim, with Giffard's agreement, ordered a general offensive. Scoones was to hold the enemy south of Imphal, establish a force at Ukhrul to cut the Japanese communications to the Chindwin and to attack *15th* and *33rd Divisions* in turn. Stopford was to hold Kohima as a starting point for an offensive to destroy *31st Division* by establishing a force in its rear in the Jessami–Kharasom area and then striking with his main force down the Imphal Road. Stilwell was to continue his advance on Mogaung and Myitkyina aided by Special Force operating from the south. There were sufficient transport aircraft left to 14th Army to maintain, after meeting its

---

[1] Each commando at full strength consisted of 600 men.
[2] See page 281.

other commitments, two brigades of XXXIII Corps and one of IV Corps. This order set the pattern of operations on the Central and Northern fronts for the next two months.

By the evening of the 9th, 5th Brigade (2nd Division) was ready to advance from its concentration area at Bokajan, 6th Brigade Headquarters and one battalion had arrived at Dimapur and 1st Burma Regiment had established a detachment at MS 32 (four miles short of Zubza) to cover the initial advance of 5th Brigade. Stopford ordered Major-General J. M. L. Grover (2nd Division) to take over operational control of the Dimapur–Kohima sector from Ranking (202 L. of C. Area) on the 10th. That morning Grover went forward to MS 32, where he learned that the road was blocked near Zubza. He sent a message to Hawkins (5th Brigade), then at Nichuguard, to get his advanced guard on the move at once and, by midday on the 11th, 7th Worcesters was in action with an enemy force strongly entrenched on a precipitous ridge astride the road at MS 37½. Frontal attack was soon found to be impossible. An infantry detachment was therefore sent by way of Sachema to by-pass the position and attack it from the rear, while a troop of medium tanks was brought forward to give close support on the axis of the road.[1] The Japanese defended tenaciously and, helped by counter-attacks, one of which got among the tanks and did considerable damage, held out for three days. The position was eventually overrun by 1st Cameron Highlanders on the 14th and contact was established with 161st Brigade.

At Kohima, the Japanese continued their efforts to capture the ridge. Identifications, obtained during the fighting on the 9th, had shown that two battalions of *58th Regiment* and one of *138th Regiment* were involved. By the 10th, D.I.S., held by a company of the West Kents and overlooked by Jail Hill, became untenable and on orders of the garrison commander was evacuated. On the 11th, the Japanese began to infiltrate on to F.S.D. and resumed their attacks on the tennis court. A counter-attack next day regained some of the ground lost on F.S.D., but it was decided not to try and regain ground towards the D.C.'s Bungalow since the mobile reserve had by this time been reduced to one company which had to be kept in hand for an emergency. By the 13th the garrison was suffering from a serious shortage of water. There was barely sufficient for drinking and urgent medical needs and, but for the discovery of a seepage on the north face of Garrison Hill which the engineers were able to enlarge, the situation might have become critical. Attempts to replenish the garrison's supply of water and mortar ammunition by air failed since

---

[1] This troop was formed from men of 150th R.A.C. brought from India and issued with medium tanks from advanced base at Dimapur.

most of the loads fell outside the perimeter, and so the Japanese, who had many captured British mortars, were able to replenish their supplies of ammunition.

A study of the map will show how closely engaged the opposing forces were, and the photographs of the battlefield show the enormous difficulties that the R.A.F. faced in giving close support and dropping supplies. In the circumstances 'a miss was as good as a mile', with perhaps a couple of thousand feet in altitude added. In order to fly low enough to ensure accuracy, the airmen risked crashing on the mountain sides or being shot at from close range by the enemy occupying them. Added to these risks was the ever-present danger of being engulfed in the sudden mists sweeping down from the surrounding mountain tops, or of being caught in the violent airpockets over the mountains—a formidable combination of dangers which needed great skill and courage to overcome.

To add to the misfortunes of the 'Black Thirteenth', as the day became known, the enemy artillery scored two direct hits on the West Kents' dressing station. Towards evening, however, there was a gleam of hope when a message from 161st Brigade was received in Kohima saying that it was hoped to start relief operations almost immediately. But no sooner had this message been sent than the Jotsoma position came under attack and Warren, with only two battalions at his disposal and involved in helping Grover clear the Zubza block, could not begin to move in any strength towards Kohima until he had either driven off the attack on Jotsoma or cleared the Zubza block.[1]

The 14th brought an intensification of sniping and mortar fire but, for the first time for ten days, Japanese infantry did not attack the ridge. This, coupled with the news that the Zubza block had been cleared, helped to revive the spirits of the garrison. Another event of some importance occurred on the 14th when Slim learned that the unlocated *124th Infantry Regiment* of *31st Division* had crossed the Chindwin on the 19th March.[2] It was improbable that the enemy columns reported to be moving towards Mokokchung were part of either *58th* or *138th Regiments*, whose whereabouts were known, but they might be part of the *124th* with the mission of cutting the railway at some point north of Dimapur. He immediately told Stopford that 23rd (L.R.P.) Brigade was entirely at his disposal. The whereabouts of *124th Regiment* was confirmed next day when 1st Essex met a strong Japanese patrol from that regiment at Phekekrima, and

---

[1] The attack on Jotsoma was made by *I/58th Battalion* which Miyazaki had sent from Maram to by-pass Kohima and attack it from the north-west.

[2] An order signed by Colonel Miyamoto (*124th Regiment*) on the 19th March on the banks of the Chindwin, showing that the regiment was about to cross the river in a trans-Chindwin offensive, was found by a column of Special Force near Banmauk when it overran a small enemy detachment guarding a supply dump.

reports were received shortly afterwards that an enemy column had entered Wokha and another was advancing towards Mokokchung. By this time, however, Perowne (23rd (L.R.P.) Brigade) had got his columns on the move with orders to make for Jessami and Kharasom.

The following day the enemy again remained inactive and the defenders learned that 2nd Division and 161st Brigade had linked up and that there was a hope of speedy relief. They had, however, still some anxious days to wait before their trials were ended. By the morning of the 16th the detachment of the West Kents at F.S.D. was so exhausted that its relief had become essential, and two platoons of Assam Rifles and one from the Assam Regiment, the only troops available, took over during the day. That evening the somewhat ominous lull in enemy activity came to an end and pressure increased at both ends of the perimeter.[1] After fierce night fighting, in which positions changed hands several times, F.S.D. was finally overrun towards the morning of the 17th. During the day patrols reported that the enemy was mustering to attack Kuki Piquet. There was no reserve available to counter-attack and that night it too was lost. Thus, by the morning of the 18th, the defenders were hemmed into the confined space of Garrison Hill, exposed to attacks from the south, north and east.

While these events were taking place urgent action was being taken to relieve the garrison. As soon as 5th Brigade had cleared Zubza and made suitable dispositions to protect the road from MS 32 to Jotsoma, Grover ordered 6th Brigade (Brigadier J. D. Shapland) to move into Jotsoma and take over its defences in order to free 161st Brigade to break through to Kohima.[2] At the same time he told Stopford that, unless he could be relieved of the responsibility for protecting the road back to Dimapur, his striking force would be inadequate. He therefore proposed to withdraw the Kohima garrison, hold the Jotsoma–Zubza area as his base of operations instead of the Kohima ridge and with the rest of his division attack Kohima from the east by way of the Merema ridge. Because a withdrawal from Kohima would tend to raise enemy morale and alarm the Nagas, Stopford did not agree to the ridge being abandoned, even though its recapture might be certain if the flank attack, to which he gave his approval, succeeded.

At daylight on the 18th April, just as the exhausted garrison of Kohima was preparing to make its 'last ditch' stand, British guns opened up on the enemy positions and shortly afterwards tanks were seen coming up the road preceded by infantry. The Japanese were

---

[1] See Sketch 13, page 346. During the 16th the medical inspection room of the hospital at the western end of Garrison Hill was hit. Two doctors were killed and one wounded, a serious loss to the garrison.

[2] See Map 8, page 360.

soon cleared from the area to the north-west of Garrison Hill and the siege was raised. A battalion of 161st Brigade then reinforced the garrison, taking over D.C.'s Bungalow spur, and all wounded and sick were evacuated. Two days later 6th Brigade took over the defence of Kohima, Richards with his headquarters and the remnants of the garrison were evacuated to Dimapur and 161st Brigade (less 4th Royal West Kents) returned to Jotsoma. The first phase of the battle of Kohima—the siege—was over.[1] There is no doubt that had Kohima ridge been lost XXXIII Corps' task of reopening the Imphal Road would have been much more difficult. The heroic defence put up by Richards and his small garrison against overwhelming odds thus played a small but very vital part in the defeat of the Japanese in the decisive battles in South-East Asia.

The second phase of the battle was about to begin with the deployment of 2nd Division, with 161st Brigade under command, to drive the Japanese from their positions around the Kohima ridge and reopen the road to Imphal. The responsibility for protecting the road back to Dimapur was given as a temporary measure to 4th Brigade, a battalion (1st Royal Scots) of which was already in action with *III/138th Battalion* in the Khabvuma area,[2] and 5th Brigade was given the task of attacking Naga Village from the north. Finding the Merema ridge clear of the enemy, it began to make its way there along the difficult jungle paths from Zubza.

During the second half of April, 23rd (L.R.P.) Brigade moving south had found elements of *124th Regiment* in position on the Merema–Bokajan track and at Wokha, and had successfully ambushed a Japanese detachment at Sakhalu on the Mokochung–Jessami track. The bulk of *124th Regiment* was in fact in the area north-east of Kohima covering the right flank of *31st Division* until the 23rd April. The regiment then moved to Aradura, leaving behind two companies which, aided by storms, dense jungle and precipitous mountains, were able to impose considerable delay on 23rd (L.R.P.) Brigade's advance towards Jessami.

During the siege of Kohima, IV Corps, having withdrawn to its prepared positions on the Imphal plain, had begun to regroup for a counter-offensive.[3] On the 5th April, Scoones laid down that the corps' task was to destroy *15th Division* and establish a force in the

---

[1] During the siege a posthumous V.C. was won by Lance-Corporal J. P. Harman, The Queen's Own Royal West Kent Regiment.

[2] The 268th Indian Brigade (the motorized brigade thrown up by the disbandment of 44th Indian Armoured Division, see pages 316–17) had been earmarked to follow up the advance of 2nd Division and take over the protection of the Dimapur–Kohima road. It was ordered to move on the 16th April and arrived at Dimapur on the 8th May.

[3] See Map 9, page 374.

Ukhrul area.[1] He ordered 5th Division to re-occupy the high ground astride the Imphal Road in the Kangpokpi area and subsequently clear the road between Kangpokpi and Imphal, and 23rd Division to clear the area south of Ukhrul and establish a strongpoint on the enemy communications to the north. These operations were to begin not later than the 11th April. Before that date 17th Division, while retaining command of 63rd Brigade at Kanglatongbi, was to take over control of operations on the Tiddim road and command of 32nd Brigade and was to hold 48th Brigade in corps reserve. This readjustment would relieve 23rd Division of all commitments except its offensive against *15th Division*. The regrouping of the corps began at once. It was not, however, to be carried out unmolested, for six battalions of the Japanese *15th Division* had reached the position north of Imphal from which they were to attack southwards in conjunction with an offensive northwards by *33rd Division*.

On the 6th, 9th Brigade, having been relieved by 63rd Brigade at Kanglatongbi, moved to Nungshigum where enemy pressure had begun to increase on the 5th.[2] Enemy pressure had also increased on Kanglatongbi, and on the 7th it became evident that the dispersed advanced base there could not be defended against either infiltration or a determined attack.[3] Scoones therefore gave permission for the base to be evacuated. Backloading to Imphal of stores most likely to be of use to the enemy began at once and by the night of the 8th, when 63rd Brigade withdrew to Sengmai, a quarter of the 4,000 tons of stores in the base had been removed. Headquarters 256 L. of C. Sub-Area moved into the 'Citadel' and most of the personnel of the base were flown back to India.

On the 7th, a company of 3/9th Jats of 9th Brigade was driven off the summit of Nungshigum hill (Point 3833) but the rest of the battalion, supported by an air strike and a regiment of artillery, quickly regained it.[4] During their brief occupation of the hill the Japanese had evidently realized its value as an observation post and a jumping-off point for an attack on Imphal and its airfield, which lay fourteen and six miles respectively to the south-west and west. On the 11th, supported by artillery fire, they secured possession of the hilltop for a second time and managed to consolidate their position. This was the nearest that any Japanese force larger than a patrol ever got to Imphal. It was within four miles of corps headquarters and was probably the most dangerous threat to Imphal which occurred during the battle. Consequently, on the 13th, the hill was bombarded

---

[1] For the disposition of IV Corps before regrouping see page 243.
[2] See pages 242–43. The Japanese *III/51st Battalion* was in this area.
[3] On the 7th, *III/60th Battalion* suffered severe casualties (including 68 killed) in an encounter with 63rd Brigade west of Kanglatongbi.
[4] For exploits during the fighting at Nungshigum, Jemadar Abdul Hafiz, 3/9th Jat Regiment, was awarded a posthumous V.C.

for one and a half hours by Vengeance dive-bombers, Hurricane fighter-bombers and artillery working to a carefully timed programme, and then attacked by a fresh battalion (1/17th Dogras from 123rd Brigade) supported by medium tanks of the Carabiniers. It was recovered but at the cost of heavy casualties including no less than five tank commanders killed, since the difficulty of the terrain forced the tanks to go into action with their turrets open.

While the struggle for Nungshigum hill raged, the regrouping of IV Corps was completed. The 37th Brigade of 23rd Division relieved 123rd Brigade of 5th Division at Yaingangpokpi in readiness to act as the pivot for 23rd Division's offensive against *15th Division*, 1st Brigade moved to Singkap in preparation for an attack on Kasom, which was reported to be the enemy's divisional headquarters, and blocks were established along the Sita–Singkap track. The relief of 123rd Brigade enabled 5th Division to prepare for its advance up the Iril valley towards Kangpokpi. At the same time 17th Division resumed responsibility for the Tiddim road, taking under command 32nd Brigade which, with a battery of field and one of mountain artillery, had been ordered to Moirang to relieve 49th Brigade which was to rejoin its own division (23rd) at Yairipok.

Mackenzie (32nd Brigade) objected to taking over the Moirang position which he considered could easily be by-passed. With Scoones' approval, Cowan accepted the objection and gave permission for the brigade to prepare and occupy positions at Bishenpur covering the junction of the Tiddim road and the Silchar track—a change of plan which was to prove sound. In consequence, 49th Brigade was ordered to remain at Moirang until the new positions were ready. The dispositions of 17th Division did not, however, deny the enemy access to the Silchar–Bishenpur track which was being improved by a strong force of engineers in the hope that it would provide an alternative line of communication to Imphal.[1] The 3 S.S. Brigade was, however, on its way from Arakan to defend Silchar and provide a mobile striking force, and two detachments from 7/10th Baluch were being sent to ensure the safety of the big suspension bridge five miles west of Tairenpokpi, which, from a captured enemy order, was known to be the objective of a Japanese raiding party.

The object of 23rd Division's offensive was to destroy that portion of *15th Division* operating on the Litan–Sangshak road. The 1st Brigade (Brigadier R. C. M. King) was to attack Kasom from the south to

---

[1] C.R.E. 461st Army Troops with 8th Battalion, I.E., a detachment of 331st Field Park Company and four companies of the Indian Pioneer Corps, as well as C.R.E., G.R.E.F. with three field companies, two R.E. Commandos and a detachment of a mechanical excavating company.

capture or destroy *Headquarters 15th Division* believed to be in the area, while 37th Brigade advanced along the main road from Yaingang-pokpi with the object of destroying all enemy forces caught between the two brigades. The 1st Brigade moved on an all-pack basis, with one battery of mountain artillery under command, while the rest of the divisional artillery, a squadron of light tanks (7th Cavalry) and a half squadron of medium tanks (Carabiniers) accompanied 37th Brigade. The 5th Division was at the same time to strike north up the Iril River valley with 123rd Brigade. This brigade was later to turn south-west towards Kanglatongbi and, in conjunction with 9th Brigade advancing north-west from Nungshigum, destroy the Japanese forces occupying the heights east of Sengmai.[1]

The 1st Brigade's plan of attack was for 1st Patalia Infantry and 1/16th Punjab to make their way during the night of the 15th/16th through the dense jungle to close all escape routes from Kasom to the north and west, while 1st Seaforth Highlanders attacked the village from the south at dawn on the 16th. The Seaforths met little resistance and, in a ravine close to the village, found dead mules, arms, equipment and documents. The area appeared to have been bombed and hurriedly evacuated. It is now known that the information that *Headquarters 15th Division* had been at Kasom was correct but, when he became aware that his communications were in danger of being cut, Yamauchi had sent an infantry detachment to Sokpao to keep the road open while his headquarters withdrew towards Ukhrul. Although fierce hand-to-hand fighting developed at Sokpao, it seems probable that by the time this began divisional headquarters had already escaped. By the 21st April, 1st and 37th Brigades had made contact, the Ukhrul road was cleared of the enemy as far as Kasom, and patrols pushing east reported that the Sangshak–Chassud track was not being used as a supply line. It was now believed that *Headquarters 15th Division* had moved to Shongpel some eight miles further north, and 23rd Division prepared to renew the chase.

The 5th Division's attempts to advance up the Iril valley met with stiff opposition and, by the 21st, 123rd Brigade had succeeded only in occupying a peak one mile east of Nungshigum. The 9th Brigade, which had meanwhile infiltrated through the hills north-west of Nungshigum, found itself faced on the 19th by strongly entrenched enemy forces in the Mapao area covering the left flank of the Japanese formations which had been unsuccessfully attacking 63rd Brigade at Sengmai since the 12th.[2] The positions at Mapao were of such strength that a carefully co-ordinated attack with strong air and artillery support was necessary to ensure success; a lull in the offensive therefore ensued while new plans were made.

---

[1] Sengmai was held by 63rd Brigade of 17th Division.
[2] The *II/60th* and *III/67th Battalions*.

The Japanese consider that the 19th April was the turning point in the operations north of Imphal, for on that day attempts to break through at Sengmai were abandoned and their forces were ordered to adopt a defensive rôle. By the 21st, Scoones realized that the threat to Imphal, which had reached its most critical stage when the Japanese gained the summit of Nungshigum hill (Point 3833), had passed, and that he had regained the initiative on the northern sector of the corps front.

To the south, however, the Japanese were still attacking. On Shenam Pass, 1st Devonshire Regiment (80th Brigade of 20th Division), supported by the whole of the divisional artillery, had on the 12th April recovered Nippon Hill and had repelled the inevitable counter-attacks.[1] On the evening of the 16th the Japanese, who had by this time been able to bring forward their artillery, opened a concentrated bombardment of Nippon Hill. When at 10 p.m. three companies of Japanese stormed the position, the company of 9/12th F.F. Regiment holding the devastated hilltop was able to offer little resistance and the enemy once more regained the summit. The same day a company of 3/1st Gurkha Rifles (80th Brigade), holding the important track junction at Sita, was surrounded and attacked by a superior force of infantry but without artillery support. The Japanese, who tried to cut the barbed wire entanglements by hand in full view of the defenders, suffered severe casualties and were repulsed. When the rest of 3/1st Gurkhas from Shenam came to the assistance of its isolated company, the attackers were driven off and 120 dead from *I/60th Battalion* were found on the perimeter. Having failed at Sita, the Japanese now concentrated on exploiting their success at Nippon Hill and attempted to break through Shenam Pass by frontal attacks supported by powerful artillery and medium tanks. After several failures they overran Crete East on the 20th and 21st. An adjacent feature known as Cyprus was, as a result, isolated and on Gracey's orders abandoned. The features known as Crete West and Scraggy now became the forward defences. They marked the limit of the Japanese advance on the Tamu–Palel road and were destined to be the scene of fighting for the next three months. There can have been few places during the war the possession of which, in proportion to their size, was more costly in human life.

On the Tiddim road, 32nd Brigade had occupied its new position covering Bishenpur by the 16th. That day 49th Brigade evacuated its position at Moirang and moved to Yairipok for a short rest and refit before taking part in 23rd Division's offensive. The 32nd Brigade's position at Bishenpur was one of great strength. Its right rested on Point 5846 on the Silchar track, its left was secured by the Imphal marshes east of Ningthoukhong and there were mutually supporting

---

[1] See page 243 and Sketch 15, page 370.

positions in depth from Potsangbum to MS 16 north of Bishenpur. The withdrawal of 49th Brigade was unmolested but an enemy force, moving unseen through the tiger grass covering the hills to the west of the road, had reached Kungpi and occupied Wireless Hill immediately to its east. But for the fact that, on the 16th, 3/8th Gurkhas (32nd Brigade) drove the enemy off the hill, 49th Brigade might have had to fight its way out. The following day the enemy once again succeeded in occupying the hill, only to be driven off it again two days later by an attack in which the Carabiniers distinguished themselves by driving their medium tanks up incredibly steep hillsides to give close support. So steep were they that one tank overturned and rolled to the foot of the hill. Except for one man the crew survived.

By this time enemy patrols were found to have infiltrated as far north as Khoirok, and from identifications obtained it appeared that *214th Regiment* was in the hills in the Point 5846 area and the bulk of *215th Regiment* astride the Tiddim road. Cowan decided to reinforce 32nd Brigade, and on the 19th sent 1/4th Gurkha Rifles from 63rd Brigade to Bishenpur and 4/12th F.F. Regiment (his divisional headquarters battalion) to Khoirok where fighting broke out at once. On the 20th it was found that an enemy force had established itself at Ningthoukhong. The artillery supporting 32nd Brigade (twelve field and four mountain guns) was quite inadequate to deal with the Japanese artillery, which included a heavy field artillery regiment. In consequence the British medium tanks, boldly handled in support of the brigade's attempt to clear the area, although superior to the Japanese tanks began to incur such heavy losses as to cause some anxiety.[1]

There had been a lull in enemy air activity during the last few days of March but, when the battle for Kohima and Imphal flared up in early April, the Japanese air force resumed the offensive by attacking ground objectives in the Imphal area. Formations of twenty to thirty fighters, sometimes accompanied by medium bombers, would usually attack out of the sun in the early morning, but by this time the R.A.F. had perfected a system of air patrols which enabled the Spitfire squadrons to be airborne in time to intercept the attackers. The most serious enemy loss was when a squadron of nine bombers was destroyed by American fighters while attempting to carry out a raid in the Assam Valley. To lessen the risk of losses, which with their dwindling bomber forces they could ill afford, the Japanese turned to

---

[1] Until the Imphal Road could be reopened they could not be replaced. So severe were the losses that the men of the squadron of 150th R.A.C. were flown out to India, handing over their few remaining tanks to make up the Carabiniers' losses.

night attack. They met with little success and in one of the earliest attacks Beaufighters of 176 Squadron shot down three light bombers over Tamu. During the third week of April enemy fighters attempted to put the airfields at Imphal, Palel and Tulihal out of action but, although casualties were inflicted, little damage was done and runways were never closed for more than a few hours at a time. During the first three weeks of April Japanese aircraft flew some 350 sorties. In the same period Spitfire and Hurricane fighters flew 1,200, and some thirty-five enemy aircraft were believed destroyed or damaged.

Close support for IV and XXXIII Corps was constantly given by Hurricane fighter-bombers and Vengeance dive-bombers. In addition to the operations already described, they attacked enemy forces on the move on the roads and tracks behind the battle front, positions at Kanglatongbi and elsewhere and supply dumps and transport in the Kabaw Valley between Mintha in the north and Kalewa in the south. Up to the 21st April the Hurricanes flew 2,000 sorties and dropped over 300 tons of bombs, while the Vengeance squadrons dropped nearly 550 tons in 1,700 sorties. The total R.A.F. loss was twenty aircraft.

By the 21st April the Japanese advance had been brought to a standstill. At Kohima the siege had been raised and both there and to the north of Imphal the enemy had been forced to give ground and turn to the defensive. To the north-east of Imphal a limited offensive had gained some success. To the south-east and south there was for the moment stalemate. Though Slim and his corps commanders were justified in their belief that the crisis was past, there was no room for complacency, for it was quite evident that the Japanese had by no means given up hope of capturing Imphal, nor could the possibility of their succeeding be entirely ruled out.

CHAPTER XXII

ADMINISTRATION AND AIR
SUPPLY
(January – July 1944)

See Maps 3, 4, 10 and 14 and Sketch 12

DURING the six months from November 1943 to April 1944 great strides had been made in overcoming the many administrative difficulties in India, and on the lines of communication to the north-east frontier, which had beset successive Commanders-in-Chief in India during 1942 and 1943.

Much had been done to improve India as a base for S.E.A.C. Reconnaissances were made by joint civil and military transportation staffs to ascertain what development of India's ports was necessary to meet future military commitments. Each port was considered in relation to the movement plan for the reception, embarkation and subsequent maintenance of the forces likely to be based on it, and the additional facilities such as berths, moorings, cranes, tugs and lighters which would be needed were calculated on the estimated peak loads. The reports submitted showed that considerable development was necessary at Calcutta, Vizagapatam and Madras, but that little was required at Bombay and Cochin.[1] Based on these reports orders were placed for equipment, and the construction of new wharves, jetties and roads and improvements to water and power supplies were put in hand, with a target date for completion of December 1944.[2]

Work, begun early in 1943, on No. 3 Reserve Base at Panagarh (near Calcutta), No. 4 at Avadi (near Madras) and the Vizagapatam transit depot had progressed sufficiently to allow their stocking to begin in December 1943, February and April 1944 respectively. Thereafter stocking kept pace with the building of accommodation and the provision of rail facilities. By April 1944 it was estimated that India base would be two-thirds complete by the end of the year, and would not meet its full target until late in 1945.

During the six months under review, India's economic position had not greatly improved. Although by the end of 1943 the effects

[1] See Map 10, page 384.
[2] See Appendix 23.

of the famine in Bengal were much less in evidence and the situation appeared to be under control, there were still grave misgivings about India's long-term prospects. To meet the increased demand for currency, Britain and America had provided considerable quantities of gold and silver, and this had temporarily stopped the rise in the price of everything except foodstuffs. Britain was, however, unable to accept the recommendations made by India at the end of October 1943 that further demands on her from overseas for war services and supplies should be reduced to safe limits.[1] By the beginning of April 1944 the strain on her industrial resources had become so serious that the Viceroy reported the country could no longer accept any more demands for war supplies, except those items peculiar to Indian troops overseas, items such as jute of which she was the sole supplier and ammunition and tyres which were specifically manufactured as part of the Allied plan of supply. These restrictions would not, however, apply to raw materials or engineering demands for India Command and S.E.A.C.

There was a good rice crop in Bengal in the autumn of 1943, but the 1943–44 Indian wheat crop had failed, and the Viceroy feared that there would be distress on a far larger scale and over a far wider area than in 1943. By reducing the civil ration of wheat and substituting where possible barley and millet something could be done, but there would still be a deficit of some 484,000 tons of wheat. He therefore asked for wheat to be imported as a matter of urgency but, because of the shortage of shipping, the War Cabinet could arrange for only some 50,000 tons to be sent from Australia. So alive were Mountbatten and Auchinleck to the dangers facing the country that in March they offered to forego a tenth of their military imports to provide shipping space for food for the civil population: twenty-five ships were thus freed to carry some 200,000 tons of wheat to India during the second and third quarters of 1944. At the end of March, however, the Viceroy was forced to give a warning that, although these imports would somewhat ease the situation, they would not solve the food problem as a whole or secure India as a military base.

During March and early April heavy rains increased the damage to the spring harvest. On the 14th April the explosion of an ammunition ship severely damaged the Victoria and Princes Docks in Bombay harbour and destroyed or severely damaged sixteen ships and most of the dockside buildings and equipment.[2] Extensive fires broke out and gutted the warehouses in an area of about one hundred acres adjacent to the docks, destroying much plant and machinery and a

---

[1] See pages 28–29.
[2] The ammunition ship was also carrying gold bars sent from England to help meet India's financial difficulties. Most of these were recovered. It was not until November 1944 that the docks were repaired and brought fully into service.

great quantity of stores, including some 36,000 tons of wheat. The Prime Minister thereupon appealed to the President to release American shipping to carry wheat from Australia to India, but because of the effect that such a diversion of shipping would have on military operations none could be spared.[1] Aware that the security of India was essential to the prosecution of the war against Japan, the Chiefs of Staff re-examined the British shipping position in June and, by making cuts in other programmes, freed another twenty-five ships to carry grain from Australia during the third quarter of the year.

By April 1944 the situation on the Indian railways had improved considerably. Of the locomotives on order, 177 out of 595 broad gauge and 433 out of 605 metre gauge had been shipped from the United Kingdom and America and all were expected to arrive in India by the end of May. This represented an increase of $3\frac{1}{2}$ per cent. in power available on the broad gauge system and 21 per cent. on the metre gauge system. In addition, a large number of both broad gauge and metre gauge trucks were coming into service. To guard against the railways to Calcutta being interrupted to the extent that they had been during the Damodar floods in the autumn of 1943, the line between Midnapore and Asansol was doubled, and, to remove the bottleneck on the railways converging on to the city, work had begun on quadrupling some 52 miles of the main line between Burdwan and Asansol.[2]

So that a reply could be given to the Secretary of State's telegram of the 11th November 1943,[3] a Sub-Committee of the War Project Co-ordination and Administration Committee was set up to discover the best method of implementing the decision that sufficient transportation facilities (whether by rail, road, inland water or coastal shipping) should be made available to maintain India's internal economy and production capacity at suitable levels, to define requirements in greater detail and to give estimates of any additional requirements in locomotives, rolling stock and shipping. It reported early in March 1944 that, although goods tonnage carried by rail in 1942–43 (the last complete year of operation) had shown a 24 per cent. increase over 1937–38, not only was the whole of the increase absorbed by military traffic but there had been a serious curtailment in the lift of civil and war supplies. The Government departments concerned in their distribution were severely affected by the unsatisfactory transport situation. Unless additional rolling

---

[1] See Ehrman, *Grand Strategy*, Volume V (H.M.S.O., 1956), pages 466–69.
[2] See Map 14, page 452. Work on the Midnapore–Asansol section was completed in September 1944 and the quadrupling of the main line in December 1944.
[3] See page 29.

stock were provided, there could be no improvement in coal supplies upon which the production of war material depended, coal exports to meet the wishes of the British Government could not be resumed, and the maintenance of an even distribution of consumer goods, on which price control depended, would not be possible. Almost all other commodities were affected to a greater or lesser degree.

The committee, after allowing for all military requirements at the existing level and for the essential coal traffic, estimated that the remaining transport was less than half of what was needed to carry the absolute minimum of civil goods required, including the raw materials and components for war supplies, if India were to fulfil her rôle as a base for operations and at the same time maintain her population.[1] They pointed out that in this calculation they had not allowed for the heavy additional load which would fall on the railways in 1945 owing to increased military demands.[2]

To meet the situation the committee assessed that India would require an extra 230,000 gross tons of shipping to restore her coastal shipping to the pre-war level, and an additional 800 broad gauge and 220 metre gauge locomotives, as well as some 40,000 broad gauge and 8,000 metre gauge wagons. This meant that, in addition to orders already placed, 206 broad gauge locomotives and 14,300 broad gauge wagons would be required. But, if no extra coastal shipping could be made available, even these numbers would be inadequate.[3] It could not be too strongly emphasized, the committee continued, that a speeding up of deliveries of locomotives and wagons was a first and vital step to putting matters on a sound footing. The gist of the sub-committee's report was sent to the Secretary of State for India on the 20th March 1944.

During the autumn of 1943, Mountbatten and Auchinleck had proposed that an Indian airborne division should be formed from 50th (P.) Brigade, a parachute brigade from the Middle East and an air landing brigade found by India Command. The War Office had approved the proposal in principle, but were unable to guarantee to find a parachute brigade from the Middle East. In March 1944 Auchinleck told the War Office, with Mountbatten's agreement, that there was no operational requirement for an armoured division in S.E.A.C. He therefore proposed to break up 44th Indian Armoured

---

[1] The requirements were 11,260 million ton-miles against an availability of 5,500 million ton-miles. See Appendix 24.

[2] To meet the additional military load in 1945, 310 broad gauge locomotives and 17,718 wagons would be needed. See Appendix 24.

[3] The figures for additional broad gauge locomotives and wagons above those already on order would be increased to 371 and 24,700 respectively. The small deficiency in metre gauge trucks (see Appendix 24) was ignored.

Division and use its headquarters and some divisional troops to form the nucleus of the airborne division. The 255th Indian Armoured Brigade (renamed 255th Tank Brigade) was to become an independent formation and be assigned to S.E.A.C., and 268th Indian (lorried) Infantry Brigade was to become General Headquarters, India, reserve. This proposal was approved and 44th Indian Armoured Division ceased to exist.

The airfield construction programme begun in 1942 had been more or less completed by April 1944, but here we are concerned only with airfields in Assam, Manipur State, eastern Bengal and Calcutta. In north-eastern Assam there was a group of ten all-weather airfields allotted to Air Transport Command which operated the air ferry to China;[1] of these, the three built in the second half of 1943 (Moran, Nazira and Golaghat) had steel plank runways and could not always be used in wet weather.[2] On the Imphal plain, in Manipur State, there were two all-weather airfields (Imphal and Palel) but both were sub-standard; the former had a single narrow runway with little hard-standing space, and the runway of the latter could not stand up to continuous use. There were, however, four fair-weather airstrips (Kangla, Tulihal, Wangjing and Sapam).[3] In eastern Bengal there were two groups of airfields: the first in the Silchar area consisted of two all-weather (Sylhet and Kumbhirgram) and two fair-weather airfields (Lalaghat and Hailakandi); the second included four all-weather airfields, capable of taking medium bomber and transport aircraft, at Agartala, Comilla, Feni and Chittagong. All these had a number of fair-weather satellites.

In the Calcutta area there was a group of some twelve all-weather airfields capable of operating heavy bombers; they were used mainly by the Strategic Air Force and the fighter squadrons allotted for the defence of the city and the surrounding industrial area. A group of five all-weather airfields was under construction near Kharagpur, some 65 miles west of Calcutta, as the main base for the American very long-range (B.29) bombers which were to operate from advanced bases in China against Japan.[4] With the aid of four American aviation engineer battalions, these five were due to be completed by the middle of May and, to supply them with the large quantities of aviation petrol required, a pipeline was laid from bulk storage depots in the port of Calcutta.

---

[1] These were Sookerating, Dinjan, Chabua, Mohanbari, Moran, Nazira, Jorhat, Golaghat, Tezpur and Misamari. See Sketch 12, page 328.
[2] See Map 4, page 53, and page 25.
[3] See Map 3, page 33.
[4] See pages 57–58. The airfields were at Kharagpur, Chakulia, Piardoba, Dudhkundi and Kalaikunda.

Great efforts were made in the early months of the year to improve the capacity of the lines of communication from Calcutta to eastern Bengal and Assam. In February the port of Calcutta was placed under the control of a civilian port director, responsible to the War Transport Department of the Government of India. He was assisted by a British and an American deputy, and a panel under military control was set up to assess the capacity of, and keep traffic moving on, the lines of communications. The port director was to regulate and control the port facilities, form a pool of labour and of lighters, assign separate dock areas to civil interests and to British and American military interests, and to take steps to overcome the prevailing congestion in the port area. The panel consisted of the Deputy Director, Movements (Calcutta) as Chairman, representing General Headquarters India, the Regional Controller of Priorities (Calcutta), representing the Government of India, two American officers, representing the American Services of Supply and the newly-arrived military railway service, two British movement officers, representing the railways and the inland water transport, and representatives of the rail and river operating companies. Its task was to estimate the capacity of the lines of communication up to twelve months ahead, to make known, a month in advance, the capacity for the succeeding month and to indicate what proportion of it was needed for civil requirements. The actual allotment of carrying space to civilian traffic and to the various Allied services was made by the Principal Administrative Officer, S.E.A.C.

From January 1944 the lines of communication to eastern Bengal and Arakan had to maintain, through the two advanced bases at Mymensingh and Chittagong, some 274,000 men and 20,000 animals.[1] The bases were supplied from Calcutta mainly by direct shipments to Chittagong, but also by rail to Tistamukh, and thence by wagon ferry to Bahadurabad or from Goalundo and Khulna by barge to Chandpur and onwards by rail.[2] By January 1944 the estimated capacity of the railway through Mymensingh had reached 525 tons a day, and that of the port of Chittagong 1,250, which was expected to reach 1,400 by the end of the month. There was, however, some congestion in the port of Calcutta which delayed the despatch of shipping to Chittagong, and to relieve the load on the port some of the shipments were transferred to Vizagapatam during February. This port was placed under military control on the 1st April, by which time it was handling some 27,000 tons a month.

On the 1st February, 14th Army took control of the port of Chittagong and the Bengal and Assam railway from there to

---

[1] 90,000 men and 8,000 animals were based on Mymensingh and 184,000 men and 12,000 animals on Chittagong.
[2] See Sketch 12, page 328.

Akhaura, subject to the proviso that General Headquarters, India, would, in consultation with S.E.A.C., remain responsible for deciding the development of the port, and would have a call upon six train paths daily northwards from Chittagong. During February, March and April, both the rail lift and the capacity of the port increased greatly. The stores carried by rail averaged just under 900 tons a day and those handled by the port just over 1,900 and, in addition, some 20,000 men and 3,000 animals passed through the port monthly.[1]

The port facilities in the Cox's Bazar area had also been improved by establishing a new terminal for barges and coastal vessels up to 200 feet in length at Ultakhali, which lay at the head of a creek six miles north-east of Cox's Bazar and only a mile and a half from the Dohazari–Tumbru road. These facilities, which were fully in use by the 1st December 1943, increased the intake capacity of the Cox's Bazar area from 400 to some 1,000 tons a day.

In January, the lines of communication to Assam were maintaining some 450,000 men (including some 100,000 Americans and Chinese) and 15,000 animals. It was estimated that by April these numbers would have increased to 620,000 men (including about 155,000 Americans and Chinese) and 18,000 animals.[2] The British proportion of this total was supplied through advanced bases at Gauhati and Dimapur, and the American and Chinese through Ledo and the river ports adjacent to airfields.

Work on the first stage of the further development of the lines of communication had begun in November 1943.[3] The proposal to build a bridge over the Brahmaputra at Amingaon was dropped, since an increase from 250 to 750 wagons a day each way on the wagon ferry between Amingaon and Pandu would enable the target figure to be reached. Work on doubling the broad gauge system southwards from Parbatipur and the metre gauge between Parbatipur and Amingaon, as well as between Lumding and Dimapur, had begun, but had made very slow progress owing to the shortage and poor quality of labour. By April the transhipment facilities at Parbatipur and at the Amingaon–Pandu ferry had been greatly improved, and additional sidings and marshalling yards at Pandu, Lumding and Mariani, as well as longer passing places along the line, had been built.

---

[1] The figures of stores carried in tons a month were:

Month	By Sea	By Rail
February	45,000	24,000
March	62,000	26,000
April	67,500	28,000

[2] This total included some 100,000 labourers and allowed for four British or Indian divisions, three Chinese divisions, an American L.R.P. brigade and corps and army troops in the forward area.

[3] For details see Appendix 5.

The British 4-inch pipeline from Chandranathpur (near Badarpur) to Dimapur was brought into operation during February 1944, and it was estimated that its extension back to Chittagong would be finished by December.[1] In June it was decided that the two American 6-inch pipelines would terminate at a tank farm at Tinsukia, and that one would be constructed from Chittagong, instead of from Calcutta, to Tinsukia, following the alignment of the 4-inch British pipeline as far as Dimapur.[2]

The proposal to run a 4-inch pipeline to China by way of Fort Hertz had been abandoned in November 1943, and, instead, work was begun on the construction of two 4-inch pipelines from Tinsukia following the alignment of the Ledo Road; one to supply petrol for vehicles operating on the road, and the other to supply airfields along the route and to supplement the 6-inch pipeline which was to be built from Chittagong by way of Tinsukia and Myitkyina to Kunming.[3]

By the end of December 1943 the metre gauge rail system east of Parbatipur was carrying some 2,700 tons a day which, with the river traffic of 600 tons, gave a total of 3,300 daily. The shoaling of the Brahmaputra near Pandu during the first fortnight of January resulted in barge traffic on the river and the rail ferry being held up, causing acute congestion on the railway system right back to Calcutta. By the 21st military traffic was down to one petrol and one stores train per day which reduced the tonnage carried in January by about 800 tons a day.[4] The opening of the British 4-inch pipeline in February eased the position a little, but it was not until the 1st March, when troops of the American military railway service took over the running of the railway from Katihar to Tinsukia (a distance of 824 miles), that the position began to improve.[5] The introduction of military control coupled with the determination that traffic should get through, regardless of economy in working the system or the need for strictly balanced running, soon produced results and tonnages carried by rail and river reached 3,500 a day in March, 4,700 in April, and by July had risen to 5,400.[6]

Between the 9th and 29th March some 22,000 non-combatants were evacuated from Imphal and 5th Indian Division was flown to the

---

[1] See Appendix 4.

[2] The reasons for this decision were that the new alignment would be shorter and would meet the need for a take-off to the Air Transport Command airfields which might have to be built in eastern Bengal, and that, by discharging oil at a sea terminal outside Chittagong harbour, a considerable saving in tankers would be effected.

[3] See Appendix 1. The maximum capacity of a 4-inch pipeline was taken to be 18,000 tons, and of a 6-inch pipeline 36,000, tons a month.

[4] Normal traffic was not resumed till the 9th February.

[5] See pages 31–32.

[6] In addition to the 4,700 tons a day of freight carried in April, the railway ran sufficient troop trains to bring all the reinforcing formations to Dimapur, other than those flown up.

Imphal plain and the Assam Valley from Arakan.[1] On the 24th, all units of the L. of C. road transport, except for traffic control posts, provost and recovery detachments, were moved to Kanglatongbi, Kohima and Dimapur, but transport was kept running night and day despite the approach of Japanese columns. When the Imphal Road was cut on the 29th, IV Corps, with a ration strength of 155,000 men and 11,000 animals, became dependent on stocks already in the Imphal area and on such supplies as could be delivered by air.[2] Thereafter there were five transport and two bulk petrol companies available to serve the Imphal plain, and fifteen transport and two bulk petrol companies in the Dimapur area, where XXXIII Corps was concentrating.

At the end of March there were sufficient stocks on the Imphal plain to enable IV Corps to operate at full scale up to the 5th May. The aircraft available to 14th Army, including those borrowed from Air Transport Command, were already fully committed until the middle of April.[3] No aircraft could therefore be spared to supply IV Corps until either some were released from their existing commitments, or the aircraft coming from the Middle East were ready to operate, which would not be until about the 18th April.[4] The corps had thus to live on its reserve stocks for the first three weeks after the Imphal Road had been cut. On the 9th, as a precaution, Scoones reduced rations for all troops and animals in the corps by about one-third and prepared to decrease the numbers to be supplied by arranging that returning aircraft would evacuate casualties and up to 26,000 labourers and non-combatants, as soon as air supply began.

Preliminary arrangements were made early in April to ensure that the necessary supplies were available at airfields in eastern Bengal, and to reinforce the air supply units at the despatching airfields. On the 17th an inter-service conference, attended by representatives of Eastern Air Command, 3rd Tactical Air Force, 11th Army Group and 14th Army, was held at Comilla to review the problem of air supply to 14th Army as a whole and to IV Corps in particular. The conference assumed that the Imphal Road would not be reopened until the end of June, but that IV Corps would retain complete control of the Imphal plain. Transport aircraft could therefore deliver supplies by landing on the Imphal group of airfields. The daily tonnage required to meet all demands on the plain at full scale was assessed at 540 tons a day (480 for IV Corps and 60 for the R.A.F.).

---

[1] See Appendix 25.

[2] When the road was cut all lorries in transit turned back to their bases and only two were lost.

[3] Their tasks were the supply of Fort Hertz, 81st (W.A.) Division, Special Force, the garrison of Kohima, and to move 5th Division and 33rd Brigade of 7th Division from Arakan, XXXIII Corps Headquarters and 4th Brigade of 2nd Division from India and 14th (L.R.P.) Brigade into Burma. See Appendix 25.

[4] See page 212.

It was agreed that, since they could not carry reserves, priority must be given to troops dependent on supply dropping; that, to reduce air maintenance to the minimum, casualties and non-combatants should be flown out by transport aircraft returning to base after unloading supplies; and that, to keep fighting units up to strength, 250 reinforcements should be flown into Imphal daily. It was evident that weather conditions and variations in the demand for air supply from other parts of the front (especially from the Chindits and Merrill's Marauders who were entirely dependent on air supply) would make a daily flat rate delivery at the assessed figure unlikely. Moreover, the newly-arrived squadrons from the Middle East, and the military organization hurriedly formed to work with them, would take time to become fully efficient.

The outcome of the conference was the 'Comilla plan' which covered the air supply needs of the whole Allied front from Arakan to Ledo. That part of the plan which dealt with the maintenance of IV Corps and the R.A.F. squadrons in the Imphal area (by air landing) was known as operation 'Stamina' and was to begin on the 18th April. Until the end of the month, all transport aircraft were to be used to build up on the Imphal plain a balanced reserve of thirty days' requirements. This would entail the delivery of 3,180 tons (2,800 of supplies, 300 of ammunition and 80 of engineer stores), a daily average delivery of 245 tons. From the 1st May deliveries were to be made daily at a rate calculated to leave IV Corps with fifteen days' reserve of supplies by the 30th June.[1] If the road to Imphal had not been reopened by July, full daily maintenance would then be undertaken, and the fifteen days' reserve kept in case of emergency.

The most convenient airfields from which to supply the Imphal plain were those in eastern Bengal. Of these, Chittagong, Comilla (with its satellite, Chandina) and Agartala were selected, all of which were on the main southern line of communications. The maintenance of some 155,000 men and 11,000 animals was thus switched from the northern to the southern line. This was made possible by the great increase in the capacity of the port of Chittagong and of the Mymensingh–Chittagong railway, and by the fact that, between the 1st April and the end of May, XV Corps was reduced from five to three divisions. By relieving the northern line, the switch also made it possible to maintain XXXIII Corps at Dimapur without difficulty.

Although the first sorties to the Imphal plain were flown on the 18th April as planned, 'Stamina' did not get off to a good start. The

[1] Up to the 1st June, 373 tons a day were to be delivered for IV Corps and 60 for the R.A.F. and thereafter 475 and 90 tons a day. Throughout the two months ten sorties a day were to be allotted to fly in reinforcements.

Tulihal airfield was to have been brought up to all-weather standard by surfacing it with bithess before the rains began, but the cutting of the Imphal Road made it impossible to bring up the material from Dimapur and it became necessary to fly it to Imphal.[1] Ten Commando aircraft were therefore diverted to Calcutta and between the 20th and 26th April delivered 368 tons of bithess to Tulihal, at the expense of supplies to IV Corps.

The Commandos proved, however, too heavy for the airfields on the Imphal plain and soon began to damage the runways. Ten were therefore returned to Air Transport Command on the 19th and the remaining ten as soon as the delivery of the bithess had been completed. The loss of the lift of the twenty Commandos, the diversion of other aircraft for emergency supply drops and the inexperience of the newly-arrived pilots and the combined army and air force teams at despatching airfields resulted in the tonnage delivered by the 30th April being only 1,926 tons, a shortfall of some 1,250 tons in the first ten days of the airlift.

Mountbatten had told the Chiefs of Staff on the 20th April that he was returning the borrowed Commandos, but said that he would like to reserve the right to call on them again during the period they had been placed at his disposal.[2] The same day he received a telegram sent on the 19th by Slim and Stratemeyer saying that, having studied the requirements in transport aircraft for the supply of 14th Army, they were both agreed that the seventy-nine Dakotas on loan from the Middle East must remain in the theatre until the 1st July. If these aircraft were removed, the forces on the Imphal plain could not be maintained and, as a result, their main line of communication to Assam might be permanently cut.

Mountbatten was assured by Giffard on the 23rd that the forces with 14th Army already in action were adequate to defeat the Japanese *15th Army*,[3] and that reliefs for the Chindits were available, but this telegram made him painfully aware that, if he returned the transport aircraft to the Middle East at the time demanded, he might not be able to supply 14th Army. On the 25th he told the Chiefs of Staff that the return of all the aircraft on loan from the Middle East might not be possible, pointed out the dangers which would arise if they were removed and asked that they might be retained until the course of the battle permitted their release.

Despite his plea, Mountbatten was told on the 28th April that all the aircraft borrowed from the Middle East would have to be returned by the middle of May. On the 1st May he warned the

---

[1] See Map 3, page 33. Bithess was hessian treated with bitumen which, laid over levelled soil in long strips with a slight overlap, produced a waterproof surface.

[2] The American Chiefs of Staff agreed on the 26th to Mountbatten's request.

[3] See page 251.

Chiefs of Staff that their withdrawal would be disastrous. It would mean either halting Stilwell's operations, or making drastic changes in the plans for the battle in the Kohima–Imphal area (such as flying out one division from the Imphal plain), or diverting some fifty Commandos from Air Transport Command from the 10th May until the end of June with a consequent large drop in the tonnage carried by the air ferry to China. He therefore again appealed for permission to keep the Middle East aircraft until the issue of the battle around Imphal was settled, or until the first seventy-nine of the four hundred transport aircraft promised by the American Chiefs of Staff had arrived in India.[1]

No reply to this having been received by the 4th, Peirse was forced to warn Giffard, Slim and Stratemeyer that all the aircraft from the Middle East would have to be withdrawn from operations by the 8th. That day Giffard, with Slim's full agreement, told Mountbatten that, if the aircraft were removed without replacement, he could not hold himself responsible for the consequences. Mountbatten thereupon told Peirse that he accepted full responsibility for a delay in the return of the seventy-nine aircraft and that they were not to go without his orders. That evening he received a telegram from the Prime Minister which read: 'Let nothing go from the battle that you need for victory. I will not accept denial of this from any quarter, and will back you to the full'.

Two days later the Chiefs of Staff told Mountbatten that the borrowed aircraft must reach the Middle East by the end of May but that the move of the first hundred Dakotas of the combat cargo group from the United States was to be accelerated so that they would reach India by the 22nd. In the event of an emergency arising as a result of any delay in the arrival of these aircraft, the twenty Commandos returned to Air Transport Command could be recalled.

This arrangement was still unsatisfactory for, even if the Dakotas did begin to arrive on the date specified, they could not be ready to operate much before the middle of June and, in order to get the Middle East aircraft to their destination by the end of the month, they would have to be withdrawn on the 24th May. This left a gap of three weeks at what might prove to be the most vital stage in the battle for Imphal. Mountbatten again warned the Chiefs of Staff of the disastrous effects which would follow from their proposal, and pointed out the folly not only of withdrawing some 150 aircraft from operations and flying them 5,000 miles in opposite directions during the height of a battle, but also of exchanging experienced for inexperienced air crews at a time when the highest level of airmanship, navigational and technical skill was required to deal with monsoon conditions. Once again he asked to be allowed to keep the

---

[1] See page 166.

seventy-nine aircraft, and suggested they should be replaced in the Mediterranean by aircraft of the combat cargo group. On the 16th May, the Chiefs of Staff replied that the return of the loaned aircraft could be delayed till the 15th June so as to allow the aircraft and crews of the combat cargo group to arrive in India and prepare for operations.[1] This arrangement assured adequate support for 14th Army's campaign, but meanwhile the Generalissimo had asked for aircraft to supply the Yunnan armies which had launched an offensive across the Salween River on the 10th May.[2] To meet this request, Mountbatten on the 17th May put a squadron of Dakotas at his disposal and replaced them by medium bombers from the Strategic Air Force, whose operations were for the time being curtailed by the pre-monsoon storms.[3]

On the 1st May, so that there should be one single authority responsible for all air supply, Troop Carrier Command was placed under the orders of Air Marshal Baldwin (3rd Tactical Air Force). Nevertheless the deliveries to IV Corps fell during the first half of the month to an average of only 100 tons a day.[4] This fall-off in deliveries was due to the diversion of aircraft to fly 89th Brigade from Arakan to Imphal, to a reduction in the numbers of sorties flown because of difficult flying conditions,[5] to aircraft not always being fully loaded because stores were not available at the despatching airfield and to the lack of refuelling facilities at airfields.[6]

To reduce the demands on the airlift to the plain, a further 5,000 non-combatants were flown out during the month and another ration cut was made which averaged 14 per cent. for the 118,000 men and 21 per cent. for the 1,000 animals still in the Imphal area. This brought down the daily requirements of IV Corps to 362 tons.[7] Six of the R.A.F. squadrons on the plain were withdrawn to airfields in Assam and eastern Bengal, thus reducing the air force requirements to 50 tons. To speed up the loading and despatch of transport aircraft, some airfields were turned into single commodity airfields. The

---

[1] The Chiefs of Staff insisted on the seventy-nine aircraft being returned to the Middle East because they were especially equipped and the crews trained for airborne operations for which the combat cargo group was not. Airborne operations were shortly to be carried out in the Mediterranean, and the presence of these aircraft in that theatre was necessary.

[2] See Chapter XXVIII.

[3] These were used from the 20th to ferry bombs from Chittagong for the squadrons operating from the Imphal plain, and to carry forward stocks of army ammunition.

[4] Deliveries to IV Corps from the 1st–16th May were some 1,700 tons as against a programme of 5,970 tons. The deficit of 4,270 tons added to that of April gave a total deficit of some 5,500 tons.

[5] The main difficulty was that dense masses of cumulus cloud built up over the mountains west of the Imphal plain during the day, even though the weather was fine both in eastern Bengal and at Imphal.

[6] See Appendices 25 and 26.

[7] The cuts in the rations were introduced between the 22nd and 29th May. The figure of 362 tons a day was made up as follows: supplies 177, P.O.L. 68, ammunition 65, ordnance 32, miscellaneous 20. Including those of the R.A.F. the total daily requirements were now 412 tons.

introduction of this system made for greater speed and efficiency as aircraft could be loaded to full capacity with one type of store at one place. Feni became the base for P.O.L., Chittagong for ammunition and Sylhet for supplies. The less bulky medical stores, mail and canteen stores as well as reinforcements were handled at three mixed commodity airfields—Jorhat, Comilla and Agartala.[1]

These measures took some time to organize and get into their stride, with the result that deliveries during the period of reorganization in the second half of May averaged only 220 tons a day. By the end of the month the deficit had risen to some 7,300 tons, IV Corps' reserves had dropped to approximately seventeen days for supplies and P.O.L. and there were shortages of some types of ammunition. As 3rd Tactical Air Force could guarantee to fly in only 363 tons a day during June, of which IV Corps' share was to be 313 tons, it was clear that by the end of June reserves would be reduced to some six or seven days instead of the stipulated fifteen. The position on the plain was beginning to cause anxiety.

Although early in June Peirse was confident that the requirements could and would be met, Mountbatten began to doubt the ability of the air force to keep IV Corps supplied. He therefore warned the Chiefs of Staff that he might have to ask for a further diversion of aircraft from Air Transport Command should the position at Imphal become so desperate that the security of the Assam line of communications was threatened. Stratemeyer was even more emphatic than Peirse that there were enough transport aircraft to meet the requirements at Imphal without further diversion of aircraft from the air ferry route. He pointed out that in any case the ground organization on the plain could not handle more aircraft and that there were no suitable airfields on which to base extra transport squadrons.

To meet the deteriorating situation, Slim had meanwhile reduced the ration strength on the plain by ordering the number of administrative boxes to be decreased and their garrisons flown out. He also accepted a proposal put forward by 3rd Tactical Air Force to move the last remaining fighter-bomber squadron from Imphal to Dimapur. Renewed efforts to increase deliveries were also being made: 3rd Combat Cargo Group was sent to Sylhet and thirty additional medium bombers were diverted to carry ammunition. To avoid aircraft having to return fully loaded to the more distant bases if they ran into really bad weather over the mountains near Imphal, a staging depot was established at Kumbhirgram airfield near Silchar. There, aircraft which met bad weather after leaving their base could dump their loads and return to base. When the weather improved, aircraft operating between Kumbhirgram and the Imphal plain had a short haul, thus saving many hours of flying time. The air base for

---

[1] See Appendix 26 for the allocation of commodities to airfields.

Special Force was also changed by degrees from Agartala and Sylhet to Dinjan. This had many advantages: flying time was considerably reduced, the new route was less vulnerable to enemy interference, better flying conditions could be expected and it would be easier for Stilwell to take over the maintenance of Special Force when it came under his command.[1]

Largely owing to the efficacy of the measures introduced by 3rd Tactical Air Force in May and early June, to the greater efficiency of the organization on the ground and in the air, and to an unexpected break in the monsoon about the middle of the month, deliveries to the plain improved during June. The daily average during the month was 362 tons, which very nearly reached the guaranteed figure of 363 tons a day, and during the last nine days reached an average of 515 tons. This was a remarkable feat, especially as Palel and Tulihal airfields broke up and could not be used once the monsoon began. All supplies from about the 22nd May had therefore to be landed on the single narrow runway at Imphal, or on the fair-weather airstrip at Kangla which drained rapidly and could be used with safety within two days of the heaviest rain.[2] Although the Imphal Road was reopened on the 22nd June, air supply was continued at the full rate until the end of the month, mainly in order to record the figures attained for a second complete month and to explore more fully the problems of air maintenance on such a scale.

From the 18th April to the 30th June, some 12,550 reinforcements and 18,800 tons of supplies were delivered to Imphal and about 13,000 sick and wounded and some 43,000 non-combatants evacuated. By the second half of June all IV Corps' needs were being met and reserves being built up again. Even if the Imphal Road had not been opened until the end of July, the corps' supply position would have still been better than it had been at any time since the airlift began on the 18th April.

The success of the Imphal airlift was made possible only by Allied air superiority which enabled transport aircraft to be used with relative safety in close vicinity of the enemy. The strain on the transport squadrons was, however, very heavy indeed. They had flown for some ten weeks, often in most difficult flying conditions and in bad weather, to the limit of endurance. By the end of June many of the air crews were completely exhausted. The great credit due to them must be shared with the R.A.F. ground crews on the airfields, and in particular those on the Imphal plain who, with no cover and often in torrential rain, succeeded in maintaining an amazingly high rate of serviceability for their aircraft.

---

[1] See Chapter XX.
[2] See Map 3, page 33. The single runway soon became congested, accidents occurred and time was wasted while loaded aircraft were kept circling awaiting permission to land.

Diagrammatic Sketch of Lines of Communication to North East

Siliguri

Bongaigaon Ran

Golakganj

Jogighopa Amin

Lalmanirhat Dhubri
Kaunia

A

Brahmaputra R.

Golapara

Parbatipur

Mokameh Ghat Katihar

Proposed Assam Access Road

Ferry

Po

Sh

EAST INDIAN RLY

Bonpara

Bahadurabad

Singhjani

Santahar

Ragannathganj Gouripur

Tistamukh

B

Mymensingh

PATHAR

Sirajganj

Ganges R.

Abdulpur

Ishurdi

Bhairab

Dumri

MADHAIGANJ

Poradha

Tangi

Ak
⊙A

Goalundo

Dacca

Comi
⊙

Asansol

DHUBALIA ⊙

GRAND TRUNK ROAD

CHARRA

Panagarh

EAST INDIAN RLY

Burdwan

Laksam

Chandpur

Jamshedpur

Ranaghat ⊙ Jessore

Bongaon

Noakhali

BENGAL NAGPUR RLY

DIGRI
SALBANI

KANCHRAPARA
BAIGACHI
BARRACKPORE
DUM DUM
CALCUTTA
RED ROAD
ALIPORE

Khulna

DELTA ARE

Kharagpur

AMARDA ROAD

Hooghly R.

BAY OF

Legend

AIRFIELDS R.A.F. U.S. .... Allweather.... ⊙ ● Fairweather....○

4" PIPELINE Completed:........ Projected:................................
(or under construction)

6" PIPELINE Completed:.... Projected:...................

ROADS (Allweather) Completed:..... Projected:............. ....

RAILWAYS BROAD GAUGE Double:....Single:

" METRE & SMALLER GAUGE Double:....Single:

A The doubling of the track between Parbatipur and Golakganj was due for completion. OCT.44

B " " " " " Abdulpur · Santahar " " " ...AUG.44

In order to give an appreciation of the area covered by this diagram a straight line drawn from Calcutta to Myitkyina would measure 590 miles

Frontier July 1944

Sookerating
MOHANBARI DINJAN
Dibrugarh
Tinsukia
CHABUA
Digboi
Namrup
Ledo
MORAN
Disangmukh
Sibsagar
Tagup
NAZIRA
Shingbwiyang
Rangapara
Balipara
Neamati
Donalgaon
Simaluguri
Misamari
Tezpur
Jorhat
Silghat
Mariani
gia
DERGAON
Maingkwan
GOLAGHAT
Furkating
gaon
Gauhati
LANKA
Lahurijan
Shadazup
Warazup
Dimapur
Chaparmukh
Lumding
Kohima
Kamaing
Myitkyina
llong
Mao
Kangpokpi
Mogaung
Kanglatongbi
y
Chandranathpur
Imphal
TULIHAL
Silchar
KUMBHIRGRAM
Surma R.
Palel
Kulaura
Badarpur
Bhamo
KANDI
Hailakandi
Lalaghat
Tamu
aura
ARTALA
Aijal
lla
Lashio
Tiddim
eni
Fort White
HATHAZARI
Chittagong
Dohazari
Mandalay
CHIRINGA
Ultakhali
Cox's Bazar
Tumbru
Bawli Bazar
Buthidaung
Maungdaw
Akyab
B E N G A L
Ramree
Toungoo

CHAPTER XXIII

THE BATTLES OF IMPHAL AND KOHIMA

The Period of Attrition

(April–May 1944)

See Maps 4, 8 and 9 and Sketches 13 and 15

AT the end of the third week of April 1944, IV Corps and XXXIII Corps had just begun a co-ordinated offensive to open the Imphal Road and destroy the Japanese *15th* and *31st Divisions* which had interposed between them. At Kohima, XXXIII Corps had relieved the garrison and was deploying 2nd British Division for an attack on the Japanese holding the heights overlooking the pass. At Imphal, IV Corps' offensive northwards against *15th Division* had achieved initial success and was developing slowly against stubborn opposition, but south of Imphal the Japanese still held the initiative, and 20th and 17th Indian Divisions were under severe pressure on Shenam Pass and at Bishenpur respectively.[1]

Aware that the attack on Imphal from the north had lost impetus, Mutaguchi had instructed *31st Division* to send a regimental group to the Kanglatongbi area so that *15th Division* could resume the offensive. Sato thereupon ordered *124th Regiment* (less *III/124th Battalion*), *I/138th Infantry* and *III/31st Mountain Artillery Battalions* to assemble at Aradura in readiness to move to Imphal under Miyazaki's command. The rest of *138th Regiment* was to hold the Cheswema–Merema area and from there harass the Dimapur–Kohima road. Naga Village was to remain the responsibility of *III/124th Battalion*, while *58th Regiment* continued to try to capture Garrison Hill.

On the 20th April a copy of Mutaguchi's order was captured on the Imphal plain. On the morning of the 21st, north of Kohima, an officer of the Cameron Highlanders came face to face with a Japanese cyclist on a track near Merema and shot him dead. Papers found on him contained orders for *I/138th Battalion* 'to proceed speedily to the south of Kohima and help in the capture of Imphal', and a very detailed description of Sato's plan for the continuance of operations at Kohima. The capture of these two documents, almost simultaneously,

---

[1] See Chapter XXI.

had significant results. Late on the 21st, Stopford received from Slim the gist of Mutaguchi's plan, together with a telephone message telling him to exert such pressure at Kohima that no Japanese force of any size could leave the area. A few hours later—at 2 a.m. on the 22nd—Stopford learnt from the papers taken at Merema not only how Sato was complying with Mutaguchi's order, but also the detail of the Japanese future plans for the Kohima operations. He lost no time.

By 6.45 a.m., at Kohima, 6th Brigade (Shapland) had received orders from Grover (2nd Division) to begin at once to clear the Japanese from their footholds on the Kohima ridge, and had been allotted a squadron of medium tanks of 149th R.A.C. and the divisional artillery to support it. An hour later Stopford told Grover that 253 L. of C. Sub-Area was being made responsible for road protection up to MS 32, and the depleted 161st Brigade forward of that point, each reinforced by a detachment of armoured cars of 11th Cavalry and light tanks of 45th Cavalry. At the same time he ordered Grover to free two brigades to clear the Kohima area, accepting all reasonable risks regarding the protection of his rearward communications. Grover accordingly ordered 4th Brigade (Brigadier W. H. Goschen), now freed from road protection duties, to move to Jotsoma, leaving one battalion as divisional reserve at Zubza, and 5th Brigade (Hawkins) to concentrate on the Merema ridge, cut all tracks to the north and prepare to attack Naga Village. No tank support could, however, be given to 5th Brigade until 6th Brigade had cleared D.C.'s Bungalow spur and secured the road junction at the summit of Kohima pass.[1]

With both Grover and Sato ordering their forward troops to gain complete possession of the Kohima ridge at the same time, it is not surprising that it became the scene of desperate fighting in which both sides suffered severely. On the afternoon of the 22nd, 6th Brigade sent two troops of tanks, supported by a detachment of 1st Royal Berkshires, to work their way eastwards along D.C.'s Bungalow spur under cover of the fire of most of the divisional artillery. Some progress was made but the tanks, operating from the road, were prevented by the steep slopes from reaching the crest of the spur and had to withdraw, leaving one tank disabled and half the accompanying infantry killed or wounded.

That night the Japanese retaliated by attacking both D.C.'s Bungalow spur and Kuki Piquet: seven companies, including the greater part of *I/138th Battalion* (part of the force due to go to Imphal), were involved in the attacks and four are said by the Japanese to have been almost wiped out. On D.C.'s Bungalow spur their attack made no

---

[1] See Sketch 13, page 346.

progress, but in the Kuki Piquet area 2nd Durham Light Infantry
had to make a counter-attack to restore the situation and suffered 105
casualties, including about a third of its officer strength. The 'dog
fight' on the Kohima ridge was destined to go on for another three
weeks.

On the 24th April, Grover, with Stopford's approval, decided to
carry out a double envelopment of Kohima. On the right, 4th Brigade,
less one battalion, was to move from Jotsoma by way of Khonoma in
a wide encircling movement and attack Kohima from the south-
west. The brigade was to be assisted by 143 S.S. Company[1], and
Naga porters and guides organized by the civil adviser at corps headquarters. To free the brigade for its advance, 161st Brigade was to
move forward to Zubza and take over the protection of Jotsoma with
one battalion, while the now reconstituted 1st Assam Regiment took
over protection of the road behind Zubza. On the left, 5th Brigade
was to clear the Naga Village area, thus completing the encirclement
from the east.

The preliminary moves for these enveloping attacks began on the
25th, but were delayed by heavy rain which made the mountain
tracks so slippery that a mile an hour was excellent progress for even
lightly armed men. While 4th and 5th Brigades were moving to their
forming-up positions, the first Vengeance dive-bombers seen in the
Kohima area began the 'softening up' of Naga Village, in preparation for 5th Brigade's attack, and the artillery moved into position.
Owing to the nature of the country observation posts were difficult
to find, and all gun positions had to be close to the Imphal Road
wherever a spur or comparatively broad re-entrant enabled the guns
to be moved off it. Their protection was undertaken by the men
of the two light batteries of the divisional artillery, for whose guns
there was so little ammunition that they were virtually out of
action.[2]

From his divisional command post on Point 5120 Sato saw enough
to make him realize that strong forces were being deployed against
him, and that, if he sent away a regimental group, he would be
unable to carry out his primary mission of capturing and holding
Kohima. Consequently on the 25th he ordered the two battalions of
124th Regiment to remain at Aradura and secure the left flank of the
division, and *I/138th Battalion* to remain under command of *58th
Regiment* which was to continue its efforts to clear the Kohima ridge.
Sato's decision not to send a regimental group to Imphal, in direct
disregard of *15th Army's* order, is considered by the Japanese to be
one of the contributory causes of their failure to press home their

---

[1] The 143 S.S. Company was originally formed by 2nd Division for amphibious reconnaissance tasks. It was retained as a commando and path-finding unit.
[2] There was a general shortage of 3.7 howizter ammunition in S.E.A.C. at this time.

attack on Imphal from the north.[1] It will be seen, however, that it was precisely the presence of *124th Regiment* in the Aradura area at the end of April which prevented 4th Brigade's enveloping attack by way of Khonoma and Pulebadze from reaching the Imphal Road behind *31st Division* and over-running G.P.T. Ridge in the first few days of May.[2] Sato's fears of what would happen if he parted with a regimental group were in fact well founded.

The impact of the battle of Kohima on operations at Imphal can be properly assessed only by a study of the events in the latter area during the last week of April and the first few days in May. On the 19th April the units of the Japanese *15th Division* north of Imphal had abandoned their attacks and dug in on the ground they had gained.[3] It is evident that Mutaguchi intended the regiment from *31st Division* to renew the offensive on its arrival at Kanglatongbi from Kohima. Had the move taken place, 63rd Brigade at Sengmai would have been hard pressed during the last few days of April but, as it was, it had little to do from the 20th April until it was relieved in the first week in May by 89th Brigade of 7th Division, which had been flown from Arakan to reinforce 5th Division.[4]

East of Sengmai, 5th Division's offensive up the Iril valley with 123rd Brigade and towards the high ground in the Molvom–Mapao area with 9th Brigade made steady progress.[5] Mapao was occupied on the 24th but, despite the help of diversionary raids by 63rd Brigade from Sengmai, the enemy clung to the heights at Molvom. By the end of the month, 9th Brigade was disposed with its left at Mapao in contact with 63rd Brigade and its right at Wakan five miles to the north-east looking down on the Iril River. There it was in contact with 123rd Brigade which, relieved of the responsibility for Nungshigum by a battalion of the reconstituted 50th (P.) Brigade, was about to strike north-west towards the main road north of Kanglatongbi.

Further east on the 26th April, Roberts (23rd Division) ordered 49th Brigade, then in divisional reserve at Kameng,[6] to take over

---

[1] As the ground provided the Japanese with good artillery positions and excellent observation, *Headquarters 31st Division* considered that, had sufficient guns with adequate supplies of ammunition been available, it would have been safe to transfer these three battalions. The *15th Army* on the other hand considered that Sato had failed to dispose his infantry to the best advantage and that, had he done so, he could have spared the battalions.

[2] Until G.P.T. Ridge was regained it was impossible to restore the Kohima water supply. The 6th Brigade was kept supplied by water lorries, which filled up at water points on the Dimapur road.

[3] See Map 9, page 374.

[4] The 89th Brigade was allotted to 5th Division to replace 161st Brigade which had been sent to Dimapur to reinforce XXXIII Corps. See page 235.

[5] See page 309.

[6] The 49th Brigade had reorganized at Yairipok after returning from the Tiddim road and had resumed command of 4/5th Mahrattas, which it had left with 50th (P.) Brigade in the Sangshak area in March.

responsibility for the road right up to Kasom, in order to leave 1st and 37th Brigades free to continue the offensive against *15th Division*, whose headquarters was now said to be at Shongpel, about eight miles north-west of Kasom.[1] By the evening of the 27th, two battalions of 1st Brigade from east and north and two of 37th Brigade from south and west were closing in on Shongpel. Early on the 28th, 1/16th Punjab, descending on the village from the 6,400-foot ridge to the east, dispersed the defenders but found no sign of a headquarters.[2] To the west 3/3rd Gurkhas dispersed an enemy column moving east and counted thirty enemy dead after the action, but apart from this the operation achieved no success. A sweep by 37th Brigade during the first week of May did, however, result in the disappearance of enemy patrols which had been active near Imphal in the Kameng and Nungshigum areas.

In the 20th Division area there had been a lull after the loss of Crete East and Cyprus on the 21st April,[3] but *II/215th Battalion* had been identified on the tracks leading to Palel to the north of the pass,[4] and a large force of the *I.N.A.* had been reported in the hills to the south between the pass and Shuganu. On the night of the 27th/28th the lull was broken by a very determined attack on Scraggy. Posts on the hill changed hands during the night in attack and counter-attack, but at dawn the enemy, identified as *III/213th Battalion*, drew off, leaving some fifty-two dead and the remnants of a company of 3/1st Gurkhas in possession. On the 29th and 30th an enemy force estimated to be a battalion unsuccessfully attacked a large supply dump some four miles north of Palel which was held by 4/3rd Madras Regiment. These attacks provided identifications of *II/51st Battalion* of *15th Division*, last heard of in the Katha area opposing the Chindits. Almost simultaneously an *I.N.A.* unit of about battalion strength was ambushed and routed in a defile in the hills south of Palel.

These enemy activities led Scoones to the conclusion that Yamamoto was attempting to by-pass Shenam and preparing to launch an offensive in that area. He did not think that *15th Divison* could resume its offensive north of Imphal unless reinforced from Kohima and, as there was no sign of this, felt he could reduce the force north-east of Imphal and leave only one brigade (49th) on the Ukhrul road. He therefore ordered 48th Brigade, in corps reserve near Imphal,[5] to move to Wangjing and clear the enemy from the Palel area. At the same time, in order to create a strong reserve within striking distance

---

[1] See page 309.

[2] It seems that there was a headquarters somewhere in the area because a Japanese wireless message in clear was intercepted which said: 'Am in face of enemy, do not open up on this group.'

[3] See page 310 and Sketch 15, page 370.

[4] There was one company of this battalion in the area; the rest of it was in the Bishenpur area.

[5] See page 307.

of the pass,[1] he ordered Roberts to place 1st Brigade in corps reserve and concentrate it at Wangjing by the 5th May. He warned him to be ready to send a second brigade to the Imphal plain at twenty-four hours' notice after the 5th.

In 17th Division's sector on the Tiddim road, the reinforced 32nd Brigade in the Bishenpur area was under considerable pressure. The Japanese *33rd Division* was disposed with *214th* and *215th Regiments* north and south of the Silchar track respectively and *II/213th Battalion* and *4th Engineer Regiment*, supported by armour and a powerful artillery force, on the main road. Their immediate objectives were Potsangbum and the water point on the Silchar track near Point 5846, which supplied the Northamptons and 1/4th Gurkhas holding the sector. In both places attack and counter-attack continued throughout the last week of April, with heavy losses on both sides. On the 24th the Japanese air force made one of its rare appearances in strength, bombers escorted by fighters attacking and setting fire to the engineers' basha camp just north of Bishenpur village. On the 25th the Japanese established a roadblock on the Silchar track near the water point, and the following day gained possession of it. Mackenzie, who had made two unsuccessful attacks on Ningthoukhong at the cost of 130 casualties, three tanks destroyed and four temporarily put out of action, was now forced to desist from his attempts to regain the village and to concentrate on regaining the vital water point.

On the 27th and 28th there was fierce hand-to-hand fighting there, during which tanks were winched up to a hill top with the help of bulldozers. It was not, however, till the evening of the 29th April that 1/4th Gurkhas, taking advantage of a violent storm, overran an enemy force holding a ridge overlooking the water point. As darkness fell the Japanese abandoned all their positions, and the Point 5846 area was cleared and the water point regained. Both sides had momentarily fought themselves to a standstill and, except for patrol clashes in the Khoirok area, there was a lull. A raid by Japanese bombers on Bishenpur village, which was empty of troops, inflicted some hundred casualties on the villagers.

While 32nd Brigade was recovering the water point, the Japanese had again begun to infiltrate at Ningthoukhong, and by the beginning of May had established themselves in Potsangbum. On the night of the 6th/7th, however, patrols reported that the village had been evacuated, but, when 9/14th Punjab moved in, it ran into serious difficulties.

On the 7th, 89th Brigade, whose move by air from Arakan had been delayed by bad weather, took over at Sengmai and came under

---

[1] The 20th Division had no reserve brigade since 32nd Brigade had been sent to Bishenpur under command of 17th Division. See page 308.

command of 5th Division. The 63rd Brigade then moved south to relieve 32nd Brigade of the responsibility for the Potsangbum area. At the same time work was begun on a new headquarters for 17th Division near Point 3094, south of Buri Bazar. Thus by the evening of the 7th, IV Corps had nearly completed its regrouping to enable it to carry out Scoones' policy of continuing the offensive northwards to clear the country as far as the line Ukhrul–Kangpokpi, standing fast on Shenam Pass and beginning a new offensive in the Bishenpur area to destroy the Japanese *33rd Division*. It was now ready to co-operate with XXXIII Corps' advance south from Kohima.

It will be recalled that at Kohima on the 25th April, 4th Brigade on the right and 5th Brigade on the left were moving into position to envelop the Japanese positions facing Garrison Hill held by 6th Brigade, while Grover (2nd Division) was making his plans for a general assault.[1] His opponent, Sato (*31st Division*), had just decided not to send a regimental group to the Imphal area, and was planning to continue the attack on Garrison Hill with a four-battalion regimental group, while smaller groups at Naga Village and Aradura secured its flanks. Detachments were operating on the tracks south from Wokha and Mokokchung to prevent any wide outflanking move from cutting the division's communications to Ukhrul and the Chindwin.[2] With ammunition and food running low and no reinforcements coming forward, the division was in an unenviable position and this fact seems to have been realized rather belatedly by Mutaguchi, who about the 28th cancelled his order for a regiment to be sent from Kohima to Imphal.

Owing to the extremely difficult country through which 4th Brigade had to pass to reach its jumping-off position, there was little Grover could do to support it and it had therefore to rely on surprise. On the other flank, where 5th Brigade's move to the Merema ridge was known to the enemy, there was no chance of surprise and he was therefore anxious to give the brigade tank support to enable it to tackle the formidable Naga Village defences. Since the only route by which tanks could get to 5th Brigade was by way of the road junction on the summit of the pass immediately east of D.C.'s Bunga-low spur, arrangements were made for 2nd Dorsets of 6th Brigade to clear the spur on the 27th April.

On the 26th, the Japanese attacked the forward troops of 5th Brigade on the Merema track, and on the Kohima ridge made a determined but unsuccessful effort to re-establish themselves on the

---

[1] See Map 8, page 360.
[2] See Map 4, page 53.

summit of Kuki Piquet.[1] So intense was the enemy fire that the Dorsets, moving forward under cover to their forming-up position on Garrison Hill, suffered considerable casualties. Enemy activity died down just before dawn on the 27th as the Dorsets' two forward companies, supported by tanks, began their attack. The right company was soon in difficulties near the Club, but the left company, moving down the north side of the spur and by-passing the tennis court and D.C.'s Bungalow, pushed steadily on and by 5 a.m. was desperately digging in on the knoll at the end of the spur overlooking the road junction. By daylight it had consolidated its position and soon afterwards an armoured force, consisting of one troop of medium tanks of 149th R.A.C., one troop of light tanks of 45th Cavalry and a Royal Engineer detachment in armoured carriers, drove up to the road junction and shot its way down the Merema track to join 5th Brigade, destroying five enemy bunkers and losing one tank on the way. Another troop of tanks, turning right at the road junction, moved along the main road to get on to the spur and help the right company of Dorsets in difficulties in the Club area, but torrential rain which had set in that morning made the hillsides so slippery that the tanks could not climb off the road. They were able to return by the way they had come, for the Japanese had not yet recovered from their surprise at seeing tanks in that area. The right company of the Dorsets withdrew later in the day, having lost half its strength, but, by attracting all the enemy's attention to itself, it had enabled the left company to reach the vital knoll above the road junction. There, magnificently supported by 25-pounders of the divisional artillery which at times put down defensive fire as close as twenty-five yards to the defences, the company hung on to its isolated, confined and exposed position with superb gallantry for five days. Had it not done so, tank support for the infantry trying to clear the Kohima ridge would have been impossible.[2] When relieved, its strength, originally about a hundred, had been reduced to three officers and twenty-nine other ranks.

By the evening of the 27th, though tanks had reached 5th Brigade on the left and 6th Brigade in the centre had gained possession of the all-important end of D.C.'s Bungalow spur, which it never lost, 4th Brigade on the right had run into difficulties. The rain which prevented the tanks from getting on to D.C.'s Bungalow spur had made the mountain paths so slippery that in places men had to crawl, but in spite of the appalling conditions the Naga porters never faltered. Their determination to help rid their country of the invader

---

[1] See Sketch 13, page 346.
[2] The company was kept supplied with ammunition, rations, water and even hot tea, and its casualties removed daily, by an armoured car of 11th Cavalry which used to come up to a defiladed re-entrant just short of the road junction.

is shown by the fact that all the able-bodied men of Khonoma village volunteered as porters, on condition that troops were sent to protect the village during their absence. On the 28th an attempt by 5th Brigade to take Firs Hill failed, and Grover decided that it should make no further attack for the moment but instead prevent the Japanese forces to the north from reinforcing their troops attacking Kohima.[1]

The same day the Japanese made a determined effort to disrupt traffic on the Dimapur–Kohima road. Guns and transport were attacked by fighter aircraft, and patrols from the Cheswema area began a series of nightly raids. Flying conditions were so bad at the time that the R.A.F. had temporarily discontinued dive-bombing attacks, and supply drops were at times going astray. Probably for the same reason the enemy air attacks caused no serious damage. The attacks on the road did, however, draw attention to the need to tighten up anti-aircraft discipline, which had become lax owing to the comparative inactivity of the Japanese air force, and to cut down 2nd Division's mechanical transport, which was causing congestion and making the road a worthwhile target. The modifications were made before any serious losses occurred.

On the 29th the two leading battalions of 4th Brigade reached Pulebadze. By this time Grover had made his fresh plan. In the centre 6th Brigade was to take F.S.D. Hill and then Jail Hill, assisted by tanks which were to get to F.S.D. by way of the road junction held by the Dorsets and the main road along the south-eastern face of Garrison Hill. On the right 4th Brigade was to occupy the Aradura spur, block the Imphal Road and attack G.P.T. Ridge from the south-west in co-operation with 161st Brigade, which was to attack the ridge from the west after occupying Two Tree and Congress Hills. On the left 5th Brigade was to capture Naga Village. As there was a general shortage of ammunition, the artillery was to concentrate on the support of 6th Brigade, only exceptionally good targets being engaged in other brigade sectors. Man-handled 'Lifebuoy' flame throwers, which now became available for the first time, were allotted to 5th Brigade to compensate for inadequate artillery support.

On the 30th, realizing that the Japanese were in strength both on G.P.T. Ridge and in the Aradura area, Grover decided to concentrate on one of them and modified 4th Brigade's task to that of attacking G.P.T. Ridge from the west on the 5th May. Led by 143 S.S. Company, the brigade moved off from Pulebadze on the 1st. A path had to be cut and the first day's advance amounted to only a mile. On the second day it was not much greater. On the 3rd, however, good progress was made with 2nd Royal Norfolk in the lead,

[1] See Map 8, page 360.

but the Royal Scots following up were delayed when an enemy column attacked and scattered the unarmed porters and attempted to establish a roadblock. An immediate counter-attack dispersed the enemy, but little further progress was made that day. Meanwhile the Japanese had been attacking and harassing the positions in the Two Tree Hill area which on the 1st had been taken over by 4/1st Gurkhas from 33rd Brigade (7th Division), recently arrived in Assam from Arakan. The *124th Regiment* was identified, and its presence on this flank explained the increase of strength which had led Grover to modify his plan of attack.

On the 4th May, the Norfolks, supported by 99th Field Regiment, established themselves on G.P.T. Ridge at a cost of seventy-seven casualties; 4th Brigade then made contact with 4/1st Gurkhas and established a supply line to Jotsoma. Although the R.A.F. bombed Jail Hill to keep down fire from there, all attempts to capture Pimple at the end of G.P.T. Ridge facing Jail Hill failed.[1] Meanwhile brigade headquarters with the Royal Scots had established a firm base between Two Tree Hill and G.P.T. Ridge, made contact with 161st Brigade on Congress Hill and reinforced the Norfolks. In co-operation with 4th Brigade's attack on G.P.T. Ridge, 2nd Durham Light Infantry of 6th Brigade attacked F.S.D. from the north, supported by tanks of 149th R.A.C. which drove round Garrison Hill along the main road, losing two tanks on the way, and joined the infantry from the south. A footing was gained on F.S.D. but the Japanese on the south side of Kuki Piquet, though now practically surrounded, held grimly on to their position. The tanks tried to assist in the fighting on G.P.T. Ridge but, unable to get past D.I.S., withdrew to their base.

The enemy's next move was to infiltrate between Two Tree Hill and G.P.T. Ridge. The 4/1st Gurkhas cleared the area, but the operation began disastrously, for Brigadier Goschen and Lieut.-Colonel I. H. Hedderwick of the Gurkhas were both killed by snipers while making a reconnaissance.

On the 5th, sixteen tanks, of which five were light tanks carrying wire and engineer stores, tried to get to F.S.D. to assist in exploiting the partial success of the day before. Three medium tanks got through to F.S.D., one of which was soon lost through slipping down a muddy hillside, and four were disabled, completely blocking the road, the crews escaping on foot to Garrison Hill. The light tanks unloaded their stores behind the block caused by the disabled tanks and, with the remaining four medium tanks, withdrew through a hail of shells and mortar bombs, losing one more on the way. By evening the Royal Berkshires and Durhams on Garrison Hill and F.S.D. had

---

[1] See Sketch 13, page 346. For exploits during this fighting Captain J. N. Randle, The Royal Norfolk Regiment, was awarded a posthumous V.C.

been so depleted that they had to be formed into a composite battalion, and 4/7th Rajput of 161st Brigade had to be sent to reinforce 6th Brigade. It was by now evident that Jail Hill, the key position on the Imphal Road, could not be taken by 6th Brigade from the Kohima ridge, and that evening Stopford decided to send forward his last reserve, 1st Queen's Royal Regiment of 33rd Brigade, to attack it from the north-west. At 9 a.m. on the 7th, a clear morning after a night of torrential rain, the Queen's moved forward from their starting point on Congress Hill and by 1 p.m. were on the north face of Jail Hill held up by an underground fortress on the hill top. All attempts to envelop it were stopped by accurate cross fire from D.I.S. and from posts dug in on the reverse slope of G.P.T. Ridge; casualties, already near three figures, were still mounting and at 3 p.m. the Queen's were withdrawn under an artillery smoke screen.

By the evening of the 7th, 4th Brigade on the right, with 4/1st Gurkhas under command and a supply line back to Jotsoma, was on G.P.T. Ridge and had almost cleared Pimple, but the enemy still held the vital Jail Hill and had small posts between 4th Brigade and the Two Tree Hill area. The 6th Brigade in the centre was slowly mopping up D.C.'s Bungalow spur and had consolidated on the summit of F.S.D., but the Japanese still held D.I.S. and the eastern slopes of both Kuki Piquet and F.S.D. The 5th Brigade, on the left, having infiltrated forward as far as Point 5120, had been unable to hold it and had consolidated on the western end of the Naga Village ridge. Wide on the left flank, a column of 23rd (L.R.P.) Brigade, whose task was to cut *31st Division's* communications with the Chindwin,[1] had meanwhile, despite heavy storms which favoured enemy delaying tactics, succeeded in cutting the Jessami track at a point some forty miles east of Kohima, but its rear columns were still clearing the area east and north-east of Cheswema.

There now followed a pause for replanning—a sure sign of a temporary stalemate. As a result, the second week of May was comparatively quiet, except for three local operations: the completion of the clearance of the Palel area by 48th Brigade, an attack at Potsangbum on the 8th by 9/14th Punjab, and an attempt by 80th Brigade on Shenam Pass to improve its hold on Scraggy by clearing an under-feature of it known as Lynch Pimple.[2] The first was completely successful. By the 8th May, 48th Brigade was back at Wangjing having suffered only forty-four casualties. Known enemy losses were two prisoners and 110 dead of whom twenty-four were from the *I.N.A.*

---

[1] See page 305.
[2] See Map 9, page 374, and Sketch 15, page 370.

and the rest from *60th Regiment*. At Potsangbum partial success was achieved in a desperate fight, in which 9/14th Punjab had 110 casualties and the Carabiniers lost eight tanks, of which six were burnt out. Two companies of 1st West Yorkshire were sent forward to help to consolidate and hold the ground gained until 63rd Brigade could arrive from Sengmai and take over responsibility for the area. The attack at Shenam failed with considerable loss, in spite of an apparently effective strike by R.A.F. fighter-bombers.

Throughout April and the first week of May, the Japanese air force made a number of harassing raids with formations of up to fifty fighters and a few light bombers. These were directed mainly on the Allied airfields on the Imphal plain, the Silchar area and those in use by Special Force within Burma. Enemy aircraft also co-operated with army formations on six occasions, the two most effective of which on the 24th at Bishenpur and on the 28th April on the Dimapur–Kohima road have been described.[1] These raids were a serious threat to the unarmed Dakotas engaged in supply-dropping duties and the airlift to the Imphal plain. To lessen the risk of their being intercepted by enemy fighters and to lighten the task of the defensive patrols, all supply aircraft approaching the Imphal plain were therefore routed by way of Silchar.

Dealing with these enemy activities did not, however, prevent Eastern Air Command from continuing the air offensive and supply dropping on an undiminished scale. At times the Strategic Air Force was used to disrupt enemy communications on the Tiddim road, especially where it traversed precipitous hillsides. In these areas a few well-placed heavy bombs could bring down hundreds of tons of earth and sweep away the road.[2] As the monsoon strengthened and the clouds became thicker and lower on the hill tops, the value of the Vengeance dive-bombers diminished, but, whenever flying was at all possible, the Hurricane fighter-bombers continued, despite the increased hazards, to give close support to the army and there were few periods when the enemy ground formations could feel safe from their attentions.

By the end of April, the administrative position at Imphal was beginning to cause Scoones some anxiety, for it was evident that the airlift (operation 'Stamina') was failing to deliver the planned tonnage of stores and that, even if full advantage were taken of the

---

[1] The six occasions were on the 10th, 17th, 24th, and 28th April and the 4th and 6th May.

[2] See Photograph 39, following page 236.

fairly good weather which might be expected up to the 21st May, the reserve held by IV Corps would have fallen to an unacceptably low level by the middle of June. Early in May he told Slim that administrative factors now dictated the date by which the Imphal Road had to be reopened. He suggested that the critical date could be deferred either by reducing the scale of rations, or by the R.A.F. flying in supplies by night as well as by day or, as a last resort, by flying out a proportion of the fighting troops. He therefore asked Slim to re-examine the administrative position and advise him on the best course to take.

Slim found this message awaiting him when he returned to his headquarters on the 4th May after his visit to Stilwell.[1] The same day he received the warning from Peirse that the transport aircraft on loan from the Middle East, on which he was dependent, had to be withdrawn by the 8th. Simultaneous receipt of two such messages at a critical moment in a battle which had to be won at all costs was sufficient to dismay any but the most determined commander. Slim was, as usual, imperturbable. With Baldwin's concurrence he sent a message to 11th Army Group and Air Headquarters, South-East Asia pointing out the disastrous effect the withdrawal of the seventy-nine transport aircraft might have on operations at Imphal and on the Northern front. As the reader will recall, Giffard fully supported him, and that afternoon Mountbatten told Peirse that no transport aircraft were to be withdrawn and that he accepted full responsibility for the decision.[2] Assured that the aircraft were to be retained, Slim felt satisfied that the Imphal supply situation would not become serious unless Stopford's advance to open the road was unduly delayed. To ensure that this would not happen, he gave orders on the 5th that the move of Headquarters 7th Division and 114th Brigade to Assam was to be carried out at once.[3] These troops would replace Stopford's last reserve, which was about to be sent into battle, and give him a balanced force of two divisions for his offensive to reopen the road.

---

[1] See page 282.

[2] See page 324.

[3] Slim had warned XV Corps on the 26th April that these formations were to go to Assam and followed this up with a warning order on the 4th May that the move was imminent.

CHAPTER XXIV

THE BATTLES OF IMPHAL
AND KOHIMA

The Imphal Road Reopened
(May – June 1944)

See Maps 3, 4, 8, 9 and 14 and Sketches 13, 14 and 15

THE replanning at the end of the first week in May was carried out against a background of a major reorganization of 14th Army's line of communication. On the 7th, Major-General C. G. G. Nicholson, with Headquarters 21st Indian Division, took over the operational commitments of 202 L. of C. Area from Dimapur and Golaghat inclusive to the rear boundary of 2nd Division (then at MS 37 on the Imphal Road), as well as the supervision of the operations of 3 S. S. Brigade at Silchar.[1] This arrangement relieved 2nd Division of protecting its own communications, 202 L. of C. Area of operational responsibilities for which it was not suited and provided a formation to take control of the line of communication along the Imphal Road which would steadily lengthen as XXXIII Corps' advance progressed.

At a conference at Jorhat on the 9th May, Slim instructed Stopford to press forward with all speed towards Imphal on a two-divisional front, as soon as Headquarters 7th Division and 114th Brigade had arrived from Arakan.[2] At Imphal, Scoones decided that the possibility of a renewed Japanese effort in the Shenam Pass area made it advisable to have a complete division there.[3] In preference to bringing 32nd Brigade back from Bishenpur, where it was heavily engaged, or placing a brigade of 23rd Division under command of 20th Division, he decided that 23rd Division from the Ukhrul sector (where the enemy was on the defensive) and 20th Division should exchange rôles. He arranged for the relief to be carried out from the 13th May, a battalion at a time.

---

[1] See Map 4, page 53. Headquarters 21st Indian Division was formed as an emergency measure out of Headquarters 44th Indian Armoured Division which had been abolished. See pages 316–17. It took command of all troops in 252 (Dibrugarh), 253 (Dimapur) and 257 (Silchar) L. of C. Sub-Areas, and 268th Brigade on its arrival in Assam. The headquarters was set up at Jorhat on the 4th May.

[2] H.Q. 7th Division was on arrival to resume command of its own 33rd Brigade and, to bring it up to full complement, take 161st Brigade under command.

[3] See Map 9, page 374, and page 333.

To the north of the Imphal plain, 5th Division's original plan for a wide outflanking move up the Iril had to be modified when unusually early monsoon storms flooded the valley.[1] Briggs' new plan was for 89th Brigade to capture the heights east of the road in a series of short outflanking attacks while 123rd Brigade, with half a squadron of medium and half of light tanks (from the Carabiniers and 7th Light Cavalry respectively), advanced straight along the road with Kanglatongbi as its first objective. The advance was to start on the 15th. The final objective was to be Kangpokpi and 89th Brigade operating in the hills was to cut the Japanese communications running eastwards to Ukhrul. Scoones' plans for a division to strike north-east towards Ukhrul in conjunction with 5th Division's northward advance had to await the completion of the changeover between 20th and 23rd Divisions.[2]

To the south of the plain, Cowan (17th Division) was planning to cut the communications of all the Japanese forces in the Bishenpur area by moving 48th Brigade, less a battalion, from Wangjing by way of Shuganu to seize and hold the Torbung defile on the Tiddim road. Once the defile was occupied, 63rd Brigade, plus a battalion, was to take Potsangbum and then drive south to destroy the Japanese forces believed to be in the plain between Potsangbum and Torbung.[3]

Like Scoones, Mutaguchi was also planning to put new impetus into the battle. He had been reinforced during April by two battalions and the remaining artillery of *15th Division*, and had ordered one (*II/51st*) to join Yamamoto at Shenam and the other (*II/67th*), together with the artillery, to rejoin its own division at Sangshak.[4] At the end of the month he was reinforced by two more battalions which he placed in army reserve.[5] His plan to revive the attack on Imphal from the north had broken down owing to the impossibility of bringing a regiment south from Kohima to reinforce *15th Division* and the formidable defences of Shenam Pass were showing no sign of breaking down under Yamamoto's attacks. In these circumstances Mutaguchi decided to switch his main effort to the Tiddim road, where *33rd Division* (the command of which was about to pass from Yanagida, in whom he had lost confidence, to Lieut.-General N. Tanaka) had reached the Bishenpur area. Having reinforced the division with armour and artillery transferred from Yamamoto's

---

[1] See page 309.
[2] See page 335.
[3] See page 311 and Sketch 14, page 352.
[4] The *II/51st Battalion* had been temporarily switched to Indaw to deal with the Chindits. See page 185 and fn.
[5] The *I/67th Battalion* (the remaining battalion of *15th Division*) and *II/154th Battalion* from *54th Division*.

command,[1] and with the two battalions from his army reserve,[2] he ordered it to try to break through to Imphal from the south.

The opening moves of 14th Army's offensive, the object of which was to destroy *15th Army*, were made by 2nd Division in the early hours of the 11th May, when 33rd Brigade (Loftus-Tottenham), with 1st Queen's on the right and 4/15th Punjab on the left, moved into position to attack Jail Hill and D.I.S.[3] A squadron of 149th R.A.C. was to move by the hazardous but only route along the main road to the F.S.D. area to assist in the final assault. After the preliminary bombardment of Jail Hill and D.I.S., which was to begin at 4.40 a.m. and continue for twenty-five minutes, the artillery was to blanket Treasury Hill while the tanks moved round the end of D.C.'s Bungalow spur. The 4/1st Gurkhas was in brigade reserve. The 4th and 6th Brigades were to co-operate by mopping up the remaining enemy posts on the reverse slope of G.P.T. Ridge and the extreme southern ends of Kuki Piquet and F.S.D., while 5th Brigade made another effort to infiltrate through Naga Village to Point 5120.

The 33rd Brigade's advance began as planned, and by 6.30 a.m. the forward troops were approaching the summits of Jail Hill and D.I.S. A little later, as they began to envelop their objectives, accurate cross-fire from G.P.T. Ridge and F.S.D. suddenly swept the line of advance and before long all movement had stopped. The tank squadron had meanwhile run into a roadblock made by the Japanese around the four disabled tanks abandoned near F.S.D. in the attack of the 5th May and was unable to take part in the assault.[4] The forward battalions were now reinforced by two companies from 4/1st Gurhkhas, but both sustained severe casualties on their way forward and could do nothing to revive the momentum of the attack. The artillery and all mortars within range were then ordered to put down smoke so that it would drift across the battlefield and hide the forward troops while they made some sort of cover.

The deep redoubts on the top of Jail Hill and D.I.S. appeared to be impervious to shell and mortar fire and by 7 p.m., with casualties still mounting and another hour of daylight to go, the situation was beginning to seem hopeless when suddenly a thick mist swept down from the mountain tops. Men could stand up to dig, the wounded were got away, ammunition and food were rushed forward and the crisis passed. During the cold wet night which followed the infantry crouched in the muddy holes they had scraped, while, in the cutting between Jail Hill and D.I.S., 77th Field Company cleared a minefield—a nightmare task in the darkness and heavy rain. At about

---

[1] The *14th Tank Regiment, II/18th Heavy Field Artillery Battalion* and *1st Anti-Tank Battalion*.
[2] To replace *15th Army* reserve, *Burma Area Army* allotted Mutaguchi *151st Regiment* (less I/*151st Battalion*) of *53rd Division* then on its way to Burma.
[3] See Map 8, page 360 and Sketch 13, page 346.
[4] See page 338.

10.30 a.m. on the 12th, the roadblock having been removed, the tanks arrived at the recently cleared cutting, ready to support the infantry at close range, and with their help 33rd Brigade gradually edged its way forward during the day. The supporting 4th and 5th Brigades on the flanks made little progress; Brigadier J. A. Theobalds, who had just taken over command of 4th Brigade, was killed, and Hawkins (5th Brigade) was severely wounded while directing mopping up operations.

At nightfall there were still Japanese left on the reverse slopes of G.P.T. Ridge, F.S.D. and Kuki Piquet, and others holding out in the formidable main redoubts on Jail Hill and D.I.S.[1] Loftus-Tottenham called on his men for one more effort. Hungry and wet, they spent a second miserable night, but before dawn on the 13th the enemy began to break. They were closely followed up by the bedraggled but triumphant attackers, who were able to take heavy toll of Japanese slipping away from their positions all along the south-east face of the Kohima ridge, with the exception of D.C.'s Bungalow spur. There the Dorsets, with the aid of a medium tank, pole charges, a 3.7-inch howitzer and a 6-pounder anti-tank gun, destroyed the remaining bunkers whose occupants fought grimly to the last. So ended an epic fight of which the losers had almost as much cause to be proud as the victors. The whole Kohima ridge was clear, but the capture of Jail Hill and D.I.S. had cost 33rd Brigade over 400 casualties. Grover now ordered it to capture Treasury Hill. During the night of the 13th/14th, 4/1st Gurkhas seized the hill with trifling loss and consolidated, in spite of shelling and counter-attacks.

The loss of Jail Hill, D.I.S. and Treasury Hill broke the Japanese hold on the pass and this, apart from the tactical gain, greatly eased the Allied supply problem, particularly for 5th Brigade on the left. With the arrival of the lorried 268th Brigade, which took over the defence of the Kohima ridge on the 16th, soon followed by 114th Brigade which moved to Zubza, congestion on the main road became so great that XXXIII Corps had to reduce the amount of transport using it. Some 1,400 vehicles were handed over for use on the Assam lines of communication and as a result 1,300 British ranks of 2nd Division became available to reinforce its rifle companies, which by now were seriously understrength. The arrival of 268th Brigade meant that brigades of 2nd Division could in turn be taken out for a short rest and refit. With one brigade resting, a guaranteed air supply for one forward brigade and a secure base on the Kohima ridge, it was now possible to renew the battle under favourable conditions.

---

[1] The Japanese had installed the steel loopholes from the Assam Rifles fortified barracks in them.

KOHIMA RIDGE

Scale of Yards

0   500

Contours at 50 feet intervals

Defended Localities ....

53 I.G.H. SPUR

To Kohima

D.C's. Bungalow

TENNIS COURT

Club

GARRISON △ HILL

KUKI △ PIQUET

Dimapur 45m.

F.S.D.

4650

4500

4750

4500

4750

D.I.S.

Jotsoma 2m

CONGRESS HILL

Jail

JAIL HILL

4600

4500

PIMPLE

Jotsoma (Jeep Track)

G.P.T. RIDGE

4750

4650

4800

4600

4500

On the Imphal plain, IV Corps' offensive against *33rd Division* began on the 13th May when 48th Brigade (Cameron), less 9th Border Regiment, marching by night and lying concealed by day, moved from Wangjing through Shuganu to block the Tiddim road at the Torbung defile.[1] At 6 a.m. on the 16th its leading battalion (2/5th Royal Gurkhas) reached Point 3404, and looked down on the road threading its way through the seven-foot high tiger grass which covered the valley floor. A supply drop that afternoon disclosed its presence, but so unexpected was the move that next morning 1/7th Gurkhas had no trouble in overrunning an enemy post on the road, and establishing a roadblock with three companies and a platoon of 70th Field Company. That night 1/7th Gurkhas drove off two counter-attacks and destroyed a column of lorries full of Japanese troops, and by the morning of the 19th had accounted for some sixty Japanese dead and destroyed two tanks for a loss of five men wounded. The Gurkhas' troubles began at 11.30 a.m. when R.A.F. fighters attacked the block in error, causing fourteen casualties and killing thirty-seven mules. From then on the problem of the disposal of bodies became worse and worse. During the night of the 19th/20th the Japanese launched their first deliberate attack on the block; it was repulsed at the cost of twenty-four casualties, the enemy leaving about a hundred dead, mostly from *I/67th Battalion*, round the perimeter. An attack on 2/5th Royal Gurkhas holding Point 3404 cost the enemy another twenty-seven dead and a prisoner, but the reserve company of 7th Gurkhas lost a quarter of its strength trying to drive a small Japanese post off Point 4358, at the south end of the Point 3404 ridge. In the absence of adequate artillery or effective tank support the defence of each side was unbreakable, and 48th Brigade, now firmly dug in, had no further need to attack.[2]

By the 20th the roadblock had created a serious situation for the Japanese, since *33rd Division's* enveloping attack on Bishenpur was to begin on the night of the 20th/21st,[3] and all its supplies, reinforcements and the divisional commander (Tanaka) were on the wrong side of the block. To make matters worse for them 63rd Brigade, having secured Potsangbum, had, in conjunction with 32nd Brigade, cleared the area south of the Silchar track as far as Sadu, thus interposing between *Headquarters 33rd Division* at Laimanai and *215th Regiment* operating to the west of Bishenpur. The Japanese attack was launched according to plan and, just as 63rd Brigade was about to begin its drive south on the 21st to mop up the enemy force believed to be between Potsangbum and Torbung,[4] it learnt that during the

---

[1] See Map 9, page 374.
[2] The Japanese tanks were unable to force their way through the tiger grass.
[3] Mutaguchi's plan to switch his main offensive to the Bishenpur area.
[4] The enemy force between Potsangbum and Torbung consisted of one infantry battalion and one engineer regiment supported by tanks and artillery. See page 334.

night the enemy had overrun 32nd Brigade's administrative area on the east side of Bishenpur, attacked Headquarters 17th Division south of Buri Bazar and established roadblocks between there and Bishenpur. Thus on the morning of the 21st each opponent had cut the other's communications and both divisional headquarters were under attack. Cowan was slightly better off than Tanaka for he at least was at his own headquarters, but neither had the comfort of being aware of the other's plight.

There was now no longer any point in 63rd Brigade driving south, for the bulk of the force it had been ordered to destroy in conjunction with 48th Brigade was quite obviously north of Bishenpur and had to be dealt with very quickly, particularly that part of it attacking 17th Division Headquarters, at this time defended only by a detachment of 7/10th Baluch Regiment. On the 21st, a troop of tanks sent by 32nd Brigade from Bishenpur broke through to divisional headquarters, and, on orders from IV Corps, 20th Division, still in process of changing rôles with 23rd Division, sent a composite battalion and a battery from the Ukhrul road sector. This heterogeneous force held off the enemy attacks for the next four days until, on the 26th, Brigadier E. G. Woods with Headquarters 50th (P.) Brigade arrived and took command of it.[1] After three more days of fierce fighting the Japanese accepted local defeat, threw many of their regimental guns into a deep pond near Oinam and, followed up by 1/4th Gurkhas, withdrew on the 29th into the hills to the west to reorganize. Meanwhile at Bishenpur 32nd Brigade had recovered its administrative area, now a ghastly shambles of hundreds of dead animals and some 150 dead Japanese from *I/214th Battalion*.[2]

To return to the story of the Torbung block. The Japanese, who had been reinforced on the 20th by *II/154th Battalion* and some more tanks, had attacked the block unceasingly for the next four days. The garrison had done what it could to bury or burn the dead, but the sanitary conditions were appalling and getting worse every day. When he sent 48th Brigade to Torbung, Cowan had left it to Cameron's discretion to decide, at the appropriate time, whether to abandon the static defence of the block and turn north to assist 63rd Brigade to mop up, or to continue to hold the block with part or all of his force, leaving the mopping up to 63rd Brigade. Cowan's instructions on this point read,

'In arriving at your decision you will bear in mind the object of your move which is to enable you to be in a position to prevent

---

[1] The force, known as Woodforce, comprised 7/10th Baluch, 9/12th F. F. Regiment, 1/4th Gurkhas, a half squadron of the Carabiniers, two troops 7th Light Cavalry and one battery 114th Jungle Field Regiment.

[2] The *III/214th Battalion* arrived too late to take an active part and its commander was relieved of his appointment. The *I/214th* and *II/214th* were almost annihilated, one battalion losing 360 out of 380 and the other 460 out of 500 men.

the enemy escaping destruction by withdrawing south, or, in the event of his remaining in his present position, to facilitate his destruction by 32 and 63 Brigades operating against him from the rear.'

On the 24th the block had been in position for a week; there was still no sign of the enemy trying to escape and 63rd Brigade had not started to move south. Cameron, in consultation with his second-in-command, decided that there was no advantage to be gained by holding the block any longer and at midday issued verbal orders for its evacuation at 7.15 p.m. that evening, and for the brigade to move north and establish a block at the road junction west of Moirang. He told Cowan of his decision, and a message approving it reached 48th Brigade at 7.12 p.m., only three minutes before 1/7th Gurkhas began its withdrawal.[1] By 9.30 p.m. the battalion had passed through 2/5th Royal Gurkhas on Point 3404 on its way to Moirang, one company being under orders to establish a roadblock at the road junction. In darkness and pouring rain and with the going difficult, companies became separated. Unknown to the rest, the one detailed to block the road was held up by a stream in spate. Two companies lost their way, one of which, escorting 6th Mountain Battery, was ambushed and cut up, the battery losing three of its four guns. That night only battalion headquarters and one company reached Moirang, where they halted and attempted to reassemble the battalion. Brigade headquarters and half of 2/5th Royal Gurkhas joined them there later.

As a result the road lay open to the Japanese from 8 p.m. on the 24th, a fact which they quickly discovered, and Tanaka was able to motor through to his headquarters with the ammunition and supply columns instead of trying to reach it by hill tracks. The 48th Brigade eventually established a roadblock west of Moirang on the evening of the 26th, by which time the road had been open for forty-eight hours. On orders from 17th Division it moved next morning to Thinunggei, where its rearguard was attacked by Japanese tanks and infantry on the 28th and driven in. On the 29th the brigade resumed its withdrawal and, after a sharp fight at Ningthoukhong, which enabled it to by-pass enemy positions to the east, made contact with 63rd Brigade at Potsangbum.

Thus by the 29th May neither Cowan nor Tanaka had succeeded in achieving his object, and the situation in the Bishenpur sector was similar to that at the beginning of the month. The operation which Wedemeyer, when he returned to S.E.A.C. Headquarters from a visit to IV Corps, had told Mountbatten would result, if vigorously implemented, in the annihilation of six Japanese battalions had come

---

[1] Scoones was at 17th Divisional Headquarters and agreed with Cowan's decision to approve Cameron's withdrawal from Torbung.

to nothing. The Japanese force which it was hoped to trap between Torbung and Bishenpur was no longer in that area, and there was therefore no point in leaving two good battalions short of food and ammunition at Torbung in danger of being overwhelmed. There was nothing to indicate the dire administrative straits that the block at Torbung had imposed on the Japanese and thus the decision to vacate it was perfectly reasonable. It is now known that the enemy force at Torbung, consisting mainly of two battalions on their way to reinforce *33rd Division,* had been reduced by casualties to the point of ineffectiveness, and that Tanaka could not reinforce it unless he brought forces back from Bishenpur.[1] Had the block stayed in position for a few more days, Tanaka might have been forced to call off his offensive towards Imphal at the end of May instead of in June, with possibly far-reaching effects on the battle.

North of Imphal, 5th Division's offensive which had begun on the 15th May made slow but steady progress. The 89th Brigade (Crowther) cleared the ridge to the east of the road in a series of sharp actions, in the course of which 1/11th Sikhs carried out a brilliant night infiltration in pouring rain to cut the enemy's communications to Ukhrul and then beat off counter-attacks by a force consisting of elements of *II/60th* and *II/67th Battalions.* The 123rd Brigade (Evans) recaptured Kanglatongbi on the 20th.[2]

No commander fighting a delaying action could wish for better country than the valley of the Imphal Turel through which runs the road from Kanglatongbi to Kangpokpi. Along the east side of the road a line of disconnected jungle-clad peaks, rising to about 800 feet, dominates the valley. Each one had to be attacked separately and before troops could reach them from the road they had to cross the Turel, which a few minutes of heavy rain could turn into a raging and unfordable torrent. Some attacks had to be called off when troops were unable to clamber up the slippery precipitous hillsides. When they did succeed in reaching the summit they were met by Japanese soldiers resolved to die rather than give way. Progress beyond Kanglatongbi was therefore very slow and laborious.

The delay in clearing the Imphal Road began to cause anxiety in London, and on the 27th May, Pownall (Mountbatten's Chief of Staff, then in London for consultations) cabled that the lack of offensive action northwards by IV Corps had been criticized by the

---

[1] The Japanese forces engaged at Torbung consisted of *I/67th* and *II/154th Battalions* and artillery, engineer and infantry details (with a total strength of about 1,100 men) supported by five medium tanks. The Japanese state that their casualties in the fighting included 280 killed.

[2] The contents of the depot were found almost intact.

Chiefs of Staff. Mountbatten immediately told Giffard of this and said:

> 'I understand that the plan was to destroy the Japanese forces to the south of Imphal first to make the maximum forces available for the offensive north. I know from the discussion that you realize the vital need for opening the Kohima–Imphal road as quickly as possible but really must ask you when you can start your offensive to the north.'

Next day Giffard explained that the security of the Imphal plain was vital to the whole battle. It would therefore be unwise to denude the plain, which was under attack by two Japanese divisions, of troops in order to reinforce a northward offensive. Slim's aim, with which he was in full agreement, was to secure the southern flank of IV Corps by so crippling the Japanese *33rd Division* that it could be contained by a small force, thus enabling the northward offensive to be reinforced. It was the task of XXXIII Corps to reopen the road, and its advance would begin on a two-division front as soon as Kohima had been cleared.[1] Meanwhile, under the most difficult conditions, 5th Division was slowly breaking through the enemy ring to the north of the plain to join hands with XXXIII Corps, and 20th Division was moving north-east towards Ukhrul.[2] The fighting everywhere, he said, was of a very savage and bitter nature. Having sent his reply Giffard flew to Imphal to discuss with Scoones how best to step up the offensive.

Stopford's plan for the resumption of XXXIII Corps' offensive was for a concentric advance on the dominating ridge at Mao (twenty miles south of Kohima) by 2nd Division on the right along the main road and by 7th Division from Naga Village by way of Chakhabama and the Kezoma and Kekrima tracks.[3] On the left 23rd (L.R.P.) Brigade on the axis Kharasom–Ukhrul was to cover the flank and cut the enemy communications to the Chindwin. Before beginning the advance 2nd Division was to shed its attached units,[4] which were to revert to corps command, and 7th Division was to take over 161st Brigade and resume command of 33rd Brigade and 25th Mountain Regiment. Since it was difficult to find gun positions, all artillery, except mountain, was to operate under corps control.

---

[1] Slim had always been quite definite that it was not the task of IV Corps to fight its way out but of XXXIII Corps to fight its way in.

[2] Unit war diaries described the appalling conditions. On one occasion it took half a company ten hours to carry two stretcher cases for four miles. On another it took a party of men (who were not carrying packs) seven hours to cover five miles on hill tracks.

[3] See Map 8, page 360.

[4] The 268th Brigade, 149th Regiment R.A.C., 24th Mountain Regiment, 1st Burma and 1st Assam Regiments and elements of 45th and 11th Cavalry.

On the 24th May, 33rd Brigade relieved 5th Brigade at Naga Village and, regrouping being complete, Stopford gave orders to 2nd Division supported by the corps artillery to attack Aradura spur on the 26th and then advance on Mao. The 7th Division was meanwhile to clear Naga Village and the Chakhabama area with a view to beginning its advance south on the 1st June. The offensive opened on the 25th with an attack by a battalion of 33rd Brigade on Point 5120. This failed with severe loss, but by next morning 4/1st Gurkhas had infiltrated from Treasury Hill on to the southern end of the Naga Village spur and had cleared much of Gun Spur in hand-to-hand fighting, with the support of mountain artillery. In spite of further attacks the Japanese clung to Point 5120.

The 2nd Division's advance did not begin till the 27th when 6th Brigade moved forward to capture the western end of the Aradura spur. When it had done so, 4th and 5th Brigades were to advance, one on each side of the road with tanks operating along it. On the morning of the 28th, a Japanese column broke into a position held by a battalion of 6th Brigade, in which brigade tactical headquarters had been established. Shapland, the fourth brigadier of 2nd Division to become a casualty in a month, was severely wounded and the advance came to a standstill. The 4th Brigade now attempted to seize Aradura by frontal attack. The tanks ran into a minefield at MS 48, one mile south of Jail Hill, and their escort and the engineers lost half their strength trying to clear it. The 1st Royal Scots and 2nd Royal Norfolks attacking the ridge on the west of the road also suffered heavy losses without making any progress, and at 4.30 p.m. the attack had to be called off.

The corps artillery now switched to support 7th Division's attack on Naga Village. With the support of the artillery and the few tanks which could operate in the confined space, 4/15th Punjab attacked Point 5120 on the 30th and 31st May, while 4/1st Gurkhas set about clearing the eastern end of the ridge. The frontal attacks again met with little success, and in one of them a company of the Punjabis came out of action only eighteen strong. On the 1st June, 161st Brigade cleared the Cheswema area, and then, coming into action against Firs Hill and McRobert Hill, reduced the heavy crossfire from that direction which had been the main cause of failure of the attacks on Point 5120. That evening 1st Queen's, taking advantage of a thick mist, moved forward and found that the Japanese had abandoned the whole of the Naga Village area.

By this time 114th Brigade (Brigadier H. W. Dinwiddie), whose task it was to lead 7th Division's advance, had relieved 33rd Brigade.[1] Orders for a general advance were issued on the 2nd and the next day

---

[1] 114th Brigade had been at Zubza preparing for the advance which entailed the organization of a jeep train to bring its supplies forward.

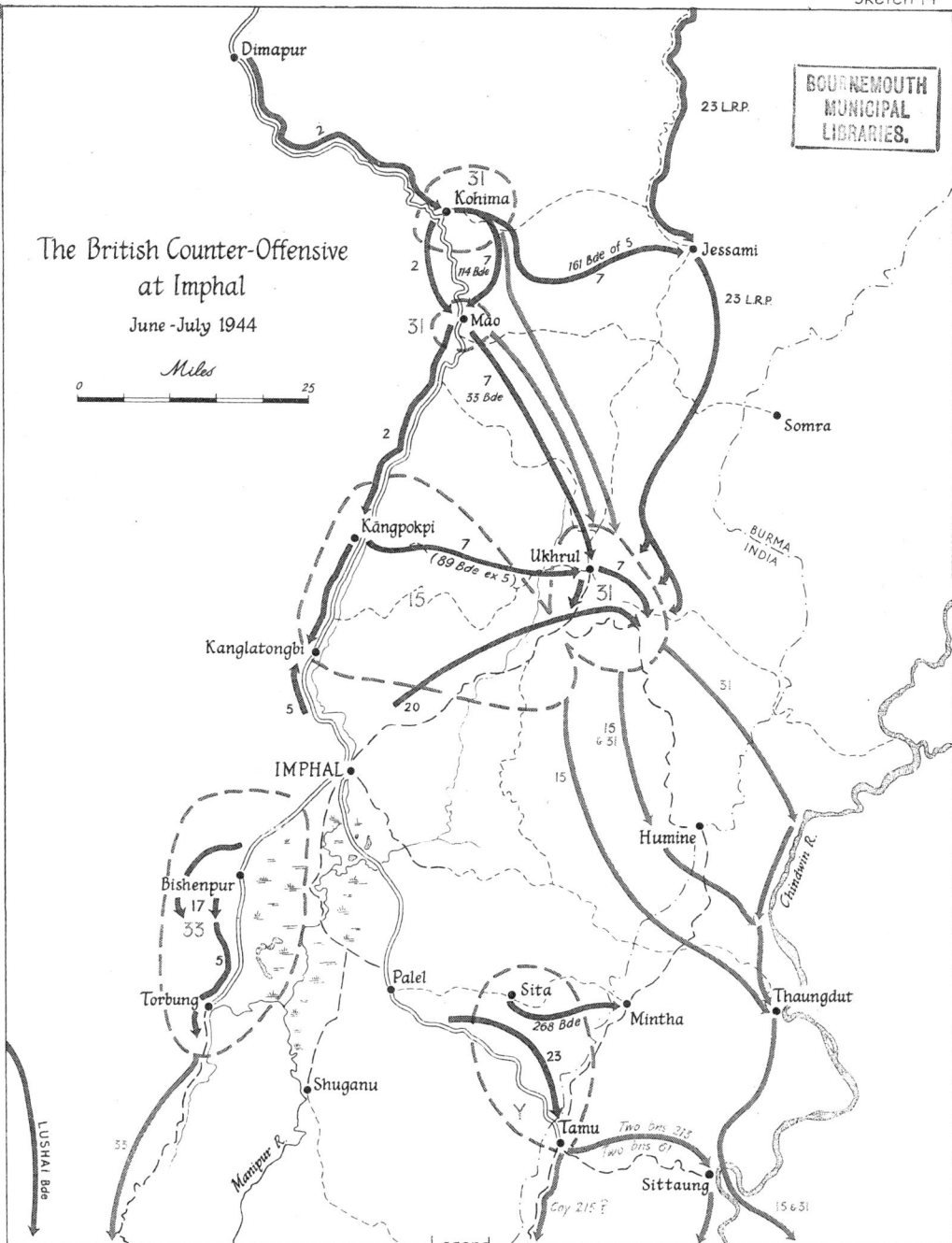

The British Counter-Offensive
at Imphal

June - July 1944

Miles

0 _____ 25

Dimapur

23 L.R.P.

31
Kohima

2

114 Bde

161 Bde of 5   Jessami

31 ● Mao

23 L.R.P.

7
33 Bde

Somra

2

BURMA
INDIA

Kăngpokpi

7
(89 Bde ex 5)   Ukhrul   7

31

Kanglatongbi

15

5

20

15

31

31

IMPHAL

15
& 31

15

Bishenpur   Humine

17
33

5

Palel

Torbung   Sita   Thaungdut

268 Bde   Mintha

23

Shuganu   Y

Tamu   Two bns 213

LUSHAI Bde   33   Two bns 61

Matipur R.   Sittaung

Coy 215 ?   15 & 61

Legend

Line of advance of British divisions......................... ➤

Position and line of retreat of Japanese divisions....   15 ➤   Roads   Allweather............
                                                                         "   Fairweather...........

                                                                 Tracks ....
Position and line of retreat of Yamamoto Detachment..   Y ➤   Rivers ....

114th Brigade, meeting only slight opposition, cleared the Chedema ridge and pushed on to Chakhabama where it contacted 161st Brigade. From there the 114th turned south for Kezoma while the 161st moved south-east along the Kekrima–Jessami track. Everywhere there were signs of a hasty retreat. Equipment and guns had been thrown into ravines, and many officers and men of the *I.N.A.* surrendered after a token resistance. Resistance, however, stiffened on the 6th June when 114th Brigade encountered a Japanese rearguard at Kezoma and 161st Brigade found Kekrima occupied.

Meanwhile in the Aradura area it was discovered on the 4th that the enemy had withdrawn and the next day 5th Brigade occupied the Phesama ridge against slight opposition and 1st Assam Regiment, covering the right flank, reported Pulebadze unoccupied. A permanent armoured component for the advanced guard was now formed to operate with whatever troops were leading the advance, and 4th Brigade prepared to leapfrog through 5th Brigade.[1]

In the middle of May the situation was far from satisfactory for the Japanese *15th Army*. The *31st Division* had failed to take Kohima and was under such pressure that not only had it been unable to spare a regiment to reinforce *15th Division* for its attack on Imphal, but it was being slowly driven from its vantage points. The attack by *15th Division* on Imphal from the north had come to a standstill, and it too was being slowly forced back. The *Yamamoto Detachment* had been unable to break through Shenam Pass, and *33rd Division* was held up south of Bishenpur. To renew the offensive Mutaguchi had ordered *33rd Division*, reinforced by two battalions, tanks and artillery, to break through to Imphal by way of Bishenpur in the second half of May.

Lieut.-General H. Hata, Assistant Chief of Staff at *Imperial General Headquarters*, Tokyo, visited *Burma Area Army* early in May in the course of a tour of inspection of all the fronts in the *Southern Army* area. When he met Hata, Kawabe mainly confined himself to stating his determination to continue his efforts to take Imphal. Hata and his staff, however, received pessimistic reports from staff officers in charge of the administrative services, and returned to Tokyo entertaining grave doubts on the possibility of success. On the 15th May, Hata was due to make a verbal report to General H. Tojo (Chief of the General Staff) at the daily routine meeting of senior staff officers at *Imperial General Headquarters*. That morning Tojo received from *Southern Army* a report on the Imphal operations which suggested that

---

[1] The permanent armoured component of the advanced guard consisted of two troops of medium tanks with a half squadron headquarters, one platoon Bombay Grenadiers and an engineer reconnaissance party, all under command of the second-in-command of 149th R.A.C.

there was still the possibility of attaining victory provided the operations were continued in a determined manner. Thus, when Hata began his report by saying that 'the Imphal operations stand little chance of success', Tojo stopped him and changed the subject.

This optimism at high level was not reflected at Kohima. Sato, under increasing pressure and extremely short of food and ammunition, began from about the middle of the month to urge *15th Army* to allow him to withdraw *31st Division* to a position where it could be properly supplied. Mutaguchi, confident that *33rd Division's* thrust would succeed provided that pressure was maintained on all fronts, refused on the ground that the fall of Imphal was imminent.

Having been ordered to hold on at Kohima, Sato made a desperate effort to do so during the second half of May. He succeeded in stopping 2nd Division's attacks at Aradura, holding 33rd Brigade's attacks on Naga Village for five days and even harassing the newly-arrived 268th Brigade by infiltrating fighting patrols on to Garrison Hill. By the end of the month, however, he realized that his division was faced with imminent destruction. On the 31st he organized a rearguard, some 600 strong, under Miyazaki to delay any advance along the Imphal Road, and ordered the remnants of his battered regiments to withdraw across country. Miyazaki held on at Aradura till the 4th June, two days after the rear parties of *124th* and *138th Regiments* in the Naga Village–Chedema–Chakhabama areas had been driven from their last positions, and then fell slowly back to Viswema.

By the end of May it was evident that *33rd Division's* attempt to break through at Bishenpur had failed, partly because the reinforcements sent it earlier in the month had been absorbed in the fighting at the Torbung defile.[1] Mutaguchi, having allotted his last reserves (*151st Infantry Regiment* less one battalion) to Tanaka to make good his losses, decided to try a new line of approach.[2] When *31st Division* began its withdrawal from Kohima without permission, he was actually considering a plan to move it into the gap between *15th Division* and the *Yamamoto Detachment* with a view to breaking through to the plain from the east. Unaware of the state of the division, he decided to take advantage of the situation, sanctioned the withdrawal and ordered Sato to concentrate east of Imphal and prepare to launch an offensive against Palel.

On the 5th June, Kawabe went to Mutaguchi's headquarters. Although he soon realized that Mutaguchi had lost his former confidence in victory, Kawabe urged him to continue his efforts to achieve success and agreed with him that the Palel offensive offered the best chance of success. He placed *I/213th Battalion* from Akyab and *61st Infantry Regiment* (less *II/61st Battalion*) together with one battalion of

---

[1] The *I/67th* and *II/154th Battalions*.

[2] The *151st Regiment* began to reach the Bishenpur front on the 19th June.

4th Artillery Regiment at the disposal of Mutaguchi who allotted them to the *Yamamoto Detachment*.[1] Next day Kawabe left for *33rd Army Headquarters* at Maymyo, from where he sent his appreciation of the situation to *Southern Army*, expressing his determination to bring the operation to a successful conclusion, and adding an urgent request for air reinforcements, in particular for fighters. The same day Mutaguchi moved his headquarters forward to Kuntaung in order to be in close touch with the proposed Palel offensive.[2]

The week from the 3rd to 9th June was perhaps the most momentous of the campaign in Burma. It saw the collapse of enemy resistance at Kohima and the beginning of the southward advance of XXXIII Corps which was to reopen the Imphal Road and lead to the destruction of the Japanese *31st Division*. On the 3rd, Mountbatten received his new directive which finally committed S.E.A.C. to a land campaign to improve the air link to China and to continue operations throughout the monsoon,[3] and on the 5th the Japanese made their decision to continue with their Imphal offensive.

On the 9th, Mountbatten issued a new directive to 11th Army Group which was to set the pattern for the final stages of the battle for Kohima and Imphal and for its exploitation. Giffard's task, as far as the Central front was concerned,[4] was defined as: firstly, to re-establish communications on the Imphal Road not later than mid-July; secondly, to clear the Dimapur–Kohima–Imphal plain–Tamanthi area of all enemy forces; and thirdly, to prepare to exploit across the Chindwin in the Yuwa–Tamanthi area after the monsoon.[5] The directive stated that 82nd (W.A.) Division would concentrate in India during August 1944, that 22nd (E.A.) Brigade would arrive in Ceylon in July, and that 19th Indian Division would be available as a relief for one British or Indian division returning to India for rehabilitation; it also confirmed that 36th Indian Division would move to the Northern front early in July and come under Stilwell's command.

It will be remembered that after he had replied to the criticism of IV Corps' operations Giffard had flown to Imphal. On the 1st June he sent Slim a message to say that he thought the Shenam defences were too strong to be broken unless the Japanese received very large

---

[1] The *61st Regiment* of *4th Division* and the battalion of *4th Artillery Regiment* had recently arrived in Burma from Sumatra. The *I/213th Battalion* reached Tamu at the end of June and the remainder on the 23rd July.
[2] See Map 3, page 33.
[3] See page 256.
[4] The directive also covered the Arakan front and Ceylon for which 11th Army Group was responsible.
[5] See Map 14, page 452.

reinforcements, and that the main threat appeared to be an offensive in the Bishenpur sector.[1] He believed that there was an opportunity to strike at Ukhrul, the nodal point of Japanese communications to Kohima and the Imphal–Kohima road, and that Scoones could do this and still keep one brigade of 23rd Division in reserve. He ended his message with the words, 'I know you agree'.

During the first week in June, Slim had his hands full, for, in addition to discussing with the commanders of 36th and 11th (E.A.) Divisions their moves to join Stilwell and 14th Army respectively, he had had to deal with an administrative crisis on the Imphal plain where the deficit in supplies and ammunition was mounting at an alarming rate.[2] While he was still dealing with these matters he was ordered by the Supreme Commander to fly to the Northern front to investigate difficulties which had arisen between Stilwell and Lentaigne over Special Force.[3] He set off on the 6th and it was not until the 9th that he was able to visit his corps commanders to co-ordinate their efforts, and not until the 12th that he got back to his headquarters at Comilla.

Meanwhile, at Supreme Headquarters, Mountbatten had been reviewing the situation on the Imphal plain in relation to the need to give the Allied forces in China the maximum assistance as quickly as possible to enable them to counter the new Japanese offensive south from Hankow which threatened the Allied airfields in south-east China.[4] On the 8th June he sent a telegram to the Chiefs of Staff, the British Military Mission in Washington, 11th Army Group and 14th Army in which he said that the best contribution S.E.A.C. could make would be to deliver the maximum supplies to China to nourish 14th U.S.A.A.F., which in turn meant maintaining the greatest possible number of aircraft on the air ferry route and relieving as quickly as possible the threat to the Assam line of communication caused by the Japanese Imphal offensive.

Mountbatten drew attention to the fact that the air transport resources at his disposal were likely to prove insufficient and that the reserves of supplies on the Imphal plain would have dropped to six days by the end of June.[5] In order to avoid making any further diversions of aircraft from Air Transport Command he intended to reopen the Imphal Road as quickly as possible and, until this was achieved, to adopt measures calculated to reduce the reliance on air supplies to the minimum, while exploiting to the maximum the existing air resources. To deal with the situation the airlift to the plain was to be intensified, if necessary by diverting aircraft from the Strategic Air

---

[1] See Map 3, page 33.
[2] See page 326.
[3] See Chapter XXIX.
[4] See Chapter XXVIII.
[5] See Chapter XXII.

Force; the offensive northwards by IV Corps was to be further developed in co-ordination with the southward drive from Kohima by
XXXIII Corps; the air evacuation of sick and non-combatants was
to be continued up to the maximum capacity of returning aircraft;
a detailed plan was to be made for increasing local resources on the
plain by requisition and by the planned slaughter of cattle; the
Bishenpur and similar tracks were to be exploited in order to augment supplies to the plain, and a plan prepared to fight a convoy
through to Imphal as early as possible. He ordered Giffard to take
action immediately on any of these items which were not already in
hand.

Slim received his copy of this telegram on returning to his headquarters on the 12th. Apart from the diversion of aircraft from the
Strategic Air Force, all the steps enumerated had been anticipated
except that of slaughtering cattle and using the Bishenpur track as a
separate line of communication. Neither of these was in fact practical: the slaughtering of cattle would on religious and economic
grounds have had a disastrous effect on the local population, and the
destruction of the great suspension bridge at MS 52 meant that the
Bishenpur track was useless until a new bridge had been built.
Nothing heavier than a jeep could use the track at the best of times
and even they could not negotiate the sharp turns on to some of the
bridges across ravines without reversing. The track was too long for
mule convoys to use without staging camps, which would take a long
time to prepare even if the material could be found on the spot.

The situation on the 12th was that in XXXIII Corps' area, 2nd
Division on the road and 114th Brigade on the Kezoma–Mao track
were in contact with the enemy rearguards firmly dug in on an east-
west line through Viswema, while 161st Brigade had cleared Kekrima and begun to push patrols along the track to Kharasom which
had already been reached by 23rd (L.R.P.) Brigade. In IV Corps' area
north of the plain, 5th Division had reached MS 111, five miles south
of Kangpokpi, and 20th Division had 80th Brigade firmly established
on the Japanese line of communication between Kangpokpi and
Ukhrul and 100th Brigade almost within striking distance of Sangshak and the track from Ukhrul to the Chindwin, where it was
encountering fierce opposition.[1] That day a deluge began, which
lasted for four days and turned every stream into a torrent, swept
away culverts, bridges and tracks and brought all operations north
of Imphal to a standstill.

In the Shenam Pass area, Yamamoto, knowing that reinforcements
were on the way, began another attempt to clear the pass as the
opening move in Mutaguchi's offensive towards Palel. A series of
attacks on Scraggy eventually achieved success and in the final attack

---

[1] See Map 9, page 374.

on the 9th June, after perhaps the most intensive bombardment ever put down by the Japanese in Burma, the detachment of 3/3rd Gurkhas holding it was almost annihilated and all counter-attacks to regain the hill failed.[1]

Apart from this, the dispositions of 23rd Division remained the same throughout June. The 37th Brigade with five battalions held the pass. The 49th Brigade (less one battalion) held the Shuganu entrance to the plain. At Wangjing 1st Brigade, less one battalion, but reinforced by the Nepalese Kalibahadur Regiment, 2nd Hyderabad Regiment, two batteries of artillery and a squadron of tanks, had the dual rôle of holding the eastern approaches to the plain from Palel northwards in order to link up with 20th Division on the Ukhrul road, and of providing the corps reserve. An engineer battalion, responsible for the maintenance of the Palel road, held a firm base on the heights at Thoubal overlooking the Yairipok road junction.

While Yamamoto continued to hammer at Shenam Pass, Tanaka (*33rd Division*), now reinforced by *151st Regiment* (less one battalion), made repeated attacks throughout June along his whole front from Potsangbum on the Tiddim road through Point 5846 on the Silchar track to Khoirok in the hills north-west of Bishenpur.[2] The 17th Division was on the defensive, partly because *33rd Division* had regained the initiative after the withdrawal of the Torbung block, and partly because priority had been given to the offensive to reopen the Imphal Road and most of the corps resources in ammunition and armour had been allotted to 5th and 20th Divisions. The division was disposed with 63rd Brigade (Burton) based on Bishenpur holding the valley astride the Tiddim road at Potsangbum–Ningthoukhong, 32nd Brigade (Mackenzie) holding Point 5846 and the Silchar track, 48th Brigade (Brigadier R. C. O. Hedley) providing the divisional reserve and garrisons of certain vital points covering the communications to forward brigades, and Woodforce, which now consisted of 17th Division's reconnaissance and defence battalions and a troop of tanks, holding the divisional headquarters area round Buri Bazar. Each brigade and Woodforce held a mobile reserve ready to attack any enemy columns attempting to infiltrate through or round the division's positions towards Imphal. The Japanese attacks, as at Shenam, made only small local gains at the cost of heavy casualties, and in general the position in the plain south of Imphal remained unaltered throughout the month.

On XXXIII Corps' front, as the four-day downpour of rain died away, 2nd Division's attack on Miyazaki's rearguard holding Viswema began to make headway on the 16th June. At the same time,

---

[1] See Sketch 15, page 370. The 3/3rd Gurkhas had some 200 casualties in this action.
[2] During this fighting Victoria Crosses were won by Sergeant H. V. Turner, The West Yorkshire Regiment and Rifleman Ganju Lama, 1/7th Gurkha Rifles.

having struggled through jungle and across torrents, 114th Brigade (7th Division) outflanked the Japanese position on the Kezoma track and began to work its way up the east end of the Mao ridge towards Viswema. Miyazaki held on for one more day but, on the morning of the 18th, forward troops of 2nd and 7th Divisions met on the Mao ridge. That day 2nd Division's advanced guard gained twelve miles until stopped at MS 77 by a blown bridge, covered by a small but determined rear party on the Maram ridge.[1] The ridge was cleared on the morning of the 19th in an attack made with great dash by 7th Worcesters.

By this time the position of *31st Division* had become desperate. Over 1,500 stretcher cases had to be got away along mountain tracks which had become quagmires on the level stretches and mudslides on the steeper slopes. All were exhausted, undernourished and hungry and many had thrown away their arms. There was nothing now that could save the division from disaster. Miyazaki's stout-hearted rear-guard effort merely postponed it. A Japanese account says that 'the Chief of Staff of the Army was astonished at the amazing, and in the Japanese Army unprecedented, spectacle of headlong retreat.'

On the 20th, 2nd Division's advanced guard reached MS 88, but it met resistance again the following day at MS 99. Opposition was half-hearted and the enemy soon withdrew to the east, leaving behind a few dead who were found to be men of *II/60th Battalion* of *15th Division*.[2] The advanced guard harboured for the night at Karong (MS 95). At 6 a.m. on the 22nd the advance was resumed with 2nd Durham Light Infantry and a troop of tanks of 149th R.A.C. leading. At 9 a.m. they reached MS 109 (three miles south of Kangpokpi) where they were ordered to halt and watch out for Indian troops of 5th Division advancing from the south. A patrol of 1/17th Dogras of 5th Division, which was soon joined by tanks of the Carabiniers, made contact with them at 10.30 a.m. in a cutting between MS 109 and 110. At 12.30 p.m. Grover met Briggs at the latter's tactical headquarters, from which he had been watching an attack by 9th Brigade on an enemy strongpoint, by-passed by the Dogras, some four miles to the south. Later in the afternoon Stopford and Scoones met and drew up a plan to cut the Japanese line of retreat. That evening the first convoy ran through to Imphal and free two-way running was resumed from the 23rd.

The battle for Imphal was over. The main concern of the British commanders now was to turn the defeat inflicted on *15th Army* into disaster.

---

[1] The task of this party was evidently to cover the track leading off the main road from Maram towards Ukhrul while the Viswema garrison got away.

[2] Japanese accounts state that *60th Regiment* and Miyazaki's rearguard were ordered to withdraw to the Ukhrul area about this date and arrived there on the 3rd and 5th July respectively.

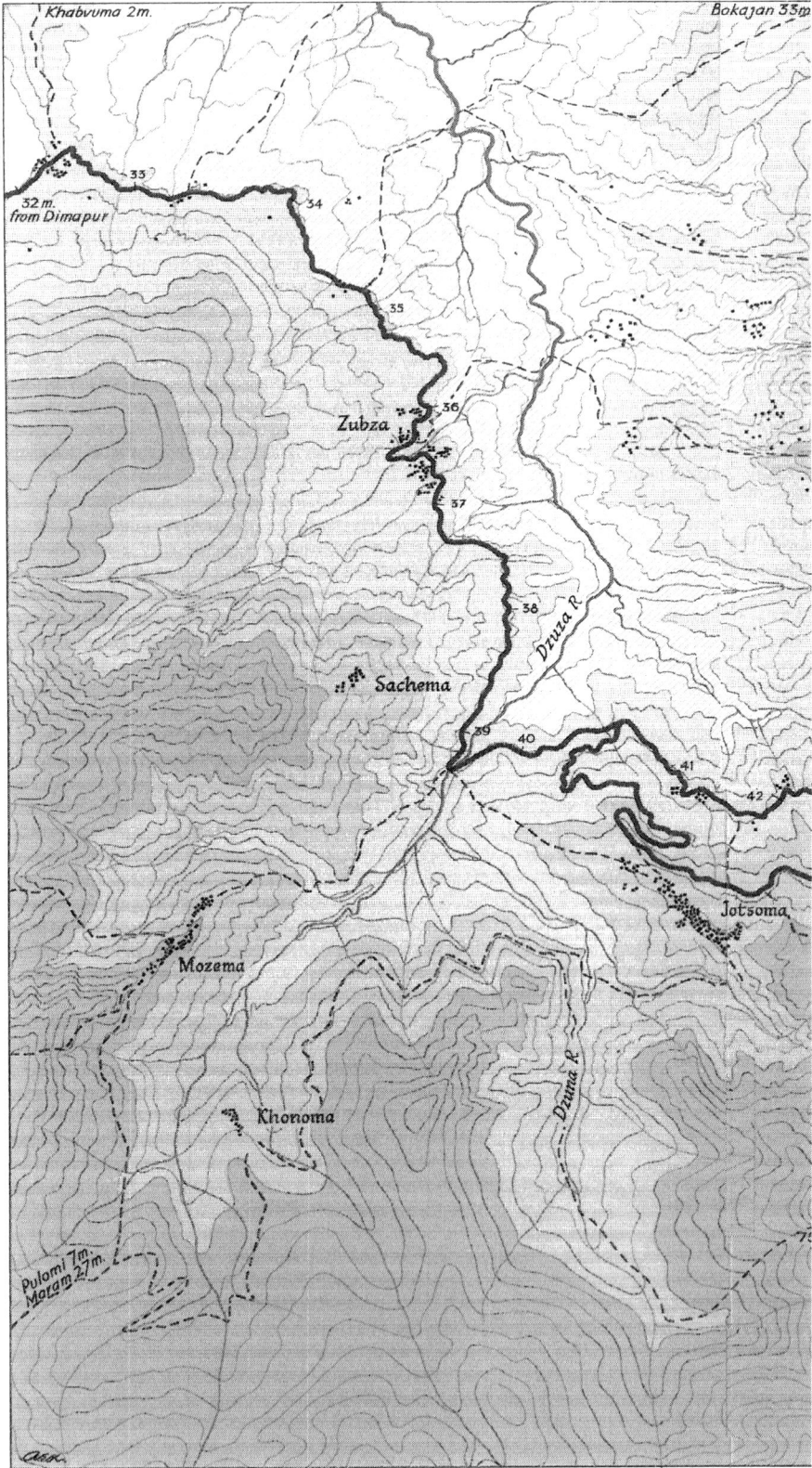

Khabvuma 2m.

Bokajan 33m.

33

32 m.
from Dimapur

34

35

36

Zubza

37

38

Druza R.

Sachema

39   40

41

42

Jotsoma

Mozema

Druma R.

Khonoma

Pulomi 7m.
Maram 27m.

Map 8

The Kohima Battlefield

Scale of Miles

0   1   2

Form lines at 250 feet intervals.   Spot heights in feet.

Cheswema

Mokokchung 63m.
Wokha 57m.J

Sano-ru R.

Pheru R.

Rekzoma

Merema

McROBERT HILL

FIRS HILL

NAGA VILLAGE

Chedema

5120

GUN SPUR

43

TREASURY HILL
46

KOHIMA

PIQUET HILL
44

GARRISON HILL

Barracks

45   F.S.D.

D.I.S.

CONGRESS HILL

47   JAIL HILL

TWO TREE HILL

G.P.T. RIDGE

48

Dzúcharu R.

Chakhabama 4 m.
Jessami 55 m.

Kezoma 9m.
Kekrima 11m.

49

Aradura

Warreo R.

Pfuchama

622
PULEBADZE

50

51   52   Phesama

Mao 15m.
Imphal 81m.

FEET
over 5000
4000
3000
1000

CHAPTER XXV

THE BATTLES OF IMPHAL
AND KOHIMA
Victory and Pursuit
(June – July 1944)

See Maps 3, 4 and 9 and Sketch 15

THE opening of the Imphal Road did not entirely remove the threat to the plain, for the Japanese *33rd Division*, which was still trying to break through at Bishenpur, had been checked but not defeated.[1] Giffard believed that Mutaguchi would not give up without making a final effort and that a new offensive in the Shenam Pass or Bishenpur area could be expected, a belief shared by Slim and Scoones. He was satisfied that both areas were too strong to be overwhelmed unless the Japanese received powerful reinforcements, and all senior commanders agreed that the surest way to prevent this happening was to destroy the Japanese *31st* and *15th Divisions*. When Scoones and Stopford met on the 22nd June, a few hours after the Imphal Road had been opened, they appreciated that the first step to bring this about must be the capture of Ukhrul, which would sever the Japanese communications to the Chindwin and between the two wings of *15th Army*. Their message to 14th Army Headquarters outlining their plan crossed one from Slim telling them to bring pressure to bear on Ukhrul as quickly as possible and maintain an offensive-defensive south of Imphal. The dividing line between IV and XXXIII Corps was to be an east-west line through Imphal, south of which IV Corps was to be responsible.

Their plan was that XXXIII Corps would encircle Ukhrul, 23rd (L.R.P.) Brigade from the east, 33rd Brigade from the north by way of the track from Maram, and 89th Brigade (now reverted to 7th Division) by way of Kangpokpi from the west. The 20th Division (less one brigade) would move on Ukhrul from the south-west and cut all the tracks leading south and south-east from it.[2] The IV Corps would be responsible for the offensive-defensive to the south and south-east of the plain where 17th and 23rd Divisions were holding

---

[1] See Map 9, page 374.
[2] The 32nd Brigade of 20th Division was with 17th Division in the Bishenpur area.

off attacks by *33rd Division* and the *Yamamoto Detachment* respectively, attacks which had increased in intensity as the plight of *15th* and *31st Divisions* worsened. This plan entailed a regrouping: 20th Division passed to XXXIII Corps, 5th Division (now rejoined by 161st Brigade) moved into IV Corps reserve near Tulihal and 2nd Division took over responsibility for protecting the road from Maram to Imphal.

Mountbatten told Giffard that, while agreeing that Ukhrul was a valuable military objective, he was concerned about the non-aggressive rôle given to IV Corps. Giffard pointed out the impossibility of doing everything simultaneously, and said he was not prepared to interfere with Slim's conduct of the battle. His views are evident from a message he sent Slim on the 29th June in which he said:

'It seems to me quite possible that *31 Div.* will be withdrawn to the south of Ukhrul and that there may be little opposition to the occupation of the Ukhrul area by us. I think it very likely that the enemy intends to make a final desperate attempt to capture Imphal from the general direction of the Tiddim and Tamu roads. I also think that we now have sufficient strength to defeat any such attempt, but to clear the enemy away altogether will be a much harder and slower business unless a real threat to his communications can be developed. You have no doubt considered whether the advance on Ukhrul might not be continued to Humine and Myothit thus giving *31 Div.* no chance to recover and presenting a threat to the communications of *15 Div.* to Thaungdut and Tamu.'

Giffard's suspicion that the enemy would make a final effort received almost immediate confirmation when on the 28th a *15th Army* order, issued by Mutaguchi on the 4th June, was captured; this spoke of withdrawing *31st Division* from Kohima, reassembling the whole army and with one great thrust capturing Imphal. A *33rd Division* order by Tanaka captured at the same time contained an exhortation which read, "On this battle rests the success or failure of the Greater South-East Asia war".

Mutaguchi had sent his Chief of Staff to *31st Division* on the 19th June with an order for Sato to stop his withdrawal immediately and send his main body to assist *15th Division* north of Imphal. Sato retorted that the failure on the part of *15th Army* to send his division either supplies or ammunition since the operation began made it impossible for his units to comply with the order, and that this automatically freed him from any obligation to obey. The morale of *31st Division* had in fact already cracked and the troops, throwing away their arms and ammunition and thinking only of their own preservation, were in headlong flight. The situation was completely out of control.

On the 26th, Mutaguchi at last recognized that success was no longer possible, and recommended to *Burma Area Army* that *15th Army* should be allowed to withdraw to a general line from the Yu River to Tiddim.[1] Kawabe, not prepared to sanction a withdrawal without first obtaining the approval of *Southern Army*, ordered *15th Army* to continue the offensive. He arranged, however, for a senior staff officer to fly to *Southern Army Headquarters* at Singapore on the 29th June to explain the situation and get permission to abandon the Imphal operation. A spell of unusually bad weather delayed the flight till the 3rd July and so the hopeless struggle was prolonged.

The start of XXXIII Corps' encirclement of Ukhrul was held up by storms and torrential rain, and it was not until the 27th June that it began, and then only under fearful difficulties. By the 28th, four columns of 23rd (L.R.P.) Brigade were moving eastwards towards Fort Keary and Layshi, and the other four, moving towards Ukhrul, were in the Kharasom–Kongai area.[2] By that date 33rd and 89th Brigades, each with a company of engineers and a detachment of mountain artillery, moving along the tracks towards Ukhrul, had reached points a few miles south-east of Maram and east of Kangpokpi respectively. Opposition was slight until the encircling columns were within sight of Ukhrul, but 20th Division, advancing along the tracks and road to the south, met fierce opposition, for the Japanese had quickly realized that this thrust was a danger to their escape route and had to be delayed, whatever the cost, until the bulk of *15th* and *31st Divisions* had passed through Ukhrul.

Except in the case of 20th Division, the main obstacle to the advance was the climate and country. The columns, struggling through blinding rain, swollen torrents, deep cloying mud and along treacherous slippery paths on the mountain sides, were often hungry, for there were periods when air supply was impossible. The physical effort of ascending and descending as much as 4,000 feet in a single march, with the temperature varying from the sub-tropical heat of the valley bottoms to the cold mists of the mountain tops, imposed a fearful strain on the fortitude of troops already beginning to suffer from undernourishment, exposure and fatigue. Dysentery, scrub typhus and skin diseases became rife and there was no comfort or shelter for the sick and wounded.

From the 3rd to the 7th July the Japanese held on grimly in the Ukhrul area. To the south *51st Regiment* fought desperately with some

[1] See Map 3, page 33.
[2] See Map 4, page 53.

success to break out of the ring drawn round it by 20th Division, while *60th Regiment* assisted by holding open an escape route through Sangshak and Sakok. Organized resistance ceased on the 8th, and 23rd (L.R.P.), 33rd and 89th Brigades began to fan out along the tracks to the Chindwin. There was no need to carry out Giffard's suggestion of pressing the pursuit to the Chindwin, since a great proportion of the men of *15th* and *31st Divisions* who had survived the battle were found dead or dying of disease and exhaustion. Bodies, guns, vehicles, and equipment lay rotting and rusting along the quagmires that had once been the tracks leading from Ukhrul— scenes of horror which compelled pity, for it was obvious that many of the dead had been sick and wounded men, who had dropped and died of starvation or been drowned in the ooze that filled every rut and pothole.[1]

It would have been foolish to have sent men, whose resistance to disease was already dangerously low, to follow the remnants of *15th* and *31st Divisions* into the notoriously malarial Kabaw Valley, or even to have kept them in the foothills along the tracks made foul by death and disease. Orders were therefore issued for 4th Brigade to take over the comparatively healthy Ukhrul area, and for 7th and 20th Divisions and 23rd (L.R.P.) Brigade, all of which had detachments operating far to the east in the foothills overlooking the Kabaw Valley and the Chindwin, to withdraw gradually.

While the troops were mopping up around and beyond Ukhrul, planning was in hand for the next phase of operations: driving the *Yamamoto Detachment* and *33rd Division* from their positions in and on the edge of the Imphal plain, and pursuing them to the Chindwin. While the advance on Ukhrul was gathering momentum, Scoones and Stopford had proposed that the inter-corps boundary should be changed from an east-west to a north-south line as soon as Ukhrul had been taken. Slim agreed and fixed the boundary as the Kohima– Imphal—Palel road (inclusive to XXXIII Corps). The effect of this decision was that IV Corps (5th and 17th Divisions, 50th (P.) and Lushai Brigades) became responsible for Bishenpur, the Tiddim road and the Lushai and Chin Hills, and XXXIII Corps (2nd, 7th, 20th and 23rd Divisions and 23rd (L.R.P.) Brigade) for Shenam Pass, the Tamu road and the tracks eastward to the Chindwin from Ukhrul and the Imphal plain.[2] Headquarters XXXIII Corps opened in Imphal on the 1st July, and the new grouping came into effect on the 7th. The rear boundary of XXXIII Corps was fixed at Maram, northward of which 21st Indian Division was placed in control of the lines of communication to Dimapur. In the first week

---

[1] The supply breakdown was due to the impossibility of distributing stocks to the scattered Japanese forces over the congested and almost unusable tracks.

[2] See Map 3, page 33.

of July its commander, Major-General Nicholson, was transferred to command of 2nd Division in place of Major-General Grover; shortly afterwards Headquarters 21st Indian Division ceased to exist as abruptly as it had begun,[1] and the control of the Imphal Road north of Maram passed to the Kohima (253) L. of C. Sub-Area.

The two corps were now in a position to begin the offensive at Shenam and Bishenpur as soon as the necessary regrouping had been completed. Slim therefore turned his attention to planning the pursuit to the Chindwin and the resumption of major operations as soon as the monsoon ended. On the 2nd July he met Mountbatten at Sylhet and proposed the 1st November as the date for a full-scale offensive, which would require no more troops than would be needed to defend the north-east frontier of India. He wished, however, to be assured that the formations now under his command would remain there and that the understrength British units would be reinforced. Mountbatten asked for the early release from Imphal of 50th (P.) Brigade for training and said that he could probably find some four to five thousand British infantry reinforcements for 14th Army by disbanding anti-aircraft artillery units. He would try to get more reinforcements from the United Kingdom, particularly for Special Force, which Stilwell had been told to evacuate to India as soon as possible.[2] He required Slim to experiment in carrying heavy anti-aircraft artillery and medium guns by air, and to consider the possibility of using heavy armoured columns in conjunction with airborne forces for the offensive.

Slim now had sufficient information on which to begin the task of preparing his army for the reconquest of Burma. He set up a tactical headquarters at Imphal from where he would be able to see the beginning of the thrust southwards to clear the Imphal plain and could at the same time be at hand to discuss with his corps commanders arrangements to rest and refit the divisions which had been in action for months on end. On the 11th July he recommended to 11th Army Group that 11th (E.A.) Division should move immediately from Chittagong to Imphal,[3] that 17th and 23rd Divisions should move back to India for rest and that 19th Division should move from India to Chittagong. All of these would remain part of 14th Army, except the 17th, which was to become the G.H.Q., India, reserve. In the event 7th Division, the early release of which had already been recommended, remained at Kohima and the 23rd

---

[1] See page 343 fn.
[2] See Chapter XXIX.
[3] The 11th (E.A.) Division had been ordered to Chittagong on the 21st April to become 14th Army reserve.

left 14th Army for good, the 19th replacing it instead of going to Chittagong. These changes made no difference in the size of the force at Slim's disposal and he was in a position to warn 3rd Tactical Air Force and his senior staff officers to be prepared to discuss plans for the capture of Mandalay and Rangoon. This was the beginning of planning for the reconquest of Burma, which will be described in the next volume.

Meanwhile there had been almost continuous fighting on Shenam Pass and in the Bishenpur sector. On the pass, attack and counter-attack added to the already formidable toll of casualties which the possession of its small underfeatures had cost both opponents. To the north of the pass Yamamoto's attempts to carry out Mutaguchi's Palel offensive met with some local, but short lived, success.[1] In the last week of June, 2/19th Hyderabad covering Palel airfield from the east lost some of its posts in the foothills and incurred over a hundred casualties, and in the first week of July a Japanese fighting patrol infiltrated to a dispersal area on the airfield and destroyed seven aircraft with hand-placed explosives.[2]

The 23rd Division was still disposed defensively with a brigade of five battalions holding the pass, and the other two, with attached unbrigaded units, covering its flanks and providing a two-battalion corps reserve.[3] On the 10th July, Roberts issued orders for it to regroup for attack, or, if the enemy showed any sign of withdrawing, for pursuit. Each brigade now resumed its normal composition. The artillery, augmented by 16th Field Regiment from 2nd Division, 1st Medium Regiment and an Indian heavy anti-aircraft battery, was grouped under command of the C.R.A. (Brigadier R. W. Andrews). Roberts' intention was to destroy the *Yamamoto Detachment* by a double envelopment. The 1st Brigade (King) on the right was to seize Nippon and Ralph Hills while 49th Brigade (Brigadier C. H. B. Rodham), less a battalion in divisional reserve, moved wide and deep round the left flank, by way of Sita to the Sibong ridge, and established a roadblock where the road cut through the end of the ridge some eight miles north-west of Moreh.[4] As soon as these forces were in posi-tion, 37th Brigade with a squadron of 149th Regiment R.A.C. was to attack down the main road. The long and difficult line of communica-tion to Sibong was to be kept open by 268th Brigade, and 5th

---

[1] See page 354.

[2] The Japanese force operating in the Palel area was the *Nukui Column*, composed of *Headquarters 213th Infantry Regiment, I/60th, II/51st Battalions* and some smaller units. The column left Tengnoupal on the 13th June but, after the action at the end of the month east of Palel, withdrew and contented itself with sending forward two sabotage parties with explosives to raid the airfield.

[3] See page 358.

[4] See Sketch 15, page 370.

Brigade of 2nd Division was to follow up 37th Brigade to mop up and be ready to pursue as soon as the enemy broke. Sudden violent storms in the mountains, which washed away tracks and brought the many mountain streams down in spate, delayed the enveloping forces. D-day for 37th Brigade's attack had therefore to be twice postponed and was finally fixed for the 24th July.

After they had been driven off the Imphal Road, and perhaps in order to try and counteract this serious setback, the Japanese had struck once again on the 21st June at the vital water point near Point 5846 in the Bishenpur sector. They got astride the Silchar track to the west of it and formed a corridor to reopen direct communication with *214th Regiment* in the Khoirok area, from where, according to captured orders, Tanaka still hoped to make a final bid to take Imphal. The situation was restored only when Cowan ordered 48th Brigade to go on the defensive at Ningthoukhong, and for its headquarters with one battalion to move to the Silchar track and clear the roadblock in co-operation with the troops already there. On the 29th June, after nearly a week of fierce fighting, 2/5th Royal Gurkhas, assisted by detachments from 1st Northamptonshire Regiment and 1/10th Gurkhas, cleared the water point and captured four enemy guns at the cost of 176 casualties.[1] From the seventy or more enemy dead found after the end of the action a firm identification of *151st Infantry Regiment* was obtained.[2]

That day Tanaka abandoned the offensive and ordered *214th Regiment* to withdraw from Khoirok. On the 5th July, 17th Divisional Intelligence staff reported that they believed that the remnants of *214th Regiment* were now all south of the Silchar track. Scoones thereupon ordered 5th Division (now commanded by Major-General Evans)[3] to take over the Bishenpur–Silchar track, clear it completely of the enemy and then be ready to advance through 17th Division as soon as it had reached the line Laimanai–Thinunggei.[4] The 5th Division was then to drive the Japanese from the western half of the Imphal plain. An armoured force of one squadron of Carabiniers and one of 7th Light Cavalry and the artillery of both divisions were to support either division as required.

The 17th Division's advance began on the 11th July when, after the enemy positions had been subjected to intensive air attacks for

---

[1] During this action Subadar Netrabahadur Thapa and Naik Agamsing Rai, both of 2/5th Royal Gurkha Rifles, gained Victoria Crosses.

[2] The *151st Infantry Regiment* of *53rd Division* (less one battalion) had joined *33rd Division* on the 19th June.

[3] Evans was promoted and assumed command when Briggs went on leave to India before taking up a new appointment.

[4] This released 32nd Brigade, which rejoined 20th Division.

some days, 48th Brigade attacked Ningthoukhong. Its garrison was not believed to be large but it was plentifully supplied with automatics and ammunition and fought to the death. It was not until the 16th, after further air and artillery bombardment, that the position was finally overrun and Thinunggei occupied. Twelve tanks dug in as pillboxes, anti-tank guns, the first Japanese flame throwers captured in Burma, and more than a hundred unburied dead were found at Ningthoukhong. That evening 63rd Brigade seized the hill above Laimanai which had for some time been the headquarters of *33rd Division*. The 17th Division having now reached its objective, 5th Division passed through it on the 18th and took up the advance to secure the Torbung defile. The 17th Division then concentrated near Imphal in readiness to move out of the battle area.

On the recommendation of *Burma Area Army*, Field-Marshal Count Terauchi (*Southern Army*) sanctioned the abandonment of the Imphal offensive on the evening of the 4th July. The following day Kawabe told Mutaguchi to prepare to withdraw, but to continue with his attack on Palel for the time being. Mutaguchi then issued orders for a final offensive: *15th Division* was to attack along the axis of the Thoubal River towards Imphal, *31st Division*, the remnants of which had by that time concentrated east of Myothit, was to move westwards and attack Palel from the north, and *214th Regiment* of *33rd Division* was to attack Palel from the south.

At the time these orders were issued, *15th Division*, with Miyazaki's rearguard under command, was endeavouring to withdraw towards the Chindwin by way of Ukhrul. In a hopeless attempt to obey Mutaguchi's instructions, Lieut.-General U. Shibata, who had taken over command from Yamauchi on the 3rd July,[1] ordered the remnants of *51st* and *67th Infantry Regiments* to concentrate at Kasom in preparation for an advance on Imphal under cover of an attack by *60th Infantry Regiment* to recover Lamu, which had just been lost.[2] The regiments were, however, fully occupied in trying to escape from the net being drawn around them and were unable to obey the order.[3] The *31st Division* (now commanded by Miyazaki) was by this time incapable of taking any action whatsoever.[4] The *33rd Division*, heavily involved in holding off attacks by 17th Division,

[1] Lieut.-General Yamauchi had been seriously ill with malaria for some time and soon after his relief died in hospital at Maymyo.
[2] Lamu was occupied by elements of 20th Division on the 4th July.
[3] See pages 363–64.
[4] Major-General Miyazaki was promoted Lieut.-General and relieved Lieut.-General Sato on the 27th June. It is interesting to note that between the 10th May and 27th June, in the middle of a battle, three divisional commanders had been relieved of their appointments.

could not disengage *214th Regiment* and thus Tanaka could not obey Mutaguchi's order.

By the 8th, it was at last evident to both Mutaguchi and Kawabe that *15th Army* was quite unable to take any further offensive action, and on the 9th Kawabe ordered it to withdraw to the general line Zibyu Taungdan–Mawlaik–Kalewa–Gangaw. Mutaguchi planned that *15th Division* would withdraw by way of Sittaung, leaving rearguards on the tracks across the watershed between the Kabaw Valley and the Chindwin, and that *31st Division* would make for Thaungdut. This was in fact sanctioning what was already taking place. The *Yamamoto Detachment* was to hold on at Shenam to cover the retreat of *15th* and *31st Divisions* and of administrative units from the Kabaw Valley. It was then to withdraw in two columns, one to Mawlaik, and the other to Yazagyo to cover the rear of *33rd Division* retiring down the Tiddim road to Kalemyo.

On the 18th July, 123rd Brigade of 5th Division passed through 17th Division, and the next day it occupied Moirang. The only opposition was from occasional small patrols and stragglers. On the 20th the brigade established itself near Toronglaobi, where a well used track led into the hills to the west. The 9th Brigade now took up the advance against gradually stiffening resistance until it encountered a strongly fortified position astride the Torbung defile at MS 33 and Point 3404, where 17th Division's roadblock had been established in May. While this advance was going on, the Lushai Brigade attacked the Japanese communications on the Tiddim road far in rear of *33rd Division*, carrying out raids in the Manipur bridge area and in the gorge where the road follows the Manipur River half way between Tongzang and Tiddim.[1]

While 5th Division advanced to the Torbung gap, 23rd Division was moving into position to surround the Japanese on Shenam Pass. At about 2.30 p.m. on the 23rd July, 49th Brigade on the left reported that it had reached Sibong, and that there was a considerable force of Japanese artillery and tanks at the bridge over the Lokchau River near Sibong. Several attempts that night to blow the bridge failed. As 49th Brigade had arrived at its destination on time, the frontal attack by 37th Brigade on the pass began according to plan at 4.30 a.m. on the 24th in driving rain and mist. By 6.30 a.m. 3/10th Gurkhas had secured Scraggy at a cost of 112 killed and

---

[1] Headquarters 14th Army suggested the establishment of a two-battalion roadblock to hold out for a month until 5th Division made contact with it, but abandoned the idea when it became clear that this involved such a great change in the operational policy of the brigade that it would be some three weeks before the block could be established and that in the meanwhile all the operations just started would have to be given up.

wounded.[1] Mopping up disclosed that there were still many Japanese in deep shelters tunnelled into the hill: some tried to break out and it was not till the engineers blew in all tunnels that resistance ceased. Japanese were now seen to be leaving Crete, which was quickly overrun. Apart from the unknown number that perished when the underground shelters were blown in, ninety dead were counted and two prisoners taken.

Meanwhile 1st Seaforth Highlanders of 1st Brigade on the right had taken Nippon Hill against only slight opposition, and had then pushed on to assist the Patiala Infantry which had been held up on Ralph Hill. The 1/16th Punjab, whose task was to cut the road to the east of Ralph Hill and destroy Yamamoto's headquarters which was believed to be there, was held up by an impassable torrent in the valley south of the road. On the 25th, 49th Brigade became involved in heavy fighting at Sibong with fresh troops, which later were found to be from *61st Infantry Regiment* of *4th Division*.[2] Throughout the day enemy medium artillery was very active and all over the area from Tengnoupal to Sibong small enemy pockets of resistance were found; since none would surrender, casualties mounted steadily.

On the evening of the 25th, plans were made for a break-through down the road next day by tanks of 149th R.A.C. and infantry of 37th Brigade to contact 1st Brigade at Ralph Hill and, if possible, 49th Brigade in the Sibong area. As soon as the road was clear a jeep convoy was to be rushed through, for supply by air and by animal transport along the tracks was precarious. At this point the monsoon intervened and a deluge during the night caused a landslide which completely blocked the road. Now relieved of any pressure from the Shenam side, the Japanese were able to concentrate their forces and break through the block which 49th Brigade had just succeeded in making on the road where it crossed the end of the Sibong ridge and withdraw towards Moreh.

Early on the 28th the road as far as Sibong was in undisputed possession of 23rd Division, and the engineers were able to begin repairing the extensive damage to the road and the Lokchau bridge caused by the monsoon and the enemy. Until their work was completed neither guns nor vehicles could be brought forward to support an attack on the prepared positions which the Japanese had taken up on the hills covering Moreh from the west. Patrols, however, infiltrated to the Kabaw Valley. Those of 268th Brigade from Sita reached Mintha, and brought back many dispirited *I.N.A.* prisoners and reports of a disorganized retreat towards the Chindwin.

The 5th Brigade of 2nd Division now moved to Tengnoupal ready

---

[1] See Sketch 15, page 370.
[2] See Map 9, page 374, and pages 354-55. This regiment (less a battalion) had reached Tamu on the 23rd July.

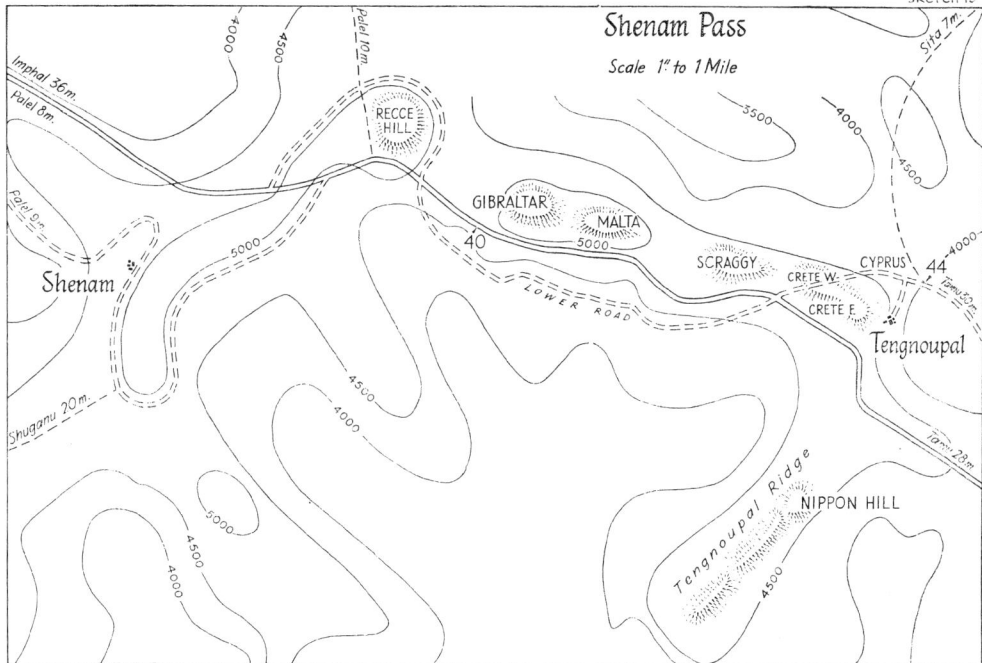

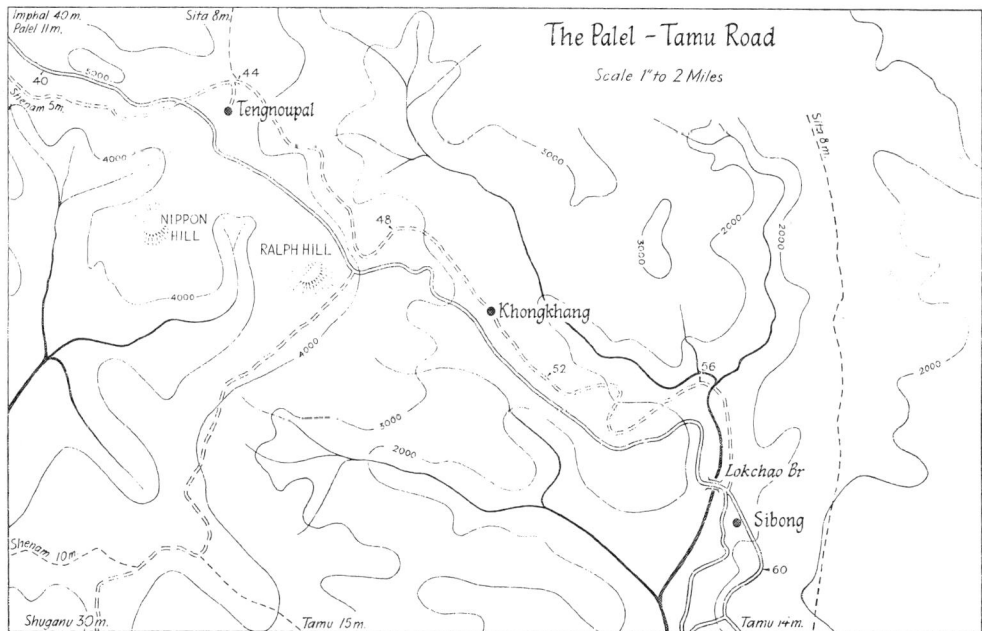

Shenam Pass

Scale 1" to 1 Mile

Imphal 36 m.
Palel 8 m.
Palel 10 m.
Palel 9 m.
Sita 7 m.

RECCE HILL

GIBRALTAR
MALTA
SCRAGGY
CRETE W.
CRETE E.
CYPRUS

Shenam

LOWER ROAD

40

5000
4500
4000
5000
4500
4000

Shuganu 20 m.

44

Tengnoupal

Tamu 30 m.
Tamu 28 m.

Tengnoupal Ridge

NIPPON HILL

4500

The Palel – Tamu Road

Imphal 40 m.
Palel 11 m.
Sita 8 m.

Scale 1" to 2 Miles

40
Shenam 5 m.
44
Tengnoupal

Sita 8 m.

NIPPON HILL
RALPH HILL

48
5000
4000
5000
2000
3000
2000

Khongkhang

52

56

Lokchao Br

Sibong

60

Shenam 10 m.

Shuganu 30 m.

Tamu 15 m.

Tamu 14 m.

Legend

ROADS	Allweather	
	Fairweather	
	Tracks	
	Mileage from Imphal	40

HILL FEATURES

Contours on the top sketch are at 500 ft interval
Contours on the lower sketch are at 1000 ft interval

to push through to Tamu as soon as the enemy had been cleared from the hills west of Moreh, and 11th (E.A.) Division at Palel began to prepare for its task of continuing the advance down the Kabaw Valley. On the 31st, before 23rd Division's attack could be launched, it was found that the Japanese had abandoned their positions in the hills covering Moreh. These were quickly occupied and 5th Brigade (Brigadier M. M. Alston-Roberts-West) moved forward ready to go through. That day 23rd Division was ordered to stand fast; it was to leave XXXIII Corps as soon as 11th (E.A.) Division (Major-General C. C. Fowkes) had moved forward and taken over operational control.

On the Tiddim road, Japanese rearguards succeeded in holding the Torbung gap throughout the 26th, but, by the morning of the 27th, 123rd Brigade had secured the defile; Headquarters 5th Division came forward to Moirang and 9th Brigade began to pass through the defile with orders to advance to MS 70. In view of the enormous difficulty of maintaining a force of any size forward of that point during the monsoon, MS 70 was intended to be the limit of the pursuit along the Tiddim road. By the 31st July, 9th Brigade, supported by a half squadron of the Carabiniers, had taken Churachandpur and its forward troops were at MS 42 in contact with a Japanese rearguard.

Late in July, Headquarters IV Corps began to leave for Ranchi to reorganize in readiness for the autumn campaign, and from midday on the 31st July XXXIII Corps (Stopford) became responsible for the whole of the Central front. The change in command and the relief of the forward division was undoubtedly responsible for the slowness in following up the retreating enemy forces at Tamu. By the time 5th Brigade finally did advance, the *Yamamoto Detachment* had withdrawn from Moreh and Tamu and broken contact. The brigade found both villages abandoned and a shambles of derelict vehicles, guns and corpses of men and animals.

By the evening of the 31st July four divisions, less some detachments, had been withdrawn to their rest areas,[1] and 23rd (L.R.P.), 50th (P.) and 3 S.S. Brigades were on their way to India. The 9th Brigade of 5th Division was preparing to attack the Japanese rearguard at MS 42 on the Tiddim road, 123rd and 161st Brigades were disposed in depth along the road behind it and the Lushai Brigade was raiding between MS 126 and MS 150. On the Tamu road, 23rd Division held the high ground overlooking Moreh from the west and north-west, 5th Brigade (2nd Division) was moving forward from Tengnoupal, 268th Brigade was on the left flank on the Sita–Mintha track and 11th (E.A.) Division was still in the early stages of its

---

[1] The 2nd at Maram (less 4th and 5th Brigades), 7th at Kohima, 17th at Imphal and 20th at Wangjing with a column in the upper Kabaw Valley.

concentration at Palel. To the north, a two-battalion column of 20th Division, known as Tarcol from its commander Lieut.-Colonel G. L. Tarver of the Baluch Regiment, was watching the tracks from the Chindwin to Kohima and Imphal, with patrols operating in the northern end of the Kabaw Valley, and Ukhrul was held by 4th Brigade (2nd Division).

British casualties during the battles at Imphal and Kohima were just under 16,700 of which approximately a quarter was incurred at Kohima.[1] The strength of *15th Army* (excluding the *I.N.A.* division of some 7,000 and 4,000 reinforcements) was 84,280. The Japanese losses were 53,505, of which 30,502 were killed, missing or died. Of the 30,775 remaining available for duty with their units, the majority were suffering either from light wounds or malnutrition or both. The Japanese *15th Army* had suffered a crushing defeat.

On the 28th July, General Giffard wrote General Slim a letter congratulating him and 14th Army on the victory. The relevant portions of this letter are quoted since they graphically sum up the difficulties faced by both sides in the battles described in this volume. It read:

My dear Slim,
    The driving of the last Japanese soldier from the Imphal plain provides me with the opportunity for which I have been waiting, to congratulate you and all ranks of Fourteenth Army upon the series of victories you have won since the beginning of the year.
    You have met, totally defeated and largely destroyed approximately five Japanese divisions or more than half the garrison of Burma. They have had 50,840 casualties killed and wounded at your hands and have lost to you over 400 prisoners, 100 guns, 20 tanks and great quantities of equipment. . . .
    Your victories have been won under the most arduous and difficult conditions of ground and weather that can be found in any theatre of war. The difficulties can hardly be equalled and are certainly not surpassed elsewhere. During the past 14 months I have seen for myself the mountains and jungles on all parts of the Fourteenth Army front at all times of the year. I know what monsoon rain can do to roads and tracks and what life under heavy continuous rain is like. I thoroughly appreciate the great physical exertions and mental strain imposed upon the troops whether they are in action forward against the enemy or struggling to bring forward supplies of every kind, repair lorries, evacuate and treat sick and wounded, etc., etc.
    Upon the infantry has fallen the greatest strain both physically and mentally, and magnificently have officers and men responded

---

[1] See Appendix 29.

to all the calls made upon them. Patrolling by night and day in dense jungle calls for high courage and great determination; attacking up steep hills in thick forest and across narrow knife edged ridges demands dash and staying power of the highest order; and defence against an enemy whose jungle craft is skilful, whose determination is great and who may come in from all sides needs steady nerves and good discipline. In all these qualities the infantry of the army has excelled, and has mastered the Japanese who were specially trained and equipped for jungle fighting and considered themselves our superiors. The infantry can be justly proud of their great successes achieved by hard and skilful fighting.

Equally distinguished in their own sphere, the 'Gunners', whether British, Indian or African, have shown once again their courage, devotion to duty and determination at all costs to support the infantry and destroy the enemy. They have fought, too, as infantry with outstanding success. The gallantry of the O.P. parties with the leading infantry has been most marked. The determination of the Regiments and Batteries to get their guns forward whatever the obstacles and difficulties, has resulted in guns of every type, including medium, coming into action in positions which in the early stages of the campaign no one would have dreamt of trying to reach.

The Royal Armoured Corps and Indian Armoured Corps, the possibility of whose usefulness in thick and mountainous country some officers were sceptical at the beginning of the campaign have silenced all their critics. The skill, courage and determination with which the tanks have been moved up and have engaged the enemy at short range has been outstanding. They have no greater admirers than the infantry whom they have supported so staunchly and with whom they have co-operated so closely and skilfully.

The versatility, courage and determination of the Engineers, British, Indian and African, have certainly never been surpassed. They have been faced with every kind of problem: bulldozing tracks under fire to get guns and tanks forward; searching for and removing mines; blowing in Japanese bunkers; making roads and airfields; building bridges; providing water; and every other kind of job which was beyond the capabilities of the other arms. They have never failed. They have as in all their former campaigns fought valiantly in the front line as infantry . . .

It is, however, as a team that an army works and it is because the Fourteenth Army is a real team, every member of which knows how to play together for the side, that it has achieved such success.

In writing this I have not forgotten the immense debt which the Army owes to the Air. It is no exaggeration to say that without the really magnificent assistance given by the Eastern Air Command, the Army could never have won its victories.

I am sure no one who watched them is likely to forget the courage, determination and skill of the aircraft pilots and crews who have flown through some of the worst weather in the world over appalling country either to attack the enemy in front of the Army and his communications in rear with bombs and machine guns, or to deliver reinforcements, supplies, ammunition, etc., to the troops isolated in the Arakan, Imphal and Central Burma.

I finally want to congratulate all commanders and staffs on their steadfastness, courage and skill under all the varying conditions of battle. Good plans and good staff work must precede good fighting. Where both are present, troops fight with confidence and courage and this they have done, as the results have shown.

The Imphal Battlefield

Scale of Miles

0 — 5 — 10 — 15 — 20

Contours at 1000 feet intervals   Spot heights in feet
AIRFIELDS *Allweather Fairweather*............◉....○

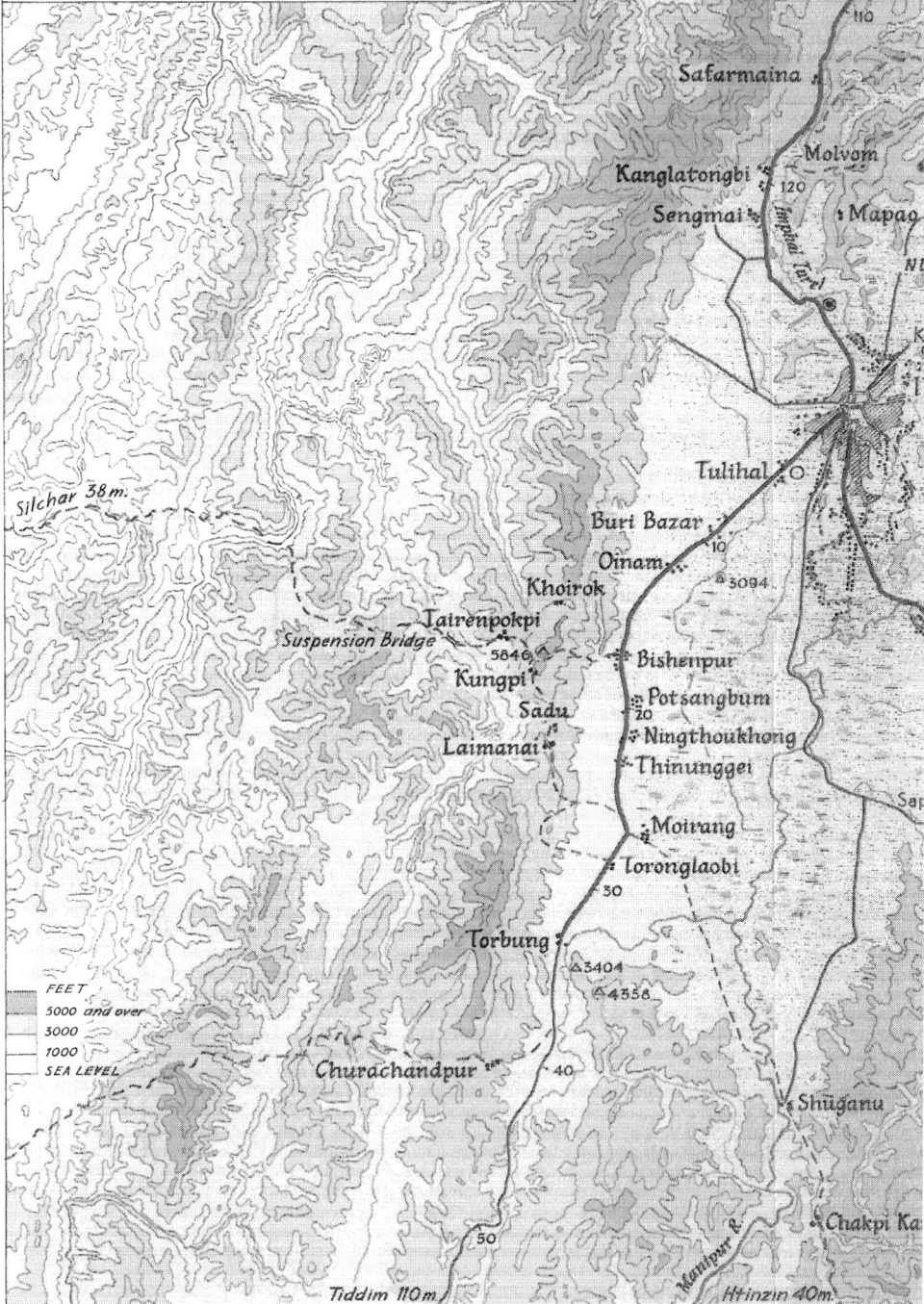

Kangpokpi

Kohima 50 m.

110

Safarmaina

Molvom

Kanglatongbi

120

Sengmai

Imphal Turel

Mapao

NI

K

Ii

Tulihal ○

Silchar 38 m.

Buri Bazar

10

Oinam

△3094

Khoirok

Tairenpokpi

Suspension Bridge

5846

Bishenpur

Kungpi

Potsangbum

20

Sadu

Ningthoukhong

Laimanai

Thinunggei

Moirang

Sap

Ioronglaobi

30

Torbung

△3404

△4358

FEET

5000 and over
3000
1000
SEA LEVEL

Churachandpur

40

Shuganu

50

Manipur

Tiddim 110 m.

Chakpi Ka

Htinzin 40 m.

Map 9

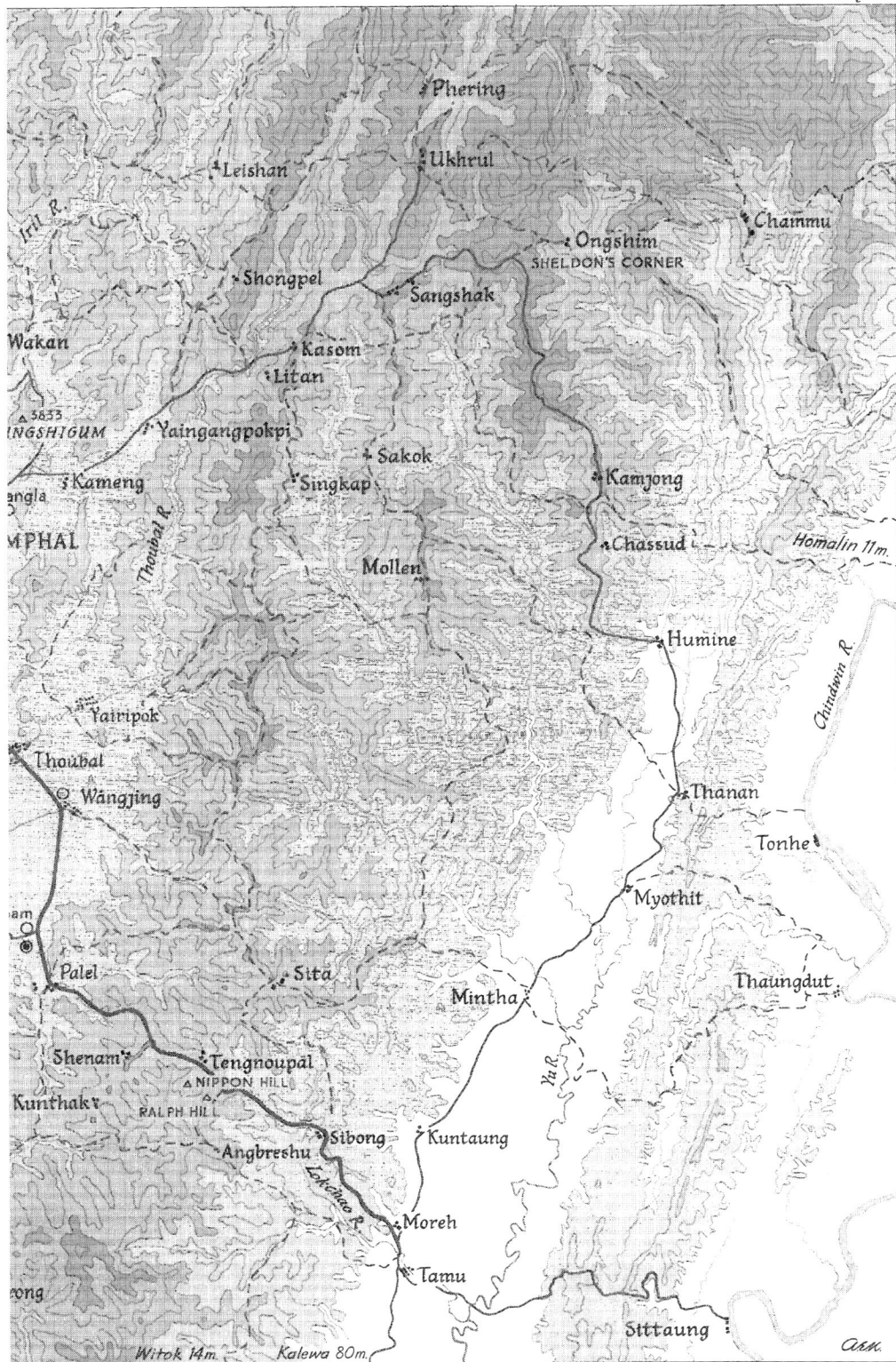

Phering

Leishan

Ukhrul

Chainmu

Ongshim
SHELDON'S CORNER

Shongpel

Sangshak

Iril R.

Wakan

5833
NGSHIGUM

Kasom

Litan

Yaingangpokpi

Sakok

Kameng

Singkap

Kamjong

ngla

MPHAL

Thoubal R.

Chassud

Homalin 11m.

Mollen

Humine

Chindwin R.

Yairipok

Thoubal

Wangjing

Thanan

Tonhe

am

Myothit

Palel

Sita

Mintha

Thaungdut

Shenam

Tengnoupal
△NIPPON HILL

Kunthak

RALPH HILL

Sibong

Kuntaung

Va R.

Angbreshu

Lokchao R.

Moreh

Tamu

ong

Witok 14m.

Kalewa 80m.

Stttaung

a.r.k.

CHAPTER XXVI

EVENTS IN THE INDIAN OCEAN
(January – July 1944)

See Maps 10, 13 and 15

ON the completion of the first phase of their plan for the conquest of the Southern Region which established a defensive perimeter running from the Kuriles through the Gilbert Islands, New Guinea and the Netherlands East Indies to Burma, the Japanese organized their defences into various fronts.[1] The area covering the Andaman and Nicobar Islands, Malaya, Sumatra, Java and Borneo became known as the 'Indian Ocean front'.[2] In 1942 the defence of the Andaman and Nicobar Islands, Malaya and Sumatra was the responsibility of *25th Army*, that of Java of *16th Army* and that of Borneo of *Borneo Garrison Army*. In March 1943 *Headquarters Southern Army* moved south from Saigon to Singapore and took over all *25th Army's* responsibilities except Sumatra.

To avoid *Headquarters Southern Army* having to deal with too many headquarters and independent units, and to provide a headquarters for the defence and administration of Malaya, *Headquarters 29th Army* was formed on the 31st January 1944 at Taiping and placed in control of Malaya, and the Andaman and Nicobar Islands. To provide a land route between the South China Sea and the Indian Ocean and reduce the sea traffic through the Strait of Malacca to Rangoon, which was under increasing attack by Allied aircraft and submarines, a railway across the Kra Isthmus from Jumbhorn to the vicinity of Victoria Point had been constructed and was brought into use in January with a capacity of four trains each way a day.[3]

When, in May 1944, the Allied offensive in the Pacific was beginning to threaten the Philippines, *Headquarters Southern Army* was moved from Singapore to Manila. At the same time *Headquarters 7th Area Army* (Lieut.-General K. Doihara) was formed at Singapore to take control of the Indian Ocean front and command of *16th*, *25th* and *29th Armies* and the *Borneo Garrison Army*.[4] Lieut.-General

---

[1] See Map 13, page 438.   [2] See Map 10, page 384.   [3] See Map 15 in end pocket.
[4] The strength of *7th Area Army* in May 1944 was:
    29th Army. Three independent mixed brigades (one of six and two of three battalions) and eight independent battalions.
    25th Army. *2nd Guards Division*, *4th Division* and two independent mixed brigades.
    16th Army. Two independent mixed brigades.
    Borneo Garrison Army. Two infantry battalions.

Doihara appreciated that the British forces based on India provided the only threat to his front and believed that their main object would be to recover the area of which Singapore was the centre. He thought that, in order to obtain forward airfields and stepping stones for an attack on Malaya, the British might take advantage of Japanese air and naval weakness in the Indian Ocean area and, in concert with their operations in Burma, attempt the recapture of the Andaman and Nicobar Islands as well as of northern Sumatra. He therefore ordered *29th Army* to provide both the Andaman and Nicobar Islands with a garrison of six battalions, and *25th Army* to dispose the greater part of its strength in northern and central Sumatra. Expecting Allied heavy bombers to attack Singapore and the main oil-bearing centres in his area, he also began to build up the air defences of Singapore, Sourabaya and the Palembang oilfields.[1]

After the Japanese raids on Ceylon and the Bay of Bengal in April 1942, the Eastern Fleet had been withdrawn to the east coast of Africa.[2] Kilindini remained its base until the 4th September 1943 when, as the threat of another Japanese incursion had receded, Admiral Somerville once again set up his headquarters at Colombo. During 1943, most of his ships had been sent to more active theatres —no less than forty-eight had been detached for service in the Mediterranean before the invasion of Sicily in July—and for a time the Eastern Fleet had been reduced below the strength even of a trade protection force. In December 1943 and January 1944, most of the effective landing craft in the Indian Ocean were recalled to take part in the coming invasion of Europe, thus ruling out any major amphibious operation until after the defeat of Germany, which it was hoped, optimistically, might take place in October 1944.

The surrender of the Italian Fleet in September 1943, followed by the destruction of the German battleship *Scharnhorst* in December, at last made possible the reinforcement of the Eastern Fleet and in the next six months it was steadily built up. By the end of January 1944, the battle cruiser *Renown*, flying the flag of Sir Arthur Power (Vice-Admiral Commanding the 1st Battle Squadron and second-in-command designate of the Eastern Fleet), with the battleships *Queen Elizabeth* and *Valiant*, the fleet carrier *Illustrious* and the aircraft carrier and repair ship *Unicorn*, had arrived in Ceylon with an escort of six destroyers. The intention of the Admiralty was by the end of April to add to these the fleet carrier *Victorious*, ten cruisers and

---

[1] See Map 10, page 384.
[2] See Volume II, Chapter VII.

twenty-four fleet destroyers, as well as a large number of long endurance escort vessels and two flotillas of submarines.

During the first nine months of 1943 the operational strength of the 4th Submarine Flotilla, the only one in the Indian Ocean, had not exceeded three submarines. During September and October it was joined by five boats from the Mediterranean. Submarines continued to arrive and by the end of March 1944 eleven were on the station and a second flotilla, the 8th, was formed. The submarines were mainly employed on patrols in the Strait of Malacca, on mine-laying and on special duties. On the 12th November 1943, the *Taurus* sank a Japanese submarine. On the 11th January 1944, the *Tally Ho* sank the light cruiser *Kuma* off Penang, and a month later a German U-boat. On the 26th January, the *Templar* torpedoed and badly damaged the cruiser *Kitagami* south-west of Penang. Few merchant ships were sunk and most of these were small craft, for larger merchantmen were scarce. Only one submarine was lost—the *Stonehenge* which sailed on the 25th February for patrol off the Nicobars and failed to return.

Early in 1944 there was a recrudescence of enemy submarine activity in the Indian Ocean. Although the surviving U-boats of the German *Monsün Group* which had been active during the latter half of 1943 had been withdrawn, they had been replaced by others and these, with some of the eight boats of the Japanese *8th Submarine Flotilla* based on Penang, opened a new offensive at the beginning of January. Convoys were reinstituted where possible, but the Eastern Fleet was desperately short of escort vessels. Destroyers, as they arrived on the station, had to be employed on escort duty and this, for a time, left the fleet practically immobilized. Air escort was given when possible to convoys during their passage through vulnerable areas, but the number of suitable aircraft was very small.

Air operations throughout the Indian Ocean other than those of the Fleet Air Arm were the responsibility of the Air Commander-in-Chief, S.E.A.C. These operations were directed by the Air Officer Commanding 222 Group (Air Vice-Marshal A. Lees), whose head-quarters were in Colombo in close touch with the Commander-in-Chief, Eastern Fleet, with a force of some ten flying-boat squadrons and nine land-based medium and long-range squadrons. Opera-tional control in distant areas was delegated to Air Headquarters, Aden, Headquarters 225 Group at Bangalore and Air Headquarters, East Africa. Owing to shortage of aircraft a system of regular patrols was in most cases impracticable, and aircraft were sent to patrol areas where submarines were known or suspected to be. Since the presence of a submarine was usually revealed only by the sinking of a ship, this method of operating often led to the rescue of survivors but seldom to the destruction of the submarine, but the mere arrival of the aircraft was a strong deterrent to further attacks on shipping in the area. The range of the flying-boats' reconnaissance was extended by operating them from anchorages in outlying bases such as the Maldive Islands, the Chagos Archipelago, the Seychelles and Socotra;[1] but the majority of reconnaissance aircraft had to be concentrated in the main shipping lanes—the Gulf of Aden, the Persian Gulf and the approaches to Bombay and Ceylon. From January to July 1944, general reconnaissance squadrons flew some 3,696 sorties on patrols in all weathers over the Indian Ocean, frequently up to the extreme endurance of the aircraft. In the course of these nine aircraft were lost.

In the first quarter of 1944, shipping losses in the Indian Ocean were heavier than in any other theatre, reaching a peak in March when 75,498 tons were sunk. These losses, though inconsiderable in proportion to the number of ships at sea, were serious in that S.E.A.C. was at the end of a long line of communications and lost cargoes took a long time to replace. Sinkings were at first heaviest in the approaches to the Gulf of Aden, the main hunting ground of the German U-boats, but later became more widespread. A particularly serious loss occurred on the 12th February when a troop convoy on its way to Ceylon, escorted by the cruiser *Hawkins* and two destroyers (the *Petard* and *Paladin*), was attacked by a Japanese submarine off the Maldive Islands, and a transport was sunk with the loss of over 1,000 lives. The submarine was subsequently destroyed by the *Petard*. The Japanese lost another submarine off the east coast of India which had also attacked an escorted convoy. In February a tanker sent out to refuel German U-boats was spotted by aircraft and then sunk by units of the Eastern Fleet and in March a second tanker was similarly dealt with. During April and May there was a lull in the U-boat offensive and no Allied ships were sunk in the Indian Ocean. In June, however, there was another recrudescence of enemy submarine activity and by the end of July eight more ships (50,000 tons) had been lost. Nevertheless, despite the great shortage of escorts and aircraft, the Royal Navy with the close co-operation of the Royal Air Force was able to keep open the line of communication in the Indian Ocean and ensure the arrival of large numbers of merchant ships at Indian ports, including Calcutta, with comparatively little loss.

Within a week or two of the arrival of the first reinforcements for the Eastern Fleet, the Japanese began to transfer some of the major units of their fleet to Singapore.[2] Although it was thought probable by the

---

[1] This resulted in a German U-boat being sunk by an aircraft on the 3rd May.

[2] By April five Japanese battleships, three fleet carriers, eighteen cruisers and about twenty-six destroyers had arrived at Singapore.

Admiralty that the move was a retreat from the east rather than an advance to the west, the possibility of a Japanese incursion in strength into the Indian Ocean could not be ruled out, and the Eastern Fleet was as yet no match for the Japanese concentration. Two more cruisers were at once ordered to join the fleet. The loan of the French battleship *Richelieu* and the American fleet carrier *Saratoga* was arranged to bridge the gap until the projected reinforcements for the fleet arrived,[1] and immediate steps were taken to increase the strength of the air defences of the fleet bases in Ceylon.

The air forces based on the island at the end of February consisted of three Hurricane fighter squadrons, two Beaufort torpedo squadrons, one Beaufighter night fighter squadron and a long-range reconnaissance squadron of Liberators, in addition to three squadrons of Catalinas.[2] Most of the Beauforts had been used for anti-submarine patrol and the escort of convoys. These were reassembled for training as a striking force and the rearming of the Hurricane squadrons with Spitfires, which had already been arranged, was accelerated. Two escort carriers (*Atheling* and *Begum*) and two aircraft transports (*Athene* and *Engadine*), which had sailed from the United Kingdom with four bomber and four fighter squadrons of the Fleet Air Arm on board, arrived in Ceylon on the 2nd April.

For a time Somerville considered withdrawing the fleet to the westward of the Maldive Islands but the Admiralty, although prepared to support him if he did so, felt that such a move would have an adverse effect on morale in India and the east, and suggested that some risks would have to be accepted if the fleet were to remain in the best strategic position. The problem soon solved itself. During March, it was learned that the Japanese fleet at Singapore had begun to carry out a docking programme and it soon became clear that the move was not linked with any offensive intentions further west. It had, in fact, been made through force of circumstances, for the capture of the Marshall Islands had brought Truk within range of American land-based bombers and the harbour had become untenable.[3] An added reason for the move was the increasing difficulty with which the Japanese had to contend in supplying oil to their fleet at their bases in the Carolines, owing to the number of tankers sunk by American submarines. Singapore was out of range of Allied air bases and near the oil stocks at Palembang and Balikpapan, and its excellent training and docking facilities were such that, in preparation for the counter-offensive against the expected American attacks in the Central and South-West Pacific, an intensive training programme could be carried out and much needed

---

[1] See pages 376–77.

[2] For performance of these aircraft see Appendix 28.

[3] The Palaus were, soon after, attacked by the U.S. Fast Carrier Force. See Map 13, page 438, and page 429.

repairs to ships executed. In an order issued to the *Combined Fleet* on the 8th March, Admiral Koga outlined his policy and made it clear that the main operations of the fleet would take place in the Pacific.[1]

The Japanese did, however, make one foray into the Indian Ocean, the first since Vice-Admiral C. Nagumo's raid of nearly two years before and the last they were to attempt. Its object was to disrupt communications and to capture and bring in ships of which, owing to the depredations of American submarines, the Japanese were alarmingly and increasingly short. Three cruisers passed through the Sunda Strait on the 1st March to raid the shipping route south of the Cocos Islands. A British merchantship, the *Behar*, on passage from Melbourne to Bombay, was shelled on the 9th. She was able to send out a distress signal and, as the presence of their force had been disclosed, the Japanese sank her and abandoned the operation. Boats from one of the cruisers picked up the survivors, fifteen of whom were landed at Batavia; the remainder, about seventy, were put to death. Apart from this one sinking the raid achieved nothing. Two Japanese cruisers leaving Lombok Strait to carry out a patrol in preparation for the return of the raiders were reported by American submarines, and for ten days shipping in the southern Indian Ocean between the meridian of 80 and 100° E. was diverted to the south and west, but that was all.

Although there had been no further evidence of raiders on the trade routes since the sinking of the *Behar*, Somerville thought it politic to make a sweep along the Australia–India ocean trade route. Destroyers were now available, the *Saratoga* was due to join his fleet towards the end of March and the operation would give his ships an opportunity to meet and work with the Americans. The fleet sailed from Ceylon on the 21st March, met the *Saratoga* and her escort of three destroyers south-west of the Cocos Islands on the 27th, and on the way home carried out exercises.

Early in April, the American Chief of Naval Operations, Admiral E. J. King, asked that the Eastern Fleet should carry out a diversionary attack on a target in the Sumatra–Andamans–Nicobars area with the object of holding as many Japanese air and surface forces as possible in the Singapore area, while MacArthur's attack on Hollandia, which was to be launched on the 22nd, was developed.[2] With Mountbatten's concurrence Somerville selected the Japanese naval base on Sabang island, off the northern tip of Sumatra, as the most profitable target. The island commanded the entrance to the Strait of Malacca and was thought to be strongly fortified; it held a radar station and an airfield. A combined ship and air bombardment was considered, but it was decided that a carrier strike only,

[1] See page 418.
[2] See Chapter XXX.

supported by the fleet, would be the more suitable operation. The main targets were to be the harbour with its installations, oil storage tanks and dockyard, and the airfield.

The fleet was organized into two forces: the carrier force consisting of the *Illustrious* and *Saratoga*, under the command of Power in the battle cruiser *Renown*, and a supporting battleship force commanded by Somerville himself, which included the *Richelieu* (which had joined the fleet on the 10th April), the *Queen Elizabeth* and the *Valiant*. The fleet sailed from Trincomalee on the 16th. At sunset on the 18th the carrier force was detached, and just before daylight on the 19th reached its flying-off position one hundred miles south-west of Sabang with the battleships twelve miles to the north-west. The wind was light and fitful and the ships had to work up a high speed to get their aircraft off the decks. The strikes from the two carriers, forty-six bombers and twenty-seven fighters in all, took off at 6.13 a.m.; at 7.0 a.m. they were over Sabang and, coming in from different directions, made low-level attacks on their targets. While the main attack was in progress, eight fighters from the *Saratoga* made an attack on Lhoknga airfield on the mainland of Sumatra twenty-five miles south of the harbour, which effectively discouraged any interference from that quarter.[1] No fighter opposition was encountered in either attack, nor did anti-aircraft fire open until the bombs began to drop. One merchant ship was sunk, another was hit and went aground, and three of the four oil tanks were set on fire. Twenty-one Japanese aircraft were claimed as having been destroyed on Sabang airfield and three at Lhoknga. All the Allied aircraft returned safely to the carriers, with the exception of one of the *Saratoga's* fighters, the pilot of which was rescued by the British submarine *Tactician*. Three Japanese torpedo-bombers which later approached the fleet were all shot down. The raid had achieved complete surprise.

The *Saratoga* was required to leave the Eastern Fleet not later than the 19th May to refit in the United States, and the opportunity was taken to make use of her in another attack on a Japanese base before she left. Admiral King proposed Sourabaya as the target and his suggestion was accepted. The naval base had already been attacked half a dozen times by land-based aircraft from western Australia and the anti-aircraft and fighter defences were expected to be on the alert. But the risk was considered worth taking, for Sourabaya was being used by the Japanese as a base for forces operating against American submarines in the Java Sea and was expected to be full of ships. Furthermore, an important oil refinery was near and could be covered by the same attack. The fleet was divided into three

---

[1] See Map 15 in pocket at end of volume.

forces: the main force, which Somerville kept under his own command, included all four capital ships, the *Queen Elizabeth*, *Valiant*,
Renown and *Richelieu*, two cruisers and eight destroyers; a carrier
force, the *Illustrious* and *Saratoga*, escorted by two cruisers and six
destroyers, under Rear-Admiral C. Moody; and a tanker force,
which comprised all six fleet oilers, and a water-distilling ship, with
an escort of two cruisers.

The fleet sailed from Ceylon on the 6th May and arrived at
Exmouth Gulf in western Australia on the 15th, the destroyers having
refuelled from the big ships on the way. The oilers had arrived the
previous day and all ships refuelled as quickly as possible and sailed
that evening for the flying-off position south of Java. Although she
lacked the speed of the carriers, the *Renown* was transferred on leaving
harbour to the carrier force in order to augment its anti-aircraft
defence. At 3.30 p.m. on the 16th the carriers were sent on ahead,
and at 4.30 a.m. next morning when 180 miles from the target began
to launch their aircraft. The air squadrons were formed up by 5.20
a.m. and set course for Sourabaya. The coast was crossed shortly
after 6 a.m. and when ten miles south-east of Sourabaya the force
split according to plan, nineteen bombers with an escort of twenty
fighters turning to attack the harbour, and twenty-six bombers with
twenty fighters to attack the oil refinery. The two attacks were well
synchronized. Once again no air opposition was encountered and
long-range high angle fire was very weak. A number of 1000-lb. and
2000-lb. bombs were dropped on the naval dockyard and the two
other docks in the harbour, and the nearby oil refinery and an
engineering works were set on fire. Twelve aircraft were claimed to
have been destroyed on the ground. All aircraft, with again the exception of one fighter from the *Saratoga* which was shot down, returned
safely to their ships. The *Saratoga* with her three destroyers parted
company on the afternoon of the 18th, and, after refuelling at
Exmouth Gulf, the fleet returned to Ceylon.

A feint towards Sabang by the *Illustrious* and the escort carrier
Atheling, screened by cruisers and destroyers, was made between the
10th and 13th June, in the hope of provoking enemy reaction, but
none was detected, nor were any aircraft sighted.

Just over a week later, the Andamans were attacked. A force
including the *Illustrious*, *Renown* and *Richelieu* left Trincomalee on the
19th under the command of Power. At first light on the 21st, when
ninety-five miles west of Port Blair, a striking force of eight Corsairs
was flown off to attack the airfield and another of fifteen Bar-
racudas escorted by sixteen Corsairs to bomb shipping in the harbour, the seaplane base and military targets on the island. Their
approach was apparently undetected; anti-aircraft fire was plentiful
during the attack but only moderately accurate. One Barracuda was

shot down and one Corsair crashed into the sea on the return journey, but the pilot was saved.

On the 5th July, the fleet carriers *Victorious* and *Indomitable* arrived at Colombo from the United Kingdom. The former, after her period of service with the American fleet in the Pacific, had taken part in attacks on the *Tirpitz* in Norway and her crew was fully trained. The latter had been newly commissioned and needed time to 'work up'.

As the enemy had shown no reaction to his carrier-borne air attacks, Somerville proposed to try the effect of a surface bombardment by the fleet on one of the outer Japanese bases, using his fighter aircraft to report the fall of shot, neutralize airfields in the vicinity and provide fighter cover. Mountbatten accepted the proposal and agreed that Sabang should again be attacked. The fleet left Trincomalee on the 22nd July and again comprised all four capital ships, the *Queen Elizabeth, Valiant, Richelieu* and *Renown*, the *Illustrious* and *Victorious*, seven cruisers and ten destroyers. Two submarines were attached for air-sea rescue duties.

The final approach to Sabang was made on the night of the 24th/25th July and the carriers, screened by a cruiser and two destroyers, were detached in time to arrive at their operating area thirty-five miles west-north-west of the harbour at 5.30 a.m. Fighters were flown off within five minutes of their arrival in the operating area: eighteen Corsairs from the *Illustrious* (eight to attack Sabang airfield and two the radar station, while the remainder provided cover for the battleships) and sixteen Corsairs from the *Victorious* (eight to attack airfields on the mainland, the remainder to give cover to the bombarding cruisers and destroyers). On arrival over the targets the fighters found the defences on the alert and were met with fierce and accurate anti-aircraft fire but made several low-flying attacks. Fires were started at many of the buildings and two enemy aircraft were reported as destroyed and two as badly damaged.

As soon as the fighters had made their attacks the fleet closed the harbour from the northward to take up its bombarding positions. Just before 7 a.m. the battleships opened fire on the harbour installations and military targets at a range of nine miles, the cruisers shelled the wireless station and engaged the shore batteries at four miles while destroyers bombarded the radar station on the north-west promontory of the island at ranges between three and one and a half miles. Fighters from the *Illustrious* spotted for the battleships, three of which used indirect fire. While the bombardment was still in progress an inshore force, composed of the Dutch cruiser *Tromp* and three destroyers under the command of Captain R. G. Onslow, R.N., steamed close in round the bay engaging such targets as offered at point-blank range. As they passed the harbour they fired some eight torpedoes through the entrance, which caused severe damage to piers and quay. 'The ships were obviously determined,' reported Somerville, 'to take full advantage of the opportunity afforded for close range fire.' The force came under fairly heavy fire from coastal batteries but, although the *Tromp* and two of the destroyers were hit, the damage was slight and casualties few.[1]

The fleet reformed after the bombardment, withdrew to the north-west and was joined by the carriers at 9.30 a.m. Two enemy shadowing aircraft which attempted to approach were shot down by fighters during the morning. In the late afternoon a force of nine or ten Japanese aircraft was detected at a distance of fifty miles and was engaged by thirteen Corsairs which shot down two and damaged another two, without loss to themselves.

The effect of a bombardment by either ships or aircraft is always difficult to assess but reports from the ships, which were later confirmed by photographic reconnaissance, indicated considerable damage. The 25th July 1944 is a notable date in the history of naval operations in the Indian Ocean, for it was then that for the first time the guns of the Eastern Fleet were brought to bear on Japanese defences.

The fleet met with no opposition in the Indian Ocean. The targets it attacked were all peripheral, and with the possible exception of Port Blair lightly defended and of no great importance. Although the air crews would have benefited from greater opposition, the raids gave valuable experience under war conditions to the newly-formed fleet, but they failed to cause any diversion of enemy forces from the Central and South-West Pacific where the Japanese needed all the strength they could muster to meet the wave of American reconquest.

---

[1] The *Tromp* was hit in her boiler-room by three 5-inch shells, none of which exploded.

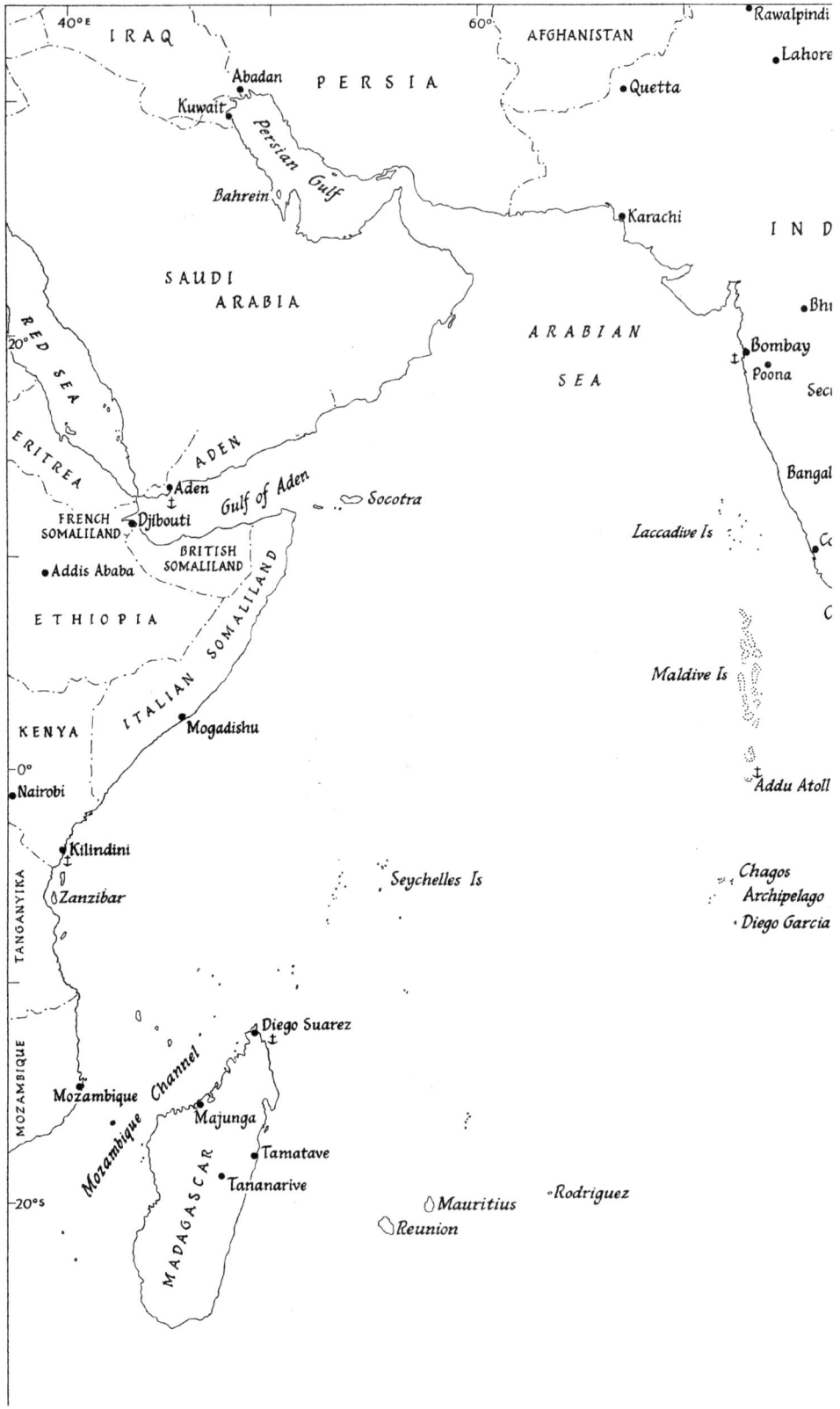

40°E   I R A Q

PERSIA

•Rawalpindi

•Lahore

•Abadan

AFGHANISTAN

60°

Kuwait•

•Quetta

Persian Gulf

Bahrein

•Karachi

I N D

S A U D I
A R A B I A

A R A B I A N

•Bhı

20°

RED SEA

SEA

‡ •Bombay
  Poona

ERITREA

ADEN

Seccı

•Aden
‡

Gulf of Aden

Bangal

FRENCH
SOMALILAND

•Djibouti

Socotra

Laccadive Is

Cc

BRITISH
SOMALILAND

•Addis Ababa

ITALIAN SOMALILAND

C

E T H I O P I A

Maldive Is

K E N Y A

•Mogadishu

0°

‡
Addu Atoll

•Nairobi

TANGANYIKA

•Kilindini
‡

Seychelles Is

*Chagos
Archipelago*

•Zanzibar

•Diego Garcia

MOZAMBIQUE

•Diego Suarez
‡

Mozambique Channel

•Mozambique

Majunga

MADAGASCAR

•Tamatave

•Tananarive

20°S

Rodriguez

Mauritius

Reunion

Map 10

T I B E T   C H I N A

80°   100°

Delhi

Chunking

Digboi

Benares

Imphal

BURMA ROAD

Kunming

Ranchi

I A

Lashio

Canton

Calcutta

Mandalay

HongKong

asawal

Akyab

B U R M A

20° N

Vizagapatam

I N D O -

HAINAN

underabad

Cocanada

B A Y

of

Rangoon

S I A M

C H I N A

CHINA

SEA

BENGAL

ore

Madras

Andaman Is

Bangkok

Port Blair

Saigon

chin

Palk Str

Kra Isthmus

Trincomalee

Nicobar Is

olombo

Kandy

CEYLON

Sabang

Penang

Taiping

Lhoknga

MALAYA

Malacca Str

Port Swettenham

S U M A T R A

Singapore

SARAWAK

B O R N E O

0°

Balikpapan

Palembang

J A V A

Batavia

Sourabaya

SEA

Sunda Str

J A V A

Lombok Str

Cocos Is

INDIAN OCEAN

1944

Fleet Base........ ‡

20° S

A U S T R A L I A

CHAPTER XXVII

THE ALLIED AIR OFFENSIVE

(January – July 1944)

See Maps 11 and 15

MOST of the operations in S.E.A.C. described in this volume, particularly those dependent on air transport or air supply, could not have been carried out successfully had not the Allies held control of the air. In the chapters dealing with military operations the description of Allied air action has in general been confined to the close support given to the army and only an occasional reference has been made to the continuous struggle for air superiority. This chapter deals with the operations to gain and maintain that superiority throughout the whole of S.E.A.C. It is not possible to describe them in detail, for they involved very large numbers of fighter sweeps and offensive patrols over enemy-occupied territory and about a hundred bomber raids.

During the British retreat from Burma in 1942 the Japanese had complete air superiority. They retained it well into 1943 while the Allied air forces in India were being expanded and re-equipped with fighters capable of defeating enemy fighters, and with bombers which had the range and power to undertake a strategic offensive. Throughout this period the Japanese based their aircraft on airfields in the Rangoon and Moulmein areas, which at that time were out of range of the British and American fighters.[1] From these secure bases they struck at targets in Assam and Bengal, staging their aircraft on the many forward airfields at their disposal in central and northern Burma. By this method their small air force was given great flexibility and, despite the constant watch by the Allies on its forward airfields, was able to achieve surprise and strike where it would. The Allied air forces were thus forced to concentrate on establishing air superiority over their own airfields and bases in north-east India with the object of making the cost of raids on Assam and Bengal prohibitive.

Although equipped with aircraft of inferior performance to those of the Japanese, the few R.A.F. fighter squadrons of Bengal Command made an attempt to seize the initiative during the 1943 monsoon.[2] The skill of the pilots and their ability to fly by instruments

---

[1] See Map 15 in pocket at end of volume.
[2] See page 43.

385

in bad weather offset the superior performance of the enemy fighters. But it was not until the British and American air forces were integrated in December 1943,[1] and armed with long-range fighters early in 1944,[2] that the Allies were in a position to make a final challenge to Japanese air superiority.

The policy to be adopted was given by Air Chief Marshal Peirse in operational directives of the 12th December 1943 and 21st January 1944. The first task of the Allied air forces was to create an air situation which would give the maximum assistance to the attainment of the military object, which at that time was to protect construction of the overland route from Ledo to Myitkyina, secure the air route from Assam to China and improve the tactical and administrative situation in Arakan. To maintain such a situation 3rd Tactical Air Force was to carry out a strong fighter offensive at all times. Fighter operations were to be undertaken in the greatest possible strength to engage and destroy enemy aircraft in the air, and, whenever favourable opportunities occurred, enemy airfields and installations were to be attacked by long-range fighters. Targets in the forward areas, such as troop concentrations, strongpoints, supply dumps, river and coastal craft and rail and road transport, were to be selected in accordance with the progress of land operations. The Strategic Air Force was given the primary task of attacking enemy airfields, particularly those where intelligence indicated that there were concentrations of aircraft. Its secondary task was to attack enemy shipping in harbour at Bangkok, Moulmein, Port Blair and Rangoon, workshops, marshalling yards and vital bridges at nodal points on the railway and lastly economic targets such as rice mills and factories. In practice the long-range fighters of 3rd Tactical Air Force were found to be so successful in dealing with enemy airfields that the Strategic Air Force was seldom used against them and so was able to concentrate on its secondary task.

At the beginning of 1944 the Japanese air force in Burma consisted of one reconnaissance, five fighter, two light and two heavy bomber air regiments, with an authorized first-line operational establishment of 220 aircraft.[3] By the time that their land offensive began in February four regiments had been sent to Japan or to other theatres, and *5th Air Division* was left with only two air brigades (*4th* and *7th*) consisting of one light and one heavy bomber, one reconnaissance and three fighter regiments with an authorized establishment of 131

---

[1] See page 48.
[2] R.A.F. Beaufighters and American Lightning (P.38) aircraft. See Appendix 28.
[3] See Appendix 7. The various regiments had an authorized establishment of 27 fighters, 20 light bombers, 15 heavy bombers and 15 reconnaissance.

aircraft, of which some 81 were fighters.[1] This number of air regiments remained constant except for a fortnight in May when an additional fighter air regiment was temporarily allotted to *5th Air Division*.

On integration in December 1943 the Allied air forces under Eastern Air Command (excluding Troop Carrier Command) consisted of some 735 operational aircraft (464 R.A.F. and 271 U.S.A.A.F.). Of these 480 were fighters, 80 light bombers, 80 medium bombers, 64 heavy bombers and the remainder were mostly reconnaissance aircraft.[2] Of this total about 100 fighters were required for the defence of the air ferry route to China and the air bases in Assam and eastern Bengal, and, as existing squadrons were constantly being re-equipped, a number of aircraft were usually out of action at any given date. Nevertheless, Eastern Air Command had some 380 fighters and 200 bombers available for offensive operations, which gave them a numerical superiority over the Japanese of about three to one. In addition to the aircraft allotted to Eastern Air Command, squadrons were available for the air defence of Ceylon and southern India, and for operations over the Indian Ocean and Bay of Bengal. Other squadrons were also being formed in India to reinforce Air Command, South-East Asia.

The 3rd Tactical Air Force (Baldwin), with headquarters at Comilla, consisted of 221 Group R.A.F. (three fighter, one fighter-reconnaissance, two fighter-bomber and three light bomber squadrons), 224 Group R.A.F. (eight fighter, one fighter-reconnaissance, two light bomber and three fighter-bomber squadrons) and Northern Air Sector Force (four U.S. fighter, three U.S. fighter-bomber and three R.A.F. fighter squadrons).[3] The Strategic Air Force (Davidson) consisted of an American heavy bomber group of four Liberator (B.24) squadrons and a medium bomber group of three Mitchell (B.25) squadrons, and a R.A.F. component of one Liberator heavy bomber and two Wellington medium bomber squadrons. The force was based in southern Bengal, chiefly on airfields in the Calcutta area. The American squadrons were normally used for day, and the British squadrons for night, operations.

The defensive operations undertaken by 3rd Tactical Air Force in December 1943 and January 1944 have been described in Chapter IX, and the operations to gain air superiority over the Arakan battlefield

---

[1] *4th Air Brigade: 50th (F.)* and *8th (L.B.) Air Regiments.*
7th Air Brigade: 64th (F.), 204th (F.), 12th (H.B.) and *81st (Recce.) Air Regiments.*
[2] For the organization of Eastern Air Command see Appendix 11.
[3] The R.A.F. squadrons were equipped with Spitfire, Hurricane, Beaufighter and Mohawk fighters, Hurricane fighter-bombers and Vengeance light bombers. The American squadrons were equipped with P.38 or P.40 fighters and P.51 fighter-bombers. The combined strength was eighteen fighter, eight fighter-bomber, five light bomber and two fighter-reconnaissance squadrons.

in February in Chapter X. During the second half of February the Japanese moved all their air regiments to airfields in central Burma to give support to their Imphal offensive. The presence of enemy aircraft in this area was soon discovered, and 3rd Tactical Air Force, assisted at times by No. 1 Air Commando, began an unremitting offensive with long-range fighters and fighter-bombers against the airfields from which *5th Air Division* was operating.

The effect on the Japanese is shown by the gradual decrease in their air effort. From the 10th to 31st March enemy aircraft operated every other day with an average of forty-one aircraft and a maximum of eighty-three; in April these figures fell to thirty-four and seventy-six and in May, although *5th Air Division* was temporarily reinforced by an extra fighter air regiment, to twenty-eight and forty-one. In June the Japanese transferred their attention to the Myitkyina and Hukawng Valley areas and operated on IV Corps front on three occasions only, ceasing altogether after the 17th June; their attacks during that month being made about every third day with an average of fifteen aircraft and a maximum of thirty-five. In July enemy air activity was confined entirely to the Northern and Salween fronts and the number of aircraft used fell to an average of twelve and a maximum of twenty-four. By the end of July, *5th Air Division* had only 49 aircraft left (36 fighters, 11 light bombers and 2 reconnaissance).

The total number of sorties flown by the Japanese from the 10th March to the 30th July was about 1,750. During the same period the R.A.F. fighter squadrons of 3rd Tactical Air Force flew 18,860 and U.S.A.A.F. fighter squadrons 10,800 sorties—a total of 29,660. Allied losses were 170 (130 R.A.F. and 40 U.S.A.A.F.) aircraft destroyed or missing.[1]

From the opening of the Japanese Imphal offensive the Allies were able to establish air superiority over any area when required and by mid-June their air superiority was absolute throughout most of Burma.

From December 1943 to July 1944 the Strategic Air Force concentrated mainly on attacking Japanese communications in southern Burma, including the Tenasserim coast, and in Siam. Since enemy shipping seldom used the Bay of Bengal, sea communications were disrupted by attacking ships in harbour and harbour installations. Nineteen major raids were made on the ports of Bangkok and Rangoon,

---

[1] These sorties exclude those of the light bomber squadrons of 3rd Tactical Air Force which are given in the appropriate chapters throughout this volume. In addition, Allied fighter squadrons flew some 7,140 sorties between September 1943 and February 1944 inclusive, in the course of which some 38 aircraft (27 R.A.F. and 11 U.S.A.A.F.) were lost.

and some forty-three on Akyab. Others were made on Mergui, Tavoy, Moulmein, Bassein, Port Blair and the Nicobars.

Liberators were extensively used on moonlight nights to lay mines in the approaches to Bangkok and Rangoon, with the result that the Japanese were forced into using only coastal vessels and other small craft for bringing supplies into Rangoon and into making increased use of the smaller ports and anchorages along the east coast of Malaya in place of Bangkok. To prevent this, mines were laid in the approaches to those known to be in use. In view of the fact that minelaying operations would be severely restricted when the monsoon began in May, a special effort was made early in the month to prolong the life of the existing minefields by adding delayed-action mines. In all 560 mines were laid by aircraft. The minelaying together with the bombing attacks on the ports proved so successful that enemy merchant ships virtually disappeared from the Bay of Bengal and the approaches to Rangoon.

The attacks on land communications were confined mainly to the railway system, and were concentrated on the large railway centres and junctions such as Bangkok, Rangoon, Pegu and Mandalay, where locomotive workshops, marshalling yards and repair depots were bombed by day and night. Second priority was given to attacks on vital bridges such as the Ava (near Mandalay) and the Sittang and those along the Siam railway from Moulmein to Bangkok in order to immobilize traffic on long sections of the railway. Once the traffic on any stretch of line had been brought to a standstill, attacks were directed on the trapped locomotives and rolling stock. The most important target on the railway system in Burma was considered to be the Sittang bridge, which had been destroyed by the British during the 1942 retreat and laboriously rebuilt by the Japanese. As soon as it was brought into use early in 1944 it was attacked by Liberators with 1000-lb. bombs, and on the 8th April two of its main spans were wrecked. Thereafter it was kept under close observation to prevent it being again repaired. The effect of all these attacks was to stop almost entirely the movement of supplies on the railways between Bangkok and Myitkyina from February to the end of May 1944.

From the 20th May a number of the Wellington and Mitchell medium bombers were temporarily diverted from the Strategic Air Force to fly ammunition and bombs to the Imphal plain,[1] and forty Wellington air crews were loaned to Troop Carrier Command to fly Dakotas and so increase the tonnage of supplies carried to IV Corps. Early in June the strength of the Strategic Air Force was further reduced when the four heavy bomber squadrons of the U.S. 7th Heavy Bomber Group were temporarily diverted to carry

---

[1] See page 325.

aviation petrol to 14th U.S.A.A.F. bases near Chengtu in China.[1] At the same time the group's medium bomber squadrons were transferred to 3rd Tactical Air Force for long-range attacks on tactical targets in central and southern Burma. The Strategic Air Force was thus reduced during June and July to two R.A.F. Liberator squadrons only, but this was of little import since at the height of the monsoon flying conditions were so bad that extensive operations over southern Burma were seldom possible and, when carried out, largely ineffective.

The contribution made by the Strategic Air Force is best illustrated by statistics. From September 1943 until the integration of the air forces in mid-December, Allied strategic bombers flew 4,650 sorties (1,290 R.A.F. and 3,360 U.S.A.A.F.) and dropped 3,800 tons of bombs. During the seven and a half months from the integration to the 31st July 1944, the Strategic Air Force flew 5,560 sorties (2,160 R.A.F. and 3,400 U.S.A.A.F.) and dropped 8,000 tons of bombs. In the course of all these operations the Allies lost twenty-nine heavy bombers (seven R.A.F. and twenty-two U.S.A.A.F.) and thirty-nine medium bombers (thirteen R.A.F. and twenty-six U.S.A.A.F).

During the period covered by this chapter some changes in organization were made in Eastern Air Command. On the 1st May Troop Carrier Command was placed under the operational control of 3rd Tactical Air Force.[2] On the 4th June it was dissolved and thereafter Headquarters 3rd Tactical Air Force controlled all transport aircraft. On the 20th June, when Stilwell and the formations on the Northern front were placed under the direct control of the Supreme Commander,[3] 10th U.S.A.A.F. was reconstituted as an entirely American operational formation with its headquarters in northern Assam and was allotted in direct support of N.C.A.C. At the same time a fighter wing of the R.A.F. was formed to defend the main air bases, including the Calcutta area, so as to relieve 3rd Tactical Air Force of that task and thus enable it to concentrate on assisting 14th Army and extending the air superiority which it had gained. From that date Eastern Air Command consisted of the Strategic Air Force, 3rd Tactical Air Force, 10th U.S.A.A.F., the Photographic Reconnaissance Force and 293 Wing R.A.F.[4]

---

[1] See Map 11, page 394, and page 393.
[2] See page 325.
[3] See pages 261–62.
[4] 293 Wing R.A.F. consisted of 607 and 155 (Spitfire) Squadrons, 176 (Beaufighter) night fighter Squadron, and two and a half balloon squadrons.

CHAPTER XXVIII

EVENTS IN CHINA

(May–July 1944)

See Maps 11, 12 and 13

THE second phase of the Japanese ('Ichi-Go') offensive in China made rapid progress since their southward advance from Hankow met with only slight opposition from 4th Chinese Army, part of IX War Area under the command of General Hseuh Yueh.[1] By the 14th June the Japanese *11th Army* had captured Liuyang, some thirty miles east of Changsha, and begun to advance on Changsha from both the north and east.[2] On the 16th the Chinese garrison hurriedly withdrew to the south-west and two days later the Japanese occupied the town. Two divisions were immediately sent forward to seize Hengyang and succeeded by the 26th in capturing the airfield outside the city. The 10th Chinese Army holding Hengyang was of a very different calibre from 4th Army which had abandoned Changsha, and two attempts by the Japanese to enter the city failed with heavy loss. By this time the Japanese lines of communication south of Hankow were under constant attack by 14th U.S.A.A.F., which delayed the arrival of reinforcements, artillery and ammunition, and the enemy was therefore unable to make a further attempt to capture the city until the 11th July. Assisted by American aircraft, the Chinese again repulsed the Japanese, who were then forced to bring up fresh formations, and it was not until the 8th August that Hengyang fell.[3]

As soon as the Japanese offensive had begun, Stilwell told Chennault that his primary task was to defend the group of airfields built near Chengtu for the long-range bombing of Japan (operation 'Matterhorn'), even at the expense of strikes against shipping and the support of the Chinese armies. Chennault submitted that the defence of Chengtu offered no problem and asked that the scope of his operations should not be limited. Stilwell agreed provided that no threat to Chengtu arose. Chennault, using one medium bomber and six fighter squadrons located on the outer ring of airfields covering

---

[1] See pages 232–33.
[2] See Map 11, page 394. For the strength of *11th Army* see page 233 fn.
[3] The operations for the capture of Changsha and Hengyang cost the Japanese 12,000 casualties as well as 7,000 sick.

Chengtu, then began a series of attacks on the bridges over the Yellow River and the Japanese lines of communications. Although these attacks did some damage, they did not affect the progress of the enemy offensive, and it seemed that the province of Honan would be overrun. Thoroughly alarmed, the Generalissimo began to press Stilwell in the middle of May to release some of the fighters and petrol from the supplies for 'Matterhorn' in order to enable 14th U.S.A.A.F. to give greater support to his armies. At the same time Chennault told Stilwell that the Chinese failure to grasp that a Japanese offensive was imminent, and the shortage of supplies, had handicapped the efforts of 14th U.S.A.A.F. to meet the situation. Although he had reinforced the fighter force at Liangshan by twelve aircraft and increased its aviation petrol supplies by some four hundred tons, poor communications and lack of airfields made it difficult for him to operate satisfactorily in the Yellow River area. Stilwell was faced with a difficult problem. He felt, like Chennault, that the greatest danger to 14th U.S.A.A.F. lay in an enemy air offensive against the Chengtu area to dispose of the threat to the Japanese homeland, but, unlike Chennault, he was unwilling to divert supplies from 'Matterhorn' for an operation which, he considered, would have little effect on the tactical situation in Honan. He told Chennault, however, that he might use some of the fighters from the Chengtu area, and began to lay plans for increasing the supplies of aviation petrol to the air force.

The situation changed when the Japanese crossed the Yangtze at the end of May and began their drive towards Changsha. On the 29th May, Chennault, believing that the Japanese advance could be stopped only by air strikes, asked to be allowed to draw on the 'Matterhorn' stocks at Chengtu, and to be allotted almost all of the tonnage reaching China across the Hump. Two days later the Generalissimo told the President that he believed the Japanese had moved six divisions from Manchuria to China and were intending to seize the Hankow–Canton railway line and all the airfields in south-east China.[1] He urged that 14th U.S.A.A.F. should be strengthened, given the whole of the air tonnage reaching China from India and allowed to use all the supplies held at Chengtu for 'Matterhorn'. On the 3rd June he demanded Stilwell's presence in Chungking for urgent discussions.

The two met on the 5th. The Generalissimo said that the situation had become so serious that the entire air force must be used to stop the Japanese offensive and repeated the requests he had made to the President. Stilwell agreed that the situation was serious but said that all the ground forces would be needed as well as the air forces. He

---

[1] Only one Japanese division had been moved to China from Manchuria, see page 232. It is probable that the formation of fourteen new independent infantry brigades in China (see page 232 fn.) led the Chinese to believe that six divisions had been brought in from Manchuria.

told Chiang Kai-shek that he had arranged to divert to Chennault all the air tonnage allotted to 20th Bomber Command for 'Matterhorn' (1,500 tons a month) and had asked Washington to allow him to use heavy bombers temporarily to fly in aviation petrol. If his request were granted, Chennault would get the 10,000 tons a month for which he had asked. The same day the American Chiefs of Staff notified Stilwell that they agreed to the diversion of tonnage to Chennault and to the temporary use of 7th Heavy Bomber Group of the Strategic Air Force in India for the transport of petrol and supplies (2,000–2,500 tons a month) to 14th U.S.A.A.F.[1]

Stilwell asked the American Chiefs of Staff for permission to release B.29s to operate against the Japanese south of Hankow, when pressed by the Generalissimo and Chennault to do so. Their refusal was immediate. They pointed out that experience in Europe showed that air attacks alone did not appreciably delay land offensives, and said that, in their view, the early use of B.29s to bomb Japan would help the situation in China much more than their use in local operations. Stilwell, who had never believed that Chennault's air forces by themselves could hold a Japanese offensive and had consistently urged the need for reorganizing and equipping the Chinese armies to meet such an offensive, welcomed this decision. He replied: 'Instructions understood, and exactly what I had hoped for. As you know, I have few illusions about power of air against ground troops. Pressure from G-MO [Generalissimo] forced the communication.'[2]

To coincide with the attack on Saipan,[3] the first air attack on the Japanese homeland since the Doolittle raid in 1942 was made on the 15th June by sixty-eight B.29 bombers from Chengtu. About 120 tons of bombs were dropped on a steelworks without doing much damage or reducing output, though considerable destruction in the surrounding industrial district was caused. Three bombers were lost on the return flight and six were damaged by anti-aircraft fire. Owing to shortage of petrol it was not until the 7th July that a second attack was launched on various targets in Kyushu by eighteen B.29s, but again little damage was caused. Two separate daylight attacks were made on the 29th July on selected industrial targets in north China and Manchuria with seventy-four and twenty-four B.29s respectively. These attacks were more successful and, at a cost of five aircraft, caused considerable damage.

On the 20th June the American Vice-President, Mr. Henry Wallace, arrived in Chungking to see the Generalissimo. After a series of interviews, he told the President that the loss of China as a base to support the American operations in the Pacific would have

---

[1] This diversion was made with the Supreme Commander's agreement.
[2] Romanus and Sunderland, page 369.
[3] See Chapter XXXI and Map 13, page 438.

to be accepted unless drastic steps were taken to stop the situation in east China from deteriorating still further. This, he suggested, could be done only by the launching of a Sino-American offensive. It seemed to him that the Generalissimo was now prepared to accept military guidance as well as military aid, and recommended that Stilwell, who, according to the Generalissimo, was unable to grasp what the Chinese called 'political considerations', should be replaced by an officer who could win his confidence.[1]

The President, accepting the advice of his Chiefs of Staff, now abandoned the belief he had held from the time of the Trident Conference in 1943 that the build-up of the air forces in China was of greater importance than the re-equipment of the Chinese armies,[2] and accepted the view that the only way to safeguard the air bases for 'Matterhorn' was to build up the strength of the Chinese armies. On the 6th July he told the Generalissimo that drastic measures would have to be taken if the situation in China were to be saved, and suggested that the power to co-ordinate all the Allied military resources in China, including those of the Chinese communists, should be placed in the hands of one man—Stilwell. 'I know of no other man', he said, 'who has the ability, the force, and the determination to offset the disaster which now threatens China and our over-all plans for the conquest of Japan.'[3]

On the 8th, Chiang Kai-shek signified his agreement in principle with the President's suggestion that Stilwell should be given, under him, the command of all Chinese and American troops in the China theatre, but said it was not advisable, for a number of reasons, to carry out such a change immediately. He asked that an influential person with full powers and 'far-sighted political vision and ability' should be sent to Chungking to represent the President, to work with him and improve his relationships with Stilwell so as to enhance the co-operation between the two countries.[4] The President's reaction was to promote Stilwell to the rank of General on the 1st August 1944, in order to give him the necessary prestige in Chinese eyes,[5] and to select a personal representative to go to Chungking.

While these events were taking place in China, the offensive by the Yunnan armies (General Wei Li-huang), ordered on the 14th April, was launched.[6] On the 10th May, the Chinese XI and XX Army Groups, consisting of twelve divisions with a strength of some 72,000

---

[1] Romanus and Sunderland, pages 376–77.
[2] See Volume II, pages 379–81.
[3] Romanus and Sunderland, page 383.
[4] Romanus and Sunderland, pages 385–86.
[5] This rank was at that time held by only four other Americans—Marshall, Mac-Arthur, Arnold and Eisenhower.
[6] See page 231.

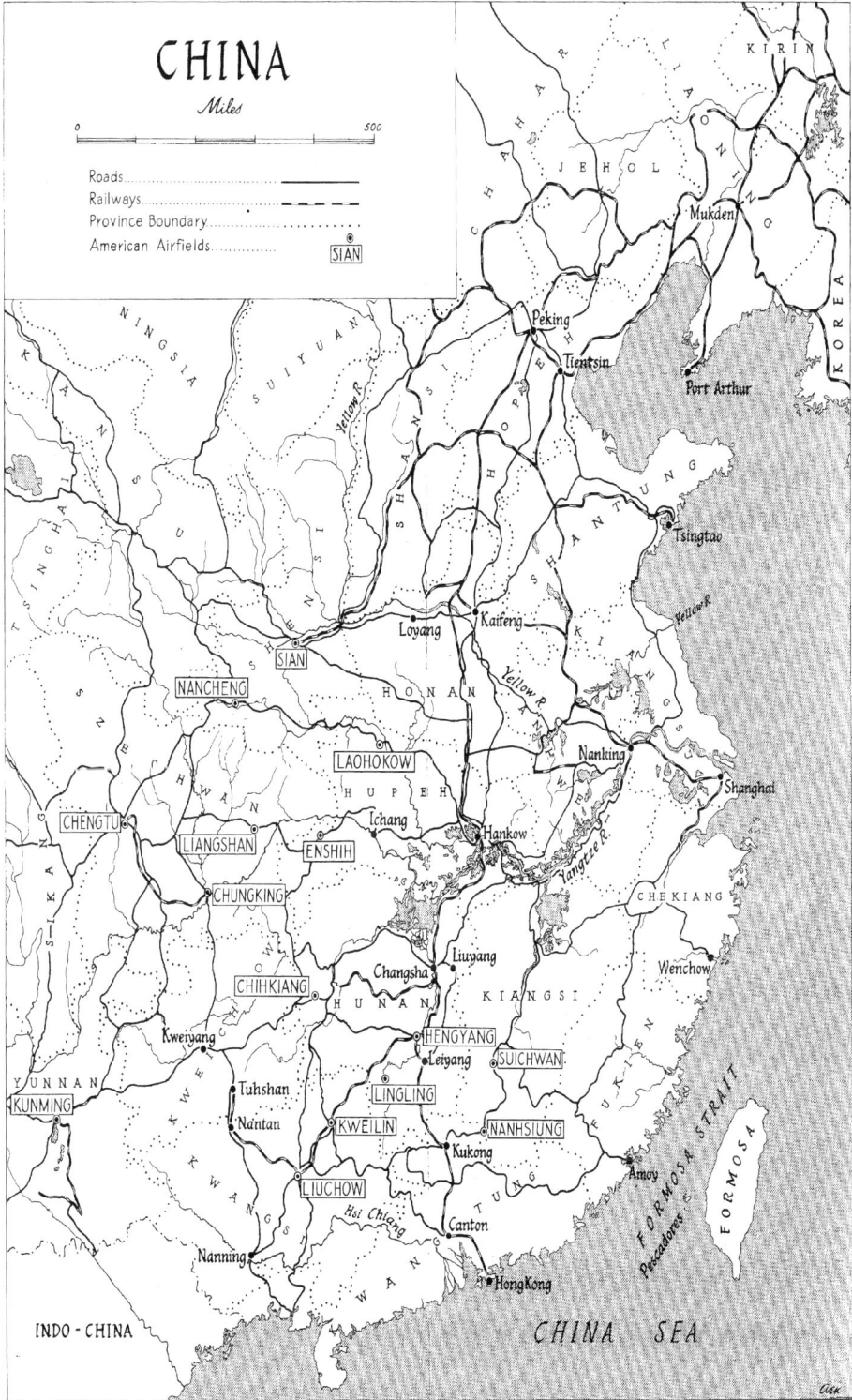

Map11

CHINA

Miles

0   500

Roads...........................
Railways......................
Province Boundary...........
American Airfields............... SIAN

KIRIN

JEHOL

C H A H A R

L I A O N I N G

Mukden

KOREA

Peking
Tientsin

Port Arthur

H O P E H

S H A N S I

S U I Y U A N

N I N G S I A

K A N S U

Yellow R.

Tsingtao

S H A N T U N G

Yellow R.

K I A N G S U

Loyang
Kaifeng

SIAN

Yellow R.

T S I N G H A I

S Z E C H W A N

NANCHENG

H O N A N

LAOHOKOW

H U P E H

Nanking

Shanghai

CHENGTU

Ichang

Hankow

LIANGSHAN
ENSHIH

Yangtze R.

CHEKIANG

CHUNGKING

S I - K A N G

CHIHKIANG

Changsha
Liuyang

KIANGSI

Wenchow

H U N A N

Kweiyang

K W E I C H O W

HENGYANG
Leiyang
SUICHWAN

F U K I E N

Y U N N A N

Tuhshan

LINGLING

KUNMING

Nantan

KWEILIN

NANHSIUNG

K W A N G S I

Kukong

Amoy

FORMOSA STRAIT

Peiscadores Is.

F O R M O S A

LIUCHOW

Hsi Chiang

K W A N G T U N G

Canton

Nanning

HongKong

INDO - CHINA

CHINA SEA

men, which was just over half their authorized establishment, crossed the Salween.[1] They were ill-supplied with artillery and their administrative organization was scarcely adequate to support them once they had crossed the Kaoli Kung Range, but tactical air support was supplied by 14th U.S.A.A.F., and 27th U.S. Troop Carrier Squadron was allotted for air supply duties.[2]

The ultimate object was the occupation of the Myitkyina–Bhamo–Lashio area. The immediate object was to seize Tengchung, Lungling and Mangshih and gain control of the Burma Road immediately west of the Salween. Wei Li-huang's plan was for XX Army Group, having crossed the Salween, to force Mamien and Tatangtzu Passes, cross the Kaoli Kung Range and then move south down the Shweli River valley on Tengchung. The XI Army Group was to advance on a broad front: 39th Division (detached from 2nd Army) was to cross the Salween north of the destroyed bridge at Hueijan, block Hungmushu Pass and attack the bridge site from the rear; 2nd Army (less 39th Division) was to cross the river south of Pingka and, after capturing the town, advance on Mangshih; 71st Army was to cross the river as soon as 2nd Army had secured the left flank and move direct to Lungling.

To meet the expected attack the Japanese had *56th Division* (Lieut.-General S. Matsuyama), which on the 10th May consisted of only six and a half infantry battalions, the divisional reconnaissance regiment and a mountain artillery regiment, with a total strength of about 11,000 men. With this division Matsuyama had to defend a front of some 250 miles from Lashio in the south to Hpimaw Pass in the north. He allotted the divisional reconnaissance regiment and two and a half battalions to hold Kunlong, Pingka, Lameng and Hpimaw Pass as pivots of manoeuvre from which counter-attacks could be launched. He placed the main body, consisting of two battalions, in the Lungling–Tengchung area with orders to hold the passes over the Kaoli Kung Range and be prepared to counter-attack the Chinese as opportunity occurred. He retained two battalions in reserve near Lungling and Bhamo respectively.[3]

---

[1] The Chinese order of battle for the operation was:
XI Army Group
    2nd Army: 9th, 33rd, 39th and 76th Division.
    71st Army: 28th, 87th and 88th Divisions.
XX Army Group
    53rd Army: 116th and 130th Divisions.
    54th Army: 2nd, 36th and 198th Divisions.
[2] See Map 12, page 398, and page 325.
[3] On the 10th May *56th Division* consisted of *113th Regiment, 148th Regiment, I/146th Battalion*, two companies of *114th Regiment* (the rest of which regiment was in the Myitkyina–Mogaung area under command of *18th Division*) and *56th Reconnaissance Regiment*. The garrisons of Kunlong, Pingka, Lameng and Hpimaw Pass were found by *56th Reconnaissance Regiment, I/146th Battalion, I/113th Battalion* and two companies of *114th Regiment* respectively. The main body consisted of *148th Infantry Regiment* (less *I/148th Battalion* which was sent to Myitkyina on the 17th May, see page 295). The *113th Infantry Regiment* (less *I/113th Battalion*) was in reserve.

The XX Army Group crossed the Salween unopposed on the 10th and, moving into the mountains, soon came in contact with the permanent defences which the Japanese had built to cover Mamien and Tatangtzu Passes. Considering his northern front the most vulnerable, Matsuyama sent his two reserve battalions to strengthen the defences of the passes. Faced by four Japanese battalions which, as usual, defended their positions to the last man and the last round, the Chinese made slow progress.

Meanwhile 2nd Chinese Army, with 88th Division of 71st Army under command, also crossed the Salween unopposed on the 10th May and by the 17th had surrounded Pingka. Leaving a formation to invest the village, 2nd Army advanced north-west and by the 9th June had established a roadblock on the Burma Road south-west of Mangshih, thus cutting the Japanese line of communications, while 88th Chinese Division moved north from Pingka and by the 7th June had reached the outskirts of Lungling. Satisfied that his left flank was secured, Wei Li-huang on the 28th May ordered 87th Division of 71st Army to cross the Salween. The crossing was delayed by a rise in the river after heavy rain, but by the 8th June the division had reached the northern and eastern outskirts of Lungling and had seized the Manlao bridge on the Lungling–Tengchung road. Attacks by both 87th and 88th Divisions between the 9th and 13th June failed, however, to capture Lungling.

Realizing that XI Army Group's advance in the south had created a serious threat to his communications, and in particular to Lungling, Matsuyama decided early in June to launch a counter-attack. Leaving *II/148th Battalion* to hold the northern passes unaided, he moved *113th Regiment* (less *I/113th Battalion*) and *III/148th Battalion* south to attack the Chinese who were surrounding Lungling. The Manlao bridge was recaptured by *113th Regiment* (1,500 strong) on the 14th and, by the 17th, the two divisions of 71st Chinese Army (totalling 10,000 men) had been driven back in some disorder into the hills to the east of Lungling. About the same time 2nd Army, owing to an alleged discrimination in the distribution of supplies within XI Army Group, abandoned its roadblock south-west of Mangshih and withdrew to the Pingka area, thus voluntarily removing the serious threat to the Japanese line of communications. In the north *II/148th Battalion* holding Mamien and Tatangtzu Passes fought desperately but by the 13th June had been driven off both. By the 22nd both wings of the Chinese XX Army Group had debouched into the Shweli River valley and begun their southward move towards Tengchung. Meanwhile 39th Division, meeting with stubborn resistance, had by the 12th June seized the eastern end of Hungmushu Pass, but instead of attacking Hueijan was sent south to attack Lameng.

By the end of June the Chinese had succeeded in investing the Japanese garrisons of Tengchung, Lameng and Pingka and were holding the hills to the east of Lungling, but their offensive had lost its momentum.

Although outnumbered by some seven to one, Matsuyama, by boldness and by taking full advantage of interior lines, had succeeded in bringing the Chinese offensive to a standstill at a cost of some 3,000 casualties. Although three of his battalions were invested in Tengchung, Lameng and Pingka, he still held the vital centre at Lungling and his line of communication was secure.

The Chinese set to work to reduce the walled cities of Tengchung, which barred the way to Myitkyina, and Lameng, which lay astride the Burma Road and their direct communications to the Lungling area. It was not, however, until the third week in July that XX Army Group with five divisions was able to close up to the walls of Tengchung. American bombers succeeded by the 2nd August in breaching the walls and, although two days later, supported by American low-flying aircraft, the Chinese gained a footing within the city, it was another month before Japanese resistance was finally overcome. The siege of Lameng followed the same pattern as that of Tengchung. Throughout July the Chinese XI Army Group launched numerous attacks, but the Japanese garrison was still resisting stubbornly at the beginning of August.

The failure of the offensive across the Salween by the Yunnan armies, which had figured so largely in the Allied plans for the reconquest of Burma, and the swift progress of the Japanese offensive in China showed only too clearly that, despite all the material aid provided by the Americans, the Chinese armies remained no match for the Japanese even when they had vast numerical superiority.

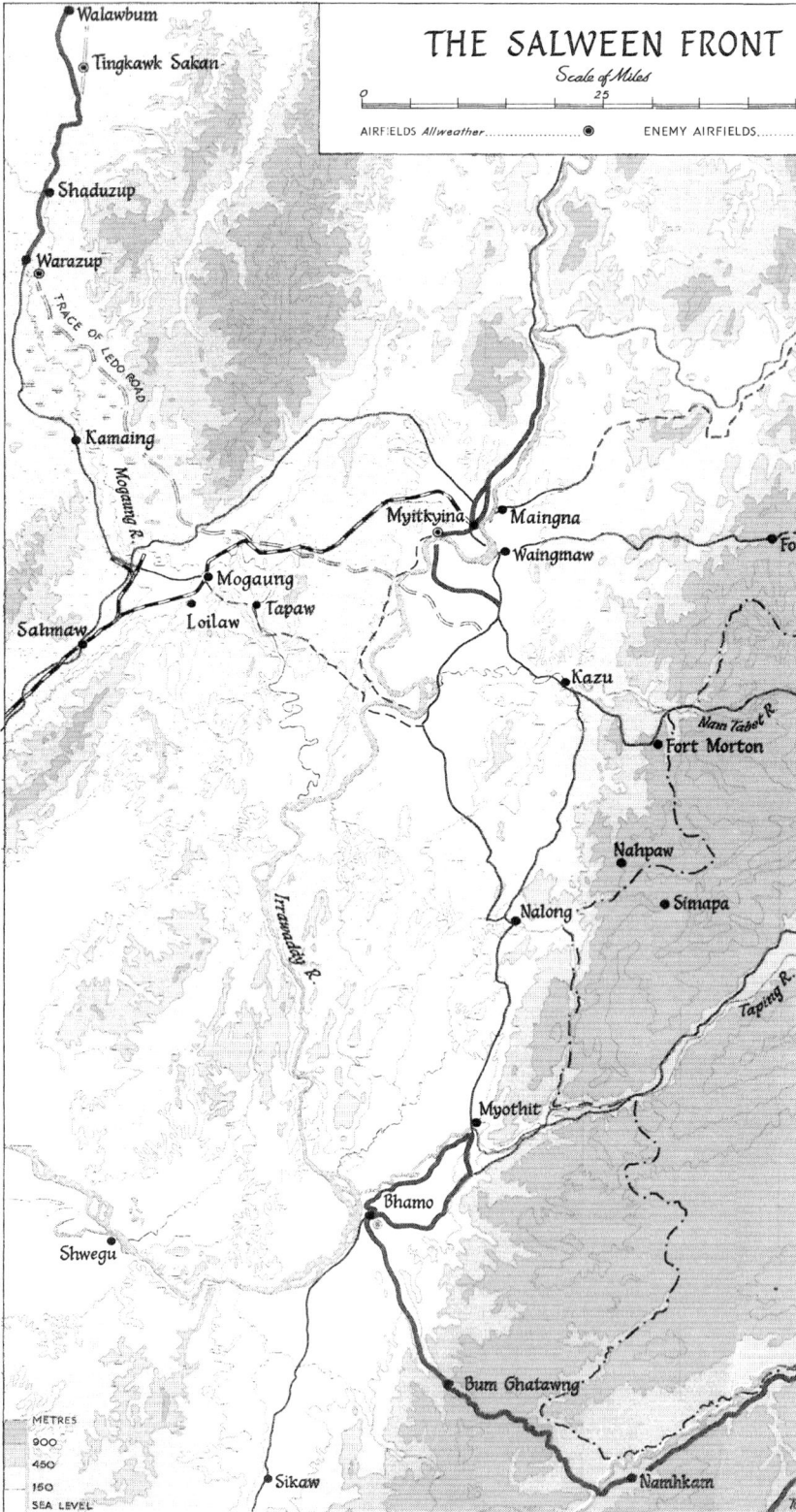

THE SALWEEN FRONT

Scale of Miles

0   25

AIRFIELDS *Allweather*....................◉   ENEMY AIRFIELDS..........

Walawbum

Tingkawk Sakan

Shaduzup

Warazup

TRACE OF LEDO ROAD

Kamaing

Mogaung R.

Myitkyina   Maingna

Mogaung   Waingmaw   Fo

Loilaw   Tapaw

Sahmaw   Kazu

Nam Tabet R.

Fort Morton

Nahpaw

Simapa

Irrawaddy R.

Nalong

Taping R.

Myothit

Bhamo

Shwegu

METRES
900
450
150   Bum Ghatawng
SEA LEVEL
                    Namhkam
Sikaw

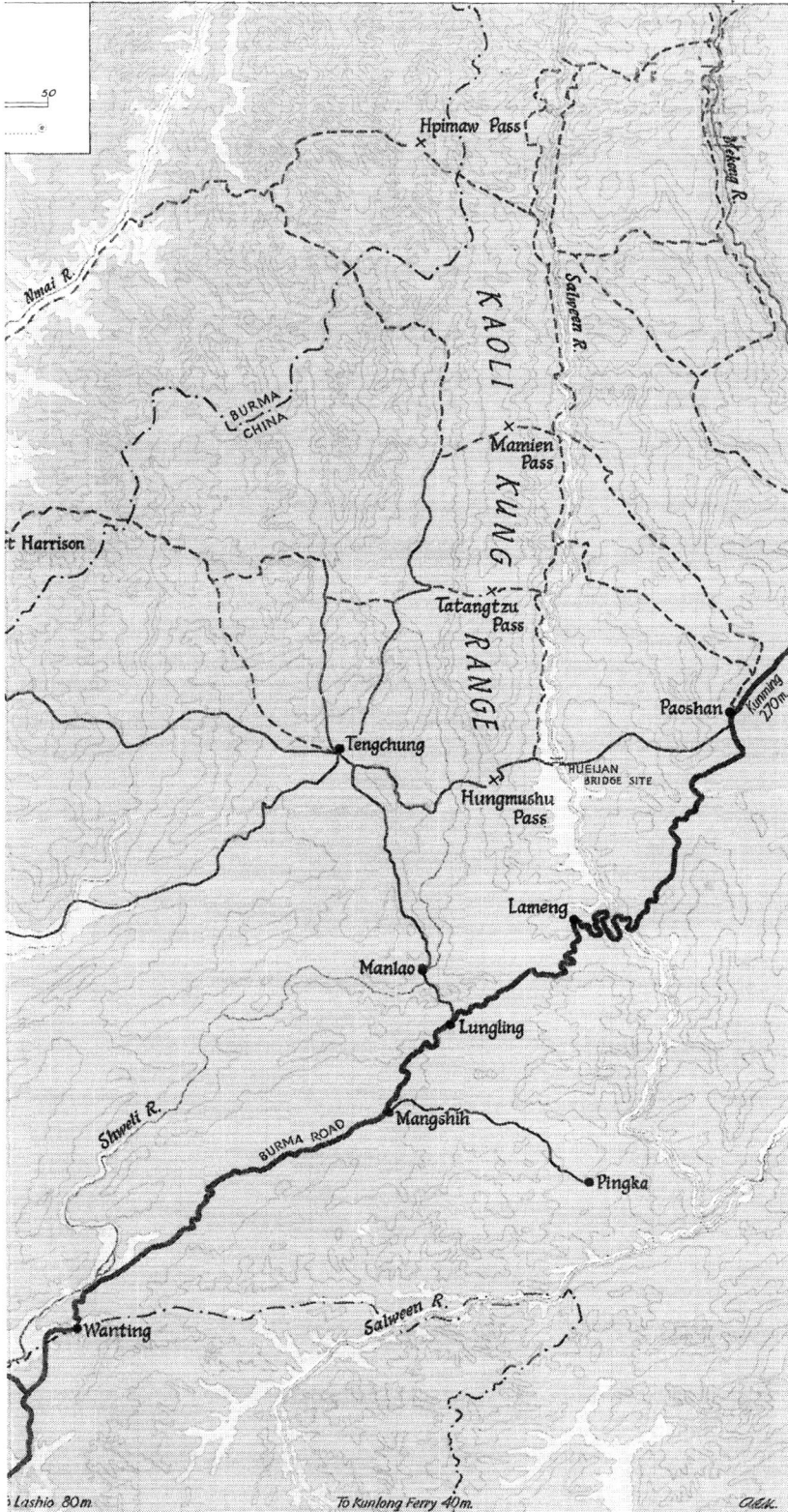

Map 12

CHAPTER XXIX

SUCCESS ON THE NORTHERN FRONT

Kamaing, Mogaung and Myitkyina Captured
(June – August 1944)

See Maps 4 and 14 and Sketches 16 and 17

STILWELL'S task was to capture Kamaing, Mogaung and Myitkyina, and continue the construction of the Ledo Road and the pipelines to Myitkyina.[1] The forces under his command were Merrill's Marauders; 22nd, 30th, 38th, 14th and 50th Chinese Divisions and a provisional tank unit;[2] and 14th, 77th, 111th Brigades, 3rd (W.A.) Brigade and Morrisforce of Special Force. Northern Air Sector Force was responsible for air support of the Northern front.[3] At the end of May he was in contact with the Japanese at all three towns: 22nd and 38th Chinese Divisions, together with 149th Regiment of 50th Division and the tank unit, were closely investing Kamaing; Special Force had three brigades in the hills west of the railway covering the evacuation of casualties from Indawgyi Lake and harassing the enemy line of communications to Mogaung, one brigade east of the railway preparing to attack Mogaung, and Morrisforce east of Myitkyina; Merrill's Marauders, 150th Regiment of 50th Chinese Division, 88th and 89th Regiments of 30th Chinese Division and part of 42nd Regiment of 14th Chinese Division were investing Myitkyina; and the remainder of 14th and 50th Chinese Divisions was in reserve.[4]

On taking over command in northern Burma, Honda (*33rd Army*) had planned to use *53rd Division* (Takeda) to relieve *18th Division* in the Kamaing area. When Myitkyina airfield was captured by Allied troops on the 17th May, he decided instead that, as soon as *53rd*

---

[1] See Map 4, page 53.
[2] Two of these divisions (14th and 50th) had only recently arrived from China. Their training was poor and their strength much less than that of the American-trained Chinese divisions.
[3] When Special Force came under Stilwell's command, No. 1 Air Commando was withdrawn for re-equipment and reorganization.
[4] See Chapter XX.

Division had overcome the Allied airborne forces in the Pinbaw–
Hopin area ('Blackpool') and had reached Mogaung, it was to
destroy the Allied forces in the Myitkyina area. On the 27th May,
Honda visited Kamaing to see for himself the situation of *18th
Division*. Tanaka reported that Kamaing could be held by his
division provided that a steady flow of supplies was guaranteed.
Honda, greatly relieved by Tanaka's attitude, thereupon confirmed
the despatch of *53rd Division* to Myitkyina, an action which was supported by *Burma Area Army*, and transferred the command of the
Myitkyina garrison from *18th Division* to *33rd Army*. Accordingly,
when *53rd Division* reached Mogaung, Takeda sent one battalion
(*I/128th*) to hold off the Chinese forces approaching from the
direction of Tumbonghka, and another (*III/128th*) to maintain
contact between *18th* and *53rd Divisions* and secure their line
of communications. With the rest of his forces, consisting of two
battalions (*I/151st* and *II/128th*), supported by a field artillery battalion and a battery of medium howitzers, he prepared to attack
Myitkyina airfield from the west.[1] At the beginning of June this
force was deployed astride the railway ready to launch its attack.

On the 28th May, 112th Chinese Regiment debouched from the
hills and occupied Seton, thus cutting *18th Division's* communications
with Mogaung.[2] This made it impossible for Honda to fulfil his
promise to supply the division, and led to a considerable discussion
within *Headquarters 33rd Army* on whether it was better to use *53rd
Division* to relieve *18th Division* or to continue with the operation to
relieve Myitkyina. The Army Chief of Staff took the view that it was
of more importance to hold Myitkyina, while others, concerned
about Tanaka's position, advocated the immediate despatch of the
division to break the block at Seton. Honda, however, decided to
carry on with the policy he had already adopted and urged Takeda
to advance on Myitkyina as quickly as possible.

Tanaka, left to fend for himself, immediately withdrew *4th Infantry
Regiment* (two battalions only) from his left flank and ordered it to
clear the roadblock from the north. At the same time he arranged
for an escape route to be cut through the hills west of the Kamaing–
Mogaung road. Not only was *4th Regiment* unable to dislodge the
Chinese from Seton, but its absence from the left flank enabled 22nd
Chinese Division's outflanking movement towards Nanyaseik to make
progress. On the 1st June, 22nd Division established a block on the
main road some seven miles north of Kamaing, thereby encircling
the greater part of *55th* and *56th Infantry Regiments*, which were holding the Japanese main position astride the road some fifteen miles

---

[1] The strength of the forces ordered to attack was about 2,600 all ranks.
[2] See page 294. The regiment captured four guns, some forty motor vehicles, one hundred horses and eight warehouses containing food and ammunition.

north of Kamaing. Further east, 113th Chinese Regiment occupied Lawa and began to move towards Zigyun and, on the 3rd, 114th Regiment entered Tumbonghka. The position of *18th Division* was becoming desperate.

On the 7th June, finding that *55th* and *56th Regiments* had lost all their artillery and had failed to break through the roadblock, Tanaka ordered them to withdraw through the hills to the south of Kamaing; this they succeeded in doing with the minimum of equipment, carrying some 500 wounded with them. In Kamaing itself, which by then was almost surrounded, rations had been cut to a fifth of the normal, petrol supplies had run out and the remaining artillery was practically without ammunition. Tanaka had no alternative but to withdraw its small garrison into the hills to the south. On the 16th June, 149th Chinese Regiment occupied the town. The first of Stilwell's three objectives had been gained.

On the 22nd June, Honda ordered *18th Division* to retreat across the hills and concentrate in the area north of Sahmaw. Tanaka recommended that his division should be allowed to remain south of Kamaing and make a final effort to clear the Seton block. Finding, however, that the supply position was considerably worse than he thought, Tanaka withdrew his recommendation, and on the 29th, with Honda's concurrence, ordered the remnants of his four regiments, now reduced by casualties and sickness to some 4,500 all ranks, to move across the hills towards Sahmaw.[1]

At Myitkyina, Stilwell's plan to capture the town by a *coup de main* before the Japanese could recover from their surprise at the sudden loss of the airfield had failed, since, after months of fighting and exhausting marches, the Marauders and the Chinese regiments with them were incapable of any sustained effort and well-trained reserve formations were not immediately available. Despite the precarious supply position, Boatner, the newly-appointed commander,[2] returned to the attack as soon as his reinforcements had arrived. The reinforcing Chinese units, however, were ill-trained, the engineering battalions, hurriedly taken from the Ledo Road and totally untrained for battle, proved at first of little value and, of the reinforcements sent up to the Marauders, many were unfit for duty and the rest were untrained. Supported by inadequate artillery, attacks on the

---

[1] By this time *18th Division* had been reduced to a strength of about 3,000 all ranks which included 1,000 in each of *55th* and *56th Infantry Regiments*. The *4th* and *146th Infantry Regiments* (a total of four battalions), attached to the division, had each lost about a third of their strength and their combined strength was some 1,500 men.

[2] See page 295. By the end of May the reserve of rations was enough for only one day for American and two days for Chinese troops, and there was a severe shortage of certain types of ammunition. On the airfield, which was only some 1,500 yards from the Japanese lines, there were thirteen wrecked transport aircraft.

31st May and the 1st June made no appreciable progress, although an enemy counter-attack was repelled. Another attack by seven Chinese battalions on the 3rd, again with poor artillery support, also failed with heavy casualties. By the 7th the wastage from casualties and sickness had reached such proportions that 89th and 150th Chinese Regiments could muster no more than 1,000 men between them, 88th and 42nd Regiments could find only one battalion each, the two engineer battalions had had to be amalgamated into one provisional regiment and the reorganized Marauders were well below strength.[1] Boatner therefore decided to pause until artillery had been flown in, his supplies of ammunition had been built up and his troops could be reorganized and given some training.

Between the 10th and 17th June another series of attacks was launched but these were equally unsuccessful except for a small gain on the left flank where the Irrawaddy was reached near Maingna.[2] Faced with continual failure and with gains out of proportion to the efforts expended, Stilwell ordered a temporary cessation of infantry attacks on the 18th and sent Brigadier-General T. F. Wessels to Myitkyina with a view to his relieving Boatner. The relief took place on the 26th June, but it was to be the end of the month before any fresh effort to capture the town could be made.[3]

Morrisforce had meanwhile done its best to comply with its orders of the 25th May to move on Myitkyina and attack Waingmaw, a task for which, like all L.R.P. forces, it was ill suited.[4] When Morris received the order, his force (already reduced to about the strength of a battalion) was engaged in attacking Kazu and had been split by a sudden rise in the Nam Tabet River. As all the bridges near Kazu had been washed away, the main body had to cross the river at Fort Morton and it was not until the 29th May that Morris was able to concentrate his force some six miles east of Waingmaw. He attacked on the 30th May and again on the 2nd June; despite the lack of artillery support his troops on each occasion broke into the Japanese positions but were unable to hold them. On the 3rd June, Boatner ordered him to move north and clear Maingna. After establishing an airstrip for light aircraft and evacuating his numerous casualties, Morris began on the 6th to infiltrate into the village only to find that it was strongly held. On the 9th he received a message from Boatner saying that his failure to capture Maingna was the reason for the failure of the Chinese to capture Myitkyina, and ordering him to attack regardless of consequences. Attacks on the 10th and 19th June failed with considerable casualties. Morrisforce, already seriously

---

[1] Up to the 4th June the Marauders had incurred 424 battle casualties and lost 1,920 men through sickness.
[2] See Sketch 17, page 414.
[3] Boatner was evacuated sick as a result of a severe attack of malaria.
[4] See page 295.

depleted by sickness and battle casualties, was now unable to launch
further attacks and could do no more than harass the Japanese and
so prevent them from taking part in the battle for Myitkyina.

At Lentaigne's request, Stilwell had called a conference on the 25th
May to consider the future action of Special Force. The discussions
at this conference are given in some detail as they marked the
beginning of a series of accusations by Stilwell against Special Force.
Lentaigne, who had at the time no knowledge of the morning's
events at 'Blackpool',[1] gave a resumé of the operations to date and
asked for permission to evacuate the block should he judge that
shortage of supplies and ammunition made it necessary for the safety
of the garrison. When Stilwell asked why he proposed to abandon
'Blackpool' when Wingate had stated categorically that blocks such
as 'Broadway' and 'Aberdeen' could be held throughout the monsoon, Lentaigne pointed out the difference between blocks sited in
areas where the enemy could not bring up artillery and those on the
enemy's main line of communication such as 'White City' and 'Blackpool'. He said that 'Blackpool' could be held if it were possible to
get supplies and ammunition there. In his opinion, however, enemy
movement northward along the road and railway could be stopped
quite as effectively by offensive action on the part of his brigades as by
holding the block. He did not therefore feel justified in prejudicing
the safety of the troops at 'Blackpool', who were now forced to fight
without adequate supplies of food and ammunition.

At first Stilwell was unwilling to give his permission for a withdrawal, but later he issued a written order in which he said that there
were insufficient data in Lentaigne's report to convince him either
that it would be safer for the 'Blackpool' garrison to attempt to break
out than to stand fast, or that enough had been done by the rest of
Special Force to disperse the enemy build-up against the block. He
drew Lentaigne's attention to his directive of the 16th May ordering
a reconnaissance in force against Mogaung, and said that 'had that
been done promptly with maximum effort, it would probably have
caused a desirable enemy reaction by now.'[2] Nevertheless, on account
of the basic limitations of L.R.P. formations and the lack of ammunition and food, he accepted Lentaigne's representations that a serious
situation existed at 'Blackpool' and gave his permission to abandon
the block in case of emergency.

On the 27th, Stilwell asked Lentaigne in writing why Morrisforce
had not arrived at Waingmaw, and later that day upbraided him,
saying that his orders were being disobeyed in that Morrisforce had

---

[1] See pages 290–91.
[2] See page 289.

not moved at once to the east bank of the Irrawaddy. Lentaigne explained the reasons for the delay and said that, despite all the difficulties and the bad weather, Morris was doing his best to execute his orders. Stilwell eventually accepted Lentaigne's explanation and his undertaking to order Morrisforce to move as rapidly as possible. They then agreed that 77th Brigade should be ordered to attack Mogaung as soon as possible with the greatest strength it could bring to bear, and that, while maintaining pressure from the west on the road and railway south of Mogaung, 14th Brigade should cover the reorganization of 111th Brigade at Mokso as well as the evacuation of casualties from the Indawgyi Lake area. As soon as 111th Brigade was reorganized, it was to be responsible for protecting the northern half, and 14th Brigade and 3rd (W.A.) Brigade the southern half, of Indawgyi Lake until all Special Force casualties had been cleared.

The same day, in a letter to Mountbatten, Stilwell again complained that the evacuation of the 'Blackpool' block had opened the door to the Japanese.[1] At the same time he requested, since the Myitkyina airfield had to be held at all costs, that British parachute troops might be put at his disposal in case bad weather continued and made it impossible for troops to be landed there. Mountbatten thereupon wrote to Giffard telling him to do everything he could to help Stilwell. Giffard replied that 14th Army was already giving Stilwell all possible assistance, Special Force had been placed under his command, anti-aircraft artillery had been flown into Myitkyina at the expense of supplies for IV Corps, the men of four transport companies had been lent to drive vehicles on the Ledo Road, and 36th Indian Division was being prepared for operations on the Northern front as early as possible.[2] No parachute battalions could be made available since both the existing battalions had been committed at Imphal and had suffered severe casualties.[3]

On the 3rd June, Mountbatten, who had heard indirectly that Stilwell was dissatisfied with Special Force on the grounds that it had not obeyed his orders, asked for a report on the matter. Stilwell replied that 77th Brigade had been ordered to make a reconnaissance in force and an attack on Mogaung but had not complied with the order, and Morrisforce, instructed to move on Waingmaw at utmost speed, had disregarded its order. He therefore asked to be relieved of the command of Special Force, but offered to give it supplies and the necessary facilities for its evacuation until it had moved out of his area. On Mountbatten's orders Giffard sent Slim to Stilwell's headquarters to investigate the matter personally and submit recommendations. On the 7th, Slim reported that he had had a satisfactory

---

[1] See page 282.
[2] See pages 252 and 355.
[3] See pages 236–38.

talk with Stilwell: good relationships had been restored and the request that Special Force should be removed had been withdrawn. Both 77th Brigade and Morrisforce were in their correct positions and working well. He recommended that, when the situation at Mogaung and Myitkyina had been stabilized, two brigades should be withdrawn and two others should remain until the arrival of 36th Indian Division.

By the beginning of June Special Force was disposed with 77th Brigade moving on Mogaung from the south, 14th and 3rd (W.A.) Brigades holding Kyusanlai Pass and guarding the southern approaches to Indawgyi Lake, and 111th Brigade, reorganized after its withdrawal from 'Blackpool', at Mokso guarding the northern approaches to the lake from which all Special Force casualties were to be evacuated by flying-boat.[1] By this time, however, the numbers to be flown out had increased to some 400, double the number for which plans had been made. The sooner evacuation began therefore the better, and on the 2nd June, despite extremely bad weather which prevented it from being escorted by fighters, a Sunderland flying-boat, relying solely on cloud cover for protection, landed on the lake.[2] Thirty-one casualties were paddled out to it in rubber dinghies and flown back to Dibrugarh.[3] By the evening of the 5th a total of 188 men had been flown out in five sorties.

In an effort to speed up the evacuation and complete it before the monsoon precluded flying, rafts capable of carrying forty casualties at a time were built on the lake and a second flying-boat was brought into service. The two Sunderlands operated between the 7th and 10th, and, in a further five sorties, evacuated 200 casualties, making a total of 388 flown out. By this time, however, a further 200 casualties had been collected at the lake and, although one Sunderland had to be returned to its normal duties in Ceylon and the other needed maintenance, it was decided to continue with the operation. The monsoon had, however, increased in intensity and, although in the following week one flying-boat attempted on three occasions to reach the lake, it could not, flying blind, clear the 11,000 ft. mountains in the turbulent air conditions and had to turn back. On the 20th, it was damaged and later sunk by a whirlwind at its moorings at Dibrugarh. Although a relief Sunderland was flown from Ceylon and reached Dibrugarh on the 26th, it was not till the 30th June that the weather improved sufficiently to enable another attempt to reach the lake to be made.

When it appeared in the middle of the month that the flying-boats might not be able to operate again and the number of casualties to

---

[1] See page 283.
[2] The Sunderland was detached from 230 Squadron R.A.F., Ceylon.
[3] See Map 14, page 452.

be evacuated still continued to mount, Lentaigne decided to attempt to move them on rafts down the Indaw chaung to Kamaing which had just been captured by Stilwell's forces. Special Force engineers therefore built a fleet of ten large rafts (capable of accommodating 400 men) using local material, and collapsible boats, outboard motors and tarpaulins dropped by Dakotas.[1] The rafts were ready towards the end of the month, but on the 29th Special Force was told that a Sunderland would make up to five more sorties early in July. Lentaigne then decided to leave 120 of the most serious cases to be flown out and to send the remainder by raft to Kamaing. Between the 30th June and the 4th July a Sunderland flew out the 120 men in three sorties, making a grand total of 508 men evacuated in thirteen sorties. After the departure of the Sunderland on the 4th, Japanese fighters machine-gunned the anchorages. The river fleet, after many vicissitudes with reed-choked channels and rapids, completed the journey to Kamaing in three days. There the casualties were transferred to boats loaned by the Americans and taken up the Mogaung River to be flown out from the airfield at Warazup.[2] All the casualties were thus safely evacuated, but the need to protect all approaches to the lake during the evacuation had immobilized about half of Special Force for a month.

With the possibility of the Japanese being forced to withdraw from both Kamaing and Mogaung, Stilwell had meanwhile given Lentaigne orders on the 8th June that 111th Brigade was to move to the Pahok–Sahmaw area to prevent enemy movement into or through that district. On the 10th, as soon as 14th Brigade had taken over the task of protecting the northern exits from the lake, 111th Brigade began to move north. The rain was incessant and much of the track was deep in mud and waist-deep in water. Exhausted and with many sick, the brigade did not reach Lakhren until the 15th.[3] It found that the track through the hills to Padiga was disused and overgrown and had to cut a new one. It was therefore not until the 19th that Masters, leaving a small force to secure Lakhren, was able to concentrate three columns in the Padiga area.

On the 11th June, Stilwell had issued an order to all formations on the Northern front in which he gave the seizure of the general line Lonkin–Taungni–Tapaw as his immediate objective. The 77th Brigade was to attack Mogaung from the south and east in conjunction with 38th Chinese Division from the north and west, 111th Brigade was to move to Sahmaw as ordered on the 8th, and 14th Brigade was to move towards Taungni as soon as the evacuation of

---

[1] Fifty 'ranger' boats, twenty outboard motors, tarpaulins, petrol and oil were dropped at the northern end of the lake. Each raft when completed was 37 ft. overall with a beam of 12 ft., and a draught of 15 ins. when fully loaded.

[2] K. M. Robertson, *Indawgyi* (R. E. Journal, 1948).

[3] During this march one column had to move for two miles waist-high in water.

casualties from the lake had been completed. On the 17th, however, Stilwell amended his original orders to 111th Brigade by adding to its task the establishment of blocks on the road and railway in the immediate vicinity of Sahmaw. This amounted to instructing the brigade, without artillery or any heavy equipment, to set up a second 'Blackpool' on the enemy's main line of communication to the south, a task which it could not possibly carry out unaided.

The same day Lentaigne took steps to readjust the disposition of 14th and 3rd (W.A.) Brigades. He ordered the former to discontinue its operations at Kyusanlai Pass and to concentrate against the railway between Taungni and Pinbaw, and the latter to move into the foothills five miles north-west of Sahmaw, with the possible rôle of establishing a defensive position on the Namyin Chaung covering Mogaung.

The 111th Brigade had meanwhile discovered that in the Padiga area the Japanese were holding all the tracks down to the valley in strength.[1] Finding that the brigade had not moved on towards Sahmaw, Lentaigne told Masters on the 23rd June that, despite the exhaustion of the men, operations against the road and railway were to begin at once. Next day Masters reported that his men had to have rest, that his units were much depleted, that the Japanese were in strength on all the tracks leading to the valley and that he was already taking grave risks in his effort to pin them down. He was not in a position to protect the ridge and the approaches to it while at the same time taking stronger offensive action, and he considered that he must hold the high ground and the approaches to it in order to cover the concentration of the other brigades of Special Force. He therefore asked to be allowed to do what he thought best. Lentaigne agreed to give him a free hand, but asked him to carry out such limited offensives as his strength permitted until further columns arrived in the area.

On the 23rd June, Lentaigne received the following signal from Stilwell:

> 'The Commanding General directs that you explain in writing what steps you have taken to comply with orders issued by this headquarters dated June 8, June 11 and June 17 as pertains to 111th Brigade. He further directs that you explain in writing why the mission assigned has not been accomplished.'

He replied by explaining why the brigade's move from Mokso to Padiga had apparently been so slow, and took the opportunity to stress once again that Special Force was not equipped and organized to capture heavily dug-in positions supported by artillery, or to hold static blocks against which artillery and mortar fire could be brought

---

[1] A Japanese post five miles east of Padiga was taken by one column after three days' fighting, but was lost again on the 23rd.

to bear. He pointed out that at 'White City' and at 'Blackpool' artillery and other weapons with their ammunition had been flown in, and that the garrisons of these blocks had been able to hold out until ordered to withdraw or, in the case of 'Blackpool', air supply had failed. The present position was very different, for not only had the enemy been reinforced with fresh troops and artillery but Special Force had been greatly weakened 'numerically, physically and in fire power.'

Before receiving its orders on the 28th May,[1] 77th Brigade had begun to move towards Mogaung and by the 1st June it had occupied Lakum and the high ground to the west, and on the 2nd it seized the ferry over the Mogaung river at Tapaw.[2] The appearance of the brigade so close to Mogaung caused Honda once again to review his policy, for the only unit in the town was a composite one formed from ordnance and field hospital units. He immediately ordered *Headquarters 128th Regiment* and *III/128th Battalion* into Mogaung and told Takeda to abandon the contemplated attack on Myitkyina and concentrate his division for the defence of Mogaung.

Meanwhile Calvert, unaware of the weakness of the Japanese garrison, had come to the conclusion that success depended largely on the speedy arrival of the Chinese troops from the north, and decided that his best action would be to make the Pinhmi–Mogaung road the axis of his attack and attempt to secure a bridgehead across the chaung near Pinhmi before the Chinese arrived. He first built an airstrip for light aircraft at Gurkha Village, and then on the 8th attacked Pinhmi. He took the village but was unable to capture the bridge.[3] Next day he crossed the Wetthauk Chaung further south, occupied Ywathitkale and Mahaung and then attempted to take the bridge from the rear. The enemy put up stiff opposition, and it was not till the 10th that it was captured.[4] The following day Court House was taken, and by the 12th the area extending to the Mogaung River and up to the outskirts of Natgyigon was cleared. But by this time the eastern defences of the town had been reinforced by *II/128th Battalion* and the southern by *I/151st Battalion* on their return from the Myitkyina area.

The 77th Brigade had by now fought itself to a standstill; it had been behind the enemy lines for fourteen weeks and the three

---

[1] See page 404.
[2] See Sketch 16, page 411, and Map 4, page 53. A defensive position was at once constructed at Tapaw, and a few days later eight boats with outboard motors and crews together with two 4.2-inch mortars and ammunition were successfully dropped to the brigade.
[3] By this time *III/128th Regiment* had organized the defences to the east of the town. In the Pinhmi area several supply and ammunition dumps and two hospitals were captured.
[4] Casualties between the 2nd and 11th June amounted to 58 killed and 179 wounded.

battalions together could muster only some 550 men fit to attack, and this number was decreasing daily from sickness. In the circumstances Calvert realized he could not hold his position indefinitely, and therefore decided to consolidate his gains and wait for the arrival of reinforcements and 114th Chinese Regiment,[1] which Stilwell had ordered to move from Tumbongkha on the 3rd June and attack Mogaung from the north. Although 114th Regiment had to cover only some fourteen miles, it was not until the afternoon of the 18th that the leading battalion, having overcome the resistance of *I/128th Battalion*, reached the Mogaung River and it was the 19th before the rest of the regiment arrived. Having taken over the protection of Calvert's left flank in a leisurely fashion, the Chinese commander decided to deploy to the south of Mogaung, and sent 2/114th Battalion to occupy Loilaw and then attack north towards the railway station and Ywathit. Because the number of his fit troops was decreasing so rapidly, Calvert could not afford to wait any longer and he made his final effort to capture the town on the 23rd. That day, after heavy bombing of the enemy positions, the attack, greatly assisted by flame throwers, was successful. By nightfall Natgyigon and the railway bridge over the Mogaung River had been captured at the cost of a further 150 casualties.[2] The same day the Chinese occupied the railway station. After a lull on the morning of the 25th, the attack was renewed and some progress into the town was made. That night the enemy withdrew to the south-west, and on the morning of the 26th June Calvert's brigade entered Mogaung. The second of Stilwell's objectives had been gained.

The 77th (L.R.P.) Brigade had been given a task for which it was neither equipped nor trained. Without the support of artillery or tanks and already exhausted by three months fighting, it had been thrown by Stilwell against the garrison of a town in prepared positions supported by artillery. Calvert's leadership and determination, and the fine fighting qualities of his men, enabled him to succeed, but at a high cost: between the 17th May, when it came under Stilwell's orders, and the 26th June the brigade suffered some 950 battle casualties and about 150 men had to be evacuated owing to sickness— approximately half the strength it had at the beginning of the period —and of those who remained only about 300 were fit for action. There was now no alternative but to withdraw the brigade to India.

With the fall of Kamaing and Mogaung, Stilwell was at last in sight of his goal, the capture of Myitkyina and the completion of the road

---

[1] The reinforcements he received were an officer and twelve men with flame throwers.
[2] During this fighting two V.C.s were gained: one (posthumous) by Lieutenant (Acting Captain) M. Allmand, Indian Armoured Corps (attached 6th Gurkha Rifles), and the other by Rifleman Tulbahadur Pun, 6th Gurkha Rifles.

link to China.[1] He had first, however, to clear the Kamaing area and the Mogaung–Myitkyina road and railway. He had already ordered Lentaigne to occupy Taungni and the high ground to the west of the railway corridor; he now ordered 22nd Chinese Division to mop up at Kamaing and clear the road to Mogaung, 38th Chinese Division to mop up the Mogaung area and infiltrate towards Sahmaw on the left flank of Special Force, and 41st Regiment of 14th Chinese Division, 149th Regiment of 50th Division and 90th Regiment of 30th Division to reinforce the troops beseiging Myitkyina.[2]

Having been forced to withdraw from Kamaing and Mogaung and with the remnants of *18th Division*, now incapable of serious resistance, falling back across the hills to Sahmaw, Takeda, reinforced early in July by *119th Regiment* (less two battalions), decided to take up a defensive position covering his communications to Indaw. He therefore disposed his division, now consisting of four battalions only,[3] astride the railway on the general line of the Sahmaw river covering Taungni. The division was supported by *1st Artillery Battalion* which now had only two field guns, all the rest having been lost in Mogaung.[4] Honda (*33rd Army*) had meanwhile moved *24th Independent Mixed Brigade* from the Indaw to the Hopin area to protect Takeda's line of communications and had ordered *18th Division*, as soon as it reached Sahmaw, to move to Indaw for rehabilitation and reorganization.

By the end of June the evacuation of the whole of Special Force had become a matter of urgency. Experience in the 1943 campaign had shown that the maximum time L.R.P. forces could operate without serious loss of health and efficiency was twelve weeks, and all ranks of the force had been told before operation 'Thursday' began that they would be relieved after that time. By this time, 77th and 111th Brigades and Morrisforce had been in Burma for some sixteen weeks.

On the 30th June, Mountbatten visited Stilwell's headquarters and discussed with him and Lentaigne the withdrawal of Special Force. Stilwell said he could not at the moment agree to the withdrawal of any troops capable of effective action. Lentaigne pointed out that in 77th and 111th Brigades there were only some 350 men capable of really effective action. It was agreed that the medical authorities should be instructed immediately to examine the troops in 77th and 111th Brigades and that all those whom they classified as unfit should

---

[1] The Ledo Road and the first 4-inch pipeline had by this time reached the vicinity of Shaduzup.
[2] These regiments reached Myitkyina on the 7th, 14th and 29th July respectively.
[3] The I/128th Battalion had lost all but 50 of its 450 men during its rearguard action south of Tumbongkha and had ceased to exist as a fighting unit.
[4] Between the 1st June and 9th July 53rd Division had suffered some 1,600 casualties.

Sketch 16

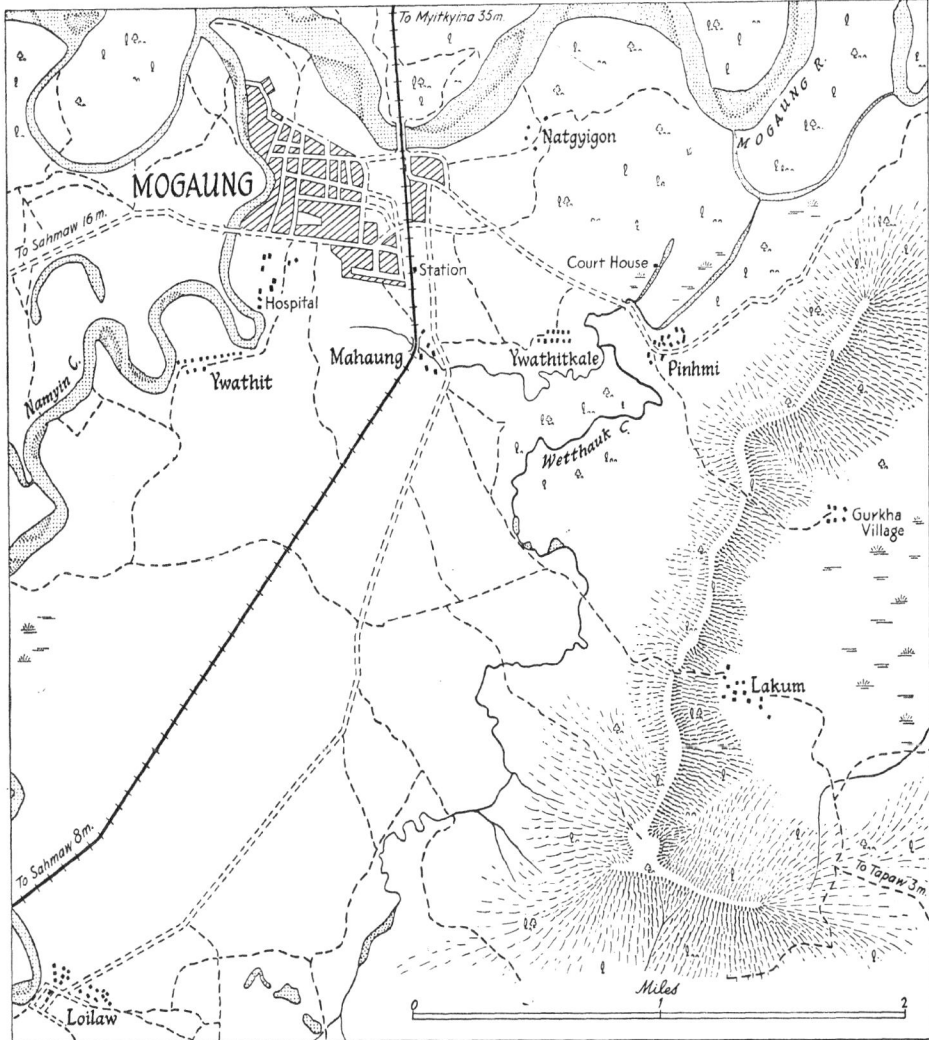

be evacuated at once, and that both brigades and Morrisforce were
to remain until the situation at Taungni had been cleared up and
Myitkyina captured. The date of the withdrawal of 3rd (W.A.) and
14th Brigades was to be left for decision later.

Lentaigne and Stilwell, however, took different views on the decisions reached. On the evening of the 30th the former issued a memorandum in which he said the Supreme Commander ruled that 77th
and 111th Brigades were to come out, the former immediately and
the latter as soon as possible after it had, in conjunction with 38th
Chinese Division, cleared up as far south as the Pahok–Sahmaw area.

He therefore informed Calvert that his brigade was to be flown out in the near future. Stilwell took the view that both brigades were to move out as soon as operations permitted, at a time to be decided by himself. When he heard that Lentaigne had ordered 77th Brigade to come out, he telegraphed Mountbatten asking that the situation might be clarified.

On the 2nd July, Mountbatten replied that it had been decided that the two brigades should 'be pulled out as soon as possible but must not be withdrawn from the immediate battle.' He went on to say that it had been agreed that 77th Brigade should be pulled out first and as soon as the situation at Taungni had been cleared up. Nevertheless, Stilwell honoured the promise Lentaigne had made to Calvert and agreed that the brigade should begin to move to Warazup on the 7th July, from where it would be flown back to India.

The rest of Special Force had by this time begun its re-deployment to carry out its tasks in the Sahmaw–Taungni area.[1] The 111th Brigade had moved forward and by the 8th July was engaged in severe fighting for Point 2171 which dominated the tracks approaching the northern end of the railway corridor. Although handicapped by the almost complete lack of air supply due to weather conditions, the reorganization of air command which affected both the method of control and the allocation of tasks, and the priority given by Stilwell to the supply of Myitkyina,[2] the brigade took the summit and held it, despite repeated counter-attacks.[3] The 3rd (W.A.) Brigade, moving north by way of Lakhren, reached Pyinbaw (three miles south of Pahok) on the 11th and occupied the area from the village to the foothills west of Sahmaw. The 14th Brigade, moving north in the hills to the east of Indawgyi Lake, and delayed by constant actions with small enemy parties, arrived at a point only some three miles west of Point 2171 on the 20th July.

Meanwhile a senior medical officer who had visited both brigades had reported on the 8th July that all ranks were physically and mentally worn out and had, on average, lost from two to three stones in weight. There were among them few men who had had fewer than three attacks of malaria and most had had as many as seven but still remained with their units. After the monsoon began the men were seldom dry and so, in addition, suffered from foot rot, septic sores and prickly heat. The incidence of death from cerebral malaria and typhus fever was rising. The general deterioration of health, loss of weight and the onset of anaemia following frequent attacks of malaria had so lowered their powers of endurance and their ability to march

---

[1] See pages 406–407.

[2] The 10th U.S.A.A.F. was now in direct support of N.C.A.C. See page 390.

[3] On the 9th July during the struggle for Point 2171, a posthumous V.C. was won by Captain (T/Major) F. G. Blaker, M.C., The Highland Light Infantry (attached 9th Gurkha Rifles).

with a sixty-pound load that, after an approach march, they were quite incapable of fighting until they had one or two days rest.

By this time Lentaigne, realizing that 111th Brigade had reached the limit of its endurance, had arranged for its relief on the arrival of 14th Brigade in the area so that medical officers could carry out a thorough examination and all unfit men could be evacuated. By the 23rd July the check had been completed and the number of men considered to be still fit for operations was just sufficient to form one company.

Lentaigne's decision to withdraw 111th Brigade from action towards the end of July led to his having a further disagreement with Stilwell who continued to hold the view that the Supreme Commander had agreed that both 77th and 111th Brigades were to remain until the Taungni situation was cleared. He therefore told Mountbatten that Lentaigne had issued orders which if carried out would nullify his own. At the same time Lentaigne submitted the plea that the withdrawal of brigades must be subservient to fitness to continue in action rather than being dependent on the consolidation of certain objectives. The 111th Brigade was wholly unfit for L.R.P. duties though a few men could still handle arms. He had therefore withdrawn it into reserve contrary to Stilwell's wishes and was prepared to accept the consequences.[1]

On receipt of these two messages Mountbatten told Stilwell that he was very much concerned at the situation disclosed by the medical report. He directed that all men of the L.R.P. brigades considered medically unfit must be evacuated without delay. He asked to be told immediately the dates Stilwell had in mind for the relief of each of the brigades, saying, 'If they are not soon relieved we may both be faced with the possible serious accusation of keeping men in battle who are unable to defend themselves. To rely on troops no longer physically fit is to court disaster.' To this Stilwell replied that there had been no restriction whatsoever on the evacuation of physically unfit men. He had already relieved 77th Brigade and Morrisforce,[2] but he required 111th, 14th and 3rd (W.A.) Brigades to assist 72nd Brigade of 36th Division to clear Taungni before he could relieve 111th Brigade. All that he was asking Lentaigne to do was to keep his fit men in action, especially as the Taungni situation should be under control in a fortnight. Mountbatten thereupon told Stilwell that 111th Brigade, which was originally due for withdrawal as early as

---

[1] Lentaigne's reasons for withdrawing 111th Brigade were stated in a letter to Mountbatten on the 23rd July. Stilwell, he said, had kept the L.R.P. brigades in and beyond the front line continuously and had made little attempt to fly in 36th Division quickly so that they could be relieved. L.R.P. brigades in close contact with the enemy and often without air or ground L. of C. could not evacuate their unfit, and, if they were to do so, had to be withdrawn out of contact with the enemy.

[2] Morrisforce, reduced in numbers to the equivalent of four platoons, was evacuated from Myitkyina airfield between the 27th and 29th July.

the 31st May, was not really fit for further action and should not be used in the operations to clear Taungni. However, since there appeared to be a misunderstanding, he proposed to send Major-General I. S. O. Playfair,[1] Wedemeyer and Merrill to discuss the matter with Stilwell and Lentaigne on the 25th. When the five met on the 25th they agreed that 111th Brigade should be evacuated as soon as 72nd Brigade had passed through the artillery positions for which it was responsible, and that 14th and 3rd (W.A.) Brigades would remain and participate in operations against Taungni, Lentaigne keeping Stilwell informed on their physical condition. This agreement was purely face-saving, for by that time 111th Brigade had been withdrawn from action and reduced to only one company. This was named 111th Company and sent to Pahok for garrison duties on the 27th. The unfit men were evacuated to India on the 30th July and 1st August.

It is of interest to examine the cause of the repeated differences of opinion which arose between Stilwell and Lentaigne. Each time that Stilwell accused Special Force of making an unsatisfactory response to his orders or of disregarding them, it is evident that Lentaigne and his brigadiers were doing their utmost to obey them, but that their efforts were nullified by the lack of time, the exhaustion of the troops, the climatic conditions and the shortage of supplies. It is understandable that Stilwell, unable to take advantage of his successful *coup de main* which had resulted in the capture of Myitkyina airfield, should suffer from exasperation as hopes of quickly capturing the town faded. He appears, however, to have lost all sense of what the troops under his command could be expected to accomplish in the prevailing conditions. Consequently he made demands on them with which even fresh troops, plentifully supplied with food and ammunition, would have found it hard to comply. The straits to which Special Force (and Merrill's Marauders) had been reduced by physical hardship and prolonged exposure on inadequate rations need not again be stressed. The willingness of the L.R.P. units to fight and go on trying in spite of the most appalling handicaps is amply proved by the story of their exploits, which completely refutes the charges made by Stilwell and Boatner.

By the 15th July, 72nd Brigade (the leading brigade of 36th Division) had begun to arrive at Myitkyina airfield. It was to concentrate at Mogaung by the 28th and attack the Japanese holding Sahmaw early in August. At the same time 14th Brigade was to reoccupy Point 2171, which had been lost during the relief, and 3rd (W.A.) Brigade was to gain control of the foothills west of the railway and be ready to take over the Sahmaw position as soon as it had been captured in order to free 72nd Brigade to advance on Taungni.

[1] General Playfair was General Giffard's Chief of Staff.

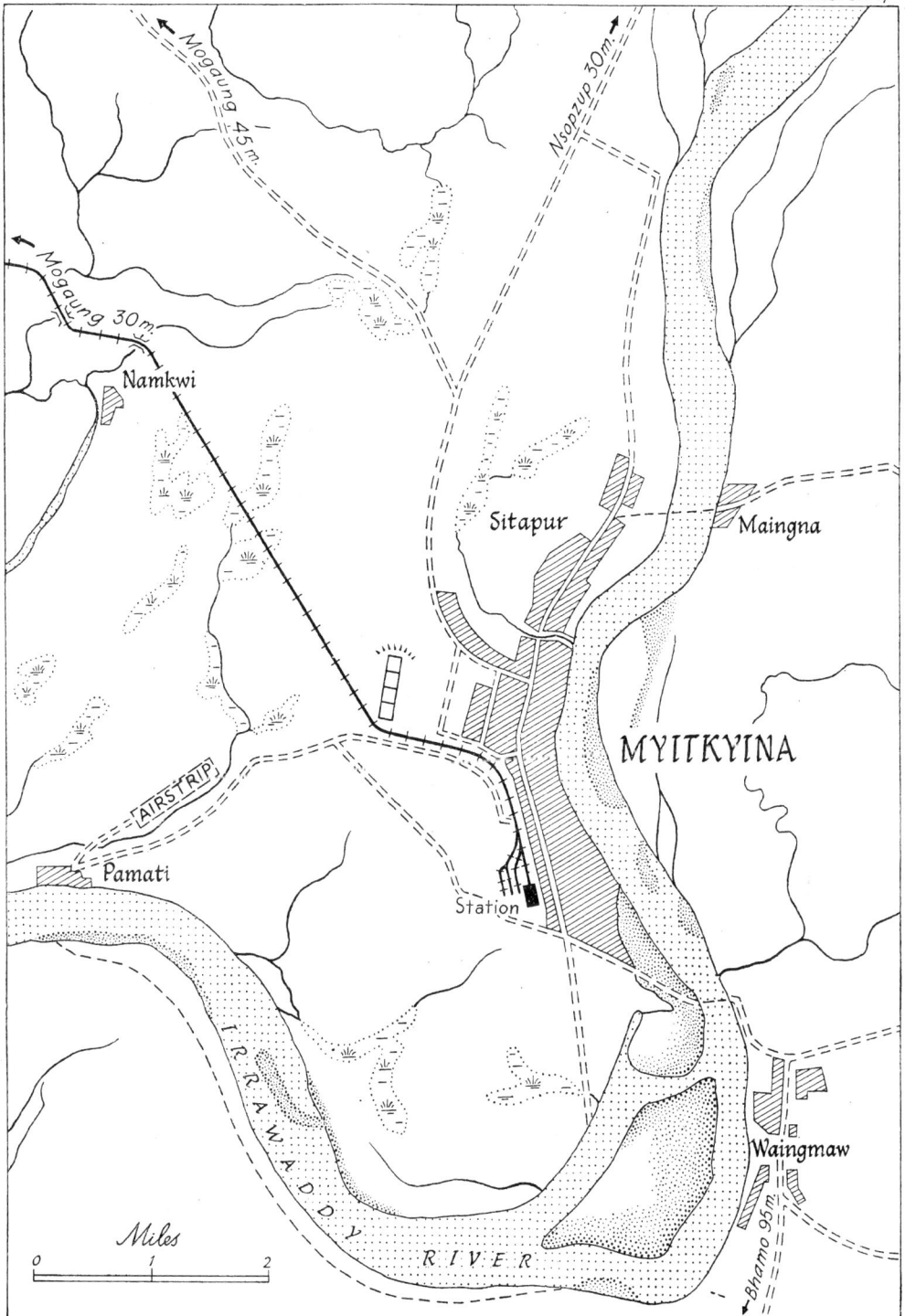

Mogaung 45m.

Mogaung 30m.

Nsopzup 30m.

Namkwi

Sitapur

Maingna

AIRSTRIP

Pamati

MYITKYINA

Station

IRRAWADDY

Waingmaw

Bhamo 95m.

RIVER

Miles

0   1   2

On the 5th August 72nd Brigade drove the Japanese from Sahmaw. The 3rd (W.A.) Brigade duly took over the position and, on the 9th, 72nd Brigade occupied Taungni. The 14th Brigade occupied all its objectives by the 12th. Both brigades of Special Force were then relieved by Chinese troops and withdrawn in preparation for their evacuation to India. The African brigade flew out from Myitkyina on the 17th and 18th August, 14th Brigade between the 19th and 26th and the remainder of Special Force on the 27th August. The battle losses of the five L.R.P. brigades involved in the operations in northern Burma amounted to 3,628 killed, wounded and missing, which was approximately eighteen per cent. of the total strength.[1]

The capture of Kamaing and Mogaung in June had cleared Stilwell's land communications and had enabled the forces attacking Myitkyina to be reinforced. The Japanese garrison could not, however, be reinforced and, although it was fighting magnificently, battle casualties and disease were steadily reducing its ability to hold out. An attempt on the 12th July to storm the defences, with powerful air support by fighters and bombers, was decisively repulsed but there were signs during the next few days that resistance was weakening. On the 1st August, Mizukami (in command of the garrison) ordered Maruyama to withdraw the remnants of his regiment and made the traditional expiation for failure by committing suicide. Thus, when on the 3rd August, Wessels launched another general attack, there was nothing in Myitkyina but a small rearguard and men too ill to move, and the town was occupied without difficulty by 3.45 p.m. According to American sources the siege of Myitkyina from the 17th May to the 3rd August cost the Allies 5,383 casualties and 1,168 sick.[2] Maruyama succeeded in extricating 800 men, and only 187 live Japanese, nearly all in hospital, were found in the town, the garrison of which had never exceeded 3,000, including non-combatants.

Stilwell had now gained all his three objectives and the way was clear, as soon as the monsoon abated sufficiently, for the Ledo Road and the two 4-inch pipelines to be driven through to Myitkyina, and for the construction of the air staging base to be begun.[3]

---

[1] See Appendix 29. The sickness rate was extremely high; for example when 77th and 111th Brigades, which bore the brunt of the fighting and were longest in Burma, were evacuated only 300 to 350 men in each brigade out of an initial strength of about 4,000 remained fit for action.

[2] Romanus and Sunderland, page 253. The total battle casualties on the Northern front between the 1st January and the 19th August 1944 were given by the Americans as 13,618 Chinese and 1,327 Americans.

[3] By early August the Ledo Road had reached Shaduzup and the first 4-inch pipeline was in operation to a point some twelve miles north of roadhead. The construction of the second 4-inch pipeline was in hand but it was not in operation beyond Ledo.

CHAPTER XXX

THE PACIFIC

The Reconquest of New Guinea

(April–July 1944)

See Maps 1, 5 and 13 and Sketch 18

THE American occupation of the Marshall Islands and the encirclement of Rabaul had spurred the Japanese on to fresh efforts to strengthen their contracted defensive zone.[1] In February, *29th Division* and some six infantry battalions were sent from Manchuria to the Marianas, and *43rd Division* in Japan was earmarked to follow them as soon as possible. Fortress units were sent to the Bonin Islands, where they eventually came under the control of *Headquarters 109th Division* which was being formed there.[2] In anticipation of an early attack on the Palaus, a regiment of *35th Division* was sent there pending the arrival of *14th Division*. In early March *Headquarters 31st Army* (Lieut.-General H. Obata) was set up in Saipan in the Marianas to exercise control, under the direction of the *Combined Fleet*, of all army units in the Central Pacific islands. Its main line of defence was that part of the new perimeter running from the Bonin Islands in the north through the Marianas, Ponape and Truk to the Palaus, where it linked up with *2nd Area Army's* zone of responsibility. The backbone of the defence of the islands was to be land-based aircraft: a new air fleet (the *14th*), formed from what was left of the *11th Air Fleet*, was being re-equipped and re-manned as fast as aircraft could be turned out and new pilots trained. At the insistence of the Army, supreme command in the Central Pacific area was given to the Navy and on the 4th April the *Central Pacific Area Fleet* was formed and placed under the command of Vice-Admiral Nagumo, the former commander of the *1st Air Fleet* which, in the opening months of the war, had laid a trail of destruction from Pearl Harbour to Ceylon. The Admiral set up his headquarters at Saipan, but his new command was a fleet in name only. It comprised the so-called *4th Fleet*, now reduced to a collection of miscellaneous small craft, the new *14th Air Fleet* and *31st Army*. Command of army formations in the field remained the responsibility of the Army.

---

[1] See pages 72–73.
[2] See Map 13, page 438.

Equally radical changes were made further south. Recognizing that *8th Area Army's* communications with New Guinea were irretrievably cut by the loss of the Admiralty Islands and that its headquarters at Rabaul could no longer exercise effective control of operations in New Guinea, *Imperial General Headquarters* in mid-March transferred *18th Army* and *4th Air Army* to *2nd Area Army's* control, leaving *8th Area Army* with *17th Army* to hold out in Rabaul and Bouganville as best it could.[1] In order to bring *18th Army* (then reorganizing at Madang and Wewak after the costly retreat from Lae and Salamaua) within its zone, *2nd Area Army's* boundary was shifted eastward to the 147th Meridian. At about the same time *32nd* and *35th Divisions* were ordered south from China to strengthen *2nd Area Army* still further.[2] The two divisions were due to arrive in Halmahera and western New Guinea respectively at the end of April.[3]

Reinforcement of the island garrisons could not hope, however, to do more than delay the American advance. As long as the Allies had control of sea communications they could always bring overpowering strength to bear when and where they chose. Admiral Koga was no doubt well aware that sooner or later he would have to meet the American fleet in action and in August 1943 had prepared plans for concentrating the Japanese fleet in readiness to engage the American fleet if it attempted to penetrate the defensive zone. On the 8th March, he issued an order to the fleet giving the general plan (operation 'Z') which was to be acted on in the event of an attempted invasion of the Carolines or Marianas. Koga did not live to see his plans materialize. In February he had transferred the main body of the *Combined Fleet* from Truk to Palau owing to the threat of air attack, but at the end of March the activities of the American carriers forced him once again to abandon his fleet base. On the last day of the month he and his staff left in two flying-boats for Davao where he intended to set up his new headquarters. The Admiral's aircraft was never heard of again; the other, carrying his staff, flew into a storm and crashed into the sea.

While the Japanese were feverishly building up their defences, the Americans were preparing to pull them down. Strategy for the Pacific during 1944 had been clearly outlined by the American Chiefs of Staff in their directive of the 12th March.[4] It will be recalled that MacArthur's South-West Pacific forces were to advance from

---

[1] Map 1, page 1.
[2] See page 97.
[3] See Map 5, page 97.
[4] See page 112.

eastern New Guinea to Hollandia in one bound, by-passing the Japanese bases at Wewak and Hansa Bay.[1] From there MacArthur was to move northwestward along the coast seizing such bases as he deemed necessary, and then, using the Halmahera group as a stepping stone, to cross to the Philippines. Nimitz's Central Pacific forces were to furnish support for the Hollandia landings and then thrust forward in two directions: northwestward towards Japan through the Marianas, and westward to the Philippines through the Palaus.

In New Guinea during March, 15th Brigade of 7th Australian Division began to advance northwards on a broad front from the crest of the Finisterre Range, and on the 21st a patrol made contact on the coast with American forces which had moved west from Saidor. The brigade entered Bogadjim on the 13th April. Madang was occupied on the 24th by 8th and 15th Brigades, the former coming up the coast in small craft from Sio. On the 25th a battalion of 8th Brigade was sent to occupy Alexishafen. In April, Headquarters 11th Australian Division (Major-General A. J. Boase) relieved Headquarters 7th Australian Division and assumed command of all units in the area. During May and June, Australian activity was confined to maintaining pressure on the enemy by active patrolling. Hansa Bay was occupied on the 16th June and patrols pushed forward as far west as the Sepik river.

Meanwhile the Americans had been preparing for the jump to Hollandia. Hollandia was a small settlement on the western arm of Humboldt Bay, the only first-class anchorage between Wewak and Geelvink Bay.[2] Twenty-five miles to the west lies Tanahmera Bay which is separated from Humboldt Bay by a mountain ridge rising steeply from the sea to 7,000 feet. South of the ridge is Lake Sentani, a narrow strip of water about fifteen miles long. In the plain between the mountains and the lake the Japanese had built three airfields and were starting a fourth further east. Hollandia, as the whole area became known to the Americans, appeared to be eminently suitable for developing into a major naval and air base. Humboldt Bay provided anchorage for the largest vessels and the Sentani plain seemed capable of almost unlimited airfield development.

In planning the operation, air support presented MacArthur with a fresh problem. For the first time in New Guinea he was advancing beyond the effective range of land-based air cover, the nearest Allied air base to Hollandia being Nadzab 500 miles to the south-east.[3] The Japanese on the other hand were known to be developing Hollandia itself as an air base and had other airfields only 125 miles away in the

---

[1] See Map 1, page 1.
[2] See Map 5, page 97.
[3] See Sketch 18, page 420.

Wakde–Sarmi area. The fast carrier groups of the U.S. 5th Fleet could provide air cover for a short time only. Carriers, however formidably defended, would be a tempting target for submarine and air attack and Nimitz was not prepared to risk them in the coastal waters of New Guinea for more than a limited period. To replace the fighters after the departure of the carriers, an airfield within effective range of Hollandia was required. Aitape, 125 miles to the east-south-east, where the Japanese already had an airstrip, was selected. The seizure of Aitape would not only solve the problem of air cover but would have the added advantage of interposing a force between Hollandia and the Japanese *18th Army* at Wewak.

Enemy strength was estimated to be about 14,000 at Hollandia and about 3,500 at Aitape, but, as the Japanese were known to be using Aitape as a staging post for troop movements between Wewak and Hollandia, the number of troops in that area might vary by as much as 3,000 men. As a result of these estimates, two and one-third assault divisions were allocated for the first phase of the operation— nearly 50,000 troops. The 1st Corps (Lieut.-General R. L. Eichelberger) of 6th U.S. Army (Lieut.-General W. Krueger) was to provide the bulk of these forces. The final plan called for three simultaneous landings: two regimental combat teams of 24th U.S. Division were to land at Tanahmera Bay and two regimental combat teams of 41st U.S. Division at Humboldt Bay. After securing their beachheads the two divisions were to drive inland on either side of the mountains, carrying out a pincer movement aimed at the rapid capture of the Sentani airfields. The third regimental combat team of 41st Division was to make the assault on Aitape, where it would be reinforced the following day by 127th Regimental Combat Team of 32nd U.S. Division. D-day was to be the 27th April.

The naval forces responsible for the landings, drawn from the U.S. 7th Fleet, were under Rear-Admiral D. E. Barbey, the commander of the 7th Amphibious Force. It was a very different fleet from the one he had commanded a year ago. He now had over 200 vessels, including a large number of the landing ships and landing craft which might have done so much to shorten the Papuan campaign. He formed three attack groups, western, central and eastern, two follow-up groups and a floating reserve. Air cover during the run-in and the landings would be provided by a task group of eight escort carriers loaned from the U.S. 5th Fleet. Two Australian heavy cruisers under Rear-Admiral Crutchley, and three cruisers under Rear-Admiral R. S. Berkey, U.S.N., each with their own screen of destroyers, would form the close escort. Finally, the Fast Carrier Force from the 5th Fleet would cover the expedition from the north and north-west against any challenge by the Japanese fleet and give air support at Hollandia.

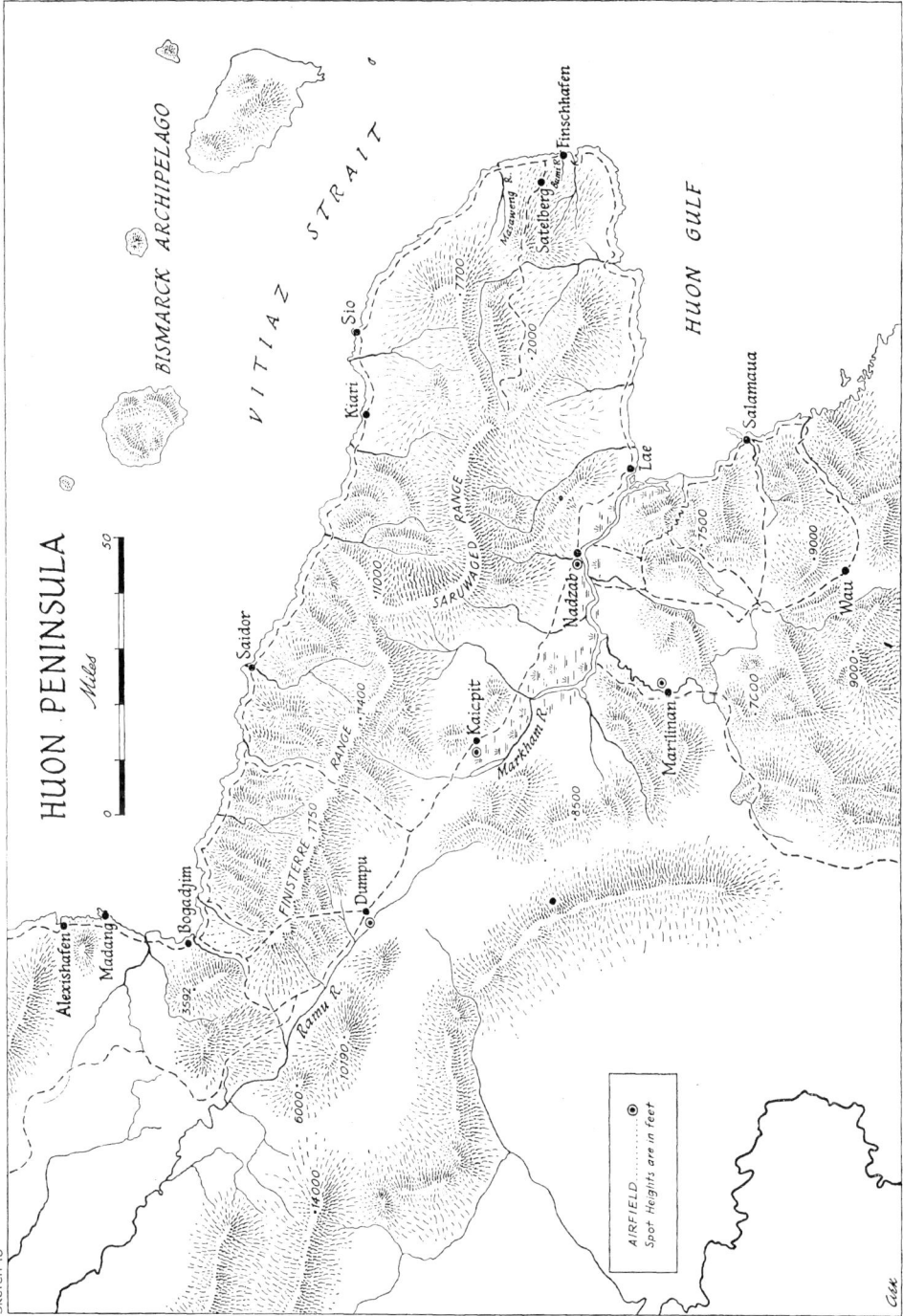

HUON PENINSULA

Miles

BISMARCK ARCHIPELAGO

VITIAZ STRAIT

HUON GULF

Sio

Kiari

Finschhafen

Satelberg

Masaweng R.

Bumi R.

.7700

.2000

Saidor

SARUWAGED RANGE

Lae

Salamaua

Nadzab

.7500

.9000

Kaicpit

FINSTERRE RANGE

.7750

Markham R.

Marilinan

Wau

.9000

.8500

.7000

.9000

Bogadjim

Dumpu

Ramu R.

.3592

Alexishafen

Madang

.6000

.10190

.14000

AIRFIELD ....◉

Spot Heights are in feet

Reduction of enemy air strength in preparation for the landings began in the second week in March. At the end of the month the Fast Carrier Force struck Palau and other islands of the western Carolines, destroying a large number of enemy aircraft. During March and April aircraft of 5th U.S.A.A.F. and the R.A.A.F. struck enemy airfields from Wewak to the Vogelkop and from Biak to Timor. From the 30th March to the 3rd April a series of devastating attacks was made on Hollandia to where the headquarters of the Japanese *4th Air Army* and *6th Air Division* had recently been transferred. In the first attack, owing largely to an inefficient radar warning system, the Japanese were taken completely by surprise and nearly one hundred aircraft were destroyed on the ground. By the 3rd April *6th Air Division* was so reduced as to be incapable of effective retaliation. The air war of attrition continued relentlessly until D-day, by which time Hollandia was ripe for the plucking.

The invasion force sailed from the embarkation ports at Goodenough Island and Finschhafen between the 16th and 18th April. So as to give no indication of their destination all convoys were routed east of the Admiralty Islands. Rendezvous with the escort carrier group was made on the morning of the 20th. During daylight the great fleet of ships made to the westward and at dusk turned south-westward towards Hollandia. During the night the eastern attack group was detached and set course for Aitape.

Tanahmera Bay was found to be undefended. A bombardment by Crutchley's cruiser squadron at dawn on the 22nd provoked no reply. No aircraft rose from the Sentani airfields to challenge the fighters flown off by the Fast Carrier Force, and the strikes which were to have been made by its aircraft were accordingly cancelled. The assault troops of 24th Division made their landing without opposition, but the two beaches were found to be unsatisfactory; a swamp thirty yards inshore prevented egress from one and the only exit from the other was a steep narrow trail impassable to vehicles. Supplies and vehicles began to pile up and on the 24th follow-up convoys were diverted to Humboldt Bay. By this time most of the two regimental combat teams had been landed, and had made their way, often in single file, along the narrow track leading to Lake Sentani and by the 26th had occupied the western airfield.

At Humboldt Bay complete surprise was achieved. When the cruisers opened their bombardments at daylight the defenders, mainly administrative troops, fled inland, rare behaviour on the part of the Japanese, and on landing 41st Division found the beach defences abandoned. The division was soon making good progress against slight opposition towards the airfields. The only untoward incident in the whole operation occurred on the night of the 23rd, when a single Japanese bomber dropped a stick of bombs which detonated a captured Japanese ammunition dump. Fires which burned for several days were started, destroying over half the division's rations and supplies landed during the previous thirty-six hours. The leading troops reached the shores of Lake Sentani on the 24th, where again slight opposition was met, but by nightfall on the 26th two of the airfields had been taken and contact made with 24th Division which had by that time secured the third.

The landing at Aitape followed much the same pattern as the other two; 163rd Regimental Combat Team of 41st Division landed on the morning of the 22nd to find that the defences had been hurriedly abandoned, and by nightfall had captured the airfield. This was quickly repaired and within forty-eight hours was in use by R.A.A.F. fighters. On the 23rd, the escort carriers which had covered the landings were sent to Hollandia to take over close support from the fast carriers which then rejoined the 5th Fleet.

The capture of Hollandia and Aitape was one operation, the largest yet undertaken by the South-West Pacific forces. As it turned out, success had been over-insured. There were in fact some 11,000 Japanese troops at Hollandia on the 22nd April, most of whom were administrative troops, instead of the 14,000 estimated. Around Aitape there were fewer, probably much fewer, than a thousand troops of the same calibre. The Japanese were caught completely unprepared. There had just been a change of command and a re-deployment of forces was taking place. The *2nd Area Army*, on taking *18th Army* under command in mid-March, had instructed Lieut.-General H. Adachi to withdraw his three divisions from Madang and Wewak to Hollandia. On the 22nd April none of his divisions was west of Wewak. No senior officer in Hollandia had been there longer than a few weeks. The commander of *6th Air Division* had just been relieved after the destruction of his forces by Allied bombers at the beginning of April. Rear-Admiral Endo, the senior naval officer, had arrived from Wewak late in March. The senior officer present was Major-General Kitazono, who had arrived in Hollandia from Wewak (where he had commanded a transport unit) only ten days before the landings. Kitazono had no time to prepare a com-prehensive defence plan, far less to co-ordinate it with the navy and air force and, even had he had time, he had neither the men nor resources to hold the area.

With the loss of Hollandia *Imperial General Headquarters* recognized that the strategic line of resistance decided on at the end of 1943, which ran through Wakde and Sarmi, was no longer tenable, and on the 2nd May ordered a withdrawal to a line Biak–Manokwari. Within a week a further withdrawal was found necessary. Attacks by Allied aircraft from the newly-won Hollandia airfields on bases in western New Guinea as far west as Biak Island made them useless either for air operations or as supply depots. Added to this, the convoy carrying *32nd* and *35th Divisions* to join *2nd Area Army* had been severely mauled by American submarines. The *32nd Division* had lost an infantry regiment and half its artillery; *35th Division* had been reduced to the equivalent of four infantry battalions and had little more than one battery of divisional artillery left. Increasing Allied air and submarine activity made it unlikely that New Guinea could be substantially reinforced or supplied, and convinced *Imperial General Headquarters* that a still further withdrawal was necessary. On the 9th May, *2nd Area Army* was ordered to prepare a new defensive line running from Sorong to Halmahera, and to hold Biak Island and Manokwari as outposts for as long as possible.

The Americans had taken the airfields at Hollandia and Aitape at small cost but holding the latter was to prove expensive. When on the 2nd May the Japanese withdrew their defensive line, *18th Army* at Wewak was ordered to by-pass Hollandia and Aitape and join *2nd Army* in western New Guinea. Adachi, knowing from bitter experience what a march of nearly 400 miles through the almost trackless hinterland of New Guinea meant, determined to throw the whole of his army against the Americans at Aitape in a do-or-die attempt at a break-through. American Intelligence got wind of his plan and by the end of June the American garrison at Aitape had been built up to a strength of nearly three divisions, and a defensive position established some seventeen miles east of the airfield. Although the Japanese attack on the 10th July found the Americans prepared, it was not until the 3rd August that, cut off from all supplies by American motor torpedo-boats and with nearly half of his 20,000 men lost, Adachi was forced to order a withdrawal.

Before the battle for Aitape had even begun, MacArthur had taken another step forward to Wakde. This island, where the Japanese had recently completed an airfield, lies two miles off the coast about 120 miles north-west of Hollandia. Opposite on the mainland lies the small village of Toem. From there the coastline runs in a north-westerly direction to Sarmi. Between Sarmi and Toem there was an airstrip and another in course of construction.

On the 17th May 163rd Regimental Combat Team of 41st Division (which had formed the spearhead of the assault on Aitape) secured a beachhead three miles west of Toem without opposition. Artillery was quickly landed and, on the following day, troops crossed the two-mile stretch of water under cover of naval and air bombardment and landed on Wakde without meeting serious opposition. On leaving the beaches, however, the troops were met with a well organized and courageous defence. Wakde is only two miles long and a mile wide, but it took the invaders over two days to secure it. By then there were only four survivors of the original garrison of about 800.

The airfields on the mainland between Toem and Sarmi were not so easily secured. Sarmi was the headquarters of the Japanese *36th Division*, and practically the whole division was in the area. General Krueger (6th U.S. Army), feeling that the retention of Wadke would be difficult with so large a number of Japanese in the vicinity, ordered a drive on Sarmi. It took over a month of bitter fighting to overcome the opposition.

On the 21st May the airstrip on Wakde was in use by fighters and a week later had been enlarged to take heavy bombers, but more room was needed by the Allied air forces. The main purpose of seizing Hollandia had been to gain an air base from which heavy bombers could reach out to Palau and Halmahera, but the Sentani airfields had proved incapable of taking anything larger than medium bombers without a great deal of heavy engineering work. Mac-Arthur had for some time had his eye on Biak Island, which held one of the two remaining groups of Japanese airfields and which gave promise of being capable of further development. It was thought to be defended by a garrison of 4,400 men of whom no more than 2,500 would be fighting troops. The island, the largest of the Schouten group, lies in the mouth of Geelvink Bay 200 miles west of Wakde and a high coral ridge runs parallel to and overlooks the southern shore. At the most southerly point in the island the ridge swings inland in an arc enclosing a plain about eight miles long and up to a mile and a half wide before reaching the shore again. On this plain the Japanese had, since the end of 1943, constructed three airfields.

The American estimate of the strength of the defence was optimistic. The garrison of the island had been reinforced in December by *222nd Infantry Regiment* (*36th Division*) from China and a company of light tanks, and in May Colonel N. Kuzume, the garrison commander, had over 11,000 troops under his command. Assuming that the airfields would be the principal Allied objective, he had concentrated his defences on the high ground overlooking the most easterly one where there were a number of caves hidden by the undergrowth and connected by subterranean passages. The entrances to the caves were ringed with pillboxes, foxholes and obstructions. When the Americans landed, Lieut.-General T. Numata, the Chief of Staff of *2nd Area Army*, happened to be on a visit of inspection and, until the 15th June, himself assumed responsibility for the defence.

While preparations for the landings were being hastily made at Hollandia, Allied bombers blasted Biak and the Japanese airfields on the mainland further west. On the 27th May, only ten days after the assault on Wakde, 162nd and 186th Regimental Combat Teams of 41st Division were landed on the south shore of Biak about eight miles east of the airfields, covered by the two cruiser squadrons of the 7th Fleet. Initial opposition was light and, as soon as a beachhead had been secured, 162nd Infantry Regiment began moving along the coastal road towards the airfields, meeting with only occasional rifle fire. It looked as if it might be a walk-over but the Japanese were biding their time. As the leading troops emerged on to the plain beyond the beaches they were brought to a halt by a deadly stream of fire from the cliffs and caves overlooking it. That evening a Japanese force, supported by tanks, cut off the leading battalion from the main American forces. It was clear that there was no hope of taking the airfields until the enemy had been driven from the high ground, and the next afternoon the isolated American troops were withdrawn by landing craft to positions further east.

On the 31st May the remainder of 41st Division (less one battalion) was brought in from Wakde, and a two-pronged attack was made on the airfields, 162nd Regiment again advancing along the coast road while 186th Regiment moved west along the inland plateau. Some of the bitterest fighting of the campaign then followed. The defenders had literally to be blasted out of their caves. It was a week before the eastern airfield was captured and another before it could be used and it was well into August before resistance on the island was finally broken.

The invasion of Biak had immediate and far-reaching consequences. When on the 9th May the Japanese line of resistance had been moved further west to Sorong and Halmahera, the garrison of Biak had been left as an outpost, without expectation of reinforcement, to hold out as best it could. The decision had been made with the full agreement of the Navy. The American landings on the 27th May at once brought about a change of attitude in naval circles in Tokyo. *Imperial General Headquarters* had issued on the 3rd May a warning order for all units of the *Combined Fleet* to start assembling for operation 'A-Go', the object of which, like Koga's operation 'Z', was to bring the American fleet to action, but with the difference that the battle was to be fought in the waters east of the Philippines. The essence of the plan was that aircraft based on the Central Pacific islands would reduce the carrier strength of the Americans before the two fleets met. *Imperial General Headquarters* soon realized, however, that in the event of an attack on the Marianas the battle might have to be fought farther north. They considered what should be done if Biak were attacked before the Marianas, and decided not to reinforce Biak and so reduce the already inadequate air strength in the north, even though it might mean losing Biak and the Vogelkop airfields. It was only when Biak was in fact invaded before the Marianas that the full implication of its loss seems to have been brought home to the Japanese Navy, which then realized that Allied aircraft using its airfields would increase the already marked disparity between the two air forces and threaten the success of 'A-Go.'

To deny the Biak airfields to the enemy the Japanese Navy took two important steps: one-third to one-half of the naval aircraft in the Central Pacific was sent south at the end of May to Halmahera and western New Guinea and placed under the command of the *23rd Air Flotilla* at Sorong; and units of the *1st Mobile Fleet*,[1] newly assembled at Tawi Tawi, were ordered to transport reinforcements to Biak.

At the same time *Imperial General Headquarters* ordered an amphibious brigade to be transferred from the Philippines to Biak. Simultaneously *2nd Area Army* ordered *35th Division* to send three infantry companies from Sorong to Biak, presumably by barge. The brigade (some 2,500 men) left Davao on the night of the 2nd June in cruisers and destroyers, escorted by a force which included one of the older battleships and two heavy cruisers. The ships were sighted by an American submarine on the morning of the 3rd and shadowed by aircraft. The same day an erroneous report was received by Admiral S. Toyoda that an American carrier was at Biak; this, combined with the knowledge that surprise had been lost, induced him to postpone the operation. The following day, when reconnaissance aircraft reported no sign of any carrier, Toyoda ordered a second attempt. The troops who had meanwhile been put ashore at Sorong were embarked in three destroyers, each with a landing barge carrying another fifty men in tow, and, escorted by three more destroyers, left for Biak on the night of the 7th June. At noon the next day the force was attacked by Allied bombers which sank one of the destroyers. Meanwhile, the two Allied cruiser forces which had been covering the Biak landings had been combined into a single force under Crutchley and now comprised three cruisers and fourteen destroyers.

The combined force was refuelling at Hollandia when the report of the approach of the Japanese destroyers was received. It was at once ordered to intercept. Radar contact was made north-west of Biak on the night of the 8th. In face of the superior force the Japanese cut their tows and turned away at high speed, pursued by Crutchley's force. His destroyers soon drew ahead of the cruisers but were unable to close the range sufficiently to make their gun-fire effective, and after three hours abandoned the chase in order to get within the shelter of friendly aircraft before daylight.

Undeterred by their two failures, the Japanese planned a third and yet more determined attempt to reinforce Biak. On the night of the 10th June a transport group, with an escort which included

---

[1] In March the *2nd* and *3rd Fleets*, which contained practically the whole of the fighting strength of the Japanese Navy, had been amalgamated and renamed the *1st Mobile Fleet*.

two of the giant 18-inch battleships (the *Yamato* and *Musashi*) and two heavy cruisers, was assembled at Batjan Bay in the Halmaheras with orders to sail for Biak on the 15th. Against a force of such strength Crutchley's force would have been powerless. It was not to be put to the test, however, for on the 11th and 12th the fast carriers of the U.S. 5th Fleet threw the whole weight of their aircraft against Guam and Saipan. It was now evident to the Japanese that the invasion of the Marianas was about to begin and that the long-awaited chance to come to grips with the American fleet had at last arrived. On the evening of the 13th, Toyoda ordered operation 'A-Go' to take place immediately. The third and final attempt to reinforce Biak was abandoned, and thereafter only sporadic attempts were made by barge, and it is probable that about 1,100 men managed to evade the American patrols and reach the island.

During the first week in June, when it seemed as if it might be some time before the Biak airfields were in use, MacArthur began to look for an airfield site further west from which protection could be given to American troops on the island until it was secured and the Allied air forces given more room for expansion. Noemfor in Geelvink Bay was chosen. The island lay half way between Biak and the head-quarters of *2nd Army* at Manokwari, and it was believed that the Japanese were using it as a staging post for reinforcements going to Biak. Though no more than fifteen miles in circumference the island contained three airfields. The strength of the garrison was estimated at about 3,000 men. During June, Japanese airfields within range of Noemfor, and in particular those on the island itself, were heavily bombed. There was little response, since on or about the 13th June all that remained of the aircraft which had been sent south to join *23rd Air Flotilla* during the attempts to reinforce Biak had been ordered north again for the defence of Saipan.[1] On the 2nd July, after an unusually lengthy and heavy bombardment by the cruiser forces of the 7th Fleet augmented by fourteen destroyers, 158th Regimental Combat Team was landed on the north-west corner of the island. Dazed by the weight of the bombardment, the enemy offered little opposition and in a few hours the north-west airfield had been captured. As a result of an exaggerated report by a Japanese prisoner-of-war that there were about 5,000 Japanese in the island, some 1,500 men of 503rd U.S. Parachute Regiment were dropped on the newly-captured airfield during the next two days. They were not needed. There was no properly organized resistance in the island and by the 6th July all three airfields were in Allied hands. The capture of Noemfor had made the eastern half of the Vogelkop untenable by the Japanese and at the end of June *35th*

---

[1] See page 430.

Division at Manokwari was ordered to move to Sorong in the extreme west.

In planning his approach to the Philippines, MacArthur had always intended to establish an air base at the western end of the Vogelkop before moving beyond New Guinea. On the 30th July, without any previous naval and air bombardment, 6th U.S. Division landed near Cape Sansapor unopposed. With the landings at Sansapor the long campaign for the control of New Guinea was over. The remnants of five Japanese divisions had been cut off from playing any further effective part in the war. They were to be mopped up in the autumn by the Australians. MacArthur was ready to make his return to the Philippines by way of the Halmaheras. Two years previously he had left them as a fugitive; he was to return as a conqueror.

CHAPTER XXXI

THE PACIFIC

The Capture of the Marianas

(April – July 1944)

Maps 5 and 13 and Sketches 19 and 20

IN the Central Pacific the three months following the capture of the Marshall Islands were a period of preparation for the advance to the Marianas, which was set for mid-June.[1] While planning went on and the tremendous logistic problems involved were being solved, the Fast Carrier Force of the U.S. 5th Fleet based on Majuro, 7th U.S.A.A.F. at Kwajalein and the American and Australian South-West Pacific air forces in New Guinea kept the enemy's by-passed airfields neutralized, and maintained a constant drain on his air strength by strikes on his operational airfields. The Fast Carrier Force, using its great speed and flexibility, attacked targets as far apart as the Bonins and the Carolines. It made its first raid on the Marianas on the 23rd February, and struck Palau and other islands in the western Carolines on the last two days of March. A month later, on its way back from supporting the Hollandia landings,[2] it made a second raid on Truk. Towards the end of May, Marcus and Wake islands, which flanked the approach to the Marianas, were attacked by one of the fast carrier groups, and during the second week in June heavy bombers from the Marshalls and Admiralties pounded Truk which held the greatest threat to the American invasion force.

The Marianas formed a vital link in the almost unbroken chain of islands extending 1,500 miles southward from Tokyo. Of the fifteen islands which comprise the group, only the four largest, Saipan, Tinian, Rota and Guam, all in the southern end of the group, were worthwhile military targets.[3] Saipan, 1,200 miles from Tokyo, was closer to Japan than any other large mandated island. Together with its neighbouring island of Tinian, three miles to the south-west, it was the key of the Marianas defence. Two airfields and a seaplane base at Saipan, and two airfields on Tinian, served as refuelling

---

[1] See Map 13, page 438.
[2] See Chapter XXX.
[3] See Sketch 20, page 437.

points on the air ferry route between Japan and the south. Guam, in addition to two airfields and a third uncompleted, had many sites suitable for the construction of airfields capable of taking the largest bombers.

After the loss of the Marshalls the Japanese had hurried reinforcements to the Marianas, but many of these fell victim to American submarines on passage. Early in June the strength of the garrison in Saipan was about 32,000, in Tinian 9,000 and in Guam about 18,000. In Saipan, the two army formations were *43rd Division* and *47th Independent Mixed Brigade*, and the total army strength was about 25,000. Naval strength was about 7,000, which included the *55th Naval Guard Unit* and the *1st Yokosuka Special Naval Landing Force*. The forces in Saipan were under command of Vice-Admiral Nagumo, but operational control of the land forces in the field was in the hands of Lieut.-General Obata, who happened to be on a tour of inspection at Guam when the Americans landed. The direction of the battle devolved upon Lieut.-General Y. Saito, the commander of *43rd Division*. The air forces were commanded by Vice-Admiral K. Kakuta, the commander of the *1st Air Fleet*, who had his headquarters at Tinian. His fleet, comprising the *61st* and *62nd Air Flotillas*, had been reorganized in Japan in July 1943, with an authorized strength of 1,600 aircraft. It was to have had at least a year's training in the homeland, but the rapidity of the Allied advance and the loss of carrier-borne aircraft at Rabaul prompted *Imperial General Headquarters* to send the bulk of the *61st Air Flotilla* to the Marianas in February. It had barely arrived there when it was called upon to defend the island against the American fast carrier raid of the 23rd February, and in doing so lost 170 of its aircraft. At the end of May one-third to one-half of the naval land-based aircraft in the Central Pacific was sent south to take part in the Biak operations, where at least half the pilots fell victim to tropical disease and losses in action took a heavy toll. In early June, however, there was still a fair number of aircraft in the Marianas, but a great many of them were destroyed during the preliminary carrier strikes. On or about 13th June, when the attempt to reinforce Biak was cancelled, the survivors from the aircraft sent south were ordered north again, but few reached even the Palaus and none, as far as is known, got back to the Marianas.[1] Thus practically the whole of the specially trained air fleet, with which the Japanese had hoped to do so much damage to the American carriers in the 'A-Go' operation, had been destroyed almost before the crucial naval battle began.

The American plan for the invasion of the Marianas called for the seizure of Saipan, Tinian and Guam. D-day for Saipan was the 15th

---

[1] See Map 13, page 438.

June. The dates for the other two landings were to depend on progress at Saipan.

Saipan is just over fourteen miles in length and six and a half miles broad at its widest point, with an area of roughly seventy-two square miles. The northern half of the island is generally hilly but the south is comparatively flat. Almost in the centre of the island Mount Tapotchau rises to 1,500 feet. The Japanese had built an airfield at Aslito on the flat land in the south, and were building another in the extreme north. An airstrip was half completed just north of the town of Charan Kanoa on the west coast. The east coast is bounded by cliffs. The west coast is low-lying and offers few natural obstacles to movement inland, but a coral reef runs parallel to it from four to two miles offshore. The beaches selected for the landings were on the southern half of the west coast, two miles either side of Charan Kanoa. A wide front was chosen to enable troops to advance rapidly inland to the first high ground. The plan was for 2nd U.S. Marine Division to seize Mount Tapotchau, while 4th Marine Division advanced across the island to the east coast, capturing Aslito airfield on the way.

Admiral Spruance, commander of the 5th Fleet, was in command of all forces taking part in the operation. Under him, Rear-Admiral Turner once again commanded the expeditionary force, Vice-Admiral M. A. Mitscher the Fast Carrier Force, and Vice-Admiral J. H. Hoover the land-based air forces. Turner organized a northern attack force, under his own command, for the capture of Saipan and Tinian, and a southern attack force under Rear-Admiral R. L. Connolly for the capture of Guam. The former was assembled at Hawaii and on the west coast of the U.S.A. and carried 2nd and 4th Marine Divisions; the latter was assembled at Guadalcanal and carried 3rd Marine Division and 1st Provisional Marine Brigade. Each force had its own bombardment and air support groups. A floating reserve carried 27th U.S. Division. The operation was by far the largest and most ambitious yet undertaken in the Pacific, involving the use of over 500 warships and auxiliaries, carrying four and a half assault divisions. The logistic difficulties were immense. The Marianas were 3,500 miles from Hawaii, 2,400 from Guadalcanal and from 1,000 to 1,500 from the nearest American bases in the Marshalls. As the Marshalls were barren of anything except cocoanut palms, everything required by the expedition had to be brought from outside.

The great armada of ships was concentrated in the Marshalls by the 8th June and sailed for Saipan on the following day. The spearhead of the attack—the four fast carrier groups—were by then already on their way, having left Majuro on the 6th June. Soon after noon on the 11th, when 200 miles east of Guam, Admiral Mitscher flew off his first strike and during the next four days his squadrons reduced enemy air strength in the Marianas to practically nothing. On the 13th, the seven fast battleships under Vice-Admiral W. A. Lee were detached from the carriers to bombard the defences of Saipan and Tinian, a task which was taken over by the older battleships of the bombardment group, with considerably more success, on their arrival the following day.

On the 15th, after the beaches had been bombed and bombarded since dawn, 2nd and 4th Marine Divisions began going ashore at 8.40 a.m. The enemy, driven from the beaches by the heavy bombardment, had retreated to commanding positions inland and the assault forces were met with heavy artillery and mortar fire and casualties were severe. Nevertheless by nightfall 20,000 marines were ashore and a beachhead had been established on a five-mile front to a depth of about 1,500 yards. That night brought Spruance news that the Japanese fleet had passed through San Bernardino Strait in the Philippines and was heading for the Marianas.[1]

It will be recalled that Toyoda, satisfied that the Fast Carrier Force's attack on the Marianas was no mere raid but the prelude to invasion, had on the 13th June cancelled the plan to reinforce Biak and ordered 'A-Go' to begin. The *1st Mobile Fleet* under Vice-Admiral J. Ozawa was at Tawi Tawi, and a force under Vice-Admiral M. Ugaki at Batjan anchorage in the Halmaheras.[2] Both forces sailed that day for a rendezvous east of the Philippines, Ozawa's force being seen and reported by an American submarine as it left harbour. The *1st Mobile Fleet* passed through the centre of the Philippine Archipelago making for San Bernardino Strait. As it emerged into the Philippine Sea at 6.35 p.m. on the 15th, it was again sighted and reported by another American submarine. About an hour later an American submarine reported Ugaki's force east of Mindanao coming north. The two forces made rendezvous at 5.0 p.m. on the 16th, and at 1 p.m. on the 17th, having concentrated and refuelled, made to the north-eastward.

On receiving the two almost simultaneous reports on the 15th, Spruance, realizing that the Japanese fleet was seeking action, cancelled the landings on Guam which were to have taken place on the 18th and ordered 27th U.S. Division, the reserve, to be landed at Saipan and all transports to be withdrawn to the eastward and to be clear of the area by dark on the 17th. He detached seven cruisers and twenty-one destroyers from Turner's fire-support groups to augment the fast carriers' screen, and sent the remainder twenty-five miles to the westward to cover Saipan in case the Japanese fleet evaded him. The two fast carrier groups which he had sent on the previous day to raid the Bonin Islands, 600–700 miles to the north-west, were ordered

[1] See Sketch 19, page 434.
[2] See Map 5, page 97.

to cut short their attacks and rendezvous with the other two groups 180 miles due west of Tinian on the 18th. Spruance himself, in the cruiser *Indianapolis*, sailed on the 17th with the ships detached from the expeditionary force to join the carriers.[1]

That evening a submarine sighted part of Ozawa's fleet steering to the eastward but, as darkness prevented the whole fleet being seen, the report still left Spruance uncertain whether the Japanese fleet was concentrated or divided. If, as seemed probable from the various reports, it was in two parts, as it had been at Coral Sea and Midway, Ozawa might be planning to by-pass him and attack his amphibious forces. Spruance considered that his first duty was to ensure the capture of Saipan. He decided, therefore, to steam west during daylight and retire to the eastward at night so as to remain in a covering position until sighting of the enemy dictated otherwise. Air searches on the 18th found no sign of the enemy and at 8.30 p.m. he altered course to the eastward.

Japanese reconnaissance had meanwhile met with more success. On the afternoon of the 18th, carrier-borne aircraft sighted Mitscher's carrier groups 160 miles west of Saipan and Ozawa altered from north-east by east to south-south-west. Having found the enemy, he intended to remain outside the range of American air search and to take advantage of the greater range of his own aircraft and the presence of Japanese airfields in Guam and Rota, where they could refuel and re-arm, and the next morning to strike with all his strength at a range of about 300 miles. To ensure full co-operation from his land-based aircraft, but unaware that the greater part had already been destroyed, he broke wireless silence to give his movements.

That night he sent Vice-Admiral T. Kurita with four battleships, three light carriers, nine cruisers and nine destroyers to take station ahead, while he himself in the fleet carrier *Taiho* followed about 100 miles astern with one battleship, five fleet carriers and one light carrier, four cruisers and nineteen destroyers. He hoped, by assuming this disposition, that the American carrier attacks, if they came, would be concentrated on the van, leaving his main forces undetected. At 3.0 a.m. he turned back to a north-easterly course and increased speed to twenty knots.

Ozawa's wireless message was picked up by an American high-frequency direction finding station, and a fix obtained and relayed to Spruance at 10.0 p.m. It placed the Japanese fleet about 300 miles west-south-west of the spot where the American fleet had altered course an hour and a half before. Mitscher at once suggested that he should turn back to the westward, which would bring him into an

---

[1] The fast carrier task force then comprised 15 carriers, 7 battleships, 20 escort carriers and 67 destroyers.

ideal position for launching a strike at daylight on the 19th. Spruance, however, doubting the accuracy of the fix and still apprehensive of an outflanking movement by the enemy and the consequent danger to the whole success of the landings, decided to continue east until the morning. Within an hour or two of his making this crucial decision, a flying-boat on patrol obtained a radar contact which confirmed the wireless fix, but for reasons unexplained the message did not reach Spruance until some seven hours later. Had he received it at the time it was made, he might have changed his mind and been in a position to strike the first blow. But if he had done so he would not have been able to deploy the whole of his fighter strength to meet the Japanese attack. Perhaps it was as well that the signal reached him too late.

A night search to the westward to a distance of 325 miles failed to find the enemy, and a dawn search of a wider sector proved equally unproductive. But the presence of one or two enemy carrier-borne aircraft showed that the two fleets could not be far apart. At 6.30 a.m. Spruance turned back to the westward, but, having constantly to turn east into the wind to fly off his aircraft, he was after a few hours little further west than he had been at daylight. As the dawn search had proved negative, Spruance ordered Mitscher to carry out a neutralizing strike on the Guam airfields then seventy miles to the south-east where there were signs of air activity. Intermittent fighting ensued over the island and accounted for a considerable number of enemy aircraft, including a last-minute group of reinforcements. By 10 o'clock, when the American fighters were recalled, Admiral Kakuta's land-based air force, on which Ozawa was counting so much for help, had virtually ceased to exist.

Ozawa so far had succeeded in doing exactly what he had intended. Having sighted the American fleet, he had avoided being sighted himself and on the morning of the 19th was in a position to engage the enemy. At 8.30 a.m. he launched the first of four heavy strikes. American radar detected the aircraft when 150 miles distant, in time for flight decks to be cleared of bombers, and fighters to be waiting in formation to intercept. In each strike it was the same. Mitscher, with the whole of his fighter strength at his disposal and plenty of warning, had always more than enough aircraft to repel each raid. The half-trained Japanese pilots were no match for their experienced American counterparts and their fighter aircraft had not the performance of the American machines. During the raids, airfields on Guam and Rota were patrolled by fighters to prevent interference from that direction, and the bombers which had been flown off the carriers to clear the flight decks blasted the runways so that enemy carrier aircraft seeking safety ashore would crash.

The 19th June was a disastrous day for the Japanese. On the 15th,

125° 130° 135°

20°N

9 am 21st

11 am 21st

Japanese Fleet (OZAWA)
9 Carriers ⎫
5 Battleships ⎬
13 Cruisers ⎬
28 Destroyers ⎭

HIYO sunk
8·30pm
21st

1pm
20th

15°

D/F Fix
of enemy
fleet
8-20pm 18th

6am
18th

San Bernardino Str.

Main body of
Japanese Fleet (OZAWA)

reports
6·35pm 15th

Samar

1pm
17th
Fuelling

3a
19t

R/V
5pm
16th

Leyte Gulf

Surigao Str.

reports
7-45pm 15th

The Kon force (UGAKI)

Mindanao

PALAU
ISLANDS
Peleliu
Angaur

125° 130° 135°

5°

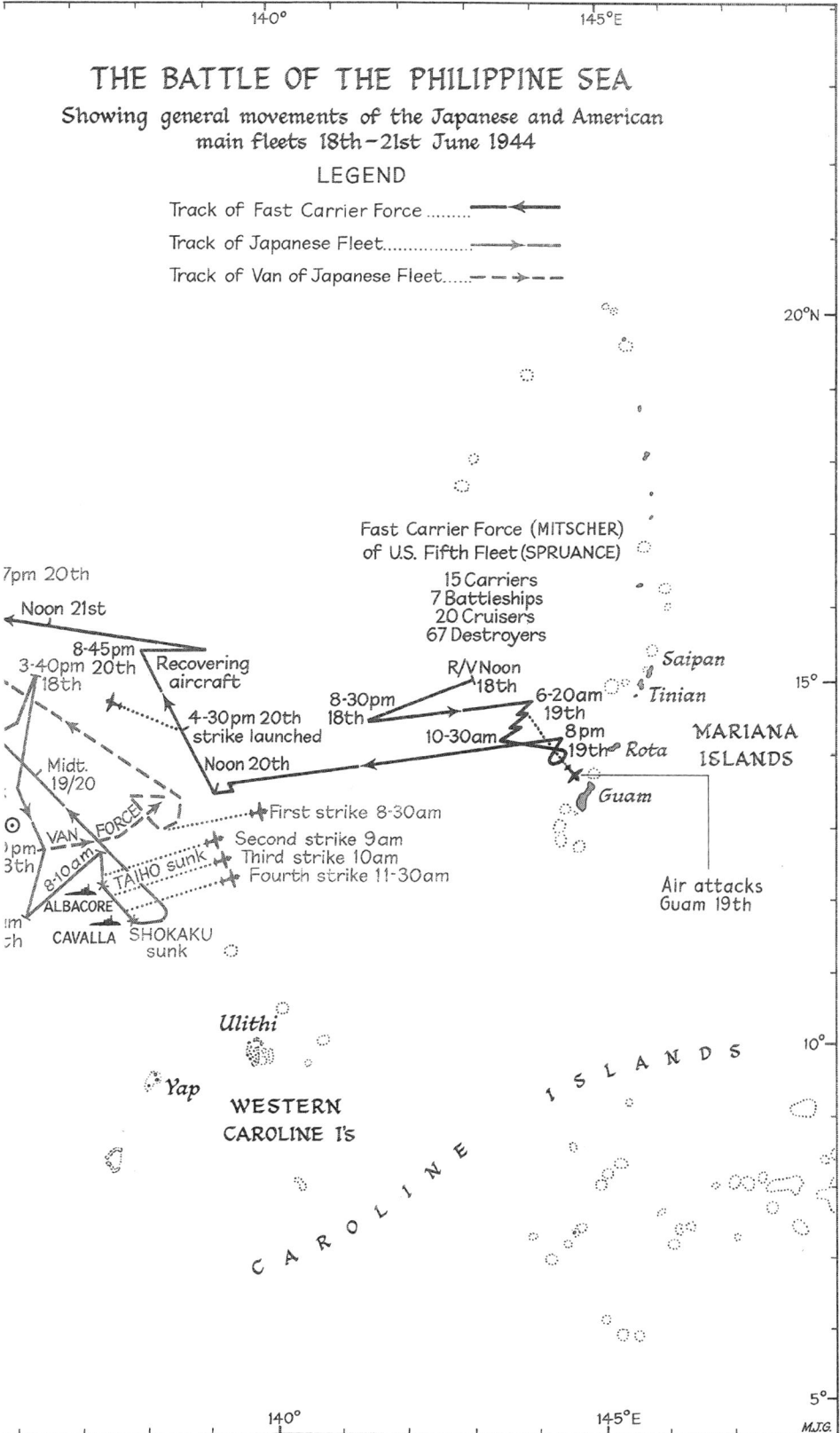

140°   145°E

THE BATTLE OF THE PHILIPPINE SEA
Showing general movements of the Japanese and American main fleets 18th–21st June 1944

LEGEND

Track of Fast Carrier Force .... ⟵━━━━
Track of Japanese Fleet................. ⟶
Track of Van of Japanese Fleet......– ⟶ – ⟶ –

20°N

Fast Carrier Force (MITSCHER)
of U.S. Fifth Fleet (SPRUANCE)

15 Carriers
7 Battleships
20 Cruisers
67 Destroyers

Saipan

15°

7pm 20th

Noon 21st

8-45pm
3-40pm 20th
18th

Recovering
aircraft

R/V Noon
18th

6-20am
19th

Tinian

8-30pm
18th

4-30pm 20th
strike launched

8pm
19th Rota

10-30am

MARIANA
ISLANDS

Noon 20th

Guam

Midt.
19/20

First strike 8-30am
Second strike 9am
Third strike 10am
Fourth strike 11-30am

Air attacks
Guam 19th

⊙
)pm
3th

VAN FORCE

8-10am

TAIHO sunk

ALBACORE

m
th

CAVALLA   SHOKAKU
                sunk

Ulithi

10°

Yap

WESTERN
CAROLINE I's

I S L A N D S

C A R O L I N E

5°

140°   145°E

M.J.G.

American submarines had been sent to patrol the area in the Philippine Sea through which it was believed that the Japanese fleet must pass. One of these, the submarine *Albacore*, torpedoed the newest fleet carrier, the 33,000-ton *Taiho*, Admiral Ozawa's flagship, just as she had flown off her aircraft for the second strike on the 19th. A petrol tank was punctured; the damage should not have been lethal, but petrol vapour was allowed to collect and at 3.30 p.m. she blew up and sank. Towards noon the submarine *Cavalla* sighted the *Shokaku*, engaged in flying on her aircraft, and put three torpedoes into her. The carrier remained afloat for some time, but shortly before the *Taiho* foundered she, too, blew up and sank. Of the 373 Japanese carrier aircraft which had taken part in the raids and searches, only 130 returned. In addition, about 50 land-based aircraft from Guam were lost, and others sank with the carriers or were lost by hazard. The total Japanese losses were about 315. By contrast, of the 300 American fighters engaged in the interceptions and in the fighting over Guam, only 29 were lost.

Ozawa did not know that two-thirds of his aircraft had been lost. The small number that returned gave no indication, for those missing might have found safety on Guam. Nor did he know that the damage to the American fleet caused by his air strikes had been almost negligible. During the afternoon he altered course to the northward, intending to refuel and resume his attacks either that day or the next, with the help of the now non-existent aircraft based on Guam.

Throughout most of the daylight hours of the 19th, Mitscher had had, perforce, to steam east into the wind to operate his aircraft. It was not until 8 p.m. on the 19th that, with all his aircraft recovered, he was able to turn to the westward in pursuit of the enemy. One of the carrier groups was left behind to keep the Mariana airfields covered. No search was sent out by Mitscher that night, and on the following day the first two searches proved negative. But at last, at 3.42 p.m. on the 20th, a report that the Japanese fleet had been sighted by an American carrier aircraft was received in the flagship. This placed the nearest enemy group about 300 miles away, heading west. Mitscher, realizing that this was the last opportunity he would have of hitting the enemy, at once informed Spruance that he intended to make an all-out strike, even though it would mean recovering his aircraft in the dark. Recovery, he calculated, would take four hours, during which time he would be steaming east into the wind and opening the distance between the two fleets at a high rate. It would be expensive, he knew, for none of his pilots was trained in night landings, but for so great a prize he was ready to accept losses. At 4.20 p.m. he turned into the wind and was back on his course again fifteen minutes later with 216 aircraft in the air.

At 6.40 p.m., just as the sun was setting, the American aircraft reached their target and began their attack. In the twenty-minute action the fleet carrier *Hiyo* was sunk, the fleet carriers *Zuikaku* (to which Ozawa had transferred his flag that afternoon) and *Junyo* were both hard hit but able to steam, the two light fleet carriers *Ryuho* and *Chiyoda*, the battleship *Haruna* and heavy cruiser *Maya* all received damage and two oilers were sunk and a third damaged.[1]

As Mitscher had foreseen, recovery of his aircraft was to prove costly. The night was very dark, some aircraft had been damaged, and all were short of fuel. The pilots, after their long flight and the excitement of the battle, were very tired. All attempts at concealment went by the board; the carriers switched on their navigation and deck landing lights. Each carrier threw up a vertical searchlight beam as a beacon to guide her aircraft home. But of 216 aircraft which had taken off, only 116 landed safely; 20 were lost in action and 80 on return. Happily, 160 airmen were rescued. Japanese losses during recovery were proportionately heavy; of the 100 aircraft, which was all Ozawa had left early that afternoon, less than half were recovered and only 35 of these were in a condition to fight again.

That evening Ozawa, on orders from Toyoda, abandoned all idea of renewing the action and made at best speed for Okinawa. Despite the damage to his fleet, all ships were able to maintain twenty knots. The Americans, of course, were not to know this and in the hope of overtaking cripples Spruance had already started a stern chase, but none was found and at 8.30 p.m. he abandoned the pursuit, turned east and steered to meet fleet oilers sent out from Saipan. Having refuelled, the carriers returned to Eniwetok, one of the groups making a strike on the Bonins for good measure on the way.

Meanwhile, ashore at Saipan, 27th Division, which had been landed during the night of the 16th/17th, passed through 4th Marine Division and advanced on Aslito airfield.[2] By the 19th the airfield and all the southern part of the island, except for a strongly-held pocket in the south-east corner, had been occupied. Leaving a part of 27th Division to clear the pocket, the three divisions began to move northward. Mount Tapotchau was captured on the 25th and on the 30th the Japanese began a general retirement to a final line of resistance across the top of the island. A salient was driven in this line by the capture of two hills on the 4th July and the Japanese were then trapped in the extreme north. Without food or water or amenities of any sort, even the Japanese could not hope to hold out for long. On the 6th July, Lieut.-General Saito and Vice-Admiral Nagumo committed suicide 'in order to encourage the troops in their final attack' and the following day the 3,000 surviving troops made a 'death or glory' charge in which almost all were killed. Two days later Turner

---

[1] For strength of the Japanese Navy on 31st August 1944 see Appendix 27.
[2] See Sketch 20.

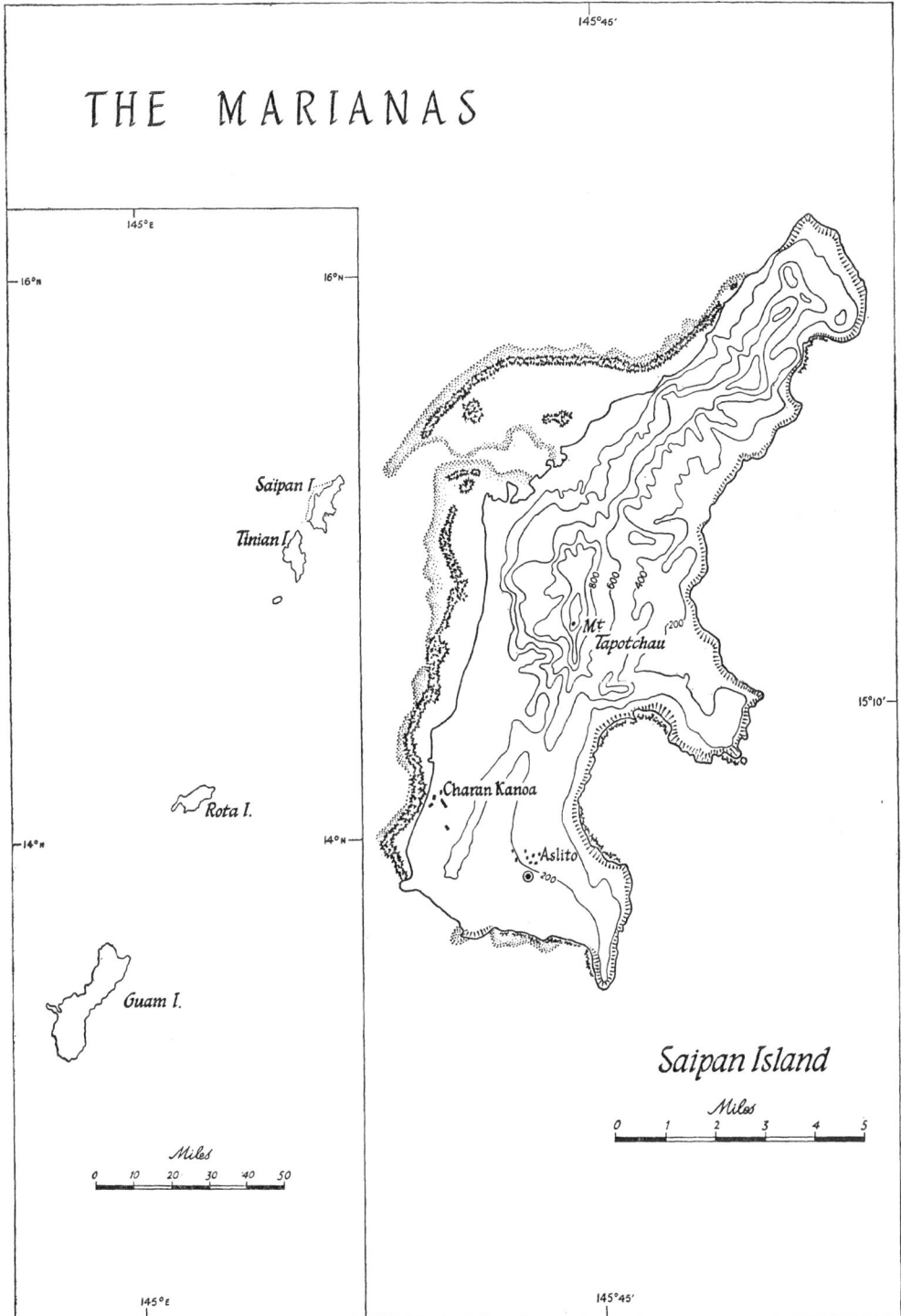

THE MARIANAS

145°45'

145°E

16°N

16°N

Saipan I.

Tinian I.

Rota I.

14°N

14°N

Guam I.

15°10'

800
600

*Mt
Tapotchau*

200

Charan Kanoa

Aslito

200

Saipan Island

Miles

0 1 2 3 4 5

Miles

0 10 20 30 40 50

145°E

145°45'

was able to announce that the island was secured. Efforts were made to induce civilians who had taken refuge in the caves at the north end of the island to give themselves up, but, poisoned by propaganda that the Americans would torture and kill them, hundreds flung themselves and their children from the cliffs on to the jagged rocks below rather than surrender. Japanse killed in the fighting numbered nearly 26,000; 1,800 prisoners were taken and 14,735 civilians interned. Until nearly the end of the war Japanese were still being rounded up.

The three American divisions lost nearly 3,500 officers and men killed and four times that number wounded. The cost was high but not too high for the results achieved. The air groups of the Japanese Navy had been destroyed. Hitherto Allied air bases (except for the tenuously held airfields in China) had been out of range of the Japanese homeland. The Americans now had an impregnable air base from which land-based bombers could strike at the very heart of Japan itself. The distance from Japan to the nearest submarine advanced base at Majuro had been halved.

When Spruance on the eve of the battle of the Philippine Sea had postponed the invasion of Guam, Conolly's Southern Attack Force had remained in a waiting area 300 miles to the east. At one time it was thought that it might be needed in Saipan, but at the end of the month it was sent back to Eniwetok where it was later joined by 77th U.S. Division from Hawaii, for the toughness of resistance at Saipan had convinced everyone that three divisions instead of two would be needed to take Guam.

Systematic bombardment began on the 8th July and for the next thirteen days at least one battleship and several cruisers poured their broadsides on to the island. It was the heaviest and most prolonged bombardment of the war in the Pacific and all coast defence emplacements in the open were destroyed. Nevertheless many of the Japanese main positions and communication installations, hidden in caves, were left untouched, and when the assault was made on the 21st July the invasion forces were met with fierce and determined resistance. The struggle was long and bitter; once again the Japanese had literally to be blasted out of the caves and defiles of the rugged island country and it was not until the 12th August that Guam was won.

The two marine divisions which had captured Saipan landed on Tinian on the 24th July, three days after the assault on Guam. The landings were made on the north-west shore, in part by ship and in part by shore-to-shore movement across the three-mile strait dividing the two islands. Progress was more rapid than on Guam and on the 1st August the island was declared secured, but hundreds of Japanese still held out in the coastal caves and for three months a complete marine regiment was engaged in mopping up. With the capture of Guam and Tinian the campaign in the Marianas was over.

Map 13

Attu

Kiska

ALEUTIAN ISLANDS

Dutch Harbour

URILE ISLANDS

THE PACIFIC

1943-44

Midway Is

HAWAIIAN ISLANDS

Marcus

Wake

Pearl Harbour

Hawaii

RIANAS Is

Eniwetok

MARSHALL Is

Kwajalein

Majuro

Truk Is

Ponape

Palmyra

ISLANDS

Nauru

GILBERT Is

Baker

Canton

IPELAGO

Rabaul

SOLOMON Is

ELLICE Is

CORAL
SEA

NEW
HEBRIDES

Samoa

FIJI Is

NEW
CALEDONIA

Noumea

FRIENDLY Is

CHAPTER XXXII

RETROSPECT

BY September 1943, when this volume begins, the period of stalemate and frustration described in the previous volume of this series was reaching its end. Most of the weaknesses arising from the rapid expansion of the Indian Army had been eradicated and there were sufficient well-trained divisions ready to make an offensive possible. A strong air force had been built up, the necessary airfields had been constructed in north-east India and the Allies were in sight of gaining air supremacy. The worst of the grave administrative problems had been solved, and the improvements in the lines of communication to Assam and eastern Bengal were such that there was a reasonable prospect of undertaking a major offensive in the coming dry season. Finally, to put new vigour into the war in South-East Asia, the Allies had decided to establish an inter-Allied command under a supreme commander.

For their part, the Japanese had decided in December 1942 to stand strictly on the defensive in Burma, but the growing threat of an Allied offensive from Assam and the realization, after the incursion of the Chindits early in 1943, that the jungles of northern Burma were not after all impenetrable had made them change their plans. Since the main base from which a powerful Allied land offensive could be launched into Burma was Imphal, they had decided to forestall such an offensive by occupying the Imphal plain, and defending it by holding the passes over the mountains giving access to it from the north and west. With both contestants preparing to take the offensive, the stage was set for the decisive battles of the war in Burma.

The setting-up of an inter-Allied command in South-East Asia under one man, with freedom from all commitments other than the energetic prosecution of the war, should have ensured complete unanimity of purpose. From the outset, however, there were difficulties which continued throughout the period covered by this volume. These difficulties sprang from two main sources. The first of these was the acquiescence by the Prime Minister and the Chiefs of Staff in the demand made by the American Chiefs of Staff, and in particular by General Marshall, that Stilwell should, in addition to his appointment as Deputy Supreme Allied Commander, retain not only the post of Chief of Staff to Generalissimo Chiang Kai-shek but also that of Commanding General of the American China–Burma–India Theatre. The second was the American unwillingness to give the Supreme Commander discretion to divert aircraft from the air ferry to China in an emergency.

The agreement which gave Mountbatten's deputy his multiple functions might have worked if some commander more co-operative than Stilwell had been appointed. Stilwell used his position as Commanding-General C.B.I. Theatre to take personal control of the operations on the Northern front;[1] this added to his many other tasks that of a corps commander and separated him from Supreme Head-quarters. Moreover, his refusal to serve under Giffard and the purely British 11th Army Group made Mountbatten's overall control of operations more difficult.[2] He also made use of the C.B.I. Headquarters, which was in fact an administrative headquarters, as a means of direct reference to the American Chiefs of Staff over matters of operational policy on which he found himself in disagreement with the Supreme Commander, with the result that comments were often passed to Washington on matters which were *sub judice* in S.E.A.C. The American Chiefs of Staff also made use of this head-quarters to pass instructions to Stilwell which affected S.E.A.C. without reference to the British Chiefs of Staff, who were, by agreement, in control of all operations in that theatre.[3] Mountbatten's authority was thus undermined. The most serious instance of this occurred when Stilwell was made the arbiter of whether Mount-batten's future plans warranted the allotment of the transport air-craft already offered by the Combined Chiefs of Staff.[4]

The American desire to retain control of Air Transport Command is understandable, since it provided the only means of sending material aid to China. Without this link with India the Generalissimo might well have been forced into making peace with Japan. But it struck at the very roots of Allied co-operation. Once they had agreed to the establishment of an Allied command, the Americans should have trusted the Supreme Commander to work loyally to an approved directive and should have placed all the resources in the theatre at his disposal. When the emergency in Arakan arose in February 1944, Mountbatten had to wait a week for authority to borrow aircraft from Air Transport Command,[5] and he was hampered in a similar way during the difficult days in March, April and May, when the outcome of the battle for Imphal depended on the quick movement of reinforcements and supplies to the Imphal plain. Twice in three months he was forced to make an arbitrary decision which he knew was likely to bring him into conflict with the American Chiefs of Staff.

When it was decided at the Sextant Conference in Cairo that the main effort against Japan should be made in the Pacific, and, owing to the needs of the European theatre, the proposed amphibious operation in the Bay of Bengal had to be postponed, it became necessary for Mountbatten to be given a directive to replace the one issued to him in October 1943.[1] A new directive was urgent because no firm plans for 1944 could be formulated without it, and, until a plan had been approved, the Americans would allot neither the necessary equipment nor the stores to carry it out. The six months' delay in the issue of this directive, which should never have been allowed to arise, was caused by differing views on strategy. Both the British and Americans were agreed on the need to increase the flow of supplies to China in order to keep her in the war and contain large enemy forces, and to use her territory as a base from which to bomb Japan and support the main drive in the Pacific. The American Chiefs of Staff believed that this could best be done by capturing upper Burma so that the Ledo Road and pipelines could be driven through to Kunming in order to supplement the existing air route. The British Chiefs of Staff, who were not convinced that the road and pipelines could be completed in time to be of use, considered that the continuance of the road beyond what was necessary for the defence of the air route would be a waste of resources. They therefore believed that the best course would be to limit operations in upper Burma to those necessary for the development, maintenance and protection of the air link. This divergence of opinion might have been quickly reconciled had not the Chiefs of Staff and the Prime Minister themselves been divided over the rôle the British forces should play in the war against Japan.[2]

To sum up: when Mountbatten assumed command in South-East Asia he found a well-organized base, lines of communication which, though not yet adequate, were rapidly improving, and sufficient well-trained formations to enable him to take the offensive. In spite of these advantages, which no previous commander in the eastern theatre had yet enjoyed, his task was beset with difficulties. The organization of S.E.A.C. did not permit him to exercise complete authority within his theatre, he was given a deputy whose allegiance was divided, and he was hampered in his handling of the decisive battles of Imphal and Kohima by not having full control over all the resources allotted to South-East Asia. Nevertheless the effect of the appointment of a Supreme Commander was far-reaching. From the outset Mountbatten insisted on being kept fully informed about

[1] See Chapter V.
[2] See Chapters XI and XVII.

everything that was taking place in the theatre. By personal visits and his fresh outlook he made his influence felt at all levels, and stimulated all he met with his own enthusiasm. Without in any way usurping the functions or weakening the authority of his Commanders-in-Chief, he succeeded in co-ordinating their actions to a degree never previously achieved in the Far East. He also made full use of the powers vested in him to ensure that commanders in the field were given the weapons and equipment, particularly transport aircraft, necessary to make victory certain.

When, in December 1943, major amphibious operations in the Bay of Bengal had to be abandoned owing to the lack of assault shipping, and Chiang Kai-shek refused to allow the Yunnan armies to co-operate in a major offensive to reoccupy northern Burma, the plans for 1943–44 had to be modified. The scope of the operations was then drastically reduced to an offensive by XV Corps in Arakan, accompanied possibly by a minor amphibious assault on Akyab, an advance by IV Corps on the Central front to gain control of the area immediately south of the Imphal–Tamu road west of the Chindwin with a view to exploitation across the river if a favourable opportunity arose, and an advance by the Chinese–American forces from Ledo down the Hukawng Valley towards Mogaung and Myitkyina. Special Force was to assist in these operations as best possible.[1]

When preparing the Army in India for the 1944 campaign, Auchinleck had intended to use the two existing L.R.P. brigades in the rôle for which they had been organized and trained. At the Quadrant Conference in August 1943, however, the Prime Minister and Chiefs of Staff, deeply impressed by Wingate's theories and claims which seemed to offer a chance of success in a theatre where there had hitherto been none, decided to increase the number of L.R.P. brigades from two to six. Auchinleck protested that their decision was uneconomical in that it entailed breaking up divisions required for the main campaign, and unsound in that L.R.P. formations alone could not achieve decisive results against organized forces of all arms. Their rôle, he said, was not to fight but to evade the enemy and to harass him by guerilla tactics, and their efforts would be largely wasted unless the main forces were strong enough to take advantage of the disorganization so caused. His arguments, which events were to prove to be sound, were rejected.[2] To increase Wingate's force from eight to twenty-three battalions, he was forced to break up his best-trained and only battle-experienced British

[1] See page 66.
[2] See Volume II, Chapter XXIV.

division, take a brigade from the newly-arrived African division, convert artillery units into infantry and, to make up the numbers, to deprive many other units of some of the best of their young British officers and men.[1] The result was that one-sixth of all the infantry at Mountbatten's disposal was locked up in L.R.P. formations suitable only for guerilla warfare.

With so great a proportion of the available infantry units incorporated in Special Force, it had to be employed in any operations planned for 1944. Thus, when the offensives in north Burma were changed from a concentric advance by IV Corps, Stilwell's forces and the Yunnan armies, assisted by guerilla action by the L.R.P. brigades, to an advance by Stilwell's forces on Myitkyina with limited advances by 14th Army, Special Force was given the specific task of helping Stilwell by cutting the enemy line of communications to the Mogaung–Myitkyina area. Wingate immediately protested that he was being asked to operate unsupported by a major operation and that his brigades might therefore be forced to disperse and withdraw as in the 1943 campaign.[2] His protest could not be upheld, for Special Force was to act in close co-operation with Stilwell's forces on the Northern front, which were of corps strength with strong armour, artillery and air support and were opposed by only one division. Moreover, the Japanese were to be kept closely engaged on both the Central and Arakan fronts. Wingate, who was still dissatisfied with the rôle allotted to Special Force, then proposed that he should be given extra infantry and artillery to protect the 'strongholds' which he intended to establish in areas inaccessible to enemy armour and heavy artillery, as pivots of manoeuvre for his columns, and as harbours to which they could withdraw to rest and refit after making raids on the enemy's communications. This conception was in the circumstances sound, and he was allotted the artillery for which he asked and such infantry units as could be spared without further disrupting the main forces.

Once his forces were committed to north Burma in March 1944, Wingate failed to carry out his own precepts.[3] That their abandonment was not forced on him by circumstances is evident from his appreciation and letters to the Supreme Commander. In these he proposed sending L.R.P. formations entirely unsupported to Pakokku and Meiktila, and suggested that more divisions should subsequently be broken up into L.R.P. groups which were then to be sent as far afield as Hanoi and Bangkok.[4] Slim had allotted Special Force an area of operations astride the enemy's line of

[1] See pages 36–37.
[2] See page 170.
[3] See Chapters I and XII.
[4] See pages 184–85 and Appendices 17 and 18.

communication south of Mogaung–Myitkyina which contained much ground suitable for guerilla operations. But Wingate, to whom the capture of Indaw airfield seems to have become an obsession, abandoned guerilla tactics and began to use his brigades as if they were equipped and organized as normal formations. He ordered his columns to attack strongly defended areas and established one of his main strongholds ('White City') in a place which was accessible to the enemy's armour and artillery.[1] But for the fact that the Japanese *15th Army* began its advance on Imphal shortly after Special Force went into north Burma, the Japanese reaction would have been much stronger and the exposed portions of Special Force might have suffered an early disaster.

The use of Special Force in a rôle for which it was unsuited resulted in the greater part of it being immobilized for a considerable time while its heavy casualties were evacuated.[2] When the force was placed under Stilwell's command it was again used in an unsuitable rôle and this, together with the accumulative effect of malaria, great physical exertion on short rations and exposure to torrential monsoon rains, caused so great a rate of wastage that it eventually became completely ineffective.

It has been shown in this volume that success or failure in 1944 turned on the outcome of the battles of Imphal and Kohima. Special Force could undoubtedly have had an effect on these battles had it been possible to use it to cut *15th Army*'s lines of communication east of the Chindwin. Its use in this way had been contemplated;[3] the idea was, however, abandoned when it was realized that the operation would be hazardous and that the Japanese were not using the lines of communication across the Zibyu Taungdan.[4] The operations of Special Force thus did little to aid 14th Army in defeating *15th Army*'s offensive. They had indeed the reverse effect, for the need to maintain five brigades of Special Force by air within Burma aggravated the shortage of aircraft which at times hampered 14th Army's conduct of the battles. Moreover, the fresh division which the Japanese brought into Burma, solely to assist in the defence of the Hukawng Valley and deal with the Chindits' interruption of their communications to Mogaung and Myitkyina, was not required in full for that purpose and provided welcome reinforcements for *15th Army*.[5]

The achievements of Special Force must therefore be gauged by the assistance it gave to the advance on the Northern front. The force completely cut the enemy's main line of communications to the

---

[1] See Chapter XIV.
[2] See Chapter XXIX.
[3] See page 247.
[4] See pages 280–81.
[5] See pages 287–88 and 345 fn.

Kamaing–Mogaung–Myitkyina area from mid-March till the end of May, and thus helped Stilwell to take Kamaing and virtually destroy the Japanese *18th Division*. The arrival of 77th (L.R.P.) Brigade at Mogaung caused the Japanese to abandon their counter-attack on Myitkyina airfield at a time when Stilwell's forces were in a state of disorganization. The capture of Mogaung, mainly brought about by the fine fighting of the brigade, opened a land line of communication to Myitkyina and made possible the reinforcement of the troops who, despite their superior numbers, had been unable to overcome the resistance of its small Japanese garrison for some two months.[1]

Without the aid of Special Force the advance on the Northern front would undoubtedly have been slower than it was and it seems probable that neither Mogaung nor Myitkyina would have been taken during the monsoon. After the failure of *15th Army's* offensive, both places would undoubtedly have fallen as soon as 14th Army began its general advance at the end of the monsoon. It is consequently open to doubt whether the gain of a few months in the establishment at Myitkyina of a staging base on the air ferry route to China, and the consequent not very significant increase in the goods carried by Air Transport Command in 1944, were worth the heavy loss of life and health in a force which contained some of the best material available to the Army in India.

The creation of the over-large Special Force appears to have been partly due to pressure from the Prime Minister, exasperated at the failure and delays in South-East Asia, and partly to the desire of the Chiefs of Staff to meet the wishes of the Americans for a quick advance into northern Burma.[2] It caught the public imagination at a time when encouraging news from South-East Asia was badly needed, but it failed to produce the results its creators hoped for. Special Force was a military misfit; as a guerilla force it was unnecessarily large and, as an air-transported force, it was too lightly armed and equipped either to capture strongly defended vital points or to hold them against attacks by forces of all arms until the arrival of the main forces.

Had the L.R.P. organization been kept at its original size, as recommended by Auchinleck, the well-trained and experienced 70th British Division would have been available to reinforce 14th Army and, with an extra division available, Slim's task of gaining a decisive victory at Imphal and Kohima would have been easier. Moreover, it must be remembered that, throughout the whole period it was operating in Burma, Special Force never contained more than about two-fifths of its own strength. This must be contrasted

[1] See Chapter XXIX.
[2] See Volume II, pages 398–404.

with the operations in Arakan of the small Japanese detachment (about half a battalion with some machine-guns) against the
Bawli–Maungdaw road, which contained superior numbers of
Allied troops at the height of a critical battle.[1] It is reasonable to
assume that the two original L.R.P. brigades could, by skilfully
handled guerilla operations, have seriously interfered with the
Japanese lines of communication to the Hukawng Valley and
Myitkyina and at the same time have contained as many of the
enemy as did the five brigades of Special Force, with far less loss and
with less than half the air effort. If to this is added the fact that
Special Force was so reduced by casualties and sickness, particularly
the latter, that its rehabilitation became virtually impossible, the
conclusion is inescapable that, in spite of the fortitude and gallantry
of the L.R.P. troops, the results achieved were not commensurate with
the resources diverted to it at the expense of 14th Army.

When the Japanese decided to launch an offensive on Imphal they
realized that they would be taking a considerable risk, but felt it would
have to be accepted, for the line of the Chindwin was indefensible
with the forces available to them in Burma.[2] Had they succeeded,
they would have forestalled an Allied general offensive, secured a
base within India, which would have had great propaganda value,
and established themselves in a strong defensive position from which
they could have seriously interfered with the Allied communications
through the Assam Valley to the forces on the Northern front, and
with the airlift to China. They might also have been able to foment,
with the aid of Bose's *Indian National Army*, a revolt in Bengal and
Bihar against British rule in India which might well have been on a
far greater scale than the riots of 1942.[3]

    Lieut.-General Ayabe, Chief of Staff of *Southern Army*, was sent
to Tokyo at the end of December 1943 to obtain sanction for the
proposed offensive. He succeeded in satisfying *Imperial General Headquarters* that *Burma Area Army* could deal successfully with any Allied
seaborne attack in the Bay of Bengal, that adequate air support
could be provided throughout the operation, that the supply position
was satisfactory, that the operational plan was sound and finally that
15th Army had sufficient strength to ensure success. He thus obtained
their assent to the operation.

    By early January 1944 *Burma Area Army* had formed a reasonably
accurate picture of the Allied dispositions, with the exception that
they had erroneously placed two or perhaps three Allied divisions in

---

[1] See Chapter X.
[2] See Chapter VI.
[3] See Volume II, pages 245–47 and 431–32.

the Shillong–Dimapur area in fairly close support of IV Corps at Imphal. Despite the assurances given by Ayabe in Tokyo, it must have been evident to *Burma Area Army* that the risks inherent in the operation were very considerable. They were woefully short of transport and administrative units and there could be no possibility of their maintaining air superiority over the battlefield. They would have to keep a considerable force to guard against an Allied amphibious attack from the Bay of Bengal, and unless *15th Army* achieved a very quick success it might have to meet up to five or possibly even six Allied divisions supported by armour on the Imphal plain. They came to the conclusion, however, that, if the Imphal plain could be captured by mid-April and time thus provided for consolidation before the monsoon broke, the risks would be offset by the fact that thereafter movement of motor transport would practically cease, and that both air support and air supply in the mountainous country near Kohima and west of Imphal would become exceedingly difficult. The monsoon, they thought, would deprive the Allies of the advantages of their air superiority and, with the Allied supply dumps and the large surplus rice crop of the Imphal plain in their possession, they themselves would be largely independent of a land line of communication, while IV Corps, bereft of its accumulated reserves, would find itself in difficulties. Finally they assumed, despite the fact that the Allies had a considerable number of transport aircraft available, that their forces once surrounded and cut off from ground supply could not hold out for long.

The *15th Army* offensive was to begin between the middle of February and early March so that the Imphal plain could be occupied by mid-April and, a short time before its launching, an attack was to be made in Arakan to contain the maximum British strength there. The relative timing of the two operations had to be such that the Allies could not bring up divisions from Arakan or elsewhere and deploy them for a counter-attack in Assam before the monsoon broke. This timing, however, went wrong. The threat of an Allied seaborne attack caused *Southern Army* to hold back *15th Division* (its sole reserve at that time) in Siam till mid-October, though *Imperial General Headquarters* had ordered it to be posted to *Burma Area Army* in June 1943. The damage inflicted on the railways in southern Burma by Allied air attacks made it necessary to move the division by road into Burma, and, despite all efforts to accelerate the move, its concentration was so delayed that the date on which *15th Army* was to cross the Chindwin had to be put back till the 15th March. In Arakan, Hanaya (*55th Division*) realized that a general offensive by XV Corps was so imminent that he had to act quickly, and therefore brought forward the date of his offensive to the 4th February, the earliest date sanctioned by the commander of *28th*

Army.[1] There was thus a much longer time lag between the two offensives than had been anticipated. This in itself would not have mattered had the Arakan offensive, as the Japanese had hoped, destroyed 7th Indian Division and thereby prevented any formations from being moved to the Central front. But although Hanaya obtained surprise he was unable to exploit it and the offensive failed to achieve the desired results. Thus, although Slim had to commit his immediately available reserves, he had sufficient time to resume the interrupted Arakan offensive and still move troops by air to the Central front in time to replace IV Corps' reserve before the Japanese reached the Imphal plain.

The *15th Army* offensive depended for its success on the speedy capture of the Imphal plain. This could be achieved only if surprise were obtained, and if IV Corps were caught dispersed and its forward formations defeated in detail, while columns moved through the mountains to the plain and cut the Imphal Road to its north. When Mutaguchi opened his offensive, he committed the whole of the forces at his disposal and kept no reserve to exploit surprise or counter the unexpected, and he so dispersed his formations that he was unable to attain superiority at the vital point. The withdrawal of IV Corps to fight on ground of its own choosing reduced the possibility of its being defeated in detail, but, as in Arakan, the Japanese succeeded in obtaining surprise and isolating 17th Indian Division in the Tiddim area. This threw 14th Army's plan for the conduct of the battle out of gear, since practically the whole of IV Corps' reserves had to be used to extricate the division, leaving Scoones without a mobile reserve. The reserve could be replaced only by withdrawing a division from Arakan, and it seemed that the Japanese might gain a rich reward for their bold offensive there. Owing, however, to the possession of air superiority, Slim was able to restore the situation quickly by flying 5th Division to the plain, while Mutaguchi, having allotted the whole of *31st Division* to the Kohima area, was unduly weak at Imphal and had no reserve to exploit the advantage he had gained. Thereafter he sent into battle piecemeal the few remaining units of his army and the reinforcements he received as they reached him and this, as could be expected, had a negligible effect.

The Japanese had accepted too lightly the considerable risks involved in taking the offensive with an overall inferiority on land and in the air, for they had failed to appreciate the greatly improved morale and fighting qualities of their opponents and the enormous potentialities of air transport. They hoped and expected to gain a quick success as in 1942 and 1943, and this led them to allow *15th Army* to take the offensive with insufficient air support and inadequate

---

[1] See page 136.

reserves and administrative arrangements. In this lay the seeds of disaster. It must be remembered, however, that from 1931 onwards the Japanese had consistently followed an aggressive policy involving considerable military risks and this had hitherto almost invariably brought them success.

Apart from the courage and excellent fighting qualities shown by the British and Indian troops under the most arduous conditions of terrain and weather, the success of the Allies in the decisive battles was due in the main to good generalship, to the fact that they had air superiority, and that they had built up a thoroughly efficient administrative organization. Thanks to Slim's foresight and the application of his new strategy,[1] as well as to the gallant defence set up by the small garrison of Sinzweya, partly composed of administrative troops, the Japanese Arakan offensive in February 1944, which, if successful, would have had a profound effect on the whole campaign, was thrown back. This victory not only deprived the Japanese of the strategic advantage they had hoped to gain for their main offensive, but had a tonic effect on the morale of 14th Army.

Slim's new strategy was also put into effect on the Central front where Scoones' plan was to withdraw on to the immensely strong pivot of manoeuvre represented by the Imphal plain, force the enemy to weaken himself by lengthening his communications, and then destroy him by launching a counter-offensive. The monsoon would, it was hoped, make the destruction complete. An essential part of this plan was that 17th Division on the Tiddim road had to make a clean break and withdraw to the plain south-west of Imphal without assistance. Meanwhile, 20th Division was to withdraw slowly from the Kabaw Valley to prepared positions on Shenam Pass while 23rd Division, with the bulk of the armour, formed a mobile reserve.

When he approved this plan on the 7th March, Slim, fearing that an unnecessary withdrawal would have a bad effect on morale, made the proviso that there was to be no retirement until the corps commander was quite certain that a major enemy offensive had begun. Though normally it would be unusual for an army commander to decide the moment at which the planned withdrawal of a corps should begin, Slim has since said that, in this instance, he should have given orders for the withdrawal of 17th Division to begin at the time he approved the plan.[2] Had he done so, the division would not have been cut off, IV Corps would not have been forced to commit its reserves to extricate it and the reinforcement crisis in the second half of March would not have arisen. But, whether Slim ordered the

---

[1] See pages 127–28.
[2] Slim, *Defeat into Victory* (Cassell, 1956) page 294.

withdrawal or left it to the corps commander, the crisis would not have occurred if IV Corps had acted on the first-hand information provided by a patrol on the 9th March that 2,000 Japanese with guns and mules had crossed the Manipur River south of Tiddim, and if 17th Division had not delayed its withdrawal for nearly twenty-four hours after it had been given permission to move. The crisis was caused by a number of individual errors made at different times, none of which in the normal course of events would have in itself been serious. It was overcome, as has been shown, by the Allies' ability to move reinforcements to Imphal by air and once this had been done the battle developed very much on the lines planned.

As is usual in battle, the commanders on both sides were faced by the unexpected. It is at such moments that generalship counts, and the commander who is able to distinguish between determination and obstinacy and between flexibility and vacillation will gain the victory or, if he is in a hopeless position, at least escape disaster. On the one hand, Giffard, as well as Slim and his corps and divisional commanders, showed, throughout the battle, determination without being in any way obstinate and, although some mistakes were made, their flexibility of mind and ability to improvise enabled them to meet and overcome each crisis as it arose. The quick decision taken in the early days of March to abandon IV Corps' advance and withdraw it to the plain was a good example of mental and operational flexibility. The move of 5th Indian Division by air from Arakan to Assam and the airlift (operation 'Stamina') to the Imphal plain again demonstrated flexibility and quick improvisation. Even with the advantage of air superiority these were no easy tasks, for with Special Force, most of Stilwell's forces and 81st (W.A.) Division on air supply, there was a serious shortage of aircraft. To overcome this, Mountbatten had on one occasion to divert aircraft from Air Transport Command at the expense of the air ferry to China without the authority to do so and on another to refuse to release aircraft ordered to the Middle East by the Chiefs of Staff. On the other hand, the Japanese, who had as usual planned their operations in meticulous detail right up to the desired conclusion, rarely showed flexibility. So intent were their commanders on following their plans to the letter that they did not adapt them to meet unexpected situations and failed to exploit such opportunities as presented themselves.

Both Giffard and Slim worked together admirably. Giffard left the conduct of the battle to Slim and remained in the background, a rock-like figure, ready to give help and support whenever needed. They were not perturbed by reverses and were confident throughout the battle that, provided sufficient transport aircraft were available, victory would be theirs. Their confidence was well justified. They realized, however, that the struggle would be long and dour, for they knew the mettle of their opponents and that they would have to drive the Japanese out of one position after another.

By the end of April, Mutaguchi knew that *31st Division* could not spare a regiment for the attack on Imphal and still retain its hold on Kohima, and that without that reinforcement *15th Division* had not the necessary punch to drive home the attack on Imphal from the north. By the middle of May, with every sign of a complete breakdown in the already inadequate administrative arrangements when the monsoon set in, and with Allied counter-attacks growing in strength on all fronts, it should have been quite plain to both Mutaguchi and Kawabe that defeat was inevitable unless large reinforcements of all arms could be sent to, and maintained on, the battlefield. Neither could be done. Nevertheless, even at that late hour, they could have averted disaster, for they had the advantage of interior lines and could have withdrawn to a shorter front where their forces could have been concentrated and properly maintained. But they refused to admit the failure of their plans and, perhaps in the belief that the fighting qualities of the Japanese soldier would somehow save the day for them, they made the fatal mistake that always leads to disaster—that of driving troops beyond the limit of human endurance. By the end of May, even the tough Japanese soldier could no longer stand up to the conditions under which he was called upon to fight. Disease and starvation took their inevitable toll and, early in June, the fierce resistance that the Allies had met, particularly around Kohima, suddenly collapsed.

The defeat of the Japanese *15th Army* was decisive. The initiative passed to the Allies and they never again lost it.

By August 1944, Japan was facing defeat. In the Pacific, American submarines, aided for the past twelve months by carrier-borne aircraft, had sunk half her merchant fleet. The losses were still mounting and the restriction of imports was having a serious effect on the production of essential war material. Her navy had lost most of its carrier-borne aircraft at the battle of the Philippine Sea and her fleet could now operate only in waters where it could be supported by what was left of its shore-based aircraft. The loss of New Guinea and the Marianas brought a threat to the Philippines and Formosa, key areas in the defence of the communications to the Southern Region. The homeland was now within range of heavy bombers from Saipan. At Imphal and Kohima, *15th Army* had been defeated and the way opened for the Allied return to Burma.

The disasters in Burma were too distant to have an immediate impact on the Japanese public, and the true facts about the naval battle of the Philippine Sea were for a time kept secret, but the fall of

Saipan was soon known to all. The significance of the loss of the Marianas was immediately realized. The blow fell at a singularly inappropriate time, for bad news had been coming in from all quarters. The first raid by long-range American bombers from bases in China had been made on Japan on the 15th June. With the loss of Saipan, heavier and more frequent raids on the homeland were to be expected and it was common knowledge that the fighting Services had thrown everything they had into the defence of the Pacific front and there was little left on which to rebuild. Normandy had been invaded, the Germans were being steadily driven back on the Russian front and the shadow of Soviet Russia loomed large. It was a gloomy and even hopeless prospect which faced Japan. On the 18th July General Tojo, Prime Minister since the beginning of the war, resigned with his entire Cabinet.

There were by this time many in Japan who realized that the war could no longer be won but, even after the fall of the Tojo Government, they dared not express their views in public. The war had therefore to continue with undiminished fury for another year until the immediate threat to her homeland at last forced the Japanese to surrender.

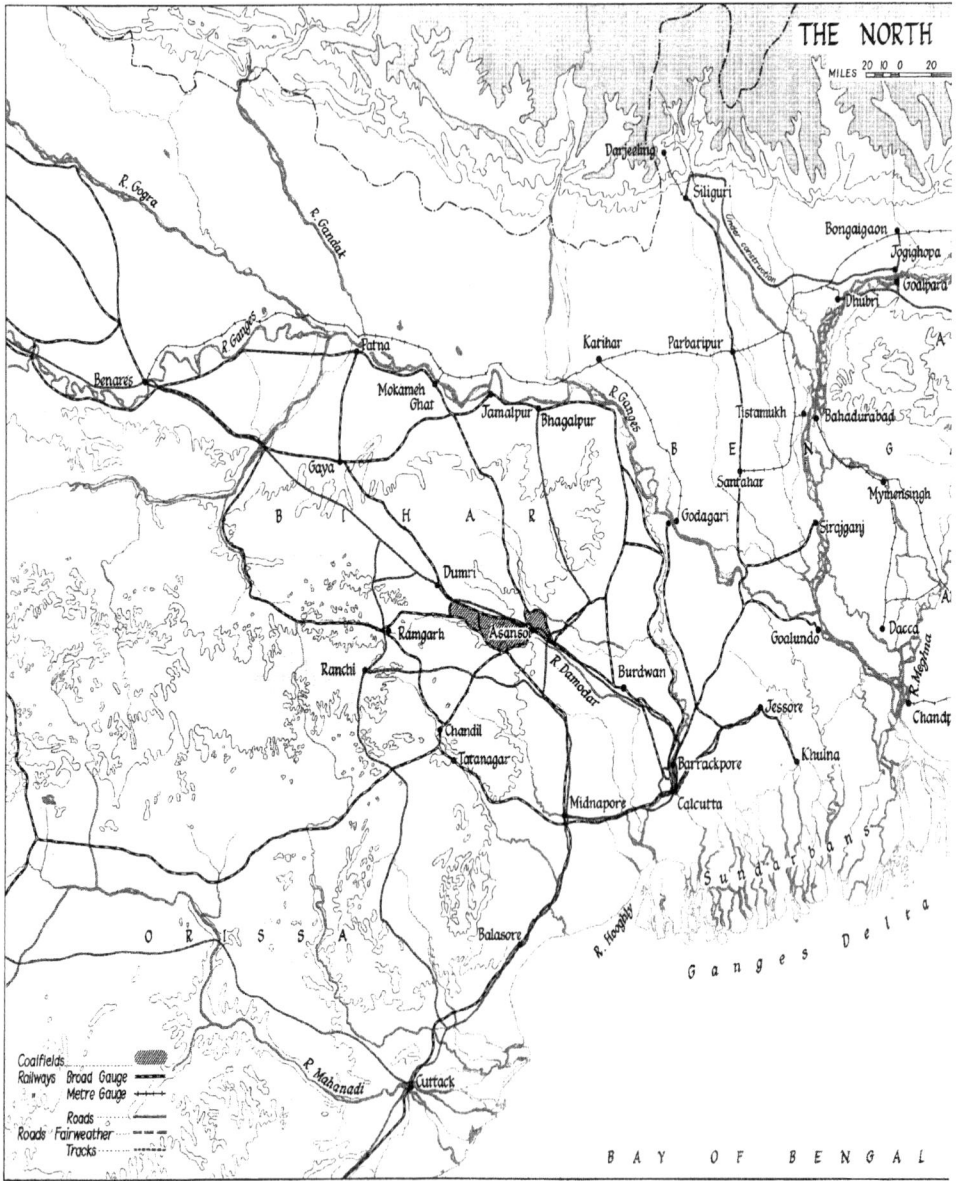

THE NORTH

MILES 20 10 0 20

Coalfields
Railways Broad Gauge
          Metre Gauge
Roads
Roads Fairweather
       Tracks

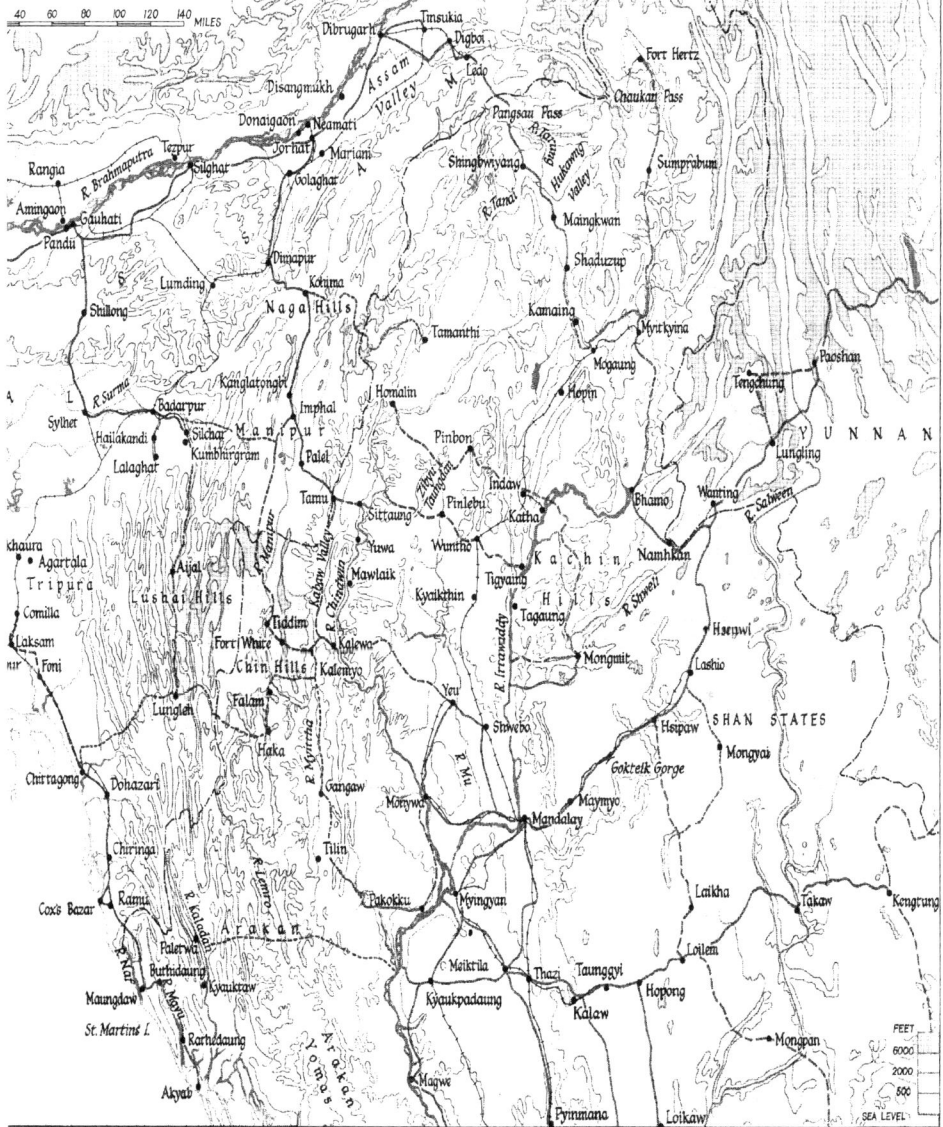

EAST FRONTIER 1943-44

APPENDIX 1

Directives to the Commander-in-Chief in India, and Supreme Commander, South-East Asia, on the Long-Term Development of the Assam Lines of Communication, 21st August 1943

Directive to the Commander-in-Chief, India, from the Chiefs of Staff

The attached directive to the Supreme Commander, S.E. Asia, has been approved by the Combined Chiefs of Staff. Pending the appointment of the Supreme Commander, you should, in consultation with the appropriate American authorities, initiate the steps necessary for the development of the N.E. India and Assam transportation systems.

Directive to the Supreme Commander, South-East Asia from the Combined Chiefs of Staff

The Combined Chiefs of Staff have approved in principle the development at the earliest possible moment, of a supply route into China from Burma, with the ultimate object of effecting delivery into China of 85,000 tons per month of general stores and up to 54,000 tons per month of petrol of which 18,000 tons of aviation spirit [will be delivered] by four inch pipeline via Fort Hertz and 36,000 tons by six inch pipeline following the road. It is envisaged that delivery of stores will be effected as to 20,000 tons monthly by air ferry, the balance passing over a rehabilitated 'Burma Road', and that all petrol will be delivered by pipelines. The prerequisite to the effective opening of the supply route to China is the development of the transportation system of N.E. India and Assam. This is a matter of urgency and you should in consultation with Commander-in-Chief India and the appropriate United States authorities in India plan your requirements and initiate the necessary action for the development of the transportation system to the following target figures:

1st November 1943	102,000 tons per month*
1st May 1944	140,000 tons per month
1st January 1945	170,000 tons per month
1st May 1945	200,000 tons per month
1st January 1946	220,000 tons per month

Note

* Plans for this have already been made by Commander-in-Chief India. U.S. Chiefs of Staff have agreed to the provision of the special personnel, equipment and stores necessary to construct and operate the route Ledo–

Kunming, and, having regard to agreed priorities, will make available such personnel, equipment and stores as may be found necessary to achieve the increase in transportation capacity, in conformity with your plan . . .

Annexure to directive to the Supreme Commander, South-East Asia

Breakdown of target tonnage

1. The ultimate target figure of 220,000 tons per month in the directive is made up as follows:

Estimated operational and administrative needs as at 1st November 1943	92,000 tons per month
Air lift as at 1st November 1943	10,000 tons per month
Estimated increase for operational forces	13,000 tons per month
Maintenance stores for the overland route	30,000 tons per month
Ultimate road delivery required into China	65,000 tons per month
Additional air lift	10,000 tons per month

Petrol

2. The intention is to deliver by two six inch pipelines from Calcutta carrying 72,000 tons per month. The United States authorities have undertaken to provide the pipelines and necessary tankage by the following dates: 1st July 1944, 1st pipeline to Ledo. 1st July 1945, 2nd pipeline to Ledo. The capacity of these pipelines is estimated to be 72,000 tons per month. The total ultimate requirements of petrol for all purposes is 96,000 tons per month of which 9,000 tons will be produced and consumed locally. There will, therefore, remain 15,000 tons per month for transport with other stores. The figure of 220,000 tons per month makes allowance for this lift.

River craft

3. The United States authorities have under provision a number of barges and towboats, and are prepared to supply the necessary supervisory personnel with a view to commencing operations by 1st April 1944 with a fleet estimated to be capable of delivering at Dibrugarh 15,000 tons P.O.L. per month and 15,000 tons general stores per month.

APPENDIX 2

Air Supply to China

Monthly Tonnage carried by the Airlift,
January 1943 – July 1944

Month	Net tonnage carried (short tons)	Remarks
1943. January	1,923	
February	3,276	At this period it was planned to increase the airlift to 4,000 tons a month.
March	3,000	
April	2,515	
May	3,147	The target was altered to 7,000 tons by July rising to 10,000 tons by September.
June	3,100	
July	4,338	
August	5,674	
September	6,719	
October	8,632	
November	7,300	
December	13,450	
1944. January	14,472	
February	14,431	
March	10,954	Tonnage carried affected by the diversion of aircraft for operational duties.
April	13,257	
May	13,686	
June	18,235	
July	25,454	

Notes:

1. These figures include tonnage carried by Air Transport Command, Troop Carrier Command and the Chinese National Aviation Corporation.
2. A short ton equals 2,000 lb.

APPENDIX 3

Directive by the Prime Minister and Minister of Defence to Admiral Mountbatten, Supreme Commander, South-East Asia Command

1. Your attention is drawn to the decisions of the Combined Chiefs of Staff at 'Quadrant' . . . which were approved by the President of the United States and by me on behalf of the War Cabinet. Pursuant to these decisions and acting in harmony with them, you will take up your appointment as Supreme Allied Commander, South East Asia, as provided for in my Memorandum . . . and, within the limits of your Command as defined therein, you will conduct all operations against Japan. In accordance with the provisions of paragraph 13 of the Memorandum and of paragraph 58 of the 'Quadrant' decisions, you will be responsible to the British Chiefs of Staff, who are authorized by the Combined Chiefs of Staff to exercise jurisdiction over all matters pertaining to operations and will be the channel through which all Directives will be issued to you.

2. Your prime duty is to engage the Japanese as closely and continuously as possible in order by attrition to consume and wear down the enemy's forces, especially his Air Forces, thus making our superiority tell and forcing the enemy to divert his forces from the Pacific theatre; and secondly, but of equal consequence, to maintain and broaden our contacts with China, both by the Air route and by establishing direct contact through Northern Burma *inter alia* by suitably organized, air-supplied ground forces of the greatest possible strength.

3. You will utilize to the full the advantages of the sea power and air power, which will be at your disposal, by seizing some point or points which (*a*) induce a powerful reaction from the enemy, and (*b*) give several options for a further stroke on your part in the light of the enemy's aforesaid reaction. For this purpose, in making your proposals for amphibious operations in 1944, you will select the point of attack which seems best calculated to yield the above conditions, and will execute the operation approved. You will also prepare plans for the second phase of your campaign in 1944, contingent upon the reaction extorted from the enemy.

4. At least four weeks before your first major amphibious operation you will be furnished by His Majesty's Government with a battlefleet to be based on Ceylon sufficient in strength to fight a general engagement with any force which, in the opinion of His Majesty's Government, it is reasonable to suppose the Japanese could afford to detach from the Pacific. The Eastern Fleet will for this purpose be equipped with at least ten escort carriers (C.V.Es.) as well as with such armoured fleet carriers as may be available.

5. You will proceed to form, as resources come to hand, a Combined Striking Force or Circus which will be available as the foundation of whatever amphibious descent is eventually chosen. This force should consist of the aircraft-carriers to provide air support, secondly of an Inshore Squadron for coastal bombardment, and further of the necessary transports, assault ships and landing craft of various classes. You will arrange, in conjunction with the Commander-in-Chief, India, for the preparation and training of the forces required by you for the special task of making opposed landings from the sea and of thus establishing bridgeheads at which reinforcements not trained for the above special work can be safely and continuously landed. You will specify such requirements for making artificial harbours, airfields, and floating runways as you may think necessary and as are within the bounds of possibility at the dates involved.

6. You will at the earliest moment report your plans, dates and requirements, bearing in mind the advantages of speed.

W. S. C.

10 Downing Street, S.W.1.
21st October, 1943.

APPENDIX 4

British Oil Pipelines Completed, under Construction and Projected, November 1943

	Size	Length in Miles	Capacity in Tons a Month	Type of Spirit	Remarks
A. River System					
1. Dhubri Station to Dhubri Ghat .	4-inch	2	10,000	Aviation	Completed
2. Tezpur–Misamari Station .	4-inch	34	10,000	Aviation	Nearing completion
3. Neamati–Jorhat . . .	4-inch	16	10,000	Aviation	Nearing completion
4. Dibrugarh–Tinsukia–Sookerating .	4-inch	55	10,000	Aviation	Nearing completion
5. Tinsukia–Dinjan . . .	4-inch	20	5,000	Aviation	Nearing completion
6. Tinsukia–Dibrugarh . .	4-inch	45	5,000	Kerosene	Nearing completion
7. Dhubri Ghat to Dhubri Station .	4-inch	2	5,000	Kerosene	Completed
B. Chittagong–Kalewa System					
8. Chittagong–Chandranathpur .	4-inch	290	15,000	Aviation and Motor	Material being collected; due for completion January 1945
9. Chandranathpur–Dimapur .	4-inch	160	13,000	Aviation and Motor	Under construction; due for completion in February 1944
10. Dimapur–Palel . . .	4-inch	178	10,000	Aviation and Motor	Projected
11. Palel–Kalewa . . .	4-inch	140	10,000	Aviation and Motor	Projected

APPENDIX 5

Phased Development of the Assam
Lines of Communication

First Stage

The following works had to be completed to give by October 1944 an estimated capacity for military stores of 4,400 tons a day (132,000 tons a month) after allowing for constructional materials:

 (a) Doubling the Abdulpur–Santahar railway (broad gauge).
 (b) Doubling the Parbatipur-Golakganj railway (metre gauge).
 (c) Parbatipur store transhipment yard.
 (d) Doubling the Lumding–Dimapur railway (metre gauge).
 (e) Provision of a railhead for the Chabua area.
 (f) Provision of additional metre gauge locomotives and rolling stock.
 (g) Completion of pipeline schemes. (These included the pipelines from Chandranathpur to Dimapur, Dhubri Station to Dhubri Ghat and various pipelines connecting railheads to airfields, but did not include the two pipelines from Calcutta and Chittagong respectively to Dibrugarh.)
 (h) Completion of 22 towing craft and 88 river flats (all new construction).
 (i) Completion of the Assam Access Road from Siliguri to Bongaigaon.
 (j) Provision of sufficient vehicles for a lift of 250 tons a day from Siliguri forward.
 (k) Conversion of the 2 ft. 6 in. railway line from Jorhat to Mariani to metre gauge.

Second Stage

The following works had to be completed to give by January 1946 an estimated capacity for military stores of 7,300 tons a day (220,000 tons a month):

 (a) Doubling the Santahar–Parbatipur railway (broad gauge).
 (b) Doubling the Golakganj–Amingaon railway (metre gauge), the Pandu–Lumding railway (metre gauge) and the Dimapur–Tinsukia railway (metre gauge).
 (c) A 4,000-ft. bridge over the Brahmaputra from Amingaon–Pandu.
 (d) A base layout at Parbatipur where there was a break of gauge, to act as a reservoir to maintain an even flow of traffic over the metre gauge railway forward to Dimapur.
 (e) A regulating station at or near Mariani.
 (f) Terminal developments as required.

459

(g) Development of the line between Chandranathpur and Lumding (the Hill Section) to carry up to 500 tons a day of traffic imported through the port of Chittagong.

Note:

No allowance was made in preparing these programmes for additional lift on the Brahmaputra since it was thought that the river craft proposed by the Americans (see Appendix 1) would prove unsuitable.

APPENDIX 6

Reorganization Proposed for Various Formations of the Army in India, June – November 1943

1. *Changes in the Indian light division*

(a) The two light brigade reconnaissance battalions, each consisting of headquarters and two mounted infantry companies and two jeep-borne companies, were to be replaced by one light divisional reconnaissance battalion, consisting of a headquarters and three mounted infantry pony companies. The new unit was to have no mechanical vehicles.[1]

(b) The British infantry battalions in the light Indian division were to remain as heretofore, with the exception that the anti-aircraft and gun platoon was to be abolished.

(c) The Indian infantry battalions in the light Indian division were to be increased by 163 Indian other ranks to enable a fourth platoon to be added to each company, making the total establishment of an Indian infantry battalion 993 all ranks. The anti-aircraft and gun platoon was to be abolished, and unit transport increased from 10 to 31 jeeps.[1]

(d) In the divisional support battalion, the gun platoon was to be replaced by a medium machine-gun platoon.

(e) A divisional artillery headquarters was to be added to the division.

2. *Changes in the divisional artillery*

(a) A mortar battery, consisting of sixteen 3-inch mortars organized in two troops of eight mortars, was to be added to each light mountain regiment in a light division.[1]

(b) In both A. & M.T. divisions and in M.T. divisions, one British field regiment was to be reorganized to consist of one battery of sixteen 3-inch mortars and two batteries each of eight 3.7-inch howitzers. These regiments were to be entirely mechanized and provided with four-wheel drive vehicles.

(c) The 3.7-inch howitzers were to be modified by the fitting of wheels with pneumatic tyres to allow of towing by motor transport.

(d) In A. & M.T. divisions, composite anti-aircraft cum anti-tank regiments were to be included instead of there being separate light anti-aircraft regiments and anti-tank regiments. These composite regiments were to have an organization similar to the composite regiments already allotted to light divisions. They were to be armed, however, with two batteries each of twelve 6-pounders and two batteries each of eighteen 20 mm. anti-aircraft guns.

3. *Changes in the Royal Indian Army Service Corps*

Consequent on the switch over to 15 cwt. trucks, the three 3-ton general purpose transport companies previously allotted to both M.T. and A. &

---

[1] These changes were not carried out.

M.T. divisions were to be changed to one 3-ton general purpose company and two 15-cwt. truck four-wheel drive companies, each of 150 vehicles.

4. *Changes in the Indian infantry battalions in M.T. and A. & M.T. divisions*

(a) These battalions were to be reorganized to consist of a battalion headquarters, a headquarters company containing signals, mortar, carrier and pioneer platoons, an administrative company containing medical and transport platoons, and four rifle companies, each of three platoons each of three sections of one N.C.O. and ten men.

(b) The establishment of these battalions was to include considerably fewer motor vehicles and none of less mobility than the four-wheel drive 15-cwt. truck. These were to be allotted for essential fighting equipment only.

5. *Changes in the British infantry battalions in M.T. and A. & M.T. divisions*

British infantry battalions allotted to M.T. and A. & M.T. divisions were to be reorganized on the same lines as Indian infantry battalions, vide paragraph 4 above.

6. *Changes in motor battalions*

All motor battalions were to be reorganized to consist of a battalion headquarters, a headquarters company, a support company of eight 6-pounder anti-tank guns and eight medium machine-guns and three companies each of three platoons and one 3-inch mortar section.

7. *Changes in the Indian machine-gun battalions*

These battalions were to be reorganized to consist of a battalion headquarters, an administrative platoon, three support companies, each of two 4.2-inch mortar platoons each of four mortars, and two medium machine-gun platoons, each of four machine-guns. The approximate strength of the battalion would then be fourteen officers and seven hundred other ranks, equipped with twenty-four mortars and twenty-four medium machine-guns.

APPENDIX 7

The Japanese Air Force in Burma, November 1943

	Type	Approximate number of operational aircraft
Headquarters 5th Air Division		
33rd Air Regiment (Fighter)	Army 1 Mark II	20
204th Air Regiment (Fighter)	Army 1 Mark II	20
4th Air Brigade		
50th Air Regiment (Fighter)	Army 1 Mark II	27
8th Air Regiment (Light Bomber)	Army 99	27
34th Air Regiment (Light Bomber)	Army 99	20
7th Air Brigade		
64th Air Regiment (Fighter)	Army 1 Mark II	30
12th Air Regiment (Heavy Bomber)	Army 97 Mark III	15
98th Air Regiment (Heavy Bomber)	Army 97 Mark III	15
81st Air Regiment (Reconnaissance)	Army 100 Mark II	15
21st Air Regiment (Fighter)	Army 2	12
	Total	201

Note:

For the attack on Calcutta on the 5th December 1943, 5th Air Division was reinforced by 9 Navy I bombers and 30 Zero fighters from 28th Air Flotilla.

APPENDIX 8

Chain of Command South-East Asia, 14th December, 1943

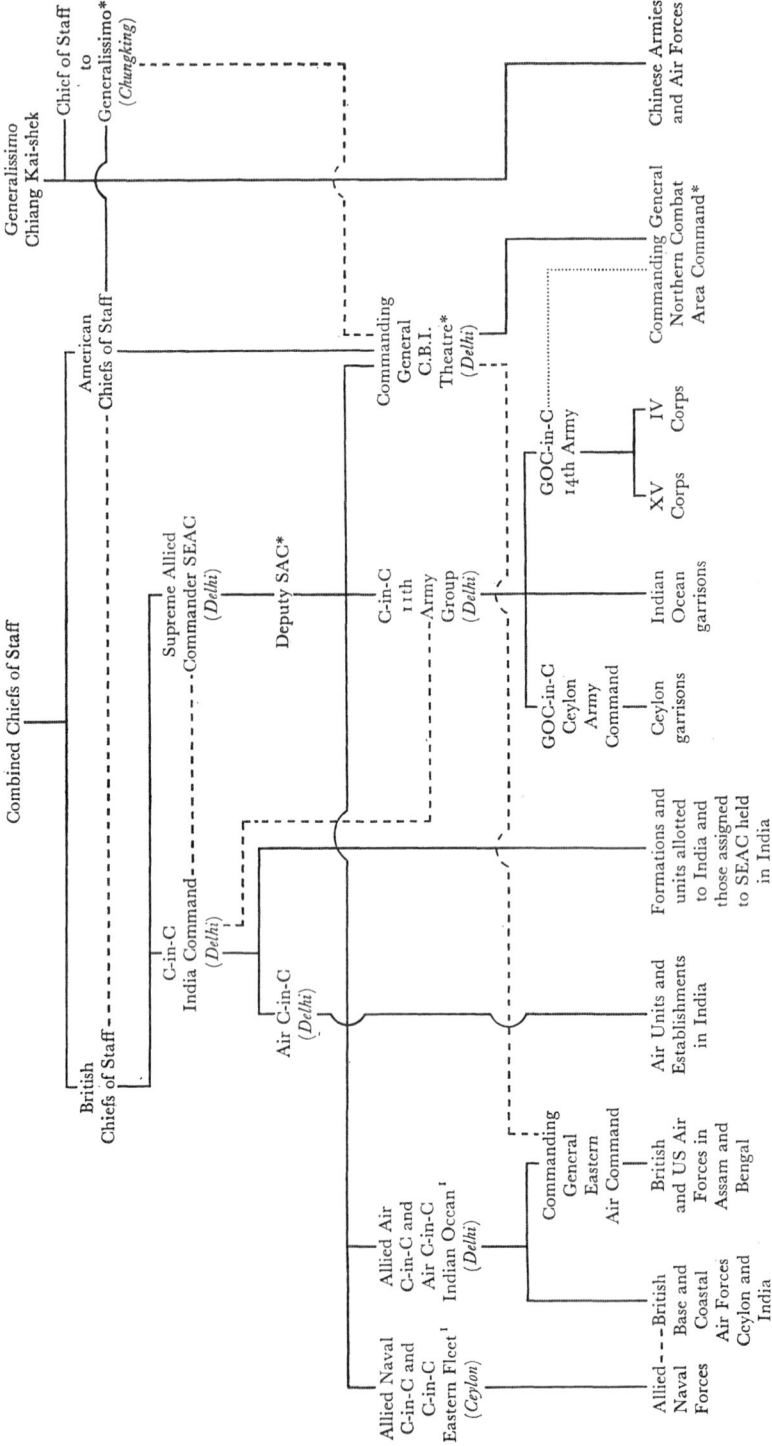

Generalissimo Chiang Kai-shek

Chief of Staff to Generalissimo* (*Chungking*)

Combined Chiefs of Staff

British Chiefs of Staff

American Chiefs of Staff

Supreme Allied Commander SEAC (*Delhi*)

Deputy SAC*

C-in-C India Command (*Delhi*)

Commanding General C.B.I. Theatre* (*Delhi*)

C-in-C 11th Army Group (*Delhi*)

Commanding General Northern Combat Area Command*

Chinese Armies and Air Forces

Air C-in-C (*Delhi*)

GOC-in-C Ceylon Army Command

GOC-in-C 14th Army

Indian Ocean garrisons

Ceylon garrisons

XV Corps

IV Corps

Formations and units allotted to India and those assigned to SEAC held in India

Air Units and Establishments in India

Allied Air C-in-C and Air C-in-C Indian Ocean[1] (*Delhi*)

Allied Naval C-in-C and C-in-C Eastern Fleet[1] (*Ceylon*)

Commanding General Eastern Air Command

British Base and Coastal Air Forces Ceylon and India

British and US Air Forces in Assam and Bengal

Allied Naval Forces

Notes: (a) All appointments marked * were held by Lieut.-General J. W. Stilwell (US Army).
(b) The officers holding the appointments marked[1] were directly responsible to the **Admiralty** and **Air Ministry** respectively for operations connected with the security of the sea communications in the Indian Ocean.

Legend: ——— Direct command
- - - - - Liaison
.... Temporary operational control

APPENDIX 9

Ships of the Eastern Fleet in the Indian Ocean,
16th November 1943

Battleship	*Ramillies*	Capt. G. B. Middleton
Escort Carrier	*Battler*	Capt. F. M. R. Stephenson
Cruisers:		
4th Cruiser Squadron	*Newcastle*	Capt. P. B. R. W. William-Powlett
	Suffolk	Capt. A. S. Russel
	Frobisher	Capt. J. W. Mudford
	Kenya	Capt. C. L. Robertson
	Ceylon	Capt. G. B. Amery-Parkes
5th Cruiser Squadron	*Danae*	Capt. J. R. S. Haines
	Emerald	Capt. F. W. Wylie
Armed Merchant	*Alaunia*	Capt. (R.N.R.) R.H.C. Crawford
Cruisers	*Chitral*	Acting-Capt. G. W. Hoare-Smith
Destroyers		Eleven (parts of the 4th, 7th and 11th Destroyer Flotillas)
Escort Vessels		Thirteen (including one Free French)
Submarines		Six (five of 4th Submarine Flotilla and one Dutch)

APPENDIX 10

Army Formations Allotted or Assigned to S.E.A.C., 16th November 1943

1. ALLOTTED

BRITISH

11th Army Group (Delhi)
14th Army (Calcutta)

XV Corps (near Cox's Bazar)
    5th Indian Division
    7th Indian Division
    81st West African Division
    (less one brigade)
IV Corps (Imphal)
    17th Indian Division
    20th Indian Division
    23rd Indian Division
Army Reserve
    26th Indian Division
    254th Indian Tank Brigade
Ceylon Army Command (Colombo)
    11th East African Division
    99th Indian Infantry Brigade
    Local forces

Indian Ocean garrisons

AMERICAN

Northern Combat Area Command
    22nd Chinese Division
    30th Chinese Division
    38th Chinese Division

2. ASSIGNED[1]

XXXIII Corps

2nd British Division ⎫ undergoing
36th Indian Division[2] ⎬ training in amphibious operations

5507th Composite Unit (Provisional)[3] attached to Special Force for training

19th Indian Division ⎫ attached to
25th Indian Division ⎬ XXXIII Corps for
50th Indian Tank Brigade ⎭ training and administration

50th Indian Parachute Brigade

---

[1] The 44th Indian Armoured Division remained under command of G.H.Q., India.
[2] This division had only two brigades (29th and 72nd).
[3] 'Merrill's Marauders'.

Special Force (3rd Indian Division)
    77th and 111th Indian (L.R.P.) Brigades
    14th, 16th and 23rd British (L.R.P.) Brigades[1]
    3rd West African (L.R.P.) Brigade

3 Special Service Brigade
    5 Commando
    44 Royal Marine Commando

---

[1] Transferred from 70th British Division.

APPENDIX 11

Air Command, South-East Asia on Integration, 12th December 1943

HEADQUARTERS, AIR COMMAND S.E.A.: New Delhi

(*Air Chief Marshal Sir Richard Peirse*)

I. EASTERN AIR COMMAND: New Delhi (for Calcutta)

(*Major-General G. E. Stratemeyer, U.S.A.A.F.*)

(a) 3RD TACTICAL AIR FORCE: Comilla (*Air Marshal Sir John Baldwin*)[1]
221 Group R.A.F.: Imphal (*Air Commodore H. V. Rowley*)

5 (F.) Squadron	Hurricane
155 (F.) Squadron	Mohawk
211 (L.R.F.) Squadron	Beaufighter
28 (F.R.) Squadron	Hurricane
34 (F.B.) Squadron	Hurricane
42 (F.B.) Squadron	Hurricane
45 (L.B.) Squadron	Vengeance
84 (L.B.) Squadron	Vengeance
110 (L.B.) Squadron	Vengeance

224 Group R.A.F.: Chittagong (*Air Commodore A. Gray*)

79 (F.) Squadron	Hurricane
136 (F.) Squadron	Spitfire
258 (F.) Squadron	Hurricane
261 (F.) Squadron	Hurricane
607 (F.) Squadron	Spitfire
615 (F.) Squadron	Spitfire
27 (N.F.) Squadron	Beaufighter
177 (N.F.) Squadron	Beaufighter
6 (F.R.) Squadron (R.I.A.F.)	Hurricane
8 (L.B.) Squadron (R.I.A.F.)	Vengeance
82 (L.B.) Squadron	Vengeance
11 (F.B.) Squadron	Hurricane
20 (F.B.) Squadron	Hurricane
60 (F.B.) Squadron	Hurricane

Northern Air Sector Force: Dinjan (*Colonel J. F. Egan, U.S.A.A.F.*)
U.S.A.A.F.

88 (F.) Squadron	Warhawk (P.40)
89 (F.) Squadron	Warhawk (P.40)

[1] On the formation of 3rd Tactical Air Force, Air Headquarters Bengal ceased to exist.

90 (F.) Squadron	Warhawk (P.40)
459 (F.) Squadron	Lightning (P.38)
528 (F.B.) Squadron	Mustang (P.51)
529 (F.B.) Squadron	Mustang (P.51)
530 F.B.) Squadron	Mustang (P.51)

R.A.F.

67 (F.) Squadron	Hurricane
146 (F.) Squadron	Hurricane
176 (N.F.) Squadron	Beaufighter

(b) STRATEGIC AIR FORCE: Calcutta (*Brig.-General H. C. Davidson, U.S.A.A.F.*)

U.S.A.A.F.

22 (M.B.) Squadron	Mitchell (B.25)
490 (M.B.) Squadron	Mitchell (B.25)
491 (M.B.) Squadron	Mitchell (B.25)
9 (H.B.) Squadron	Liberator (B.24)
436 (H.B.) Squadron	Liberator (B.24)
492 (H.B.) Squadron	Liberator (B.24)
493 (H.B.) Squadron	Liberator (B.24)

R.A.F.[1]

99 (M.B.) Squadron	Wellington
215 (M.B.) Squadron	Wellington
159 (H.B.) Squadron	Liberator

(c) TROOP CARRIER COMMAND: Calcutta (for Comilla) (*Brig.-General W. D. Old, U.S.A.A.F.*)

U.S.A.A.F.

| 1 (T.C.) Squadron | Dakota (C.47) |
| 2 (T.C.) Squadron | Dakota (C.47) |

R.A.F.

31 (Tpt.) Squadron	Dakota
62 (Tpt.) Squadron	Dakota
117 (Tpt.) Squadron	Dakota
194 (Tpt.) Squadron	Hudson

(d) PHOTOGRAPHIC RECONNAISSANCE FORCE: Comilla (*Group Captain S. G. Wise, R.A.F.*)

U.S.A.A.F.

10 (P.R.) Squadron	Lightning (P.38)
21 (P.R.) Squadron	Lightning (P.38)
99 (P.R.) Squadron	Lightning (P.38)

[1] Organized as 231 Group R.A.F., Calcutta.

R.A.F.

681 (P.R.) Squadron	Spitfire
684 (P.R.) Squadron	Mosquito

2. DIRECTLY UNDER COMMAND OF AIR HEADQUARTERS S.E.A.C.

222 Group R.A.F.: Colombo (*Air Vice-Marshal A. Lees*)

17 (F.) Squadron	Hurricane
30 (F.) Squadron	Hurricane
273 (F.) Squadron	Hurricane
89 (N.F.) Squadron	Beaufighter
22 (T.B.) Squadron	Beaufort
217 (T.B.) Squadron	Beaufort
205 (Fg. Bt.) Squadron	Catalina
321 (Fg. Bt.) Squadron (Netherlands)	Catalina
413 (Fg. Bt.) Squadron (R.C.A.F.)	Catalina
160 (G.R.) Squadron	Liberator

225 Group R.A.F.: Bangalore (*Air Commodore P. H. Mackworth*)

4 (F.R.) Squadron (R.I.A.F.)	Hurricane
212 (Fg. Bt.) Squadron	Catalina
240 (Fg. Bt.) Squadron	Catalina

3. NON-OPERATIONAL SQUADRONS

U.S.A.A.F.

20 (Tac. R.) Squadron	Warhawk (P.40)
24 (C.M.) Squadron	Liberator (F.7)
34 (C.M.) Squadron	Liberator (F.7)
40 (P.R.) Squadron	Lightning (F.5)
118 (Tac. R.) Squadron	Mustang (P.51)
426 (F.) Squadron	Northrop (P.61)

R.A.F.[1]

81 (F.) Squadron	Spitfire
123 (F.) Squadron	Hurricane
134 (F.) Squadron	Hurricane
135 (F.) Squadron	Hurricane
152 (F.) Squadron	Spitfire
113 (L.B.) Squadron	Bisley
355 (H.B.) Squadron	Liberator
356 (H.B.) Squadron	Liberator
203 (G.R.) Squadron	Wellington
353 (G.R.) Squadron	Hudson
354 (G.R.) Squadron	Liberator
191 (Fg. Bt.) Squadron	Catalina

R.I.A.F.[1]

2 (F.) Squadron	Hurricane
3 (F.R.) Squadron	Audax

Note:

Abbreviations: F.—Fighter; F.B.—Fighter-Bomber; F.R.—Fighter-Reconnaissance; L.R.F.—Long-Range Fighter; Fg. Bt.—Flying Boat; G.R.—General Reconnaissance; L.B.—Light Bomber; M.B.—Medium Bomber; H.B.—Heavy Bomber; N.F.—Night Fighter; P.R.—Photographic Reconnaissance; T.C.—Troop Carrier; C.M.—Combat Mapping; Tpt.—Transport; Tac.R.—Tactical Reconnaissance; T.B.—Torpedo-Bomber.

---

[1] These squadrons in varying stages of re-equipment and training were located in 225 Group and Air H.Q. India areas.

APPENDIX 12

The Distribution of the Japanese Army, August 1943

Location	Army Formation	Remarks
A. Japan · · · ·	General Defence Command: Five divisions	1st Guards, 4th, 46th, 52nd and 53rd Divisions
B. Korea · · ·	Korea Army: Two divisions	19th and 30th Divisions
C. Manchuria · ·	Kwantung Army: 2nd, 3rd, 4th, 5th, 6th and 20th Armies, comprising fifteen divisions and two air divisions	1st, 8th, 9th, 10th, 11th, 12th, 14th, 23rd, 24th, 25th, 27th, 28th, 29th, 57th and 71st Infantry Divisions 1st and 2nd Armoured Divisions 2nd and 4th Air Divisions
D. China · · ·	China Expeditionary Army: 1st, 11th, 12th, 13th and 23rd Armies and Mongolia Garrison, comprising twenty-five divisions, one tank division and one air division	3rd, 13th, 22nd, 26th, 32nd, 34th, 35th, 36th, 37th, 39th, 40th, 58th, 59th, 60th, 61st, 62nd, 63rd, 64th, 65th, 68th, 69th, 70th, 104th, 110th, and 116th Divisions 3rd Armoured Division 3rd Air Division
E. North-East Front · ·	Northern Army: One division and one air division	7th Division and 1st Air Division. This front included the Kurile Islands, Sakhalin and Hokkaido
F. Central Pacific ·	Garrison units	
G. Formosa · ·	Formosa Army	
H. Philippines · ·	14th Army: Two divisions	2nd and 16th Divisions
I. South-East Pacific ·	8th Area Army: 17th and 18th Armies comprising six divisions 4th Air Army, comprising two air divisions	6th, 17th, 20th, 38th, 41st and 51st Divisions 6th and 7th Air Divisions

Location	Army Formation	Remarks
J. Southern Operations controlled by	Southern Army (Field-Marshal Count H. Terauchi) 3rd Air Army	
(1) Northern Australia Front .	19th Army: Two divisions	5th and 48th Divisions. This front covered Celebes, Amboina, Timor and western New Guinea
(2) Java . . .	16th Army	Consisted of only two mixed brigades
(3) Indian Ocean Front .	25th Army: One division	2nd Guards Division. This front included Malaya and Sumatra
(4) Burma .	Burma Area Army: 15th Army, comprising six divisions	18th, 31st, 33rd, 55th and 56th Divisions and 5th Air Division. The 54th Division was en route to Burma. The 15th Division had been allotted to Burma by Imperial General Headquarters, but for the time being was held by Southern Army in Siam
(5) Siam .	Siam Garrison Army: One division and garrison units	15th Division
(6) Indo-China .	One division and garrison units	21st Division
(7) Borneo .	Borneo Garrison Army	Garrison units

Notes:

1. This appendix should be compared with Volume I, pages 94–95 and Appendix 5. The Japanese military forces, which in 1941 consisted of 51 operational divisions and 5 air divisions, had by August 1943 been expanded to 67 operational divisions, 3 armoured divisions and 7 air divisions.
2. This appendix does not show any Japanese formation below a division.

APPENDIX 13

Specific Operations in 1944 for the Defeat of Japan Approved by the Combined Chiefs of Staff at the Sextant Conference

Target Date	Central Pacific	South-West Pacific Area	South-East Asia and China
1st–31st January	Seizure of the Marshalls, including Eniwetok	Complete seizure of W. New Britain, continue neutralization of Rabaul	
15th January–5th March		Seizure of Hansa Bay Area (1st February), capture of Kavieng (20th March)	Operations in upper Burma, Arakan and China
20th April		Seizure of Manus	
1st May	Seizure of Ponape		Initiate V.L.R. bombing of Japanese 'Inner Zone' from China bases
1st June		Seizure of Hollandia (Humboldt Bay)	
20th July	Seizure of eastern Carolines (Truk area)	Initiate V.L.R. bombing of vital targets in the N.E.I.	
15th August		Advance westward along north coast of New Guinea to include Vogelkop	
1st October	Seizure of Guam and Japanese Marianas		
1st November (end of monsoon)			Intensification of offensive operations in S.E.A.C.
31st December	Initiate V.L.R. bombing of vital targets in Japanese 'Inner Zone' from bases in the Marianas		

APPENDIX 14

Losses of Japanese Merchant Vessels of over 500 tons, December 1941 – July 1944

Month	Number of ships lost	Gross tonnage lost including tankers	Tankers — Number lost	Tankers — Gross tonnage	Remarks
December 1941	12	57,758	—	—	
January 1942	17	73,865	—	—	
February	9	37,291	—	—	
March	20	103,095	1	8,636	Pistols on American torpedoes found to be unreliable
April	9	42,796	—	—	
May	24	105,128	1	902	
June	10	38,519	—	—	
July	12	62,331	—	—	
August	23	114,281	—	—	Solomons and Papua campaigns, 7th August 1942–2nd February 1943
September	14	54,478	—	—	
October	36	176,997	—	—	
November	30	168,253	—	—	
December	25	88,364	—	—	
Total 1941/2	241	1,123,156	2	9,538	
January 1943	34	158,885	1	10,023	
February	21	92,662	—	—	
March	37	147,540	3	9,370	Air battle of Bismarck Sea
April	26	132,724	1	17,579	
May	34	134,661	2	17,570	
June	26	105,108	1	3,000	
July	25	84,361	—	—	Central Solomons campaign, 30th June–7th October
August	24	100,064	—	—	
September	45	178,966	3	19,876	
October	39	158,093	2	8,589	Reliable pistols fitted to American torpedoes
November	70	320,807	7	62,460	Capture of Gilberts
December	53	207,048	3	21,024	
Total 1943	434	1,820,919	23	169,491	

Month	Number of ships lost	Gross tonnage lost including tankers	Tankers		Remarks
			Number lost	Gross tonnage	
January 1944	95	355,368	9	64,365	Capture of Marshalls and carrier raid on Truk
February	112	518,697	14	114,490	Carrier raid on Palau
March	67	263,805	10	73,116	
April	38	128,328	1	5,244	
May	64	258,591	3	32,785	
June	71	278,484	8	46,765	
July	66	251,921	7	37,884	
Total 1944 (7 months)	513	2,055,194	52	374,649	

The total losses from December 1941 to July 1944 were 1,188 ships of 4,999,269 tons, including 77 tankers of 553,678 tons.

APPENDIX 15

Outline Order of Battle of XV Corps, January – July 1944

XV CORPS HEADQUARTERS

Lieut.-General A. F. P. Christison

Corps Troops

    Armoured Group   *Colonel S. H. Perse*
        25th Dragoons
        One troop 401st Field Squadron, I.E.
        One company 3/4th Bombay Grenadiers (motorized)
        Detachment 254th Bridging Troop, I.E.
        81st (West African) Reconnaissance Regiment
        3rd Gwalior Lancers I.S.F. (less horsed wing)

    Artillery   *Brigadier L. Harris*
        6th Medium Regiment, R.A.
        8th (Belfast) Heavy Anti-Aircraft Regiment, R.A.
        36th Light Anti-Aircraft Regiment, R.A.
        5th Mahratta Anti-Tank Regiment

    Engineers   *Brigadier L. I. Jacques*
        73rd Field Company, I.E.
        483rd Field Company, I.E.
        Malerkotla Field Company, I.S.F.
        408th Field Park Company, I.E.
        853rd Bridging Company, I.E.
        11th Bridging Section, I.E.
        23rd Battalion, I.E.
        24th Battalion, I.E.

Signals
    XV Corps Signals

Infantry
        12th Frontier Force Regiment Machine-Gun Battalion
        79th Indian Infantry Company

Commandos
        3 Special Service Brigade   *Brigadier W. I. Nonweiler, R.M.*
          5 Commando
          44 Royal Marine Commando

APPENDIX 15

5TH INDIAN INFANTRY DIVISION[1]

Major-General H. R. Briggs

Major-General G. C. Evans (from 1/7/44)

Artillery   *Brigadier E. C. R. Mansergh*

    4th Field Regiment, R.A.
    28th Jungle Field Regiment, R.A.
    56th Light Anti-Aircraft/Anti-Tank Regiment, R.A.
    24th Indian Mountain Regiment

Engineers

    2nd Field Company, I.E.
    20th Field Company, I.E.
    74th Field Company, I.E.
    44th Field Park Company, I.E.
    1st Bridging Section, I.E.

Signals

    5th Indian Divisional Signals

Divisional H.Q. Infantry Battalion

    3/2nd Punjab Regiment

Infantry

    9th Indian Infantry Brigade
                    Brigadier G. C. Evans
                    Brigadier J. A. Salomons (from 25.2.44)
      2nd West Yorkshire Regiment
      3/9th Jat Regiment
      3/14th Punjab Regiment

    123rd Indian Infantry Brigade
                    Brigadier T. J. Winterton
                    Brigadier G. C. Evans (from 25.2.44)
                    Brigadier E. J. Denholm-Young (from 1.7.44)
      2nd Suffolk Regiment
      2/1st Punjab Regiment
      1/17th Dogra Regiment

    161st Indian Infantry Brigade[2]
                    Brigadier D. F. W. Warren
      4th Queen's Own Royal West Kent Regiment
      1/1st Punjab Regiment
      4/7th Rajput Regiment

Medical

    10th Indian Field Ambulance
    45th Indian Field Ambulance
    75th Indian Field Ambulance

---

[1] To IV Corps on 19th March.
[2] To XXXIII Corps.

Major-General F. W. Messervy

Divisional Reconnaissance

    Horsed wing of 3rd Gwalior Lancers, I.S.F.

Artillery   *Brigadier A. F. Hely*

    136th Field Regiment, R.A.

    139th Jungle Field Regiment, R.A.

    24th Light Anti-Aircraft/Anti-Tank Regiment, R.A.

    25th Indian Mountain Regiment

Engineers

    62nd Field Company, I.E.

    77th Field Company, I.E.

    421st Field Company, I.E.

    303rd Field Park Company, I.E.

    17th Bridging Section, I.E.

Signals

    7th Indian Divisional Signals

Divisional H.Q. Infantry Battalion

    1/11th Sikh Regiment (later replaced by 7/2nd Punjab Regiment)

Infantry

    33rd Indian Infantry Brigade[2]

                       Brigadier F. J. Loftus-Tottenham

      1st Queen's Royal Regiment (West Surrey)

      4/15th Punjab Regiment

      4/1st Gurkha Rifles

    89th Indian Infantry Brigade[3]

                       Brigadier W. A. Crowther

      2nd King's Own Scottish Borderers

      7/2nd Punjab Regiment (later 1/11th Sikh Regiment)

      4/8th Gurkha Rifles

    114th Indian Infantry Brigade

                       Brigadier M. R. Roberts

                       Brigadier H. W. Dinwiddie (from 23.6.44)

      1st Somerset Light Infantry

      4/14th Punjab Regiment

      4/5th Royal Gurkha Rifles

Medical

    44th Indian Field Ambulance

    54th Indian Field Ambulance

    66th Indian Field Ambulance

---

[1] To XXXIII Corps on 15th May.
[2] To XXXIII Corps between 5th and 9th April.
[3] To IV Corps between 1st and 6th May.

APPENDIX 15

Major-General H. L. Davies

Artillery   *Brigadier R. O'Carrol-Scott*

    8th Field Regiment, R.A.
    27th Jungle Field Regiment, R.A.
    5th Indian Field Regiment
    7th Indian Light Anti-Aircraft/Anti-Tank Regiment

Engineers

    63rd Field Company, I.E.
    93rd Field Company, I.E.
    425th Field Company, I.E.
    16th Bridging Section, I.E.

Signals

    25th Indian Divisional Signals

Divisional H.Q. Infantry Battalion

    8/19th Hyderabad Regiment

Infantry

    51st Indian Infantry Brigade   *Brigadier T. H. Angus*
        8th York and Lancaster Regiment
        17/5th Mahratta Light Infantry
        16/10th Baluch Regiment

    53rd Indian Infantry Brigade   *Brigadier G. A. P. Coldstream*
        9th York and Lancaster Regiment
        2/2nd Punjab Regiment
        4/18th Royal Garhwal Rifles

    74th Indian Infantry Brigade   *Brigadier J. E. Hirst*
        6th Oxfordshire and Buckinghamshire Light Infantry
        14/10th Baluch Regiment
        3/2nd Gurkha Rifles

Medical

    55th Indian Field Ambulance
    58th Indian Field Ambulance
    61st Indian Field Ambulance

---

[1] In relief of 5th Indian Division, March 1944.

26TH INDIAN DIVISION[1]

Major-General C. E. N. Lomax

Artillery   *Brigadier C. J. G. Dalton*
    160th Jungle Field Regiment, R.A.
    30th Indian Mountain Regiment
    7th Indian Field Regiment
    1st Indian Light Anti-Aircraft/Anti-Tank Regiment

Engineers
    28th Field Company, I.E.
    72nd Field Company, I.E.
    98th Field Company, I.E.
    7th Bridging Section, I.E.

Signals
    26th Indian Divisional Signals

Divisional H.Q. Infantry Battalion
    5/9th Jat Regiment

Infantry
    4th Indian Infantry Brigade   *Brigadier A. W. Lowther*
        1st Wiltshire Regiment
        2/13th Frontier Force Rifles
        2/7th Rajput Regiment

    36th Indian Infantry Brigade   *Brigadier L. G. Thomas*
        8/13th Frontier Force Rifles
        5/16th Punjab Regiment
        1/8th Gurkha Rifles

    71st Indian Infantry Brigade   *Brigadier G. G. C. Bull*
        1st Lincolnshire Regiment   *Brigadier R. C. Cotterell-Hill*
        5/1st Punjab Regiment   (from 28.1.44)
        1/18th Royal Garhwal Rifles

Medical
    1st Indian Field Ambulance
    46th Indian Field Ambulance
    48th Indian Field Ambulance

---

[1] Originally 14th Army reserve. Relieved 7th Indian Division in March 1944.

36TH INDIAN INFANTRY DIVISION

Major-General F. W. Festing

Armour
    'C' Squadron 149th Regiment, R.A.C.

Artillery   *Brigadier C. E. Barrington*

    130th Assault Field Regiment, R.A.
    178th Assault Field Regiment, R.A.
    122nd Light Anti-Aircraft/Anti-Tank Regiment, R.A.

Engineers
    324th Field Park Company, I.E.
    12th Bridging Section, I.E.
    Two companies 15th Battalion, I.E.
    One section 99th Field Company, I.E.

Signals
    36th Indian Divisional Signals

Divisional H.Q. Infantry
    One company 2nd Manchester Machine-Gun Battalion

Medical
    22nd Casualty Clearing Station

29th Infantry Brigade Group   *Brigadier H. C. Stockwell*

  Engineers
    236th Field Company, R.E.

  Signals
    29th Infantry Brigade Signals

  Infantry
    1st Royal Scots Fusiliers
    2nd Royal Welch Fusiliers
    2nd East Lancashire Regiment
    2nd South Lancashire Regiment

  Medical
    154th Field Ambulance

72nd Indian Infantry Brigade Group   *Brigadier A. R. Aslett*

  Engineers
    30th Field Company, I.E.

  Signals
    72nd Indian Infantry Brigade Signals

  Infantry
    6th South Wales Borderers
    10th Gloucestershire Regiment
    9th Royal Sussex Regiment

  Medical
    69th Indian Field Ambulance

81ST WEST AFRICAN DIVISION

Major-General C. G. Woolner

Artillery   *Brigadier T. A. H. Coltan*

    1st (W.A.) Light Anti-Aircraft/Anti-Tank Regiment
    3rd, 4th and 6th Independent (W.A.) Light Batteries

Engineers

    5th (W.A.) Field Company
    6th (W.A.) Field Company
    8th (W.A.) Field Park Company

Signals

    81st (W.A.) Divisional Signals

Infantry

    5th West African Infantry Brigade   *Brigadier N. H. Collins*
        5th Gold Coast Regiment
        7th Gold Coast Regiment
        8th Gold Coast Regiment
    6th West African Infantry Brigade   *Brigadier J. W. A. Hayes*
        4th Nigeria Regiment   *Brigadier R. N. Cartwright*
        1st Gambia Regiment   *(from 26.3.44)*
        1st Sierra Leone Regiment

Divisional Reconnaissance

    11th (E.A.) Divisional Scout Battalion

Auxiliary Porter Groups

    1st (W.A.) Auxiliary Group
    3rd (W.A.) Auxiliary Group
    4th (W.A.) Auxiliary Group

Medical

    5th and 6th (W.A.) Field Ambulances

404 L. OF C. AREA

Brigadier T. R. Henry

Artillery

    13th Anti-Aircraft Brigade, R.A.

Infantry

    1st Bihar Regiment
    7/16th Punjab Regiment[1]
    2nd Baroda Regiment, I.S.F.
    1st Tripura Rifles, I.S.F.

---

[1] Attached 81st (W.A.) Division from December 1943 to June 1944.

APPENDIX 16

Outline Order of Battle of Special Force
(3rd Indian Division)

Column
Nos.

Special Force Headquarters *Major-General O. C. Wingate*

Major-General W. D. A. Lentaigne (from 27.3.44)

14th Infantry Brigade (*Brigadier T. Brodie*)	59
54th Field Company, R.E.	
1st Bedfordshire and Hertfordshire Regiment	16/61
7th Leicestershire Regiment	47/74
2nd Black Watch	73/42
2nd York and Lancaster Regiment	84/65
Medical detachment	
16th Infantry Brigade (*Brigadier B. E. Fergusson*)	99
2nd Field Company, R.E.	
51st/69th Field Regiment, R.A.[1]	51/69
2nd Queen's Royal Regiment (West Surrey)	21/22
2nd Leicestershire Regiment	17/71
45th Reconnaissance Regiment[1]	45/54
Medical detachment	
23rd Infantry Brigade (*Brigadier L. E. C. M. Perowne*)	32
12th Field Company, R.E.	
60th Field Regiment, R.A.[1]	60/88
2nd Duke of Wellington's Regiment	33/76
4th Border Regiment	34/55
1st Essex Regiment	44/56
Medical detachment	
77th Indian Infantry Brigade (*Brigadier J. M. Calvert*)	25
Mixed Field Company, R.E./I.E.	
1st King's Regiment (Liverpool)	81/82
1st Lancashire Fusiliers	20/50
1st South Staffordshire Regiment	38/80
3/6th Gurkha Rifles	36/63
Medical and veterinary detachments	
111th Indian Infantry Brigade (*Brigadier W. D. A. Lentaigne*)[2]	48
Mixed Field Company, R.E./I.E.	

[1] Employed as long-range penetration infantry.
[2] See page 279 fn.

2nd King's Own Royal Regiment (Lancaster)	41/46
1st Cameronians	26/90
3/4th Gurkha Rifles	30/40
4/9th Gurkha Rifles	49/94
Medical and veterinary detachments	

3rd West African Brigade (*Brigadier A. H. Gillmore*)   10
   7th West African Field Company
   6th Nigeria Regiment   39/66
   7th Nigeria Regiment   29/35
   12th Nigeria Regiment   12/43
   3rd West African Field Ambulance

Divisional Troops
   219th Field Park Company, R.E.
   Detachment 2nd Burma Rifles
   145th Brigade Company, R.A.S.C.
   61st Air Supply Company, R.A.S.C.
   2nd Indian Air Supply Company, R.I.A.S.C.

Attached Troops
   Four troops 160th Field Regiment, R.A.
   Four troops 69th Light Anti-Aircraft Regiment, R.A.
   3/9th Gurkha Rifles   57/93

APPENDIX 17

Appreciation of the Prospect of Exploiting Operation 'Thursday' by Major-General O. C. Wingate for the Supreme Commander, South-East Asia, 10th February 1944

OBJECT

To exploit to the maximum extent any gains, or prospect of gain, which may result from Operation 'THURSDAY'.

FACTORS

(a) *L.R.P. Troops now available*

77, 111 and 16 Brigades are actually employed in the opening stages of Operation 'THURSDAY'. In addition, certain Garrison Troops, amongst which are columns of the 3 WA Brigade, will also be employed in the opening stages. Prediction of dates is to some extent guess-work, but in order to illustrate what is said, an attempt will be made to phase the Operation giving dates.

Phase I

Phase I began on 6th February with the entry of 16 Brigade from LEDO. At present, this Brigade is experiencing great difficulties in passing the precipitous mountain tracks separating it from . . . HKAMTI. There is, however, reason to hope that it will cross the Chindwin by the 25th February.

Phase I, therefore, will have begun about the 6th of February and may be expected to end early in May.

During this Phase, I intend to concentrate three Brigades within a circle of 40 miles radius, whose centre is INDAW; and four Garrisons, each consisting of one battalion and two troops of Artillery, will be introduced into the circle to form Strongholds in areas inaccessible to Artillery and tanks.

These operations, if successful, may well compel the enemy to evacuate BURMA North of the 24th Parallel.

It is possible that it may be necessary in April to introduce two more columns of 14 Brigade to break the line BHAMO–MYITKYINA to which the enemy may well switch his communications with 18th Division.

A prominent feature of Phase I will be the bold employment of glider patrols to exploit and develop the general threat to the enemy's communications in Northern Burma.

Phase II

Phase II will overlap Phase I to some extent, and the exact date cannot be predicted. It may never occur at all.

486

It will begin as soon as the enemy gives evidence of having been defeated by the operations in Phase I. Phase II may be described as the Phase of Exploitation.

Apart from the introduction of the two columns referred to above, (which might take place in any case in order to complete the cutting off of 18th Division), in the event of marked success the introduction of the whole of 14 and 23 Brigades might be desirable to intrude into the monsoon period in the Dry Zone and to encourage an advance on the part of the Chinese on the line LASHIO–MAYMYO. If this introduction of 14 and 23 Brigades were carried out, it would be my intention to withdraw 77 and 16 Brigades as soon as possible to permit of their use on future occasions.

Since I purpose to do this, in any case, Phase II would merely mean the introduction of 14 and 23 Brigades to relieve at an earlier date than I would contemplate in the case of a smaller degree of success. However, it should be understood that in the case of a smaller degree of success, I would endeavour to relieve all three brigades; 16, 77 and 111, with one Brigade only, viz. 14, which, together with the Garrison Brigade, would hold the necessary areas for the monsoon.

Phase III

The third Phase will begin with the end of the Monsoon in October 1944, when free movement is possible, without getting malaria. The Japanese may be expected to prepare an offensive for this season and it will be necessary to forestall them. The only way I can see in which this might be done is to stage an airborne L.R.P. operation, designed to strike at their communications South of MANDALAY, possibly in the area THAZI. Such an operation would require a minimum of three L.R.P. brigades, of which one might be American, and two British. By this time it may be hoped that the YOKE [Yunnan] Forces would be disposed to play a necessary part in the follow-up.

Thus the operations as planned would leave two brigades available for CULVERIN even on the existing planning.

(b) *Troops Available for Increasing L.R.P. Resources*

It is highly desirable that we should form L.R.P. Brigades from the best elements in our army and not leave it to the other nations to produce these forces, although we will, of course, welcome all such Brigades that other nations are prepared to produce. In this connection it is interesting that the Generalissimo has just intimated his intention of sending in the immediate future 50 CHINESE Majors to my headquarters to learn the Science of L.R.P. He is also sending a considerable number of CHINESE ORS.

In INDIA there are a number of Divisions which, should Operation 'THURSDAY' prove successful, it would be wrong not to be made available for L.R.P.

The first of these is, of course, the Parachute Brigade and any other portion of the PHANTOM Airborne Division which may, by that time, have come to light.

The Parachute Brigade is obsolete in as much as there is now no function for parachutists in War. They have not been trained to fight the Japanese in warfare, because they have not been trained by the people with the necessary experience. They still require to be introduced to, and to study, the methods of L.R.P. They are, however, available to be turned into an L.R.P. Brigade.

Secondly, there are both British and Indian divisions in INDIA which should be turned over to be converted to L.R.P.

It does not seem to be realised that if Operation 'THURSDAY', which is being carried out by unsupported L.R.P. Brigades, succeeds in driving the Japanese out of Northern BURMA, the superiority of L.R.P. to normal formations in a normal operation (including normal airborne formations), will have been abundantly proved, and there will no longer be any grounds for claiming that normal Divisions have any function in South East Asia. They should instead be broken up into L.R.P. Brigades (Airborne), Assault Brigades, and Airport Garrison Brigades, organized into larger formations corresponding to divisions and corps but with rather different scope and functions.

I do not, however, claim, at this juncture, that L.R.P. Brigades will be capable of this degree of success. I only point out that if they *are* capable of it the proper inference must be drawn and we must not shrink from applying measures to save life and gain victory.

The number of L.R.P. Brigades that are required purely to exploit the Operation in Northern BURMA in November 44 is a minimum of three and a maximum of six. If the more rewarding HANOI operation is contemplated another six are needed of which three would be taken from BURMA where further offensive would be redundant. The number required for CULVERIN is a minimum of two, a maximum of three. This latter figure may be greatly increased if Operation 'THURSDAY' is a complete success. Thus, we may need a maximum of say fifteen L.R.P. Brigades by next November, and a minimum of five.

At present there are in existence five L.R.P. Brigades of which one is being used for Garrisons and two will definitely not be available for operations in November 44. This leaves three, which means that on the minimum estimate another two will be required to be raised.

If Operation 'THURSDAY' is a complete failure L.R.P. will lapse. If, however, it has any measure of success, another good Division now in INDIA should be turned over to L.R.P. This Division may well be supplied by 14th Army which can hardly be expecting ever to operate beyond the mountain barrier with its present establishment after the experiences of the past two years.

(c) *Proposals Should* CULVERIN *be Abandoned*. (See also attached note on Operations against THAILAND AND INDO-CHINA)

Should CULVERIN be abandoned the best prospect for the INDIA Command will be to concentrate on progressing to HANOI and BANGKOK, by the use of the Airborne L.R.P. Brigades, building up behind them at suitable distances defended airports. The latter require normal garrison troops. In the van will be the deeply penetrating columns, a mass of enemy between them and territory occupied by us. The operations of these columns will progressively force the enemy to withdraw. In territory from which the enemy has withdrawn, normal communications may be built up, and strong garrisons living in fortifications introduced. At certain distances behind the forward wave of penetration will come defended airports. In the van with the L.R.P. Brigades will be Strongholds with their Garrisons.

A campaign of this nature would require some 20 to 25 L.R.P. Brigades in being, a total strength of 100,000 infantry of good calibre. This is a small enough force to carry out such an operation, in all conscience. If measures are taken in time a proportion of it can be found from British Artillery, etc. now in INDIA, although indeed much of this Artillery will be needed to be flown in to garrison L.R.P. Strongholds and defended airports. It remains to be seen whether West Africans have the qualities required (or rather if their British Officers have these qualities) for L.R.P. If so, some can be found from these sources. In the main, they should be found from British Infantry Divisions. Airborne divs. are suitable provided they first undergo three months training with Special Force.

If CULVERIN is off and 'THURSDAY' has been successful there can be no argument against at least the 2nd Division and any other British division in INDIA being used for this purpose, plus the existing element of the airborne division.

Good Indian troops such as Gurkhas and Sikhs could also be employed.

Once the view had gained acceptance that L.R.P. was an excellent way to beat the Japanese, there would be no difficulty in obtaining the necessary enthusiasm and confidence, and units which I might at present deem unfit, might become fit.

All this could be done by the India Command without any further assistance from the U.K. were CULVERIN to be abandoned.

The capture of BANGKOK and HANOI may well result in the giving of an amphibious role to the India Command (Nov. 45) and the L.R.P. thrust would then continue to carry a chain of defended airports across CHINA to the coast where it would meet up with the seaborne forces.

Some such operation is highly desirable if the War is to be shortened.

PLAN

Lay down that Operation 'THURSDAY' will be exploited with all the forces of L.R.P. that are available in INDIA, with a view to creating the maximum success possible.

In the event of a qualified success two brigades of L.R.P. will be withdrawn and prepared for CULVERIN. In the event of an unqualified success arrangements will be made to raise at once many more L.R.P. brigades from good Divisions now in INDIA, and all existing plans for future operations against the Japanese will be revised in the light of this success.

The whole of 14 and 23 Brigades will be used only in the event of a degree of success being obtained in Operation 'THURSDAY'. If the Operation is uniformly unsuccessful they will not be used.

Should 77 Brigade and 111 Brigade succeed in holding out in the

INDAW Area and cutting the Japanese lines of communication for a considerable period this would be a sufficient measure of success to justify the introduction of two columns of 14 Brigade to cut the BHAMO–MYITKYINA Road. Should the operations of L.R.P. Brigades result in a Japanese withdrawal permitting the LEDO Force to gain the line MOGAUNG–MYITKYINA that would be a measure of success justifying a large increase in the number of L.R.P. Brigades.

Should the action of L.R.P. Brigades result in the enemy evacuating BURMA North of the 24th Parallel this would be a great measure of success justifying turning over many existing Divisions to L.R.P.

The number of SD Aircraft requisite for the supply of the L.R.P. Force in the field will be guaranteed and will not be cut down on any consideration whatsoever without the agreement of the L.R.P. Force Commander.

Should very favourable opportunities for flying in columns, further to confuse the enemy and exploit opportunities, occur, every endeavour will be made to supply additional transport aircraft to allow this to be done.

The scale on which it is intended to create new L.R.P. Brigades will be decided by the degree of success of 'THURSDAY'. This will be apparent by May 15th 1944.

Should it be decided to go ahead turning divisions into L.R.P.Gs, the machine exists at GWALIOR. This machine will be capable of taking on the training of six to ten Brigades at a time. Each batch requires three months complete from date of arrival with animals to date of entraining for operations.

APPENDIX 18

Note by Major-General O. C. Wingate on L.R.P. Operations against Siam and Indo-China, 11th February 1944

1. OBJECT

To seize HANOI and BANGKOK.

2. FACTORS

(a) *Supply Limitations*

An Airborne L.R.P. Brigade can readily be introduced and maintained more economically than any equivalent striking force. The radius at which it can operate from its Air Base is up to a maximum of 300 miles. Thus, an Air Base at KUNMING could support the operations of L.R.P. up to 70 miles of HANOI. It would be best, therefore, first to establish an Air Base 100 miles South of KUNMING to permit of introducing L.R.P. Brigades capable of reaching the coast in the Gulf of TONGKING.

(b) *Method of Operating and Numbers Required*

The number of L.R.P. Brigades required to paralyse the enemy forces in French Indo-China would be six. This would require an additional allotment of three Brigades of Garrison Troops with supporting artillery. The whole could be assembled at KUNMING without difficulty provided Northern BURMA were in our hands by say March 45.

The process of conquest would probably follow the lines which are to be worked out in Operation 'THURSDAY', i.e. severing of communications, establishing Strongholds in areas inaccessible to wheeled transport, introducing Garrisons into areas evacuated by the enemy, which will become defended airports, and in this way gaining control of the whole territory.

(c) *The Number of Transport Aircraft Required to Lay on the Entire Operation*

The total number in the Force proposed amounts to some 40,000 all ranks of which 24,000 only are L.R.P.

The maintenance of this force requires 40 DAKOTA sorties daily. Thus, at least, 100 DAKOTAS should be earmarked for this purpose. In addition a large number of aircraft must be allotted for the airborne side of the Operation. Another 150 DAKOTAS should be allotted for this purpose, making a total of 250 DAKOTAS which should be available from six weeks before the Operation until its completion.

COMMENT

It should be apparent from the above that a very small number of aircraft would be required to complete the operation, which, by any other means, would cost up to 1,000 million pounds sterling to bring off.

The capture of HANOI might well prove decisive in this theatre especially if some seaborne operation could be staged to take advantage of it. Success in the South Pacific might render it unnecessary to capture SINGAPORE.

This operation would appear to be worth while and to be within the powers of the INDIA COMMAND without assistance from elsewhere, except in the matter of transport aircraft.

BANGKOK

A similar campaign could equally readily be staged against THAILAND but with less advantage. Details can be supplied on demand.

APPENDIX 19

Outline Order of Battle of IV Corps,
January – July 1944

Corps Troops
    Armour
        H.Q. 254th Indian Tank Brigade   *Brigadier R. L. Scoones*
            3rd Carabiniers
            7th Cavalry
            'C' Squadron 150th Regiment, R.A.C.
            401st Field Squadron, I.E. (less one troop)
            3/4th Bombay Grenadiers, less one company (motorized)

    Artillery   *Brigadier P. S. Myburgh*
        8th Medium Regiment, R.A.
        67th Heavy Anti-Aircraft Regiment, R.A.
        28th Light Anti-Aircraft Regiment, R.A.
        78th Light Anti-Aircraft Regiment, R.A.
        15th Punjab Anti-Tank Regiment
        One battery 2nd Survey Regiment

    Engineers   *Brigadier H. Williams*
        75th Field Company, I.E.
        424th Field Company, I.E.
        94th (Faridkot) Field Company, I.S.F.
        305th Field Park Company, I.E.
        854th Bridging Company, I.E.
        16th Battalion, I.E.
        336th Forestry Company, I.E.
        3rd West African Field Company

Signals
    IV Corps Signals

Infantry
        9th Jat Machine-Gun Battalion
        15/11th Sikh Regiment
        Chin Hills Battalion, Burma Army
        3rd Assam Rifles
        4th Assam Rifles
        78th Indian Infantry Company
        Kalibahadur Regiment (Nepalese)
        One company Gwalior Infantry, I.S.F.

5TH INDIAN INFANTRY DIVISION

Major-General H. R. Briggs

Under command from 19th March 1944, less 161st Infantry Brigade with XXXIII Corps (for details see Appendix 15).

89TH INDIAN INFANTRY BRIGADE

Brigadier W. A. Crowther

From 7th Indian Division under command from 7th May (for details see Appendix 15).

17TH INDIAN LIGHT DIVISION

Major-General D. T. Cowan

Artillery   *Brigadier The Baron de Robeck*

    21st Indian Mountain Regiment
    29th Indian Mountain Regiment
    129th Light Field Regiment, R.A.
    82nd Light Anti-Aircraft/Anti-Tank Regiment, R.A.

Engineers

    60th Field Company, I.E.
    70th Field Company, I.E.
    414th Field Park Company, I.E.

Signals

    17th Indian Divisional Signals

Divisional Infantry

    1st West Yorkshire Regiment (divisional support battalion)
    4/12th Frontier Force Regiment (divisional headquarters battalion)
    7/10th Baluch Regiment (divisional reconnaissance battalion)

Infantry

    48th Indian Infantry Brigade   *Brigadier R. T. Cameron*
      9th Border Regiment   *Brigadier R. C. O. Hedley*
      2/5th Royal Gurkha Rifles   (from 31.5.44)
      1/7th Gurkha Rifles

    63rd Indian Infantry Brigade   *Brigadier A. E. Cumming, V.C.*
      1/3rd Gurkha Rifles   *Brigadier G. W. S. Burton*
      1/4th Gurkha Rifles   (from 13.1.44)
      1/10th Gurkha Rifles

Medical

    23rd Indian Field Ambulance
    37th Indian Field Ambulance

20TH INDIAN INFANTRY DIVISION

Major-General D. D. Gracey

Artillery   *Brigadier J. A. E. Hirst*

> 9th Field Artillery Regiment, R.A.
> 114th Jungle Field Regiment, R.A.
> 23rd Indian Mountain Regiment
> 55th Light Anti-Aircraft/Anti-Tank Regiment, R.A.

Engineers

> 92nd Field Company, I.E.
> 422nd Field Company, I.E.
> 481st Field Company, I.E.
> 309th Field Park Company, I.E.
> 9th Bridging Section, I.E.

Signals

> 20th Indian Divisional Signals

Divisional H.Q. Infantry Battalion

> 4/3rd Madras Regiment

Infantry

> 32nd Indian Infantry Brigade   *Brigadier D. A. L. Mackenzie*
> > 1st Northamptonshire Regiment
> > 9/14th Punjab Regiment
> > 3/8th Gurkha Rifles

> 80th Indian Infantry Brigade   *Brigadier S. Greeves*
> > 1st Devonshire Regiment
> > 9/12th Frontier Force Regiment
> > 3/1st Gurkha Rifles

> 100th Indian Infantry Brigade   *Brigadier W. A. L. James*
> > 2nd Border Regiment
> > 14/13th Frontier Force Regiment
> > 4/10th Gurkha Rifles

Medical

> 42nd Indian Field Ambulance
> 55th Indian Field Ambulance
> 59th Indian Field Ambulance

23RD INDIAN INFANTRY DIVISION

Major-General O. L. Roberts

Artillery   *Brigadier R. W. Andrews*

    158th Jungle Field Regiment, R.A.
    3rd Indian Field Regiment
    28th Indian Mountain Regiment
    2nd Indian Light Anti-Aircraft/Anti-Tank Regiment

Engineers

    68th Field Company, I.E.
    71st Field Company, I.E.
    91st Field Company, I.E.
    323rd Field Park Company, I.E.
    10th Bridging Section, I.E.

Signals

    23rd Indian Divisional Signals

Divisional H.Q. Infantry Battalion

    2/19th Hyderabad Regiment

Infantry

    1st Indian Infantry Brigade   *Brigadier R. C. McCay*
        1st Seaforth Highlanders   *Brigadier R. C. M. King*
        1/16th Punjab Regiment   (from 25.2.44)
        1st Patiala Infantry, I.S.F.

    37th Indian Infantry Brigade   *Brigadier H. V. Collingridge*
        3/3rd Gurkha Rifles   *Brigadier J. F. Marindin*
        3/5th Royal Gurkha Rifles   (from 15.6.44)
        3/10th Gurkha Rifles

    49th Indian Infantry Brigade   *Brigadier F. A. Esse*
        4/5th Mahratta Light Infantry
        6/5th Mahratta Light Infantry
        5/6th Rajputana Rifles

Medical

    24th Indian Field Ambulance
    47th Indian Field Ambulance
    49th Indian Field Ambulance

50TH INDIAN PARACHUTE BRIGADE

Brigadier M. R. J. Hope-Thompson

Brigadier E. G. Woods (from 22.5.44)

Engineers

411th (Parachute) Field Squadron, I.E.

Infantry

152nd Indian Parachute Battalion
153rd Gurkha Parachute Battalion
50th Indian Parachute Machine-Gun Company

Medical

80th Indian Field Ambulance

APPENDIX 20

Composition of Japanese Columns for
The Attack on Imphal

31st Division (*Lieut.-General K. Sato*)

    Right column   III/138th Battalion
                          One battery 31st Mountain Artillery Regiment
                          One platoon 31st Engineer Regiment
                          Signal and medical detachments

Centre column

    Advanced guard   138th Infantry Regiment (less III/138th Battalion)
                          I/31st Mountain Artillery Battalion (less one battery)
                          One company 31st Engineer Regiment
                          Signal and medical detachments (including a field
                             hospital)

    Main body   Headquarters 31st Division
    (divisional   124th Infantry Regiment
    reserve)   31st Mountain Artillery Regiment
                             (less two battalions)
                          31st Engineer Regiment (less two companies)
                          Divisional signal unit
                          Divisional medical unit (including a field hospital)
                          31st Transport Regiment (less one company)

    Left column   Headquarters 31st Infantry Group
                             (*Major-General M. Miyazaki*)
                          58th Infantry Regiment
                          II/31st Mountain Artillery Battalion
                          One company 31st Engineer Regiment
                          Signal and medical detachments

15th Division (*Lieut.-General M. Yamauchi*)

    Advanced guard   III/67th Battalion (less two companies)
                          Detachment 15th Engineer Regiment
                          Regimental gun company 67th Infantry Regiment

    Right Column   60th Infantry Regiment (less one battalion and two
                             companies)
                          21st Field Artillery Regiment (less two battalions)
                          Two platoons 15th Engineer Regiment
                          Half of a field hospital

    Centre column   51st Infantry Regiment (less one battalion and two
                             companies)
                          III/21st Field Artillery Battalion
                          Detachment 15th Engineer Regiment

Left Column	I/60th Battalion (less one company) One section 21st Field Artillery Regiment Detachment 15th Engineer Regiment
Divisional reserve	Headquarters 15th Division Seven infantry companies One composite infantry company 15th Engineer Regiment (less detachments) Medical detachment Half of a field hospital

33rd Division (*Lieut.-General G. Yanagida*)

Right column	Headquarters 33rd Infantry Group (*Major-General T. Yamamoto*) 213th Infantry Regiment (less I/213th Battalion) One company I/215th Battalion 14th Tank Regiment (less one company) 1st Anti-Tank Battalion (less two companies) II/33rd Mountain Artillery Battalion 3rd Heavy Field Artillery Regiment (less one battalion and one battery) II/18th Heavy Field Artillery Battalion One company 33rd Engineer Regiment
Centre column	214th Infantry Regiment (less headquarters and two companies III/214th Battalion) I/33rd Mountain Artillery Battalion Detachment 33rd Engineer Regiment H.Q. 33rd Division
Left column	215th Infantry Regiment (less two companies) III/33rd Mountain Artillery Battalion Detachment 33rd Engineer Regiment
Reserve (Fort White) Column	One company 215th Infantry Regiment One company 14th Tank Regiment 33rd Engineer Regiment (less two companies) 4th Independent Engineer Regiment 18th Heavy Field Artillery Regiment (less one battalion) Detachment 3rd Heavy Artillery Regiment
Falam—Haka Garrison	III/214th Battalion (less two companies)

APPENDIX 21

Outline Order of Battle of XXXIII Corps,
April–July 1944

XXXIII CORPS HEADQUARTERS

Lieut.-General M. G. N. Stopford

Corps Troops

Armour

149th Regiment, R.A.C. (less one squadron)
Detachment 150th Regiment, R.A.C.
11th Cavalry (armoured cars)
45th Cavalry (light tanks)

Artillery   *Brigadier D. J. Steevens*

1st Medium Regiment, R.A.
50th Indian Light Anti-Aircraft/Anti-Tank Regiment
24th Indian Mountain Regiment (attached from 5th Indian
    Division)

Engineers   *Brigadier J. F. D. Steedman*

429th Field Company, I.E.
44th Field Park Company, I.E.
10th Battalion, I.E.

Infantry

1st Burma Regiment, Burma Army
1st Chamar Regiment
1st Assam Regiment
Shere Regiment (Nepalese)
Mahindra Dal Regiment (Nepalese)

2ND INFANTRY DIVISION

Major-General J. M. L. Grover

Major-General C. G. G. Nicholson (from 5.7.44)

Artillery   *Brigadier H. S. J. Bourke*

    10th Assault Field Regiment, R.A.
    16th Assault Field Regiment, R.A.
    99th Assault Field Regiment, R.A.
    100th Light Anti-Aircraft/Anti-Tank Regiment, R.A.

Engineers

    5th Field Company, R.E.
    208th Field Company, R.E.
    506th Field Company, R.E.
    21st Field Park Company, R.E.

Signals

    2nd Divisional Signals

Divisional Infantry

    2nd Reconnaisance Regiment
    2nd Manchester Machine-Gun Battalion (less one company with
        36th Indian Division)
    143 Special Service Company

Infantry

    4th Infantry Brigade   *Brigadier W. H. Goschen*
      1st Royal Scots   *Brigadier J. A. Theobalds*
      2nd Royal Norfolk Regiment (from 7.5.44)
      1/8th Lancashire Fusiliers *Brigadier R. S. McNaught*
      4th Field Ambulance   (from 4.6.44)

    5th Infantry Brigade   *Brigadier V. F. S. Hawkins*
      7th Worcestershire Regiment *Brigadier M. M. Alston-Roberts-West*
      2nd Dorsetshire Regiment   (from 16.5.44)
      1st Queen's Own Cameron Highlanders
      5th Field Ambulance

    6th Infantry Brigade   *Brigadier J. D. Shapland*
      1st Royal Welch Fusiliers *Brigadier W. G. Smith* (from 30.5.44)
      1st Royal Berkshire Regiment
      2nd Durham Light Infantry
      6th Field Ambulance

APPENDIX 21

7TH INDIAN INFANTRY DIVISION

Major-General F. W. Messervy

less 89th Indian Infantry Brigade plus 161st Indian Infantry Brigade
(for details see Appendix 15)

23RD (L.R.P.) INDIAN INFANTRY BRIGADE

Brigadier L. E. C. M. Perowne

(for details see Appendix 17)

268TH BRIGADE

Brigadier G. M. Dyer

2/4th Bombay Grenadiers
5/4th Bombay Grenadiers
17/7th Rajput Regiment

3 SPECIAL SERVICE BRIGADE

Brigadier W. I. Nonweiler

(for details see Appendix 15)

LUSHAI BRIGADE

Brigadier P. C. Marindin

1st Royal Battalion, Jat Regiment (from 202 L. of C. Area)
8/13th Frontier Force Regiment
7/14th Punjab Regiment (from 202 L. of C. Area)
1st Bihar Regiment
One company 77th Field Ambulance

202 L. OF C. AREA

Major-General R. P. L. Ranking

251, 252, 253, 256, 257 L. of C. Sub-Areas.

APPENDIX 22

Order of Battle of 221 Group R.A.F., March–June 1944

	Name	Type	Location			
			March	April	May	June
Headquarters 221 Group	—	—	Imphal	Imphal	Imphal	Imphal
168 Wing	—	—	Kumbhirgram	Kumbhirgram	Kumbhirgram	Kumbhirgram
7 Squadron R.I.A.F.	Vengeance	Light Bomber	Kumbhirgram	Kumbhirgram	Kumbhirgram	Kumbhirgram
84 Squadron R.A.F.	Vengeance	Light Bomber	Kumbhirgram	Kumbhirgram	Kumbhirgram	Kumbhirgram
110 Squadron R.A.F.	Vengeance	Light Bomber	Kumbhirgram	Kumbhirgram	Kumbhirgram	To India for re-equipment
170 Wing	—		Imphal	Imphal	Imphal	Imphal
1 Squadron R.I.A.F.	Hurricane	Fighter-Reconnaissance	Imphal	Imphal	Imphal	Imphal
5 Squadron R.A.F.	Hurricane	Fighter	Wangjing	Patharkandi	Lanka	Dergaon with 243 Wing
11 Squadron R.A.F.	Hurricane	Fighter-Bomber	Tulihal	Tulihal to Lanka	Lanka	Imphal
28 Squadron R.A.F.	Hurricane	Fighter-Reconnaissance	Imphal	Imphal to Jorhat	Jorhat with 243 Wing	Jorhat with 243 Wing
34 Squadron R.A.F.	Hurricane	Fighter-Bomber	Palel	Palel to Dergaon	Dergaon with 243 Wing	Dergaon with 243 Wing
42 Squadron R.A.F.	Hurricane	Fighter-Bomber	Palel	Palel	Kangla	Kangla
113 Squadron R.A.F.	Hurricane	Fighter-Bomber	Tulihal	Silchar	Patharkandi	Palel
81 Squadron R.A.F.	Spitfire VIII	Fighter	Tulihal	Kumbhirgram	Kumbhirgram	Kumbhirgram
136 Squadron R.A.F.	Spitfire VIII	Fighter	Wangjing	Wangjing	To 224 Group at Chittagong	—
Detachments from						
176 Squadron R.A.F.	Beaufighter VIII	Night Fighter	Kangla	Kangla	Kangla	Kangla
607 Squadron R.A.F.	Spitfire VIII	Fighter	—	—	Imphal	Imphal

	Name	Type	Location — March	April	May	June
189 Wing	—	—	Silchar	Silchar	Silchar	Silchar
9 Squadron R.I.A.F.	Hurricane	Fighter	Kulaura	Silchar	Kulaura	Comilla
123 Squadron R.A.F.	Hurricane	Fighter	Patharkandi	Patharkandi	Patharkandi	To India for re-equipment
243 Wing	—	—	—	—	Dergaon	Dergaon
28 Squadron R.A.F.	Hurricane	Fighter-Reconnaissance	—	—	Jorhat	Jorhat
34 Squadron R.A.F.	Hurricane	Fighter-Bomber	—	—	Dergaon	Dergaon
60 Squadron R.A.F.	Hurricane	Fighter-Bomber	—	—	Dergaon	Dergaon
615 Squadron R.A.F.	Spitfire VIII	Fighter	—	Tulihal with 170 Wing	Dergaon	Palel with 170 Wing

Notes: (i) 243 Wing was established at Dergaon on 28th April for close support of XXXIII Corps.

(ii) Squadrons withdrawn from the Imphal area were 5, 11, 28, 34, 81, 113 and 136. Those remaining on the Imphal plain throughout the period were 1, 42 and dets. 176 and 607.

APPENDIX 23

Improvements to Indian Ports in 1944

Calcutta

Provision of four import and two tanker berths, two personnel and M.T. jetties, four loading berths for barges and two loading hards for L.S.T.s.

Development of watering facilities, power plants and road and rail communications within the port area.

Vizagapatam

Provision of two lighter wharfs, a loading basin and quay for bulk petroleum, a loading hard for L.S.T.s and a lay-up berth for lighters.

Development of watering facilities and road and rail communications within the port area.

Madras

Provision of an oil mooring berth, a coal discharging berth and a loading hard for L.S.T.s.

Development of watering facilities and road and rail communications.

Cochin

Extension of the existing wharfage to give three additional 500 ft. berths and the construction of a new oil fuel jetty.

Bombay

Provision of a new small craft pier, an ammunition wharf and loading hards for ten L.S.T.s, and the development of an extra 4,500 ft. of lightering frontage.

To equip the new wharfs, jetties and so on, and to enable the enlarged ports to operate efficiently, the following equipment was ordered: 52 Portal cranes, 21 rail mounted cranes, 103 mobile cranes, 497 harbour craft and 114 fork lift trucks.

APPENDIX 24

The Minimum Additional Transportation Required to Maintain India's Internal Economy and War Production, and to Meet the Increased Military Load Arising out of the Decisions of the Quadrant Conference

1. At the end of 1943 a Sub-Committee of the War Projects Co-ordination and Administrative Committee of the War Department in India was set up to examine the best method of implementing the decision that sufficient transportation facilities, whether by rail, road, inland water or coastal shipping, should be made available to maintain India's internal economy and production capacity at suitable levels; to define the requirements in greater detail; and to give estimates of any additional requirements in locomotives, rolling stock and shipping.

2. To arrive at a solution of the problem set them the sub-committee had first to examine carefully the many novel problems facing the Indian transport system in coping with additional traffic arising from war conditions. They realized that these problems could be solved only by a redistribution of traffic and that a simple increase in train and ton mileages along established routes would prove to be no answer. The following were the major factors which had to be examined:

(a) Transport of coal

In 1939 about 1 million tons of coal were mined in the Indian coalfields, some 100 to 150 miles inland from Calcutta, exported through that port and carried by coastal shipping to ports along the east and west coasts of the continent. The transfer of a great part of the coastal shipping overseas or to other wartime activities forced the transfer of coal traffic to the railways. This resulted in the rail-borne tonnage across India increasing by 570 per cent. to Bombay and by 120 per cent. to Karachi. This constituted some 46 per cent. of the total net mileage on India's broad gauge system, and more than treble the pre-war wagon and locomotive usage between the collieries and Calcutta.

(b) Construction of airfields

The enormous airfield construction programme had necessitated special arrangements being made on a priority basis for the carriage of immense tonnages of construction material to and from places, which, from the point of view of rail transport, were often inconveniently and uneconomically sited.

(c) Carriage of petrol and oil products

In 1942 all the pre-war trade channels for the distribution by rail of P.O.L. had assumed a new pattern. The loss of the Netherlands East Indies and Burma oilfields, and increased military operational requirements had resulted in greater movements of P.O.L. (bulk and packed) from west to east. Although the Bombay–Bhusaval pipeline had gone some way towards relieving the shortage of tank wagons, to meet the military demands it had become essential to run special trains carrying maximum loads of P.O.L. and worked by heavy goods locomotives.

(d) Military special trains

The number of military special trains in a normal pre-war year was between 300 and 400. The railways now had to deal with approximately three times that number in a single month. Many of the specials covered well over 1,000 miles and a few over 2,000 miles (the average haul being approximately 600), and all required heavy goods engines.

(e) Military depots

The great increase in the number of military depots had resulted in a considerable volume of traffic moving outside the established routes, with an ensuing dislocation of the normal flow of loaded and empty trucks.

(f) Food shortages

The incidence of food shortages in many parts of India, and actual famine conditions in certain areas in eastern and southern India, had forced a reorientation of food distribution throughout the country. Large tonnages of essential foodstuffs had to be carried from surplus to deficit areas, which often involved hauls of over 1,000 miles and cross-running of different types of staple foods.

3. *Road and internal water transport systems.* The railways could expect no help from road transport, since not only was the road system inadequate but, owing to the requisition of used vehicles from the comparatively small civilian fleet and of most of the new vehicles which would normally have become available for civil purposes, the small fraction of the total volume of goods and passengers carried pre-war by road had been reduced to a negligible amount. The same applied to the inland water services on the Ganges and Brahmaputra. The sub-committee had therefore to leave both road and inland water transport systems out of their calculations.

4. *Coastal shipping.* Excluding coastal trade with Burma, the Indian coastal fleet carried in a pre-war year $3\frac{1}{2}$ million tons deadweight or 300,000 tons a month, of which about 50 per cent. was coal. From January to September 1943 the average tonnage carried by coastal shipping was only 150,000 tons a month, half the pre-war figure. Allowing for the slow

turn round caused by war conditions, it was estimated that 150,000 additional gross shipping tonnage was necessary to bring the coastal fleet up to its pre-war carrying capacity. But in 1943 a considerable quantity of military tonnage, which could more conveniently be moved by coastal shipping, had to be refused owing to lack of space. The sub-committee estimated that to enable the military demands to be met an extra 75,000 tons of shipping would be required. Thus, allowing a further 5,000 tons for certain essential passenger traffic, the sub-committee considered that 230,000 tons of additional coastal shipping should be made available to meet the demand.

5. *Rail transport*. The sub-committee's first problem was to decide what level of transport would be required to maintain India's internal economy. They selected 1937–38 as a basis on which to work since that year was a fair average, neither a slump nor a bumper year. The operational performance in 1937–38 had, however, to be adjusted to allow for certain factors that had come into operation during the war. These included:

(a) Export from India was now rigidly controlled and therefore the transport required was fairly easily calculable.
(b) Certain commodities, such as cement, iron, steel and metallic ores, were in the main required for war purposes and were not generally available to the public.
(c) The population of India had increased by 4 per cent.
(d) Despite the severe restriction in passenger traffic available to the public, an increase over the 1937–38 figures in train miles of about $9\frac{1}{2}$ per cent. on the broad gauge and 11 per cent. on the metre gauge systems had to be allowed for because of the great increase in the number of military special trains.

After allowing for all military requirements (assessed at 10,150 million ton miles) and for the additional traffic (assessed at 2,000 m.t.m.) forced on to the railways by the shortage of coastal shipping, there was a balance of 15,550 m.t.m. for purely civil traffic. Of this 10,500 was required for coal traffic, leaving only 5,050 m.t.m. for civil goods. It was assessed that, including a proportion of raw materials and components for war supplies, the civil requirements amounted to 11,260 m.t.m., a deficit of 6,210 m.t.m. If the amount of coastal shipping were increased to enable it to carry its normal share of traffic, thus relieving the railways, the deficit could be reduced to 4,210 m.t.m. The maximum deficit amounted to 22 per cent. of the total broad gauge and 14 per cent. of the total metre gauge traffic carried in 1942–43, and the minimum deficit to 15 per cent. of the broad gauge and 9 per cent. of the metre gauge.

6. *Additional military requirements*. The sub-committee had to allow for an increase in the military load during 1945. This was assessed in conjunction with General Headquarters, India, as 310 broad gauge and 70 metre gauge locomotives, and some 18,000 broad gauge and 4,000 metre gauge wagons.

7. The sub-committee's estimation of the additional locomotives required to meet existing deficits was:

(a) On the basis of a deficit of 6,210 million ton miles.

	B.G.	M.G.
(i) For troop and military trains	104	68
(ii) Additional goods ton miles at 22 per cent. increase for broad gauge and 14 per cent. for metre gauge	359	74
(iii) Additional for shunting at 33⅓ per cent. of (ii)	120	25
Total	583	167
(iv) 12½ per cent. for locomotives under repair	73	21
Total	656	188
(v) For additional military equipment for 1945	310	70
Total	966	258

(b) On the basis of a deficit of 4,260 million ton miles.

	B.G.	M.G.
(i) For troop and military trains	104	68
(ii) Additional goods ton miles at 15 per cent. increase for broad gauge and 9 per cent. for metre gauge	249	48
(iii) Additional for shunting at 33⅓ per cent. of (ii)	83	16
Total	436	132
(iv) 12½ per cent. for locomotives under repair	55	17
Total	491	149
(v) For additional military equipment for 1945	310	70
Total	801	219

	B.G.	M.G.
(c) Wagons on basis of 6,210 million ton miles deficit	32,600	6,520
(d) Wagons on basis of 4,210 million ton miles deficit	22,230	4,190

8. The sub-committee gave the following approximate deficiencies to meet the additional military load during 1945 and to maintain India's internal economy and production capacity at suitable levels:

(a) Locomotive requirements (civil and military)

	B.G.	M.G.
To meet deficit of 6,210 million ton miles	966	258
Number on order	595	310
Additional requirements	371	Nil

To meet deficit of 4,210 million ton miles	801	219
Number on order	595	310
Additional requirements	206	Nil

(b) Wagon requirements (civil and military)

To meet deficit of 6,210 million ton miles	50,318	10,250
Number on order	25,649	7,155
Additional requirements	24,669	3,095
To meet deficit of 4,260 million ton miles	39,948	7,920
Number on order	25,649	7,155
Additional requirements	14,299	765

APPENDIX 25

Fly-in of Formations to the Central Front,

March – May 1944

Date	Formation	Route
March 19th–22nd	123rd Indian Infantry Brigade (5th Division)	Dohazari to Tulihal and Palel
March 23rd–26th	9th Indian Infantry Brigade (5th Division)	One battalion from Dohazari to Dimapur and two battalions to Palel
	H.Q. 5th Indian Division and divisional troops	Dohazari to Palel
March 26th–29th	161st Indian Infantry Brigade (5th Division)	Dohazari to Dimapur and Jorhat
March 30th	15/11th Sikhs	Agartala to Imphal
March 31st	XXXIII Corps Signals	Comilla and Amarda Road to Jorhat

By the 31st March, the transport aircraft had been ferrying troops non-stop for 12 days, and a pause for maintenance was essential. Between the 1st and 4th April, only commanders, senior staff officers and key men of XXXIII Corps were flown to Jorhat.

April 5th–9th	33rd Indian Infantry Brigade (7th Division)	Chittagong and Dohazari to Jorhat
April 10th–15th	4th Infantry Brigade (2nd Division)	Amarda Road to Dimapur and Jorhat
May 4th–12th	89th Indian Infantry Brigade (7th Division)	Dohazari to Imphal (Bad weather interfered with this move)

Note:

A number of miscellaneous units were also flown in; these included 50th Indian Parachute Brigade Signals, a squadron 150th R.A.C., an army-air support control unit and R.A.F. personnel.

APPENDIX 26

Air Supply in South-East Asia, February – August 1944

1. The major air transport operations carried out within the command were:

(a) Routine supply-dropping missions to British detachments in the Chin Hills and at Fort Hertz, including the stocking of supplies at Tiddim.

(b) The maintenance of 81st West African Division in the Kaladan Valley.

(c) The maintenance of 7th Indian Division in Arakan between the 8th February and 6th March.

(d) The maintenance of Special Force in Burma.

(e) The move by air of 5th Indian Division and two-thirds of 7th Indian Division from Arakan to Imphal and Dimapur together with a proportion of their heavy equipment, including artillery.

(f) The move by air of one brigade of 2nd British Division from Calcutta to Jorhat.

(g) The maintenance of 17th Indian Division during its retreat along the Tiddim road.

(h) The maintenance of IV Corps on the Imphal plain from the 18th April to 30th June, together with the evacuation of casualties and some 43,000 non-combatants from Imphal. The maintenance of part of XXXIII Corps in Assam.

(i) The maintenance of the Americans and Chinese operating on the Northern and Yunnan fronts.

(j) The maintenance of the Lushai Brigade.

2. Tonnages landed, or dropped each month, excluding the maintenance of IV Corps (operation 'Stamina'):

Destination	Landed	Dropped	Total	Number of Sorties
Deliveries in Long Tons				
February 1944				
N.C.A.C. (U.S.)[1] . .	715	3,485	4,200	1,491
Chin Hills[1] . .	—	662	662 ⎤	
Kaladan[1] . . .	—	1,074	1,074 ⎟	
Fort Hertz . . .	20	149	169 ⎬	1,520[2]
Special Force . .	—	254	254 ⎟	
Arakan[3] . . .	—	1,636	1,636 ⎦	
Total	735	7,260	7,995	3,011

[1] Inclusive of 'V' Force.
[2] Approximate.
[3] 7th Indian Division.

512

2. (*Contd.*)

Deliveries in Long Tons				
Destination	Landed	Dropped	Total	Number of Sorties
March 1944				
N.C.A.C. (U.S.)[1]. .	910	3,620	4,530	1,542
Chin Hills[1, 4] . .	—	519	519 ⎫	
Kaladan . . .	1	1,113	1,114 ⎪	
Fort Hertz . . .	37	138	175 ⎬	1,240[2]
Special Force . .	107	929	1,036 ⎪	
Arakan[3] . . .	—	263	263 ⎭	
Total	1,055	6,582	7,637	2,782
April 1944				
N.C.A.C. (U.S.)[1]. .	2,240	4,660	6,900	2,553
Chin Hills[1, 4] . .	—	1,255	1,255 ⎫	
Kaladan[1] . . .	—	1,316	1,316 ⎪	
Fort Hertz . . .	24	246	270 ⎬	1,897[2]
Special Force . .	316	1,457	1,773 ⎪	
XXXIII Corps . .	—	94	94 ⎭	
Total	2,580	9,028	11,608	4,450
May 1944				
N.C.A.C. (U.S.)[1]. .	1,850	3,350	5,200	1,868
Kaladan[1] . . .	34	1,047	1,081 ⎫	
Fort Hertz[1]. . .	10	139	149 ⎪	
Special Force . .	50	929	979 ⎬	1,072[2]
Lushai Brigade . .	—	405	405 ⎪	
XXXIII Corps . .	—	175	175 ⎭	
Total	1,944	6,045	7,989	2,940
June 1944				
N.C.A.C. (U.S.)[1]. .	1,575	2,700	4,275	1,940
Kaladan[1] . . .	—	376	376 ⎫	
Fort Hertz . . .	4	149	153 ⎪	
Special Force . .	18	1,803	1,821 ⎬	1,040[2]
Lushai Brigade . .	—	266	266 ⎪	
XXXIII Corps . .	—	7	7 ⎭	
Total	1,597	5,301	6,898	2,980
July 1944				
N.C.A.C. (U.S.)[1]. .	5,425	3,575	9,000	3,898
Kaladan[1] . . .	—	130	130 ⎫	
Fort Hertz . . .	30	248	278 ⎪	
Special Force . .	58	2,132	2,190 ⎬	1,682[2]
Lushai Brigade . .	—	387	387 ⎪	
XXXIII Corps . .	—	1,235	1,235 ⎭	
Total	5,513	7,707	13,220	5,580

[1] Inclusive of 'V' Force.
[2] Approximate.
[3] 7th Indian Division.
[4] Inclusive of 17th Indian Division.

2. (*cont.*)

Deliveries in Long Tons

Destination	Landed	Dropped	Total	Number of Sorties
August 1944				
N.C.A.C. (U.S.)[1] .	8,100	4,450	12,550	5,499
Kaladan[1] . . .	—	58	58 ⎤	
Fort Hertz . . .	23	175	198 ⎟	
Special Force . .	35	478	513 ⎟	
Lushai Brigade . .	—	327	327 ⎬	1,631[2]
XXXIII Corps . .	—	1,981	1,981 ⎟	
36th Division . .	2	911	913 ⎟	
Myitkyina (civil) . .	86	—	86 ⎦	
Total	8,246	8,380	16,626	7,130
Grand Total for 7 months	21,670	50,303	71,973	28,873

[1] Inclusive of 'V' Force.   [2] Approximate.

3. Deliveries in long tons to IV Corps on the Imphal plain during operation 'Stamina', 18th April to 30th June:

Period	Target		Attainment		Shortages on Target		Average daily delivery
	Stocks	Reinforcements	Stocks	Reinforcements	Stocks	Reinforcements	
18th–30th							
April	3,180	3,250	1,926	1,479	1,254	1,771	148 tons
May	13,423	7,750	6,040	5,011	7,383	2,739	194·8 tons
June	10,890	7,500	10,858	6,071	32	1,429	362 tons
Total	27,493	18,500	18,824	12,561	8,669	5,939	

Note: On their return flights the transport aircraft evacuated some 13,000 casualties and 43,000 non-combatants.

4. Transport aircraft available to 14th Army, February to August 1944:

Month	Squadrons	Type of aircraft	Establishment	Total
February	R.A.F.: 31, 62, 117, 194	Dakota	100 ⎤	126
	U.S.: 1, 2	Dakota	26 ⎦	
March	R.A.F.: 31, 62, 117, 194	Dakota	100 ⎤	152
	U.S.: 1, 2, 27, 315	Dakota	52 ⎦	
April				
1st–17th	As for March	Dakota	152	152
18th–30th	R.A.F.: 31, 62, 117, 194, 216[1]	Dakota	100 ⎤ 15 ⎟	
	U.S.: 1, 2, 27, 315, 4[1], 16,[1] 17,[1] 18,[1] 35[1]	Dakota	52 ⎬ 65 ⎦	232
	On loan from Air Transport Command	Commando	20(30)[2]	30

Notes: [1] On loan from Middle East.
    [2] 20 Commandos were equivalent in lift to 30 Dakotas.

4. (*cont.*)

Month	Squadrons	Type of aircraft	Establish-ment	Total
May	As for April 18th–30th, less the Commandos	Dakota	232	232
June				
1st–15th	As for May	Dakota	232	232
15th–30th	R.A.F.: 31, 62, 117, 194	Dakota	100 ⎫	
	U.S.: 1, 2, 11, 315	Dakota	52 ⎬	191
	U.S. Combat Cargo Groups:			
	9, 10, 12	Dakota	39 ⎭	
July	R.A.F.: 31, 62, 117, 194	Dakota	100 ⎫	
	U.S.: 1, 2, 315	Dakota	39 ⎬	191
	U.S. Combat Cargo Groups:			
	9, 10, 11, 12	Dakota	52 ⎭	
August	R.A.F.: 62, 117, 194	Dakota	75 ⎫	
	U.S.: 1, 2, 315	Dakota	39 ⎬	166
	U.S. Combat Cargo Groups:			
	9, 10, 11, 12	Dakota	52 ⎭	
	Non-operational R.A.F.: 31	Dakota	25	
	R.C.A.F.: 435, 436	Dakota	50	

5. Total number of sorties flown:

Supply-dropping and landing (excluding operation 'Stamina')		28,873
Operation 'Stamina': Reinforcements	360[1] ⎫	7,360
Supplies	7,000[2] ⎭	
Fly-in of troops to Central front, March/April 1944:		
5th Division	760 ⎫	
7th Division (33rd and 89th Brigades)	397 ⎬	1,540
2nd Division (4th Brigade)	285	
Miscellaneous[3]	98 ⎭	
Total . .		37,773

Notes:

[1] It is not possible from records to give the exact number of sorties flown with reinforcements. It was customary for small parties of troops to be flown as opportunity offered in aircraft carrying supplies. The number flown in on supply aircraft, however, was probably no more than 10 per cent. of the total.

[2] The total number of sorties is based on an average load of 2½ tons per sortie as no exact figure can be obtained from the available records. No allowance has been made for abortive sorties due to weather or other causes; these were estimated at the time as about one-fifth of the total sorties flown, or approximately 1,400.

[3] Includes 50th Parachute Brigade Signals, XXXIII Corps Signals, a squadron 150th R.A.C., 15/11th Sikhs, an army-air support control unit and R.A.F. personnel.

6. Ground organization to handle supplies:

(a) In February 1944 there were one British and five Indian air supply companies under command of 14th Army. These were located at:

No. 1 Company R.I.A.S.C. Comilla   } to supply XV Corps in
No. 5   ,,   ,,   Chittagong } Arakan
No. 2.   ,,   ,,   } { to supply the Chin
No. 4   ,,   ,,   } Agartala { Hills and Special
No. 61   ,,   R.A.S.C. }   { Force

Detachment
No. 3 Company   Tinsukia-Dinjan to supply Fort Hertz

(b) In March Nos. 2 and 61 Companies moved to Sylhet to supply Special Force, leaving No. 4 at Agartala to supply IV Corps.

(c) During operation 'Stamina', Feni and Jorhat airfields were brought into use. These were served by No. 5 Company, leaving No. 1 Company at Comilla (later moved forward to Hathazari), and the existing companies were reinforced by additional sections.

(d) During 'Stamina' these air supply companies had, in addition to their normal duties, to act as a link between the army and the R.A.F. station commander. This proved to be unsatisfactory. Later a Rear Airfield Maintenance Organization (R.A.M.O.), made up of a small headquarters with staff and service representatives and a variable number of service units according to the quantity and range of stores to be handled, was introduced.

7. Allocation of commodities to airfields:

In order to facilitate stocking and the adjustment of priorities, and to economize in man-power and stores, the army made attempts to standardize the daily lift from individual airfields as far as was compatible with the availability of aircraft and the priority of demands from IV Corps. The air force preferred mixed commodity bases, on the grounds that aircraft stationed at a single commodity airfield would have to be switched to another airfield if that particular commodity did not provide sufficient lift for all aircraft based there. A workable compromise was reached by the time 'Stamina' was in full swing. The final lay-out in use throughout June was:

Single Commodity Airfields:
   Chittagong (until flooded in mid-June)   Ammunition
   Feni   P.O.L.
   Sylhet   Supplies

Mixed Commodity Airfields:
   Agartala   Supplies
                                                  Ordnance stores
                                                  Signal stores
                                                  Mail

Comilla

Reinforcements
Medical
Ordnance
Ammunition
(after mid-June)

Jorhat

Canteen stores
Mail
Reinforcements
Ordnance stores

APPENDIX 27

Comparative Strength and Losses of the United States and Japanese Naval Forces in the Pacific, December 1941–August 1944

	Battleships American	Battleships Japanese	Aircraft Carriers Fleet American	Aircraft Carriers Fleet Japanese	Aircraft Carriers Light American	Aircraft Carriers Light Japanese	Aircraft Carriers Escort American	Aircraft Carriers Escort Japanese	Cruisers Heavy American	Cruisers Heavy Japanese	Cruisers Light American	Cruisers Light Japanese	Destroyers American	Destroyers Japanese	Submarines American	Submarines Japanese
Strength Dec. 1941	7	10	3	6	—	4	—	—	13	18	11	21	78	112	52	65
Additions Dec. 1941 to Aug. 1943	9	2	6	2	3	1	11	3	3	—	11	2	107	21	69	39
Total	16	12	9	8	3	5	11	3	16	18	22	23	185	133	121	104
Losses Dec. 1941 to Aug. 1943	1(1)	3	4	4	—	2	—	—	6	4	5(2)	3	51(24)	46	17(2)	35
Strength 31st May 1943	15	9	5	4	3	3	11	3	10	14	17	20	134	87	104	69
Additions Aug. 1943 to Aug. 1944	2	—	7	3	6	2	39	2	3	—	8	1	124	22	72	32
Total	17	9	12	7	9	5	50	5	13	14	25	21	258	109	176	101
Losses Aug. 1943 to Aug. 1944	—	—	—	3	—	1	3(2)	2	—	—	—	10	9(5)	36	21(3)	53
Strength 31st Aug. 1944	17	9	12	4	9	5	47	3	13	14	25	11	249	73	155	48

Note: The figure of losses 3(2) denotes that one ship was lost by enemy action and two were transferred to the Atlantic.

APPENDIX 28

Some Particulars of British, American and Japanese Aircraft in Use in South-East Asia During the Period Covered by this Volume

The figures in these tables are no more than a general guide to the characteristics and capabilities of each type of aircraft. The performance was affected by the climate, the skill of the pilot, the accuracy of navigation and by the uncertainties of flying in the presence of the enemy. For these reasons the operational range—not to be confused with the radius of action—was always much less than the still air range. Broadly speaking, after allowing for the running of the engines on the ground and for the climb to the height quoted, the still air range was the distance that could be flown in still air until the tanks were empty.

Notes (i) The most economical cruising speed was the speed at which the greatest range was achieved.
(ii) The height given in column IV was the optimum height for the maximum speed.

FIGHTER AIRCRAFT

BRITISH AND AMERICAN

Aircraft	Fuel and Still Air Range at Most Economical Cruising Speed		Most Economical Cruising Speed in Miles per Hour	Maximum Speed in Miles per Hour	Gun Armament	Remarks
	Gals.	Miles				
Beaufighter Mk. VI Twin engine monoplane Crew 2	550	1,810	210 at 15,000 ft.	361 at 18,000 ft.	4 × 20 mm. 6 × ·303 in.	British. Long-range fighter. With special equipment was also used for night fighter interception.
Corsair Single engine monoplane Crew 1	192	673	251 at 20,000 ft.	374 at 23,000 ft.	6 × ·50 in.	American. A naval fighter which was also used by the Fleet Air Arm.
Hurricane Mk. II Single engine monoplane Crew 1	97 183 (2 × 43)	480 970	200 at 15,000 ft.	342 at 22,000 ft.	12 × ·303 in. 4 × 20 mm.	British. Below 10,000 ft. the Hurricane was less manoeuvreable than the Japanese Zero fighter but above 20,000 ft. proved to be superior. This aircraft was also developed as an effective fighter-bomber.

FIGHTER AIRCRAFT
BRITISH AND AMERICAN

Aircraft	Fuel and Still Air Range at Most Economical Cruising Speed (Gals.)	(Miles)	Most Economical Cruising Speed in Miles per Hour	Maximum Speed in Miles per Hour	Gun Armament	Remarks
Warhawk (P.40) Single engine monoplane Crew 1	123	670	200 at 15,000 ft.	350 at 15,000 ft.	6 × ·50 in.	American. This aircraft was an improved version of the earlier Tomahawk.
Lightning (P.38) Twin engine monoplane Crew 1	250	790	190 at 15,000 ft.	357 at 16,000 ft.	4 × ·50 in. 1 × 20 mm.	American. In practice this fighter proved particularly effective in low-level attacks on airfields.
Mohawk Single engine monoplane Crew 1	132	900	170 at 15,000 ft.	300 at 14,000 ft.	6 × ·303 in.	American. This aircraft was an earlier version of the Tomahawk. It was obsolete in 1941 but was retained in use by the R.A.F. in India.
Mustang (P.51) Single engine monoplane Crew 1	140	685	225 at 15,000 ft.	390 at 8,000 ft.	4 × ·50 in. 4 × ·30 in.	American. A version of this aircraft was developed as an effective fighter-bomber.
Spitfire Mk. VIII Single engine monoplane Crew 1	120	660	220 at 20,000 ft.	408 at 25,000 ft.	4 × ·303 in. 2 × 20 mm.	British. This high-performance aircraft proved superior to the Japanese Zero and Oscar fighters.

BOMBER AIRCRAFT
(including torpedo-bomber and reconnaissance)
BRITISH AND AMERICAN

Aircraft	Still Air Range with Associated Bomb-load		Most Economical Cruising Speed in Miles per Hour	Maximum Speed in Miles per Hour	Gun Armament	Remarks
	Miles	Bomb-load				
Barracuda Single engine monoplane Crew 2	1,010	1 torpedo or 1,600 lb.	138 at 6,000 ft.	249 at 9,000 ft.	1 × ·303 in.	British. Torpedo-bomber used by the Fleet Air Arm.
Beaufort Mk. II Twin engine monoplane Crew 4	1,390	1 torpedo or 1,650 lb.	160 at 5,000 ft.	236 at 5,000 ft.	4 × ·303 in.	British. R.A.F. land-based torpedo-bomber.
Liberator Mk. II (B.24) Four engine monoplane Crew 8	1,940 2,730	8,000 lb. 4,500 lb.	156 at 15,000 ft.	228 at 14,000 ft.	5 × ·50 in. 4 × ·303 in.	American. Heavy bomber used extensively by both U.S.A.A.F. and R.A.F. primarily for strategic bombing by day and night. It was also used for mine-laying and with special equipment for general reconnaissance and anti-submarine operations.
Mitchell (B.25) Twin engine monoplane Crew 5	1,150	3,000 lb.	210 at 15,000 ft.	295 at 15,000 ft.	4 × ·50 in. 1 × ·30 in.	American. Medium bomber. It proved particularly effective in attacking tactical targets.

BOMBER AIRCRAFT
(*including torpedo-bomber and reconnaissance*)
BRITISH AND AMERICAN

Aircraft	Still Air Range with Associated Bomb-load		Most Economical Cruising Speed in Miles per Hour	Maximum Speed in Miles per Hour	Gun Armament	Remarks
	Miles	Bomb-load				
Mosquito Mk. IV Twin engine monoplane Crew 2	1,620	2,000 lb.	265 at 15,000 ft.	380 at 14,000 ft.	4 × ·303 in.	British. Light bomber. A special unarmed version of the Mosquito was used for long-range high-altitude photographic reconnaissance.
Superfortress (B.29) Four engine monoplane Crew 8	2,970	16,500 lb.	240 at 25,000 ft.	340 at 25,000 ft.	8 × ·50 in.	American. Very long-range bomber used exclusively by the U.S.A.A.F. primarily for raids on Japan from advanced bases in China and the Pacific.
Vengeance Single engine monoplane Crew 2	915	1,500 lb.	187 at 15,000 ft.	258 at 11,500 ft.	6 × ·303 in.	American. Light bomber used exclusively by the R.A.F. It proved most effective as a dive-bomber against tactical targets.
Wellington Mk. X Twin engine monoplane Crew 6	1,325	4,500 lb.	180 at 15,000 ft.	255 at 14,500 ft.	6 × ·303 in.	British. Medium bomber chiefly used for strategic bombing by night. With special equipment the Wellington was also used for general reconnaissance and anti-submarine operations.

GENERAL RECONNAISSANCE AND TRANSPORT AIRCRAFT
BRITISH AND AMERICAN

Aircraft	Still Air Range with Associated Bomb-load		Most Economical Cruising Speed in Miles per Hour	Maximum Speed in Miles per Hour	Gun Armament	Remarks
	Miles	Bomb-load				
Catalina Twin engine flying-boat Crew 9	1,395 2,950	2,000 lb. Nil	123 at 5,000 ft.	177 at 5,000 ft.	2 × ·303 in. 2 × ·50 in.	American. Was used extensively by the R.A.F.
Sunderland Mk. III Four engine flying-boat Crew 10	2,500 3,120	1,900 lb. Nil	143 at 5,000 ft.	212 at 1,500 ft.	7 × ·303 in.	British. Used by the R.A.F. in conjunction with the Catalina primarily for long-range seaward reconnaissance.
Dakota (C.47) Twin engine monoplane Crew 3 or 4	1,910	26 troops with full equipment or 6,000 lb. freight	160 at 10,000 ft.	220 at 10,000 ft.	None	American. The Dakota became the standard Allied transport aircraft. It proved to be invaluable for air supply and airborne operations.
Commando (C.46) Twin engine monoplane Crew 3	1,600	35 troops with full equipment or 10,000 lb. freight	183 at 14,000 ft.	267 at 15,000 ft.	None	American. Used exclusively by the U.S.A.A.F. It was the standard type of transport aircraft on the India–China air route. Less manoeuvreable than the Dakota, the Commando was not suitable for supply-dropping.

FIGHTER AIRCRAFT
JAPANESE

Aircraft	Fuel and Still Air Range at Most Economical Cruising Speed — Gals.	Miles	Most Economical Cruising Speed in Miles per Hour	Maximum Speed in Miles per Hour	Gun Armament	Remarks (and Allied Code Name)
Navy Zero Mk. II Single engine monoplane Crew 1	112	885	160 at 18,000 ft.	335 at 18,500 ft.	2 × 7·7 mm. 2 × 20 mm.	'ZEKE 2'. Standard Naval fighter, both carrier-borne and land-based.
Army I Mk. II Single engine monoplane Crew 1	126	950	155 at 18,000 ft.	325 at 18,500 ft.	2 × 12·7 mm.	'OSCAR 2'. Standard Army fighter.

BOMBER AIRCRAFT
(including torpedo-bomber and reconnaissance)
JAPANESE

Aircraft	Still Air Range with Associated Bomb-load — Miles	Bomb-load	Most Economical Cruising Speed in Miles per Hour	Maximum Speed in Miles per Hour	Gun Armament	Remarks (and Allied Code Name)
Navy I Twin engine monoplane Crew 7	3,075	2,200 lb. or 1 torpedo	145 at 15,000 ft.	283 at 13,800 ft.	3 × 7·7 mm. 2 × 20 mm.	'BETTY.' Standard Navy bomber (land-based).
Navy 97 Mk. II Single engine monoplane Crew 2	1,220	1,000 lb. or 1 torpedo	130 at 13,000 ft.	222 at 15,000 ft.	4 × 7·7 mm.	'KATE.' Standard torpedo-bomber, carrier-borne.

BOMBER AIRCRAFT
(including torpedo-bomber and reconnaissance)
JAPANESE

Aircraft	Still Air Range with Associated Bomb-load		Most Economical Cruising Speed in Miles per Hour	Maximum Speed in Miles per Hour	Gun Armament	Remarks (and Allied Code Name)
	Miles	Bomb-load				
Army 97 Mk. III Twin engine monoplane Crew 7	1,635	2,200 lb.	150 at 13,000 ft.	294 at 15,500 ft.	6 × 7·7 mm. or 5 × 7·7 mm. plus 1 × 12·7 mm. 1 × 20 mm.	'SALLY.' Army heavy bomber.
Army 99 Twin engine monoplane Crew 2	1,030	660 lb.	180 at 12,000 ft.	250 at 12,000 ft.	3 × 7·7 mm.	'SONIA.' Army light bomber.
Army I Mk. II Twin engine monoplane Crew 2	1,405	None	219 at 15,000 ft.	365 at 21,000 ft.	1 × 7·7 mm.	'DINAH.' Specially developed for high-altitude photographic reconnaissance.
Navy 2 Four engine flying-boat Crew 10	4,370	4,400 lb.	210 at 5,000 ft.	296 at 5,000 ft.	5 × 20 mm. 4 × 12·7 mm.	'EMILY.' Largest Japanese flying-boat for long-range seaward reconnaissance.

Notes: (i) The Japanese system of numbering each type of aircraft was related to the year of issue. Type numbers correspond to the last one or two digits of the year of issue according to the Japanese calendar, by which the year 1940 was the Japanese year 2600. Thus aircraft brought into service in 1939 were designated 'Type 99' and those issued in 1940 were 'Type 0'. To simplify reference to particular types the Allies allotted a code name to each.

(ii) The Japanese did not introduce basically new types of aircraft during the course of the war. Modified versions of types in production in 1941 or earlier were made, resulting in improved performance in some types. Variations in armament were also made. In general, however, the types of aircraft with which squadrons were equipped remained unchanged.

(iii) Japanese aircraft were not normally fitted with self-sealing petrol tanks or protective armour, nor were the air crews equipped with parachutes. For these reasons their losses, particularly of aircraft damaged in action, may have been greater than they otherwise would have been.

APPENDIX 29

British Battle Casualties, November 1943–July 1944

This period covers the battles of north Arakan, Ngakyedauk Pass, Kohima and Imphal, and the action of the Chindits

A. ARAKAN FRONT

(1) North Arakan (up to 3rd February 1944)

5th Indian Division	617	
7th Indian Division	466	
	——	
		1,083

(2) Ngakyedauk Pass

Corps troops (XV Corps)	204	
7th Indian Division	1,579	
5th Indian Division	993	
26th Indian Division	612	
36th Indian Division	118	
	——	
		3,506

(3) North Arakan (March–July 1944)

Corps troops (XV Corps)	10	
26th Indian Division	1,705	
25th Indian Division	916	
81st (W.A.) Division	431	
7th Indian Division	181 (to April only)	
36th Indian Division	119 (to May only)	
	——	
		3,362

Total for Arakan	7,951

B. CENTRAL FRONT

(1) Operations before the battles of Kohima and Imphal

17th Indian Division	604	
20th Indian Division	316	
		920

(2) Kohima

Corps troops (XXXIII Corps)	95	
2nd Division	2,125	
7th Indian Division (less 89th Brigade)	623 (from 7th May)	
161st Indian Brigade (5th Division)	462	
Kohima Garrison (less Royal West Kents)	401	
23rd (L.R.P.) Brigade	158	
1st Assam Regiment (Jessami & Kharasom)	200 (estimate)	
	——	
		4,064

(3) Imphal

Corps troops (IV Corps)	677	
17th Indian Division	4,134	
20th Indian Division	2,887	
23rd Indian Division	2,494	
5th Indian Division (less 161st Indian Brigade)	1,603	
89th Indian Brigade (7th Division)	219 (from 7th May)	
50th Indian Parachute Brigade	589	
	——	12,603
Total for Central front		17,587

C. SPECIAL FORCE (less 23rd Brigade)

14th, 16th, 77th, 111th, 3rd (W.A.) Brigades	3,628
GRAND TOTAL	29,166

APPENDIX 30

Code Names Used in the Text

ALLIED

Anakim[1]   First plan for the reoccupation of Burma
Anvil   Landing in the south of France
Buccaneer[1] Operation against the Andaman Islands
Bulldozer[1] Capture of Akyab in conjunction with 'Cudgel'
Bullfrog[1] First plan for the capture of Akyab
Cudgel   Limited land advance in Arakan
Culverin[1] Occupation of northern Sumatra
Gripfast   Modified 'Tarzan'
Matterhorn Long-range bombing of Japan from China
Overlord   Liberation of north-west Europe
Pigstick[1] Landing on the Mayu Peninsula
Quadrant   The First Quebec Conference, August 1943
Sextant   The Cairo Conference, November–December 1943
Stamina   Maintenance by air of IV Corps and the R.A.F. squadrons on the Imphal plain
Tarzan[1]   Plan for the airborne capture of the Indaw-Katha area in conjunction with a major land advance
Thursday   Second Chindit Expedition
Trident   The Second Washington Conference, May 1943

JAPANESE

A-Go   Plan to bring the American fleet to action east of the Philippines
Ha-Go   Diversionary offensive in Arakan, as a preliminary to 'U-Go'
Ichi-Go   Offensive in China
U-Go   Offensive on the Imphal front
Z   Plan to engage the American fleet in the event of an attempted invasion of the Carolines or Marianas

---

Note: [1] These operations were not carried out.

Index

INDEX

Note : Formations and units of the British, Commonwealth and Indian Armies, and of the Burma and Colonial military forces, are indexed under 'Army'. British infantry battalions are in order of regimental seniority.

531

12404

Wt. 3525   K 32   H.W.V. Ltd.

S.O. Code No. 63-111-23-6*

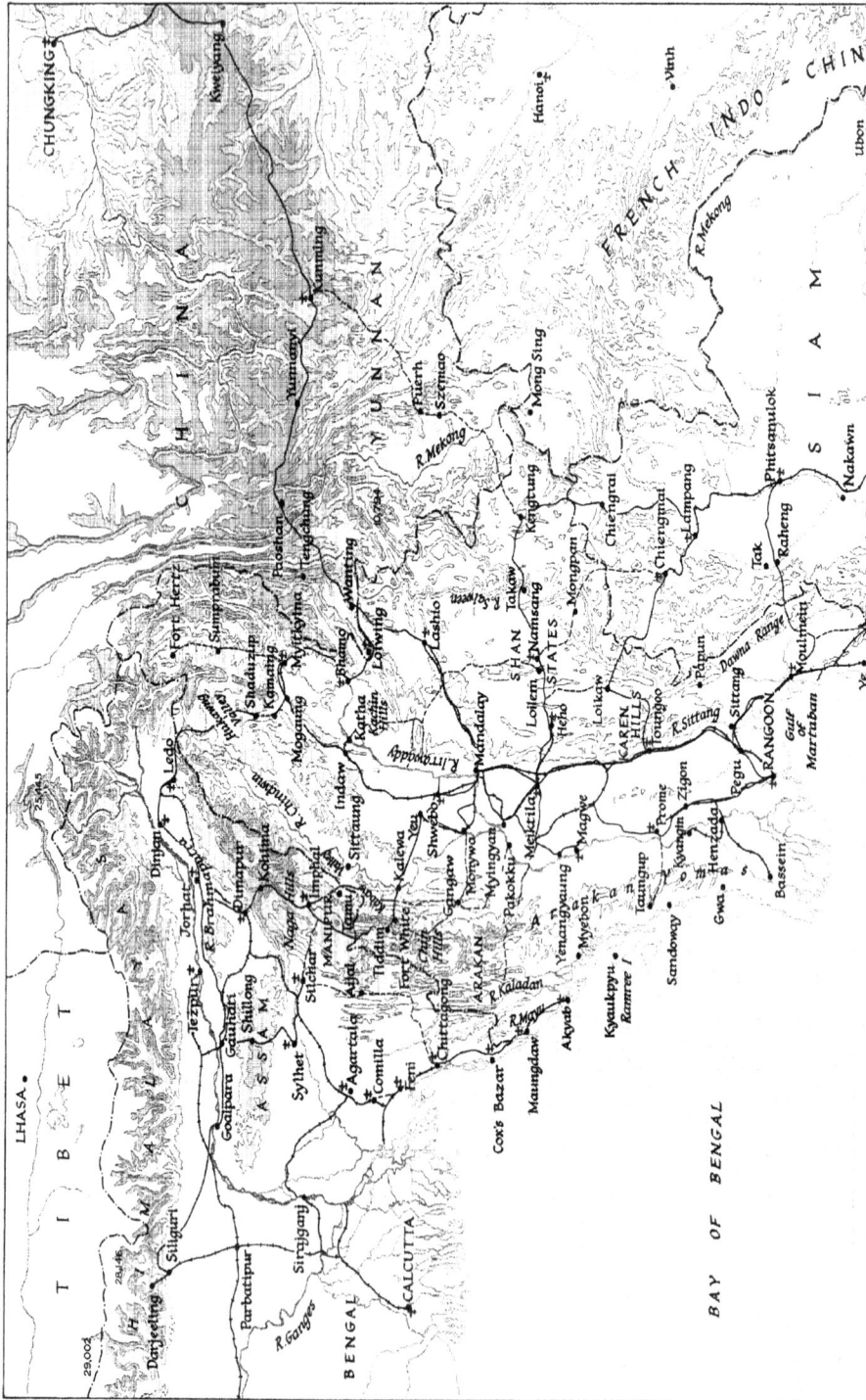

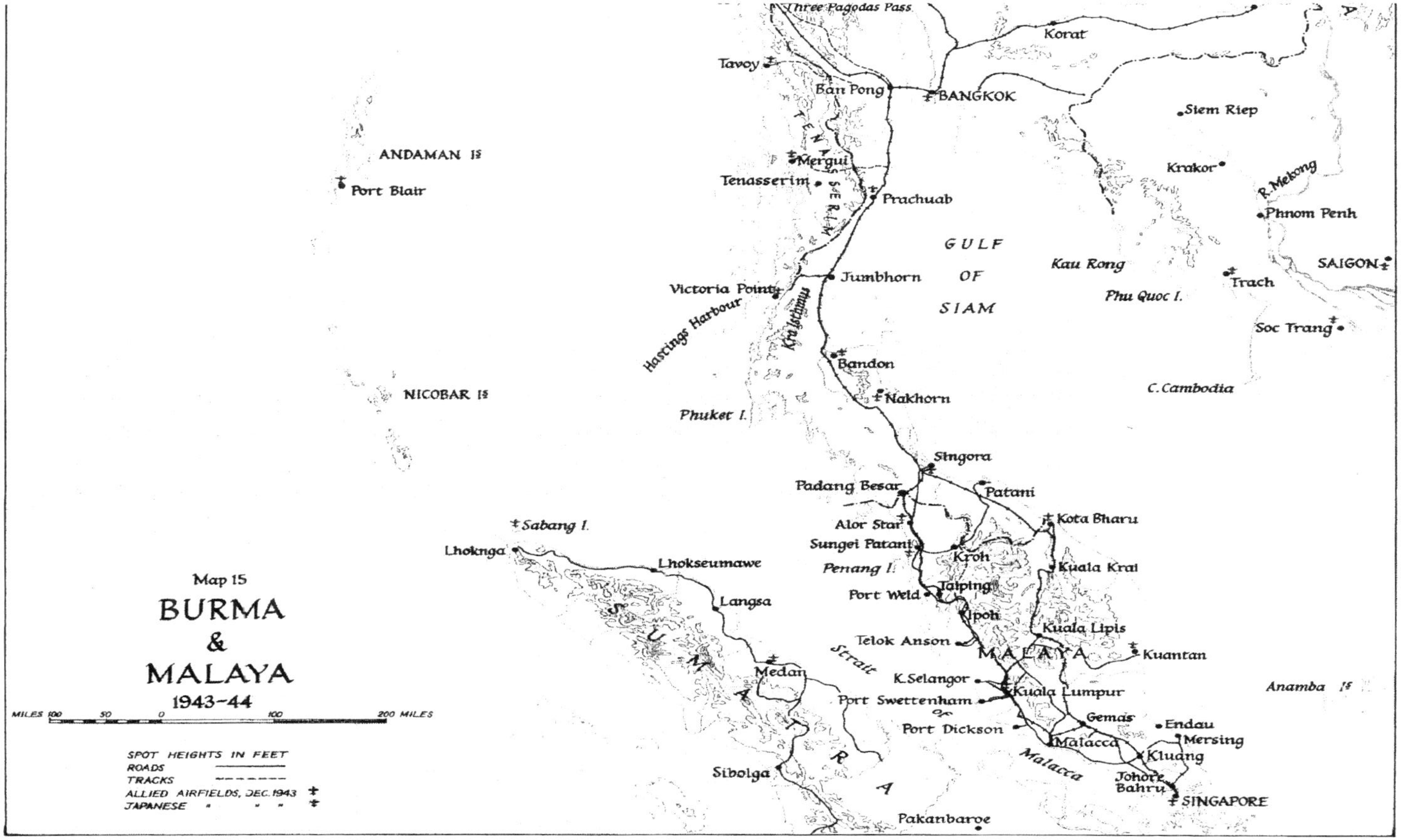

Map 15

BURMA
&
MALAYA
1943-44

MILES 600   50   0   100   200 MILES

SPOT HEIGHTS IN FEET
ROADS
TRACKS
ALLIED AIRFIELDS, DEC. 1943 ✝
JAPANESE   „   „   „   ✝

HISTORY OF THE SECOND WORLD WAR
UNITED KINGDOM MILITARY SERIES

Reprinted by the Naval & Military Press in twenty two volumes with the permission of the Controller of HMSO and Queen's Printer for Scotland.

THE DEFENCE OF THE UNITED KINGDOM

Basil Collier

Official history of Britain's home front in the Second World War, from the Phoney War, through the Battle of Britain and the Blitz to victory in Europe.
ISBN: 1845740556
Price £22.00

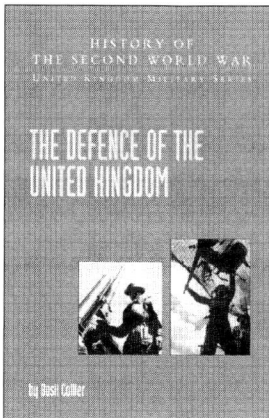

THE CAMPAIGN IN NORWAY

T. H. Derry

The catastrophic 1940 campaign which caused the downfall of Neville Chamberlain and brought Winston Churchill to power.
ISBN: 1845740572
Price: £22.00

THE WAR IN FRANCE AND FLANDERS 1939-1940

Major L. F. Ellis

The role of the BEF in the fall of France and the retreat to Dunkirk.
ISBN: 1845740564
Price £22.00

VICTORY IN THE WEST
Volume I: The Battle of Normandy

Major L. F. Ellis

The build-up, execution and consequences of D-Day in 1944.
ISBN: 1845740580
Price: £22.00

Volume II: The Defeat of Germany

Major L. F. Ellis

The final stages of the liberation of western Europe in 1944-45.
ISBN: 1845740599
Price £22.00

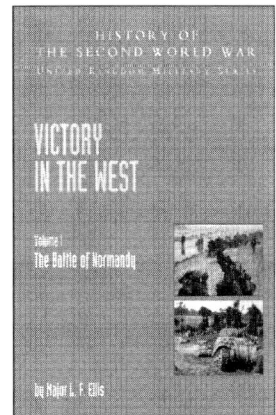

THE MEDITERRANEAN AND MIDDLE EAST

Volume I: The Early Successes against Italy (to May 1941)

Major-General I. S. O. Playfair

Britain defeats Italy on land and sea in Africa and the Mediterranean in 1940.
ISBN: 1845740653
Price: £22.00

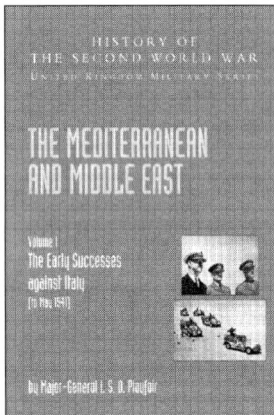

Volume II: The Germans Come to the Help of their Ally (1941)

Major-General I. S. O. Playfair

Rommel rides to Italy's rescue, Malta is bombarded, Yugoslavia, Greece and Crete are lost, and Iraq and Syria are secured for the Allies.
ISBN: 1845740661
Price: £22.00

Volume III: (September 1941 to September 1942) British Fortunes reach their Lowest Ebb

Major-General I. S. O. Playfair

Britain's darkest hour in North Africa and the Mediterranean, 1941-42.
ISBN: 184574067X
Price: £22.00

Volume IV: The Destruction of the Axis Forces in Africa

Major-General I. S. O. Playfair

The battle of El Alamein and 'Operation Torch' bring the Allies victory in North Africa, 1942-43.
ISBN: 1845740688
Price: £22.00

Volume V: The Campaign in Sicily 1943 and the Campaign in Italy — 3rd Sepember 1943 to 31st March 1944

Major-General I. S. O. Playfair

The Allies invade Sicily and Italy, but encounter determined German defence in 1943-44.
ISBN: 1845740696
Price: £22.00

Volume VI: Victory in the Mediterranean Part I: 1st April to 4th June 1944

Brigadier C. J. C. Molony

The Allies breach the Gustav, Hitler and Caesar Lines and occupy Rome.
ISBN: 184574070X
Price: £22.00

Volume VI: Victory in the Mediterranean Part II: June to October 1944

General Sir William Jackson

The 1944 Italian summer campaign breaches the Gothic Line but then bogs down again.
ISBN: 1845740718
Price: £22.00

Volume VI: Victory in the Mediterranean Part III: November 1944 to May 1945

General Sir William Jackson

The messy end of the war in Italy, Greece, and Yugoslavia.
ISBN: 1845740726
Price: £22.00

THE WAR AGAINST JAPAN

Volume I: The Loss of Singapore

Major-General S. Woodburn Kirby

The fall of Hong Kong, Malaya and Singapore in 1941–42.
ISBN: 1845740602
Price: £22.00

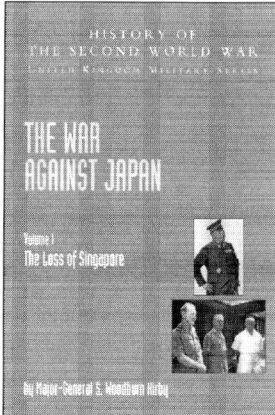

Volume III: The Decisive Battles

Major-General S. Woodburn Kirby

Turning the tide in the war against Japan at the battles of Kohima, Imphal and the Chindit campaigns.
ISBN: 1845740629
Price: £22.00

Volume IV: The Reconquest of Burma

Major-General S. Woodburn Kirby

The reconquest of Burma by Bill Slim's 'forgotten' 14th Army.
ISBN: 1845740637
Price: £22.00

Volume V: The Surrender of Japan

Major-General S. Woodburn Kirby

Victory in South-East Asia in 1945 - from Rangoon to Nagasaki.
ISBN: 1845740645
Price: £22.00

Volume II: India's Most Dangerous Hour

Major-General S. Woodburn Kirby

The loss of Burma and Japan's threat to India in 1941–42.
ISBN: 1845740610
Price: £22.00

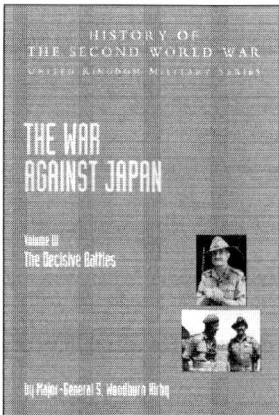

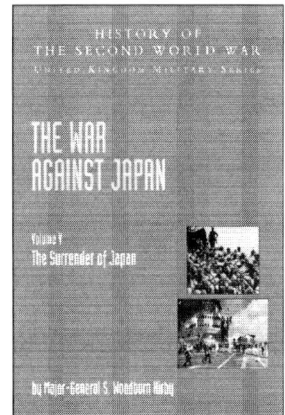

THE WAR AT SEA - 1939—1945

Captain Roskill has long been recognised as the leading authority on The Royal Navy's part in the Second World War. His official History is unlikely ever to be superceded. His narrative is highly readable and the analysis is clear. Roskill describes sea battles, convoy actions and the contribution made by technology in the shape of Asdic & Radar.

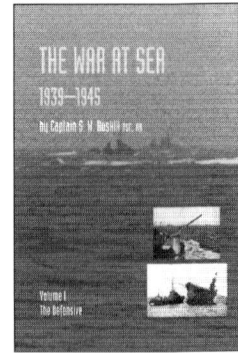

Volume I: The Defensive

Captain S. W. Roskill, D.S.C., R.N.

2004 N&MP reprint (original pub 1954).
SB. xxii + 664pp with 43 maps and numerous contemporary photos.
ISBN: 1843428032
Price: £32.00

Volume II: The Period of Balance

Captain S. W. Roskill, D.S.C., R.N.

2004 N&MP reprint (original pub 1956).
SB. xvi + 523pp with 42 maps and numerous contemporary photos.
ISBN: 1843428040
Price: £32.00

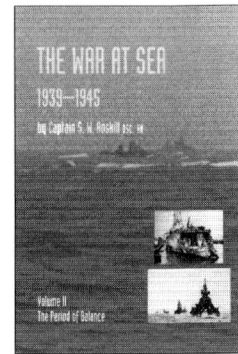

Volume III: Part I The Offensive
1st June 1943–31 May 1944

Captain S. W. Roskill, D.S.C., R.N.

2004 N&MP reprint (original pub 1960).
SB. xv + 413pp with 21 maps and numerous contemporary photos.
ISBN: 1843428059
Price: £32.00

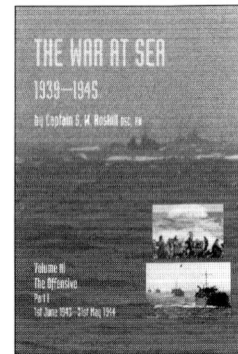

Volume III: Part 2 The Offensive
1st June 1944–14th August 1945

Captain S. W. Roskill, D.S.C., R.N.

2004 N&MP reprint (original pub 1961).
SB. xvi + 502pp with 46 maps and numerous contemporary photos.
ISBN: 1843428067
Price: £32.00

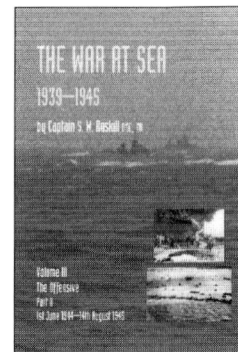

Printed in Great
Britain
by Amazon